Object Categorization

This edited volume presents a unique multidisciplinary perspective on the problem of visual object categorization. The result of a series of four highly successful workshops on the topic, the book gathers many of the most distinguished researchers from both computer and human vision to reflect on their experience, identify open problems, and foster a cross-disciplinary discussion with the idea that parallel problems and solutions have arisen in both domains.

Twenty-seven of these workshop speakers have contributed chapters, including fourteen from computer vision and thirteen from human vision. Their contributions range from broad perspectives on the problem to more specific approaches, collectively providing important historical context, identifying the major challenges, and presenting recent research results. This multidisciplinary collection is the first of its kind on the topic of object categorization, providing an outstanding context for graduate students and researchers in both computer and human vision.

Sven J. Dickinson is Professor of Computer Science at the University of Toronto. From 1994 until 2000, he was Assistant Professor at Rutgers University, where he held joint appointments in the Department of Computer Science and the Rutgers Center for Cognitive Science. He was cochair of the 1997, 1999, 2004, and 2007 IEEE International Workshops on Generic Object Recognition and Categorization and cochair of the First International Workshop on Shape Perception in Human and Computer Vision in 2008.

Aleš Leonardis is a Full Professor and Head of the Visual Cognitive Systems Laboratory at the University of Ljubljana and Adjunct Professor at the Faculty of Computer Science, Graz University of Technology. He was a researcher and visiting professor at the University of Pennsylvania, Vienna University of Technology, Swiss Federal Institute of Technology, and University of Erlangen.

Bernt Schiele is Full Professor of Computer Science at TU Darmstadt, Germany. He obtained his Ph.D. from INPG in Grenoble, France. He was a researcher at Carnegie Mellon University and visiting Assistant Professor at Massachusetts Institute of Technology, as well as Assistant Professor at the Swiss Federal Institute of Technology in Zurich (ETH Zurich).

Michael J. Tarr is the Co-Director of the Center for the Neural Basis of Cognition and a Professor of Psychology at Carnegie Mellon University. From 1989 to 1995, he was an Assistant Professor of Psychology and Computer Science at Yale University. From 1995 to 2009, he was a Professor of Cognitive and Linguistic Sciences at Brown University. While at Brown he also served as the Co-Director of the Center for Vision Research.

Object Categorization

Computer and Human Vision Perspectives

Edited by

Sven J. Dickinson

University of Toronto

Aleš Leonardis

University of Ljubljana

Bernt Schiele

Darmstadt University of Technology

Michael J. Tarr

Carnegie Mellon University

CAMBRIDGE
UNIVERSITY PRESS

CAMBRIDGE UNIVERSITY PRESS
Cambridge, New York, Melbourne, Madrid, Cape Town, Singapore,
São Paulo, Delhi, Dubai, Tokyo

Cambridge University Press
32 Avenue of the Americas, New York, NY 10013-2473, USA

www.cambridge.org
Information on this title: www.cambridge.org/9780521887380

© Sven J. Dickinson, Aleš Leonardis, Bernt Schiele, and Michael J. Tarr 2009

First published 2009

Printed in the United States of America

A catalog record for this publication is available from the British Library.

Library of Congress Cataloging in Publication data

Object categorization : computer and human vision perspectives / edited
by Sven J. Dickinson . . . [et al.].
     p.   cm.
Includes bibliographical references and index.
ISBN 978-0-521-88738-0
1. Computer vision – Congresses.   2. Pattern recognition systems – Congresses.
I. Dickinson, Sven J.   II. Title.
TA1634.O25   2009
006.3′7–dc22   2009026893

ISBN   978-0-521-88738-0 Hardback

Contents

Preface

The recognition of object categories has a rich history in computer vision. In the 1970s, generic object recognition systems sought to model and recognize objects based on their coarse, prototypical shape. These early systems employed complex 3-D models, which offered invariance to viewpoint (including image translation, rotation, and scale), articulation, occlusion, and minor within-class shape deformation. Despite powerful modeling paradigms, however, these early systems lacked the low- and intermediate-level segmentation, grouping, and abstraction machinery needed to recover prototypical shapes from real images of real objects. Over the next two decades, the recognition community began to back away from this "holy grail" of recognition, bringing new models closer to the image in an effort to reduce the representational gap between extractable image features and model features. During this time, the community migrated from the CAD-based vision era, in which exact 3-D geometry was specified, to the appearance-based vision era, in which exact 2-D photometry was specified (either globally, or locally at interest points). Almost in parallel, approaches to biological vision have followed a roughly similar path; that is, there has been a migration from CAD-inspired structural models comprised of 3-D parts, to image-based models preserving much of an object's input appearance, to, most recently, hybrid fragment-based models that rely on hierarchies of more localized image features.

Over this period, the recognition problem was sometimes reformulated from generic object recognition to exemplar recognition. For the first time, real object exemplars, with full texture and complex shape, could be recognized. However, it became apparent that these techniques for exemplar recognition did not scale up to generic objects (alternatively called classes or categories). Moreover, as is abundantly clear from the study of biological vision, the generic recognition of object categories is the predominant mode of how we interact with our visual environments. Thus, over the last decade, the mainstream object recognition pendulum has started to swing back toward object categorization. Armed with new features, new segmentation techniques, new optimization and matching techniques, new machine learning methods, and new a understanding of behavioral and neural phenomena, the community is far better prepared to tackle this important problem. Of course, because categorization was absent from the mainstream for so long, there is a tendency not to look back at earlier problem formulations, challenges, and solutions. We feel that this historical disconnect has not served the community well, and, in many instances, we are facing today's challenges, including the quests for more categorical features (shape vs. appearance), viewpoint invariance, articulation invariance, occlusion invariance, and invariance to within-class structural change, without the clear hindsight of the community's earlier experience.

In an effort to foster greater communication between researchers from disparate disciplines, and to help bridge this historical disconnect, we organized international workshops on generic object recognition at many venues, including CVPR 97 (Ram Nevatia and Sven J. Dickinson, co-chairs), ICCV 99 (Gerard Medioni and Sven J. Dickinson, co-chairs), CVPR 04 (Aleš Leonardis, Bernt Schiele, and Sven J. Dickinson, co-chairs), and ICCV 2007 (Aleš Leonardis, Bernt Schiele, and Sven J. Dickinson, co-chairs). The workshops all had an identical format: bring together ten to twelve of the community's most prominent researchers, whose research spans the evolution of the field, to share their perspectives on the problem. Importantly, these researchers have been drawn from both the biological and computer vision communities with the idea that parallel problems and solutions have arisen in both domains. Moreover, we adhere to the integrative, multidisciplinary approach perhaps best articulated in the seminal work of David Marr. To stimulate discussion, we often purposely chose researchers with opposing viewpoints. We have found that beyond representing all perspectives of a problem, creating a forum for a diversity of views leads to more meaningful and more productive exchanges of ideas. As an added benefit, many of the workshop attendees were graduate students; thus, a broad treatment of the problem, with broad historical context, is particularly important. Speakers were encouraged not to simply present their latest work, but rather to provide a perspective on their experience working on the problem, and to talk about the challenges, successes, and failures. The workshops have been a great success, and attendance has been very high, in some cases outdrawing all other workshops at the conference!

To mark the tenth anniversary of the first such workshop, we decided to invite all the contributors from the four workshops to submit a chapter to what we hope will become a valuable collection of perspectives, from both human and computer vision, on the problem of object categorization. There are many reasons why we believe the time is right for such a collection. As mentioned, the historical disconnect continues to grow at the same time as more researchers enter the recognition community; an institutional memory refresh is especially important for today's researchers and students if we are to maximally benefit from the community's prior work. Perhaps a more compelling reason for assembling such a collection is a renewed interest from computer vision researchers in results originating from cognitive neuroscience, neuroscience, and psychology. In particular, the advent of functional neuroimaging, as well as new neurophysiological methods, has rejuvenated the study of object categorization in humans. Some of the best new researchers from these disciplines are represented in this volume. Even more promising is that there have been, of late, several successful algorithms that are biologically inspired or motivated. By bringing together researchers from different vision subcommunities, we hope to foster interdisciplinary awareness and collaboration, both of which will ultimately help to shed light on the problem of object categorization.

What you hold in your hands is a collection of twenty-seven chapters from some of the top human and computer vision researchers in the field of categorization. Some have worked on the problem for many years (decades) and have a unique perspective to offer researchers and students alike on what trends and issues have shaped the field, the progress we've made, and the challenges we face. Others have been in the field for a decade or less and offer fresh perspectives on old problems. Like our workshops, this volume is aimed at offering a unique, multidisciplinary view that strives to cover this important problem from all sides rather than promote a particular paradigm. Such a perspective is essential for new researchers attempting to understand the broader landscape of the problem so that they can build on a firm foundation. We hope you find the collection as exciting and as useful as we do.

When we sat down to organize the chapters by topic, we quickly found that many chapters defied categorization in that they addressed many topics. Our attempts to cluster chapters into sections led to uneven clusters of chapters, and decisions to put a chapter in one section versus another seemed rather arbitrary. There was also a tendency to cluster human vision chapters together and computer vision chapters together, which defeated our goal of bridging and integrating the two communities. As a result, we decided on a flat (sectionless) structure, with alternating human and computer vision chapters clustered by theme when appropriate. It is our hope that this lack of structure will avoid the biases associated with particular topics and encourage the reader to explore the unique contributions and perspectives offered by each chapter. Moreover, we hope that the interleaved format will naturally encourage human and computer vision researchers to explore each other's community.

Finally, there are a number of people we would like to thank for helping to make this volume possible. Ram Nevatia and Gerard Medioni co-chaired the first and second workshops, in 1997 and 1999, respectively. Heather Bergman, from Cambridge University Press, has been incredibly supportive of the volume and very patient with the editors, and her colleague, David Jou, has been extremely helpful on the editorial side. Mario Fritz, from the Darmstadt University of Technology, maintained a wonderful website for the collection and provided valuable technical support. We would also like to thank our sponsors for their generous financial support: ECVision, the European research network for cognitive computer vision systems, sponsored the workshop in 2004, and EuCognition, the European network for the advancement of artificial cognitive systems, and Toyota Europe sponsored the workshop in 2007. Our sincere thanks to you all.

Sven J. Dickinson
University of Toronto

Aleš Leonardis
University of Ljubljana

Bernt Schiele
Darmstadt University of Technology

Michael J. Tarr
Carnegie Mellon University

Contributors

Cecilia Ovesdotter Alm
University of Illinois at
    Urbana-Champaign

Benjamin Balas
Department of Brain and Cognitive
    Sciences
Massachusetts Institute of Technology

Moshe Bar
Martinos Center for Biomedical
    Imaging at MGH
Harvard Medical School

Marlene Behrmann
Department of Pyschology
Carnegie Mellon University

Tamara Berg
SUNY Stony Brook

Marko Boben
University of Ljubljana, Slovenia

Jasmine Boshyan
Martinos Center for Biomedical
    Imaging at MGH
Harvard Medical School

Kevin Bowyer
University of Notre Dame

Scott L. Brincat
Department of Brain and Cognitive
    Sciences
Massachusetts Institute of Technology

Heinrich H. Bülthoff
Max Planck Institute for Biological
    Cybernetics

Charles E. Connor
Department of Neuroscience
Johns Hopkins University

James J. DiCarlo
Department of Brain and Cognitive
    Sciences
Massachusetts Institute of Technology

Sven J. Dickinson
University of Toronto

Shimon Edelman
Department of Psychology
Cornell University

Ali Farhadi
University of Illinois at
    Urbana-Champaign

Sanja Fidler
University of Ljubljana, Slovenia

D.A. Forsyth
University of Illinois at
   Urbana-Champaign

Mario Fritz
Darmstadt University of Technology

Kalanit Grill-Spector
Department of Pyschology and
   Neuroscience
Stanford University

Martial Hebert
Carnegie Mellon University

Julia Hockenmaier
University of Illinois at
   Urbana-Champaign

Donald D. Hoffman
University of California, Irvine

Kate Humphreys
Institute of Psychiatry

David W. Jacobs
University of Maryland

Benjamin B. Kimia
Division of Engineering
Brown University

Zoe Kourtzi
University of Birmingham

Kestutis Kveraga
Martinos Center for Biomedical
   Imaging at MGH
Harvard Medical School

Svetlana Lazebnik
University of North Carolina at
   Chapel Hill

Tai Sing Lee
Carnegie Mellon University

Aleš Leonardis
University of Ljubljana, Slovenia

Marius Leordeanu
Carnegie Mellon University

Nicolas Loeff
University of Illinois at
   Urbana-Champaign

Gérard Medioni
University of Southern California

Yuri Ostrovsky
Department of Brain and Cognitive
   Sciences
Massachusetts Institute of Technology

Anitha Pasupathy
Department of Biological Structure
University of Washington

Pietro Perona
California Institute of Technology

Stephen Pizer
University of North Carolina at
   Chapel Hill

Jean Ponce
LIENS, Ecole Normale Superieure

Jake Porway
University of California, Los Angeles

Brian Potetz
Carnegie Mellon University

Maximilian Riesenhuber
Department of Neuroscience
Georgetown University
   Medical Center

Edmund T. Rolls
Department of Experimental
   Psychology
University of Oxford

Jason Samonds
Carnegie Mellon University

K. Suzanne Scherf
Department of Pyschology
Carnegie Mellon University

Bernt Schiele
Darmstadt University of Technology

Cordelia Schmid
INRIA Grenoble

Kaleem Siddiqi
Centre for Intelligent Machines
McGill University

Pawan Sinha
Department of Brain and Cognitive
    Sciences
Massachusetts Institute of
    Technology

Louise Stark
University of the Pacific

Tom Stepleton
Carnegie Mellon University

Rahul Sukthankar
Intel Research, Pittsburgh

Melanie Sutton
University of West Florida

Shimon Ullman
Weizmann Institute of Science

Siavash Vaziri
Department of Biomedical Engineering
Johns Hopkins University

Christian Wallraven
MPI for Biological Cybernetics

Gang Wang
University of Illinois at
    Urbana-Champaign

Jonas Wulff
RWTH Aachen University, Germany

Benjamin Yao
University of California, Los Angeles

Song Chun Zhu
Lotus Hill Research Institute

CHAPTER 1

The Evolution of Object Categorization and the Challenge of Image Abstraction

Sven J. Dickinson

1.1 Introduction

In 2004, I was a guest at the Center for Machine Perception at the Czech Technical University. During my visit, a graduate student was kind enough to show me around Prague, including a visit to the Museum of Modern and Contemporary Art (Veletržní Palác). It was there that I saw the sculpture by Karel Nepraš entitled "Great Dialogue," a photograph of which appears in Figure 1.1. The instant I laid eyes on the sculpture, I recognized it as two humanoid figures seated and facing each other; when I've presented a 2-D image (Fig. 1.1) of the sculpture to classroom students and seminar audiences, their recognition of the two figures was equally fast. What's remarkable is that at the level of local features (whether local 2-D appearance or local 3-D structure), there's little, if any, resemblance to the features constituting real 3-D humans or their 2-D projections. Clearly, the local features, in terms of their specific appearance or configuration, are irrelevant, for individually they bear no causal relation to humans. Only when such local features are grouped, and then *abstracted*, do the salient parts and configuration begin to emerge, facilitating the recognition of a previously unseen exemplar object (in this case, a very distorted statue of a human) from a known category (humans).

The process of image (or feature) abstraction begins with the extraction of a set of image features over which an abstraction can be computed. If the abstraction is parts-based (providing the locality of representation required to support object recognition in the presence of occlusion and clutter), the local features must be perceptually grouped into collections that map to the abstract parts. For the features to be groupable, nonaccidental relations [152] must exist between them. Although such relations could be appearance-based, such as color and texture affinity, appearance is seldom generic to a category. Had the statue been painted a different color or textured with stripes or spots, for example, recognition would have been unaffected. Clearly, we require more powerful grouping cues that reflect the shape regularities that exist in our world – cues that have long been posited by the perceptual organization community [131, 265, 42, 43].

The ability to group together shape-based local features, such as contours or regions, is an important first step that has been acknowledged by shape-based object

Figure 1.1. The two shapes depicted in this statue clearly represent two humanoid figures seated and facing each other. At the level of local features, the figures are unrecognizable. At a more abstract level, however, the coarse parts of the figures begin to emerge, which, along with their relations, facilitate object categorization. The local features that constitute the abstract parts were not learned from training examples (they don't exist on a real human), nor were they grouped/abstracted using a prior target (human) model. This sculpture by Karel Nepraš, entitled "Great Dialogue," is found in the Museum of Modern and Contemporary Art (Veletržní Palác), in Prague. Image reproduced with permission. (See color plate 1.1.)

recognition researchers since the 1960s [198]. However, the grouping of causally (i.e., nonaccidentally) related features is necessary but not sufficient for object categorization. Returning to Figure 1.1, the grouping of the various local features that make up the torso of one of the figures is indeed an extremely challenging and important problem. Having recovered and grouped a set of salient shape features, a typical recognition system would proceed to establish one-to-one correspondence between salient image features (in the grouping) and salient model features. But herein lies the problem. The assumption that a one-to-one correspondence exists between local image features, such as points, patches, contours, or even regions, constrains the model to be little more than a template of the image.

The true correspondence between the collection of local features making up the torso and the torso "part" on any intuitive model of a human lies not at the level of local image features but at a more abstract level of shape features. For example, one such abstraction of the seated human model is shown in Figure 1.2, which includes an elliptical part corresponding to the torso.[1] Under a one-to-one correspondence

---

[1] This is not meant to imply that the abstraction process is necessarily 2-D. Many, including Biederman [27] and Pizlo [184], would argue that such abstraction is 3-D. In that case, the ellipses in Figure 1.2 might be interpreted as the projections of ellipsoids.

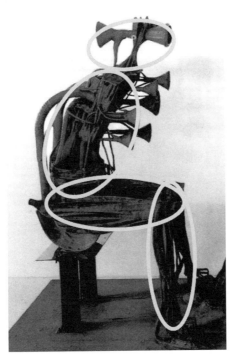

Figure 1.2. A shape abstraction of the seated humanoid on the left in Figure 1.1. Note that the boundaries of the shape abstraction do not map one-to-one to (or align well with) local features (e.g., contours) in the image. (See color plate 1.2.)

assumption, the myriad local features making up the statue torso (including many long, "salient" contours) must be abstracted before correspondence with the model torso can be established. It is important to note that this abstraction does not live explicitly in the image; that is, it is not simply a subset of the grouped image features. Moreover, although such an abstraction clearly requires a model (in this case, an elliptical shape "prior"), the model assumes no object- or scene-level knowledge.

The problem of abstraction is arguably the most important and most challenging problem facing researchers in object categorization. This is not a new problem, but one that was far more commonly acknowledged (but no more effectively solved) by early categorization researchers whose models captured object shape at high levels of abstraction. Over the last four decades, our inability to recover effectively such abstractions from real images of real objects has led us to increasingly specific object recognition domains that require little or no abstraction. Understanding this evolution not only brings the abstraction problem into focus, but helps to identify the many important contributions made by categorization researchers over the last four decades.

1.2 Avoiding the Abstraction Problem: A Historical Trend

The evolution of object recognition over the past 40 years has followed a very clear path, as illustrated in Figure 1.3. In the 1970s, the recognition community focused on generic

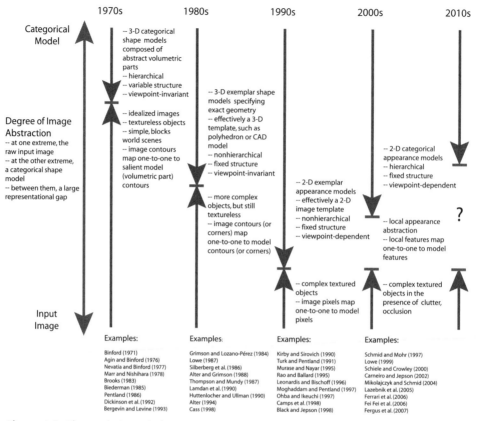

Figure 1.3. The evolution of object categorization over the past four decades (see text for discussion).

(alternatively, prototypical, categorical, or coarse) 3-D shape representations in support of object categorization. Objects were typically modeled as constructions of 3-D volumetric parts, such as generalized cylinders (e.g., [29, 2, 169, 45]), superquadrics (e.g., [176, 91, 229, 107, 238, 143, 144]), or geons (e.g., [27, 72, 74, 73, 24, 191, 40]). Figure 1.4 illustrates an example output from Brooks' ACRONYM system, which recognized both categories and subcategories from the constraints on the projections of generalized cylinders and their relations. The main challenge facing these early systems was the *representational gap* that existed between the low-level features that could be reliably extracted and the abstract nature of the model components. Rather than addressing this representational gap through the development of effective abstraction mechanisms, the community effectively eliminated the gap by bringing the images closer to the models. This was accomplished by removing object surface markings and structural detail, controlling lighting conditions, and reducing scene clutter. Edges in the image could then be assumed to map directly (one-to-one) to the occluding boundaries (separating figure from background) and surface discontinuities of the high-order volumetric parts making up the models.

The results left many unsatisfied, as the images and objects were often contrived (including blocks world scenes), and the resulting systems were unable to deal with real objects imaged under real conditions. Nevertheless, some very important principles

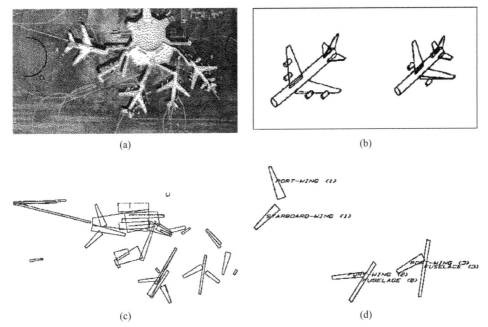

Figure 1.4. Brooks' ACRONYM system [45] recognized 3-D objects by searching for the projections of their volumetric parts and relations: (a) input image; (b) 3-D models composed of generalized cylinders; (c) extracted ribbons from extracted edges; and (d) recognized objects. Images courtesy of Rod Brooks.

emerged in the 1970s, many of which are being rediscovered by today's categorization community:

1. the importance of shape (e.g., contours) in defining object categories;
2. the importance of viewpoint-invariant, 3-D shape representations;
3. the importance of symmetry and other nonaccidental relations in feature grouping;
4. the need for distributed representations composed of shareable parts and their relations to help manage modeling complexity, to support effective indexing (the process of selecting candidate object models that might account for the query), to support object articulation, and to facilitate the recognition of occluded objects;
5. the need for hierarchical representations, including both part/whole hierarchies and abstraction hierarchies;
6. the need for scalability to large databases – that is, the "detection" or target recognition problem (as it was then known) is but a special case of the more general recognition (from a large database) problem, and a linear search (one detector per object) of a large database is unacceptable; and
7. the need for variable structure – that is, the number of parts, their identities, and their attachments may vary across the exemplars belonging to a category.

The 1980s ushered in 3-D models that captured the exact shape of an object. Such models, inspired by CAD models, were effectively 3-D templates (e.g., [106, 225, 116, 152, 153, 240, 60, 5, 57, 61]). Figure 1.5 illustrates an example output from Lowe's SCERPO system, which recognized a 3-D polyhedral template of an

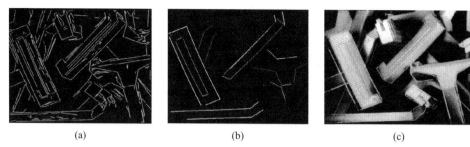

(a)   (b)   (c)

Figure 1.5. Lowe's SCERPO system [152] used perceptual grouping to prune hypothesized correspondences between image contours and polyhedral edges: (a) extracted edges; (b) extracted perceptual groups; and (c) detected objects and their poses. Images courtesy of David Lowe. (See color plate 1.5.)

object from nonaccidental groupings of features comprising its projection. Provided that such models could be acquired for a real object (requiring considerable overhead), the community found that it could build object recognition systems capable of recognizing real (albeit restricted) objects – a very important development indeed. Although object models were still viewpoint-invariant (since they were 3-D), hierarchical representations became less common as the models became less coarse-to-fine. This time, the representational gap was eliminated by bringing the model closer to the imaged object, which required the model to capture the exact geometry of the object. Moreover, because the presence of texture and surface markings seriously affected the search complexity of these systems, once again the objects were texture-free, so that a salient image edge mapped to, for example, a polyhedral edge. Again, there was dissatisfaction, because the resulting systems were unable to recognize complex objects with complex surface markings. Moreover, the overhead required to construct a 3-D model, either by hand or automatically from image data, was significant.

It is important to note that although both the generations of systems just discussed assumed a one-to-one correspondence between salient image features and model features, there was a dramatic redefinition of the problem from category recognition to exemplar recognition. In earlier systems, the bottom-up recovery of high-level volumetric parts and their relations, forming powerful indexing structures, meant that models could accommodate a high degree of within-class shape variation. However, as the scope of indexing structures later retreated to individual lines, points, or small groups thereof, their indexing ambiguity rose dramatically, and extensive verification was essential to test an abundance of weak model hypotheses. The need for 3-D model alignment, as a prerequisite for verification, required that models were essentially 3-D templates that modeled the shape of an exemplar rather than a category (although some frameworks supported the articulation of rigid parts). Still, at the expense of backing down from the more challenging categorization problem, recognition had begun to penetrate real industrial domains, providing real solutions to real problems.

Most object recognition systems up to this point employed 3-D models and attempted to recognize them in 2-D images (3-D from 2-D). However, a number of researchers (e.g., [102, 23, 213, 251, 47, 263, 75, 20]) began to study the invariant properties of views and their application to view-based 3-D object recognition (2-D from 2-D). Inspired by the early aspect graph work of Koenderink and van Doorn [129], a large

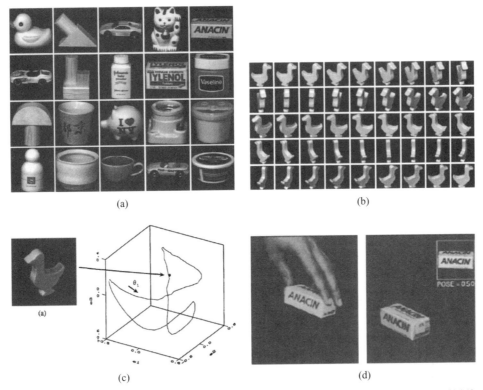

Figure 1.6. Murase and Nayar's appearance-based (view-based) recognition system [166]: (a) a database of objects; (b) a dense set of views is acquired for each object; (c) the views trace out a manifold in low-dimensional space, with each view lying on the manifold; (d) recognizing a query object. Images reproduced from [166] with permission of the *International Journal of Computer Vision*, Springer.

community of researchers began to explore the properties of aspect graphs in support of view-based object recognition [118, 132, 185, 76, 206, 233, 74, 73, 79, 70, 77, 101, 100, 217, 230]. Although view-based methods were gaining momentum, they still lagged behind the 3-D from 2-D methods, which were now shifting toward the use of geometric invariants to enable recognition from larger object databases [136, 165, 94].

In the early 1990s, a number of factors led to a major paradigm shift in the recognition community, marking the decline of 3-D shape models in favor of appearance-based recognition. Faster machines could now support the high throughput needed to accommodate the multitude of image templates required to model a 3-D object. Moreover, no 3-D modeling (including software and trained personnel) was required for model acquisition; a mere turntable and camera would suffice. More importantly, by focusing on the explicit pixel-based appearance of an object, the complex, error-prone problem of segmentation could be avoided. For the first time, recognition systems were constructed that could recognize arbitrarily complex objects, complete with texture and surface markings (e.g., [128, 250, 166, 193, 142, 162, 170, 49, 32]). Figure 1.6 illustrates an example output from the appearance-based (view-based) 3-D object recognition system of Murase and Nayar, which used PCA and nearest-neighbor search to reduce drastically the complexity of image correlation over a large database.

(a)   (b)

Figure 1.7. Learning scale-invariant parts-based models from examples (from Fergus et al. [87]): (a) Learned motorcycle model with ellipses representing part covariances and labels representing probability of occurrence; (b) example model detections in query images, with colored circles representing matched part hypotheses. Images reproduced from [87] with permission of the *International Journal of Computer Vision*, Springer. (See color plate 1.7.)

This time, the representational gap was eliminated by bringing the models all the way down to the image, which yielded models that were images themselves. The resulting systems could therefore recognize only exemplar objects, which were specific objects that had been seen at training time. Despite a number of serious initial limitations of this approach, including difficulties in dealing with background clutter, illumination change, occlusion, translation, rotation, and scaling, the approach gained tremendous popularity, and some of these obstacles were overcome [142, 49, 21, 141, 19]. But the templates were still global, and invariance to scale and viewpoint could not be achieved.

To cope with these problems, the current decade (2000s) has seen the appearance model community turn to the same principles adopted by their shape-based predecessors: a move from global to local representations (parts), and the use of part representations that are invariant to changes in translation, scale, image rotation, illumination, articulation, and viewpoint (e.g., [154, 155, 261, 262, 50, 1, 53, 52, 161, 137, 130, 210]). Whereas early systems characterized collections of such features as either overly rigid geometric configurations or, at the opposite extreme, as unstructured "bags," later systems (e.g., [209, 256, 51, 52, 89, 90, 82, 87, 189]) added pairwise spatial constraints, again drawing on classical shape modeling principles from the 1970s and 1980s. For example, Figure 1.7 illustrates the system of Fergus et al. [87], in which a scale-invariant, parts-based object model is learned from a set of annotated training examples and is used to detect new instances of the model in query images. Unlike the systems of the 1970s and 1980s, today's systems are applied to images of cluttered scenes containing complex, textured objects. Yet something may have been lost in our evolution from shape to appearance, for today's appearance-based recognition systems are no more able to recognize yesterday's line drawing abstractions than were yesterday's systems able to recognize today's images of real objects.

Like the models of the 1990s, today's models have been brought close to the image; however, this trend is clearly reversing and starting to swing back. Unlike the previous three decades, the representational gap has not been completely eliminated. The scope of a local feature has expanded from a single pixel to a scale-invariant patch. Moreover, the patch representation encodes not the explicit pixel values but rather a weak abstraction of these values (e.g., the gradient histograms found in SIFT [155] or the radial distribution of mass found in the shape context of Belongie et al. [22]). The increased level of abstraction offered by these local features supports an increased amount of within-class variation of a category's appearance. This proved to be sufficient to handle some restricted categories whose exemplars do indeed share the same local features. Such categories, including cars, faces, people, and motorcycles, can be characterized as geometrically regular configurations of recurring, distinctive, local features. However, such categories are likely to be the exception rather than the rule, for local features are seldom generic to a shape category. In fact, for most categories, it's quite possible for two exemplars to not share a single local appearance-based feature.

If one extrapolates this upward trajectory in (decreasing) feature specificity, one might first predict a return to those image contours that encode the shape (occluding boundaries or surface discontinuities) of an object – features that are far more generic to a category than appearance.[2] Yet the cost of more generic features is their increased ambiguity, for a small fragment of contour (e.g., resulting from a curve partitioning process that parses contours at curvature discontinuities or inflections) carries very little category-specific information. As proposed decades earlier, the solution lies in grouping together causally related, nearby contours into more distinctive structures.

How distinctive depends entirely on the problem. In a detection (or target recognition) task, for which model selection is provided, the need for complex, bottom-up contour grouping to yield distinctive indexing structures is absent in the presence of a strong template; rather, only minimal grouping is required to test a particular model. This is precisely the approach taken in recent work (e.g., [167, 172, 87, 145, 88]) which builds relational models of contour fragments in support of object detection. However, in a more general recognition task, more ambitious domain-independent grouping, which clearly introduces additional complexity, is essential. To help manage this complexity, feature hierarchies have reemerged, in combination with powerful learning tools, to yield exciting new categorization frameworks [7, 6, 179, 41, 241, 92, 171, 4, 242, 273].[3] Figure 1.8 illustrates the system of Todorovic and Ahuja [242], in which a region-based hierarchical object model is learned from training examples and used to detect new instances of the model in query images.

But what of the more general categorization problem of recognition from a large database? Continuing our trajectory of working with image contours, we will have to group them into larger, more distinctive indexing structures that can effectively prune a large database down to a few candidates.[4] If we want our models to be articulation invariant, then our indexing structures will map naturally to an object's parts. Moreover,

---

[2] In all fairness, appearance-based methods (based on explicit pixel values) implicitly encode both shape and nonshape information, but cannot distinguish between the two. Hence, they are less invariant to changes in appearance when shape is held constant.

[3] In fact, Tsotsos [247, 248, 249] proved that such hierarchies are essential for managing the complexity of visual recognition.

[4] Indexing can take many forms, including hashing (e.g., [136, 93, 94]), decision trees (including kd-trees) e.g. [118, 102, 20, 214, 215], and coarse-to-fine model hierarchies, (e.g., [45]). All assume that the query object is unknown and that a linear search of the database is unacceptable (or intractable).

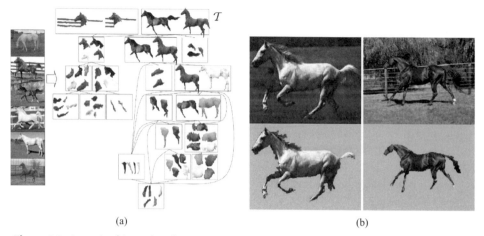

(a)   (b)

Figure 1.8. Learning hierarchical segmentation tree-based models from examples (from Todorovic and Ahuja [242]): (a) learned hierarchical tree-union model (right) from examples (left), capturing the recursive containment and spatial layout of regions making up the model; (b) example model detections (below) in query images (above). Images reproduced from [242], ©2008 IEEE with permission.

if we want to reduce the dimensionality of the parts to allow part sharing across categories, then we somehow have to boost the power of our indexing structures to offset the increased ambiguity of our parts. That means grouping parts together until the resulting indexing structures are sufficiently powerful. Interestingly enough, this is exactly the original framework proposed in the 1970s, meaning that if our prediction holds, we will have come full circle. If we do revisit this paradigm, we will do so with vastly faster machines, more powerful inference and search algorithms, and a desire to learn representations rather than to handcraft them. Yet has this convergence of machine learning and object categorization led to deeper representational insight?

The trend over the last four decades is clear. Rather than developing mechanisms for image and shape abstraction that are required to bridge the representational gap between our favorite "salient" image features and true categorical models, we have consistently and artificially eliminated the gap, originally by moving the images up the abstraction hierarchy (simulating the abstraction) and later by moving the models down the abstraction hierarchy (making them less categorical). Driven by a desire to build recognition systems that could solve real problems, the evolution of recognition from category to exemplar was well-motivated. But the community is clearly headed back toward categorization. Although our models are slowly creeping back up the abstraction hierarchy, image features are still tightly coupled to model features, and the critical problem of abstraction continues to receive little attention. Until this important problem is addressed, progress in more general categorization seems unlikely.

1.3 The Abstraction of Shape

In the 1970s, there was no shortage of abstract shape representations. For example, Binford's generalized cylinder (GC) [29] (see Fig. 1.4) was a powerful, symmetry-based

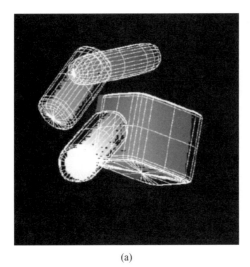
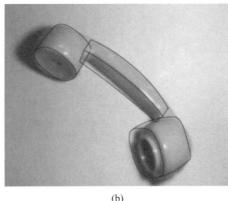

(a) (b)

Figure 1.9. Two powerful 3-D shape abstractions evolved from the generalized cylinder (GC), each retaining a powerful symmetry property and each restricting the GC in a different way: (a) superquadric ellipsoids [17] were typically recovered from 3-D range data (from Leonardis et al. [144], ©1997 IEEE); (b) geons [27] were typically recovered from 2-D image data (from Pilu and Fisher [181]; image reproduced with permission of Springer).

part model whose complexity was unbounded.[5] To manage the complexity of bottom-up shape recovery, a number of restrictions were introduced that arguably strengthened the fundamental role of symmetry. Such restrictions included, for example, a straight axis, a homogeneous sweep function, a linear sweep function, or a rotationally symmetric cross-section [169, 2, 159, 45, 253, 272, 188, 31, 133, 186, 160, 30, 157, 59]. Although an abstract object model composed of restricted GCs and their spatial relations could support powerful categorization, recovering such parts and relations from images of real objects was the stumbling block. When image contours mapped one-to-one to the occluding boundaries or surface discontinuities of restricted GCs, such recovery was indeed possible. However, when the projected model contours were not a subset of the observed image contours, part recovery was not possible. Abstraction mechanisms for mapping observed image contours to abstract model contours were simply not available at that time.

In the 1980s, two powerful symmetry-based, volumetric shape abstractions emerged; they were founded on the symmetry axis concept, but each took a very different approach to restricting the complexity of the GC. Superquadric ellipsoids [17, 176, 229, 107, 91, 143, 144, 71] provided a rich set of deformations with a small set of parameters. Although most successful superquadric ellipsoid recovery lived in the range data domain (see Fig. 1.9(a)), where a surface model could often be abstracted from a cloud of 3-D shape points, their recovery from 2-D images was far more challenging and far less successful, because of the lack of abstraction mechanisms to map observed image contours to abstract model contours [69].

---

[5] The generalized cylinder is defined by axis, cross-section, and sweep functions, each of which can be arbitrarily complex.

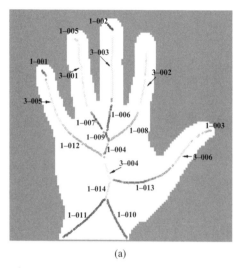 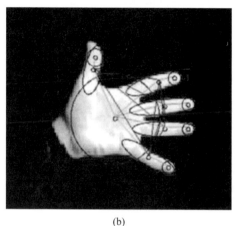

(a) (b)

Figure 1.10. Two powerful 2-D qualitative shape abstractions: (a) the shock graph (from Siddiqi et al. [223]), whose parts represent a qualitative partitioning of Blum's medial axis transform [35], and whose edges span adjacent parts, directed from larger to smaller (image reproduced from [223] with permission of the *International Journal of Computer Vision*, Springer); (b) the blob graph (from Shokoufandeh et al. [218]), whose parts capture elongated symmetric structure at different scales, and whose edges capture parent-child (topological=green) and sibling (geometric=red) relationships between parts (image reproduced from [218] with permission of *Computer Vision and Image Understanding*, Elsevier). (See color plate 1.10.)

Biederman's geons [27, 28] represented a qualitative partitioning of the space of GCs according to simple dichotomous and trichotomous properties that humans could distinguish effortlessly. Although this psychological theory inspired a subcommunity of categorization researchers to develop computational models for geon recovery [25, 24, 191, 192, 268, 66, 181] (see Fig. 1.9(b)), including more general qualitative volumetric part models [72, 74, 73, 67], these models faced the same challenge as their GC ancestors: salient image contours do not necessarily map one-to-one to abstract model contours. Although proponents of GCs, restricted GCs, superquadric ellipsoids, and geons were well motivated in attempting to model an object's abstract parts and their relations, their assumption that the features comprising these models could be directly observed in the image was unrealistic. Instead of pursuing the abstraction mechanisms that would allow such modeling frameworks to be further explored, the frameworks were abandoned owing to their inability to recognize real images of real objects.

Blum's medial axis transform (MAT) [35, 36, 37] is a 2-D axial symmetry-based shape description that, much like Binford's GC that followed it, spawned an entire shape subcommunity. Just as geons imposed a qualitative partitioning of the space of GCs, shock graphs [223] (see Fig. 1.10(a)) imposed a qualitative partitioning on the branches of the MAT. Moreover, just as geons inspired a community of geon-based recognition systems, shock graphs inspired a community of shock graph–based recognition systems [223, 174, 212], and 3-D medial surfaces (analogous to medial axes) led to medial surface graph–based recognition systems [224] (the mathematics, algorithms, and applications of medial representations are detailed in [222]). However, just as GC-based systems assumed that salient contours in the image map one-to-one to contours generated by the GC model, the medial axis–based community assumed that salient contour points (i.e., *all* points on an object's silhouette) map one-to-one to points generated by the MAT model. For either framework to succeed on real images of real objects, image abstraction must yield a set of abstract contours that, in turn, map to the features of an abstract categorical model.

One might ask to what extent abstract shape recovery can be purely bottom-up. Part models like the unrestricted GC in 3-D and a medial branch in 2-D impose no mid-level shape priors (i.e., shape constraints) to help regularize their recovery from real images of real objects. As a consequence, too much stock is placed in features arising from simple bottom-up segmentation, such as contours or regions, and the assumption that they map one-to-one to salient model features. If one looks back at the geon-based recognition systems, one sees that geons provided a powerful set of regularizing constraints on the data, but were never used as the basis for an image abstraction process. Shock graphs offered a similar set of constraints, but have also not yet been effectively used as the basis for image abstraction, although there have been efforts to regularize, in a bottom-up sense, the MAT [8, 236, 255, 83, 10].

The mid-level shape prior of symmetry has been used, albeit with limited success, as a basis for such image abstraction. Multiscale blobs, including the work of Crowley [62, 63], Lindeberg [148, 149], Blostein and Ahuja [34], and Shokoufandeh et al. [220, 218] all employ ridge and/or blob models (see Fig. 1.10(b)) as symmetry-based mid-level part constraints. Even though these models provide excellent regularization and have led to powerful hierarchical shape representations for recognition, they have not been successfully recovered from textured objects. Moreover, it's not clear whether they provide a rich enough shape description, for unlike shock graphs or geons, the parts cannot bend or taper.

Symmetry is an invariant in all these approaches, and has its roots in Gestalt psychology. The symmetry-based abstractions (superquadrics, geons, and shock graphs) represent but a small fraction of a much broader community working with symmetry-based shape models for object categorization, both in 3-D (e.g., [164, 177, 178, 239]) and in 2-D (e.g., [147, 200, 211, 95, 274, 3, 126, 271, 9]). Although symmetry provides a basis for perceptual grouping of image structure, such as contours, it's important to realize that in general (at least for real images of real objects), the groups may not be in a form suitable for direct matching to an abstract model. Rather, the groups must be abstracted and regularized to yield a set of abstract features that only then can be matched to an abstract model. It is highly unlikely for such features to exist explicitly in the image; rather, they must be inferred from appropriate groupings of local features that we can extract. For example, in Figure 1.2, the elliptical contour defining any of the part abstractions does not exist explicitly in the image, but rather defines the extent of an elliptical cluster of local features that are causally related.

Finally, despite the community's focus on exemplar (or restricted category) recognition over the last 15 to 20 years, it is important to acknowledge that there has been an active community that is committed to the problems of shape abstraction and categorization. Apart from the symmetry-based frameworks described earlier, important shape abstractions include shape contexts [22], inner-distance [150] in 2-D and shape distributions [173] in 3-D, multiscale boundary-based methods (e.g., [97]), parameterized blob models (e.g., [122]), deformable models [18, 86, 269], and articulated models (e.g., [119, 194, 85, 264]). It is also important to acknowledge the work of the content-based image retrieval (CBIR) community [226]. Although they have focused less on the problems of segmentation, grouping, and shape abstraction, they have focused on powerful (typically global) abstractions of appearance that are appropriate for many image-retrieval tasks. One such image abstraction consists of simply representing an entire image at low (e.g., 32×32) resolution, the minimum resolution at which human subjects can correctly interpret images of natural scenes [244]. If the model database contains enough correctly labeled, low-resolution model images (e.g., 80,000,000 in [244]), the space of real images of real objects can be sampled densely enough to facilitate surprisingly effective, albeit restricted, forms of object categorization.

1.4 The Abstraction of Structure

Successful image abstraction into a set of abstract shape primitives is only part of the problem, for a recovered primitive configuration may still not match the configuration of the correct model. For example, a chair that has one leg has a very different part configuration than a chair that has four legs. In fact, for most categories, part structure is variable and must somehow be parameterized. Although the current recognition community is focused on strategies that assume a one-to-one correspondence between local image and model features, the need for models that accommodate variable structure was acknowledged long ago by, for example, Fu [96] and Rosenfeld [180, 202]. Brooks' ACRONYM system also parameterized structure, which allowed variable numbers of parts in an elaborate constraint manipulation system [45]. As the need to model structural variability is once again acknowledged, grammar-based methods, including AND/OR graphs, are beginning to reemerge, for example, in work by Zhu and Mumford [275] (see Fig. 1.11), Jin and Geman [123], and by Levinshtein et al. [146]. To the extent that the rewrite rules in a grammar can model the coarse-to-fine appearance of an object,[6] a grammar can provide an effective structural abstraction [146]. Other exciting categorization frameworks that support structural variability are also emerging, such as the hidden state shape models (HSSMs) of Wang et al. [259].

There have been other approaches to dealing with variable structure. One approach is to develop representations for structural abstraction, so that two configurations (or graphs) that have similar structure have similar structural abstractions. For example, in the domain of hierarchical structures, representing coarse-to-fine feature hierarchies that are ubiquitous in computer vision, Shokoufandeh et al. [219] draw on spectral graph theory to compute a low-dimensional abstraction of a directed acyclic graph (DAG). The eigenvalues of a DAGs antisymmetric adjacency matrix characterize the degree distribution of the graph's nodes, and are combined to define a low-dimensional vector description of the "shape" of a graph. This structural abstraction forms a basis for both indexing (nearest-neighbor search) as well as matching, unifying these two important problems in a common representational framework. However, the approach

---

[6] Recall Marr's famous coarse-to-fine representation of a human being with a single cylinder at the most abstract end of the modeling spectrum, and a detailed configuration down to the fingers at the least abstract end [158].

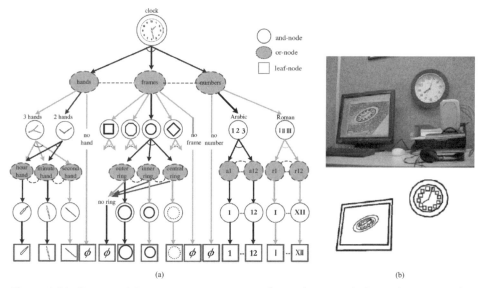

Figure 1.11. Parameterizing structure represents a form of structural abstraction, supporting less brittle object categories having variable structure. Drawing on the classical shape grammars of the 1960s and 1970s and on stochastic grammars from the computational linguistics community, Zhu and Mumford have rekindled interest in shape grammars. In this example, taken from [275], the clock grammar shown in (a) is used to recognize the two clocks (real and display) in the image shown in (b). Images reproduced from [275], courtesy of Now Publishers. (See color plate 1.11.)

implicitly assumes that an effective grouping process has been used to generate the hierarchy.

In the absence of a strong set of grouping rules, a given set of extracted features may give rise to an exponential number of possible abstraction hierarchies. For example, consider the number of region adjacency graphs that can be abstracted from a single region adjacency graph by contracting an edge (merging two regions) to yield a new graph, and repeating. However, in a supervised setting, two exemplar graphs, which may not share a single node in correspondence, may be known to represent the same category. Keselman [127] searched for the *lowest common abstraction* of a set of exemplar graphs – that is, the most informative graph derivable from each of the exemplars. Although the technique was able to abstract a categorical model from a set of examples for which input feature correspondence might not exist, the method provided little insight into generating appropriate abstractions for a single image, because it was too dependent on "evidence" provided by other images known to belong to the same category.

Keselman's approach sought to group features to support one-to-one correspondence at some higher level, representing a many-to-many correspondence at the original level. An alternative strategy, proposed by Demirci et al. [64], computes an explicit many-to-many node correspondence between the original edge-weighted graphs. Drawing on recent work from the graph embedding community, the graphs are embedded with low distortion into a vector space, where shortest-path distances between nodes in a graph are reflected in the geometric distances between the nodes' corresponding points in the embedding space. The resulting points are matched many-to-many using the

Earth Mover's Distance (EMD) algorithm, in which the computed flows specify the many-to-many node correspondences between the original graphs.

The approach cleverly transforms an intractable combinatorial problem into a tractable geometric problem, but it relies on assigning an appropriate set of edge weights in the original graphs. If an edge weight is small, the two nodes (spanned by the edge) are embedded nearby to one another, and will likely receive flow from a common source in the EMD solution. A small edge weight can be thought of as a high probability that the features are nonaccidentally related. Therefore, the approach is only as successful as the perceptual grouping heuristics used to generate the graph and its edge weights. Moreover, the many-to-many solution yields only corresponding collections, not corresponding abstractions. Still, it does acknowledge the need to overcome the popular assumption that for every salient image feature, there exists a corresponding model feature. In fact, the need for many-to-many matching is acknowledged by a growing subcommunity. Important approaches have been proposed based on graph-edit distance [46, 212, 199], spectral methods [48], tree-union [241], association graph methods [175], and the emerging grammar-based methods mentioned earlier.

Finally, a discussion of shape and structural abstraction is incomplete without a reference to functional object descriptions [201, 99, 267, 254], which can be thought of as the highest form of shape abstraction. Many categories of objects exhibit a high degree of shape and structural variability; for such categories, explicit geometric models are too brittle. One might argue that even shape grammars, in their attempt to explicitly encode the possible structural variations, might be too unwieldy if the within-class structural variability is too high. In response to such categories, Stark and Bowyer [231, 232] proposed a number of functional predicates that are designed to test the essential functional features of a model whose structural variability could be infinite. Although these features could be described as functional (e.g., a chair provides horizontal support, vertical support, foot clearance, etc), such functional primitives could, in fact, be thought of as highly abstract geometric primitives (which were, in fact, computed from 3-D shape data). Rivlin et al. [197] suggested that reasoning about function first requires the extraction of high-order shape primitives, and that the mapping from shape primitives to functional primitives was many-to-one. Putting these two ideas together, such a many-to-one mapping could be considered a further form of shape abstraction. Unfortunately, neither the mechanisms for high-level primitive shape extraction nor the ability to abstract shape to the level of functional primitives were available. As a result, functional models lost popularity during the mid-1990s.

1.5 Segmentation, Grouping, and the Role of Models: Beyond Target Recognition

Today's categorization community has clearly acknowledged the deficiency of appearance-based region segmentation to correctly separate figure from ground, and the need for some sort of prior knowledge to overcome this deficiency. Although the perceptual organization community sought to inject mid-level, object-independent knowledge into the process, there has been a tendency recently to by-pass mid-level knowledge and inject object-dependent knowledge into the process

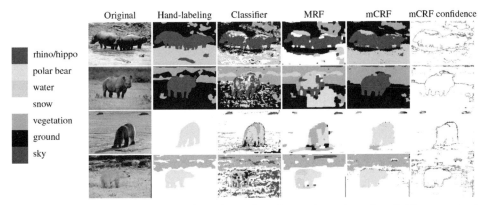

Figure 1.12. Image labeling results from the multiscale conditional random field approach of He et al. [110]. From labeled training images, knowledge of an object's appearance, position, size, and background can be learned and applied to the segmentation of test images. Image reproduced from [110], ©2004 IEEE with permission. (See color plate 1.12.)

(e.g., [39, 252, 140, 270, 234, 151, 163, 243, 266, 260, 38, 111]) (see Fig. 1.12). Cast as a knowledge-based (or top-down) segmentation problem, it is important to note that this bears a close resemblance to classical target (or model-based) recognition, in which an individual object model (whether exemplar or category) is used to constrain image segmentation. In any classical target recognition task, the target was typically aligned with its detected instance, with the alignment defining (as a by-product) a figure/ground separation (including a parsing of the object into parts if the representation was parts-based). Although target recognition was an important problem, particularly in military applications, knowing exactly which object to search for in the image, and, hence, which constraints to apply, was considered a special case of the more general problem of recognition from a large database.

Today's knowledge-based systems are superior to their early predecessors, particularly in terms of their ability to learn such constraints from training data. Once again however, the problem of mid-level shape abstraction has been avoided through the use of overly strong model assumptions. If the image to be labeled or segmented can contain any of 10,000 object categories (with arbitrary viewpoint, scale, articulation, occlusion, etc.), such techniques clearly don't scale up, and an indexing mechanism is required to prune all but a few promising candidates. Local features will have to be grouped and abstracted into mid-level primitives to support articulation, occlusion, and within-class shape deformation. Given a small vocabulary of such primitives, primitive extraction defines a tractable recognition task in its own right. When an extracted ("recognized") primitive is combined with a few other nearby primitives, they together yield a highly distinctive indexing structure. Somehow, the more specific detection problem has, in recent years, drawn the community's attention away from the more general categorization problem. In doing so, the need for mid-level, generic parts and relations in the presence of a strong, top-down model is greatly diminished, just as it was in the classical verification-oriented recognition systems of the 1980s.

Although the detection problem may have drawn attention away from the bottom-up perceptual grouping and mid-level shape abstraction problems, it has nonetheless led to some very powerful abstraction mechanisms based on local image statistics. Such statistics, computed over some appropriate area, can take the form of distributions of semilocal features, with overlapping spatial support and some degree of spatial flexibility, ranging from total flexibility in a bag-of-features model [78] to multiple levels of spatial flexibility in a multiresolution, multilevel histogram pyramid [104]. Multi-level bag-of-feature models are by no means the only way to build representations with multiple levels of spatial selectivity. Biologically inspired architectures like Hier-archical Model and X (HMAX) [216] or convolutional neural networks [138] construct hierarchical representations by alternating successive layers of convolution (template matching to prototypes) and rectification (max pooling operations over afferent unit responses) in order to progressively build descriptors with increased invariance to scale, image rotation, and position. Local image statistics can also be used as inputs for train-ing predictive models (complex, potentially multivalued, or one-to-many mappings) of 3-D abstractions, such as planar structures [112] or human poses [26, 228, 227, 125].

Although these approaches focus primarily on appearance and less on shape, they clearly acknowledge the need for flexible, abstract models that are robust to within-class variation. However, because they operate in a detection environment, the problem of segmentation is typically avoided by simply running the detector at all locations, orientations, and scales, until the image statistics inside a window match that of the target. Such an approach, which effectively tries all possible segmentations (over which the feature distribution is computed), simply does not scale up to either general view-point invariance or recognition from large databases. Perceptual grouping mechanisms (perhaps based on feature statistics, e.g., [196, 195]) must first group together causally related features into parts without regard to object class. Only then should shape statis-tics over the part (i.e., feature group) be computed, offering a powerful part abstraction mechanism.

1.6 Expanding Model Scope: Objects to Scenes

During the golden years of (Defense Advanced Research Projects Agency) DARPA-funded image understanding research in the United States, much of the object recog-nition community was devoted to *knowledge-based vision systems* (sometimes called *expert vision systems* [203], or *context-based vision systems*), which exploited scene-specific, contextual knowledge to provide additional evidence with which to disam-biguate poorly segmented objects (see Fig. 1.13). Early seminal work by researchers such as Tenenbaum and Barrow [237] and Hanson and Riseman [108] in the late 1970s popularized the integration of segmentation and interpretation. Over the next 10 to 15 years, the knowledge-based vision community manually constructed models that mapped functional or semantic relationships between objects in a scene to geometric relationships among their projections in the image. The resulting systems were ap-plied to such diverse problems as aerial photo interpretation (e.g., [117, 109, 124]), autonomous road following (e.g., [68]), mechanical system image analysis (e.g., [44]), medical image analysis (e.g., [246, 103]), perceptual grouping (e.g., [207]), or more general contexts (e.g., [235]).

Although the idea that domain-specific knowledge must play an important role was widely adopted by those seeking solutions to practical problems, there were those who

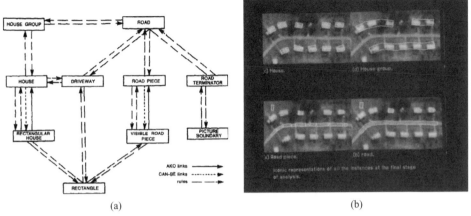

(a)   (b)

Figure 1.13. The SIGMA image understanding system of Hwang et al. [117]: (a) a contextual model of a suburban housing development; (b) detecting instances of the contextual model's components in an image. Contextual constraints can help overcome poor segmentation and spurious hypotheses. Images reproduced from [117] with permission of *Computer Vision, Graphics, and Image Processing*, Elsevier.

dismissed knowledge-based vision systems as ad hoc or overly specific. Such systems were typically very slow and largely unsuccessful, for the problems they addressed were often extremely difficult. Moreover, encoding domain knowledge in a system required significant overhead, and the fact that knowledge of one domain rarely lent itself to the next domain did not encourage their widespread adoption. When appearance-based vision appeared on the scene in the early 1990s, coupled with a decreasing DARPA presence, knowledge-based vision systems all but disappeared. They would make a comeback, however, just as shape-based categorization has reemerged in the mainstream.

The first hints at a return to knowledge-based vision have come in the form of encoding scene context using simple spatial image statistics *without* requiring explicit segmentation or grouping (e.g., [58, 245, 110, 134]) (see Fig. 1.14). Although appropriate for the recognition of very broad contexts (e.g., label a scene as containing people vs. furniture), the lack of segmentation prevents the localization of individual objects that might comprise a more specific context. Moreover, contexts whose components differ in shape (rather than appearance) cannot be addressed without segmentation. Still, unlike earlier generations of context-based or knowledge-based systems, contextual knowledge is learned automatically from annotated training examples, which makes such a framework far easier to transport to other domains. In more recent work, the community is returning to the classical ideas of combining object recognition and 3-D scene understanding, with notions of scene context capturing high-level relationships among objects (e.g., the fact that cars are typically found on roads and people are not typically detected on the sides of a building [113]).

When an object's identity is ambiguous, it makes little sense to ignore the contextual clues offered by nearby objects. If a context is too strictly specified (i.e., components appear at particular locations, scales, and orientations in an image), then context-based vision amounts to little more than brittle object detection. Interacting with a complex environment means explicitly recognizing its objects, whose number, location,

(a)   (b)

Figure 1.14. From a set of labeled training images, Torralba [245] learns the correlation between context and object properties based on low-level image feature statistics computed over
annotated training images: (a) test images for which $p(vehicles|v_c) < 0.05$, where v_c is a vector
of contextual features derived from statistics computed over low-level image features; (b) test
images for which $p(vehicles|v_c) > 0.95$. Images reproduced from [245] with permission of the
International Journal of Computer Vision, Springer.

orientation (in both the image and in depth), scale, shape, and appearance may be highly
variable. The fact that objects are coupled to form contexts (or environments, such as
streetscapes, dining rooms, offices, or army barracks) means that large object databases
can be partitioned into smaller, context-specific databases. Determining what context
(database) you're looking at requires that you first segment, group, and index into a
set of contexts. The most likely context, in turn, defines the context-specific database
with which to constrain the recognition of the unidentified or ambiguous objects in
the scene. Because contextual indexing lies at the object level, and because the objects
making up a context are typically categorical, we're back to the same problem of shape
and configuration abstraction in support of object recognition. Contexts are to their
component objects as objects are to their component parts. In either case, we must start
with the segmentation, abstraction, and grouping of an object's parts.

Finally, on the topic of increasing model scope, one might imagine moving beyond
purely visual (shape-based or appearance-based) models toward more semantic models,
which couple visual and semantic information. Learning the associations between
visual features and nouns in training image captions has led to augmented models
that combine visual appearance with an object name, supporting automatic image
annotation (e.g., [56, 15, 11, 16, 13, 33, 12, 258, 55, 120, 121, 54, 14, 190]) (see
Fig. 1.15). The linguistic knowledge exploited by such approaches is minimal, however,
and the unrealized potential for object names to invoke powerful semantic knowledge
to guide image segmentation and scene interpretation is enormous. Although some
efforts (e.g., [115, 114]) have exploited the restricted semantic information captured
in WordNet's IS-A hierarchy [84], little work has tapped into more general semantic
knowledge that may be captured through statistical analysis of text corpora.

1.7 Managing Search Complexity: The Case for 3-D Models

Early categorization systems typically modeled objects in 3-D and sought to infer
3-D model features from 2-D image features. In the words of the distinguished vision

| Toronto Maple Leafs vs. Montreal Canadiens | Florida's Olli Jokinen gets bumped by Alexei Ponikarovsky of the Maple Leafs | Mats Sundin of the Toronto Maple Leafs misses a scoring chance against Ryan Miller of the Buffalo Sabres | "Maple Leafs" |

(a)   (b)

Figure 1.15. Learning structured appearance models for image annotation (from Jamieson et al. [121]): (a) Sample input image-caption collection, in which each image contains hundreds of local (SIFT) features (yellow crosses). From the input training collection, associations between structured subsets of local features and particular nouns are learned (discovered); (b) sample output, in which one of the objects learned during training (representing the Maple Leafs logo) is detected (shown with red features and green relationships in a yellow box), and annotated with its name ("Maple Leafs"). (See color plate 1.15.)

researcher, Jan-Olof Eklundh, "We need to build vision systems that look at the world, not at images." When 3-D models gave way to appearance models in the early 1990s, the need for viewpoint invariance in a recognition system translated from a single viewpoint-invariant 3-D model to a dense collection of 2-D views. However, The appearance-based community was not the first to propose view-based 3-D object recognition, for the view-based [102, 23, 213, 251, 47, 263, 75, 20] and aspect graph–based [129, 118, 132, 185, 76, 206, 233, 74, 73, 70, 77, 101, 100, 217, 230] communities had studied both the theoretical as well as the practical implications of the approach.

The cost of transforming the 3-D recognition problem into a 2-D one is significant [79]. Plantinga and Dyer [185] proved that for a *rigid* polyhedron with n faces, the complexity of its aspect graph, in terms of the number of distinct configurations of features observed as the viewing sphere is traversed, is $O(n^9)$. For articulating or deformable categories, the complexity becomes even more prohibitive. One way out of this dilemma is to apply the classical parts-based approach, using aspects to model not the entire objects, but rather the views of a small number of 3-D parts, which, in turn, could be combined to form an infinite number of 3-D objects [74, 73, 70]. Thus, the number of views is fixed, and independent of the number of objects in the database. Moreover, because the parts are simple (having low complexity in terms of surfaces), their aspect graphs are similarly simple.

The evolution of appearance-based categorization saw a curious movement away from viewpoint invariance (which would reduce the number of views required to model a 3-D object) to a focus on particular views of categories, such as the sides of cars, the fronts of faces, the sides of motorcycles, or the sides of horses (effectively ignoring all but a few of the views required to model a 3-D object). The earlier view-based recognition assumption of having to recognize all possible views of a 3-D object did not translate into a multitude of detectors, one per view class. Surprisingly, the current categorization community has only recently begun to return to the roots of view-based 3-D recognition, seeking view-based descriptions that offer greater viewpoint invariance.

(a)   (b)

Figure 1.16. Recovering 3-D surface layout from a single image (from Hoeim et al. [112]): (a) input image. (b) recovered surface layout: colors reflect class labels (green=support red=vertical; blue=sky), whereas subclass labels are indicated by markings (left/up/right arrows for planar left/center/right; "O" for porous, "X" for solid). Image reproduced from [112] with permission of the *International Journal of Computer Vision*, Springer. (See color plate 1.16.)

We are starting to see representations that bear a strong resemblance to the aspect graphs of the 1980s and 1990s (e.g., [204, 135, 208]). As the community returns to shape modeling (as reflected in recent work on contour-based representations, e.g., [221, 172, 87, 145]), it may well rediscover that for complex, articulating shape models, the number of aspects is intractable. The problem is further compounded when the community moves beyond object detectors to the more general problem of unexpected object recognition. The road back to 3-D is once again on the horizon, with exciting new work on learning to infer 3-D shape from 2-D appearance [112] (see Fig. 1.16), and on the perception of 3-D shape from 2-D contours using a 3-D compactness constraint [184].[7] As contours once again become fashionable, one might expect a return to the problem of 3-D shape-from-contour. As we move from the narrow problem of detection toward the more general problem of unexpected object recognition, the need to extract local (occlusion resistant) viewpoint- and articulation-invariant indices will focus shape-from-contour at the part level (rather than at the object level). After 40 years, we may once again be faced with the problem of recovering a vocabulary of higher-order, 3-D part models and their relations. Once again, the major challenge will be the abstraction of such part models from real images of real objects.

1.8 Identifying Our Shortcomings: The Need for New Benchmarks

Early work in categorization was rarely evaluated thoroughly, but rather demonstrated on a small set of anecdotal images. The weaknesses of the approaches were rarely

---

[7] Our ability to perceive 3-D objects is largely unaffected by the absence of such "direct" depth cues as binocular disparity or motion [183, 184]. This suggests that perceptual grouping operates on a single 2-D image. Although adding more images will always improve 3-D interpretation, it will not change the way shapes are found in, and abstracted from, the images. This chapter has focused on the case of categorization (and abstraction) from a single 2-D image, but it does not imply that binocular reconstruction and structure from motion, when available, cannot contribute to the processes of 3-D shape recovery and abstraction.

discussed or illustrated in detail, and one was left to wonder on what domains a reported method might be successful. It was not the case that early categorization researchers did not appreciate the importance of evaluation. Rather, a number of factors conspired to make systematic evaluation a challenge: (1) the models were primarily 3-D and a standard representation had not been adopted by the community; (2) image and/or model databases were unavailable; and (3) computing power was extremely limited, with a single image taking minutes or hours to interpret.

Not until the 1990s, with the advent of appearance-based recognition (where the model was the image) and faster machines, did evaluation benchmarks begin to emerge. The most prominent was the Columbia COIL-100 database [168], followed by the ETH database [139], and more recently the Amsterdam Library of Object Images [98], Caltech-101 [81], Caltech-256 [105], the MIT "tiny" image database [244], the LabelMe database [205], the ESP dataset [257], and a variety of other databases contained in the PASCAL Object Recognition Database Collection [78]. These databases were long overdue, and provide a means for more uniform evaluation and comparison of our work. They also provide a wealth of real-world images with which to learn object models automatically.

The evaluation of categorization algorithms has improved dramatically since the early 1990s. Although we can now compare each other's algorithms on a standard dataset, it's not clear whether these datasets reflect the strengths and weaknesses of our algorithms [187, 182]. Even though early databases tested invariance to viewpoint (since they exhaustively enumerated a large set of views of an object), they did not test invariance to scale, image rotation, occlusion, significant articulation, clutter, or significant within-class shape deformation. Conversely, although more recent databases test significant within-class appearance and shape deformation, they do not systematically test invariance to scale, image rotation, occlusion, clutter, and articulation. It's not that such transformations do not exist in the database collections, it's that they are not systematically parameterized so that the failure modes of our algorithms can be clearly identified.

In some sense, our benchmarks are either too simple or too complex. When they're too simple, we run the risk of ignoring important invariance goals in our categorization system design because such goals are not reflected in the data. When a system reports good results on such a dataset, we have no way of knowing how it will fare under conditions not reflected in the dataset. Conversely, when the benchmarks are too complex, the invariance goals become obfuscated by the data. When a system reports good (or better) results on such a dataset, we don't know which conditions are handled well and which are not. The performance indicators simply don't yield critical insight into what aspects of the problem need improvement.

The community clearly needs a dataset that isolates the various conditions that we need to address. Such a database may take the form of a sequence of image suites that progress from exemplars imaged under very controlled conditions to categories imaged under very challenging conditions, with a full spectrum of suites in between. For example, suite-0 might fix a number of object imaging conditions – for example, single scale, fixed illumination, fixed articulation, fixed appearance (i.e., an exemplar), no occlusion, and no clutter. The only free parameter would be viewpoint. Suite-0 would therefore be used to evaluate your algorithm's invariance to viewpoint change, and nothing else. Next up would be suite-1, which fixes all conditions except, for example, image scale, enabling you to evaluate the scale-invariance of your algorithm. Each successive suite, in turn, would test a different condition. Moreover, each condition would be systematically parameterized, so that where you fail on a particular suite would tell you exactly *how* invariant you are to that suite's condition(s). Early databases, such as COIL-100 [168] and the Amsterdam Image Library [98] parameterized viewpoint and illumination. One recent database [65], created from the COIL-100 database, systematically parameterizes degree of occlusion.

As the suites progress toward the "human vision" suite, exemplars would give way to categories, rigid objects would give way to deformable objects, and uniform backgrounds would give way to cluttered backgrounds. Categories in earlier suites would exhibit very little within-class appearance or shape deformation, and in later suites would exhibit significant structural variability. Further suites could then combine conditions, leading to many subsets of conditions that might tease out limitations of particular algorithms. To evaluate your algorithm would then amount to starting at suite-0 and reporting your results on each suite up to the conditions to which you claim to be invariant. Such a set of suites would need to be designed by a consortium with no disposition toward a particular recognition paradigm. In fact, to be paradigm-invariant, 3-D data of the imaged objects should also be provided, which would allow for the automatic construction of 3-D models, which some may prefer to view-based models.

The existence of such a set of suites would allow our algorithms to evolve in a clear direction, ever more invariant to increasingly challenging conditions but never losing sight of the need to address the fundamental conditions. Without the carefully designed intermediate suites, testing on only the most challenging suites, which combine many conditions (akin to today's popular databases), may contribute little to our understanding of categorization. If such databases become more performance- than diagnostic-oriented, they may, in fact, end up distracting the categorization community from focusing on those particular issues that deserve attention. It is here that we can take a cue from our human vision colleagues, as the problem of designing proper experiments to test the performance of a vision system and to evaluate competing models has existed for a long time in the form of psychophysics. The first formal presentation of psychophysical methods can be found in Fechner [80]. A recent review that emphasizes the use of signal detection theory can be found in Macmillan and Creelman [156], and examples of the application of psychophysical methodology to the study of 3-D shape perception is presented by Pizlo [184].

1.9 Conclusion

The problem of object categorization has been around since the early 1970s. The legacy left by that original community was a set of rich object representations that modeled the coarse, prototypical, 3-D shape of an object. Although important concepts such as viewpoint invariance, hierarchical representations, structural variability, indexing, and symmetry are rooted in this early work, the lack of image abstraction mechanisms restricted these systems to contrived images of contrived scenes. Instead of incrementally building on these rich representational ideas, models became gradually stronger, first in terms of shape and then appearance, thereby avoiding the need for image abstraction mechanisms. The resulting recognition systems began to be useful, first solving real exemplar-based industrial recognition problems under tightly controlled conditions, and, more recently, solving real exemplar-based recognition problems in the real world.

Having made enormous progress on the problem of exemplar recognition, the community is now eager to return to the categorization problem. However, the gradual redefinition of the recognition problem from categories to exemplars, followed by a representational movement from shape to appearance, has unfortunately displaced a rich history of categorization from our community's memory. The sudden popularity of object recognition in the early 2000s is due in part to the fact that an image can now be mapped to a set of very distinctive local feature vectors without having to engage in the classical, unsolved problems of segmentation and grouping. This has drawn a new generation of computer vision and machine learning researchers into the ring. Our progress will clearly benefit from both the increased popularity of the problem as well as the influx of new techniques from other communities. However, a much smaller portion of this new community will have witnessed the evolution of categorization, which further serves to separate the categorization community from its roots.

Today's categorization community has moved quickly to apply exemplar-based appearance models to more categorical tasks. Ultimately, these are destined to fail, for local appearance is seldom generic to a category. This is reflected in a recent shift back to shape, along with a recent rediscovery of the importance of viewpoint invariance.[8] This is a very positive development, for our computers, our inference engines, our ability to deal with uncertain information, and our ability to learn a system's parameters rather than hand-code them represent enormous improvements over previous generations. As such, our return to earlier problems will lead to vastly more effective solutions. Without a doubt, we are heading in the right direction again.

One invariant, however, has survived the pendulum-like journey of our community: our tendency to avoid the difficult problem of image (or shape) abstraction. Once we acknowledge this important problem, we must be patient and not expect results too soon. We must understand the history of the research in our community, build on important representational ideas and concepts from the past, and not dismiss earlier work just because it did not deal with real images. Each generation of categorization researchers has made important contributions, and we must incrementally build on the foundations laid by our predecessors. When we do develop solutions, they must be carefully evaluated under controlled conditions that can provide us with the most constructive feedback. Finally, we must reconnect with our human vision colleagues, so that we can maximally benefit from their research on the most impressive categorization system of them all: the human vision system.

Acknowledgments

I am indebted to the following individuals who provided thoughtful feedback on and corrections to this chapter: Narendra Ahuja, Ronen Basri, Gustavo Carneiro, Larry

---

[8] Note that viewpoint invariance is equally important in the study of human vision, where it is usually referred to as "shape constancy."

Davis, Afsaneh Fazly, Gertruda Grolinger, Mike Jamieson, Allan Jepson, Anatoliy Kats, Yakov Keselman, Alex Levinshtein, David Lowe, Diego Macrini, Stefan Mathe, Zygmunt Pizlo, Pablo Sala, Stan Sclaroff, Linda Shapiro, Ali Shokoufandeh, Kaleem Siddiqi, Cristian Sminchisescu, Suzanne Stevenson, Babak Taati, Alireza Tavakoli Targhi, Sinisa Todorovic, John Tsotsos, and Steve Zucker. My sincerest thanks to you all.

Bibliography

1. Agarwal S, Awan A, Roth D. 2004. Learning to detect objects in images via a sparse, part-based representation. *IEEE Trans Pattern Anal Mach Intell* 26(11):1475–1490.
2. Agin G, Binford TO. 1976. Computer description of curved objects. *IEEE Trans Comp* C-25(4):439–449.
3. Ahuja N, Chuang J-H. 1997. Shape representation using a generalized potential field model. *IEEE Trans Pattern Anal Mach Intell* 19(2):169–176.
4. Ahuja N, Todorovic S. 2007. Learning the taxonomy and models of categories present in arbitrary images. In Proceedings of the IEEE international conference on computer vision, Rio de Janeiro, Brazil.
5. Alter TD. 1994. 3-d pose from 3 points using weak-perspective. *IEEE Trans Pattern Anal Mach Intell* 16(8):802–808.
6. Amit Y, Geman D. 1997. Shape quantization and recognition with randomized trees. *Neural Comput* 9:1545–1588.
7. Amit Y, Geman D, Wilder K. 1997. Joint induction of shape features and tree classifiers. *IEEE Trans Pattern Anal Mach Intell* 19:1300–1305.
8. August J, Siddiqi K, Zucker SW. 1999. Ligature instabilities in the perceptual organization of shape. *Comput Vis Image Und* 76(3):231–243.
9. Bai X, Latecki LJ. 2008. Path similarity skeleton graph matching. *IEEE Trans Pattern Anal Mach Intell* 30(7):1282–1292.
10. Bai X, Latecki LJ, Liu W. 2007. Skeleton pruning by contour partitioning with discrete curve evolution. *IEEE Trans Pattern Anal Mach Intell* 29(3):449–462.
11. Barnard K, Duygulu P, de Freitas N, Forsyth D. 2002. Object recognition as machine translation – part 2: Exploiting image database clustering models. In Proceedings of the European conference on computer vision.
12. Barnard K, Duygulu P, Forsyth D, de Freitas N, Blei D, Jordan M. 2003. Matching words and pictures. *J Mach Learn Res* 3:1107–1135.
13. Barnard K, Duygulu P, Guru R, Gabbur P, Forsyth D. 2003. The effects of segmentation and feature choice in a translation model of object recognition. In Proceedings of the IEEE conference on computer vision and pattern recognition.
14. Barnard K, Fan Q. 2007. Reducing correspondence ambiguity in loosely labeled training data. In Proceedings of the IEEE conference on computer vision and pattern recognition.
15. Barnard K, Forsyth D. 2001. Learning the semantics of words and pictures. In Proceedings of the international conference on computer vision.
16. Barnard K, Gabbur P. 2003. Color and color constancy in a translation model for object recognition. In Proceedings of the eleventh color imaging conference.
17. Barr AH. 1981. Superquadrics and angle-preserving transformations. *IEEE Comput Graph* 1(1).
18. Basri R, Costa L, Geiger D, Jacobs D. 1998. Determining the similarity of deformable shapes. *Vision Rese* 38:2365–2385.

19. Basri R, Jacobs DW. 2003. Lambertian reflectance and linear subspaces. *IEEE Trans Pattern Anal Mach Intell* 25(2):218–233.

20. Beis JS, Lowe D. 1999. Indexing without invariants in 3d object recognition. *IEEE Trans Pattern Anal* 21(10):1000–1015.

21. Belhumeur PN, Kriegman DJ. 1996. What is the set of images of an object under all possible lighting conditions? In proceedings of the IEEE conference on computer vision and pattern recognition, 270–277.

22. Belongie S, Malik J, Puzicha J. 2002. Shape matching and object recognition using shape contexts. *IEEE Trans Pattern Anal Mach Intell* 24(4):509–522.

23. Ben-Arie J. 1992. The probabilistic peaking effect of viewed angles and distances with application to 3-D object recognition. *IEEE Trans Pattern Anal Mach Intell* 12(8):760–774.

24. Bergevin R, Levine MD. 1992. Part decomposition of objects from single view line drawings. *Comput Vis Image Und* 55(1):73–83.

25. Bergevin R, Levine MD. 1993. Generic object recognition: Building and matching coarse 3d descriptions from line drawings. *IEEE Trans Pattern Anal Mach Intell* 15:19–36.

26. Beymer D, Poggio T. 1996. Image representations for visual learning. *Science 28*, 272 (5270):1905–1909.

27. Biederman I. 1985. Human image understanding: recent research and a theory. *Comput Vision Graph* 32:29–73.

28. Biederman I. 1987. Recognition-by-components: a theory of human image understanding. *Psychol Rev* 94:115–147.

29. Binford TO. 1971. Visual perception by computer. In Proceedings of the IEEE conference on systems and control, Miami, FL.

30. Binford TO, Levitt TS. 2003. Evidential reasoning for object recognition. *IEEE Trans Pattern Anal Mach Intell* 25(7):837–851.

31. Binford TO, Levitt TS, Mann WB. 1989. Bayesian inference in model-based machine vision. In UAI' 87: Proceedings of the 3rd annual conference on uncertainty in artificial intelligence, Philadelphia: Elsevier, 73–96.

32. Black MJ, Jepson A. 1998. Eigentracking: robust matching and tracking of articulated objects using a view-based representation. *Int J Comput Vis* 26(1):63–84.

33. Blei D, Jordan M. 2003. Modeling annotated data. Proceedings of the international conference on research and development in information retrieval.

34. Blostein D, Ahuja N. 1989. A multiscale region detector. *Comput Vision Graph* 45:22–41.

35. Blum H. 1967. *A transformation for extracting new descriptors of shape*. In *Models for the perception of Speech and visual form* ed. W Wathen-Dunn, 362–380. Cambridge: MIT Press.

36. Blum H. 1973. Biological shape and visual science. *J Theor Biol* 38:205–287.

37. Blum H, Nagel RN. 1978. Shape description using weighted symmetric axis features. *Pattern Recog* 10:167–180.

38. Borenstein E, Malik J. 2006. Shape guided object segmentation. In Proceedings of the IEEE conference on computer vision and pattern recognition, 969–976.

39. Borenstein E, Ullman S. 2002. Class-specific, top-down segmentation. In Proceedings of the european conference on computer vision, 109–124.

40. Borges D, Fisher R. 1997. Class-based recognition of 3d objects represented by volumetric primitives. *Image Vision Comput* 15(8):655–664.

41. Bouchard G, Triggs B. 2005. Hierarchical part-based visual object categorization. In *Proceedings of the IEEE conference on computer vision and pattern recognition*, 710–715.

42. Boyer KL, Sarkar S. 1999. Perceptual organization in computer vision: status, challenges, and potential. *Comput Vis Image Und* 76(1):1–5.

43. Boyer KL, Sarkar S. 2000. *Perceptual organization for artificial vision systems*. Boston: Kluwer.

44. Brand M. 1997. Physics-based visual understanding. *Comput Vis Image Und* 65(2):192–205.

45. Brooks R. 1983. Model-based 3-D interpretations of 2-D images. *IEEE Trans Pattern Anal Mach Intell* 5(2):140–150.

46. Bunke H. 1997. On a relation between graph edit distance and maximum common subgraph. *Pattern Recogn Lett* 18(8):689–694.

47. Burns J, Weiss R, Riseman E. 1993. View variation of point-set and line-segment features. *IEEE Trans Pattern Anal Mach Intell* 15(1):51–68.

48. Caelli T, Kosinov S. 2004. An eigenspace projection clustering method for inexact graph matching. *IEEE Trans Pattern Anal Mach Intell* 26(4):515–519.

49. Camps O, Huang C, T Kanungo. 1998. Hierarchical organization of appearance based parts and relations for object recognition. In Proceedings of the IEEE conference on computer vision and pattern recognition, 685–691. Santa Barbara, CA.

50. Carneiro G, Jepson AD. 2002. Phase-based local features. In Proceedings of the European conference on computer vision, 282–296.

51. Carneiro G, Jepson AD. 2004. Flexible spatial models for grouping local image features. In Proceedings of the IEEE conference on computer vision and pattern recognition, 747–754.

52. Carneiro G, Jepson AD. 2007. Flexible spatial configuration of local image features. *IEEE Trans Pattern Anal Mach Intell* 29(12):2089–2104.

53. Carneiro G, Lowe D. 2006. Sparse flexible models of local features. In Proceedings of the European conference on computer vision, 29–43.

54. Carniero G, Chan AB, Moreno P, Vasconcelos N. 2007. Supervised learning of semantic classes for image annotation and retrieval. *IEEE Trans Pattern Anal Mach Intell* 29(3):394–410.

55. Carniero G, Vasconcelos N. 2005. Formulating semantic image annotation as a supervised learning problem. In Proceedings of the IEEE conference on computer vision and pattern recognition.

56. La Cascia M, Sethi S, Sclaroff S. 1998. Combining textual and visual cues for content-based image retrieval on the World Wide Web. In Proceedings of IEEE workshop on content-based access of image and video libraries.

57. Cass TA. 1998. Robust affine structure matching for 3d object recognition. *IEEE Trans Pattern Anal Mach Intell* 20(11):1265–1274.

58. Cheng H, Bouman CA. 2001. Multiscale bayesian segmentation using a trainable context model. *IEEE Trans Image Process* 10(4):511–525.

59. Chuang J-H, Ahuja N, Lin C-C, Tsai C-H, Chen C-H. 2004. A potential-based generalized cylinder representation. *Comput Graph* 28:907–918.

60. Clemens DT, Jacobs DW. 1991. Space and time bounds on indexing 3d models from 2d images. *IEEE Trans Pattern Anal Mach Intell* 13(10):1007–1017.

61. Costa MS, Shapiro LG. 2000. 3d object recognition and pose with relational indexing. *Comput Vis Image Und* 79(3):364–407.

62. Crowley J, Parker A. 1984. A representation for shape based on peaks and ridges in the difference of low-pass transform. *IEEE Trans Pattern Anal Mach Intell* 6(2):156–169.

63. Crowley J, Sanderson AC. 1987. Multiple resolution representation and probabilistic matching of 2–D gray–scale shape. *IEEE Trans Pattern Anal Mach Intell* 9(1):113–121.

64. Demirci MF, Shokoufandeh A, Keselman Y, Bretzner L, Dickinson S. 2006. Object recognition as many-to-many feature matching. *Int J Comput Vis* 69(2):203–222.

65. Denton T, Novatnack J, Shokoufandeh A. 2005. Drexel object occlusion repository (door). Technical Report DU-CS-05-08, Drexel University.

66. Dickinson S, Bergevin R, Biederman I, Eklundh J-O, Jain A, Munck-Fairwood R, Pentland A. 1997. Panel report: the potential of geons for generic 3-D object recognition. *Image Vision Comput* 15(4):277–292.

67. Dickinson S, Christensen H, Tsotsos J, Olofsson G. 1997. Active object recognition integrating attention and viewpoint control. *Comput Vis Image Und* 67(3):239–260.

68. Dickinson S, Davis L. 1990. A flexible tool for prototyping alv road following algorithms. *IEEE J Robotic Autom* 6(2):232–242.

69. Dickinson S, Metaxas D. 1994. Integrating qualitative and quantitative shape recovery. *Int J Comput Vis* 13(3):1–20.

70. Dickinson S, Metaxas D. 1997. Using aspect graphs to control the recovery and tracking of deformable models. *Int J Pattern Recogn Artif Intell* 11(1):115–142.

71. Dickinson S, Metaxas D, Pentland A. 1997. The role of model-based segmentation in the recovery of volumetric parts from range data. *IEEE Trans Pattern Anal Mach Intell* 19(3):259–267.

72. Dickinson S, Pentland A, Rosenfeld A. 1990. A representation for qualitative 3-D object recognition integrating object-centered and viewer-centered models. In Vision: a convergence of disciplines, ed. K Leibovic. New York: Springer-Verlag.

73. Dickinson S, Pentland A, Rosenfeld A. 1992. From volumes to views: an approach to 3-D object recognition. *Comput Vis Image Und* 55(2):130–154.

74. Dickinson S, Pentland A, Rosenfeld A. 1992. 3-D shape recovery using distributed aspect matching. *IEEE Trans Pattern Anal Mach Intell* 14(2):174–198.

75. Dickinson S, Wilkes D, Tsotsos JK. 1999. A computational model of view degeneracy. *IEEE Trans Pattern Anal Mach Intell* 21(8):673–689.

76. Eggert D Bowyer K. 1990. Computing the orthographic projection aspect graph of solids of revolution. *Pattern Recogn Lett* 11:751–763.

77. Eggert D, Bowyer K, Dyer C, Christensen H, Goldgof D. 1993. The scale space aspect graph. *IEEE Trans Pattern Anal Mach Intell* 15(11):1114–1130.

78. Everingham M, Zisserman A, Williams CKI, Van Gool LJ, Allan M, Bishop CM, Chapelle O, Dalal N, Deselaers T, Dorkó G, Duffner S, Eichhorn J, Farquhar JDR, Fritz M, Garcia C, Griffiths T, Jurie F, Keysers D, Koskela M, Laaksonen J, Larlus D, Leibe B, Meng H, Ney H, Schiele B, Schmid C, Seemann E, Shawe-Taylor J, Storkey AJ, Szedmák S, Triggs B, Ulusoy I, Viitaniemi V, Zhang J. 2005. The 2005 pascal visual object classes challenge. In *Machine Learning Challenges Workshop*, 117–176.

79. Faugeras O, Mundy J, Ahuja N, Dyer C, Pentland A, Jain R, Ikeuchi K, Bowyer K. 1992. Why aspect graphs are not (yet) practical for computer vision. *CVGIP Image Und* 55(2):212–218.

80. Fechner G. 1860/1966. *Elements of psychophysics*. New York: Holt, Rinehart & Winston.

81. Fei-Fei L, Fergus R, Perona P. 2004. Learning generative visual models from few training examples: an incremental bayesian approach tested on 101 object categories. In Proceedings of the IEEE workshop on generative-model based vision, Washington, D.C.

82. Fei-Fei L, Fergus R, Perona P. 2006. One-shot learning of object categories. *IEEE Trans Pattern Anal Mach Intell* 28(4):594–611.

83. Feldman J, Singh M. 2006. Bayesian estimation of the shape skeleton. *Proc Nat Acad Sci* 103:18,014–18,019.

84. Fellbaum C, ed. 1998. *WordNet: an electronic lexical database*. Cambridge: MIT Press.

85. Felzenszwalb P, Huttenlocher D. 2005. Pictorial structures for object recognition. *Int J Comput Vision* 61(1):55–79.

86. Felzenszwalb PF. 2005. Representation and detection of deformable shapes. *IEEE Trans Pattern Anal Mach Intell* 27(2):208–220.

87. Fergus R, Perona P, Zisserman A. 2007. Weakly supervised scale-invariant learning of models for visual recognition. *Int J Comput Vis* 71(3):273–303.

88. Ferrari V, Jurie F, Schmid C. 2007. Accurate object detection with deformable shape models learnt from images. In Proceedings of the IEEE conference on computer vision and pattern recognition.

89. Ferrari V, Tuytelaars T, Van Gool LJ. 2004. Simultaneous object recognition and segmentation by image exploration. In Proceedings of the European conference on computer vision, 40–54.

90. Ferrari V, Tuytelaars T, Van Gool LJ. 2006. Simultaneous object recognition and segmentation from single or multiple model views. *Int J Comput Vis* 67(2):159–188.

91. Ferrie F, Lagarde J, Whaite P. 1993. Darboux frames, snakes, and super-quadrics: geometry from the bottom up. *IEEE Trans Pattern Anal Mach Intell* 15(8):771–784.

92. Fidler S, Leonardis A. 2007. Towards scalable representations of object categories: learning a hierarchy of parts. In Proceedings of the IEEE conference on computer vision and pattern recognition.

93. Flynn P, Jain A. 1992. 3D object recognition using invariant feature indexing of interpretation tables. *Comput Vis Image Und* 55(2):119–129.

94. Forsyth DA, Mundy JL, Zisserman A, Coelho C, Heller A, Rothwell C. 1991. Invariant descriptors for 3d object recognition and pose. *IEEE Trans Pattern Anal Mach Intell* 13(10):971–991.

95. François ARJ, Medioni GG. 1996. Generic shape learning and recognition. In Proceedings of the object representation in computer vision II, international workshop, Cambridge, UK, 287–320.

96. Fu KS. 1974. *Syntactic methods in pattern recognition*. New York: Academic Press.

97. Gdalyahu Y, Weinshall D. 1999. Flexible syntactic matching of curves and its application to automatic hierarchical classification of silhouettes. *IEEE Trans Pattern Anal Mach Intell* 21(12):1312–1328.

98. Geusebroek J-M, Burghouts G, Smeulders A. 2005. The Amsterdam library of object images. *Int J Comput Vis* 61(1):103–112.

99. Gibson J. 1979. *The ecological approach to visual perception*. Boston: Houghton Mifflin.

100. Gigus Z, Canny JF, Seidel R. 1991. Efficiently computing and representing aspect graphs of polyhedral objects. *IEEE Trans Pattern Anal Mach Intell* 13(6):542–551.

101. Gigus Z, Malik J. 1990. Computing the aspect graph for line drawings of polyhedral objects. *IEEE Trans Pattern Anal Mach Intell* 12(2):113–122.

102. Goad C. 1983. Special purpose automatic programming for 3D model-based vision. In Proceedings of the DARPA image understanding workshop, 94–104, Arlington, VA.

103. Gong L, Kulikowski CA. 1995. Composition of image analysis processes through object-centered hierarchical planning. *IEEE Trans Pattern Anal Mach Intell* 17(10):997–1009.

104. Grauman K, Darrell T. 2006. Unsupervised learning of categories from sets of partially matching image features. In Proceedings of the IEEE conference on computer vision and pattern recognition, 19–25.

105. Griffin G, Holub A, Perona P. 2007. Caltech-256 object category dataset. Technical Report 7694, California Institute of Technology.

106. Grimson W, Lozano-Pérez T. 1984. Model-based recognition and localization from sparse range or tactile data. *Int J Robot Res* 3(3):3–35.

107. Gupta A, Bajcsy R. 1993. Volumetric segmentation of range images of 3d objects using superquadric models. *Comput Vis Image Und* 58(3):302–326.

108. Hanson A, Riseman E. 1978. Visions: a computer vision system for interpreting scenes. In *Computer vision systems*, ed. A Hanson and E Riseman 303–334. New York: Academic Press.

109. Harwood D, Prasannappa R, Davis L. 1988. Preliminary design of a programmed picture logic. In *Proceedings of the image understanding workshop*, vol. 2, 745–755. Science Applications International Corp.

110. He X, Zemel RS, Carreira-Perpiñán MÁ. 2004. Multiscale conditional random fields for image labeling. In *Proceedings of the IEEE conference on computer vision and pattern recognition*, 695–702.

111. He X, Zemel RS, Ray D. 2006. Learning and incorporating top-down cues in image segmentation. In Proceedings of the European conference on computer vision, 338–351.

112. Hoiem D, Efros A, Hebert M. 2007. Recovering surface layout from an image. *Int J Comput Vis* 75(1):151–172.

113. Hoiem D, Efros AA, Hebert M. 2006. Putting objects in perspective. In Proceedings of the IEEE conference on computer vision and pattern recognition, 2137–2144.

114. Hoogs A, Collins R. 2006. Object boundary detection in images using a semantic ontology. In Proceedings of the twenty-first national conference on artifical intelligence and the eighteenth innovative applications of artifical intelligence conference, Boston, MA: AAAI Press.

115. Hoogs A, Rittscher J, Stien G, Schmiederer J. 2003. Video content annotation using video analysis and a large semantic knowledgebase. In Proceedings of the IEEE conference on computer vision and pattern recognition.

116. Huttenlocher D, Ullman S. 1990. Recognizing solid objects by alignment with an image. *Int J Comput Vis* 5(2):195–212.

117. Hwang V, Davis LS, Matsuyama T. 1986. Hypothesis integration in image understanding systems. *Comput Vision Graph* 36(3):321–371.

118. Ikeuchi K, Kanade T. 1988. Automatic generation of object recognition programs. *Proc IEEE* 76:1016–1035.

119. Ioffe S, Forsyth D. 2001. Probabilistic methods for finding people. *Int J Comput Vis* 43(1):45–68.

120. Jamieson M, Dickinson S, Stevenson S, Wachsmuth S. 2006. Using language to drive the perceptual grouping of local image features. In Proceedings of the IEEE conference on computer vision and pattern recognition.

121. Jamieson M, Fazly A, Dickinson S, Stevenson S, Wachsmuth S. 2007. Learning structured appearance models from captioned images of cluttered scenes. In Proceedings of the international conference on computer vision.

122. Jepson AD, Fleet DJ, Black MJ. 2002. A layered motion representation with occlusion and compact spatial support. In Proceedings of the European conference on computer vision, 692–706.

123. Jin Y, Geman S. 2006. Context and hierarchy in a probabilistic image model. In Proceedings of the IEEE conference on computer vision and pattern recognition, 2145–2152.

124. McKeown Jr. DM, Harvey WA, Wixson LE. 1989. Automating knowledge acquisition for aerial image interpretation. *Comput Vision Graph* 46(1):37–81.

125. Kanaujia A, Sminchisescu C, Metaxas DN. 2007. Semi-supervised hierarchical models for 3d human pose reconstruction. In Proceedings of the IEEE conference on computer vision and pattern recognition. IEEE Computer Society.

126. Katz RA and Pizer SM. 2003. Untangling the blum medial axis transform. *Int J Comput Vis* 55(2–3):139–153,

127. Keselman Y, Dickinson S. 2005. Generic model abstraction from examples. *IEEE Trans Pattern Anal Mach Intell* 27(7):1141–1156.

128. Kirby M, Sirovich L. 1990. Application of the karhunen-loeve procedure for thecharacterization of human faces. *IEEE Trans Pattern Anal Mach Intell* 12(1):103–108.

129. Koenderink J, van Doorn A. 1979. The internal representation of solid shape with respect to vision. *Biol Cybern* 32:211–216.

130. Koenderink JJ, van Doorn AJ. 1987. Representation of local geometry in the visual system. *Biol Cybern* 55:367–375.

131. Koffka K. 1935. *Principles of gestalt psychology*. New York: Harcourt, Brace.

132. Kriegman D, Ponce J. 1990. Computing exact aspect graphs of curved objects: solids of revolution. *Int J Comput Vis* 5(2):119–135.

133. Kriegman DJ, Ponce J. 1990. On recognizing and positioning curved 3-d objects from image contours. *IEEE Trans Pattern Anal Mach Intell* 12(12):1127–1137.

134. Kumar S, Hebert M. 2006. Discriminative random fields. *Int J Comput Vis* 68(2):179–201.

135. Kushal A, Schmid C, Ponce J. 2007. Flexible object models for category-level 3d object recognition. In Proceedings of the IEEE conference on computer vision and pattern recognition, Minneapolis, MN.

136. Lamdan Y, Schwartz J, Wolfson H. 1990. Affine invariant model-based object recognition. *IEEE Trans Robotic Autom* 6(5):578–589.

137. Lazebnik S, Schmid C, Ponce J. 2005. A sparse texture representation using local affine regions. *IEEE Trans Pattern Anal Mach Intell* 27(8):1265–1278.

138. LeCun Y, Bottou L, Bengio Y, Haffner P. 1998. Gradient-based learning applied to document recognition. *Proc IEEE* 86(11):2278–2324.

139. Leibe B, Schiele B. 2003. Analyzing appearance and contour based methods for object categorization. In Proceedings of the IEEE conference on computer vision and pattern recognition, 409–415.

140. Leibe B, Schiele B. 2003. Interleaved object categorization and segmentation. In Proceedings of the British machine vision conference, Norwich, UK.

141. Leonardis A, Bischof H. 2000. Robust recognition using eigenimages. *Comput Vis Image Und* 78(1):99–118.

142. Leonardis A, Bischoff H. 1996. Dealing with occlusions in the eigenspace approach. In Proceedings of the IEEE conference on computer vision and pattern recognition, 453–458, San Francisco, CA.

143. Leonardis A, Gupta A, Bajcsy R. 1995. Segmentation of range images as the search for geometric parametric models. *Int J Comput Vis* 14(3):253–277.

144. Leonardis A, Jaklic A, Solina F. 1997. Superquadrics for segmenting and modeling range data. *IEEE Trans Pattern Anal Mach Intell* 19(11).

145. Leordeanu M, Hebert M, Sukthankar R. 2007. Beyond local appearance: Category recognition from pairwise interactions of simple features. In Proceedings of the IEEE conference on computer vision and pattern recognition.

146. Levinshtein A, Sminchisescu C, Dickinson S. 2005. Learning hierarchical shape models from examples. In Proceedings of the EMMCVPR, 251–267.

147. Leyton M. 1988. A process-grammar for shape. *Artif Intell* 34(2):213–247.

148. Lindeberg T. 1993. Detecting salient blob-like image structures and their scales with a scale-space primal sketch: a method for focus-of-attention. *Int J Comput Vis* 11:283–318.

149. Lindeberg T. 1998. Edge detection and ridge detection with automatic scale selection. *Int J Comput Vis* 30(2):117–154.

150. Ling H, Jacobs DW. 2007. Shape classification using the inner-distance. *IEEE Trans Pattern Anal Mach Intell* 29(2):286–299.

151. Liu L, Sclaroff S. 2004. Deformable model-guided region split and merge of image regions. *Image Vis Comput* 22(4):343–354.

152. Lowe D. 1985. *Perceptual organization and visual recognition*. Norwell, MA: Kluwer Academic Publishers.

153. Lowe D. 1987. Three-dimensional object recognition from single two-dimensional images. *Artif Intell* 31:355–395.

154. Lowe D. 1999. Object recognition from local scale-invariant features. In Proceedings of the international conference on computer vision 1150–1157.

155. Lowe D. 2004. Distinctive image features from scale-invariant keypoints. *Int J Comput Vis* 60(2):91–110.

156. Macmillan NA, Creelman CD. 2005. *Detection theory: a user's guide*. Mahwah, NJ: Lawrence Erlbaum.

157. Mann WB. 1995. Three dimensional object interpretation of monocular grey-scale images, PhD thesis, Stanford University.

158. Marr D. 1982. *Vision*. San Francisco: WH. Freeman.

Plate 1.1. The two shapes depicted in this statue clearly represent two humanoid figures seated and facing each other. At the level of local features, the figures are unrecognizable. At a more abstract level, however, the coarse parts of the figures begin to emerge, which, along with their relations, facilitate object categorization. The local features that constitute the abstract parts were not learned from training examples (they don't exist on a real human), nor were they grouped/abstracted using a prior target (human) model. This sculpture by Karel Nepraš, entitled "Great Dialogue," is found in the Museum of Modern and Contemporary Art (Veletržní Palác), in Prague. Image reproduced with permission.

Plate 1.2. A shape abstraction of the seated humanoid on the left in Figure 1.1. Note that the boundaries of the shape abstraction do not map one-to-one to (or align well with) local features (e.g., contours) in the image.

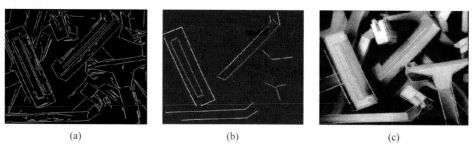

(a)   (b)   (c)

Plate 1.5. Lowe's SCERPO system [152] used perceptual grouping to prune hypothesized correspondences between image contours and polyhedral edges: (a) extracted edges; (b) extracted perceptual groups; and (c) detected objects and their poses. Images courtesy of David Lowe.

(a)   (b)

Plate 1.7. Learning scale-invariant parts-based models from examples (from Fergus et al. [87]): (a) Learned motorcycle model with ellipses representing part covariances and labels representing probability of occurrence; (b) example model detections in query images, with colored circles representing matched part hypotheses. Images reproduced from [87] with permission of the *International Journal of Computer Vision*, Springer.

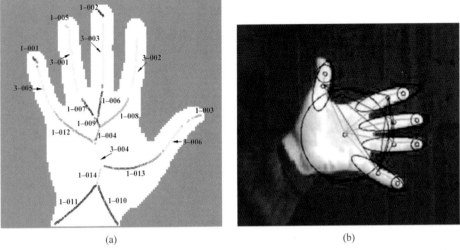

(a)　　　　　　　　　　　　(b)

Plate 1.10. Two powerful 2-D qualitative shape abstractions: (a) the shock graph (from Siddiqi et al. [223], whose parts represent a qualitative partitioning of Blum's medial axis transform [35], and whose edges span adjacent parts, directed from larger to smaller (image reproduced from [223] with permission of the *International Journal of Computer Vision*, Springer); (b) the blob graph (from Shokoufandeh et al. [218]), whose parts capture elongated symmetric structure at different scales, and whose edges capture parent-child (topological=green) and sibling (geometric=red) relationships between parts (image reproduced from [218] with permission of *Computer Vision and Image Understanding*, Elsevier).

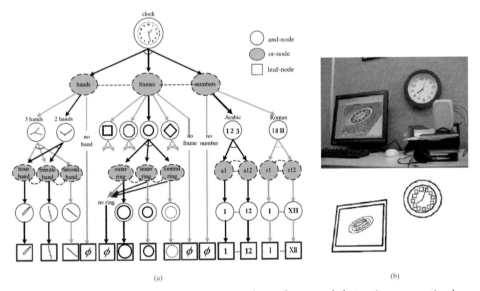

(a)　　　　　　　　　　　　(b)

Plate 1.11. Parameterizing structure represents a form of structural abstraction, supporting less brittle object categories having variable structure. Drawing on the classical shape grammars of the 1960s and 1970s and on stochastic grammars from the computational linguistics community, Zhu and Mumford have rekindled interest in shape grammars. In this example, taken from [275], the clock grammar shown in (a) is used to recognize the two clocks (real and display) in the image shown in (b). Images reproduced from [275], courtesy of Now Publishers.

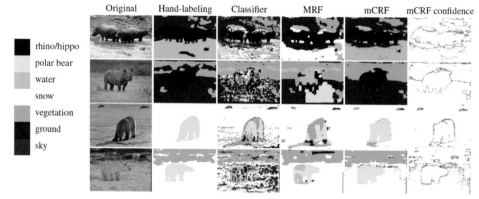

Plate 1.12. Image labeling results from the multiscale conditional random field approach of He et al. [110]. From labeled training images, knowledge of an object's appearance, position, size, and background can be learned and applied to the segmentation of test images. Image reproduced from [110], ©2004 IEEE with permission.

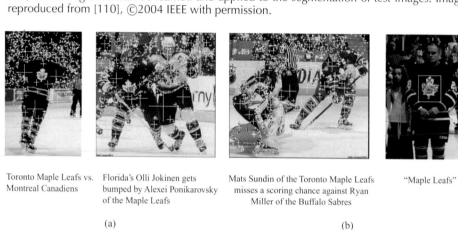

Toronto Maple Leafs vs. Montreal Canadiens

Florida's Olli Jokinen gets bumped by Alexei Ponikarovsky of the Maple Leafs

Mats Sundin of the Toronto Maple Leafs misses a scoring chance against Ryan Miller of the Buffalo Sabres

"Maple Leafs"

(a)   (b)

Plate 1.15. Learning structured appearance models for image annotation (from Jamieson et al. [121]): (a) Sample input image-caption collection, in which each image contains hundreds of local (SIFT) features (yellow crosses). From the input training collection, associations between structured subsets of local features and particular nouns are learned (discovered); (b) sample output, in which one of the objects learned during training (representing the Maple Leafs logo) is detected (shown with red features and green relationships in a yellow box), and annotated with its name ("Maple Leafs").

(a)   (b)

Plate 1.16. Recovering 3-D surface layout from a single image (from Hoeim et al. [112]): (a) input image. (b) recovered surface layout: colors reflect class labels (green=support red=vertical; blue=sky), whereas subclass labels are indicated by markings (left/up/right arrows for planar left/center/right; "O" for porous, "X" for solid). Image reproduced from [112] with permission of the *International Journal of Computer Vision*, Springer.

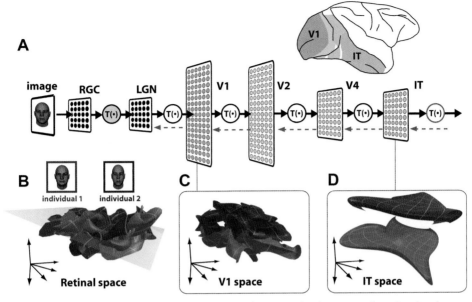

Plate 2.2. *A*, In our best model of the human visual system, the rhesus monkey, the visual areas have been mapped, and organized hierarchically, and the ventral visual stream is known to be critical for complex object discrimination (colored areas in brain inset, adapted from Felleman and Van Essen 1991). We conceptualize each stage of the ventral stream as a new population representation. The lower panels schematically illustrate these populations at successively higher stages across the ventral visual stream. Any pattern of photons from the world (here a face) is transduced into neuronal activity at the retina and is progressively and rapidly transformed and re-represented in each population, perhaps by a common canonical cortical transform (T, see text). Solid arrows indicate the direction of visual information flow based on neuronal latency (∼100 ms latency in IT), but this does not preclude fast feedback both within and between areas (dashed arrows). *B–D*, In each neuronal population space, each cardinal axis is one neuron's activity (e.g., firing rate over a ∼200-ms interval), the dimensionality is the number of neurons, and a given visual image is one point. Although such high-dimensional spaces cannot be visualized, the 3-D views portrayed here provide intuition. Owing to changes in identity-preserving variables such as position, scale, and pose, each object can produce an infinite number of different points in each space. Those points arise from its low-dimensional object identity manifold embedded in the space. Here two objects are shown (two faces) along with their simulated object identity manifolds (here two-dimensional sheets resulting from the manipulation of two degrees of freedom in pose). The left panel shows pixel (retina-like) manifolds generated from 3-D face models (14,400-dimensional data). The display axes were chosen to be the projections that best separate identity, pose azimuth, and pose elevation. Even though this simple example only exercises a fraction of typical real-world variation, the object manifolds are hopelessly tangled and not separable with simple decision functions (e.g., hyperplane in green). As visual information progresses through the ventral visual pathway, it is progressively re-represented (untangled) in each visual area and becomes better and better at directly supporting object recognition. A population of 500 V1 neurons was simulated as a bank of Gabor filters with firing thresholds (still tangled). In contrast, a population of 500 simulated IT neurons gives rise to object manifolds that are easily separated. In addition, such a representation also allows one to recover information about identity-preserving variables, such as object position, size, and pose (see text). Figure adapted from DiCarlo and Cox 2007; please see for details.

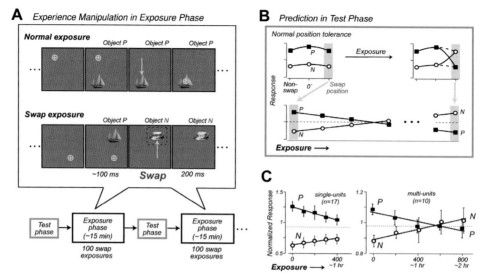

Plate 2.3. Targeted manipulation of the natural temporal continuity of object image experience produces rapid, unsupervised changes in IT neuronal tolerance (invariance). *A*, IT responses were tested in *test phases* (green boxes), which alternated with 15-minute *exposure phases*. During each *exposure phase*, objects initially appeared at 3 degrees above and 3 degrees below the center of gaze, and primates spontaneously made an eye movement (saccade) toward each presented object. In a normal exposure, the object remained unchanged during the saccade. In a "swap" exposure, the normal temporal contiguity of object image experience was altered by swapping the initial object for another object during that saccade. Each *exposure phase* consisted of 100 normal exposures and 100 "swap" exposures. *B*, If the visual system builds tolerance using temporal contiguity (here driven by saccades), the swap exposure should cause incorrect grouping of two different object images (here *P* and *N*). Thus, the predicted effect is a decrease in object selectivity at the swap position that increases with increasing exposure (in the limit, reversing object preference), and little or no change in object selectivity at the non-swap position. *C*, Response data to objects *P* and *N* at the swap position for single neurons (*left*) and multiunit sites (*right*) tested for the longest exposure time. The plot shows the mean normalized response to objects *P* and *N* as a function of exposure time (compare with *B*). No change in selectivity was observed at the equally eccentric control (non-swap) position, and no change in selectivity was observed among other object pairs not shown during the *exposure phase* (not shown). Adapted from Li and DiCarlo 2008, please see details there.

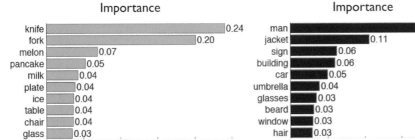

Plate 3.5. Different objects in an image have different "importance" for human observers. Importance here is measured as the probability that a human observer producing a list of objects in the scene will mention a given object first (Spain and Perona 2008).

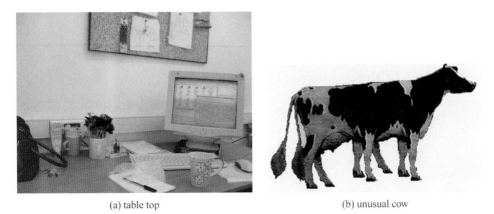

(a) table top   (b) unusual cow

Plate 5.1. Generic object recognition involves recognizing objects that might never have been observed before.

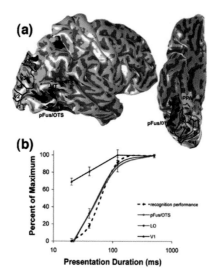

Plate 6.1. Object-, face-, and place-selective cortex. (a) Data of one representative subject shown on her partially inflated right hemisphere: lateral view (*left*); ventral view (*right*). *Dark gray* indicates sulci. *Light gray indicates* gyri. *Black lines* delineate retinotopic regions. *Blue regions* delineate object-selective regions (objects > scrambled objects), including LO and pFus/OTS ventrally as well as dorsal foci along the intraparietal sulcus (IPS). *Red regions* delineate face-selective regions (faces > non-faces objects), including the FFA, a region in LOS and a region in posterior STS. *Magenta regions* delineate overlap between face- and objects-selective regions. *Green regions* delineate place-selective regions (places > objects), including the PPA and a dorsal region lateral to the IPS. *Dark green regions* delineate overlap between place- and object-selective regions. All maps thresholded at $P < 0.001$, voxel level. (b) LO and pFus/OTS (but not VI) responses are correlated with recognition performance (Grill-Spector et al. 2000). To superimpose recognition performance and fMRI signals on the same plot, all values were normalized relative to the maximum response for the 500-ms duration stimulus.

For fMRI signals (blue, red, and orange lines) $= \dfrac{\% \, signal(condition)}{\% \, signal(500 \, ms)}$. For recognition perfor-

mance (black) $= \dfrac{\% \, correct(condition)}{\% \, correct(500 \, ms)}$.

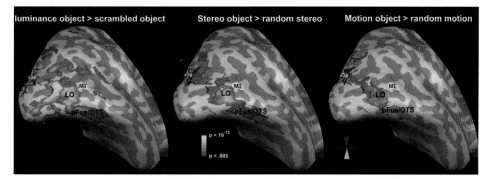

Plate 6.2. Selective responses to objects across multiple visual cues across the LOC. Statistical maps of selective response to object from luminance, stereo and motion information in a representative subject. All maps were thresholded at $P < 0.005$, voxel level, and are shown on the inflated right hemisphere of a representative subject. (a) Luminance objects > scrambled objects. (b) Objects generated from random dot stereograms versus structureless random dot streograms (perceived as a cloud of dots). (c) Objects generated from dot motion versus the same dots moving randomly. Visual meridians are represented by *red* (upper), *blue* (horizontal), and *green* (lower) *lines*. *White contour* indicates a motion-selective region, or MT. Adapted from Vinberg and Grill-Spector 2008.

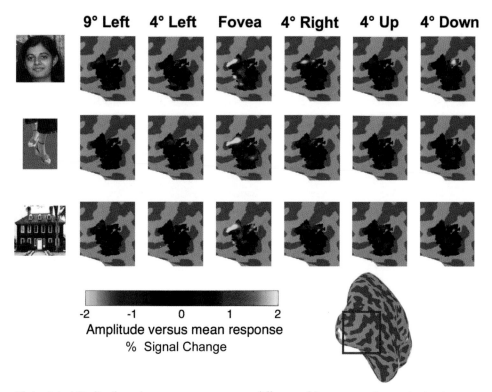

Plate 6.4. LO distributed response patterns to different object categories and stimulus positions. Data are shown on the lateral aspect of the right hemisphere cortical surface for a representative subject. Each panel shows the distributed LO fMRI amplitudes after subtracting from each voxel its mean response. *Red and yellow,* Responses that are higher than the voxel's mean response. *Blue and cyan,* Responses that are lower than the voxel's mean response. *Inset,* Inflated right cortical hemisphere, with red square indicating the zoomed region. Note that pattern changes significantly across columns (positions) and to a lesser extent across rows (categories). Adapted from Sayres and Grill-Spector 2008.

Plate 9.2. Images returned by (*top*) Berg and Forsyth's method, and (*bottom*) Wang and Forsyth's method on a set of test images for the "bear," "dolphin," and "frog" categories. Most of the top classified images for each category are correct and display a wide variety of poses, depictions, and species ("leopard," heads or whole bodies) and even multiple species ("penguins"). Returned "bear" results include "grizzly bears," "pandas," and "polar bears." False-positives are indicated by red squares.

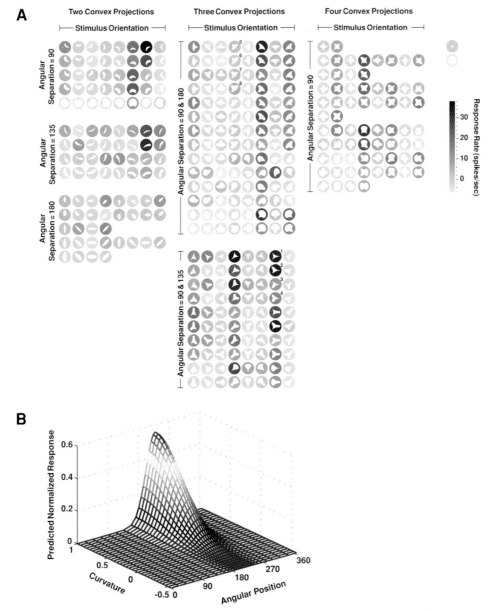

Plate 10.1. V4 shape tuning. *A*, Responses of a V4 neuron to stimuli constructed by factorial combination of boundary fragments. Spike activity of well-isolated individual neurons was recorded from the lower-field V4 representations of rhesus macaque monkeys performing a fixation task to stabilize eye position. Stimuli were flashed in the neuron's RF for 500 ms each in random order. Average responses across five repetitions are indicated by the background color for each stimulus. (The circular background was not part of the display.) This neuron was tuned for boundary fragments defined by sharp convexities facing to the lower left (225°) adjacent to shallow concave curvature facing downward (270°). *B*, Best-fitting Gaussian tuning function captures the neuron's sensitivity to convexity at 225°. Tuning domain axes represent angular position and curvature of boundary elements. Vertical axis and surface color represent normalized response predicted by the tuning function. To determine the best-fitting function, each shape was first decomposed into component boundary elements characterized by their curvatures and angular positions with respect to object center. Curvature runs from −1.0 (for sharp concavities) through 0.0 (for straight edges) to 1.0 for (sharp convexities). Predicted response for each stimulus depended on the value of the tuning function at domain points corresponding to its constituent surface fragments. Nonlinear regression was used to find the 2-D Gaussian function that minimized the sum of squared errors between predicted and observed responses. From Pasupathy and Connor, 2001; used with permission from the *Journal of Neurophysiology*.

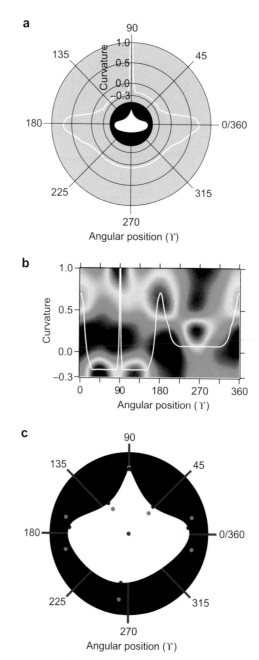

Plate 10.2. Shape reconstruction from V4 neural population response. (**a**) The original stimulus shape is shown at the center of a plot of boundary curvature (radial axis) as a function of angular position (polar axis) (white line). (**b**) Estimated V4 population response across the curvature × position domain (colored surface) with the veridical curvature function superimposed (white line). (**c**) Reconstruction of stimulus shape from the population surface in (b). From Pasupathy and Connor 2002.

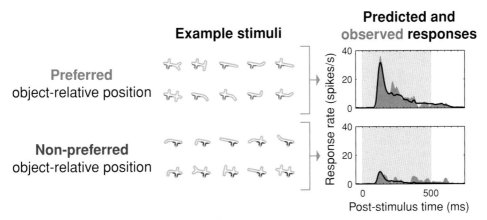

Plate 10.3. PIT tuning for object-centered position. These results are a subset from an experiment in which PIT neural responses were recorded from awake, fixating monkeys. Stimuli were constructed by factorial combination of boundary fragments. This neuron was highly selective for a configuration of opposed concavities positioned to the left of object center, as in the top panel. For these stimuli, the average response is high, as shown by the peristimulus-time response histogram at the right. In the stimuli shown in the bottom panel, the identical double-concavity configuration is positioned to the right of object center, and average response is low.

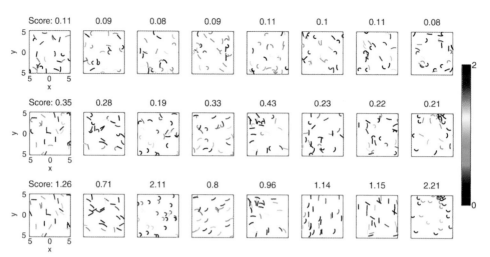

Plate 10.4. Hidden layer tuning in a shape identification network. A three-layer, feedforward neural network was trained using back-propagation to discriminate between 196 2-D shapes (Brincat and Connor 2004) in a position-invariant manner, across 36 random positions spanning 10 × 10 arbitrary units (average stimulus length = 3 units). Stimuli were described as combinations of contour fragments, with each fragment defined by its curvature, orientation, and x,y-position (Brincat and Connor 2004). Thus, the input corresponding to each stimulus was a set of 4-D vectors representing its contour components. Each V4-like input layer unit was modeled as a product of 4 Gaussian tuning functions, in the curvature, orientation, and x,y-position dimensions (Pasupathy and Connor 2001; Brincat and Connor 2004). The input unit's response to a contour fragment was the amplitude of the 4-D Gaussian at that point in the stimulus domain. The input unit's overall response to a given stimulus was the sum of Gaussian amplitude values for all the contour fragments making up that stimulus.

Each of the 30 hidden units received feedforward connections from 25 input units. (Simulations with fewer hidden units suffered substantial decrements in performance.) Input-layer tuning was not fixed; instead, the tuning parameters for all 25 inputs to each hidden unit were adjusted during training. This made it possible to simulate input from a much larger potential pool of input units. The output layer consisted of eight nodes constrained to represent stimulus identity (regardless of position) with an arbitrary binary code. (Similar results were obtained with other output conditions, including simple maximization of Euclidean distance between output layer activation patterns.) Each hidden unit provided feedforward connections to all eight output nodes. Each connection was modulated by a sigmoidal nonlinearity.

Back-propagation (Rumelhart et al. 1986) was used to adjust input-layer tuning parameters (Gaussian means and standard deviations in the contour curvature, orientation, and position dimensions), connection weights, and sigmoidal output function slopes and offsets. The cost function minimized during training was the mean sum of squared differences between the target and actual responses of the output nodes across all training stimuli (batch algorithm). The cost function included additive penalty terms that constrained the range of network parameters. The training criterion was failure to improve identification performance (nearest neighbor classification) on a validation stimulus set (same shapes at 36 newly generated random positions) across 20 consecutive iterations. Classification accuracy (averaged over 10 separate runs) was 90 +/− 2% on the training stimuli and 84 +/− 3% on the validation stimuli, indicating good generalization to stimulus positions outside the training set

Top row, Typical hidden unit connection patterns for eight training runs (*columns*). In each panel, the curvatures, orientations, and positions of the contour icons represent the 4-D Gaussian tuning peaks for the 25 V4-like inputs to the hidden unit. Color represents input connection strength (see scale at right). Due to the high variability in structural tuning (curvature and orientation) across positions, the structural coding scores (given above each panel; see text) for these hidden units were low (0.08 to 0.11). In each case, the unit chosen for illustration had the structural coding score closest to the mean for that run. *Middle row,* Hidden units with maximum structural coding scores in each run. The structural coding scores for these units ranged from 0.19 to 0.43. *Bottom row,* Idealized hidden units exemplifying robust structural coding. In each case, the observed hidden unit from the middle row was adjusted to produce consistent structural signals across the position domain. This was achieved by identifying input functions in the top quartile of partial structural coding scores, and replacing all other input functions with curvature/orientation values drawn from this top quartile. These hypothetical units exhibit much higher structural coding scores ranging from 0.71 to 2.21.

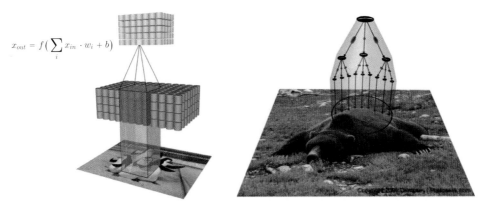

$$x_{out} = f\left(\sum_i x_{in} \cdot w_i + b\right)$$

Plate 11.1. *Left,* A traditional (convolutional) neural network. *Right,* A compositional hierarchy.

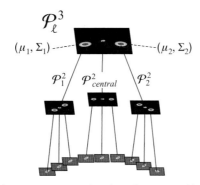

Plate 11.2. Example of an $\mathcal{L}_3$ composition.

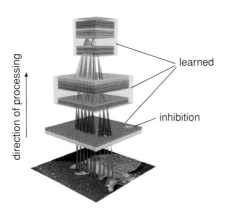

Plate 11.3. The hierarchical recognition architecture.

Plate 11.4. The learned hierarchical library of parts is applied in each image point (robustness to position of objects) and several image scales (robustness to objects' size).

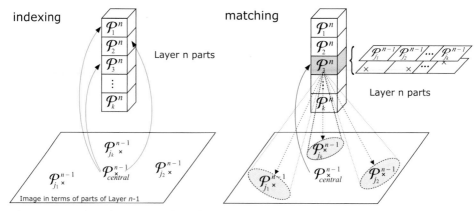

Plate 11.5. *Left,* Indexing – evoking higher-level composite hypotheses. *Right,* Matching – verification of a composite library part.

159. Marr D, Nishihara H. 1978. Representation and recognition of the spatial organization of three-dimensional shapes. *R Soc Lond B* 200:269–294.

160. Medioni G, Rao K. 1992. Generalized cones: Useful geometric properties. *Comput Vision Graph* 10(3):185–208.

161. Mikolajczyk K, Schmid C. 2004. Scale & affine invariant interest point detectors. *Int J Comput Vis* 60(1):63–86.

162. Moghaddam B, Pentland A. 1997. Probabilistic visual learning for object representation. *IEEE Trans Pattern Anal Mach Intell* 19(7):696–710.

163. Mori G, Ren X, Efros AA, Malik J. 2004. Recovering human body configurations: combining segmentation and recognition. In Proceedings of the IEEE conference on computer vision and pattern recognition, 326–333.

164. Mulgaonkar P, Shapiro L, Haralick R. 1984. Matching "sticks, plates and blobs" objects using geometric and relational constraints. *Image and Vision Comput* 2(2):85–98.

165. Mundy J, Zisserman A, eds. 1992. *Geometric invariance in computer vision*. Cambridge: MIT Press.

166. Murase H, Nayar S. 1995. Visual learning and recognition of 3-D objects from appearance. *Int J Comput Vis* 14:5–24.

167. Nelson R, Selinger A. 1998. A cubist approach to object recognition. In Proceedings of the IEEE international conference on computer vision, Bombay, India.

168. Nene S, Nayar S, Murase H. 1996. Columbia object image library (coil-100). Technical Report CUCS-006-96, Columbia University.

169. Nevatia R, Binford TO. 1977. Description and recognition of curved objects. *Artif Intell* 8:77–98.

170. Ohba K, Ikeuchi K. 1997. Detectability, uniqueness, and reliability of eigen windows for stable verification of partially occluded objects. *IEEE Trans Pattern Anal Mach Intell* 19(9):1043–1048.

171. Ommer B, Buhmann JM. 2007. Learning the compositional nature of visual objects. In Proceedings of the IEEE conference on computer vision and pattern recognition.

172. Opelt A, Pinz A, Zisserman A. 2006. Incremental learning of object detectors using a visual shape alphabet. In Proceedings of the IEEE conference on computer vision and pattern recognition, 3–10.

173. Osada R, Funkhouser TA, Chazelle B, Dobkin DP. 2002. Shape distributions. *ACM Graphic* 21(4):807–832.

174. Pelillo M, Siddiqi K, Zucker S. 1999. Matching hierarchical structures using association graphs. *IEEE Trans Pattern Anal Mach Intell* 21(11):1105–1120.

175. Pelillo M, Siddiqi K, Zucker SW. 2001. Many-to-many matching of attributed trees using association graphs and game dynamics. In IWVF, 583–593.

176. Pentland A. 1986. Perceptual organization and the representation of natural form. *Artif Intell* 28:293–331.

177. Pentland A. 1990. Automatic extraction of deformable part models. *Int J Comput Vis* 4:107–126.

178. Pentland A, Sclaroff S. 1991. Closed-form solutions for physically based shape modeling and recognition. *IEEE Trans Pattern Anal Mach Intell* 13(7):715–729.

179. Perrin B, Ahuja N, Srinivasa N. 1998. Learning multiscale image models of 2d object classes. In Proceedings of the Asian conference on computer vision, 323–331.

180. Pfaltz JL, Rosenfeld A. 1969. Web grammars. In Proceedings of the international joint conference on artificial intelligence, 609–620.

181. Pilu M, Fisher RB. 1996. Recognition of geons by parametric deformable contour models. In Proceedings of the European conference on computer vision, 71–82.

182. Pinto N, Cox DD, DiCarlo JJ. 2008. Why is real-world visual object recognition hard? *PLoS Comput Biol* 4(1:e27).

183. Pizlo Z. 2001. Perception viewed as an inverse problem. *Vision Res* 41:3145–3161.

184. Pizlo Z. 2008. *3D shape: its unique place in visual perception*. Cambridge: MIT Press.

185. Plantinga H, Dyer C. 1990. Visibility, occlusion, and the aspect graph. *Int J Comput Vis* 5(2):137–160.

186. Ponce J. 1990. Straight homogeneous generalized cylinders: differential geometry and uniqueness results. *Int J Comput Vis* 4(1):79–100.

187. Ponce J, Berg TL, Everingham M, Forsyth DA, Hebert M, Lazebnik S, Marszalek M, Schmid C, Russell BC, Torralba A, Williams CKI, Zhang J, Zisserman A. 2007. Toward category-level object recognition. In *Springer-Verlag Tecture Notes in Computer Science*, ed. J Ponce, M Hebert, C Schmid, A Zisserman. New York: Springer-Verlag.

188. Ponce J, Chelberg D. 1987. Finding the limbs and cusps of generalized cylinders. *Int J Comput Vis* 1(3):195–210.

189. Quack T, Ferrari V, Leibe B, Van L Gool. 2007. Efficient mining of frequent and distinctive feature configurations. In Proceedings of the international conference on computer vision, Rio de Janeiro, Brazil.

190. Quattoni A, Collins M, Darrell T. 2007. Learning visual representations using images with captions. In Proceedings of the IEEE conference on computer vision and pattern recognition.

191. Raja N, Jain A. 1992. Recognizing geons from superquadrics fitted to range data. *Image Vision Comput* 10(3):179–190.

192. Raja N, Jain A. 1994. Obtaining generic parts from range images using a multi-view representation. *Comput Vis Image Und* 60(1):44–64.

193. Rao RPN, Ballard DH. 1995. An active vision architecture based on iconic representations. *Artif. Intell.* 78(1-2):461–505.

194. Rehg J, Morris D, Kanade T. 2003. Ambiguities in visual tracking of articulated objects using two- and three-dimensional models. *Int J Robot Res* 22(6):393–418,

195. Ren X, Fowlkes CC, Malik J. 2005. Scale-invariant contour completion using conditional random fields. In Proceedings of the tenth international conference on computer vision, vol. 2, 1214–1221.

196. Ren X, Fowlkes CC, Malik J. 2006. Figure/ground assignment in natural images. In Proceedings of the nineth European Conference Computer Vision, vol 2, 614–627.

197. Rivlin E, Dickinson S, Rosenfeld A. 1995. Recognition by functional parts. *Comput Vis Image Und* 62(2):164–176.

198. Roberts L. 1965. Machine perception of three-dimensional solids. In *Optical and electro-optical information processing*, ed. J Tippett et al., 159–197. Cambridge: MIT Press.

199. Robles-Kelly A, Hancock ER. 2005. Graph edit distance from spectral seriation. *IEEE Trans Pattern Anal Mach Intell* 27(3):365–378.

200. Rom H, Medioni G. 1993. Hierarchical decomposition and axial shape description. *IEEE Trans Pattern Anal Mach Intell* 15(10):973–981.

201. Rosch E, Mervis C, Gray W, Johnson D, Boyes-Braem. P. 1976. Basic objects in natural categories. *Cognit Psychol*, 8:382–439.

202. Rosenfeld A. 1979. *Picture languages: formal models for picture recognition*. New York: Academic Press.

203. Rosenfeld A. 1986. Expert vision sytems: some issues. *Comput Vision Graph* 34(1):99–102.

204. Rothganger F, Lazebnik S, Schmid C, Ponce J. 2006. 3d object modeling and recognition using local affine-invariant image descriptors and multi-view spatial constraints. *Int J Comput Vis* 66(3):231–259.

205. Russell B, Torralba A, Murphy K, Freeman W. 2008. Labelme: a database and web-based tool for image annotation. *Int J Comput Vis* 77(1-3):157–173.

206. Sallam M, Bowyer K. 1991. Generalizing the aspect graph concept to include articulated assemblies. *Pattern Recogn Lett* 12:171–176.

207. Sarkar S, Boyer KL. 1995. Using perceptual inference networks to manage vision processes. *Comput Vis Image Und* 62(1):27–46.

208. Savarese S, Fei-Fei L. 2007. 3d generic object categorization, localization and pose estimation. In Proceedings of the IEEE international conference on computer vision.

209. Schiele B, Crowley JL. 2000. Recognition without correspondence using multidimensional receptive field histograms. *Int J Comput Vis* 36(1):31–50.

210. Schmid C, Mohr R. 1997. Local grayvalue invariants for image retrieval. *IEEE Trans Pattern Anal Mach Intell* 19(5):530–535.

211. Sclaroff S, Pentland A. 1995. Modal matching for correspondence and recognition. *IEEE Trans Pattern Anal Mach Intell* 17(6):545–561.

212. Sebastian T, Klein PN, Kimia B. 2004. Recognition of shapes by editing their shock graphs. *IEEE Trans Pattern Anal Mach Intell* 26(5):550–571.

213. Seibert M, Waxman A. 1992. Adaptive 3-D object recognition from multiple views. *IEEE Trans Pattern Anal Mach Intell* 14(2):107–124.

214. Sengupta K, Boyer KL. 1995. Organizing large structural modelbases. *IEEE Trans Pattern Anal Mach Intell* 17(4):321–332.

215. Sengupta K, Boyer KL. 1998. Modelbase partitioning using property matrix spectra. *Comput Vis Image Und* 70(2):177–196.

216. Serre T, Wolf L, Bileschi S, Riesenhuber M, Poggio T. 2007. Object recognition with cortex-like mechanisms. *IEEE Trans Pattern Anal Mach Intell* 29(3):411–426.

217. Shimshoni I, Ponce J. 1997. Finite-resolution aspect graphs of polyhedral objects. *IEEE Trans Pattern Anal Mach Intell* 19(4):315–327.

218. Shokoufandeh A, Bretzner L, Macrini D, Demirci MF, Jönsson C, Dickinson S. 2006. The representation and matching of categorical shape. *Comput Vis Image Und* 103(2):139–154.

219. Shokoufandeh A, Macrini D, Dickinson S, Siddiqi K, Zucker SW. 2005. Indexing hierarchical structures using graph spectra. *IEEE Trans Pattern Anal Mach Intell* 27(7):1125–1140.

220. Shokoufandeh A, Marsic I, Dickinson S. 1999. View-based object recognition using saliency maps. *Image Vis Comput* 17(5-6):445–460.

221. Shotton J, Blake A, Cipolla R. 2005. Contour-based learning for object detection. In Proceedings of the international conference on computer vision 503–510.

222. Siddiqi K, Pizer S. 2008. *Medial representations: mathematics, algorithms, and applications.* New York: Springer Verlag.

223. Siddiqi K, Shokoufandeh A, Dickinson S, Zucker S. 1999. Shock graphs and shape matching. *Int J Comput Vis* 30:1–24.

224. Siddiqi K, Zhang J, Macrini D, Shokoufandeh A, Bioux S, Dickinson S. 2008. Retrieving articulated 3-d models using medial surfaces. *Mach Vis Appl* 19(4):261–275.

225. Silberberg T, Harwood DA, Davis LS. 1986. Object recognition using oriented model points. *Comput Vis Graph* 35(1):47–71.

226. Smeulders WMA, Worring M, Santini S, Gupta A, Jain R. 2000. Content-based image retrieval at the end of the early years. *IEEE Trans Pattern Anal Mach Intell* 22(12):1349–1380.

227. Sminchisescu C, Kanaujia A, Metaxas D. 2007. "bm^3e: Discriminative density propagation for visual tracking". *IEEE Trans Pattern Anal Mach Intell* 29(11): 2030–2044.

228. Sminchisescu C, Kanaujia A, Metaxas DN. 2006. Learning joint top-down and bottom-up processes for 3d visual inference. In Proceedings of the IEEE conference on computer vision and pattern recognition, 1743–1752.

229. Solina F, Bajcsy R. 1990. Recovery of parametric models from range images: the case for superquadrics with global deformations. *IEEE Trans Pattern Anal Mach Intell* 12(2):131–146.

230. Sripradisvarakul T, Jain R. 1989. Generating aspect graphs for curved objects. In Proceedings of the IEEE workshop on interpretation of 3D Scenes, 109–115, Austin, TX.

231. Stark L, Bowyer K. 1991. Achieving generalized object recognition through reasoning about association of function to structure. *IEEE Trans Pattern Anal Mach Intell* 13(10):1097–1104.

232. Stark L, Bowyer K. 1994. Function-based generic recognition for multiple object categories. *Comput Vis Image Und* 59(1):1–21.

233. Stewman J, Bowyer K. 1990. Direct construction of the perspective projection aspect graph of convex polyhedra. *Comput Vis Graph* 51:20–37.

234. Storkey AJ, Williams CKI. 2003. Image modeling with position-encoding dynamic trees. *IEEE Trans Pattern Anal Mach Intell* 25(7):859–871.

235. Strat TM, Fischler MA. 1991. Context-based vision: recognizing objects using information from both 2d and 3d imagery. *IEEE Trans Pattern Anal Mach Intell* 13(10):1050–1065.

236. Telea A, Sminchisescu C, Dickinson S. 2004. Optimal inference for hierarchical skeleton abstraction. In Proceedings of the international conference on pattern recognition, 19–22.

237. Tenenbaum JM, Barrow HG. 1977. Experiments in interpretation-guided segmentation. *Artif Intell* 8(3):241–274.

238. Terzopoulos D, Metaxas D. 1991. Dynamic 3D models with local and global deformations: deformable superquadrics. *IEEE Trans Pattern Anal Mach Intell* 13(7):703–714.

239. Terzopoulos D, Witkin A, Kass M. 1987. Symmetry-seeking models and 3D object recovery. *Int J Comput Vis* 1:211–221.

240. Thompson D, Mundy J. 1987. Three-dimensional model matching from an unconstrained viewpoint. In Proceedings of the IEEE international conference on robotics and automation, 4:208–220.

241. Todorovic S, Ahuja N. 2006. Extracting subimages of an unknown category from a set of images. In Proceedings of the IEEE conference on computer vision and pattern recognition, 927–934.

242. Todorovic S, Ahuja N. 2008. Unsupervised category modeling, recognition, and segmentation in images. *IEEE Trans Pattern Anal Mach Intell* 30(12):2158–2174.

243. Todorovic S, Nechyba MC. 2005. Dynamic trees for unsupervised segmentation and matching of image regions. *IEEE Trans Pattern Anal Mach Intell* 27(11):1762–1777.

244. Torralba A, Fergus R, Freeman WT. 2007. Tiny images. Technical report, Computer Science and Artificial Intelligence Lab, Massachusetts Institute of Technology.

245. Torralba AB. 2003. Contextual priming for object detection. *Int J Comput Vis* 53(2):169–191.

246. Tsotsos JK. 1985. Knowledge organization and its role in representation and interpretation for time-varying data: the alven system. *Comput Intell* 1:16–32.

247. Tsotsos JK. 1988. A "complexity level" analysis of immediate vision. *Int J Comput Vis (Marr Prize Special Issue)* 2(1):303–320.

248. Tsotsos JK. 1990. Analyzing vision at the complexity level. *Behav Brain Sci* 13(3):423–445.

249. Tsotsos JK. 1992. On the relative complexity of passive vs. active visual search. *Int J Comput Vis* 7(2):127–141.

250. Turk M, Pentland A. 1991. Eigenfaces for recognition. *J Cognitive Neurosci* 3(1):71–86.

251. Ullman S, Basri R. 1991. Recognition by linear combinations of models. *IEEE Trans Pattern Anal Mach Intell* 13(10):992–1006.

252. Ullman S, Vidal-Naquet M, Sali E. 2002. Visual features of intermediate complexity and their use in classification. *Nature Neurosci* 5(7):1–6.

253. Ulupinar F, Nevatia R. 1993. Perception of 3-D surfaces from 2-D contours. *IEEE Trans Pattern Anal Mach Intell* 15:3–18.

254. Vaina L, Jaulent M. 1991. Object structure and action requirements: a compatibility model for functional recognition. *Int J Intell Syst* 6:313–336.

255. van Eede M, Macrini D, Telea A, Sminchisescu C, Dickinson S. 2006. Canonical skeletons for shape matching. In Proceedings of the international conference on pattern recognition, 64–69.

256. Viola P, Jones M. 2004. Robust real-time face detection. *Int J Comput Vis* 57(2):137–154.

257. von Ahn L, Dabbish L. 2004. Labeling images with a computer game. In ACM conference on human factors in computing systems, 319–326.

258. Wachsmuth S, Stevenson S, Dickinson S. 2003. Towards a framework for learning structured shape models from text-annotated images. In HLT-NAACL03 workshop on learning word meaning from non-linguistic data.

259. Wang J, Athitsos V, Sclaroff S, Betke M. 2008. Detecting objects of variable shape structure with hidden state shape models. *IEEE Trans Pattern Anal Mach Intell* 30(3):477–492.

260. Wang W, Pollak I, Wong T-S, Bouman CA, Harper MP, Mark Siskind J. 2006. Hierarchical stochastic image grammars for classification and segmentation. *IEEE Trans Image Process* 15(10):3033–3052.

261. Weber M, Welling M, Perona P. 2000. Towards automatic discovery of object categories. In Proceedings of the IEEE conference on computer vision and pattern recognition, 2101–2108.

262. Weber M, Welling M, Perona P. 2000. Unsupervised learning of models for recognition. In Proceedings of the European conference on computer vision, 18–32.

263. Weinshall D, Werman M. 1997. On view likelihood and stability. *IEEE Trans Pattern Anal Mach Intell* 19(2):97–108.

264. Weiss I, Ray M. 2005. Recognizing articulated objects using a region-based invariant transform. *IEEE Trans Pattern Anal Mach Intell* 27(10):1660–1665.

265. Wertheimer M. 1938. Laws of organization in perceptual forms. In *Source book of Gestalt psychology*, ed. W. Ellis. New York: Harcourt, Brace.

266. Winn JM, Jojic N. 2005. Locus: learning object classes with unsupervised segmentation. In Proceedings of the international conference on computer vision, 756–763.

267. Winston P, Binford T, Katz B, Lowry M. 1983. Learning physical description from functional descriptions, examples, and precedents. In Proceedings of the AAAI, 433–439, Palo Alto, CA.

268. Wu K, Levine MD. 1997. 3-d shape approximation using parametric geons. *Image Vis Comput* 15(2):143–158.

269. Wu YN, Si ZZ, Gong HF, Zhu SC. 2009. Active basis for deformable object modeling, learning and detection. *Int J Comput Vis* (in press).

270. Yu SX, Shi J. 2003. Object-specific figure-ground segregation. In Proceedings of the IEEE conference on computer vision and pattern recognition, 39–45.

271. Zerroug M, Medioni GG. 1994. The challenge of generic object recognition. In Object representation in computer vision, international workshop, 217–232, New York, NY.

272. Zerroug M, Nevatia R. 1996. Volumetric descriptions from a single intensity image. *Int J Comput Vis* 20(1/2):11–42.

273. Zhu L, Chen Y, Yuille A. 2009. Unsupervised learning of probabilistic grammar-markov models for object categories. *IEEE Trans Pattern Anal Mach Intell* (in press).

274. Zhu S, Yuille AL. 1996. Forms: a flexible object recognition and modelling system. *Int J Comput Vis* 20(3):187–212.

275. Zhu S-C, Mumford D. 2006. A stochastic grammar of images. *Found Trends Comput Graph Vision* 2(4):259–362.

CHAPTER 2

A Strategy for Understanding How the Brain Accomplishes Object Recognition

James J. DiCarlo

2.1 Introduction

It is an exciting time to be working on the problem of visual object recognition. The fields of visual neuroscience, cognitive science, and computer vision are rapidly converging; they are beginning to speak the same language and define the same set of problems. This chapter is not a scholarly review of any of those fields, and I apologize to the authors of a great deal of work that is relevant to this discussion but is not mentioned here. Instead, my chapter is an attempt to give our perspective on key questions at the intersections of these fields. I use the term "our" because the opinions expressed derive not only from myself but also from the hard work of my students, post-docs, and collaborators. Along the way, I briefly mention some recent research results relevant to this discussion, but mostly refer the reader to the original citations. Although I will not be providing the final answers here, I hope that our perspective among the others in this book will encourage agreement on what those answers might look like and a strategy for finding them.

The authors of the chapters in this book share a strong common interest. Loosely stated, we all want to understand how visual object recognition (categorization and identification) "works." We have a goal in the mist – there is a mountain out there, and we would like to climb it together. Let's stop hiking for a moment and talk about three key questions that we need to answer to reach that goal:

1. What problem are we trying to solve?
2. What do good forms of visual representation to solve this problem look like?
3. What brainlike algorithms can produce such representations?

In this chapter, I give our perspective on each question. The most important thing is not who is right and who is wrong, but that we keep asking these three questions of ourselves and each other so that we keep our compass pointed in the right direction.

2.2 What Problem Are We Trying to Solve? The Importance of Having a Goal

In the machine vision community focused on object recognition, a tremendous amount of effort is being expended on exploring algorithms that may support general object recoagnition. This is fun and it pays the bills, because one can hold up an actual "product" and give performance numbers, which feels like progress. Indeed, to the newly initiated, it often sounds as if such algorithms have solved the problem of object recognition, because successes are highlighted more than failures. Various algorithms come in and out of favor, each typically claiming some good level of performance on some particular image database. We do not wish to impugn the very creative work in the community; certainly, this is an understandable attempt to focus on smaller problems that may not have been solved, while setting aside problems that may have been solved. However, it is not clear that such a piecemeal approach will lead us to a general theory of object recognition, and the short-term goal of succeeding on limited problems may distract us from the crux computational issues (i.e., natural image variability, or invariance; see Pinto et al. 2008 for a further discussion on this issue).

In the neuroscience community working on the brain processing pathway implicated in object recognition, neurophysiologists and cognitive neuroscientists have clear phenomena, such as the very remarkable spiking patterns of individual neurons (and fMRI voxels), especially at high levels of the visual system, where individual neurons/voxels can be selective for particular objects or categories, such as faces (Downing et al. 2001; Kanwisher et al. 1997; Logothetis and Sheinberg 1996; Rolls 2000; Tanaka 1996). This naturally makes the experimentalist set the implicit goal as one of understanding what makes each neuron "go"; therefore, much effort has been expended on seeking the stimuli that each neuron "likes," sometimes in a systems identification framework (Brincat and Connor 2004; Kayaert et al. 2003; Pasupathy and Connor 2001; Pollen et al. 2002; Tanaka 1996; Tsunoda 2001; Yamane et al. 2006). Although a complete understanding of the transfer function (image input to neuronal response) of many high-level single neurons could help us reach our goal of understanding object recognition, it is probably intractable, given the dimensionality of the input space and nonlinearity of the system, and it may not even expose the key underlying computational principles at work.

In short, these lines of work have, individually, contributed a great deal to the knowledge base from which we can now draw. However, it is not at all clear that continuing or either or both of these paths is the way to achieve our goal. It is time for us to step back and consider our overall strategy.

2.3 Can We Agree on the Overarching Goal?

We all have intuition about our goal, which is to "understand" object recognition. We want to understand how a visual system (biologic or synthetic) can take incoming visual input (retinal images) and report the identities or categories of objects in the scene. Intuition alone, however, does not provide the traction needed to reach our goal. How will we know when we have attained this understanding? This difficulty is known to many in the field, but was perhaps best articulated by Marr (1982), when he pointed out that there are different levels of understanding in vision and that it might be necessary to understand each level (these levels roughly parallel the three questions I posed at the beginning of this chapter).

Even with this notable history in our field, we do not all agree on the goal. Some workers primarily aim to build a good recognition system, even if it looks nothing like the real brain and even if they have not uncovered any deep general principles; they just want a computational system that works. Others primarily want to understand how the brain solves this problem, and they may not care if what they discover ever leads to working machine systems, as long as they understand the gist of the computational processes at work in the brain and something about the instantiation of those processes in the brain wetware. Many such workers are driven by a notion of pure, academic understanding, perhaps that which will support the treatment of brain disorders that impact the perceptual system (e.g., agnosias, Alzheimer's disease, dyslexia, autism, etc.) or the development of neural prosthetics.

Others (myself and perhaps most of the other authors in this book) believe that all these motivations are not only valuable but inextricably linked. Artificial recognition systems define the hypotheses to be tested (competing against each other for computational supremacy), and brain experimentation (behavior, physiology, and anatomy) aims to rule out computationally viable hypotheses and to discover new clues that lead to new hypotheses (new artificial systems). In short, we believe that the key insights will be discovered by approaches that are savvy to *both* the computational hypotheses and the brain wetware.

Why is it critical to define the goal of the system that we aim to understand/build/emulate? From an engineering perspective, goals are explicit constraints on the form of the solution – the tighter the constraints, the more likely they are to help us arrive at the "true" solution (i.e., the solution actually at work in the brain). Ideally, the goal (or goals) should be specified as an explicit definition of the problem we are trying to solve, and should contain concrete benchmarks that engage that problem. To put it bluntly, no team of engineers would be put to work on a project without an explicit description from the project manager of the desired functionality of the product and a set of tests to gauge the team's progress.

So how do we begin working on this functional description of visual object recognition (Arathorn et al. 2007)? More broadly, what is the Turing (1950) test of vision? At the very top level, the only test that biologic vision systems must pass is survival (and reproduction) in real-world environments. Although this very top-level goal has led to new lines of interesting work (e.g., embodied systems; see Brooks 1987; Pfeifer and Scheier 1999), such a goal is probably not a powerful enough constraint to guide progress on the problem of vision, generally, or object recognition, particularly. Thus, although it is often not explicitly stated, I and others speculate that at least some aspects of vision can be considered as relatively independent of other sensory systems and behavioral goals, such as, for example, a general-purpose object recognition subsystem that provides powerful object representations as a "front end" to guide ongoing decision and action. Some neuropsychology data support this viewpoint (Farah 1990), and we take it as a working assumption so that we can make progress by narrowing the domain we aim to understand.

2.4 The Key, Near-Term Goal: Core Recognition

We define the functional goal of object recognition as the ability (1) to discriminate accurately each named object (identification) or set of objects (categorization) from all other possible objects, materials, textures, and so on; (2) to do this over a range of identity-preserving transformations of the retinal image of that object (e.g., position, size, pose, etc.). We concentrate on what we believe to be the core of the brain's recognition system, which is the ability to report rapidly the identity or category of an object after a single brief glimpse of visual input (<300 ms) (Hung et al. 2005; Potter 1976; Thorpe et al. 1996). To be more concrete, think of black and white images that contain one or more objects briefly presented to one eye without any prior instruction. This paradigm avoids color, binocularity, and attentional cueing of any type, yet our object recognition abilities in that situation are remarkably impressive. We term this ability and the computations that support it "core recognition." We do not claim that this is all of object recognition, and, looking ahead, it will be important to understand and quantify how much of real-world object recognition is accomplished in that manner. Regardless, we believe that this piece of the larger problem is the right size to bite off and chew (i.e., it is important *and* defined), and we aim to see how far a clear focus on this problem will take us.

2.5 Establishing Benchmarks for Core Recognition

Note that my definition of core object recognition provided in the preceding section still lacks teeth. Concretely, we must specify expected performance on sets of real images (i.e., benchmark tests). The development of such benchmarks is clearly necessary so that we can assess whether we have succeeded or whether, at the very least, we know more today than we did yesterday. Indeed, instantiated computational object recognition models are the only way to explore the complex hypothesis space that must be navigated, and appropriate benchmarks can act as an evolutionary-like selection force to negotiate that terrain.

Although some have strongly advocated for such benchmarks, it turns out that establishing them is far from straightforward (Pinto, Cox, and DiCarlo 2008; Ponce et al. 2006). Many small, specialized object recognition benchmarks have existed for many years, but their use has typically remained restricted to the groups that designed them and the problems they were meant to test. Thus, it is laudable that the work of several groups has recently encouraged more standardized, freely available, and widely used benchmarks (Li et al. 2004; The PASCAL object recognition database collection). This development is a step forward in setting up the aforementioned evolutionary selection force for two reasons. First, it enforces the idea that all real models must work on real images; that is, widely adopted benchmarks define a playing field, and models that cannot produce predictions on any given real-world image are appropriately ushered off that playing field (although they may still shout out important suggestions from the grandstands). Second, it implicitly encourages the comparison of different models (i.e., friendly competition), which allows the field to learn which ideas work and which ideas do not.

The establishment of these competitive selection forces carries the potential risk that the "surviving" models will be led in the wrong direction. For example, we have recently found that, on some ostensibly natural recognition benchmarks, simple forms of visual representation that are not good object recognition systems can nonetheless perform as well as many state-of-the-art systems (Pinto, Cox, and DiCarlo 2008) (Fig. 2.1). This certainly does not imply that those state-of-the-art systems are faulty or misguided (indeed, many of them are tested on other benchmarks that could be more suitable). It also does not imply that benchmarks are a bad idea. Instead, it points out that establishing good benchmarks is not easy. Although some benchmarks may seem useful at first glance, they can be poorly suited at separating good ideas from less interesting ones.

Going forward, much more work is needed to ensure that our benchmarks capture the computational crux of the problem of object recognition, which is the ability to identify and categorize objects in each image in the face of natural variability (i.e., the invariance problem) (DiCarlo and Cox 2007). Only in doing so will those benchmarks provide the right kind of evolutionary pressure on models of how the ventral visual stream represents images to support object recognition. Given the remarkable abilities of modern machine-learning methods to sniff out any advantage they can gain in a data set, we do not advocate for a fixed set of benchmark images. Instead, the best benchmark strategy may be one in which images rendered by computer graphics allow full control of parameters of interest, such as the amount of variation in object position, scale, pose, and so on, as well as control of backgrounds, other objects, and temporal statistics (i.e., movies). Although approaches in which ground truth is known and controlled have been used in the past, because algorithms developed in such environments did not generalize well to real images (see Chap. 1), ground-truth approaches have been displaced by an emphasis on natural recognition problems, which typically means images pulled off the web (Li et al. 2004; The PASCAL object recognition database collection). Interestingly, this same debate between natural images and parametric control of simple images has been raging in the experimental neuroscience community (e.g., Rust et al. 2005). However, given the remarkable power in computer graphics technology for building realistic visual worlds, the parametric, ground-truth approach should allow us to have our cake and eat it too (i.e., the creation of natural images even with a high level of experimental control). Because this approach is parametric, it has the advantage of allowing us to ratchet up gradually the evolutionary pressure (i.e., amount of invariance that is needed) on competing models of visual representation and to diagnose quickly where models are weak.

Other potential benchmark approaches are those that aim to explicitly capture real-world image variation in photographs (Lecun et al. 2004), and those that might implicitly capture that variation in large labeled sets of real-world images (e.g., Ahn et al. 2006; Bileschi 2006; Huang et al. 2007; Russell et al. 2008). Regardless of the benchmark strategy, the use of well-established forms of visual representations (e.g., primary visual area, V1; Fig. 2.1) should be used to calibrate each benchmark by setting the bar against which models must compete (Pinto, Cox, and DiCarlo 2008; Pinto, DiCarlo, and Cox 2008).

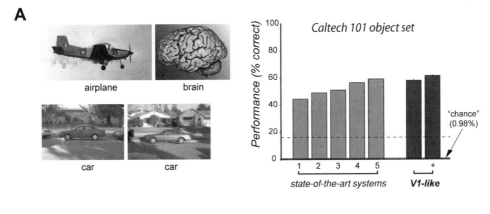

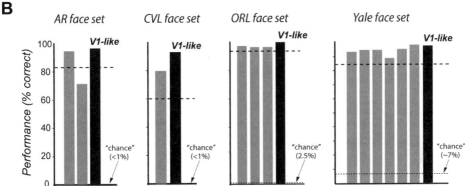

Figure 2.1. Using a simple neuroscientist "null" model of object representation (primary visual area, V1) to calibrate various benchmarks. *A*, When tested on an ostensibly natural standard object recognition benchmark (Caltech 101), a V1-like model performs as well as some state-of-the-art artificial object recognition systems. *Left*, Example images from the database and their category labels, including two example images from the "car" category. *Right*, Cross-validated performance of five different state-of-the-art computational object recognition systems on this "natural" database are shown in gray (fifteen training examples were used to train each system). The performance of the simple V1-like model is shown in black (+ is with ad hoc features; see [1]). Although the V1-like model is extremely simple and lacks any explicit invariance-building mechanisms, it performs as well as, or better than, the state-of-the-art object recognition systems. *B*, Cross-validated performance of the same V1-like model on four different benchmarks of face detection. Various models using those databases to judge performance are shown in gray. Values are near ceiling, but again, the V1-like model performs as well as, or better than, other models. Dashed lines in all panels indicate performance obtained from pixel representations. That does not imply that the recognition systems shown here are without value, but that benchmarks must be developed that can better weed out less interesting forms of representation (such as this simple V1 model). Adapted from Pinto Cox, and DiCarlo 2008; Pinto, DiCarlo, and Cox 2008. Please see details there, including benchmark suggestions.

2.6 What Computational Processes Must Be at Work to Accomplish Core Recognition?

We now turn away from the (unfinished) business of defining the problem we are trying to solve and focus on the strategy the brain might use to solve it. We have previously discussed this at length (DiCarlo and Cox 2007) and only briefly review here. To solve a recognition task, a subject must use some internal neuronal representation of the visual scene (population pattern of activity) to make a decision (e.g., Ashby and Gott 1988; Johnson 1980): "Is object **A** present in the image or not?" Computationally, the brain must apply a decision function (Johnson 1980) to divide an underlying neuronal representational space into regions where object **A** is present and regions where it is not (one function for each object to be potentially reported). Because brains compute with neurons, the subject *must* have neurons somewhere in its nervous system (read-out neurons) that can successfully report if object **A** was present (Barlow 1995). There are many relevant *mechanistic* issues, such as the number of neurons involved in computing the decision at this location in the brain, whether their operation is fixed or dynamically created with the task at hand, and how choices are coded in their spikes. In contrast, the central *computational* questions are: What is the format of the representation used to support the decision (the substrate on which the decision functions directly operate)? What *kinds* of decision functions (i.e., read-out tools) are applied to that representation?

These two central computational issues are two sides of the same coin. Object recognition can be described as the problem of finding very complex decision functions (highly nonlinear) that operate on the retinal image representation, or as the problem of finding operations that progressively *transform* that retinal representation into a new form of representation, followed by the application of relatively simple decision functions (e.g., linear classifiers; Duda et al. 2001). At a pure mathematical level, the difference is only terminology, but we and others (e.g., Hung et al. 2005; Johnson 1980) argue that the latter viewpoint is more productive because it starts to take the problem apart in a way that is consistent with the architecture and response properties of the ventral visual stream (Fig. 2.2), and because such simple decision functions are easily implemented in biologically plausible neurons (a thresholded sum over weighted synaptic inputs). This view also meshes well with the conventional wisdom on pattern recognition, which is that the choice of representation is often more important than the strength of the decision rule (classifier) that is used.

What do we mean by visual representation? During each glimpse of the world, a visual image is projected into the eye, transduced by $\sim$100 million retinal photoreceptors, and conveyed to the brain in the spiking activity pattern of $\sim$1 million retinal ganglion cells. We conceptualize that initial retinal image representation as a high-dimensional representation in which each axis of the space is the spiking response rate of one retinal ganglion cell (e.g., Roweis and Saul 2000; Tenenbaum et al. 2000; Fig. 2.2).

Consider the face of one particular person. All the possible retinal images that face could ever produce (e.g., due to changes in its pose, position, size, etc.) arise from a continuous, low-dimensional, curved surface inside the retinal image representation (an object identity manifold; e.g., Edelman 1999; Roweis and Saul 2000; Tenenbaum et al. 2000). Different objects have different identity manifolds that generally do not cross or superimpose in the retinal image representation; they are like sheets of paper crumpled together. Thus, although the retinal representation cannot directly support recognition, it *implicitly* contains the information to distinguish which of the two individuals was seen. We argue that this describes the computational crux of everyday recognition: the problem is typically *not* a lack of information or noisy information, but that the information is badly formatted, or tangled, in the retinal representation. One way of viewing the overarching computational goal of the brain's object recognition machinery, then, is as an untangling transformation from neuronal population representations that are

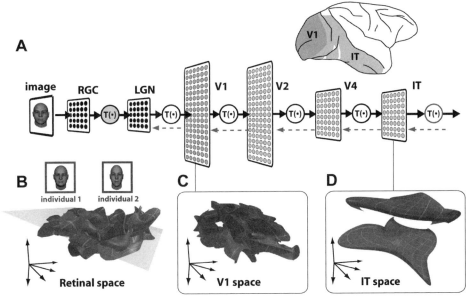

Figure 2.2. *A,* In our best model of the human visual system, the rhesus monkey, the visual areas have been mapped, and organized hierarchically, and the ventral visual stream is known to be critical for complex object discrimination (colored areas in brain inset, adapted from Felleman and Van Essen 1991). We conceptualize each stage of the ventral stream as a new population representation. The lower panels schematically illustrate these populations at successively higher stages across the ventral visual stream. Any pattern of photons from the world (here a face) is transduced into neuronal activity at the retina and is progressively and rapidly transformed and re-represented in each population, perhaps by a common canonical cortical transform (T, see text). Solid arrows indicate the direction of visual information flow based on neuronal latency (~100 ms latency in IT), but this does not preclude fast feedback both within and between areas (dashed arrows). *B–D,* In each neuronal population space, each cardinal axis is one neuron's activity (e.g., firing rate over a ~200-ms interval), the dimensionality is the number of neurons, and a given visual image is one point. Although such high-dimensional spaces cannot be visualized, the 3-D views portrayed here provide intuition. Owing to changes in identity-preserving variables such as position, scale, and pose, each object can produce an infinite number of different points in each space. Those points arise from its low-dimensional object identity manifold embedded in the space. Here two objects are shown (two faces) along with their simulated object identity manifolds (here two-dimensional sheets resulting from the manipulation of two degrees of freedom in pose). The left panel shows pixel (retina-like) manifolds generated from 3-D face models (14,400-dimensional data). The display axes were chosen to be the projections that best separate identity, pose azimuth, and pose elevation. Even though this simple example only exercises a fraction of typical real-world variation, the object manifolds are hopelessly tangled and not separable with simple decision functions (e.g., hyperplane in green). As visual information progresses through the ventral visual pathway, it is progressively re-represented (untangled) in each visual area and becomes better and better at directly supporting object recognition. A population of 500 V1 neurons was simulated as a bank of Gabor filters with firing thresholds (still tangled). In contrast, a population of 500 simulated IT neurons gives rise to object manifolds that are easily separated. In addition, such a representation also allows one to recover information about identity-preserving variables, such as object position, size, and pose (see text). Figure adapted from DiCarlo and Cox 2007; please see for details. (See color plate 2.2.)

easy to build (e.g., the set of center-surround filters in the retina) but are not easily decoded, into new neuronal population representations that we do not yet know how to build (e.g., the set of all inferior temporal cortex neurons) but that are easily decoded (see Fig. 2.2). The general idea of representational transformation is not new (2 1/2-D sketch, feature selection, etc.; Duda et al. 2001; Johnson et al. 1995; Mann 1982), but the untangling perspective suggests the *kinds* of computational principles the ventral visual system might employ (see Fig. 2.2).

2.7 What Does a Good Representation to Support Core Recognition Look Like?

In human beings and other primates, these representations are thought to be built by the ventral visual stream, culminating in its highest level, the inferior temporal cortex (IT) (for reviews, see (Logothetis and Sheinberg 1996; Tanaka 1996; Rolls 2000). Many individual IT neurons respond selectively to particular classes of objects, such as faces or other complex shapes, yet show some tolerance to changes in object position and size, pose, illumination, and low-level shape cues (see Serre et al. 2007 for recent related results in humans). We, and others (Felleman and Van Essen 1991; Riesenhuber and Poggio 1999), consider the ventral visual stream to be a progressive series of visual re-representations, from V1 to V2 to V4 to IT. As outlined previously, we argue that object identity manifolds are gradually "untangled" by iterated computational principles at work at each stage of that stream (Fig. 2.2; DiCarlo and Cox 2007). To date, we have focused on characterizing the initial wave of neuronal population images that are successively produced along the ventral visual stream as the retinal image is transformed and re-represented on its way to IT (Fig. 2.2). For example, we have recently found that population representations in IT can support at least some core recognition. Specifically, simple linear classifiers can rapidly (within <300 ms from image onset) and accurately decide an object's category from reading the firing rates of an IT population of ~200 neurons, despite object position and size variation (Hung et al. 2005).

Although we do not yet know how the ventral visual stream builds this powerful form of visual representation, it is helpful to think about what the elements of such representation should look like. Given the definitions provided, a neuronal population representation that is "good" must easily support the benchmark recognition tasks that we develop (which reminds us that such human performance should ideally be tested using the same benchmarks (e.g., Serre et al. 2007). Does this population constraint tell us what the individual elements (single neurons) of the representation should ideally be doing?

The simple textbook conception of IT suggests that each IT neuron should have both high shape selectivity and high invariance to identity-preserving image transformations. However, the contemporary experimental data show that IT neurons do not typically have large invariance to identity-preserving image changes. For example, IT neurons have only limited position, size, and pose tolerance (DiCarlo and Maunsell 2003; Logothetis and Pauls 1995; Logothetis et al. 1995) and their responses are strongly affected by the presence of nonpreferred objects ("clutter") (Chelazzi et al. 1998; Miller et al. 1993; Rolls and Tovee 1995; Sato 1989; Zoccolan et al. 2005; Zoccolan et al. 2007).

Do such data reflect the limitations of IT neurons? We believe not, because populations of such neurons can still support position- and clutter-tolerant object recognition (Li et al. 2009). Indeed, population representations are more than their individual parts. For example, when individual IT neurons have appropriate joint tuning for object identity (shape) and object position, scale and pose (properties they do seem to have; Ito et al. 1995; Logothetis et al. 1995; Op de Beeck and Vogels 2000; Zoccolan et al. 2005), and they are distributed such that the population has sufficiently "tiled" the space (of natural shapes, positions, scales, and pose), that results in a very powerful population representation. It not only allows straightforward report of object category and identity (see benchmarks cited previously), but also allows report of information about object position, scale, and pose (Li et al. 2006). Thus, it allows the populations to avoid numerous forms of the "binding problem" (Edelman 1999; Hang et al. 2005; Riesenhuber and Poggio 1999) and to report the answers to questions such as, "Which object is on the left?" and "Is the book on top of the table?" These ideas about good forms of representation are known in parts of the computational vision community (Edelman 1999; Riesenhuber and Poggio 1999) and are now influencing the cognitive neuroscience community (Schwarzlose et al. 2008) (see Chap. 6). From the untangling perspective, this amounts to population representations in which object identity manifolds are flat and coordinated (DiCarlo and Cox 2007) (Fig. 2.2D).

From a mechanistic point of view, however, much work remains to be done. The appreciation of the power of this form of representation and the empirical evidence that the ventral visual stream may have adopted it do not tell us how to build it or how the brain builds it. This information does clarify the problem, however: it points out that the key property that single neurons should try to achieve is not the *amount* of tolerance (invariance) to object position, scale, and pose, but instead the *separation* of selectivity for identity-related image changes (changes in "shape") and identity-preserving image changes (e.g., changes in object position, scale, and pose). Indeed, we argue that this single neuron separability tuning is a better description of the implicit goal of the ventral visual stream. It is also a more refined computational goal, because it motivates one to think about how a brainlike system learned to distinguish between identity-related and identity-preserving image changes (Li et al. 2006).

2.8 How Might the Ventral Visual Stream Build Good Representation?

We do not know how the brain constructs representation for core recognition; however, work from a number of groups is beginning to reveal some key principles.

The first principle is the idea of using dimensionality expansion to help untangle object identity manifolds. In one of its earliest processing steps, the visual system projects incoming information into an even higher-dimensional, overcomplete space (e.g., ~100 times more V1 neurons than retinal ganglion neurons). If nonlinearities are involved (e.g., neuronal thresholds), this helps untangle because it "spreads out" the data in a much larger space (e.g., Lewicki and Sejnowski 2000). The additional constraint of sparseness can reduce the size of the subspace that any given incoming visual image "lives" in and thus make it easier to find projections where object manifolds are flat and separable (Olshausen and Field 2004, 2005). In the language of computer science, this is a memory-intensive strategy, which means that it fundamentally relies on many (nonlinear) elements rather than complex computations within each element.

The second principle is the idea that the ventral visual stream employs a canonical computational strategy that is iterated at each of the cortical steps. With respect to the global problem of object recognition (i.e., untangling object identity manifolds), this computational strategy does not need to swallow the problem whole. Instead, it can untangle object manifolds progressively, in a series of rapidly executed, successive steps (consistent with anatomic and physiologic data along the ventral stream; Rolls 2000). Flattening at local, small scales can ultimately produce flattening at a global scale. Indeed, V1 neurons in a local neighborhood only "see" the world through a small aperture (cannot see whole objects), but they can perform untangling operations with respect to their inputs; V2 can do the same on its V1 inputs, and so on. Even though no single cortical stage or local ensemble within a stage would "understand" its global role, we imagine the end result to be globally flattened, coordinated object manifolds with preserved shape selectivity. Thus, we believe that the most fruitful computational algorithms will be those that a visual system (natural or artificial) could apply locally and iteratively at each cortical processing stage, and some of the leading biologically inspired computational approaches adopt this iterative, hierarchical strategy (Bengio et al. 1995; Fukushima 1980; Heeger et al. 1996; Lecun et al. 2004; Riesenhuber and Poggio 1999; Serre et al. 2007).

The third principle is the related idea that these canonical computational principles may not be best described as hardwired transfer functions but as more fundamental ideas about how those transfer functions may be learned by each cortical stage based on the incoming data (e.g., how does V2 learn to process its inputs from V1?). At least two types of learning relevant to this discussion have been proposed. One is that the ventral visual stream should not waste its processing resources encoding images that do not occur often and that are not biologically relevant (i.e., do not bother encoding the white-noise patterns that make up the vast majority of theoretically possible images). That is, the neuronal tuning functions on inputs from the previous stage may be allocated (perhaps learned) in a way that matches the distribution of visual information encountered in the real world (e.g., Serre et al. 2007; Simoncelli 2008; Ullman et al. 2002). When done in the context of normalization (e.g., Olshausen and Field 2005; Schwartz and Simoncelli 2001) this would increase the effective overcompleteness of visual representations of real-world objects and, thus, help untangle object manifolds, as discussed previously.

Another potentially fundamental learning principle is the idea that time implicitly supervises manifold untangling. Several theorists have noted that the temporal evolution of a retinal image provides clues for learning which image changes are identity-preserving transformations (Edelman 2002; Foldiak 1991; Liand Clark 2004; Masquelier and Thorp 2007; Ullman and Solovier 1999; Wallis and Rolls 1997; Wiskottand Sejnowski 2002). In the manifold untangling context, temporal image evolution spells out the degrees of freedom of object identity manifolds and, thus, may be a powerful,

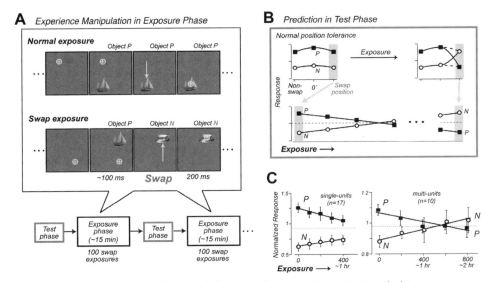

Figure 2.3. Targeted manipulation of the natural temporal continuity of object image experience produces rapid, unsupervised changes in IT neuronal tolerance (invariance). *A,* IT responses were tested in *test phases* (green boxes), which alternated with 15-minute *exposure phases.* During each *exposure phase,* objects initially appeared at 3 degrees above and 3 degrees below the center of gaze, and primates spontaneously made an eye movement (saccade) toward each presented object. In a normal exposure, the object remained unchanged during the saccade. In a "swap" exposure, the normal temporal contiguity of object image experience was altered by swapping the initial object for another object during that saccade. Each *exposure phase* consisted of 100 normal exposures and 100 "swap" exposures. *B,* If the visual system builds tolerance using temporal contiguity (here driven by saccades), the swap exposure should cause incorrect grouping of two different object images (here *P* and *N*). Thus, the predicted effect is a decrease in object selectivity at the swap position that increases with increasing exposure (in the limit, reversing object preference), and little or no change in object selectivity at the non-swap position. *C,* Response data to objects *P* and *N* at the swap position for single neurons (*left*) and multiunit sites (*right*) tested for the longest exposure time. The plot shows the mean normalized response to objects *P* and *N* as a function of exposure time (compare with *B*). No change in selectivity was observed at the equally eccentric control (non-swap) position, and no change in selectivity was observed among other object pairs not shown during the *exposure phase* (not shown). Adapted from Li and DiCarlo 2008, please see details there. (See color plate 2.3.)

invisible teacher of how to untangle those manifolds. Indeed, human studies in our lab (Cox et al. 2005) and others (Wallis and Bulthoff 2001) have begun to connect this computational idea with biological vision, showing that invariant object recognition can be predictably manipulated by the temporal statistics of the environment. Recently, we have discovered that the tolerance (invariance) properties of IT neurons in monkeys can be changed with visual experience (Cox et al. 2005), and, in parallel to the human studies, can be manipulated in an unsupervised manner by altering the natural temporal image statistics that spell out object identity manifolds (Li and DiCarlo 2008). These learned changes in neuronal invariance are exactly what is expected if time is used to teach the ventral stream how to untangle those object identity manifolds (Fig. 2.3), and are a promising new doorway into the underlying computational mechanisms and their instantiation in the brain.

2.9 A Strategy for Understanding Visual Object Recognition

This is an exciting time to be working on the problem of visual object recognition because the previously disparate fields of neuroscience, cognitive science, and computer vision are rapidly becoming intertwined, which creates new opportunities for progress. Although we are still far from understanding how the brain constructs the neuronal representations that support object recognition and many disparate ideas appear to be in play, we hope that we can at least agree on a strategy for approaching this question. That strategy should have three main components.

First, much more effort must be devoted to defining the problem we are trying to solve. Also, we must establish concrete benchmarks that are not simply collections of images, but that force us to engage the computational crux of the problem – dealing with identity-preserving image variation, or invariance.

Second, although a number of workers have led the way in building instantiated computational models that are constrained by the known anatomy and physiology of the ventral visual stream (e.g., Fukushima 1980; Heeger et al. 1996; Riesenhuber and Poggio 1999), much more work is needed in this area. To be called a real "model" of object recognition, a system must pass two tests: it must answer object identification and categorization questions on arbitrary images, and its performance on concrete benchmarks should be above well-known baseline models. These instantiated models explore the complex hypothesis space of interest, and the most important models are those that perform well on benchmarks and can be falsified by new experimental data. Theorists should not be afraid to highlight the failures of their models more than the successes, because computational failures show us when ideas do not work and keep us focused on the truly hard problems. The corollary of this is that models that do not work on real images and, thus, can never be falsified should be shunned, because they only serve to confuse the issue.

Third, although instantiated computational models may discover potentially useful ways to create good forms of visual representation for object recognition, only experimental data will reveal which model is at work in the brain. Thus, one of the key roles of neuroscience is to conduct targeted experiments to distinguish among those models (hypotheses) and to develop new methods to obtain more powerful data. In parallel with developing concrete benchmarks of object recognition, much more psychophysical effort must be aimed at collecting human performance data on the same tests. These data will set the relevant upper limit for all our models and tell us how far (or near) we are to the reaching our goal. Finally, even with all our hypothesis-testing framework experimentalists should still do what they often do best – keep their eyes open for anomalies in their data. There may still be a role for serendipity, even if it is only to get us out of bed to do more experiments.

In this chapter, we have outlined our opinion on how to approach the task of understanding how the brain accomplishes object recognition. We discussed the importance of clear goals and concrete benchmarks, the critical role of instantiated computation models to embody concretely the alternative hypotheses, and the use of experiments to distinguish among these hypotheses and to uncover new ideas or constraints. We doubt that any reader would take issue with the spirit of these overarching ideals, and some may even consider them as obvious. However, a good strategy is meaningless if it is not well executed, and we hope this chapter, along with the others in this book, will encourage all of us to get to work on that execution.

Acknowledgments

I would especially like to thank my first graduate student, David Cox, for helping to develop many of the ideas expressed in this chapter and for Figure 2.2. I also thank my MIT colleagues Tomaso Poggio and Nancy Kanwisher for many insightful discussions, Nicolas Pinto and Nuo Li for Figures 2.1 and 2.3; and Nuo Li and Nicole Rust for helpful comments on this text. Support was provided by The National Eye Institute (NIH-R01-EY014970) and The McKnight Foundation.

Bibliography

Ahn LV, Liu R, Blum M. 2006. Peekaboom: a game for locating objects in images. In Proceedings of the SIGCHI conference on human factors in computing systems.

Arathorn D, Olshausen B, DiCarlo J. 2007. Functional requirements of a visual theory . COSYNE workshop.

Ashby FG, Gott RE. 1988. Decision rules in the perception and categorization of multidimensional stimuli. *J Exp Psychol Learn Mem Cogn* 14: 33–53.

Barlow H. 1995. The neuron doctrine in perception. In *The cognitive neurosciences*, ed. MS Gazzaniga. Cambridge: MIT Press, 415–435.

Bengio Y, LeCun Y, Nohl C, Burges C. 1995. LeRec: a NN/HMM hybrid for on-line handwriting recognition. *Neural Comput* 7: 1289–1303.

Bileschi SM. 2006. *Streetscenes: towards scene understanding in still images.* PhD Thesis, MIT.

Brincat SL, Connor CE. 2001. Underlying principles of visual shape selectivity in posterior inferotemporal cortex. *Nat Neurosci* 7: 880–886.

Brooks R. 1987. Intelligence without representation. *Arti Intell* 47: 139–159.

Chelazzi L, Duncan J, Miller EK, Desimone R. 1998. Responses of neurons in inferior temporal cortex during memory-guided visual search. *J Neurophysiol* 80: 2918–2940.

Cox DD, DiCarlo JJ. 2008. Does learned shape selectivity in inferior temporal cortex automatically generalize across retinal position? *J Neurosci* 28: 10045–10055.

Cox DD, Meier P, Oertelt N, DiCarlo JJ. 2005. "Breaking" position-invariant object recognition. *Nat Neurosci* 8: 1145–1147.

DiCarlo JJ, Cox DD. 2007. Untangling invariant object recognition. *Trends Cogn Sci* 11: 333–341.

DiCarlo JJ, Maunsell JHR. 2003. Anterior inferotemporal neurons of monkeys engaged in object recognition can be highly sensitive to object retinal position. *J Neurophysiol* 89: 3264–3278.

Downing PE, Jiang Y, Shuman M, Kanwisher N. 2001. A cortical area selective for visual processing of the human body. *Science* 293: 2470–2473.

Duda RO, Hart PE, Stork DG. 2001. *Pattern classification.* New York: Wiley–Interscience.

Edelman S. 1999. *Representation and recognition in vision.* Cambridge: MIT Press, 1999.

Edelman S. 2002. Multidimensional space: the final frontier. *Nat Neurosci* 5: 1252–1254.

Farah MJ. 1990. *Visual agnosia : disorders of object recognition and what they tell us about normal vision.* Cambridge: MIT Press.

Felleman DJ, Van Essen DC. 1991. Distributed hierarchical processing in the primate cerebral cortex. *Cereb Cortex* 1: 1–47.

Foldiak P. 1991. Learning invariance from transformation sequences. *Neural Comput* 3: 194–200.

Fukushima K. 1980. Neocognitron: a self-organizing neural network model for a mechanism of pattern recognition unaffected by shift in position. *Biol Cybern* 36: 193–202.

Heeger DJ, Simoncelli EP, Movshon JA. 1996. Computational models of cortical visual processing. *Proc Natl Acad Sci USA* 93: 623–627.

Huang GB, Ramesh M, Berg T, Learned-Miller E. 2007. Labeled faces in the wild: a database for studying face recognition in unconstrained environments. Technical Report, 07-49, University of Massachusetts.

Hung CP, Kreiman G, Poggio T, DiCarlo JJ. 2005. Fast readout of object identity from macaque inferior temporal cortex. *Science* 310: 863–866.

Ito M, Tamura H, Fujita I, Tanaka K. 1995. Size and position invariance of neuronal responses in monkey inferotemporal cortex. *J Neurophysiol* 73: 218–226.

Johnson KO. 1980. Sensory discrimination: decision process. *J Neurophysiol* 43: 1771–1792.

Johnson KO, Hsiao SS, Twombly IA. 1995. Neural mechanisms of tactile form recognition. In *The cognitive neurosciences*, ed. MS, Gazzaniga. Cambridge: The MIT Press.

Kanwisher N, McDermott J, Chun MM. 1997. The fusiform face area: a module in human extrastriate cortex specialized for face perception. *J Neurosci* 17: 4302–4311.

Kayaert G, Biederman I, Vogels R. 2003. Shape tuning in macaque inferior temporal cortex. *J Neurosci* 23: 3016–3027.

Lecun Y, Huang F, Bottou L. 2004. Learning methods for generic object recognition with invariance to pose and lighting. In Proceedings of the conference on computer vision and pattern recognition.

Lewicki MS, Sejnowski TJ. 2000. Learning overcomplete representations. *Neural Comput* 12: 337–365.

Li M, Clark JJ. 2004. A temporal stability approach to position and attention-shift-invariant recognition. *Neural Comput* 16: 2293–2321.

Li N, Cox DD, Zoccolan D, DiCarlo JJ. 2009. What response properties do individual neurons need to underlie position and clutter "invariant" object recognition? *J Neurophysiol* (in press).

Li N, DiCarlo JJ. 2008. Unsupervised natural experience rapidly alters invariant object representation in visual cortex. *Science* 321: 1502–1507.

Li F, Fergus R, Perona P. 2004. Learning generative visual models from few training examples: an incremental Bayesian approach tested on 101 object categories. In IEEE Computer Society Conference on Computer Vision and Pattern Recognition, 178.

Logothetis NK, Pauls JP. 1995. Psychophysical and physiological evidence for viewer-centered object representation in the primate. *Cereb Cortex* 5: 270–288.

Logothetis NK, Pauls J, Poggio T. 1995. Shape representation in the inferior temporal cortex of monkeys. *Curr Biol* 5: 552–563.

Logothetis NK, Sheinberg DL. 1996. Visual object recognition. *Ann Rev Neurosci* 19: 577–621.

Marr D. 1982. *Vision: a computational investigation into the human representation and processing of visual information.* New York: Henry Holt.

Masquelier T, Thorpe SJ. 2007. Unsupervised learning of visual features through spike timing dependent plasticity. *PLoS Comput Biol* 3:e31.

Miller EK, Gochin PM, Gross CG. 1993. Suppression of visual responses of neurons in inferior temporal cortex of the awake macaque by addition of a second stimulus. *Brain Res* 616: 25–29.

Olshausen BA, Field DJ. 2004. Sparse coding of sensory inputs. *Curr Opin Neurobiol* 14: 481–487.

Olshausen BA, Field DJ. 2005. How close are we to understanding v1? *Neural Comput* 17: 1665–1699.

Op de Beeck H, Vogels R. 2000. Spatial sensitivity of macaque inferior temporal neurons. *J Comp Neurol* 426: 505–518.

Pasupathy A, Connor CE. 2001. Shape representation in area V4: position-specific tuning for boundary conformation. *J Neurophysiol* 86: 2505–2519.

Pfeifer R, Scheier C. 1999. *Understanding intelligence.* Cambridge: MIT Press. Pinto N, Cox DD, DiCarlo JJ. 2008. Why is real-world visual object recognition hard? *PLoS Comput Biol.* 4:(:e27).

Pinto N, DiCarlo JJ, Cox DD. 2008. Establishing benchmarks and baselines for face recognition. In *ECCV 2008 faces in real life workshop.*

Pollen DA, Przybyszewski AW, Rubin MA, Foote W. 2002. Spatial receptive field organization of macaque V4 neurons. *Cereb Cortex* 12: 601–616.

Ponce J, Berg TL, Everingham M, et al. 2006. Dataset issues in object recognition. toward category-level object recognition. In *Springer-Verlag lecture notes in computer science.*

Potter MC. 1976. Short-term conceptual memory for pictures. *J Exp Psychol [Hum Learn]* 2: 509–522.

Quiroga RQ, Reddy L, Kreiman G, Koch C, Fried I. 2005. Invariant visual representation by single neurons in the human brain. *Nature* 435: 1102–1107.

Riesenhuber M, Poggio T. 1999. Are cortical models really bound by the "binding problem"? *Neuron* 24: 87–93, 111–125.

Riesenhuber M, Poggio T. 1999. Hierarchical models of object recognition in cortex. *Nat Neurosci* 2: 1019–1025.

Rolls ET. 2000. Functions of the primate temporal lobe cortical visual areas in invariant visual object and face recognition. *Neuron* 27: 205–218.

Rolls ET, Tovee MJ. 1995. The responses of single neurons in the temporal visual cortical areas of the macaque when more than one stimulus is present in the receptive field. *Exp Brain Res* 103: 409–420.

Roweis ST, Saul LK. 2000. Nonlinear dimensionality reduction by locally linear embedding. *Science* 290: 2323–2326.

Russell BC, Torralba A, Murphy KP, Freeman WT. 2008. LabelMe: a database and web-based tool for image annotation. *Int J Comput Vis* 77: 157–173.

Rust NC, Schwartz O, Movshon JA, Simoncelli EP. 2005. Spatiotemporal elements of macaque V1 receptive fields. *Neuron* 46: 945–956.

Sato T. 1989. Interactions of visual stimuli in the receptive fields of inferior temporal neurons in awake macaques. *Exp Brain Res* 77: 23–30.

Schwartz O, Simoncelli EP. 2001. Natural signal statistics and sensory gain control. *Nat Neurosci* 4: 819–825.

Schwarzlose RF, Swisher JD, Dang S, Kanwisher N. 2008. The distribution of category and location information across object-selective regions in human visual cortex. *Proc Natl Acad Sci USA* 105: 4447–4452.

Serre T, Oliva A, Poggio T. 2007. A feedforward architecture accounts for rapid categorization. *Proc Natl Acad Sci USA.* 104: 6424–6429.

Serre T, Wolf L, Bileschi S, Riesenhuber M, Poggio T. 2007. Robust object recognition with cortex-like mechanisms. *IEEE Trans Pattern Anal Mach Intell* 29: 411–426.

Simoncelli EP. 2008. Vision and the statistics of the visual environment. *Curr Opin Neurobiol* 13: 144–149.

Tanaka K. 1996. Inferotemporal cortex and object vision. *Ann Rev Neurosci* 19: 109–139.

Tenenbaum JB, Silva V, Langford JC. 2000. A global geometric framework for nonlinear dimensionality reduction. *Science* 290: 2319–2323.

The PASCAL object recognition database collection. Visual object classes challenge. http://www.pascal-network.org/challenges/VOC.

Thorpe S, Fize D, Marlot C. 1996. Speed of processing in the human visual system. *Nature* 381: 520–522.

Tsunoda K. 2001. Complex objects are represented in macaque inferotemporal cortex by the combination of feature columns. *Nat Neurosci* 4: 832–838.

Turing AM. 1950. Computing machinery and intelligence. *Mind* 49: 433–460.

Ullman S, Soloviev S. 1999. Computation of pattern invariance in brain-like structures. *Neural Netw* 12: 1021–1036.

Ullman S, Vidal-Naquet M, Sali E. 2002. Visual features of intermediate complexity and their use in classification. *Nat Neurosci* 5: 682–687.

Wallis G, Bulthoff HH. 2001. Effects of temporal association on recognition memory. *Proc Natl Acad Sci USA* 98: 4800–4804.

Wallis G, Rolls ET. 1997. Invariant face and object recognition in the visual system. *Prog Neurobiol* 51: 167–194.

Wiskott L, Sejnowski TJ. 2002. Slow feature analysis: unsupervised learning of invariances. *Neural Comput* 14: 715–770.

Yamane Y, Tsunoda K, Matsumoto M, Phillips AN, Tanifuji M. 2006. Representation of the spatial relationship among object parts by neurons in macaque inferotemporal cortex. *J Neurophysiol* 96: 3147–3156.

Zoccolan D, Cox DD, DiCarlo JJ. 2005. Multiple object response normalization in monkey inferotemporal cortex. *J Neurosci* 25: 8150–8164.

Zoccolan D, Kouh M, Poggio T, DiCarlo JJ. 2007. Trade-off between object selectivity and tolerance in monkey inferotemporal cortex. *J Neurosci* 27: 12,292–12,307.

CHAPTER 3

Visual Recognition Circa 2008

Pietro Perona

3.1 Introduction

Allow me to pose a few questions on the nature of visual recognition. Why do we bother studying it? What are the "things" we recognize? How many things is it useful to recognize? What is the nature of different recognition tasks? What have we learned so far? What are the open problems that face us? I am assuming that the reader has some familiarity with the technical aspects of vision and visual recognition. This is not a survey, and the references are meant to exemplify an idea or an approach; they are not meant to give proper credit to the many excellent people who work in the field. Also, some of the interesting technical issues are not visible from the mile-high perspective I take here and are therefore not mentioned.

3.2 What?

What is it that we recognize in images? We recognize both the component elements and the overall scene: materials and surface properties ("leather," "wet"), objects ("frog," "corkscrew") and the gist of the ensemble ("kitchen," "prairie"). We recognize things both as individuals ("Gandhi," "my bedroom") and as members of categories ("people," "mountainscape"). These distinctions are important because the visual statistics of materials are different from those of objects and scenes. Also, the visual variability of individual objects is different from that of categories; different approaches may be needed to model and recognize each. In the following text, for brevity, when referring to the thing to be recognized, I will often call it "object," although it could be a material or a scene, an individual or a category.

What are "categories"? This is not easy to define. The reason why we are interested in recognizing categories is that we wish to generalize. Having learned the properties of one object (e.g., "it will break if I let it drop," or "it is good to eat"), we will attribute them to objects that look similar. Why would the looks of an object be related to its properties? The reason is that often form determines function (e.g., you need a sharp tip to be able to pierce; you need to be spongy to be soft); thus, paying attention to form will tell us something useful about function. Another reason is that the form of things often carries a memory of the process that brought them into existence, and things that are generated by similar processes often have similar properties, thus, again form is linked to other physical properties.

All this tells us that we should pay attention to visual similarities (Malisiewicz and Efros 2008). So, again, why make the extra step and worry about categories? The reason is purely statistical: often the things we see are organized naturally into separate groups. "Wolves" are distinct from "dogs" and "foxes," and we do not easily find a continuum between them (in terms of genome, habitat and behavior). The same for "airplanes" and "helicopters." This is because living organisms are organized into discrete species, and man-made objects are often designed with a specific function in mind, made by a specific company, assembled from a selected set of parts. We do find, exceptions, of course: dogs may be organized into distinct breeds, but we can produce mutts that share properties of different breeds; also, there is now a continuum between "cameras" and "cell phones" because of market demands. "Old man," "middle-aged man," and "young man" do overlap, and it would not make sense to try and define a clear distinction; these categories are probably forced on us by language, rather than by our senses, and we may prefer regression, rather than categories, to model "visual" age. Therefore, some categories are "real" and useful, whereas others are somewhat arbitrary and may not be terribly useful in helping us with generalization from visual properties.

3.3 Why?

Why worry about visual recognition? I can see two reasons, each one compelling in its own right. The first is that we wish to understand how visual recognition works in biologic systems. It is one of the wonders of nature that we can see at all. Understanding vision in computational terms brings us closer to understanding how the brain works. The second reason is that machines whose visual systems approach human ability would be extremely useful in a great number of applications: science, medicine, human-machine interfaces, searching and indexing into image and video collections, security, manufacturing, monitoring the environment. If we could build such machines, our lives would probably be better (caveat: these machines could be used to build surveillance systems that limit our privacy as well as to build weapons). It is useful to reflect on a few of these applications to understand what forms of visual recognition are potentially most useful, and how to measure a system's performance. I will focus here on two.

The first application is analyzing and indexing large collections of photographs and video. Cameras and video sensors are becoming more affordable and better by the year. Storage space is similarly becoming abundant and inexpensive. As a consequence, large amounts of images are captured and stored – vastly more images than can be inspected, indexed, and organized by humans. Images and video are quickly becoming a sort of "dark matter" that takes the large majority of the storage space reserved for data but is rarely seen and used. Automating the process of associating keywords with images, linking meaningful visual patches in images with other patches and with text, discovering interesting content – all would help make these image collections more useful. The complexity of image collections varies widely. An astronomical survey of a section of the sky might contain few, possibly fewer than one hundred, distinct categories, because most items are being seen against a plain background. The collection of movies owned by a major film house likely contains tens of thousands of categories, as we shall see later, with each item being variously occluded and seen against a complex and unmodeled background.

A second interesting and useful application is autonomous driving in urban/suburban traffic. How much recognition is needed? One could reasonably take two opposite and extreme points of view. The minimalistic point of view says that no recognition is needed: all that a vehicle needs to know is the 3-D shape of its immediate environment, and this information will be sufficient for successful navigation if synchronized with readily available street maps (e.g. GPS and inertial sensors). On the other hand, one could set the ambitious goal of "flawless driving," in which autonomous vehicles will never cause a traffic accident. To achieve this goal, any information that is useful at predicting the behavior of pedestrians, vehicles, animals, and other obstacles must be available to the system. According to this second point of view, recognition of thousands of categories is vital.

3.4 Which?

Under the umbrella name of "visual recognition" I distinguish five recognition tasks. I present them in order of difficulty (with the exception of 2 and 3, which I would not know how to rank):

1. **Verification.** A patch of the image has been selected. Is a given object/category there or not? The automated concierge at the entrance of a building is an example of this: a person stands in front of the camera and punches Sally Jean's PIN. Do I see Sally Jean's face in the picture? Yes or no?

2. **Detection and localization.** A complex image is presented. It may contain an exemplar of a given category. Is it there? Where? Finding human faces in the pictures from a wedding party is an example of this.

3. **Classification.** Given an image (or a specific patch of an image) can we classify it into one of a number of categories? An example of this is classifying all the faces found by a face detector (see "Detection") in the the pictures I have on my hard drive: 353 pictures of my first child, 233 of my second child, 3 of uncle Joe. Another example is classifying vacation pictures into "beach," "city," "hotel room," "airport lounge," "museum," "portrait."

4. **Naming.** Given a complex image, name and locate all objects that are present out of a (possibly large) number of categories. If we wanted to associate keywords to images (e.g., to allow word-based indexing without requiring humans to do it by hand), we would want to automate naming.

5. **Description.** Given an image, describe it: What is the environment? What are the objects and actions you see? What are their relationships? A typical example would be preparing text summaries for a collection of images, so that it may be searched using complex queries: "Find all pictures showing the pope kissing a child." This is also called "scene

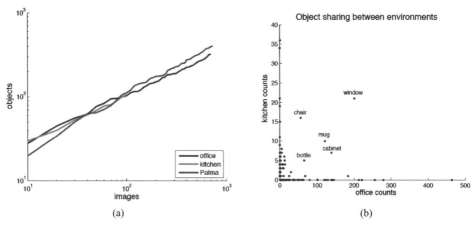

Figure 3.1. How many things do we recognize? (a) The total number of words reported by human observers when looking at pictures taken in three environments: offices, kitchens, and Palma de Mallorca. The number of words increases proportionally to the square root of the number of pictures. There is no sign of saturation even when the number of pictures approaches 10^3. This suggests that, even in fairly restricted environments, there is a large number of different things that may be recognized. (b) Different environments share few recognizable things. Each dot in the plot is associated to an "object" that was detected in pictures of offices and kitchens. The two axes show us how many times the object was detected in each of the two collections. Amongst many hundreds of objects, only "bottle," "chair," "cabinet," "mug," and "window" appear often in both kitchens and offices. Adapted from Spain and Perona 2007.

understanding." I suspect that we will discover a further variety of tasks within image understanding, once we get there.

Which ones of these tasks have been attempted so far? Much of the recent work in visual recognition is in classification. For instance, Caltech-101 and Caltech-256 images typically contain a single object and little clutter. The task is then one of classifying the entire image as belonging to a given category. It might seem intuitive that, as soon as we have solved classification, we can move quickly on to naming by simply shifting windows of different sizes across the image and classifying each such region of interest. Similarly, one could think of solving detection and localization by running a verification algorithm on each window of the image. Unfortunately, this intuition is deceiving, as I will argue in section 3.5. There has been considerable activity in detection/localization as well. Work in this area has mostly focused on three categories: human faces, pedestrians, and automobiles. Recently, the PASCAL consortium has published datasets containing 20 categories, which will help us make progress on this task.

3.5 How Many? How Fast?

What is the size of the problem we are trying to solve? If our goal is to emulate, and perhaps surpass, human abilities, then we should gear up for 10^5 to 10^6 categories. Biederman (Biederman et al. 1982) estimates that there are $3 \cdot 10^3$ Entry-level categories and $3 \cdot 10^4$ visual categories overall (Fig. 3.1). These numbers make sense:

if educated Chinese can recognize up to 10^4 different characters, it is reasonable to presume that they would recognize at least as many categories outside reading. We estimated that we recognize more than one thousand categories in fairly limited domains (kitchen, office) and that these domains do not share many categories (see Fig. 3.1). Suppose that we operated in twenty to thirty different domains (city streets, country-side, people, foods, indoor scenes, the seaside, biology, animals, etc.), then we would end up with an estimate that is similar to Biederman's: between 10^4 and 10^5. Arguably, an automatic system could integrate the visual knowledge of many people, each one an expert in a different domain (medicine, paleontology, car mechanics, botany, e.g.) and thus might recognize far more categories than any human being would: thus, the target of "more than 10^5, fewer than 10^6."

Is emulating human abilities the right way to formulate the problem? If you are looking at the problem from the point of view of an engineer, the answer is clearly "no." Whereas humans work on a variety of tasks across many different environments, machines are designed for specific environments and tasks. Going back to the example of autonomous driving, an automobile will operate in cities, suburbs, open landscape, and freeways, but it will never enter a kitchen or look at MRI images. Thus, a machine's ability to recognize will not need to approach the versatility of humans (matching and surpassing human accuracy and speed in specific domains will be more useful). Furthermore, precise naming of many objects that might be visible from a vehicle (e.g., an ice cream parlor, a larch tree) might be irrelevant for the task of driving safely down the road. To give another example, a machine carrying out anatomic annotation of brain slices will need to recognize a few tens of neurons, but not rifles and blue jays. We do not yet have good estimates of the number of categories that are relevant for a representative palette of well-defined tasks. Even for an important task, such as autonomous driving, we only have a fuzzy idea: the lower bound might be ten to twenty categories (pedestrians, three to four types of vehicles, traffic signs, road markings). The upper bound might sometimes exceed 10^3: a good driver will recognize a toy ball, which will tell him that an oblivious child may soon be running after it. Also, a good driver will distinguish between similar-sized obstacles, such as a shoebox, a cinderblock, a crow, and a cat; each will behave differently when the car approaches, and, if run over, each will inflict different amounts of damage to the vehicle.

However, we could argue the opposite point of view: a general-purpose machine for recognition might be useful, too. Think of classifying by content all images and video one finds on the web. More generally, think how useful it would be to have a visual encyclopedia or "Visipedia," a machine that could identify any image we supplied and connect us with the relevant encyclopedia page or human expert. It is likely that we will need to design different machines that are optimized for a broad range of task complexities, from 1 to, say, 10^5 categories.

How fast should the task be accomplished? In some cases, time is of the essence (think of the autonomous driving vehicle). It would be nice to be able to detect and locate 10 to 10^3 categories in real time. What about annotating and organizing large image collections? At first blush, one could convince oneself that a large batch process that takes days or weeks to process a few thousand images (e.g., organizing the pictures I have on my hard drive) would be good enough. However, we must remember that some collections of images are indeed extremely large and are updated frequently;

computation sometime comes at a premium; and fast turnaround is important. Think of a planetary orbiter with a tenuous downlink, collecting thousands of high-resolution pictures every day and having to prioritize which images to send to earth. Consider a TV soap opera, in which each episode needs to be annotated and put on line as soon as it is aired.

In conclusion, although visual recognition is already useful for a number of applications, current classification speeds (a few pictures per minute when classifying 1 out of 10^2 categories) are not good enough for most uses. It would be highly desirable to achieve naming of, say, 10^3 categories on many frames per second on a single CPU. We are many orders of magnitudes away from achieving this goal. More ambitious goals are also reasonable, so it seems we have enough to keep us busy for a couple of decades.

3.6 Scaling

One could think that the more complex tasks could be solved by decomposing them into simpler ones. For example, classification could be obtained by combining the output of multiple verification modules, one per category. Furthermore, detection could be built out of verification; consider all rectangular windows in an image (sampling scale and position), and run verification on each. Will this work? Unfortunately, there are a number of difficulties. First, good verification performance in any one category does not predict good classification performance over thousands of categories; the more choices there are, the easier it is to make mistakes. Performance drops precipitously with the number of categories (Fig. 3.2). Second, in a straight-out implementation, the computational cost would be horrendous: linear both in the number of categories and in the number of test windows, which, depending on the sampling scheme, could be 10 multiplied by the number of pixels. Third, the probability of any category being present in any given window is small (e.g., 10^{-7}–10^{-8} in a typical scenario); thus, one would be forced to choose high detection thresholds in order not to be swamped by false alarms, and this would likely decrease detection rates to unacceptable levels. In summary, the answer is "no"; verification does not scale easily to detection, and classification does not scale easily to naming. New ideas are necessary to focus computational resources only where they are needed (Fleuret and Geman 2001; Viola and Jones 2004).

3.7 The State of the Art

Are we close to having solved any of the tasks that we have defined? How many have we tackled credibly?

Most researchers so far have focused on *classification*. The typical benchmark datasets are Caltech-101 and Caltech-256 (Griffin et al. 2007). Images from Caltech-101 and Caltech-256 were culled from the web using Google images and other equivalent search engines. Most of these images contain only one object, and the object is rather central in the picture and the viewpoint is conventional (Griffin et al. 2007). Most algorithms that are tested on Caltech-101 and Caltech-256 are designed to classify the

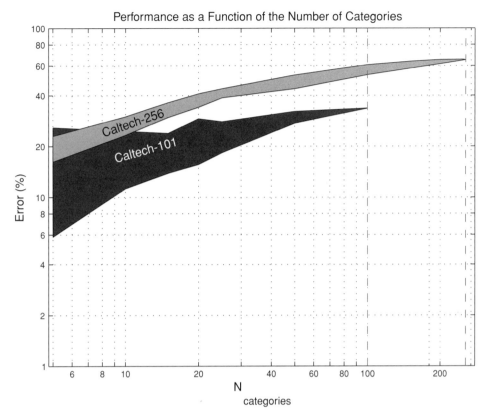

Figure 3.2. Classification error increases quickly with the number of categories. The curves show the log % error (y-axis) in classifying N categories (x-axis) using a standard method with 30 training examples. The thickness of the lines indicates the variation between different choices of categories from the Caltech-101 and Caltech-256 collections. Adapted from Griffin et al. 2007, 30 training examples.

entire image, without separating foreground from background, and therefore do not generalize to the task of *naming* in large images where the position of the object is unknown. Classification is improving steadily, as one may clearly see from Figure 3.3 (left). How close are we to good performance in classification? It is apparent that there is much progress every year. However, it is clear from Figure 3.3 (right) that we are far from human-level performance (it is reasonable to assume 1% error rate for comparison, although an accurate measurement of human performance on Caltech-101 and Caltech-256 is not yet available). New datasets are becoming available for detection and naming, such as the PASCAL Challenge annotated image collections (Everingham et al. 2005). We should expect equally robust progress on those tasks.

During the past 10 years we have made much progress, both practically and in our understanding of the problem:

1. We have started paying attention to categorical recognition, as opposed to recognition of specific objects, which was the dominant recognition problem until the 1990s.
2. We have understood that good category representations are built out of "constellations" (Burl and Perona 1996) of "image patches," "visual words," or "textons," which may be

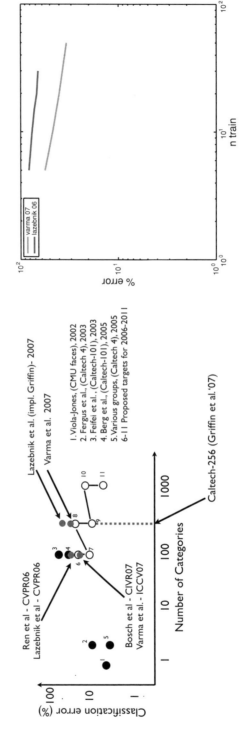

Figure 3.3. How well are we doing? *Left*, Classification performance has seen steady improvement in the last few years, both in the number of categories on which algorithms are tested and in classification error rates. *Right*, Performance of the best 2006 (Lazebnik et al. 2006) and the best 2007 algorithm (Varma 2007) are compared here (classification error rates vs number of training examples). One may notice the significant yearly progress (see also left panel). Extrapolation enthusiasts may calculate that 10^8 training examples would be sufficient to achieve 1% error rates with current algorithms. Furthermore, if the pace of yearly progress is constant on this log scale chart, 1% error rates with 30 training examples will be achieved in 8 to 10 years.

shared across categories (Torralba et al. 2004) and whose shape may be either modeled (Burl et al. 1998), or ignored (Dorkó and Schmid 2003).

3. We have realized that image segmentation is not a necessary preliminary step to visual recognition (Burl et al. 1998); rather, it may be seen as part of the recognition process (Leibe et al. 2008).

4. We have realized that it is possible to learn categories without much human supervision, directly from the data (Weber et al. 2000b; Fergus et al. 2003).

5. Algorithms are now tested for a variety of appearance statistics. Bonsai trees look different from baseball bats. Also, their pattern of variability is rather different. We may find out which approaches are specific to a category (e.g., faces) and which approaches generalize to multiple categories.

6. We have become aware that learning categories from a small number of training examples is a crucial problem (Fei-Fei et al. 2004).

7. Ideas have come about for speeding up classification and naming (Grauman and Darrell 2005).

Although we should be happy about the good clip of progress of classification on datasets such as Caltech-256, we should be aware of limitations to the current approaches and the challenges that lay ahead of us:

1. We are still far from "good performance." Error rates of 1% on Caltech-256 are not around the corner, and naming with 10^5 categories is not even in sight. Similarly, currently detection/localization algorithms miss 10 to 30% of faces, automobiles, and pedestrians with false alarm rates of about one per image. In order to help autonomous driving and many other applications, one should aim for 1% miss rates with virtually no false alarms on the same benchmark datasets.

2. This is still a "classification" task, not a "naming" task. Localization, as well as occlusion and clutter, remain challenging problems.

3. There is no reason to believe that current approaches generalize across viewpoint: Once we learn "car" from the side, our algorithms will not recognize "car" when viewed frontally. Scale-invariance remains a challenge (Savarese and Fei-Fei 2007).

4. Current algorithms will not scale well with the number of categories. Their cost increases linearly at best. We need to design algorithms with sublinear growth (Griffin and Perona 2008).

5. Current algorithms do not scale well with the size in the image. Again, scaling is linear or superlinear at the moment.

6. We suspect that learning should be "generative" for distant categories and "discriminative" for similar categories (Holub et al. 2008b), but we do not yet have a principled way to think about this problem and design hybrid algorithms.

3.8 Visual Learning

Whether our goal is verification or full-fledged scene understanding, models of visual categories must be acquired from examples and human expertise. Unlike stereoscopy, motion, and shape perception, in which geometry and physics constrain the problem, there is little to tell us a-priori what a frog and a cell phone should look like. A vast amount of information has to be learned either from experts or from training examples.

The knowledge that may be acquired from training examples goes beyond phenomenological models of objects, materials, and scenes. An overall organization, or taxonomy, of our visual knowledge is desirable, as are the statistics of co-occurrence of environments, objects, and materials.

Depending on the context in which learning takes place, different learning strategies are called for. A great number of tantalizing challenges face us:

1. One-shot learning. Learning new categories from a handful training examples would be very useful, for pretraining examples are difficult to come by. As Don Geman is fond of saying, "The interesting limit is $n \rightarrow 1$." Bayesian (Fei-Fei et al. 2004, 2005) and other approaches (Holub et al. 2008b) seem promising.

2. Incremental learning. Although most efforts have understandably focused on batch learning, it is clear that both animal and machine are better off if they can improve their knowledge of the world as new training examples come along (Gomes et al. 2008). An additional benefit is that incremental approaches often offer faster learning algorithms.

3. Category formation. When do we have enough evidence to form a new category? How do we bootstrap knowledge about related categories in forming a new one?

4. Taxonomization. How do we organize our visual knowledge? Can we discover the relationship between different categories and group them into broader categories (Bart et al. 2008)? Can we take advantage of shared properties to make learning more effective, to speed up categorization and naming, to simplify the front-end of a visual system by sharing related mechanisms (Torralba et al. 2004)?

5. Human-machine interfaces. Humans are expert recognizers, but their time is precious. A machine ought to harvest information from human experts without wasting their time (Kapoor et al. 2007; Holub et al. 2008a). Could existing human-provided information (e.g., the Google image search engine) be harvested for useful training information (Barnard et al. 2003; Fergus et al. 2005)?

6. Unsupervised learning. Can machines learn from collections of complex images and movies (e.g., the entire archive of all TV soap operas) without any further help (Weber et al. 2000a; Russell et al. 2006)?

3.9 Towards Scene Understanding

Is the task of image understanding well-defined? One might take a hard-nosed point of view and say that visual recognition is irrelevant unless it is directed at some goal (e.g., feeding, fighting, mating). In that case, one could claim that there is no such thing as "scene understanding"; rather, there is preparation for an action. According to this line of thinking, visual recognition cannot be studied in the abstract, but it ought to be understood as part of a complete perception-action loop. However, I would argue that it is not necessary to consider specific perception-action tasks in order to

107ms   500ms

This is outdoors. A black, furry dog is running/walking towards the right of the picture. His tail is in the air and his mouth is open. Either he had a ball in his mouth or he was chasing after a ball. (Subject EC)

I saw a black dog carrying a gray frisbee in the center of the photograph. The dog was walking near the ocean, with waves lapping up on the shore. It seemed to be a gray day out. (Subject JB)

inside a house, like a living room, with chairs and sofas and tables, no ppl. (Subject HS)

A room full of musical instruments. A piano in the foreground, a harp behind that, a guitar hanging on the wall (to the right). It looked like there was also a window behind the harp, and perhaps a bookcase on the left. (Subject RW)

Figure 3.4. Human observers find it natural to provide a few sentences describing what they saw in a complex image. This is true even when the image is seen only briefly. Adapted from Fei-Fei et al. 2007.

make progress in visual recognition. For humans it is easy and natural to give accurate verbal descriptions of images even when no task is specified and when images are shown for a brief moment (Fig. 3.4). This suggests that a category-level description of the scene may be useful for carrying out a diverse set of unrelated tasks. Therefore, producing informative general-purpose high-level scene descriptions is a worthwhile goal. Solving this task will entail understanding the nature of these descriptions, as well as knowing how to produce them.

What does a task-independent image description look like? We do not know. Language provides a degree of guidance, but it is likely that such a description might be more informative than what can be easily verbalized. A first step toward this is naming; or producing the full list of "things" we see in a scene, and where they are. That would include "global" labels (such as "office" and "kitchen") as well as objects (such as "penguin" and "inkwell") and materials (such as "leather" and "sand"). But naming is clearly just the beginning. We also need to be able to compute and express properties, actions, and relationships (i.e., we need not only names, but also verbs, adjectives, and adverbs), and we need to combine all these together into meaningful descriptions.

Researchers currently working on recognition largely ignore the geometry of the environment. At some point, both geometry and recognition must come together for proper scene understanding. Coming up with the simple statement "an apple is on the table" will require both.

The relative importance of different statements that one can make about a scene is also an issue that needs to be understood (Fig. 3.5). The description "sky above ground" or "ceiling above floor" is short and accurate, and it accounts for most pixels of most

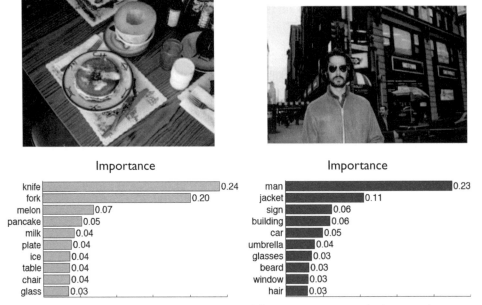

Figure 3.5. Different objects in an image have different "importance" for human observers. Importance here is measured as the probability that a human observer producing a list of objects in the scene will mention a given object first (Spain and Perona 2008). (See color plate 3.5.)

images; however, it is hardly informative. How do we select the most informative subset of the exceedingly large number of statements one could make about a scene?

3.10 Conclusion

Visual recognition is one of the most exciting and useful challenges of modern engineering. Understanding the computational foundations of visual recognition helps us understand the brain. Machines endowed with visual recognition would enable unprecedented applications and change our lives. Approaching visual recognition makes us think hard about fundamental and diverse issues, such as the geometry and photometry of visual representations, the statistical properties of the world, unsupervised learning, categorization and model selection, efficient approximate optimization and search, human language, and the link between perception and cognition.

We have made progress in the recent past. It is fair to say that now we have some understanding of the problem, as well as ideas about how to approach it. This was not the case just 10 years ago. We are still far from addressing many of the "known unknowns": naming, sublinear scaling with image size and number of categories, viewpoint and lighting invariance, extrapolation to novel views, faster and more accurate algorithms.

There are also "unknown unknowns." Many believe that "scene understanding" is the grand goal, but we do not yet know what form scene descriptions should take, or how to approach producing such descriptions. Similarly, taxonomies that organize our visual knowledge and relate similar categories are believed to be useful, but we do not yet have a clear view of the organizing principles for these taxonomies and of possible algorithms for producing them.

Bibliography

Barnard K, Duygulu P, Forsyth DA, de Freitas N, Blei DM, Jordan MI. 2003. Matching words and pictures. *J Mach Learn Res* 3:1107–1135.

Bart E, Porteous I, Perona P, Welling M. 2008. Unsupervised learning of visual taxonomies. Proceedings of the IEEE conference on computer vision and pattern recognition.

Biederman I, Mezzanotte R, Rabinowitz J. 1982. Scene perception: detecting and judging object undergoing relational violations. *Cogn Psychol* 14:143–147.

Burl M, Perona P. 1996. Recognition of planar object classes. IEEE Conference on Computer Vision and Pattern Recognition, 223–230.

Burl M, Weber M, Perona P. 1998. A probabilistic approach to object recognition using local photometry and global geometry. European conference on computer vision (ECCV), II:628–641.

Dorkó G, Schmid C. 2003. Selection of scale-invariant parts for object class recognition. IEEE international conference in computer vision, 634–640.

Everingham M, Zisserman A, Williams CKI, Gool LJV, Allan M, Bishop CM, Chapelle O, Dalal N, Deselaers T, Dorkó G, Duffner S, Eichhorn J, Farquhar JDR, Fritz M, Garcia C, Griffiths T, Jurie F, Keysers D, Koskela M, Laaksonen J, Larlus D, Leibe B, Meng H, Ney H, Schiele B, Schmid C, Seemann E, Shawe-Taylor J, Storkey AJ, Szedmák S, Triggs B, Ulusoy I, Viitaniemi V, Zhang J. 2005. The 2005 Pascal visual object classes challenge. First PASCAL machine learning challenges workshop, 117–176.

Fei-Fei L, Fergus R, Perona P. 2004. Learning generative visual models from few training examples: An incremental bayesian approach tested on 101 object categories. IEEE CVPR workshop of generative model-based vision.

Fei-Fei L, Fergus R, Perona P. 2005. One-shot learning of object categories. *IEEE Trans Pattern Anal.*

Fei-Fei L, Iyer A, Koch C, Perona P. 2007. What do we perceive in a glance of a real-world scene? *J Vision* 7(1):Art. No. 10.

Fergus R, Fei-Fei L, Perona P, Zisserman A. 2005. Learning object categories from google's image search. IEEE international conference in computer vision, 1816–1823.

Fergus R, Perona P, Zisserman A. 2003. Object class recognition by unsupervised scale-invariant learning. IEEE computer society conference on computer vision and pattern recognition, vol 2, 264.

Fleuret F, Geman D. 2001. Coarse-to-fine face detection. *Int J Comput Vis* 41(1-2):85–107.

Gomes R, Welling M, Perona P. 2008. Incremental learning of nonparametric bayesian mixture models. Proceedings of IEEE international conference on computer vision and pattern recognition.

Grauman K, Darrell T. 2005. The pyramid match kernel: discriminative classification with sets of image features. Proceedings of the IEEE International Conference on Computer Vision, Beijing, China.

Griffin G, Holub A, Perona P. 2007. Caltech-256 object category dataset. Technical Report CNS-TR-2007-001, California Institute of Technology.

Griffin G, Perona P. 2008. Learning and using taxonomies for fast visual categorization. IEEE conference on computer vision and pattern recognition.

Holub A, Burl M, Perona P. 2008a. Entropy-based active learning for object recognition. IEEE conference on computer vision and pattern recognition. Second IEEE workshop on online learning for classification.

Holub A, Welling M, Perona P. 2008b. Hybrid generative-discriminative visual categorization. *Int J Comput Vis*.

Kapoor A, Grauman K, Urtasun R, Darrell T. 2007. Active learning with gaussian processes for object categorization. IEEE international conference on computer vision.

Lazebnik S, Schmid C, Ponce J. 2006. Beyond bags of features: spatial pyramid matching for recognizing natural scene categories. IEEE conference on computer vision and pattern recognition, vol. 2, 2169–2178.

Leibe B, Leonardis A, Schiele B. 2008. Robust object detection with interleaved categorization and segmentation. *Int J Comput Vis* 77(1-3):259–289.

Malisiewicz T, Efros A. 2008. Recognition by association via learning per-exemplar distances. Proceedings of the IEEE computer society conference on computer vision and pattern recognition.

Russell BC, Freeman WT, Efros AA, Sivic J, Zisserman A. 2006. Using multiple segmentations to discover objects and their extent in image collections. IEEE conference on computer vision and pattern recognition, 1605–1614.

Savarese S, Fei-Fei L. October, 2007. 3d generic object categorization, localization and pose estimation. IEEE international conference in computer vision.

Spain M, Perona P. 2007. Measuring and predicting importance of objects in our visual world. Caltech CNS Technical Report 2007-002, California Institute of Technology.

Spain M, Perona P. 2008. Some objects are more equal than others: Measuring and predicting importance. Proceedings of the European conference on computer vision.

Torralba AB, Murphy KP, Freeman WT. 2004. Sharing features: efficient boosting procedures for multiclass object detection. IEEE conference on computer vision and pattern recognition, vol. 2, 762–769.

Varma M. 2007. Entry in the caltech 256 competition. Visual recognition challenge workshop.

Viola P, Jones MJ. 2004. Robust real-time face detection. *Int J Comput Vis* 57(2):137–154.

Weber M, Welling M, Perona P. 2000a. Towards automatic discovery of object categories. Proceedings of the conference on computer vision and pattern recognition, Hilton Head Island, USA.

Weber M, Welling M, Perona P. 2000b. Unsupervised learning of models for recognition. Proceedings of the 6th European conference on computer vision-part I, 18–32. London: Springer-Verlag.

CHAPTER 4

On What It Means to See, and What We Can Do About It

Shimon Edelman

Seeing is forgetting the name of the thing one sees.

PAUL VALÉRY (1871–1945)

If you are looking at the object, you need not think of it.[1]

LUDWIG WITTGENSTEIN (1889–1951)

4.1 Introduction

A decisive resolution of the problems of high-level vision is at present impeded not by a shortage of computational ideas for processing the array of measurements with which vision begins, but rather by certain tacit assumptions behind the very formulation of these problems.

Consider the problem of object recognition. Intuitively, recognition means determining whether or not the input contains a manifestation of a known object, and perhaps identifying the object in question. This intuition serves well in certain contrived situations, such as character recognition in reading or machine part recognition in an industrial setting – tasks that are characterized first and foremost by only involving objects that come from closed, well-defined sets. An effective computational strategy for object recognition in such situations is to maintain a library of object templates and to match these to the input in a flexible and efficient manner (Basri and Ullman 1988; Edelman et al. 1990; Huttenlocher and Ullman 1987; Lowe 1987).

In categorization, in which the focus of the problem shifts from identifying concrete shapes to making sense of shape *concepts*, this strategy begins to unravel – not because flexible template matching as such cannot keep up with the demands of the task, but rather because the template library is no longer well-defined at the levels of abstraction on which the system must operate. The established approaches to both recognition and categorization are thus seen to suffer from the same shortcoming: an assumption that

---

[1] *Philosophical Investigations*, (Wittgenstein 1958, II,xi).

the input is fully interpretable in terms of a finite set of well-defined visual concepts or "objects."

In this chapter, I argue that forcing a specific and full conceptual interpretation on a given input may be counterproductive not only because it may be a wrong conceptual interpretation, but also because the input may best be left altogether uninterpreted in the traditional sense. Nonconceptual vision is not widely studied, and yet it seems to be the rule rather than the exception among the biological visual systems found on this planet, including human vision in its more intriguing modes of operation (Chap. 5 in Edelman 2008).

To gain a better understanding of natural vision, and to make progress in designing robust and versatile artificial visual systems, we must therefore start at the beginning, by carefully considering the range of tasks that natural vision has evolved to solve. In other words, we must sooner rather than later face up to the question of what it means to see.

4.2 Seeing vs. "Seeing As"

In his epochal book *Vision*, David Marr (1982) offered two answers to the question of what it means to see: one short and intuitive, the other long, detailed, and computational. Briefly, according to Marr, to see means "to know what is where by looking" – a formulation that expresses the computational idea that vision consists of processing images of a scene so as to *make explicit* what needs to be known about it. On this account, "low-level" vision has to do, among other things, with recovering from the stimulus the positions and orientations of visible surfaces (perhaps in the service of navigation or manipulation), and "high-level" vision with determining which of the known objects, if any, are present in the scene.

The research program initiated by Marr and Poggio (1977), now in its fourth decade, spurred progress in understanding biological vision and contributed to the development of better machine vision systems. Most of the progress has, however, been confined to the understanding of vision *qua* interpretation, rather than of vision *per se*. The difference between the two is best introduced with a selection of passages from Wittgenstein (1958), who distinguished between "seeing" and "seeing as":

> Two uses of the word "see."
> The one: "What do you see there?" – "I see *this*" (and then a description, a drawing, a copy). The other: "I see a likeness between these two faces" [. . .]
> I contemplate a face, and then suddenly notice its likeness to another. I *see* that it has not changed; and yet I see it differently. I call this experience "noticing an aspect." [. . .]
> I suddenly see the solution of a puzzle-picture. Before, there were branches there; now there is a human shape. My visual impression has changed and now I recognize that it has not only shape and color but also a quite particular 'organization.' [. . .]
> Do I really see something different each time, or do I only interpret what I see in a different way? I am inclined to say the former. But why? – To interpret is to think, to do something; seeing is a state.
>
> – Wittgenstein (1958, part II, section xi)

A little reflection reveals that the two kinds of seeing – I'll call the first one "just seeing" to distinguish it from "seeing as" – are related to each other. Informally, the ultimate level of "just seeing" would be attained by a system that can see any possible scene "as" anything at all – that is, a system that can parse differences among scenes in every conceivable way, by varying the labels it attaches to each discernible "aspect" of the input, to use Wittgenstein's expression (these aspects need not be spatial).[2]

Semi-formally, the power of a visual system can be quantified by treating scenes as points in some measurement space, $s \in S$, which are to be distinguished from one another by being classified with respect to a set of concepts C. A system is powerful to the extent that it has both a high-resolution measurement front end and a sophisticated conceptual back end (a 12-megapixel digital camera and a person with low vision are both not very good at seeing, for complementary reasons). If, however, the dimensionality of the measurement space is sufficiently high, the system in question will be able at least to *represent* a very large variety of distinct scenes.[3] Let us, therefore, assume that the dimensionality of the measurement space is in the mega-pixel range (as indeed it is in the human retina) and proceed to examine the role of conceptual sophistication in seeing.

This can be done by formalizing the visual system's conceptual back end as a classification model. The model's power can then be expressed in terms of its Vapnik-Chervonenkis (VC) dimension (Vapnik 1995; Vapnik and Chervonenkis 1971). Consider a class of binary concepts $f \in C$ defined over a class of inputs (i.e., measurements performed over scenes from S), such that $f : S \rightarrow \{0, 1\}$. The VC dimension $VCdim(C)$ of the class of concepts (i.e., of the model that constitutes the categorization back end of the visual system) quantifies its ability to *distinguish* among potentially different inputs. Specifically, the $VCdim$ of a concept class C is defined as the cardinality of the largest set of inputs that a member concept can shatter.[4]

Because classifying a scene as being an instance of a concept amounts to seeing it *as* something, we have thus effectively formalized the notion of "seeing as." We are now ready to extend this framework to encompass the ability to "just see." The key observation is this: among several conceptual systems that happen to share the same measurement space, the one with the highest VC dimension is the most capable of distinguishing various subtle aspects of a given input. In other words, to progressively more complex or higher-$VCdim$ visual systems, the same scene would appear richer and more detailed – a quality that translates into the intuitive notion of a progressively better ability to "just see."

---

[2] Although intuition is never to be trusted blindly, we must use it as a starting point in a process of formalization, because the notion of seeing is itself inherently intuitive rather than formal to begin with. In that, it is similar to the notion of effective computation, which is invoked by the Church-Turing Thesis.

[3] For a discussion of the nominal dimensionality of continuous measurement spaces and the actual dimensionality of data sets mapped into such spaces, see Edelman (1999). The same topics are treated in terms of persistent homology theory by Fekete et al., "Arousal increases the representational capacity of cortical tissue" (2008, submitted).

[4] A set S is shattered by the binary concept class C if for each of the $2^{|S|}$ subsets $s \subseteq S$ there is a concept $f \in C$ that maps all of s to 1 and $S - s$ to 0. The analytical machinery of VC dimension can be extended to deal with real-valued concepts: for a class of real-valued function $g : S \rightarrow \mathbb{R}$, the VC dimension is defined to be that of the indicator class $\{I(g(s) - \beta > 0)\}$ where β takes values over the range of g (Hastie et al. 2001). An extension to multiple-valued concepts is also possible (Bradshaw 1997).

It is worth recalling that the VC dimension of a class of visual concepts determines its learnability: the larger $VCdim(\mathcal{C})$, the more training examples are needed to reduce the error in generalizing $\mathcal{C}$ to new instances below a given level (Blumer et al. 1986; Edelman 1993). Because in real-life situations training data are always at a premium (Edelman and Intrator 2002), and because high-$VCdim$ classifiers are too flexible and are therefore prone to overfitting (Baum and Haussler 1989; Geman et al. 1992), a purposive visual system should always employ the simplest possible classifier for each task that it faces. For this very reason, purposive systems that are good at learning from specific experiences are likely also to be poor general experiencers: nonconceptual and purposeless experience of "just seeing" means being able to see the world under as many as possible of its different aspects, an ability that corresponds to having a high $VCdim$.[5]

To clarify this notion, let us now imagine some examples. A rather extreme one would be a pedestrian-avoidance system installed in a car, which sees any scene s that's in front of it either *as* an instance of a class $C_1 = \{s \mid endangered\_pedestrian(s) = 1\}$ or *as* an instance of $C_2 = \{s \mid endangered\_pedestrian(s) = 0\}$. Note that C_2 is a rather broad category: it includes elephants, ottoman sofas, and heaps of salted pistachios, along with everything else in the universe (except, of course, some pedestrians). I would argue that the ability of such a pedestrian avoidance system to "just see" is very limited, although it is not to be dismissed: it is not blind, merely egregiously single-minded.

In contrast, the ability of a human driver to "just see" is far more advanced than that of a pedestrian-avoidance module, because a human can interpret any given scene in a greater variety of ways: he or she can harbor a much larger number of concepts and can carry out more kinds of tasks. The human ability to "just see" is, however, very far from exhausting the range of conceivable possibilities. Think of a super-observer whose visual system is not encumbered by an attention bottleneck and who can perceive in a typical Manhattan scene (say) the location and disposition of every visible building and street fixture and can simultaneously track every unattached object, including chewing gum wrappers and popcorn kernels, as well as discern the species and the sex of every animal within sight, including pigeons, pedestrians, and the occasional rat.

A being with such powers of observation would be very good at "seeing as": for instance, should it have had sufficient experience in outer space travel, it may be capable of seeing the street scene *as* a reenactment of a series of collisions among rock and ice fragments in a particular cubic kilometer of the Oort cloud on January 1, 0800 hours UTC, 2008 CE, which it happened to have viewed while on a heliopause cruise. Equally importantly, however, it would also be very good at "just seeing" – a non-action[6] in which it can indulge merely by letting the seething mass of categorization processes that in any purposive visual system vie for the privilege of interpreting the input *be* the representation of the scene, without allowing any one of them to gain the upper hand.[7]

---

[5] A fanciful literary example of a cognitive system crippled by its own enormous capacity for individualizing concepts can be found in the short story "Funes the Memorious" by Jorge Luis Borges (1962); a real case has been described by A. Luria in *The Mind of a Mnemonist* (Harvard: 1968).

[6] For the concept of non-action, or *wu wei*, see Loy (1985).

[7] Because the activation levels of conceptual representations are graded, there exists a continuum between "just seeing" and "seeing as" (I am grateful to Melanie Mitchell for pointing out to me this consequence of the approach to vision outlined in this paper). A distributed conceptual system (e.g., the Chorus of Prototypes

Note that although the evolution of visual systems may well be driven by their role in supporting action and by their being embodied in active, purposive agents (Noë 2004), once the system is in place no action is required for it to "just see" (Edelman 2006). When not driven by the demands of a specific task, the super-observer system just imagined may see its surroundings *as* nothing in particular, yet its visual experience would be vastly richer than ours, because of the greater number of aspects made explicit in (and therefore potential distinctions afforded by) its representation of the scene.

This brings us to a key realization: rather than conceptual, purposive, and interpretation-driven, visual experience, whether rich or impoverished, is representational. As Wittgenstein (1958) noted, "To interpret is to think, to do something; seeing is a state."[8] We are now in a position to elaborate on this observation: seeing is a *representational* state (Edelman 2002; for a detailed discussion, see Edelman 2008, sections 5.7 and 9.4).

4.3 A Closer Look at "Seeing As"

The foregoing discussion suggests that to understand the computational nature and possible range of pure visual experience, or "just seeing," we must first understand the nature of conceptual vision, or "seeing as," of which "just seeing" is a kind of by-product (at least in evolved rather than engineered visual systems). In the early years of principled computational study of vision, the efforts to understand "seeing as" focused on charting the possible paths leading from raw image data to seeing the world as a spatial arrangement of surfaces, volumes, and, eventually, objects (Aloimonos and Shulman 1989; Marr 1982; Marr and Nishihara 1978). The key observation, due to Marr, was that this goal could be approached by processing the input so as to *make explicit* (Marr 1982, pp. 19–24) the geometric structure of the environment that is implicitly present in the data. This research program thus amounts to an attempt to elucidate how the geometry of the world could be reconstructed from the visual input.

Both the feasibility of and the need for an explicit and sweeping reconstruction of the geometry of the visual world have been subsequently questioned (Aloimonos et al. 1988; Bajcsy 1988). Noting that biological vision is purposive and active, researchers proposed that computer vision too should aim at serving certain well-defined goals such as navigation or recognition rather than at constructing a general-purpose representation of the world. Moreover, a visual system should actively seek information that can be used to further its goals. This view rapidly took over the computer vision community. At present, all applied work in computer vision is carried out within the purposive framework; the role of active vision is especially prominent in robotics.

From the computational standpoint, this development amounted to shifting the focus of research from "inverse optics" approaches (Bertero et al. 1988), which aim to recover

model of visual recognition and categorization; Edelman 1999) may position itself along this continuum by controlling its dynamics – in the simplest case, a single "temperature" parameter (Hofstadter and Mitchell 1995).

[8] Wittgenstein's observation concerning the nature of vision may have been anticipated by Aristotle in *Metaphysics* (350 B.C.E., IX,8): "In sight the ultimate thing is seeing, and no other product besides this results from sight."

the solid geometry of the viewed scene, to managing feature-based evidence for task-specific hypotheses about the input (Edelman and Poggio 1989). This shift occurred in parallel with the gradual realization that the prime candidate framework for managing uncertainty – graphical models, or Bayes networks – is ubiquitous in biological vision (Kersten et al. 2004; Kersten and Yuille 2003; Knill and Richards 1996), as it is, indeed, in cognition in general (Chater et al. 2006). Importantly, the Bayesian framework allows for a seamless integration of bottom-up data with prior assumptions and top-down expectations, without which visual data are too underdetermined to support reliable decision-making (Marr 1982; Mumford 1996). Such integration is at the core of the most promising current approaches to object and scene vision (Fei-Fei et al. 2003; Freeman 1993; Torralba et al. 2003), including the explicitly generative "analysis by synthesis" methods (Yuille and Kersten 2006).[9]

4.4 The Problems with "Seeing As"

Both major approaches to vision – scene reconstruction and purposive processing – run into problems when taken to the limit. On the one hand, vision considered as reconstruction is problematic because complete recovery of detailed scene geometry is infeasible, and because a replica of the scene, even if it were available, would not in fact further the goal of conceptual interpretation – seeing the scene as something (Edelman 1999). On the other hand, extreme purposive vision is problematic because a system capable of performing seventeen specific tasks may still prove to be effectively blind when confronted with a new, eighteenth task (Intrator and Edelman 1996). To better appreciate the issues at hand, let us consider three factors in the design of a visual system: the role of the task, the role of the context in which a stimulus appears, and the role of the conceptual framework within which vision has to operate.

4.4.1 The Role of the Task

Given that biological visual systems are selected (and artificial ones engineered) not for contemplation of the visible world but for performance in specific tasks, it would appear that the purposive approach is the most reasonable one to pursue – provided that the list of visual tasks that can possibly matter to a given system is manageably short. Deciding whether the purposive approach is feasible as a general strategy for vision reduces, therefore, to answering the question "What is vision for?" In practice, however, the need to develop a taxonomy of visual tasks has not been widely recognized in vision research (the works of Marr 1982, Ballard 1991; Aloimonos 1990; and Sloman 1987, 1989, 2006 are some of the rare exceptions).

---

[9] A related generative approach to scene interpretation, which also integrates top-down guesses with bottom-up data, aims at developing stochastic visual grammars, similar to those proposed by some computational linguists as a solution to natural language generation and parsing (Zhu and Mumford 2006). Seeing how poorly the idea of a stochastic rule-based grammar has fared in computational linguistics (Berwick et al. 2007; Sandbank et al. 2008), I doubt that importing it into vision holds promise over and above the simpler, exemplar- rather than rule-driven generative methods (Yuille and Kersten 2006).

The unavailability of a thorough, let alone complete, taxonomy of visual tasks has a reason other than the sheer tediousness of taxonomic work. The reason is this: insofar as vision is to be useful to an active agent (biological or engineered) in confronting the real world, it must be *open-ended*. Specifying ahead of time the range of tasks that a visual system may need to face is impossible because of a very general property of the universe: the open-endedness of the processes that generate complexity – especially the kind of complexity that pervades the biosphere (Clayton and Kauffman 2006).

The relentless drive toward higher complexity in ecosystems can be illustrated by the simple example of a situation in which a predator must decide between two species of prey: inedible (toxic) "models," and edible "mimics" (Tsoularis 2007). The resort to mimicry by the edible prey presents a computational challenge to the predator, whose perceptual system must learn to distinguish among increasingly similar patterns presented by the prey, on the pain of indigestion, starvation, and possibly death.[10] The mimic species faces a similar perceptual challenge (albeit dissimilar consequences of a wrong decision) in mate choice.[11] Crucially for the evolution of a visual system that is thrown into the midst of such a computational arms race, mimicry situations typically involve "rampant and apparently easy diversification of mimetic patterns" (Joron 2003).

Note that counting new perceptual distinctions as new "tasks" in the preceding example falls squarely within the computational complexity framework based on VC dimension, which is all about counting ways to classify the data into distinct categories. Complexity theory is neutral with respect to the actual methods whereby classification can be learned and progressively finer perceptual distinctions supported. Of the many such methods (Hastie et al. 2001), I mention here one of the simplest, the Chorus of Prototypes (Edelman 1998, 1999). According to this method, the representation space into which new stimuli are cast and in which the categorization decision is subsequently made is spanned by the outputs of filter-like units tuned to some of the previously encountered stimuli (the "prototypes") – a representation that can be learned simply by "imprinting" units newly recruited one after another with select incoming filter patterns.

Employing the terminology introduced earlier, we may observe that a stimulus presented to such a system is thereby simultaneously "seen as" each of the existing prototypes (in a graded rather than all-or-none sense, because the responses of the prototype units are graded). The denser the coverage of a given region of the stimulus space by prototypes, the finer the discrimination power that is afforded in that region to the system by the vector of similarities to the prototypes (and the higher the VC dimension of the system). Crucially, if discrimination is deferred, the mere representation of the stimulus by the outputs of the prototype-tuned filters still amounts to "just seeing" it – that is, to having a visual experience whose richness is determined by the dimensionality and, very importantly, by the spatial structure and the prototype composition of the representation space.

---

[10] Famous last words of a mistaken predator: "Oops, it sure *looked* tasty."

[11] Famous last words of a too undiscriminating sex partner seeker: "Care for a dance, mate?", spoken to a trigger-happy alien that *looked* like a member of one's opposite sex.

Why do the structure and the composition of the representation space spanned by the system's conceptual back-end matter so much? Although any input scene is necessarily also represented in the front end (as a vector of pixel values or photoreceptor activities), this more primitive representation does not make explicit various behaviorally and conceptually consequential aspects of the scene. The human visual system harbors both raw (pixel-like) representations and a great variety of structured ones, whereas a pedestrian detection system may only need the former; this is why a human is much better not only at seeing the visual world *as* a profusion of objects, but also at "just seeing" it (insofar as he or she can make sure that "seeing as" does not get in the way).[12]

4.4.2 The Role of Context

The runaway proliferation of visual tasks, which as noted above include the distinctions that need to be made among various stimuli, stems not only from the complexity of the stimuli by themselves, but also from the diversity of the contexts in which they normally appear. This latter, contextual complexity figures prominently in what Sloman (1983, p. 390) called "the horrors of the real world" that beset computer vision systems.

One problem posed by real-world scenes is that recognizable objects, if any, tend to appear in the wild against highly cluttered backgrounds (Oliva and Torralba 2007). I illustrate this point with two photographs: Figure 4.1 (top) shows an urban scene in which some common objects (a car, a cat, a house) appear at a medium distance; Figure 4.1 (bottom) shows a close-up of a rain-forest floor centered on a snail clinging to a rotting mango. Reliable detection (let alone recognition) of objects in such scenes was impossible until recently in computer vision. Highly purposive systems limited to dealing with a small number of object classes are now capable of finding their target objects in cluttered scenes, by employing Bayesian methods that combine bottom-up and top-down cues (Torralba et al. 2003; Weber et al. 2000; Yuille and Kersten 2006).

Being class-specific, these methods cannot, however, solve the wider problem posed by real-world clutter: the impossibility of constructing an exhaustive and precise description of any scene that is even halfway interesting. The best that a targeted recognition system can hope for is attaining a sparse, conceptual description, as when the arid pasture scene of Figure 4.2 (top) is mapped into the set of spatially anchored labels shown at the bottom of the figure. By now, computer vision researchers seem to have realized that reconstructing the detailed geometry of such scenes, in which the shape and pose of every pebble and the disposition of every blade of grass is made explicit

---

[12] The distinction between the kinds of experience afforded by low-level, pixel-like representations and high-level ones spanned by similarities to prototypes is crucial for understanding how the so-called "hard problem" of consciousness (Chalmers 1995), which pertains to visual qualia, is fully resolved by Smart (2004): "Certainly walking in a forest, seeing the blue of the sky, the green of the trees, the red of the track, one may find it hard to believe that our qualia are merely points in a multidimensional similarity space. But perhaps that is what *it is like* (to use a phrase that can be distrusted) to be aware of a point in a multidimensional similarity space." Briefly, qualia that exist as points in a *structured* space (such as the one spanned by a set of prototype-tuned units; Edelman, 1999) can pertain to any and all aspects of the stimulus (over and above mere local intensities represented at the "pixel" level). Smart's insight thus accounts in a straightforward computational manner for the supposedly mysterious nature of perceptual experience.

Figure 4.1. Two real-world scenes. *Top,* An urban environment, mid-distance. *Bottom,* A natural environment, close-up.

(as in the $2\frac{1}{2}D$ sketch of Marr (1982) or the intrinsic images of Barrow and Tenenbaum (1978)), is not feasible (Barrow and Tenenbaum 1993; Dickinson et al. 1997).

Our visual experience would be impoverished indeed if we were capable of seeing the scenes of Figures 4.1 and 4.2 only "as" parked car, rotting mango, or grazing goat, respectively.[13] These photographs[14] strike us as replete with visual details. Most of these details are, however, "just seen," not "seen as" anything; computer vision systems too need not attempt the humanly impossible when confronted with real-world scenes. Matching the complexity of a human experience of the visual world is a realistic goal, and is challenging enough. As we saw earlier, representations that would make such a match possible are also likely to support highly sophisticated purposive vision.

---

[13] The approach to scene "description" illustrated in Figure 4.2 has been lampooned by René Magritte in paintings such as *From One Day to Another* and *The Use of Speech* (Edelman 2002).

[14] High-resolution originals of the photographs in Figures 4.1 and 4.2 are available from the author by request.

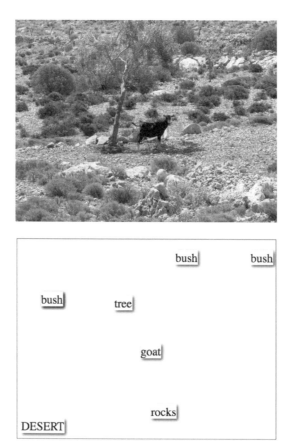

Figure 4.2. Two versions of a real-world scene. *Top,* A natural environment. *Bottom,* The same natural scene, represented by spatially anchored conceptual labels.

4.4.3 The Role of Conceptual Knowledge

As just noted, purposive visual systems can only deliver scene descriptions that are (1) sparse, and (2) conceptual. The second of these properties, or rather limitations, is no less important than the first one (which I discussed briefly above). Restricting the representations derived from scenes to being conceptual amounts to imposing a severe handicap on the visual system. At the level of description with which human "just seeing" resonates, the natural visual world is *ineffable*, in that a vast majority of its "aspects" are not statable in a concise linguistic form; indeed, most are nonconceptual (Clark 2000, 162).[15] Correspondingly, philosophers point out that "Perceptual experience has a richness, texture and fineness of grain that [conceptual] beliefs do not and cannot have" (Bermúdez 1995; see also Akins 1996; Villela-Petit 1999).

   When a set of conceptual labels is applied to a visual scene and is allowed to take over the representation of that scene, the ineffability issue gives rise to two sorts of

---

[15] To the extent that nonhuman animals and prelinguistic infants are capable of conceptual cognition (Smith and Jones 1993; Vauclair 2002), concepts need not be linguistic. If and when available, language does, of course, markedly boost the ability to think conceptually (Clark 1998; Dennett 1993).

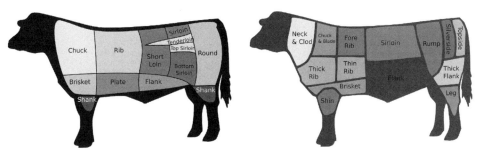

Figure 4.3. Concepts that may affect scene segmentation are not necessarily universal, as illustrated metaphorically by these butchers' diagrams, which compare the US cuts of beef (*left*) to the British cuts (*right*). Ask an English butcher for a piece of beef tenderloin, and you will not be understood.

problems. The first problem stems from the poverty of conceptual labels; earlier in this section I used Figure 4.2 to illustrate the extent to which a conceptual interpretation of a scene is impoverished relative to its image. The second problem arises when one tries to decide where exactly to place the boundary between areas corresponding to each two adjacent labels – precisely the task with which users of interactive scene labeling applications such as LabelMe (Russell et al. 2007) are charged.

The common mistake behind various attempts to develop the ultimate algorithm for scene segmentation, whether using image data or input from a human observer, is the assumption that there is a "matter of fact" behind segmentation.[16] For natural scenes, segmentation is in the eye of the beholder: the same patch may receive different labels from different users or from the same user engaged in different tasks (Figure 4.3), or no label at all if it is too nondescript or if it looks like nothing familiar.[17] To a visually sophisticated observer, a complex natural scene would normally appear as continuous canvas of rich experience, rather than as a solved puzzle with labeled pieces. Even if nothing in the scene is "seen as" something familiar, the whole, and whatever fleeting patterns that may be discerned in it, can always be "just seen" in the sense proposed above.

To summarize, the major challenges that arise in the design of an advanced visual system – adapting to diverse tasks, dealing with realistic contexts, and preventing vision from being driven exclusively by conceptual knowledge – can all be met in the same way. This middle way, which calls for fostering properly structured intermediate representations while avoiding the symmetrical excesses of full geometric reconstruction and full conceptual interpretation, corresponds precisely to "just seeing." Somewhat paradoxically, therefore, it is "just seeing" that saves the day for "seeing as."

---

[16] The Platonist notion that there exists an absolute truth about the conceptual structure of world "out there" that only needs to be discovered is not peculiar to theories of vision: it has been the mainstay of theoretical linguistics for decades. This notion underlies the distinction made by Householder (1952) between what he termed "God's truth" and "hocus-pocus" approaches to theorizing about the structure of sentences, the former one being presumably the correct choice. Although it still survives among the adherents of Chomsky's school of formal linguistics, the idea that every utterance possesses a "God's truth" analysis seems to be on its way out (Edelman and Waterfall 2007).

[17] The few exceptions to this general pattern are provided by scenes in which a prominent object is foregrounded by a conjunction of several cues, as when a horse is seen galloping in a grassy field; such images figure prominently in computer vision work on scene segmentation (e.g., that of Borenstein and Ullman 2002).

4.5 Some Parallels with Biological Vision

In computer vision, the discussion of what it means to see can afford to be normative, in suggesting what a good visual system should be doing. In biological vision, in contrast, the first order of business is finding out what it is that living visual systems actually do. What a visual system does depends on the animal in which it is embodied and on the ecological niche in which the animal resides. For instance, in the behavioral repertoire of the bay scallop, escaping danger by rapidly pulling the shell shut occupies a prominent place. The scallop's visual system, which is fed information from the many tiny eyes that line the rim of its mantle, triggers the escape reflex in response to the onset of a shadow (Hartline 1938; Wilkens and Ache 1977).

Even when the shadow is in fact cast by a cuttlefish on the prowl, it would be unparsimonious to assume that the scallop sees it *as* a manifestation of the concept cuttlefish: scallops are simply wired to propel themselves away from shadows (just as frogs are preset to snap at dark moving dots that may or may not be flies, and flies are compelled to chase other dark moving dots).[18] Near the other end of the spectrum of visual sophistication, the primate visual system (Kremers 2005) incorporates, in addition to a multitude of reflexes, a variety of classification- and action-related functions.

The now familiar contrast between "just seeing" and "seeing as" can be interpreted in terms of a major distinction that exists among the various functions of the primate visual system. In anatomical terms, it corresponds to the distinction between mesencephalic (midbrain) and telencephalic (forebrain) visual systems. A key part of the former is the superior colliculus (King 2004): a structure in the midbrain's "roof" or tectum, where sensory (visual, auditory, and somatic), motor, and motivational representations are brought together in the form of spatially registered maps (Doubell et al. 2003).

With only a slight oversimplification, it may be said that the superior colliculus (SC) is the engine of purposive vision: if the animal is motivated to reach out to a stimulus that its eyes fixate, the action is coordinated by SC neurons (Stuphorn et al. 2000). It is the sparing of subcortical structures including the thalamus and the SC that supports blindsight (Stoerig and Cowey 1997) and makes possible the persistence of a primitive kind of visual consciousness (Merker 2007) in patients with severe cortical damage.

The association networks of concepts (visual and other) that make primate cognition so powerful are distilled from long-term memory traces of the animal's experiences. Because these networks reside in the forebrain (Merker 2004), mesencephalic vision, which bypasses the isocortical structures in primates, is nonconceptual, although the purposive behavior that it can support may be quite flexible (insofar as its planning involves integrating information from multiple sources, including context and goals). As such, the midbrain visual system is not good at "just seeing" – a function that, as I argued earlier, is built on top of the capacity for "seeing as."

In primates, the capacity for "seeing as" is supported by isocortical structures that consist of the primary visual areas in the occipital lobe and the high-level areas in the

---

[18] In contrast to scallops, which can act on what they see but not classify it in any interesting sense, the HabCam computer vision system built by Woods Hole marine biologists, which carries out a high-resolution scan of the ocean floor (Howland et al. 2006), can classify and count scallops in the scenes that it registers. This undoubtedly qualifies it as capable of seeing scallops *as* such.

temporal and parietal lobes (Rolls and Deco 2001), and the frontal lobe, the visual functions of which include exerting contextual influence on the interpretation of the viewed scene (Bar 2004) and active vision or foresight (Bar 2007). In computational terms, the cortical visual system represents the scene by the joint firing of banks of neurons with graded, overlapping receptive fields, which are coarsely tuned to various "objects" (which may be conceptually quite sophisticated) and are modulated by top-down signals (Edelman 1999). By virtue of having a cortical visual system – over and above (literally) the vertebrate standard-issue one in the midbrain – primates can see the world *as* so many different things, as well as just see it.

4.6 Conclusions

We find certain things about seeing puzzling, because we do not find the whole business of seeing puzzling enough.[19]

LUDWIG WITTGENSTEIN (1889–1951)

Contrary to the widespread but tacit assumption in the sciences of vision, having a well-developed sense of sight corresponds to more than the ability to recognize and manipulate objects and to interpret and navigate scenes. The behavioral, neurobiological, and computational insights into the workings of primate vision that emerged in the past two decades go a long way toward characterizing the component that has hitherto been missing from most accounts of vision. The missing component is the capacity for having rich visual experiences.

In a concrete computational sense, visual experience is not merely an epiphenomenon of visual function. A profound capacity for perceptual contemplation goes together with the capacity for seeking out flexible, open-ended mappings from perceptual stimuli to concepts and to actions. In other words, the ability to see the world *as* an intricate, shifting panoply of objects and affordances – an oft-discussed mark of cognitive sophistication (Hofstadter 1995) – is coextensive with the ability to "just see."

From a computational standpoint, this ability requires that the visual system maintain versatile intermediate representations that (1) make explicit as wide as possible a variety of scene characteristics, and (2) can be linked in a flexible manner to a conceptual system that is capable of growing with need and experience. These requirements transcend the traditional goals of high-level vision, which are taken to be the ability to recognize objects from a fixed library and to guess the gist of scenes. The visual world is always more complex than can be expressed in terms of a fixed set of concepts, most of which, moreover, only ever exist in the imagination of the beholder.

Luckily, however, visual systems need not explain the world – they only need to resonate to it in various useful ways (Gibson 1979; Sloman 1989). Anticipating the idea of O'Regan (1992) and O'Regan and Noë (2001), who argued that the world is its own best representation, Reitman et al. (1978, p. 72) observed that "the primary function of perception is to keep our internal framework in good registration with that

---

[19] *Philosophical Investigations*, Wittgenstein 1958, II,xi.

vast external memory, the external environment itself." To be able to resonate with the virtually infinite perceivable variety of what's out there – quoting William Blake, "to see a world in a grain of sand" – an advanced visual system should therefore strive for the richness of the measurement front end, the open-endedness of the conceptual back end,[20] and the possibility of deferring conceptualization and interpretation in favor of just looking.[21]

Acknowledgments

Thanks to Melanie Mitchell for inviting me to a Santa Fe Institute workshop ("High-Level Perception and Low-Level Vision: Bridging the Semantic Gap," organized by M. Mitchell and G. Kenyon) that prompted me to rethink answers to questions in the computational neurophenomenology of vision that preoccupied me for some time. Thanks also to Tony Bell and to David Ackley for their remarks following my talk at SFI, and to Melanie, Tomer Fekete, and Catalina Iricinschi for commenting on a draft of this chapter.

Bibliography

Akins K. 1996. Of sensory systems and the 'aboutness' of mental states. *J Philos* 93:337–372.

Aloimonos JY. 1990. Purposive and qualitative vision. In Proceedings of the AAAI-90 workshop on qualitative vision, 1–5, San Mateo, CA. Morgan Kaufmann.

Aloimonos JY, Shulman D. 1989. *Integration of visual modules: an extension of the Marr paradigm*. Boston: Academic Press.

Aloimonos JY, Weiss I, Bandopadhay A. 1988. Active vision. *Intl J Comput Vision* 2:333–356.

Aristotle (350 B.C.E.). Metaphysics. Available online at http://classics.mit.edu/Aristotle/metaphysics.html.

Bajcsy R. 1988. Active perception. *Proc IEEE* 76(8):996–1005. Special issue on computer vision.

Ballard DH. 1991. Animate vision. *Artif Intell* 48:57–86.

Bar M. 2004. Visual objects in context. *Nat Rev Neurosci* 5:617–629.

Bar M. 2007. The proactive brain: using analogies and associations to generate predictions. *Trends Cogn Sci* 11:280–289.

Barrow HG, Tenenbaum JM. 1978. Recovering intrinsic scene characteristics from images. In eds. AR Hanson and EM Riseman, *Computer vision systems*, 3–26. New York: Academic Press.

Barrow HG, Tenenbaum JM. 1993. Retrospective on "interpreting line drawings as three-dimensional surfaces." *Artif Intell* 59:71–80.

Basri R, Ullman S. 1988. The alignment of objects with smooth surfaces. In Proceedings of the 2nd international conference on computer vision, 482–488, Tarpon Springs, FL. Washington, DC: IEEE.

Baum EB, Haussler D. 1989. What size net gives valid generalization? *Neural Comput* 1:151–160.

---

[20] An intriguing computational mechanism that seems capable of implementing an open-ended representational system is the liquid-state machine of Maass et al. (2003) (for a recent review, see Maass 2007). The power of LSMs to support classification is related to that of support-vector machines (Cortes and Vapnik 1995).

[21] With regard to the virtues of "just looking," consider the following piece of inadvertent propaganda for *wu wei*: "Don't just do something, stand there!" – White Rabbit to Alice in the film *Alice in Wonderland* (1951).

Bermúdez JL. 1995. Non-conceptual content: from perceptual experience to subpersonal computational states. *Mind Lang* 10:333–369.

Bertero M, Poggio T, Torre V. 1988. Ill-posed problems in early vision. *Proc IEEE* 76:869–889.

Berwick RC, Coen M, Fong S, Niyogi P. 2007. The great (Penn Treebank) robbery: when statistics is not enough.

Blumer A, Ehrenfeucht A, Haussler D, Warmuth M. 1986. Classifying learnable geometric concepts with the Vapnik-Chervonenkis dimension. In 18th annual ACM symposium on theory of computing, 273–282.

Borenstein E, Ullman S. 2002. Class specific top down-segmentation. In Proceedings of the European conference on computer vision, ed. A Heyden. vol 2351, Lecture notes in computer science, 110–122.

Borges JL. 1962. *Ficciones*. Translated by A. Bonner in collaboration with the author. New York: Grove Press.

Bradshaw NP. 1997. The effective VC dimension of the n-tuple classifier. In Proceedings of artificial neural networks – ICANN'97, vol 1327, Lecture notes in computer science, 511–516. Berlin: Springer.

Chalmers DJ. 1995. Facing up to the problem of consciousness. *J Conscious Stud* 2:200–219.

Chater N, Tenenbaum JB, Yuille A. 2006. Probabilistic models of cognition: conceptual foundations. *Trends Cogn Sci*, 10:287–291.

Clark A. 1998. Magic words: how language augments human computation. In *Language and thought: interdisciplinary themes*, eds. P Carruthers and J Boucher, 162–183. Cambridge: Cambridge University Press.

Clark A. 2000. *A theory of sentience*. Oxford: Oxford University Press.

Clayton P, Kauffman SA. 2006. Agency, emergence, and organization. *Biol Philos* 21:501–521.

Cortes C, Vapnik V. 1995. Support-vector networks. *Mac Learn*, 20:273–297.

Dennett DC. 1993. Learning and labeling. *Mind Lang* 8:540–547.

Dickinson S, Bergevin R, Biederman I, Eklundh J, Munck-Fairwood R, Jain A, Pentland A. 1997. Panel report: the potential of geons for generic 3-d object recognition. *Image Vis Comput* 15:277–292.

Doubell TP, Skaliora T, Baron, J, King AJ. 2003. Functional connectivity between the superficial and deeper layers of the superior colliculus: an anatomical substrate for sensorimotor integration. *J Neurosci* 23:6596–607.

Edelman S. 1993. On learning to recognize 3D objects from examples. *IEEE Trans Pattern Anal* 15:833–837.

Edelman S. 1998. Representation is representation of similarity. *Behav Brain Sci* 21:449–498.

Edelman S. 1999. *Representation and recognition in vision*. Cambridge: MIT Press.

Edelman S. 2002. Constraining the neural representation of the visual world. *Trends Cogn Sci* 6:125–131.

Edelman S. 2006. Mostly harmless. Review of *Action in perception* by Alva Noë. *Artif Life* 12:183–186.

Edelman S. 2008. *Computing the mind: how the mind really works*. New York: Oxford University Press.

Edelman S, Intrator N. 2002. Models of perceptual learning. In *Perceptual learning*, eds. M Fahle and T Poggio, 337–353. Cambridge: MIT Press.

Edelman S, Poggio T. 1989. Representations in high-level vision: reassessing the inverse optics paradigm. In Proceedings of the DARPA image understanding workshop, 944–9, San Mateo, CA. Morgan Kaufman.

Edelman S, Ullman S, Flash, T. 1990. Reading cursive handwriting by alignment of letter prototypes. *Intl J Comput Vision* 5:303–331.

Edelman S, Waterfall HR. 2007. Behavioral and computational aspects of language and its acquisition. *Physics Life Rev* 4:253–277.

Fei-Fei L, Fergus R, Perona P. 2003. A Bayesian approach to unsupervised one-shot learning of object categories. In Proceedings of the ICCV-2003.

Freeman WT. 1993. Exploiting the generic view assumption to estimate scene parameters. In Proceedings of the 3rd international conference on computer vision, 347–356, Washington, DC. IEEE.

Geman S, Bienenstock E, Doursat R. 1992. Neural networks and the bias/variance dilemma. *Neural Comput*, 4:1–58.

Gibson JJ. 1979. *The ecological approach to visual perception*. Boston: Houghton Mifflin.

Hartline HK. 1938. The discharge of impulses in the optic nerve of *Pecten* in response to illumination of the eye. *J Cell Comp Physiol* 2:465–478.

Hastie T, Tibshirani R, Friedman J. 2001. *Elements of statistical learning: data mining, inference and prediction*. New York: Springer.

Hofstadter DR. 1995. On seeing A's and seeing As. *Stanford Humanit Rev* 4:109–121.

Hofstadter DR, Mitchell M. 1995. The Copycat project: a model of mental fluidity and analogy-making. In *Fluid concepts and creative analogies*, ed. DR Hofstadter, chapt. 5, 205–265. New York: Basic Books.

Householder FW. 1952. Review of methods in structural linguistics by ZS Harris. *Int J Am Linguist* 18:260–268.

Howland J, Gallager S, Singh, H, Girard A, Abrams L, Griner C, Taylor R, and Vine N. 2006. Development of a towed survey system for deployment by the fishing industry. *Oceans*: 1–5.

Huttenlocher DP, Ullman S. 1987. Object recognition using alignment. In Proceedings of the 1st international conference on computer vision, 102–111, London, England. Washington, DC: IEEE.

Intrator N, Edelman S. 1996. How to make a low-dimensional representation suitable for diverse tasks. *Connect Sci* 8:205–224.

Joron M. 2003. Mimicry. In *Encyclopedia of insects*, eds. RT Cardé and VH Resh, 714–26. New York: Academic Press.

Kersten D, Mamassian, P, Yuille, A. 2004. Object perception as Bayesian inference. *Annual Rev Psychol* 55:271–304.

Kersten D, Yuille, A. 2003. Bayesian models of object perception. *Curre Opin Neurobiol* 13:1–9.

King AJ. 2004. The superior colliculus. *Curr Biol* 14:R335–R338. A primer.

Knill D, Richards W, ed. 1996. *Perception as Bayesian inference*. Cambridge: Cambridge University Press.

Kremers J, ed. 2005. *The primate visual system*. New York: John Wiley & Sons.

Lowe DG. 1987. Three-dimensional object recognition from single two-dimensional images. *Artif Intell* 31:355–395.

Loy D. 1985. Wei-wu-wei: nondual action. *Philos East West*, 35:73–87.

Maass W. 2007. Liquid computing. In Proceedings of the CiE'07 conference: computability in Europe 2007. Lecture notes in computer science. Berlin: Springer-Verlag.

Maass W, Natschläger T, Markram H. 2003. Computational models for generic cortical microcircuits. In *Computational neuroscience: a comprehensive approach*, ed. J Feng, chapt. 18, 575–605. Boca Raton: CRC-Press.

Marr D. 1982. *Vision*. San Francisco: WH. Freeman.

Marr D, Nishihara HK. 1978. Representation and recognition of the spatial organization of three dimensional structure. *Proc R Soc Lond B* 200:269–294.

Marr D, Poggio T. 1977. From understanding computation to understanding neural circuitry. *Neurosci Res Prog Bull* 15:470–488.

Merker B. 2004. Cortex, countercurrent context, and dimensional integration of lifetime memory. *Cortex* 40:559–576.

Merker B. 2007. Consciousness without a cerebral cortex: a challenge for neuroscience and medicine. *Behavi Brain Sci* 30:63–81.

Mumford D. 1996. Pattern theory: a unifying perspective. In *Perception as Bayesian inference*, ed. D Knill and W Richards. Cambridge: Cambridge University Press.

Noë A. 2004. *Action in Pepception*. Cambridge: MIT Press.

Oliva A, Torralba A. 2007. The role of context in object recognition. *Trends Cogn Sci* 11:520–527.

O'Regan JK. 1992. Solving the real mysteries of visual perception: the world as an outside memory. *Can J Psychol* 46:461–488.

O'Regan JK, and Noë A. 2001. A sensorimotor account of vision and visual consciousness. *Behav Brain Sci*, 24:883–917.

Reitman W, Nado R, Wilcox B. 1978. Machine perception: what makes it so hard for computers to see? In *Perception and cognition: issues in the foundations of psychology*, ed. CW Savage, vol. IX, *Minnesota studies in the philosophy of science*, 65–87. Minneapolis: University of Minnesota Press.

Rolls E, Deco G. 2001. *Computational neuroscience of vision*. New York: Oxford University Press.

Russell B, Torralba A, Murphy K, Freeman WT. 2007. LabelMe: a database and web-based tool for image annotation. *Int J Comput Vision*. DOI: 10.1007/s11263-007-0090-8.

Sandbank B, Berant J, Edelman S, Ruppin E. 2008. From context to grammar: inferring rich grammatical structure from raw text. Submitted.

Sloman A. 1983. Image interpretation: the way ahead? In *Physical and biological processing of images*, eds. OJ Braddick and AC Sleigh. Springer Series in Information Sciences, 380–401. New York: Springer-Verlag.

Sloman A. 1987. What are the purposes of vision? CSRP 066, University of Sussex.

Sloman A. 1989. On designing a visual system (towards a Gibsonian computational model of vision). *J Exp Theoret Artif Intell*, 1:289–337.

Sloman A. 2006. Aiming for more realistic vision systems? COSY-TR 0603, University of Birmingham, School of Computer Science.

Smart JJC. 2004. The identity theory of mind. In *Stanford encyclopedia of philosophy*, ed. EN Zalta. Stanford University. Available online at http://plato.stanford.edu/archives/fall2004/entries/mind-identity/.

Smith LB, Jones S. 1993. Cognition without concepts. *Cogn Dev* 8:181–188.

Stoerig P, Cowey A. 1997. Blindsight in man and monkey. *Brain* 120:535–559.

Stuphorn V, Bauswein E, Hoffmann KP. 2000. Neurons in the primate superior colliculus coding for arm movements in gaze-related coordinates. *J Neurophysiol* 83:1283–1299.

Torralba A, Murphy, KP, Freeman WT, Rubin MA. 2003. Context-based vision system for place and object recognition. In Proceedings of the IEEE international conference on computer vision, 273–281, Nice, France.

Tsoularis A. 2007. A learning strategy for predator preying on edible and inedible prey. *Acta Biotheoret* 55:283–295.

Vapnik V. 1995. *The nature of statistical learning theory*. Berlin: Springer-Verlag.

Vapnik V, Chervonenkis A. 1971. On the uniform convergence of relative frequencies of events to their probabilities. *Theory of Prob Appl* 16:264–280.

Vauclair J. 2002. Categorization and conceptual behavior in nonhuman primates. In *The cognitive animal*, eds. M Bekoff, C Allen, and G Burghardt, 239–245. Cambridge: MIT Press.

Villela-Petit M. 1999. Cognitive psychology and the transcendental theory of knowledge. In *Naturalizing phenomenology: issues in contemporary phenomenology and cognitive science*, eds. J Petitot, FJ Varela, B Pachoud, and J-M Roy, 508–524. Stanford: Stanford University Press.

Weber M, Welling M, Perona P. 2000. Unsupervised learning of models for recognition. In Proceedings of the European conference on computer vision, ed. D Vernon, vol. 1842, Lecture notes in computer science, 18–32, Berlin: Springer.

Wilkens LA, Ache BW. 1977. Visual responses in the central nervous system of the scallop *Pecten ziczac*. *Cell Mol Life Sci* 33:1338–1340.

Wittgenstein L. 1958. *Philosophical investigations*. 3rd ed. Englewood Cliffs, NJ: Prentice Hall. Translated by G. E. M. Anscombe.

Yuille A, Kersten D. 2006. Vision as Bayesian inference: analysis by synthesis? *Trends Cogn Sci* 10:301–308.

Zhu SC, Mumford D. 2006. A stochastic grammar of images. *Found Trends in Comput Graph Vision* 2:259–362.

CHAPTER 5

Generic Object Recognition by Inference of 3-D Volumetric Parts

Gérard Medioni

5.1 Introduction

Recognizing 3-D objects from a single 2-D image is one of the most challenging problems in computer vision; it requires solving complex tasks along multiple axes. Humans perform this task effortlessly, and have no problems describing objects in a scene, even if they have never seen these objects before. This is illustrated in Figure 5.1. The first task is to extract a set of features from the image, thus producing descriptions of the image different from an array of pixel values. A second task involves defining a model description, and producing a database of such models. One must then establish correspondences between descriptions of the image and those of the models. The last task consists of learning new objects, and adding their descriptions to the database. If the database is large, then an indexing scheme is required for efficiency.

Although these tasks seem clear and well-defined, no consensus has emerged regarding the choice and level of features (2-D or 3-D), the matching strategy, the type of indexing used, and the order in which these tasks should be performed. Furthermore, it is still not established whether all these tasks are necessary for recognizing objects in images.

The early days of computer vision study were dominated by the dogma of the 2 1/2-D sketch (Marr 1981). Consequently, it was "obvious" that the only way to process an image was to extract features such as edges and regions to infer a description of the visible surfaces, from which 3-D descriptions should be inferred. The preferred embodiments of these descriptions were generalized cylinders, which can indeed be generated from 2-D images under imperfect and realistic viewing conditions, making them suitable for shape abstraction of large classes of complex 3-D objects.

The path was clearly defined, and the chosen representation scheme presented a number of attractive properties, such as invariance to viewpoint, robustness to occlusion, and articulation. Unfortunately, the implementation of the algorithmic chain turned out to be immensely more complex than expected, and success was limited to small, restricted subsets of real world scenes. The field, possibly starving for success, turned its attention to recognition of *specific* objects, which requires knowledge of the exact geometry or appearance of the object. A variety of hypotheses and verification methods have been proposed for this purpose (a review can be found in Grimson et al. 1990). All these object recognition approaches can be roughly classified into three groups:

- *3-D shape-based approaches* model the object categories as collections of high-level, volumetric parts, such as generalized cylinders (Binford 1971; Brooks 1983; Marr 1981). Part-based abstractions of objects are extracted and used for recognition. These methods were demonstrated mostly on idealized, textureless images. In this context, deriving deformation invariant shape abstractions from real images remains the main issue.

- *3-D model-based approaches* require an available 3-D CAD-like model. They use prior knowledge of shape and appearance of specific objects to find a best fit of that 3-D model to matching 2-D image features. The problem is solved as a calibration/pose estimation, one with respect to a reference 3-D (Kollning and Nagel 1997). Alternatively, one may compute, from the model, a set of view classes in the aspect-graph approach (Gigus and Malik 1990; PetitJean et al. 1992). The main issues involved are model reconstruction, class generalization, occlusion, and articulation.

- *2-D appearance-based approaches* do not construct an explicit 3-D model; they use multiple views instead. Object descriptions are learned by observations under various conditions, such as pose and illumination. In the absence of occlusion, global methods work well. A very successful example is SLAM (Murase and Nayer 1995), which addresses indexing in a large space and also considers the lighting effects. Class generalization and occlusions remain the main problems in such approaches.

The past ten years or so have seen renewed interest in recognition of generic objects under new names such as "object class recognition" or "object category recognition." These are motivated by applications requiring nonrigid object recognition as well as content-based image retrieval, in which exact object geometry is not an option. These methods, unlike the ones just described, rely on local appearance. They proceed by extracting and matching descriptors (Lowe 2003; Rothganger et al. 2006) such as scale and rotation invariant key-points (Lowe 1995) and local affine-invariant descriptors (Zerroug and Nevatia 1996; Demirci et al. 2006; Everingham et al. 2006; Li et al. 2004, 2006; Rothganger et al. 2006).

With early success and with the creation of benchmark-annotated databases (Everingham 2007; Li et al. 2006), a number of groups are producing interesting and valuable results for detecting (or segmenting) various class of objects (Schneiderman and Kanada 2000; Viola and Jones 2002; Griffin et al. 2007). These methods, however, seem to suffer from a ceiling in performance, as they are inherently view-sensitive.

We first review in detail one of the early approaches proposed on generic object recognition, and make the case that it is still quite attractive. Then, we posit that a possible way to move the field forward is to combine this principled bottom-up approach with top-down detectors, whose recent success is truly remarkable. This work is based on an invited oral talk presented at ICPR in 2000, and at a CVPR workshop in Washington, D.C., in 2005.

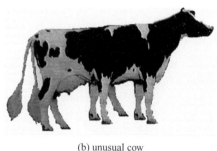

(a) table top   (b) unusual cow

Figure 5.1. Generic object recognition involves recognizing objects that might never have been observed before. (See color plate 5.1.)

5.2 A Principled Approach to Generic Object Recognition

Generic object recognition involves recognition of an object that might never have been observed before and for which no exact model is available (see Fig. 5.1). In this context, the necessary components of an object recognition system are description, matching, and learning.

- *Description* consists of a transformation (and interpretation) of the image data into higher level features, which ideally are components of an objects.
- *Matching* consists of assigning a label to elements of the preceding descriptions, a process that involves accessing stored models and comparing them at the feature level.
- *Learning* consists of generating descriptions for objects not previously known to the system, and describing both similarities and differences with existing known objects. This third component is often ignored in many systems, or performed by the user.

These three tasks make extensive use on the representation scheme used. It drives the strategies for the description process, the way models are accessed and compared, and the methods for learning. The specific representation also affects the complexity of each of the aforementioned tasks. Thus, choosing a good representation scheme is a fundamental issue.

We argue that an appropriate way to solve all of the previous tasks is to generate and use high-level representations in terms of volumetric parts, their hierarchy, and their arrangement. We further propose that part-based representations based on subsets of generalized cylinders constitute a suitable means for shape abstraction of large classes of complex 3-D objects, and that these descriptions can indeed be generated from 2-D images under imperfect and realistic viewing conditions.

In section 5.3, we make the case for generic, high-level, volumetric part-based descriptions. We show how such descriptions can be computed from real images in section 5.4. In section 5.5, we show how to use the obtained descriptions for learning and recognition. Section 5.6 offers a few remarks on achieving progress towards generic object recognition.

5.3 Description Issues

Extraction of generic descriptions requires an adequate representation scheme. Such a scheme becomes itself a generic model from which description methods are derived. However, there is no universal representation scheme that can deal with arbitrary objects. Thus, one must derive generic shape representations that allow one to capture a large class of objects.

The desirable characteristics of a representation scheme for the purposes of generic shape analysis and recognition include local support, stability, discriminatory power, and unambiguity (Nevatia and Binford 1977; Marr 1981). The extraction of descriptions from an image (or a set of images) under realistic imaging effects also requires these characteristics.

A good representation should be able to handle changes in the scene properties, including small irregularities on an object's surface, sensor noise, illumination changes, and, especially, changes in viewpoint. Even if its appearances are relatively different, descriptions of the same object should be similar. Another issue is the degree of detail that might be needed by different tasks. Some tasks may require only coarse-level shape information, whereas others requires some finer details. Hence, a good representation scheme should also allow the control of what is represented in an object. Representing an object's shape hierarchically is a natural way to control the representation scale.

Geometric invariants have been used by researchers to characterize point-sets and certain curves (Mundy and Zisserman 1992). This approach requires visibility and selection of key points on an object, which may not be stable or discriminatory enough. Another approach was to derive higher-level viewpoint-tolerant properties of generic shape representations schemes, such as generalized cylinders (Binford 1971). Higher-level structures provide more stability and expressiveness, leading us to use a high-level representation scheme from which such structures can be identified in the image.

5.3.1 Part-Based Representations

Objects are often made up of a number of components. Although a part-based representation may be difficult for some objects (such as bushes, terrain, face features), it is evident for many others. For instance, one would clearly describe a teapot as consisting of a main body, a spout, a handle, and a lid. For such objects, an explicit representation in terms of parts allows one to capture their rich structure, which is important for the image interpretation process. This way, one can represent an object even if some components are missing. A part-based representation is also useful for reasoning about function (Stark and Bowyer 1991; Rivlin et al. 1994).

Part-based representations include a hierarchical design, in which parts can themselves be decomposed into subcomponents. Therefore, it becomes easy to control the description scale during image interpretation and object recognition; which also allows

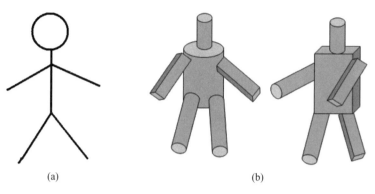

(a) (b)

Figure 5.2. (a) Volumetric part-based descriptions support natural shape abstraction. (b) Volumetric representations are more suited to shape comparison.

judging the similarity of objects in a coarse-to-fine fashion. However, there are many issues involved in generating such descriptions, as indicated later.

Psychological studies of human perception and recognition of 3-D objects from their line drawings also indicate the strong influence of the structured nature of objects on the perception performance of subjects (Biederman 1987). The findings also show that simple geometric primitives and their interactions provide substantial viewpoint-invariant object shape information. Although this theory does not account for textured or highly irregular objects, it accounts for a large set, including new objects, not known a priori to the observer.

5.3.1.1 Volumes vs. Surfaces

Volumes and surfaces are the two main representations for capturing the structured nature of an object. Volumetric representations provide the correct level of abstraction for viewpoint-tolerant descriptions. Volumes constitute a more natural abstraction of an object's shape than surfaces do. For instance, a stick figure using only the axes of generalized cylinders is often a good abstraction of the structure of a complex object (e.g., human; Figure 5.2 (a)). However, abstraction from a surface-based representation is unclear in this case. Surface attributes can be easily determined from a volumetric description, whereas the reverse is not as direct. Also, surface-based descriptions do not provide the differences between the shapes of the two objects directly at a symbolic level.

By decoupling the volumetric representation into a set of attributes, one can easily compare objects and analyze the shape similarities according to several criteria (for each of the intrinsic functions of the volumetric description). Consider the two objects in Figure 5.2(b). Despite their surface differences, they have a similar structure. Although the corresponding parts of the objects have quite different surface representations, we are still able to judge their similarities (sizes along the parts axes and cross-sections), and differences (circular vs. polygonal cross-sections). In this case, the representation is symbolic and discriminative. This type of analysis is essential for recognition and learning.

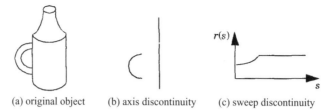

(a) original object   (b) axis discontinuity   (c) sweep discontinuity

Figure 5.3. Segmentation of the handle (a) is based on the discontinuity of its axis with the other axes (b), whereas the segmentation between the top part and the central one is based on the (first order) discontinuity of the sweep function (c), their axes being continuously connected. Adapted from Zerroug and Medioni 1995.

Generalized cylinders (GCs) are of particular interest here; since they possess many of the aforementioned characteristics. They can capture a large number of both real and artificial objects. Generalized cylinders have recently been used in many studies at one or more of the steps in generic object recognition (Nevatia and Binford 1977; Brooks 1983; Pentland 1987; Ponce et al. 1989; Sato and Binford 1993; Mundy et al. 1994; Dickinson et al. 1997). However, without any restrictions, GCs are too general to be practical. Rather, well-defined subclasses of GCs are needed to be practical yet general enough to capture a large set of objects. Examples of such subclasses of GCs are straight homogeneous generalized cylinders (SHGCs) (Ponce et al. 1989; Sato and Binford 1993; Nevatia and Zerroug 1994), planar right constant generalized cylinders (PRCGCs) (Ulupinar and Nevatia 1993), and circular planar right generalized cylinders (circular PRGCs) (Zerroug and Nevatia 1996).

5.3.1.2 Segmentation into Parts

An issue that naturally arises at this point is the definition of a part. In the case of GCs, a definition consists of delimiting parts at discontinuities of any of the intrinsic functions, the axis, the sweep, or the cross-section (Nevatia and Binford 1977) (Fig. 5.3). This definition can be used both to partition a 3-D model and to segment the image of an object. The discontinuities in the intrinsic functions create discontinuities in the image (i.e., in symmetry relationships) and thus provide generic criteria by which to decompose shape. This way, a natural decomposition of parts can be captured at articulation joints, where, owing the relative motion of parts, discontinuities in their shape are produced (e.g., axis-orientation discontinuities, as between the upper and lower legs of a human).

5.4 Computation of Part-Based Descriptions

The derivation of generic descriptions from an imperfect image in a data-driven fashion is a challenging problem in computer vision. One can use the principles of perceptual grouping to implement a promising method. However, this gives rise to many issues,

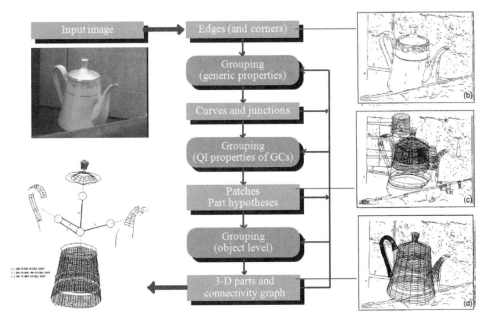

Figure 5.4. From image to 3-D description (adapted from Zerroug and Medioni 1995). The description module starts from an intensity image and ends at a level where structured representations in terms of parts (generalized cylinders) and their relationships are obtained. This representation includes information about the 3-D shape of each complex object so detected.

because the derivation of grouping (segmentation) and description methods should work not only on imperfect images, but for large classes of objects as well.

5.4.1 Organization

There is a direct link between the hierarchical nature of the representations and the organization of the description process. The latter should proceed in successive stages, in which features are detected and then grouped to form higher-level descriptions. In this regard, the feature groups of one level become themselves features of a higher level type, which in turn can be grouped, and so on. This way, the scope of the interpretation process increases at each step owing to the geometric context built by previous feature groups. Thus, feedback loops can be used from higher levels to lower ones in order to refine the features or their groupings based on the information gathered from the increased scope.

This organization is illustrated in Figure 5.4. Although the description module seems to be a pure bottom-up process, it makes use of expectations about image properties, which can be viewed as top-down generic knowledge.

5.4.2 Generating Descriptions

Three tasks need to be performed at each feature level: feature extraction, grouping, and selection (and refinement) of feature groups. The main issues to be considered

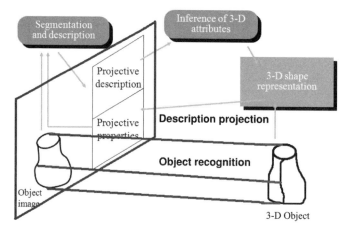

Figure 5.5. The description extraction process (adapted from Zerroug and Medioni 1995). The 3-D representation scheme relies on a set of projective properties. The segmentation and description process exploits the projective properties while extracting relevant descriptions from the image features, and finds image features that satisfy these properties. This results in image (projective) descriptions from which 3-D attributes of the detected object's shape are inferred.

here consist of which features to extract, what criteria to use for grouping them into meaningful clusters, and how to decide whether a cluster is indeed meaningful.

Generic shape representation scheme plays an important role at this process. As we go higher in the hierarchy, the content of this scheme provides the derivation of generic constraints (in the form of expectations) in most of the aforementioned tasks to overcome noise and other image imperfections. Some of these constraints are image properties that any element of the class of objects captured by the shape scheme must satisfy if it is observed. These properties allow the description extraction process to take explicitly into account the shape representation (the desired output of the system), including its dimensionality. In case of 3-D representations, the desired outputs include the projective properties, which hold the 3-D attributes of the shape of the object. As illustrated in Figure 5.5, a 3-D object projects onto an image object (a set of features to be extracted).

5.4.3 A Hierarchy

A typical hierarchy for the description process includes boundaries, surface patches volumetric parts, and compound objects. All the tasks at these levels are pertinent to each other. A robust system should perform all levels of grouping in a concurrent manner. This is not an easy task, however, and in most of the recent systems, this process is linear, with little (or no) feedback, which makes higher levels sensitive to errors at lower levels.

Recently, perceptual edge detection methods have been introduced by enforcing continuity and co-curvilinearity generic constraints to improve the detection of contours (Medioni et al. 2000). However, because they do not incorporate important higher-level information in the segmentation (and description) process, they cannot fully solve the contour extraction problem. The next step after extracting partial contours is to infer surface patches from them. Using symmetry constraints is an adequate approach as long as they cover the characteristics outlined for the shape representation scheme. One would naturally choose symmetries intuitively, but then they would not provide information about the presence of relevant scene objects. However, these constraints should be viewpoint-tolerant properties of the shape representation scheme itself. One would also expect them to be stable, not only to imperfections in object shape but to approximations of the viewing geometry as well.

In an attempt to derive and use *invariant* and *quasi-invariant properties* of certain generalized cylinders, Ponce et al. (1989) proposed a perspective invariant property of SHGCs. It asserts that the intersection of tangent lines at corresponding (symmetric) points of the outline is a straight line, which is the projection of the SHGC axis. Quasi-invariants are relaxed versions of invariants that have a small range of variation over a large portion of the viewing sphere (Binford et al. 1987). For example, a quasi-invariant property of circular PRGCs derived by Zerroug and Nevatia (1996) affirms that the segments joining the projection of co–cross-sectional points of the outline and the locus of their midpoints are very close to forming a right ribbon under most viewing directions. Parallel and skew symmetries have also been used, which apply to certain subclasses of GCs but require more research to derive more general properties (Ulupinar and Nevatia 1993). Therefore, we propose to use quasi-invariance, because invariant properties are rare or so general as to be useless.

Once the surface patches are inferred, they need to be pieced together to form volumetric part hypotheses. This process involves merging both the surface fragments of the same part surface and different surfaces of a part into a single-part hypothesis. The grouping criteria must be rigorous and derived from the properties of the shape scheme. The same criteria apply for object-level grouping. One should exploit the projective properties of the shape representation scheme while grouping different parts that are likely to belong to the same object into a single-object hypothesis and inferring the 3-D shape attributes of each object.

5.5 Recognition Using Part-Based Descriptions

The recognition process involves the manipulation of extracted image descriptions (part-based, volumetric, or hierarchical). New objects must be stored in the database in such a way that they can be retrieved efficiently when a candidate description is proposed for recognition. There are two main issues to be considered: the organization of the database (indexing based on high-level representations) and the retrieval methodology (matching high-level representations).

Our generic object recognition module relies on the following four principles, which have also been applied for 2-D shapes in François and Medioni (1996):

- Hierarchical object description
- Symbolic part description
- Hierarchical database organization
- Partial-match hypotheses generation, followed by interpretation and validation

The described approach does not provide any information about pose or geometric reasoning. We still need to invoke them once the object has been recognized. Therefore, the purpose is to estimate pose as well as emphasize differences with existing stored models.

5.5.1 Symbolic, Hierarchical Descriptions

For the purpose of attaining hierarchy, the connectivity graph is transformed to a mono-rooted directed acyclic graph. Only a small number of the main parts of an object appear at the first level of the hierarchy; more detailed descriptions are stored in deeper levels. For instance, the size of the parts would be a good criterion for orienting the edges in the description graph. We infer the symbolic part descriptions from the resultant quantitative descriptions extracted. The intrinsic geometrical properties thus encoded are similar to that of geons (Biederman 1987). Geometrical relationships between connected parts are also implied by the description.

5.5.2 Learning: Dynamic Database Organization

Efficient database retrieval can be achieved by an original indexing mechanism. The most natural and efficient data structure for indexing hierarchical object descriptions for retrieval is a hierarchy. To achieve this, we need to define a partial order on the descriptions, which can be inferred from the description graph properties. The indexing of a description hierarchy is based on its structure, complemented by a characteristic subset of qualitative part attributes. We call the assessed qualitative partial description an I-Structure.

We assign exactly one I-Structure to each node of the index, by which the node is associated with the actual descriptions. The nodes are themselves organized into a specialization hierarchy, based on a partial order on the I-Structures. Figure 5.6 illustrates an example of hierarchical indexing of hierarchical structures built from three types of parts.

By using such an indexing mechanism, a new description can be added to the database at anytime without any re-computation of the existing structure. Consequently, one can start either with an important list of descriptions that already appear in the database or with a minimum database that is updated incrementally when new shapes are encountered.

5.5.3 Recognition: Object Description Retrieval

Recognition starts by retrieving similar descriptions in the database. Partial matches should be considered at the retrieval step for possible occlusions and uncertainty. The partial matching relies on a similarity/dissimilarity metric among shape descriptions and qualitative information about the comparison.

5.5.3.1 Defining Similarities

We define the dissimilarity between two shapes as a transition cost between them. Transition cost can be computed from the cost of the assumption that two different symbolic objects (parameter values, parts, descriptions) have been obtained from the

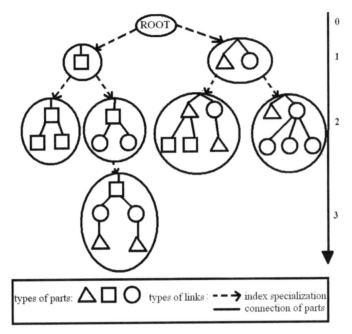

Figure 5.6. Hierarchical organization of the database for dynamic learning and efficient retrieval. The first level of the index hierarchy represents a coarse filter, whereas the deeper levels allow one to focus and refine the early recognition hypotheses.

same real object, variation of the observation conditions, and so on. We define a transition cost for each part description parameter.

To compute the transition cost among part description, we built a comparison graph based on the correspondence hierarchy between two shape descriptions. Each node in this graph points to two matching parts of the considered shapes, and its position in the correspondence hierarchy matches that of the parts it links in their respective description hierarchies. We store the transition cost between two paired parts in the correspondence node. A transition cost is then defined as the aggregation of transition costs between parts. Consequently, one can compute transition costs incrementally and perform a symbolic, qualitative comparison of objects descriptions.

5.5.3.2 Retrieval

The retrieval process is an NP-complete, subgraph isomorphism problem. To solve this problem, we propose an algorithm that exploits the index and the correspondence structures. We compute a partial match between the new description and the possible candidates incrementally at each level. Therefore, the comparison structures are built level by level, keeping at each stage only the structures that point to a compatible description for the current level. The first step of the retrieval process is to select compatible nodes on the first level of the index, and build the first level of the comparison structure for all the descriptions pointed by these nodes and the nodes in their subtrees. Then, we select the partially compatible subnodes of the previously selected nodes and the process is repeated. This iterative process increases the precision of matching.

The algorithm stops after processing the last level of the proposed shape, or after all candidates are processed. Finally, we classify the new description by using the selected retrieved descriptions.

Using both an incremental process and hierarchical indexing allows a reduction in the average complexity of the retrieval process, because fewer and fewer shapes remain to be processed at each step. Therefore, our retrieval process is nearly independent of the number of descriptions in the database. Finally, we should point out that the dynamic organization of the database provides a very powerful and flexible way of manipulating knowledge, especially with the open world and adaptability assumptions, which are required for generality.

5.6 The Way Forward

This "principled approach to generic object recognition" is certainly attractive, but far from accepted. It is thus important to discuss its limitations and ways they can be overcome.

*   *Generality.* A fundamental criticism of this part-based approach is that it fails to represent many objects. This is indeed the case. We need to keep in perspective that the shape description methodology presented here captures shape only, not appearance, owing to photometric properties. Trying to recognize objects by shape only is necessarily limited. Even considering shape only, some objects are better represented as surfaces than volumes. Also, some objects (trees, bushes) that may be better described by statistical features are not well represented with this approach.
*   *Parts are semantic.* The idea that parts naturally emerge at discontinuities of one of the functions describing a GC is certainly attractive, but it has not been fully proven. Parts are labeled as such for other reasons, such as functionality, and may not be easily distinguished by the process just described. For example, a face is naturally described in terms of well-defined parts, such as nose, chin, cheeks, and forehead, but these are not the parts emerging from a GC decomposition.
*   *Efficiency and robustness issues.* The attraction of high-level features is that they greatly reduce the complexity of the comparison and matching processes. The counterpart is that the higher the description level, the higher the cost of a missed detection. Generating the decomposition from Figure 5.4 is not stable with respect to the parameters involved and requires significant computational resources.

One of the most remarkable advances in the field of computer vision in recent years is, in my opinion, the development of detectors for specific object classes, such as pedestrians, cars, or faces. Face detectors are now integrated into consumer cameras and produce very reliable results. The methods used are context-free, in the sense that images are scanned uniformly and do not require additional information. Many implementations, including the freely available OpenCV one, are based on Viola and Jones (2002). They proposed a fast and efficient face-detection algorithm by first computing image features using integral images and then selecting a subset of key features based on AdaBoost. Another approach uses a deformable template consisting of a few keypoints (Elagin et al. 1998).

The presence of a face in an image provides useful context to find the other elements of a human body, such as limbs, torso, and so on. This was documented by Lee in his work on 3-D pose estimation from a single image (Lee and Cohen 2006), and then by others (Mokhtarian and Nevatia 2005). This suggest a constructive path to address the problem of generic object recognition. Specialized, context-free detectors, for tens of objects or elements, should continue to be developed. These detectors provide strong hypotheses for the presence of objects. They also provide context to look for other parts, in order to verify the original hypothesis and to generate more hypotheses. The parts can be found using the bottom-up grouping methodology described in earlier sections.

5.7 Conclusion

We have discussed the issues and challenges involved in generic object recognition, based on an invited talk at ICPR in Barcelona in 2000, and a presentation at the generic object recognition workshop in Washington, D.C., in 2005. We have reviewed in detail one of the early approaches proposed on generic object recognition. The approach derives volumetric descriptions from images and can be used for recognition and learning, resulting in a full recognition system. Although attractive, this approach has not been widely adopted and does suffer from a number of limitations. We have sketched a proposal for moving the field forward by combining the approach with object detectors that only use low-level image information. The current efforts on object category recognition can be regarded as developing such detectors, which need to be complemented with a detailed analysis of image-derived components. Hopefully, the image in Figure 5.1 can then be described as a cow with seven legs and two tails, as opposed to simply a cow.

Bibliography

Biederman I. 1987. Recognition-by-components: a theory of human image understanding. *Psychol Rev* 94(2):115–147.

Binford T. 1971. Visual perception by computer. In Proceedings of the IEEE systems and controls, Miami, FL, December.

Binford T, Levitt T, Mann W. 1987. Bayesian inference in model-based machine vision. In Proceedings of the AAAI uncertainty workshop.

Brooks R. 1983. Model-based three dimensional interpretation of two dimensional images. *IEEE Trans Pattern Anal* 5(2):140–150.

Demirci MF, Shokoufandeh A, Keselman Y, Bretzner L, Dickinson S. 2006. Object recognition as many-to-many feature matching. *Int J Comput Vis* 69(2):203–222.

Dickinson S, Bergevin R, Biederman I, Eklundh J, Munck-Fairwood R, Jain A, Pentland A. 1997. Panel report: the potential of geons for generic 3-d object recognition. 277–292. [Online]. Available: citeseer. ist.psu.edu/diskinson97panel.html.

Elagin E, Steffens J, Neven H. 1998. Automatic pose estimation system for human faces based on bunch graph matching technology. In Proceedings of the 3rd international conference on face and gesture recognition, Nara, Japan, April 14–16, 1998, 136–141.

Everingham M, Gool LV, Williams CKI, Winn J, Zisserman A. 2007. The PASCAL visual object classes challenge 2007 (VOC2007) results. http://www.pascal-network.org/challenges/VOC/voc2007/workshop/index.html.

Everingham M, Zisserman A, Williams C., Gool LV, Allan M, Bishop CM, Chapelle O, Dalal N, Deselaers T, Dorko G, Duffner S, Eichhorn J, Farquhar J, Fritz M, Garcia C, Griffiths T, Jurie F, Keysers D, Koskela M, Laaksonen J, Larlus D, Leibe B, Meng H, Ney H, Schiele B, Schmid C, Seemann E, Shawe-Taylor J, Storkey A, Szedmak S, Triggs B, Ulusoy I, Viitaniemi V, Zhang J. 2006. Recognition-by-components: A theory of human image understanding. *Lecture Notes Comput Sci*, 3944/2006:117–176.

François RJ, Medioni G. 1996. Generic shape learning and recognition. In *ECCV '96: Proceedings of the international workshop on object representation in computer vision II*, 287–320, London: Springer-Verlag.

Gigus Z, Malik J. 1990. Computing the aspect graph for line drawings of polyhedral objects. *IEEE Trans Pattern Anal* 12(2):113–122.

Griffin G, Holub A, Perona P. 2007. Caltech-256 object category dataset.

Grimson W, Perez T, Huttenlocher D. 1990. *Object recognition by computer: the role of geometric constraints*. Cambridge: MIT Press.

Kollnig H, Nagel H. 1997. 3d pose estimation by directly matching polyhedral models to gray value gradients. *Int J Comput Vis* 23(3):283–302.

Lee MW, Cohen I. 2006. A model-based approach for estimating human 3d poses in static images. *IEEE Trans Pattern Anal Mach Intell* 28(6):905–916.

Li FF, Fergus R, Perona P. 2004. Learning generative visual models from few training examples: an incremental bayesian approach tested on 101 object categories. *Proc IEEE Comput Soc Conf Comput Vis Patlern Recognit* 12: 178.

Li FF, Fergus R, Perona P. 2006. One shot learning of object categories. *IEEE Trans Pattern Anal* 28(4): 594–611.

Lowe D. 2003. Distinctive image features from scale-invariant keypoints. *Int J Comput Vis* 20:91–110.

Marr D. 1981. *Vision*. WH. Freeman.

Medioni G, Lee M-S, Tang C-K. 2000. *Computational framework for segmentation and grouping*. New York: Elsevier Science.

Mundy JL, Huang C, Liu J, Hoffman W, Forsyth DA, Rothwell CA, Zisserman A, Utcke S, Bournez O. 1994. MORSE: A 3D object recognition system based on geometric invariants. In *Image understanding workshop*, ed. M Kaufmann. Moueterey, CA, II:1393–1402 [Online]. Available: citesser.ist.psu.edu/87837.html.

Mundy JL, Zisserman A. ed. 1992. *Geometric invariance in computer vision*. Cambridge: MIT Press.

Mun Wai Lee, Nevatia R. 2005. Integrating component cues for human pose tracking. In *2nd Joint IEEE International Workshop on Visual Surveillance and Performance Evalution of Tracking and Surveillance*, 41–48.

Murase H, Nayar SK. 1995. Visual learning and recognition of 3-d objects from appearance. *Int. J. Comput. Vis* 14(1):5–24.

Nevatia R, Binford T. 1977. Description and recognition of complex curved objects. *Artif Intell* 8(1):77–98.

Nevatia R, Zerroug M. 1994. From an intensity image to 3-d segmented descriptions. In Proceedings of the 12th IAPR international conference on pattern recognition, 1994. VOl, 1, Conference A: Computer Vision and Image Processing, 108–113.

Pentland A. 1987. Recognition by parts. In Proceedings of ICCV, 612–620.

PetitJean S, Ponce J, Kriegman DJ. 1992. Computing exact aspect graphs of curved objects: algebraic surfaces. *Int J Comput Vis* 9(3):231–255.

Ponce J, Chelberg D, Mann W. 1989. Invariant properties of straight homogeneous generalized cylinders and their contours. *IEEE Trans Pattern Anal* 11(9):951–966.

Rivlin E, Dickinson SJ, Rosenfeld A. 1994. Object recognition by functional parts. In Proceedings of DARPA image understanding workshop, Monterey, CA, 1531–1539.

Rothganger F, Lazebnik S, Schmid C, Ponce J. 2006. 3d object modeling and recognition using local affine-invariant image descriptors and multi-view spatial constraints. *Int J Comput Vis* 66(3):231–259.

Sato H, Binford TO. 1993. Finding and recovering shgc objects in an edge image. *Comput Vis Image Und.* 57(3):346–358.

Schneiderman H Kanade T. 2000. A statistical method for 3d object detection applied to faces and cars. *CVPR* 1:1746.

Stark L, Bowyer K. 1991. Achieving generalized object recognition through reasoning about association of function to structure. *IEEE Trans Pattern Anal* 13(10):1097–1104.

Ulupinar F, Nevatia R. 1993. Perception of 3-d surfaces from 2-d contours. *IEEE Trans Pattern Anal Mach Intell* 15(1):3–18.

Viola P, Jones M. 2002. Robust real-time object detection. *Int J Comput Vis*. [Online]. Available: citesser.ist.psu.edu/viola01robust.html.

Zerroug M, Medioni G. 1995. The challenge of generic object recognition. In *Proceedings of the international NSF-ARPA workshop on object representation in computer vision*, 217–232. London: Springer-Verlag.

Zerroug M, Nevatia R. 1996. Three-dimensional descriptions based on the analysis of the invariant and quasi-invariant properties of some curved-axis generalized cylinders. *IEEE Trans Pattern Anal Mach Intell* 18(3):237–253.

Zerroug M, Nevatia R. 1996. Volumetric descriptions from a single intensity image. *Int J Comput Vis* 20(1-2):11–42.

CHAPTER 6

What Has fMRI Taught Us About Object Recognition?

Kalanit Grill-Spector

6.1 Introduction

Humans can effortlessly recognize objects in a fraction of a second despite large variability in the appearance of objects (Thorpe et al. 1996). What are the underlying representations and computations that enable this remarkable human ability? One way to answer these questions is to investigate the neural mechanisms of object recognition in the human brain. With the advent of functional magnetic resonance imaging (fMRI) about 15 years ago, neuroscientists and psychologists began to examine the neural bases of object recognition in humans. Functional magnetic resonance imaging (fMRI) is an attractive method because it is a noninvasive technique that allows multiple measurements of brain activation in the same awake behaving human. Among noninvasive techniques, it provides the best spatial resolution currently available, enabling us to localize cortical activations in the spatial resolution of millimeters (as fine as 1 mm) and at a reasonable time scale (in the order of seconds).

Before the advent of fMRI, knowledge about the function of the ventral stream was based on single-unit electrophysiology measurements in monkeys and on lesion studies. These studies showed that neurons in the monkey inferotemporal (IT) cortex respond to shapes (Fujita et al. 1992) and complex objects such as faces (Desimone et al. 1984), and that lesions to the ventral stream can produce specific deficits in object recognition, such as agnosia (inability to recognize objects) and prosopagnosia (inability to recognize faces, Farah 1995). However, interpreting lesion data is complicated because lesions are typically diffuse (usually more than one region is damaged), typically disrupt both a cortical region and its connectivity, and are not replicable across patients. Therefore, the primary knowledge gained from fMRI research was which cortical sites in the normal human brain are involved in object recognition. The first set of fMRI studies of object and face recognition in humans identified the regions in the human brain that respond selectivity to objects and faces (Malach et al. 1995; Kanwisher et al. 1997; Grill-Spector et al. 1998b). Then a series of studies demonstrated that activation in object- and face-selective regions correlates with success at recognizing object and faces, respectively, providing striking evidence for the involvement of these regions in

102

recognition (Grill-Spector et al. 2000; Bar et al. 2001; Grill-Spector et al. 2004). Once researchers found which regions in the cortex are involved in object recognition, the focus of research shifted to examining the nature of representations and computations that are implemented in these regions to understand how they enable efficient object recognition in humans.

In this chapter I will review fMRI research that provided important knowledge about the nature of object representations in the human brain. I chose to focus on this topic because results from these experiments provide important insights that can be used by computer scientists when they design artificial object recognition systems. For example, one of the fundamental problems in recognition is how to recognize an object across variations in its appearance (invariant object recognition). Understanding how a biological system has solved this problem may give clues for how to build a robust artificial recognition system. Further, fMRI is more adequate for measuring object representations than the temporal sequence of computations en route to object recognition because the time scale of fMRI measurements is longer than the time scale of the recognition process (the temporal resolution of fMRI is in the order of seconds, whereas object recognition takes about 100–250 ms). Nevertheless, combining psychophysics with fMRI may give us some clues about what kind of visual processing is implemented in distinct cortical regions. For example, finding regions whose activation is correlated with success at some tasks, but not others, may suggest the involvement of particular cortical regions in one computation, but not another.

In discussing how fMRI has impacted our current understanding of object representations, I will focus on results pertaining to two aspects of object representation:

- How do the underlying representations provide for invariant object recognition?
- How is category information represented in the ventral stream?

I have chosen these topics because (i) they are central topics in object recognition for which fMRI has substantially advanced our understanding. (ii) Some findings related to these topics stirred considerable debate (see sect. 6.7), and (iii) some of the fMRI findings in humans are surprising given prior knowledge from single-unit electrophysiology in monkeys. In organizing the chapter, I will begin with a brief introduction of the functional organization of the human ventral stream and a definition of object-selective cortex. Then I will describe research that elucidated the properties of these regions with respect to basic coding principles. I will continue with findings related to invariant object recognition, and end with research and theories regarding category representation and specialization in the human ventral stream.

6.2 The Functional Organization of the Human Ventral Stream

The first set of fMRI studies on object and face recognition in humans was devoted to identifying the regions in the brain that are object- and face-selective. Electrophysiology research in monkeys suggested that neurons in higher-level regions respond to shapes and objects more than simple stimuli such as lines, edges, and patterns (Desimone et al. 1984; Fujita et al. 1992; Logothetis et al. 1995). Based on these findings, fMRI studies measured brain activation when people viewed pictures of objects compared to

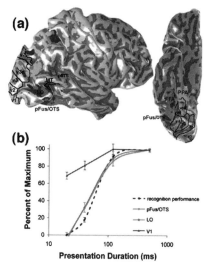

Figure 6.1. Object-, face-, and place-selective cortex. (a) Data of one representive subject shown on her partially inflated right hemisphere: lateral view (*left*); ventral view (*right*). *Dark gray* indicates sulci. *Light gray indicates* gyri. *Black lines* delineate retinotopic regions. *Blue regions* delineate object-selective regions (objects > scrambled objects), including LO and pFus/OTS ventrally as well as dorsal foci along the intraparietal sulcus (IPS). *Red regions* delineate face-selective regions (faces > non-faces objects), including the FFA, a region in LOS and a region in posterior STS. *Magenta regions* delineate overlap between face- and objects-selective regions. *Green regions* delineate place-selective regions (places > objects), including the PPA and a dorsal region lateral to the IPS. *Dark green regions* delineate overlap between place- and object-selective regions. All maps thresholded at $P < 0.001$, voxel level. (b) LO and pFus/OTS (but not VI) responses are correlated with recognition performance (Grill-Spector et al. 2000). To superimpose recognition performance and fMRI signals on the same plot, all values were normalized relative to the maximum response for the 500-ms duration stimulus.

For fMRI signals (blue, red, and orange lines) $= \dfrac{\% \, signal(condition)}{\% \, signal(500 \, ms)}$. For recognition performance (black) $= \dfrac{\% \, correct(condition)}{\% \, correct(500 \, ms)}$. (See color plate 6.1.)

scrambled objects (have the same local information and statistics, but do not contain an object) or texture patterns (e.g., checkerboards, which are robust visual stimuli, but do not elicit a percept of a global form). These studies found a constellation of regions in the lateral occipital cortex (or the lateral occipital complex, LOC), beginning around the lateral occipital sulcus, posterior to MT, and extending ventrally into the occipitotemporal sulcus (OTS) and the fusiform gyrus (Fus), that respond more to objects than controls. The LOC is located lateral and anterior to early visual areas (V1–V4), (Grill-Spector et al. 1998a; Grill-Spector et al. 1998b) and is typically divided into two subregions: LO, a region in the lateral occipital cortex, adjacent and posterior to MT; and pFus/OTS; a ventral region overlapping the OTS and posterior fusiform gyrus (Fig. 6.1).

The lateral occipital complex (LOC) responds similarly to many kinds of objects and object categories (including novel objects) and is thought to be in the intermediate- or high-level stages of the visual hierarchy. Importantly, LOC activations are correlated with subjects' object recognition performance. High LOC responses correlate with successful object recognition (hits), and low LOC responses correlate with trials in which objects are present but not recognized (misses) (Fig. 6.1(b)). Object-selective regions are also found in the dorsal stream (Grill-Spector 2003; Grill-Spector and Malach 2004), but activation of these regions does not correlate with object recognition performance (Fang and He 2005). These regions may be involved in computations related to visually guided actions toward objects (Culham et al. 2003). However, a comprehensive discussion of the role of the dorsal stream in object perception is beyond the scope of this chapter.

In addition to the LOC, researchers found several ventral regions that show preferential responses to specific object categories. The search for regions with categorical preference was motivated by reports that suggested that lesions to the ventral stream can produce very specific deficits, such as the inability to recognize faces or the inability to read words, while other visual (and recognition) faculties remain preserved. By contrasting activations to different kinds of objects, researchers found ventral regions that show higher responses to specific object categories: including lateral fusiform regions that respond more to animals than tools, and medial fusiform regions that respond to tools more than animals (Martin et al. 1996; Chao et al. 1999)), a region in the left OTS that responds more strongly to letters than textures (the visual word form area, or VWFA) (Cohen et al. 2000); several foci that respond more strongly to faces than to other objects (Kanwisher et al. 1997; Haxby et al. 2000; Hoffman and Haxby 2000; Grill-Spector et al. 2004), including the well known fusiform face area (FFA) (Kanwisher et al. 1997), regions that respond more strongly to houses and places than faces and objects (including a region in the parahippocampal gyrus, the parahippocampal place area (PPA) (Epstein and Kanwisher 1998); regions that respond more strongly to body parts than faces and objects, including a region near MT called the extrastriate body area (EBA) (Downing et al. 2001); and a region in the fusiform gyrus (the fusiform body area, or FBA) (Schwarzlose et al. 2005)). Nevertheless, many of these object-selective and category-selective regions respond to more than one object category and also respond strongly to object fragments (Grill-Spector et al. 1998b; Lerner et al. 2001; Lerner et al. 2008). This suggests that one must be cautious when interpreting the nature of the selective responses. It is possible that the underlying representation is perhaps of object parts, features, and/or fragments and not of whole objects or object categories.

Findings of category-selective regions in the human brain initiated a fierce debate about the principles of functional organization in the ventral stream. Are there regions in the cortex that are specialized for any object category? How abstract is the information represented in these regions (e.g., is category information represented in these regions, or low-level visual features that are associated with categories)? I will address these questions in detail in section 6.7.

6.3 Cue-Invariant Responses in the LOC

Although findings of object-selective responses in the human brain were suggestive of the involvement of these region in processing objects, there are many differences between objects and scrambled objects (or objects and texture patterns). Objects have

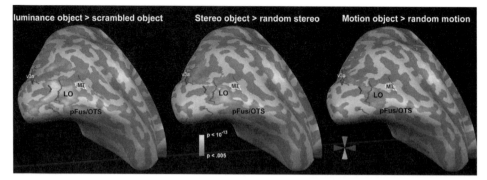

Figure 6.2. Selective responses to objects across multiple visual cues across the LOC. Statistical maps of selective response to object from luminance, stereo and motion information in a representative subject. All maps were thresholded at $P < 0.005$, voxel level, and are shown on the inflated right hemisphere of a representative subject. (a) Luminance objects > scrambled objects. (b) Objects generated from random dot stereograms versus structureless random dot streograms (perceived as a cloud of dots). (c) Objects generated from dot motion versus the same dots moving randomly. Visual meridians are represented by *red* (upper), *blue* (horizontal), and *green* (lower) *lines. White contour* indicates a motion-selective region, or MT. Adapted from Vinberg and Grill-Spector 2008. (See color plate 6.2.)

shapes, surfaces, and contours; they are associated with a meaning and semantic information; and they are generally more interesting than texture patterns. Each of these factors may affect the higher fMRI response to objects than controls. Differences in low-level visual properties across objects and controls may be driving some of these effects as well.

Converging evidence from several studies revealed an important aspect of coding in the LOC: it responds to object shape, not low-level visual features. Several studies showed that all LOC subregions (LO and pFus/OTS) are activated more strongly when subjects view objects independent of the type of visual information that defines the object form (Grill-Spector et al. 1998a; Kastner et al. 2000; Kourtzi and Kanwisher 2000, 2001; Gilaie-Dotan et al. 2002; Vinberg and Grill-Spector 2008) (Fig. 6.2). The lateral occipital complex (LOC) responds more strongly to (1) objects defined by luminance than to luminance textures; (2) objects generated from random dot stereograms than to structureless random dot stereograms; (3) objects generated from structure from motion than to random (structureless) motion; and (4) objects generated from textures than to texture patterns. The response of the LOC to objects is also similar across object format[1] (gray-scale, line drawings, and silhouettes), and it responds to objects delineated by both real and illusory contours (Mendola et al. 1999; Stanley and Rubin 2003). Kourtzi and Kanwisher (Kourtzi and Kanwisher 2001) also showed that there was fMRI-adaptation (fMRI-A, indicating a common neural substrate), when objects had the same shape but different contours, but that there was no fMRI-A when the shared contours were identical but the perceived shape was different, suggesting that the LOC responds to global shape rather than to local contours (see also Lerner et al. 2002; Kourtzi et al. 2003). Overall, these studies provided fundamental knowledge

---

[1] Selective responses to faces and houses across stimulus format (photographs, line drawings, and silhouettes) have also been shown for the FFA and PPA, respectively.

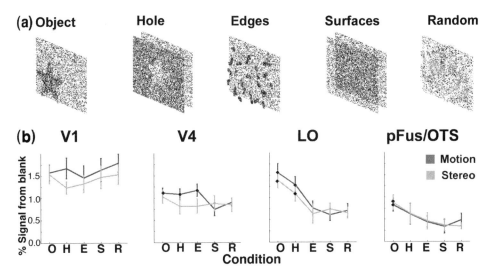

Figure 6.3. Responses to shape, edges, and surfaces across the ventral stream. (a) Schematic illustration of experimental conditions. Stimuli were generated from either motion or stereo information alone and had no luminance edges or surfaces (except for the screen border, which was present during the entire experiment, including blank baseline blocks). For illustration purposes, darker regions indicate front surfaces. From left to right: *Object* on the front surface in front of a flat background plane. *Hole* on the front surface in front of a flat background. Disconnected *edges* in front of a flat background. Edges were generated by scrambling the shape contours. *Surfaces*, Two semitransparent flat surfaces at different depths. *Random* stimuli with no coherent structure, edges, global surfaces, or global shape. Random stimuli had the same relative disparity or depth range as other conditions. See examples of stimuli: http://www-psych.stanford.edu/~kalanit/jnpstim/. (b) Responses to objects, holes, edges, and global surfaces across the visual ventral-processing hierarchy. Responses: mean ± SEM across eight subjects. *O*, object; *H*, hole; *S*, surfaces; *E*, edges; *R*, random; *diamonds,* significantly different than random at $P < 0.05$. Adapted from Vinberg and Grill-Spector 2008.

by showing that activation of the LOC is driven by shape rather than by the low-level visual information that generates form.

In a recent study, we examined whether the LOC response to objects is driven by their global shape or their surface information and whether LOC subregions are sensitive to border ownership. One open question in object recognition is whether the region in the image that belongs to the object is first segmented from the rest of the image (figure-ground segmentation) and then recognized, or whether knowing the shape of an object aids its segmentation (Peterson and Gibson 1994b, 1994a; Nakayama et al. 1995). To address these questions, we scanned subjects when they viewed stimuli that were matched for their low-level information and generated different percepts: (1) a percept of an object in front of a background object, (2) a shaped hole (same shape as the object) in front of a background, (3) two flat surfaces without shapes, (4) local edges (created by scrambling the object contour) in front of a background, or (5) random dot stimuli with no structure (Fig. 6.3(a)) (Vinberg and Grill-Spector 2008). We repeated the experiment twice, once with random dots that were presented stereoscopically and once with random dots that moved. We found that LOC responses (both LO and pFus/OTS) were higher for objects and shaped holes than for surfaces, local edges, or random stimuli (Fig. 6.3(b)). These results were observed for both motion and stereo cues. In contrast, LOC responses were not higher for surfaces than for random stimuli and were not higher for local edges than for random stimuli. Thus, adding either local edge information or global surface information does not increase LOC response. Adding a global shape, however, does produce a significant increase in LOC response. These results provide clear evidence that cue-invariant responses in the LOC are driven by object shape, rather than by global surface information or local edge information.

Interestingly, recent evidence shows that the LOC is sensitive to border ownership/figure-ground segmentation) (Appelbaum et al. 2006; Vinberg and Grill-Spector 2008). We found that the LO and pFus/OTS responses were higher for objects (shapes presented in the foreground) than for the same shapes when they had defined holes in the foreground. The only difference between the objects and the holes was the assignment of the figure region (or border ownership of the contour defining the shape). This higher response to objects than to holes was a unique characteristic of LOC subregions and did not occur in other visual regions (Fig. 6.3). This result suggests that the LOC prefers shapes (and contours) when they define the figure region. One implication of this result is that the same brain machinery may be involved in both recognizing objects and in determining which region in the visual input contains the figure region. Thus, one consideration for computer scientists is that an effective object recognition algorithm should determine both what is the the object in the scene as well as which region in the scene corresponds to the object.

6.4 Neural Bases of Invariant Object Recognition

The literature reviewed so far provides evidence that the LOC is involved in the recognition and processing of object form. Given the LOC's role in object perception, one may consider, how it deals with variability in an object's appearance. Many factors can affect the appearance of objects. Changes in an object's appearance can occur as a result of the object being at different locations relative to the observer, which will affect it's retinal projection of objects in terms of size and position. Also, the 2-D projection of a 3-D object on the retina varies considerably owing to changes in its rotation and viewpoint relative to the observer. Other changes in appearance occur because of differential illumination conditions, which affect an object's color, contrast, and shadowing. Nevertheless, humans are able to recognize objects across large changes in their appearance, which is referred to as *invariant object recognition*.

A central topic of research in the study of object recognition is understanding how invariant recognition is accomplished. One view suggests that invariant object recognition is accomplished because the underlying neural representations are invariant to the appearance of objects. Thus, this view suggests that there neural responses will remain similar even when the appearance of an object changes considerably. One means by which this can be achieved is by extracting from the visual input features or fundamental elements (such as geons (Biederman 1987) that are relatively insensitive to changes in objects' appearance. According to one influential model (recognition by components, or RBC; Biederman 1987), objects are represented by a library of geons, which are easy to detect in many viewing conditions, and by their spatial relations. Other theories suggest that invariance may be generated through a sequence of computations across a hierarchically organized processing stream in which the level of invariance increases from one level of the processing to the next. For example, at the lowest level of the processing stream, neurons code local features; at higher levels of the processing stream, neurons respond to more complex shapes and are less sensitive to changes in position and size (Riesenhuber and Poggio 1999).

Neuroimaging studies of invariant object recognition found differential sensitivity across the ventral stream to object transformations such as size, position, illumination, and viewpoint. Intermediate regions, such as LO, show higher sensitivity to image transformations than higher-level regions, such as pFus/OTS. Notably, evidence from many studies suggests that at no point in the ventral stream are neural representations *entirely* invariant to object transformations. These results support an account in which invariant recognition is supported by a pooled response across neural populations that are sensitive to object transformations. One way in which this can be accomplished is by a neural code that contains independent sensitivity to object information and object transformation (DiCarlo and Cox 2007); for example, neurons may be sensitive to both object category and object position. As long as the categorical preference is retained across object transformations, invariant object information can be extracted.

6.5 Object and Position Information in the LOC

One variation that the object recognition system needs to deal with is variation in the size and position of objects. Size and position invariance are thought to be accomplished in part by an increase in the size of neural receptive fields along the visual hierarchy (i.e., as one ascends the visual hierarchy, neurons respond to stimuli across a larger part of the visual field). At the same time, a more complex visual stimulus is necessary to elicit significant responses in neurons (e.g., shapes instead of oriented lines). Findings from electrophysiology suggest that even at the highest stages of the visual hierarchy, neurons retain some sensitivity to object location and size although electrophysiology reports vary significantly about the degree of position sensitivity of IT neurons (Op De Beeck and Vogels 2000; Rolls 2000; DiCarlo and Maunsell 2003). A related issue is whether position sensitivity of neurons in higher visual areas manifests as an orderly, topographic representation of the visual field. Researchers have examined position and size sensitivity in the LOC and nearby cortex (such as PPA and FFA) using measurements of the mean response across a region of interest; fMRI-A, in which they measured sensitivity to changes in object size or position; and examination of the distributed response across the ventral stream to the same object or object category across sizes and positions.

Several studies documented sensitivity to both eccentricity and polar angle in distinct ventral stream regions. Both object-selective and category-selective regions in the ventral stream respond to objects presented at multiple positions and sizes. However, the amplitude of response to object varies across different retinal positions. The LO and pFus/OTS as well as category-selective regions (e.g., FFA, PPA) respond more strongly to objects presented in the contralateral versus ipsilateral visual field (Grill-Spector et al. 1998b; Hemond et al. 2007; McKyton and Zohary 2007). Some regions (LO and EBA) also respond more strongly to objects presented in the lower visual field (Sayres and Grill-Spector 2008; Schwarzlose et al. 2008). Responses also vary with eccentricity: LO, FFA, and the VWFA respond more strongly to centrally presented stimuli, and the PPA responds more strongly to peripherally presented stimuli (Levy et al., 2001; Hasson et al. 2002; Hasson et al. 2003; Sayres and Grill-Spector 2008).

Using fMRI-A, my colleagues and I have shown that pFus/OTS, but not LO, exhibits some degree of insensitivity to an object's size and position (Grill-Spector et al. 1999). The fMRI-A method allows one to characterize the sensitivity of neural representations to stimulus transformations at a subvoxel resolution. fMRI-A is based on findings from single-unit electrophysiology that show that when objects repeat, there is a stimulus-specific decrease in the response of IT cells to the repeated image but not to other object images (Miller et al. 1991; Sawamura et al. 2006). Similarly, fMRI signals in higher visual regions show a stimulus-specific reduction (fMRI-A) in response to repetition of identical object images (Grill-Spector et al. 1999; Grill-Spector and Malach 2001; Grill-Spector et al. 2006a). We showed that fMRI-A can be used to test the sensitivity of neural responses to object transformation by adapting cortex with a repeated presentation of an identical stimulus and then examining adaptation effects when the stimulus is changed along an object transformation (e.g., changing its position). If the response remains adapted, it indicates that neurons are insensitive to the change; however, if responses return to the initial level (recover from adaptation), it indicates sensitivity to the change (Grill-Spector and Malach 2001).

Using fMRI-A we found that repeated presentation of the same face or object at the same position and size produces reduced fMRI activation or fMRI-A. This is thought to reflect stimulus-specific neural adaptation. Presenting the same face or object in different positions in the visual field or at different sizes also produces fMRI-A in pFus/OTS and FFA, indicating insensitivity to object size and position (Grill-Spector et al. 1999; see also Vuilleumier et al. 2002). This result is consistent with electrophysiology findings that showed that IT neurons that respond similarly to stimuli at different positions in the visual field also show adaptation when the same object is shown in different positions (Lueschow et al. 1994). In contrast, LO recovers from fMRI-A to images of the same face or object when presented at different sizes or positions. This indicates that LO is sensitive to object position and size.

Recently, several groups examined the sensitivity of the distributed response across the visual stream to object category and object position (Sayres and Grill-Spector 2008; Schwarzlose et al. 2008) and also object identity and object position (Eger et al. 2008). These studies used multi-voxel pattern analyses and classifier methods developed in machine learning to examine what information is present in the distributed responses across voxels in a cortical region. The distributed response can carry different information from the mean response of a region of interest when there is variation across voxels' responses.

In order to examine sensitivity to position information, several studies examined whether distributed response patterns to same object category (or object exemplar) is the same (or different) when the same stimulus is presented in a different position in the visual field. In multi-voxel pattern analyses researchers typically split the data into two independent sets and examine the cross-correlation between the distributed responses to the same (or different) stimulus in the same (or different) position across the two datasets. This gives a measure of the sensitivity of distributed responses to object information and position. If responses are position-invariant, there will be a

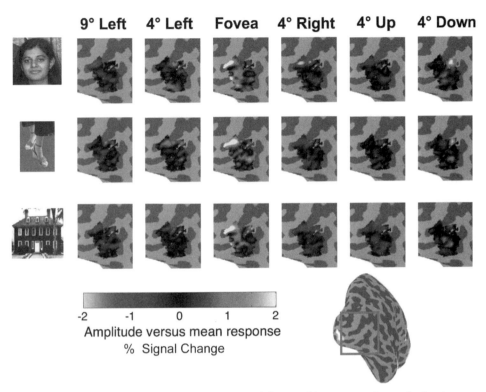

Figure 6.4. LO distributed response patterns to different object categories and stimulus positions. Data are shown on the lateral aspect of the right hemisphere cortical surface for a representative subject. Each panel shows the distributed LO fMRI amplitudes after subtracting from each voxel its mean response. *Red and yellow,* Responses that are higher than the voxel's mean response. *Blue and cyan,* Responses that are lower than the voxel's mean response. *Inset,* Inflated right cortical hemisphere, with red square indicating the zoomed region. Note that pattern changes significantly across columns (positions) and to a lesser extent across rows (categories). Adapted from Sayres and Grill-Spector 2008. (See color plate 6.4.)

high correlation between the distributed responses to the same object category (or exemplar) at different positions. If responses are sensitive to position, there will be a low correlation between responses to the same object category (or exemplar) at different positions.

Figure 6.4 illustrates distributed LO responses to three categories: houses, limbs, and faces at six visual locations (fovea; 4° up, right, down, or left from the fovea; 9° left of fovea). Activation patterns for the same object category presented at different positions vary considerably (compare the response patterns in the same row across the different columns in Fig. 6.4). There is also variation (but to a lesser extent) across different object categories when presented at the same retinal position (same column, different rows, in Fig. 6.4). Surprisingly, position effects in LO were larger than category effects – that is, showing objects from the same category, but at a different position, reduced the correlation between activation patterns (Fig. 6.5, first vs. third bars) more significantly than changing the object category in the same position (Fig. 6.5, first vs. second bar). Importantly, position and category effects were independent, as there were no significant interactions between position and category

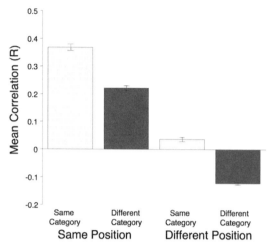

Figure 6.5. Mean cross-correlations between LO distributed responses across two independent halves of the data for the same or different category at the same or different position in the visual field. *Position effects*: LO response patterns to the same category were substantially more similar if they were presented at the same position versus different positions (first and third bars, $P < 10^{-7}$). *Category effects*: The mean correlation was higher for same-category response patterns than for different-category response patterns when presented in the same retinotopic position (first two bars, $P < 10^{-4}$). Error bars indicate SEM across subjects. Adapted from Sayres and Grill-Spector 2008.

(all F values < 1.02, all P values > 0.31). Thus, changing both object category and position produced maximal decorrelation between distributed responses (Fig. 6.5, fourth bar).

We also examined whether position sensitivity in LO is manifested as an orderly topographic map (similar to retinotopic organization in lower visual areas), by measuring retinotopic maps in LO using standard traveling wave paradigms (Wandell 1999; Sayres and Grill-Spector 2008). We found a continuous mapping of the visual field in LO both in terms of eccentricity and polar angle. This topographic map contained an over-representation of the contralateral and lower visual field (more voxels preferred these visual field positions than the ipsilateral and upper visual fields). Although we did not consistently find a single visual field map (a single hemifield or quarterfield representation) in LO, this analysis suggests that there is preserved retinotopic information in LO that may underlie the position effects observed in analyses of distributed LO responses.

Overall, our data show that different object categories produce relatively small changes to both the mean and distributed response across LO (categorical effects are larger in the fusiform and parahippocampal gyri). In comparison, a modest $4°$ change in an object's position produces signal changes in LO that are as large or larger than the category modulation. This $4°$ displacement is well within the range for which humans can categorize and detect objects (Thorpe et al. 2001). This indicates a difference between the position sensitivity of recognition behavior and that of neural populations in LO. However, it is possible that performance in recognition tasks that require fine-grain discrimination between exemplars is more position sensitive, and limited by the degree of position sensitivity in LO.

A related recent study examined position sensitivity using multi-voxel pattern analysis more broadly across the ventral stream and provided additional evidence for a hierarchical organization across the ventral stream (Schwarzlose et al. 2008). Schwarzlose and colleagues found that distributed responses to a particular object category (faces, body parts, or scenes) was similar across positions in ventrotemporal regions (e.g., pFus/OTS and FBA) but changed across positions in occipital regions (e.g., EBA and LO). Thus, evidence from both fMRI-A and multi-voxel pattern analysis studies suggests a hierarchy of representations in the human ventral stream through which representations become less sensitive to object position as one ascends the visual hierarchy.

6.5.1 Implications for Theories of Object Recognition

It is important to relate imaging results to the concept of position-invariant representations of objects and object categories. What exactly is implied by the term "invariance" depends on the scientific context. In some instances, this term is taken to reflect a neural representation that is abstracted so as to be independent of viewing conditions. A fully invariant representation, in this meaning of the term, is expected to be completely independent of information about retinal position (Biederman and Cooper 1991). In the context of studies of visual cortex, however, the term is more often considered to be a graded phenomenon, in which neural populations are expected to retain some degree of sensitivity to visual transformations (like position changes) but in which stimulus *selectivity* is preserved across these transformations (Kobatake and Tanaka 1994; Rolls and Milward 2000; DiCarlo and Cox 2007). In support of this view, a growing literature suggests that maintaining local position information within a distributed neural representation may actually aid invariant recognition in several ways (Dill and Edelman 2001; DiCarlo and Cox 2007; Sayres and Grill-Spector 2008). First, maintaining separable information about position and category may also allow on to maintain information about the structural relationships between object parts (Edelman and Intrator 2000). Indeed some experiments suggest that LO may contain both object-based (McKyton and Zohary 2007) and retinal-based reference frames (Sayres and Grill-Spector 2008). The object-based reference frame may provide a basis for structural encoding. Second, separable position and object information may provide a robust way for generating position invariance by using a population code. Under this model, objects are represented as manifolds in a high-dimensional space spanned by a population of neurons. The separability of position and object information may allow for fast decisions based on linear computations (e.g., linear discriminant functions) to determine the object identity (or category) across positions see (DiCarlo and Cox 2007). Finally, separable object and position information may allow concurrent localization and recognition of objects (i.e., recognizing what the object is and determining where it is).

6.6 Evidence for Viewpoint Sensitivity Across the LOC

Another source of change in object appearance that merits separate consideration is change across rotation in depth. In contrast to position or size changes, in which invariance may be achieved by a linear transformation, the shape of objects changes with depth rotation. This is because the visual system receives 2-D retinal projections of 3-D objects. Some theories suggest that view-invariant recognition across object rotations is accomplished by largely view-invariant representations of objects (generalized cylinders', Marr 1980; recognition by components', or RBC', Biederman 1987); that is, the underlying neural representations respond similarly to an object across its views. Other theories, however, suggest that object representations are view-dependent, that is, they consist of several 2-D views of an object (Ullman 1989; Poggio and Edelman 1990; Bulthoff and Edelman, 1992; Edelman and Bulthoff 1992; Bulthoff et al. 1995; Tarr and Bulthoff 1995). Invariant object recognition is accomplished by interpolation across these views (Ullman 1989; Poggio and Edelman 1990; Logothetis et al. 1995) or by a distributed neural code across view-tuned neurons (Perrett et al. 1998).

Single-unit electrophysiology studies in primates indicate that the majority of neurons in monkey inferotemporal cortex are view-dependent (Desimone et al. 1984; Logothetis et al. 1995; Perrett 1996; Wang et al. 1996; Vogels and Biederman 2002) with a small minority (5–10%) of neurons showing view-invariant responses across object rotations (Logothetis et al. 1995; Booth and Rolls 1998).

In humans, results vary considerably. Short-lagged fMRI-A experiments, in which the test stimulus is presented immediately after the adapting stimulus (Grill-Spector et al. 2006a), suggest that object representations in the LOC are view-dependent (Fang et al. 2007; Gauthier et al. 2002; Grill-Spector et al. 1999; but see Valyear et al. 2006). However, long-lagged fMRI-A experiments, in which many intervening stimuli occur between the test and adapting stimulus (Grill-Spector et al. 2006a), have provided some evidence for view-invariant representations in ventral LOC, especially in the left hemisphere (James et al. 2002; Vuilleumier et al. 2002) and the PPA (Epstein et al. 2008). Also, a recent study showed that the distributed LOC responses to objects remained stable across 60° rotations (Eger et al. 2008). Presently, there is no consensus across experimental findings in the degree to which ventral stream representations are view-dependent or view-invariant. These variable results may reflect differences in the neural representations depending on object category and cortical region, and/or methodological differences across studies (e.g., level of object rotation and fMRI-A paradigm used).

We addressed these differential findings in a recent study in which we used a parametric approach to investigate sensitivity to object rotation and a computational model to link putative neural tuning and resultant fMRI signals (Andresen et al. 2008, 2009). The parametric approach allows a richer characterization of rotation sensitivity because, rather than characterizing representations as invariant or not invariant, it measures the degree of sensitivity to rotations. Using fMRI-A we measured viewpoint sensitivity as a function of the rotation level for two object categories – animals and vehicles. Overall, we found sensitivity to object rotation in the LOC, but there were differences across categories and regions. First, there was higher sensitivity to vehicle rotation than to animal rotation. Rotations of 60° produced a complete recovery from adaptation for vehicles, but rotations of 120° were necessary to produce recovery from adaptation for animals (Fig. 6.6). Second, we found evidence for overrepresentation of the front view of animals in the right pFus/OTS: its responses to animals were

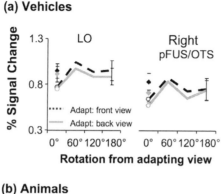

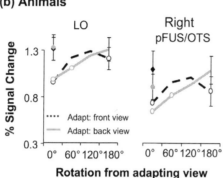

Figure 6.6. LO responses during fMRI-A experiments of rotation sensitivity. Each line represents response after adapting with a front (dashed black) or back view (solid gray) of an object. The nonadapted response is indicated by the diamonds (black for front view, and gray for back view). The open circles indicate significant adaptation, lower than nonadapted, $P < 0.05$, paired t-test across subjects. (a) Vehicle data. (b) Animal data. Responses are plotted relative to a blank fixation baseline. Error bars indicate SEM across eight subjects. Adapted from Andreson, Vinberg, and Grill-Spector (2009).

higher for the front view than the back view (compare black and gray circles in Fig. 6.6(b) right). In addition fMRI-A effects across rotation varied according to the adapting view (Fig. 6(b) right). When adapting with the back view of animals, we found recovery from adaptation for rotations of 120° or larger, but when adapting with the front view of animals, there was no significant recovery from adaptation across rotations. One interpretation is that there is less sensitivity to rotation when adapting with front views than back views of animals. However, the behavioral performance of subjects in a discrimination task across object rotations showed that they are equally sensitive to rotations (performance decreases with rotation level) whether rotations are relative to the front or back of an animal (Andresen et al. 2008), which suggests that this interpretation is unlikely. Alternatively, the apparent adaptation across a 180° rotation relative to a front animal view, may just reflect lower responses to a back animal view.

To better characterize the underlying representations and examine which representations may lead to our observed results, we simulated putative neural responses and predicted the resultant fMRI responses in a voxel. In the model, each voxel contains a mixture of neural populations, each of which is tuned to a different object view

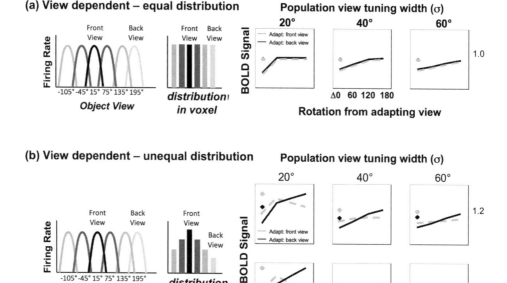

Figure 6.7. Simulations predicting fMRI responses of putative voxels containing a mixture of view-dependent neural populations. *Left,* Schematic illustration of the view tuning and distribution of neural populations tuned to different views in a voxel. For illustration purposes we show a putative voxel with 4 neural populations. *Right,* Result of model simulations illustrating the predicted fMRI-A data. In all panels, the model includes 6 Gaussians tuned to specific views around the viewing circle, separated 60° apart. Across columns, the view tuning width varies. Across rows, the distribution of neural populations preferring specific views varies. *Diamond,* Responses without adaptation (black for back view, and gray for front view). *Lines,* Response after adaptation with a front view (dashed gray line) or back view (solid black line). (a) Mixture of view-dependent neural populations that are equally distributed in a voxel. Narrower tuning (left) shows recovery from fMRI-A for smaller rotations than wider view tuning (right). This model predicts the same pattern of recovery from adaptation when adapting with the front or back view. (b) Mixture of view-dependent neural populations in a voxel with a higher proportion of neurons that prefer the front view. The number on the right indicates the ratio between the percentages neurons tuned to the front versus the back view. Top row, ratio = 1.2. Bottom row, ratio = 1.4. Because there are more neurons tuned to the front view in this model, it predicts higher BOLD responses to frontal views without adaptation (gray vs. black diamonds) and a flatter profile of fMRI-A across rotations when adapting with the front view. Adapted from Andreson, Vinberg, and Grill-Spector (in press).

(Fig. 6.7 and Andresen et al. 2008, in press). fMRI responses were modeled to be proportional to the sum of responses across all neural populations in a voxel. We simulated the fMRI responses in fMRI-A experiments for a set of putative voxels that varied in the view-tuning width of neural populations, the preferred view of different neural populations, the number of different neural populations, and the distribution of populations tuned to different views within a voxel. Results of the simulations indicate that two main parameters affected the pattern of fMRI data: (1) the view-tuning width of the neural population, and (2) the proportion of neurons in a voxel that prefer a specific object view.

Figure 6.7(a) shows the response characteristics of a model of a putative voxel that contains a mixture of view-dependent neural populations that are tuned to different object views, in which the distribution of neurons tuned to different views is uniform. In this model, narrower tuning (left) shows recovery from fMRI-A for smaller rotations than wider view tuning (right). Responses to front and back views are identical when there is no adaptation (Fig. 6.7(a), diamonds), and the pattern of adaptation as a function of rotation is similar when adapting with the front or back views (Fig. 6.7(a)). Such a model provides an account of responses to vehicles across object-selective cortex (as measured with fMRI) and for animals in LO. Thus, this model suggests that the difference between the representation of animals and vehicles in LO is likely due to a smaller population view tuning for vehicles than for animals (a tuning width of $\sigma < 40°$ produces complete recovery from adaptation for rotations larger than $60°$, as observed for vehicles). Figure 6.7(b) shows the effects of neural distributions on fMRI signals. Simulations predict that when there are more neurons in a voxel that are tuned to the front view, there will be higher BOLD responses to frontal views without adaptation (gray vs. black diamonds) and a flatter profile of fMRI-A across rotations when adapting with the front view, as observed in pFus/OTS for animals.

6.6.1 Implications for Theories of Object Recognition

Overall, our results provide empirical evidence for view-dependent object representation across human object-selective cortex that is evident with standard fMRI as well as fMRI-A measurements. These data provide important empirical constraints for theories of object recognition and highlight the importance of parametric manipulations for capturing neural selectivity to any type of stimulus transformation.

Given the evidence for neural sensitivity to object view, how is view-invariant object recognition accomplished? One appealing model for view-invariant object recognition is that objects are represented by a population code in which single neurons may be selective to a particular view, but the distributed representation across the entire neural population is robust to changes in object view (Perrett et al. 1998).

Does the view-specific approach necessitate a downstream view-invariant neuron? One possibility is that perceptual decisions may be performed by neurons outside visual cortex and these neurons are indeed view-invariant. Examples of such view-invariant neurons have been found in the hippocampus, perirhinal cortex, and prefrontal cortex (Freedman et al. 2001, 2003; Quiroga et al. 2005; Quiroga et al. 2008). Alternatively, operations based on the population code (or a distributed code) across view-tuned neurons may be sufficient for view-invariant decisions based on view-sensitive neural representations.

6.7 Debates About the Nature of Functional Organization in the Human Ventral Stream

So far we have considered general computational principles that are required by any object recognition system. Nevertheless, it is possible that some object classes or domains require specialized computations. The rest of this chapter examines functional specialization in the ventral stream that may be linked to these putative "domain-specific" computations.

As illustrated in Figure 6.1, several regions in the ventral stream exhibit higher responses to particular object categories, such as places, faces, and body parts, compared to other object categories. The discovery of category-selective regions initiated a fierce debate about the principles of functional organization in the ventral stream. Are there regions in the cortex that are specialized for any object category? Is there something special about computations relevant to specific categories that generates specialized cortical regions for these computations? In other words, perhaps some general processing is applied to all objects, but some computations may be specific to certain domains and may require additional brain resources. We may also ask about how these category-selective regions come about: Are they innate, or do they require experience to develop?

Four prominent views have emerged to explaining the pattern of functional selectivity in the ventral stream. The main debate centers on the question of whether regions that elicit maximal response for a category are a module for the representation of that category, or whether they are part of a more general object recognition system.

6.7.1 Limited Category-Specific Modules and a General Area for All Other Objects

Kanwisher and coworkers (Kanwisher 2000; Op de Beeck et al. 2008) suggested that ventral temporal cortex contains a limited number of modules specialized for the recognition of special object categories such as faces (in the FFA), places (in the PPA), and body parts (in the EBA and FBA). The remaining object-selective cortex (LOC), which shows little selectivity for particular object categories, is a general-purpose mechanism for perceiving any kind of visually presented object or shape. The underlying hypothesis is that there are few domain-specific modules that perform computations that are specific to these classes of stimuli beyond what would be required from a general object recognition system. For example, faces, like other objects, need to be recognized across variations in their appearance (a domain-general process). However, given the importance of face processing for social interactions, there are aspects of face processing that are unique. Specialized face processing may include identifying faces at the individual level (e.g., John vs. Harry), extracting gender information, evaluating gaze and expression, and so on. These unique, face-related computations may be implemented in face-selective regions.

6.7.2 Process Maps

Tarr and Gauthier (2000) proposed that object representations are clustered according to the type of processing that is required, rather than according to their visual attributes. It is possible that different levels of processing may require dedicated computations that are performed in localized cortical regions. For example, faces are usually recognized at the individual level (e.g., "That is Bob Jacobs"), but many objects are typically recognized at the category level (e.g., "That is a horse"). Following this reasoning, and evidence that objects of expertise activate the FFA more than other objects

(Gauthier et al. 1999; Gauthier et al. 2000), Gauthier, Tarr, and their colleagues have suggested that the FFA is not a region for face recognition, but rather a region for subordinate identification of any object category that is automated by expertise (Gauthier et al. 1999; Gauthier et al. 2000; Tarr and Gauthier 2000).

6.7.3 Distributed Object-Form Topography

Haxby and colleagues (2001) posited an "object-form topography," in which the occipitotemporal cortex contains a topographically organized representation of shape attributes. The representation of an object is reflected by a distinct pattern of response across all ventral cortex, and this distributed activation produces the visual perception. Haxby and colleagues showed that the activation patterns for eight object categories were replicable and that the response to a given category could be determined by the distributed pattern of activation across all ventrotemporal cortex. Further, they showed that it is possible to predict what object category the subjects viewed, even when regions that show maximal activation to a particular category (e.g., the FFA) were excluded (Haxby et al. 2001). Thus, this model suggests that the ventrotemporal cortex represents object category information in an overlapping and distributed fashion.

One of the reasons that this view is appealing is that a distributed code is a combinatorial code that allows representation of a large number of object categories. Given Biederman's rough estimate that humans can recognize about 30,000 categories (Biederman 1987), this provides a neural substrate that has a capacity to represent such a large number of categories. Second, this model posited a provocative view that when considering information in the ventral stream, one needs to consider the weak signals as much as the strong signals, because both convey useful information.

6.7.4 Topographic Representation

Malach and colleagues (2002) suggested that eccentricity biases underlie the organization of ventral and dorsal stream object-selective regions because they found a correlation between category preference (higher response to one category over others) and eccentricity bias (higher response to a specific eccentricity than to other eccentricities (Levy et al. 2001; Hasson et al. 2002; Hasson et al. 2003). Regions that prefer houses to other objects also respond more strongly to peripheral stimulation than to foveal stimulation. In contrast, regions that prefer faces or letters respond more strongly to foveal stimulation than to peripheral stimulation. Malach and colleagues (Malach et al. 2002) proposed that the correlation between category selectivity and eccentricity bias is driven by spatial-resolution needs. Thus, objects whose recognition depends on analysis of fine details are associated with foveal representations, and objects whose recognition requires large-scale integration are associated with peripheral representations. To date, however, there is no clear evidence that eccentricity biases in the FFA are also coupled with better representation of high spatial frequency or smaller receptive fields or, conversely, that the PPA prefers low spatial frequencies or contains neurons with larger receptive fields.

Presently, there is no consensus in the field about which account best explains the functional organization of the ventral stream. Much of the debate centers on the degree to which object processing is constrained to discrete modules or involves distributed computations across large stretches of the ventral stream (Op de Beeck et al. 2008). The debate is about the spatial scale on which computations for object recognition occur as well as the fundamental principles that underlie specialization in the ventral stream.

On the one hand, domain-specific theories need to address findings of multiple foci that show selectivity. For example, multiple foci in the ventral stream respond more strongly to faces than to objects; thus, a strong modular account of a single "face module" for face recognition is unlikely. Also, the spatial extent of these putative modules is undetermined, and it is unclear whether each of these category-selective regions corresponds to a visual area. Further, high-resolution fMRI (1–2 mm on a side) shows that the spatial extent of category-selective regions is smaller than that estimated with standard fMRI (3–4 mm on a side) and that these regions appear more patchy (Schwarzlose et al. 2005; Grill-Spector et al. 2006b).

On the other hand, a potential problem with very distributed and overlapping account of object representation in the ventral stream is that, in order to resolve category information, the brain may need to read out information present across the entire ventral stream (which is inefficient). Further, the fact that there is information in the distributed response does not mean that the brain uses the information in the same way that an independent classifier does. It is possible that activation in localized regions is more informative for perceptual decisions than the information available across the entire ventral stream (Grill-Spector et al. 2004; Williams et al. 2007). For example, FFA responses predict when subjects recognize faces and birds but do not predict when subjects recognize houses, guitars, or flowers (Grill-Spector et al. 2004).

6.8 Differential Development of Category Selectivity from Childhood to Adulthood

One research direction that can shed light on these debates is an examination of the development of ventral stream functional organization. What is the role of experience in shaping category selectivity in the ventral stream?

6.8.1 fMRI Measurements of the Development of the Ventral Stream

To address these questions, our lab (Golarai et al. 2007) identified face-, place-, and object-selective regions within individual children (7–11 years old), adolescents (12–14 years old), and adult subjects (18–35 years old) while subjects fixated and reported infrequent events when two consecutive images were identical (one-back task). We found a prolonged development of the right FFA (rFFA) and left PPA (lPPA) that manifested as an expansion of the spatial extent of these regions across development from age 7 to adulthood (Fig. 6.8). The rFFA and lPPA were significantly larger in adults than in children, with an intermediate size of these regions in adolescents. Notably, the rFFA of children was about a third of the adult size, but it was still evident in 85% of children. These developmental changes could not be explained by smaller anatomical cortical volumes of the fusiform gyrus or the parahippocampal

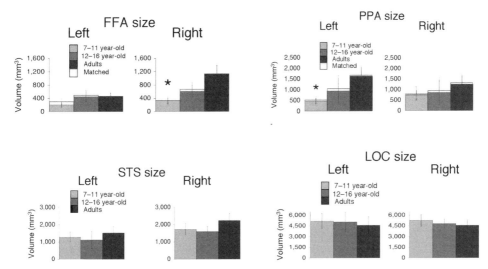

Figure 6.8. Volume of the rFFA, lPPA, STS, and LOC across children, adolescents, and adults. Filled bars indicate average volume across all subjects, which include 20 children, 10 adolescents, and 15 adults. Open bars indicate the average volumes for the subset of subjects that were matched for BOLD-related confounds and include 10 children, 9 adolescents, and 13 adults. Error bars indicate SEM across subjects. Asterisks indicate significantly different than adult, $P < 0.05$. Note that different panels have different scales on the y-axis. Adapted from Golarai et al. 2007.

gyrus (Golarai et al. 2007), which were similar across children and adults, or higher BOLD-related confounds in children (i.e., larger fMRI-related noise or larger subject motion; see Golarai et al. 2007; Grill-Spector et al. 2008) because results remained the same for a subset of subjects that were matched for fMRI-related confounds across ages. These developmental changes were specific to the rFFA and lPPA, because we found no differences across ages in the size of the LOC or the size of the pSTS face-selective region. Finally, within the functionally defined FFA, PPA, and LOC, there were no differences across ages in the level of response amplitudes to faces, objects, and places.

We also measured recognition memory outside the scanner and found that that face- and place-recognition memory increased from childhood to adulthood (Golarai et al. 2007). Further, face-recognition memory was significantly correlated with rFFA size (but not the size of other regions) in children and adolescents (but not adults), and place-recognition memory was significantly correlated with lPPA size (but not the size of other regions) in each of the age groups (Fig. 6.9). These data suggest that improvements in face- and place-recognition memory during childhood and adolescence are correlated with increases in the size of the rFFA and lPPA, respectively.

Another recent study (Scherf et al. 2007) examined the development of the ventral stream in children (5–8 years old), adolescents (11–14 years old), and adults using movie clips that contained faces, objects, buildings, and navigation. Using group analysis methods, they reported the absence of face-selective activations (vs. objects, buildings, and navigation) in 5- to 8-year-old children in both the fusiform gyrus and the pSTS. The lack of FFA in young children in the group analysis may be due to the smaller and more variable FFA location in children, which would affect its detection

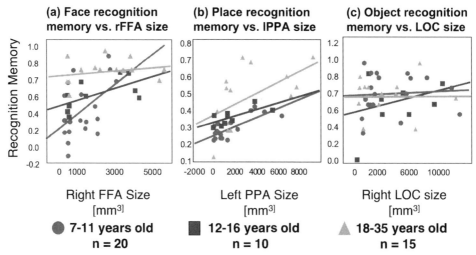

Figure 6.9. Recognition memory versus size of rFFA, iPPA, and LOC. (a) Recognition memory accuracy for different categories across age groups. Recognition memory for faces was significantly better in adults than children (*P < 0.0001) or adolescents (**P < 0.03). Adolescents' memory for faces was better than children's (**P < 0.03). Recognition memory for places was better in adults than in children ([†] P < 0.0001). Adolescents' memory for places was better than children's ([‡] P < 0.01). Recognition accuracy for objects was not different across age groups. Error bars indicate SEM. (b) Recognition memory for faces versus FFA size. Correlations are significant within children and adolescents (r > 0.49, P < 0.03), but not adults. (c) Recognition memory of places versus PPA size. Correlations are significant within each age group (r > 0.59, P < 0.03). (d) Recognition memory for objects versus LOC size. No correlations were significant (P > 0.4). Adapted from Golarai et al. 2007.

in a group analysis. Indeed when Scherf and colleagues performed individual subject analysis, they found face-selective activations in 80% of their child subjects, but the extent of activations was smaller and more variable in location compared to those in adults. Like Golarai and colleagues, they found no difference in the spatial extent or level of response amplitudes to objects in the LOC. Unlike Golorai and colleagues, they reported no developmental changes in the PPA. The variant results may be due to differences in stimuli (pictures vs. movies), task (one-back task vs. passive viewing), and analysis methods (single subject vs. group analysis) across the two studies. For example, Golarai and colleagues instructed subjects to fixate and perform a one-back task. In this task, children had the same accuracy as adults but were overall slower in their responses, with no differences across categories. In the Scherf study, subjects watched movies, and performance was not measured during the scan. It is possible that the children had differential different eye movements or levels of attention than the adults, and this affected their findings.

6.8.2 Implications of Differential Development of Visual Cortex

Overall, fMRI findings suggest differential developmental trajectories across the human ventral visual stream. Surprisingly, these data suggest that more than a decade is necessary for the development of an adult-like rFFA and lPPA. This suggests that experience over a prolonged time may be necessary for the normal development of these regions. This result is surprising, especially because there is evidence for preferential viewing of face-like in newborn babies and evidence for face-selective ERPs within the first 6 to 12 months (for a review, see Johnson 2001). One possibility suggested by Johnson and colleagues is that face processing has an innate component that may be implemented in subcortical pathways (e.g., through the superior colliculus), which biases newborns to look at faces. However, cortical processing of faces may require extensive experience (Gauthier and Nelson 2001; Nelson 2001) and may develop later.

The reasons for differential development across ventral stream regions are unknown. Importantly, it is difficult to disentangle maturational components (genetically programmed developmental changes) from experience-related components, because both are likely to play a role during development. One possibility is that the type of representations and computations in the rFFA and lPPA may require more time and experience to mature than those in the LOC. Second, different cortical regions may mature at different rates owing to genetic factors. Third, the FFA may retain more plasticity (even in adulthood) than the LOC, as suggested by studies that show that FFA responses are modulated by expertise (Gauthier et al. 1999; Tarr and Gauthier 2000). Fourth, the neural mechanisms underlying experience-dependent changes may differ among LOC, FFA, and PPA.

6.9 Conclusion

In sum, neuroimaging research in the past decade has advanced our understanding of object representations in the human brain. These studies have identified the functional organization of the human ventral stream, shown the involvement of ventral stream regions in object recognition, and laid fundamental stepping stones in understanding the neural mechanisms that underlie invariant object recognition.

Many questions remain, however. First, what is the relationship between neural sensitivity to object transformations and behavioral sensitivity to object transformations? Do biases in neural representations produce biases in performance? For example, empirical evidence shows overrepresentation of the lower visual field in LO. Does this lead to better recognition in the lower visual field than in the upper visual field? A second question is related to the development of the ventral stream: To what extent is experience (vs. genes) necessary for shaping functional selectivity in the ventral stream? Third, do object representations remain plastic in adulthood? If so, what is the temporal scale of plasticity, and are experience-induced changes long-lasting? Fourth, what computations are implemented in the distinct cortical regions that are involved in object recognition? Does the "aha" moment in recognition involve a specific response in a particular brain region, or does it involve a distributed response across a large cortical expanse? Combining experimental methods such as fMRI and MEG will provide both high spatial and temporal resolution, which is critical to addressing this question. Fifth, what is the pattern of connectivity between ventral stream visual regions? Although the connectivity in monkey visual cortex has been explored extensively (Van Essen et al. 1990; Moeller et al. 2008), we know little about the connectivity between cortical visual areas in the human ventral stream. This knowledge is necessary for building a model of hierarchical processing in humans and any neural network model of object recognition. Approaches that combine methodologies, such as psychophysics with fMRI, MEG with fMRI, or DTI with fMRI, will be instrumental in addressing these fundamental questions.

Acknowledgments

I thank David Andresen, Golijeh Golarai, Rory Sayres, and Joakim Vinberg for their contributions to the research summarized in this chapter. David Andresen, for his contributions to understanding viewpoint-sensitive representations in the ventral stream. Golijeh Golarai, for spearheading the research on the development of the ventral study. Rory Sayres, for his contributions to research on position invariance and distributed analyses of the ventral stream. Joakim Vinberg, for his dedication to researching cue-invariant and figure-ground processing in the ventral stream. I thank David Remus, Kevin Weiner, Nathan Witthotft, and two anonymous reviewers for comments on this manuscript. This work was supported by National Eye Institute Grants 5 R21 EY-016199-02 and Whitehall Foundation Grant 2005-05-111-RES.

Bibliography

Andresen DR, Vinberg J, Grill-Spector K. 2009. The representation of object viewpoint in the human visual cortex. *Neuroimage* 45(2):522–536. E pub Nov, 25, 2008.

Appelbaum LG, Wade AR, Vildavski VY, Pettet MW, Norcia AM. 2006. Cue-invariant networks for figure and background processing in human visual cortex. *J Neurosci* 26:11,695–11,708.

Bar M, Tootell RB, Schacter DL, Greve DN, Fischl B, Mendola JD, Rosen BR, Dale AM. 2001. Cortical mechanisms specific to explicit visual object recognition. *Neuron* 29:529–535.

Berl MM, Vaidya CJ, Gaillard WD. 2006. Functional imaging of developmental and adaptive changes in neurocognition. *Neuroimage* 30:679–691.

Biederman I. 1987. Recognition-by-components: a theory of human image understanding. *Psychol Rev* 94:115–147.

Biederman I, Cooper EE. 1991. Evidence for complete translational and reflectional invariance in visual object priming. *Perception* 20:585–593.

Booth MC, Rolls ET. 1998. View-invariant representations of familiar objects by neurons in the inferior temporal visual cortex. *Cereb Cortex* 8:510–523.

Bulthoff HH, Edelman S. 1992. Psychophysical support for a two-dimensional view interpolation theory of object recognition. *Proc Natl Acad Sci USA* 89:60–64.

Bulthoff HH, Edelman SY, Tarr MJ. 1995. How are three-dimensional objects represented in the brain? *Cereb Cortex* 5:247–260.

Chao LL, Haxby JV, Martin A. 1999. Attribute-based neural substrates in temporal cortex for perceiving and knowing about objects. *Nat Neurosci* 2:913–919.

Cohen L, Dehaene S, Naccache L, Lehericy S, Dehaene-Lambertz G, Henaff MA, Michel F. 2000. The visual word form area: spatial and temporal characterization of an initial stage of reading in normal subjects and posterior split-brain patients. *Brain* 123 (Pt 2):291–307.

Culham JC, Danckert SL, DeSouza JF, Gati JS, Menon RS, Goodale MA. 2003. Visually guided grasping produces fMRI activation in dorsal but not ventral stream brain areas. *Exp Brain Res* 153:180–189.

Desimone R, Albright TD, Gross CG, Bruce C. 1984. Stimulus-selective properties of inferior temporal neurons in the macaque. *J Neurosci* 4:2051–2062.

DiCarlo JJ, Cox DD. 2007. Untangling invariant object recognition. *Trends Cogn Sci* 11:333–341.

DiCarlo JJ, Maunsell JH. 2003. Anterior inferotemporal neurons of monkeys engaged in object recognition can be highly sensitive to object retinal position. *J Neurophysiol* 89:3264– 3278.

Dill M, Edelman S. 2001. Imperfect invariance to object translation in the discrimination of complex shapes. *Perception* 30:707–724.

Downing PE, Jiang Y, Shuman M, Kanwisher N. 2001. A cortical area selective for visual processing of the human body. *Science* 293:2470–2473.

Edelman S, Bulthoff HH. 1992. Orientation dependence in the recognition of familiar and novel views of three-dimensional objects. *Vision Res* 32:2385–2400.

Edelman S, Intrator N. 2000. (Coarse coding of shape fragments) + (retinotopy) approximately = representation of structure. *Spat Vis* 13:255–264.

Eger E, Ashburner J, Haynes JD, Dolan RJ, Rees G. 2008. fMRI activity patterns in human LOC carry information about object exemplars within category. *J Cogn Neurosci* 20:356–370.

Epstein R, Kanwisher N. 1998. A cortical representation of the local visual environment. *Nature* 392:598–601.

Epstein RA, Parker WE, Feiler AM. 2008. Two kinds of fMRI repetition suppression? Evidence for dissociable neural mechanisms. *J Neurophysiol* 99(6):2877–2886.

Fang F, He S. 2005. Cortical responses to invisible objects in the human dorsal and ventral pathways. *Nat Neurosci* 8:1380–1385.

Fang F, Murray SO, He S. 2007. Duration-dependent FMRI adaptation and distributed viewer-centered face representation in human visual cortex. *Cereb Cortex* 17:1402–1411.

Farah MJ. 1995. *Visual agnosia*. Cambridge: MIT Press.

Freedman DJ, Riesenhuber M, Poggio T, Miller EK. 2001. Categorical representation of visual stimuli in the primate prefrontal cortex. *Science* 291:312–316.

Freedman DJ, Riesenhuber M, Poggio T, Miller EK. 2003. A comparison of primate prefrontal and inferior temporal cortices during visual categorization. *J Neurosci* 23:5235–5246.

Fujita I, Tanaka K, Ito M, Cheng K. 1992. Columns for visual features of objects in monkey inferotemporal cortex. *Nature* 360:343–346.

Gauthier I, Hayward WG, Tarr MJ, Anderson AW, Skudlarski P, Gore JC. 2002. BOLD activity during mental rotation and viewpoint-dependent object recognition. *Neuron* 34:161–171.

Gauthier I, Nelson CA. 2001. The development of face expertise. *Curr Opin Neurobiol* 11:219–224.

Gauthier I, Skudlarski P, Gore JC, Anderson AW. 2000. Expertise for cars and birds recruits brain areas involved in face recognition. *Nat Neurosci* 3:191–197.

Gauthier I, Tarr MJ, Anderson AW, Skudlarski P, Gore JC. 1999. Activation of the middle fusiform 'face area' increases with expertise in recognizing novel objects. *Nat Neurosci* 2:568–573.

Gilaie-Dotan S, Ullman S, Kushnir T, Malach R. 2002. Shape-selective stereo processing in human object-related visual areas. *Hum Brain Mapp* 15:67–79.

Golarai G, Ghahremani DG, Whitfield-Gabrieli S, Reiss A, Eberhardt JL, Gabrieli JD, Grill-Spector K. 2007. Differential development of high-level visual cortex correlates with category-specific recognition memory. *Nat Neurosci* 10:512–522.

Grill-Spector K. 2003. The neural basis of object perception. *Curr Opin Neurobiol* 13:159–166.

Grill-Spector K, Golarai G, Gabrieli J. 2008. Developmental neuroimaging of the human ventral visual cortex. *Trends Cogn Sci* 12:152–162.

Grill-Spector K, Henson R, Martin A. 2006a. Repetition and the brain: neural models of stimulus-specific effects. *Trends Cogn Sci* 10:14–23.

Grill-Spector K, Knouf N, Kanwisher N. 2004. The fusiform face area subserves face perception, not generic within-category identification. *Nat Neurosci* 7:555–562.

Grill-Spector K, Kushnir T, Edelman S, Avidan G, Itzchak Y, Malach R. 1999. Differential processing of objects under various viewing conditions in the human lateral occipital complex. *Neuron* 24:187–203.

Grill-Spector K, Kushnir T, Edelman S, Itzchak Y, Malach R. 1998a. Cue-invariant activation in object-related areas of the human occipital lobe. *Neuron* 21:191–202.

Grill-Spector K, Kushnir T, Hendler T, Edelman S, Itzchak Y, Malach R. 1998b. A sequence of object-processing stages revealed by fMRI in the human occipital lobe. *Hum Brain Mapp* 6:316–328.

Grill-Spector K, Kushnir T, Hendler T, Malach R. 2000. The dynamics of object-selective activation correlate with recognition performance in humans. *Nat Neurosci* 3:837–843.

Grill-Spector K, Malach R. 2001. fMR-adaptation: a tool for studying the functional properties of human cortical neurons. *Acta Psychol (Amst)* 107:293–321.

Grill-Spector K, Malach R. 2004. The human visual cortex. *Annu Rev Neurosci* 27:649–677.

Grill-Spector K, Sayres R, Ress D. 2006b. High-resolution imaging reveals highly selective nonface clusters in the fusiform face area. *Nat Neurosci* 9:1177–1185.

Hasson U, Harel M, Levy I, Malach R. 2003. Large-scale mirror-symmetry organization of human occipito-temporal object areas. *Neuron* 37:1027–1041.

Hasson U, Levy I, Behrmann M, Hendler T, Malach R. 2002. Eccentricity bias as an organizing principle for human high-order object areas. *Neuron* 34:479–490.

Haxby JV, Gobbini MI, Furey ML, Ishai A, Schouten JL, Pietrini P. 2001. Distributed and overlapping representations of faces and objects in ventral temporal cortex. *Science* 293:2425–2430.

Haxby JV, Hoffman EA, Gobbini MI. 2000. The distributed human neural system for face perception. *Trends Cogn Sci* 4:223–233.

Hemond CC, Kanwisher NG, Op de Beeck HP. 2007. A preference for contralateral stimuli in human object- and face-selective cortex. *PLoS ONE* 2:e574.

Hoffman EA, Haxby JV. 2000. Distinct representations of eye gaze and identity in the distributed human neural system for face perception. *Nat Neurosci* 3:80–84.

James TW, Humphrey GK, Gati JS, Menon RS, Goodale MA. 2002. Differential effects of viewpoint on object-driven activation in dorsal and ventral streams. *Neuron* 35:793–801.

Johnson MH. 2001. Functional brain development in humans. *Nat Rev Neurosci* 2:475–483.

Kanwisher N. 2000. Domain specificity in face perception. *Nat Neurosci* 3:759–763.

Kanwisher N, McDermott J, Chun MM. 1997. The fusiform face area: a module in human extrastriate cortex specialized for face perception. *J Neurosci* 17:4302–4311.

Kastner S, De Weerd P, Ungerleider LG. 2000. Texture segregation in the human visual cortex: a functional MRI study. *J Neurophysiol* 83:2453–2457.

Kobatake E, Tanaka K. 1994. Neuronal selectivities to complex object features in the ventral visual pathway of the macaque cerebral cortex. *J Neurophysiol* 71:856–867.

Kourtzi Z, Kanwisher N. 2000. Cortical regions involved in perceiving object shape. *J Neurosci* 20:3310–3318.

Kourtzi Z, Kanwisher N. 2001. Representation of perceived object shape by the human lateral occipital complex. *Science* 293:1506–1509.

Kourtzi Z, Tolias AS, Altmann CF, Augath M, Logothetis NK. 2003. Integration of local features into global shapes: monkey and human FMRI studies. *Neuron* 37:333–346.

Lerner Y, Epshtein B, Ullman S, Malach R. 2008. Class information predicts activation by object fragments in human object areas. *J Cogn Neurosci* 20:1189–1206.

Lerner Y, Hendler T, Ben-Bashat D, Harel M, Malach R. 2001. A hierarchical axis of object processing stages in the human visual cortex. *Cereb Cortex* 11:287–297.

Lerner Y, Hendler T, Malach R. 2002. Object-completion effects in the human lateral occipital complex. *Cereb Cortex* 12:163–177.

Levy I, Hasson U, Avidan G, Hendler T, Malach R. 2001. Center-periphery organization of human object areas. *Nat Neurosci* 4:533–539.

Logothetis NK, Pauls J, Poggio T. 1995. Shape representation in the inferior temporal cortex of monkeys. *Curr Biol* 5:552–563.

Lueschow A, Miller EK, Desimone R. 1994. Inferior temporal mechanisms for invariant object recognition. *Cereb Cortex* 4:523–531.

Malach R, Levy I, Hasson U. 2002. The topography of high-order human object areas. *Trends Cogn Sci* 6:176–184.

Malach R, Reppas JB, Benson RR, Kwong KK, Jiang H, Kennedy WA, Ledden PJ, Brady TJ, Rosen BR, Tootell RB. 1995. Object-related activity revealed by functional magnetic resonance imaging in human occipital cortex. *Proc Natl Acad Sci USA* 92:8135–8139.

Marr D. 1980. Visual information processing: the structure and creation of visual representations. *Philos Trans R Soc Lond B Biol Sci* 290:199–218.

Martin A, Wiggs CL, Ungerleider LG, Haxby JV. 1996. Neural correlates of category-specific knowledge. *Nature* 379:649–652.

McKyton A, Zohary E. 2007. Beyond retinotopic mapping: the spatial representation of objects in the human lateral occipital complex. *Cereb Cortex* 17:1164–1172.

Mendola JD, Dale AM, Fischl B, Liu AK, Tootell RB. 1999. The representation of illusory and real contours in human cortical visual areas revealed by functional magnetic resonance imaging. *J Neurosci* 19:8560–8572.

Miller EK, Li L, Desimone R. 1991. A neural mechanism for working and recognition memory in inferior temporal cortex. *Science* 254:1377–1379.

Moeller S, Freiwald WA, Tsao DY. 2008. Patches with links: a unified system for processing faces in the macaque temporal lobe. *Science* 320:1355–1359.

Nakayama K, He ZJ, Shimojo S. 1995. Visual surface representation: a critical link between low-level and high-level vision. In *An invitation to cognitive sciences: visual cognition*, ed. SM Kosslyn and DN Osherson. Cambridge: MIT Press.

Nelson CA. 2001. The development and neural bases of face recognition. *Infant Child Develop* 10:3–18.

Op de Beeck HP, Haushofer J, Kanwisher NG. 2008. Interpreting fMRI data: maps, modules and dimensions. *Nat Rev Neurosci* 9:123–135.

Op De Beeck H, Vogels R. 2000. Spatial sensitivity of macaque inferior temporal neurons. *J Comp Neurol* 426:505–518.

Perrett DI. 1996. View-dependent coding in the ventral stream and its consequence for recognition. In *Vision and movement mechanisms in the cerebral cortex*, ed. R Camaniti, KP Hoffmann, and AJ Lacquaniti, 142–151. Strasbourg: HFSP.

Perrett DI, Oram MW, Ashbridge E. 1998. Evidence accumulation in cell populations responsive to faces: an account of generalisation of recognition without mental transformations. *Cognition* 67:111–145.

Peterson MA, Gibson BS. 1994a. Must shape recognition follow figure-ground organization? An assumption in peril. *Psychol Sci* 5:253–259.

Peterson MA, Gibson BS. 1994b. Object recognition contributions to figure-ground organization: operations on outlines and subjective contours. *Percept Psychophys* 56:551–564.

Poggio T, Edelman S. 1990. A network that learns to recognize three-dimensional objects. *Nature* 343:263–266.

Quiroga RQ, Mukamel R, Isham EA, Malach R, Fried I. 2008. Human single-neuron responses at the threshold of conscious recognition. *Proc Natl Acad Sci USA* 105:3599–3604.

Quiroga RQ, Reddy L, Kreiman G, Koch C, Fried I. 2005. Invariant visual representation by single neurons in the human brain. *Nature* 435:1102–1107.

Riesenhuber M, Poggio T. 1999. Hierarchical models of object recognition in cortex. *Nat Neurosci* 2:1019–1025.

Rolls ET. 2000. Functions of the primate temporal lobe cortical visual areas in invariant visual object and face recognition. *Neuron* 27:205–218.

Rolls ET, Milward T. 2000. A model of invariant object recognition in the visual system: learning rules, activation functions, lateral inhibition, and information-based performance measures. *Neural Comput* 12:2547–2572.

Sawamura H, Orban GA, Vogels R. 2006. Selectivity of neuronal adaptation does not match response selectivity: a single-cell study of the FMRI adaptation paradigm. *Neuron* 49:307–318.

Sayres R, Grill-Spector K. 2008. Relating retinotopic and object-selective responses in human lateral occipital cortex. *J Neurophysiol* 100(1):249–267, Epub May 7, 2008.

Scherf KS, Behrmann M, Humphreys K, Luna B. 2007. Visual category-selectivity for faces, places and objects emerges along different developmental trajectories. *Dev Sci* 10:F15–30.

Schwarzlose RF, Baker CI, Kanwisher NK. 2005. Separate face and body selectivity on the fusiform gyrus. *J Neurosci* 25:11055–11059.

Schwarzlose RF, Swisher JD, Dang S, Kanwisher N. 2008. The distribution of category and location information across object-selective regions in human visual cortex. *Proc Natl Acad Sci USA* 105:4447–4452.

Stanley DA, Rubin N. 2003. fMRI activation in response to illusory contours and salient regions in the human lateral occipital complex. *Neuron* 37:323–331.

Tarr MJ, Bulthoff HH. 1995. Is human object recognition better described by geon structural descriptions or by multiple views? Comment on Biederman and Gerhardstein (1993). *J Exp Psychol Hum Percept Perform* 21:1494–1505.

Tarr MJ, Gauthier I. 2000. FFA: a flexible fusiform area for subordinate-level visual processing automatized by expertise. *Nat Neurosci* 3:764–769.

Thorpe S, Fize D, Marlot C. 1996. Speed of processing in the human visual system. *Nature* 381:520–522.

Thorpe SJ, Gegenfurtner KR, Fabre-Thorpe M, Bulthoff HH. 2001. Detection of animals in natural images using far peripheral vision. *Eur J Neurosci* 14:869–876.

Ullman S. 1989. Aligning pictorial descriptions: an approach to object recognition. *Cognition* 32:193–254.

Ungerleider LG, Mishkin M, Macko KA. 1983. Object vision and spatial vision: two cortical pathways. *Trends Neurosci* 6:414–417.

Valyear KF, Culham JC, Sharif N, Westwood D, Goodale MA. 2006. A double dissociation between sensitivity to changes in object identity and object orientation in the ventral and dorsal visual streams: a human fMRI study. *Neuropsychologia* 44:218–228.

Van Essen DC, Felleman DJ, DeYoe EA, Olavarria J, Knierim J. 1990. Modular and hierarchical organization of extrastriate visual cortex in the macaque monkey. *Cold Spring Harb Symp Quant Biol* 55:679–696.

Vinberg J, Grill-Spector K. 2008. Representation of shapes, edges, and surfaces across multiple cues in the human visual cortex. *J Neurophysiol* 99:1380–1393.

Vogels R, Biederman I. 2002. Effects of illumination intensity and direction on object coding in macaque inferior temporal cortex. *Cereb Cortex* 12:756–766.

Vuilleumier P, Henson RN, Driver J, Dolan RJ. 2002. Multiple levels of visual object constancy revealed by event-related fMRI of repetition priming. *Nat Neurosci* 5:491–499.

Wandell BA. 1999. Computational neuroimaging of human visual cortex. *Annu Rev Neurosci* 22:145–173.

Wang G, Tanaka K, Tanifuji M. 1996. Optical imaging of functional organization in the monkey inferotemporal cortex. *Science* 272:1665–1668.

Williams MA, Dang S, Kanwisher NG. 2007. Only some spatial patterns of fMRI response are read out in task performance. *Nat Neurosci* 10:685–686.

CHAPTER 7

Object Recognition Through Reasoning About Functionality: A Survey of Related Work

Kevin Bowyer, Melanie Sutton, and Louise Stark

7.1 Recognition Based on Functionality

Minsky (1991) is one of several well-known researchers who have argued for the necessity of representing knowledge about functionality:

> ... it is not enough to classify items of information simply in terms of the features or structures of those items themselves. This is because we rarely use a representation in an intentional vacuum, but we always have goals – and two objects may seem similar for one purpose but different for another purpose. Consequently, we must also take into account the functional aspects of what we know, and therefore we must classify things (and ideas) according to what they can be used for, or which goals they can help us achieve. Two armchairs of identical shape may seem equally comfortable as objects for sitting in, but those same chairs may seem very different for other purposes, for example, if they differ much in weight, fragility, cost, or appearance. ... In each functional context we need to represent particularly well the heuristic connections between each object's internal features and relationships, and the possible functions of those objects.

The early part of this quote contrasts the approach of representing (only) features or structure of objects with the approach of representing knowledge about how an object functions to achieve a goal. Particularly in computer vision, objects have traditionally been represented by their shape or their appearance. Object recognition based on reasoning about functionality stands in contrast to these more traditional approaches, with the aim of achieving recognition at a more generic level. The middle part of this quote illustrates the ideas in the context of the object category `chair`. Figure 7.1 depicts a variety of typical chairs. Chair seems to be a favorite object category for research in this area and is the example that we started within the Generic Recognition Using Form and Function (GRUFF) project. The last part of this quote highlights the point that there is some relationship between the features and structure of an object and how that object may be used to achieve a particular function. From the computer vision perspective, it should be possible to analyze the shape or appearance of an object to

Figure 7.1. Typical chairs with varied shape and appearance. Object recognition based purely on representing shape and/or appearance would have great difficulty encompassing all of these objects in one model. The essence of a representation based on functionality is that each object would be recognized as a chair by reasoning that it has a sittable surface, back support, and arm support that could be used together.

find features and/or structures that make it possible to infer a potential function of the object.

The purpose of this chapter is to review work in this area over the last two decades. Our viewpoint is primarily that of a computer vision researcher wanting to enable object recognition at a generic, or category, level (see Rosch et al. 1976 for a discussion of object categories). However, sensing of shape and/or appearance is generally sufficient only to determine potential functionality. Actual functionality typically depends on material properties that are best determined by interacting with the object, and this level of reasoning about functionality involves both vision and robotics. Additionally, as object functionality becomes more complex, the representations used need to become correspondingly more systematic and powerful. Thus, object recognition based on functionality eventually incorporates elements of artificial intelligence, computer vision, and robotics. This chapter will touch on each of these areas, and we will attempt to show how they contribute to a greater whole.

The remainder of the chapter is organized as follows. Section 7.2 summarizes the development of the GRUFF approach pioneered by Stark and Bowyer (1991). Section 7.3 explores uses of function in artificial intelligence, computer vision, and robotics, as well as related research in cognitive psychology that impacts functionality-based object recognition research. Finally, Section 7.4 proposes research lines to be explored in the next generation of systems based on reasoning about the functionality of objects.

7.2 Development of the GRUFF Approach

The GRUFF project began in the late 1980s (Stark and Bowyer 1989), and work has continued now for approximately two decades. The initial work focused on demonstrating reasoning about the functionality of 3-D shapes as exemplars of the category `chair` (Stark and Bowyer 1990, 1991). This was quickly followed by generalizations to additional object categories whose exemplars could be described by rigid 3-D shapes (Stark and Bowyer 1994; Sutton et al. 1994) and by articulated 3-D shapes (Green et al. 1995). Another line of generalization moved away from analyzing ideal 3-D shape descriptions and into the segmentation and analysis of sensed range images of real objects (Stark et al. 1993; Hoover et al. 1995). Still another effort looked at using machine learning techniques to simplify the construction of functional representations (Woods et al. 1995). A later line of work, which still continues, began to explore robotic interaction with a sequence of sensed shape descriptions to confirm actual functionality and drive additional bottom-up processing (Stark et al. 1996; Sutton et al. 1998, 2002; Sutton and Stark 2008).

7.2.1 Reasoning about Static 3-D Shapes

Early versions of GRUFF took an ideal 3-D shape as the starting point for reasoning about functionality. The shape models were simple boundary representations of polyhedral objects, of the type common in "CAD-based vision" efforts of that time. These shape descriptions were idealized in that they did not have any of the noise, artifacts, occlusion, or other problems that occur with 3-D sensing of real scenes. Also, the types of objects considered were ones that could reasonably be described by a rigid 3-D shape; for example, chairs and tables, or cups and plates.

The first GRUFF system reasoned about 3-D shapes to determine whether they satisfied the functionality of the object category `chair` (Stark and Bowyer 1991). The definition of the simplest category of chair could be given as:

```
Conventional Chair
  = Provides Sittable Surface + Provides Stable Support
```

The properties named in the definition are called *knowledge primitives*. Each is implemented as a procedure call that takes the 3-D shape description as input, possibly with features identified by previous knowledge primitives, and performs computations to determine if the named property can be satisfied by the shape. For example, the knowledge primitive `Provides Sittable Surface` looks for planar surfaces, or approximately co-planar groups of surfaces, that cover an area of the appropriate size to be a seating surface. The execution of the knowledge primitive provides a list of the candidate surfaces found on the shape. The knowledge primitive `Provides Stable Support` then takes these candidates and performs computation to determine if the object will rest stably on a support plane when the seating surface is oriented up and force is applied to it. The result is a list of surfaces on the object that can be oriented upward and serve as stable seating surfaces. This first GRUFF system had multiple categories of chair, including `straight-back chair`, `arm chair`, `balans chair`, `lounge chair`, and `high chair`. All of these were elaborations or variations on the same basic idea of using functional primitives to process a 3-D shape to determine how it might serve a specific function.

Experimental results were shown for the first GRUFF system processing 101 different 3-D shapes created as 38 intended chair exemplars and 63 intended non-chair exemplars. The system declared that 37 of the 38 intended chair exemplars satisfied the functionality of a chair, and that 46 of the 63 intended non-chair exemplars could not satisfy the functionality of a chair. The disagreement on the intended non-chair exemplars came from the system determining that in fact they could serve as a chair if used in some novel orientation. The disagreement on the intended chair exemplar came from the fact that the exemplar only marginally met the requirements of individual knowledge primitives and slipped below the threshold for recognition. The system did not actually give a binary chair/non-chair result, but it did provide a measure that reflected how well the aggregate functionality was satisfied, with a threshold for a chair/non-chair decision.

The basic ideas used in the initial version of GRUFF proved sufficient to represent a much broader range of object classes than just `chair`. The system was relatively easily extended to various categories of furniture objects (Stark and Bowyer 1994), and also to various categories of dishes and cups (Sutton et al. 1994). Common themes in all these efforts are that the functionality involved rigid shape, and the models processed by the system were boundary representations of polyhedral shapes.

7.2.2 Functionality Requiring Articulated Shape

One generalization of GRUFF dealt with reasoning about objects whose functionality is realized by articulated motion of 3-D parts (Green et al. 1995). The input to this problem is a time sequence of shape models with no information about parts or articulation. This sequence is assumed to encompass the full range of motion of the underlying articulated object. GRUFF first infers a 3-D model of parts and their ranges of articulated motion, based on the sequence of observed 3-D shapes. GRUFF then uses knowledge primitives to determine the functionality of the recovered articulated model. The object category explored in this work is `Scissors`, and the high-level definition of its functionality is given as:

```
Scissors = Provides Opposing Finger Grasp
         + Provides Opposing Cutting Blades
         + Closing Grasp Causes Cutting
```

Experimental evaluation was done with time sequences of shape instances from twenty-four objects, including various "near miss" type objects. The evaluation confirms that the GRUFF approach can model the functionality of simple hand tools with articulated parts.

7.2.3 Shape Models from Sensed Range Images

An important line of generalization of GRUFF was to reason about functionality starting with sensed range images of real objects (Stark et al. 1993). This involves constructing "object plus unseen space" shape models from range images (Hoover et al. 1995). These models allow reasoning about both the surfaces of the shape that have been seen and the limits to the parts that have not yet been seen. The need for better segmentation of sensed range images spawned a separate project that focused on how to evaluate and compare segmentations of range images objectively (Hoover et al. 1996). The theme of dealing with real sensor input that provides partial and imperfect information about object shape and appearance is one that still confronts researchers today.

7.2.4 Robotic Interaction with Objects

Reasoning about partial object shape highlighted the fact that complete recognition often requires additional images from a selected viewpoint and/or interaction with the object to confirm possible functionality (Sutton et al. 1998). This version of GRUFF added an interaction-based reasoning subsystem to the shape-based reasoning capabilities of previous versions. The shape-based reasoning about functionality could, for an object category such as cup, suggest an approach to grasping the object and an enclosed volume that should hold liquid. The interaction-based reasoning would guide an attempt to use the object as a cup, sensing the scene to observe the results at appropriate points. For instance, after pouring a substance into the cup, a visual check is made for leaks. This theme of interaction with the object to confirm functionality suggested by shape or appearance is another that still confronts researchers today.

Major conclusions from the interaction-based version of GRUFF include: (1) metrically accurate representations of the world can be built and used for higher level reasoning; (2) shape-based reasoning prior to interaction-based reasoning provides an efficient methodology for object recognition; and (3) interaction-based reasoning can be used to confirm the functionality of a categorized object without explicitly determining the object's material composition (Sutton et al. 1998). One noted limitation of this approach in 1998 was its dependence on isolated objects in a scene as well as a single parameter set utilized to minimize the average residual error between the true range data and resulting values after segmentation and model-building to construct 3-D models. In 2002, the use of context-based reasoning was applied to deal with more complex scenes involving multiple objects (Sutton et al. 2002). In a later work, Sutton and Stark also proposed recovering the 20 to 30 percent loss of usable data or models in each subsystem (model-building, shape-based reasoning, and interaction-based reasoning) by exploring parameter set selection driven by functional analysis of initial extracted surfaces from coarse and then refined segmentations (Sutton and Stark 2008).

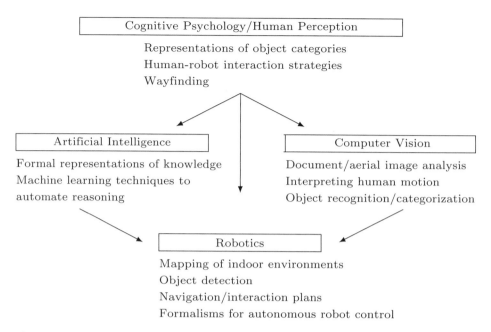

Figure 7.2. Research fields employing function-based approaches. Function-based approaches have been developed in various contexts across the disciplines, with robotics employing best practices from all fields as systems have increased in complexity.

7.3 Functionality in Related Disciplines

The following subsections summarize research on functionality within the fields of artificial intelligence (AI), computer vision, robotics, and other closely related disciplines. Figure 7.2 provides a brief overview of major research areas within each of these fields. Early in the development of functionality-based research, AI and computer vision often pulled directly from research in cognitive psychology and human perception. Examples include perception-inspired low-level image processing and representations for object categorization supporting generic object recognition. Robotics incorporated image analysis early on as part of its array of sensors, and benefited from advances in this area in early computer vision systems. As problem complexity has increased and software/hardware costs have decreased, multisensor robotics systems have continued to draw from computer vision, as well as lessons learned in related AI systems employing function-based approaches. In the following sections, we explore historical and recent trends in each of these areas and then summarize the open problems that remain.

7.3.1 Functionality-Related Work within AI

There are at least two different areas within AI that impact research on constructing systems that recognize objects by their functionality. One of these areas is the work on formal representations of knowledge about functionality. The other is the application of machine learning techniques to automate the process of constructing systems that reason about object functionality.

As might be expected, research in AI concerned with reasoning about functionality of objects has developed greater formalism and depth than that in computer vision, and research in computer vision has been much more concerned with how to extract information about functionality from the sensed data of a scene. As efforts in robotics and vision tackle more complicated scenes and object functionalities, more complex representations will likely be needed.

Chandrasekaran (1994) reviews the development of his functional representation (FR) line of work, and the differences between it and related efforts in AI. Functional representation is an approach to describing the function, structure, and causal processes of a device. This allows for representing a more complicated object functionality than is present in simple objects such as chairs (Stark and Bowyer 1991), but that might be used by object categories such as tools with articulated parts (Green et al. 1995).

Hodges (1995) presents the functional ontology for naive mechanics (FONM) representation theory. The system takes advantage of causal relationships between the structure, behavior, and function of an object. Function is represented "in terms of its low-level structure and behavior and in terms of its use in problem-solving contexts" (Hodges 1995).

Chandrasekaran and Josephson (1997) make a useful distinction between three types of knowledge about functionality: "(i) what the device is intended to do (function), (ii) the causal process by which it does it, and (iii) how the process steps are enabled by the functions of the components of the device...." They also make a distinction between the function of a device and the behavior of a device. This work is important for bringing out some of the complexity needed in formal systems for reasoning about device functionality.

Mukerjee and colleagues consider "conceptual descriptions" that use "linguistic" terms, as in the example "There is a hedge in front of the bench" (Mukerjee et al. (2000). The immediate context of the work is more in visualization of a conceptually described scene rather than recognition from image data. The idea of a continuum field is used as a means to represent the description given in linguistic terms. Experiments are performed with human subjects and placement of objects in a graphic scene in order to determine a preferred interpretation of linguistic terms. The connection of this work to reasoning about function is rather tenuous. In fact, Stark and Bowyer (1991) is cited as an example of "parameterized geometric models." However, the concepts in this work are potentially useful in reasoning about function, if the criteria for functionality are not crisply defined but instead involve what this work terms "linguistic" descriptions.

More recently, Gurevich et al. (2006) tackle the problem of learning how to recognize generic objects as seen in range images. They focus on how to generate negative examples automatically that are "near-misses" of positive examples of an object. Rules are introduced to transform a positive example into a near-miss negative example. This allows the user to, in effect, focus the learning algorithm on the important elements of an object definition. Experiments are performed with 200 range images of positive examples of each of the categories stool, chair, and fork. The experiments verify that the learning is more efficient with the near-miss negative examples than with general negative examples. This work is important as an example of how to automate elements of the construction of a recognition system.

7.3.2 Functionality-Based Computer Vision

Computer vision researchers have pushed the concepts of functionality-driven object recognition in several directions. Perhaps the most surprising of these is the use of functionality in document image analysis. Another area that is very different from the GRUFF work is the recognition of roads and buildings in aerial images.

Doermann et al. (1998) apply the concept of functionality to document image analysis. Document functional organization is defined as "organization in information transfer terms" with the analogy "between components of a document, which is a device for transferring information, and the parts of a tool, which is a device for transferring force" (Doermann et al. 1998). Documents can be defined by their layout structure, as in how the information is organized and presented, and their logical structure, as in what the document is trying to convey (i.e., semantic or conceptual organization). The functional level is an intermediate level "that relates to the efficiency with which the document transfers its information to the reader." As an example, a block of text might have a geometry description that includes its size and position on the page. Based on the geometry of a particular block in relation to other text, the functionality of the block may be classified as that of a "header." A further categorization of "title" would be a semantic labeling of the block. In one experiment, documents are classified according to use, as a reading document, a browsing document, or a searching document, based on the number and size of text blocks. Also, a functionality-driven approach is outlined for classifying the type of a document as journal article, newspaper article, or magazine article, and the pages of a journal article as title, body, or references. Beyond its contribution in the area of document analysis, this paper is interesting for how it shows that concepts of functionality can be applied to object classes very different from those studied in earlier research on functionality.

Mayer (1999) surveys work in the area of extracting buildings from aerial images and proposes a model and approach that incorporates elements of functionality. In this model, "the general parts of the model are: characteristic properties [that] are often the consequence of the function of objects. Importantly, they integrate knowledge about the 3D real world into the model. Typical examples for knowledge sources are, apart from constraints concerning the usefulness for humans (Stark and Bowyer 1991), construction instructions for different types of buildings and roads. For large parts of the knowledge about function it seems to be enough to take them into consideration for modeling . . .".

Baumgartner et al. (1997) consider the perspective of functionality in developing a system to extract roads automatically from aerial images – "In the real world, the characteristics of roads can be described as consequences of their function for human beings." Texture analysis is used to describe context regions such as open-rural, forest, and suburban. Relations between background objects, such as buildings or trees, and parts of roads may vary with the type of context region. Image analysis for edges is done at both a coarse and a fine resolution. Road parts are aggregated into a road network.

Mirmehdi et al. (1999) outline a feedback-control strategy for processing images to recognize generic objects based on functionality. The essential idea is that initial processing would be computationally cheap and fast, serving to generate candidates that would then be explored further and, finally, leading to confirmed instances of objects. The initial, or lower-level, processing of the image is "very closely linked to the modeling and representation of the target objects." In the more interesting examples in this paper, which focus on detecting bridges in infrared images of large-scale outdoor scenes, the reasoning is based on edges detected in the image. The generic model of bridges used for interpretation is functionality-based "unlike normal model-based object recognition systems in which the knowledge of an object's appearance is provided by an explicit model of its shape, we adopt a signature and a stereotype of the object as image and model representations, respectively, with both being very loose and generic descriptions of the object based on their functionality after Stark and Bowyer (1991)." Examples are shown of various bridges that can be recognized in terms of sets of edges representing the roadway and the support columns.

Zerroug and Medioni (1995) and Medioni and Francois (2000) propose to approach the problem of generic object recognition by extracting 3-D volumetric primitives from 2-D images. The 3-D volumetric primitives are particular restricted subclasses of generalized cylinders. Objects are represented as a composition of volumetric primitives. Segmentation is proposed to use perceptual grouping and quasi-invariant properties of primitives/regions. This is a modern proposal related to older work by Marr (1982), Bierderman (1987), and others. This approach is related to reasoning about functionality in the sense that it is aimed at extracting generalized object models from images, which could potentially be followed by or accompanied by reasoning about functionality.

Peursum et al. (2003, 2004) analyze the pattern of activity in a video of a person interacting with a scene, in order to label parts of the scene according to their functionality. The emphasis on observing the pattern of human activity rather than reasoning directly about an object distinguishes their approach from that of Stark and Bowyer (1991): "Our premise is that interpreting human motion is much easier than recognizing arbitrary objects because the human body has constraints on its motion" (Peursum et al. 2004). An "interaction signature" between the person and a part of the scene is what characterizes a particular type of functionality. In experiments, pixels in an image are classified as representing an instance of either chair or floor in the scene. The accuracy of characterizing parts of the scene as floor is substantially higher than the accuracy for chair. In some ways, this work is like a realization of ideas explored in simulation in Stark et al. (1996), but with less emphasis on reasoning about object shape, and more of an emphasis on reasoning about human activity patterns in video.

In a similar vein, work by Duric and colleagues (1996) addresses the problem: "Given a model of an object, how can we use the motion of the object, while it is being used to perform a task, to determine its function?" The authors note that motion and form are required. Motion analysis is used to produce motion descriptors. A known set of motion-to-function mappings in the form of motion descriptors can be used to identify the action (function) taking place in the image sequence.

Finally, Wunstel and Moratz (2004) report on results of generic object recognition from range images using a functionality-based approach. They are interested in an office-like context that contains instances of objects such as chair, door, table, and other such objects. They aim to deal with more general object shapes than were experimented with in GRUFF (Stark and Bowyer 1996). "Stark's original form and function algorithm [as described in section 7.2.1] contains a segmentation work step within the 2 1/2-D data, which is finally based on geometric limitations of the allowed objects. They only used objects composed of cuboids with sharp corners. In our environment, scenario freeform objects (preliminarily restricted to tables and chairs) have to be identified. A three-dimensional segmentation based approach is not suitable or necessary as we neither have nor need fully defined three dimensional object model descriptions" (Wunstel and Moratz 2004). By taking slices through the sensed 3-D model of the scene at particular heights and orientations, and processing these as 2-D images, they are able to recognize objects without creating an explicit segmentation into 3-D shapes or models. Example results are presented for an office scene. Froimovich et al. (2007) similarly have applied function-based object classification to raw range images. Data from 150 images from object instances from 10 categories are provided in this work, with examples provided for dealing with cluttered environments.

7.3.3 Reasoning about Functionality in Robotics

As highlighted in Figure 7.2, the evolution of robotics-based systems that employ function-based approaches has been buoyed by incorporating best practices gleaned from other fields. In the following sections we examine parts of this evolution, from research in service robots and generalized navigational systems to function-driven manipulation in various environments.

Moratz and Tenbrink (2007) define affordances as the "visually perceivable functional object aspects shared by the designer of the recognition module and the prospective robot user or instructor." Their model for an affordance-based recognition system is based on the need to build service robots that deal more effectively with coarse, underspecified knowledge. They propose that their system is more scalable than traditional systems, even when the robot encounters occlusion, sensor error, or detection difficulties, because their linguistic module will allow nonexpert users to be able to specify instructions relative to previously recognized function-based objects.

Kim and Nevatia (1994, 1998) use a functionality-driven approach in having a mobile robot map out an indoor environment. They consider a functionality-driven approach because of its inherent ability to handle a broad variety of instances of a class of objects: "The most generic representation of an object is probably in terms of its functionality." Their system creates an "s-map" of an indoor environment, that marks the presence of objects such as doors and desks. Object categories such as these are defined in terms of surfaces that are important to their functionality, possibly with multiple surfaces at different levels of importance to the functionality. The implemented system uses planar surfaces in its modeling of functionality, and assumes that objects are encountered in a standard or typical pose. Experimental results show the ability to recognize substantially different instances of the object category "desk." This work illustrates how a mobile robot might recognize objects in its environment in terms of categories of relevant functionality.

Wixson (1992) studies the problem of having a mobile robot with a camera "head" explore a defined space for the presence of particular types of objects. In this context, he notes the limitations of simpler object modeling techniques and the potential advantage of a functionality-based approach. "Unfortunately, the great majority of objects that we might consider to be intermediate objects, such as desks, countertops, sofas, chairs, and bookshelves are ill-suited for recognition by traditional machine-vision algorithms. As noted in (Strat and Fischler 1990) and (Stark and Bowyer 1991) such algorithms assume that the object to be recognized is either: (a) definable by an explicit geometric model, or (b) has characteristic homogeneous and locally measurable features such as color or texture.... These assumptions are not valid for most of the large-scale 'generic' objects just mentioned, although we do believe that it should be possible to extend methods related to assumption 2. Further research must be performed on recognizing large-scale generic objects" Wixson (1992). This report does not present results of any object recognition or classification experiments.

Rivlin et al. (1995) blend elements of a GRUFF-like approach with part-whole definitions of what constitutes an object. "Comparing this approach to that of Stark and Bowyer for searching the image for a 'chair kind of support,' we would like to reason about a set of chair legs, a seat and a back, rather than a set of simple planar surfaces or 3D points." They develop the notion of "functional parts" and model simple functional parts by superquadrics. This approach to recognition is illustrated with a range image of a scene that has a mallet lying on a table. The range image can be segmented into regions, superquads fit to the regions, and the superquadric models then interpreted as functional parts. It is acknowledged that this approach is "appropriate for objects composed of simple volumetric parts" and that "we support only functionality that is defined in terms of an object's shape."

Rivlin and Rosenfeld (1995) discuss functionalities that objects in the environment can have for a navigating agent, or mobile robot. In the context of a hallway-cleaning task, objects in the environment of the mobile robot function as objects to be intercepted, objects to be avoided, or objects to be used as landmarks. These are very general categories of object functionality, defined relative to a particular task. Rivlin and Rosenfeld outline the image-processing operations needed for a mobile robot to categorize objects into these categories.

Cooper et al. (1995) look at knowledge representation meant to support robotic interaction with a scene: "What knowledge about a scene does a robot need in order to take intelligent action in that scene?" They seek a representation that embeds a causal understanding of the scene, because "understanding the world in causal terms is what permits intelligent interaction with that scene." Causal representations of scenes is based on naive or qualitative physics. One instance of the approach outlined by Cooper et al. (1995) generates causal explanations of stacks of blocks in an image, given a starting point and assuming blocks are represented as rectangular regions in the image. Another version generates explanations of a stereo pair of images of a scene of link-and-junction (tinker-toy) objects, including inference of extensions of occluded portions of links. A third instance of this approach is aimed at picking up coffee mugs with a robotic gripper. One important contribution of this work is showing how a causal explanation, or functional plan, of a scene can be generated based on image analysis and a set of qualitative physics rules.

Bogoni and Bajcsy (1995) make distinctions between intended, imposed, and intrinsic functionality, and construct a representation of functionality that combines elements of object structure, the context of the actor involved in the context of the function, and the application of the function. The formalism used for representing functionality in this work is based on discrete event systems. Conceptually, this work differs from that of Stark and Bowyer (1991) in that it emphasizes a representation of functionality that goes beyond reasoning about shape alone. It is more similar to that of Stark and colleagues (1996), except that Bogoni and Bajcsy's experimental work involves the use of robotic manipulators and vision. The experimental context is the general hand tools category of objects, and particular experiments involve the functionality of an object being used as a tool to pierce a material. This work is one of a small number to blend robotics and vision in its experiments.

Further work by Bogoni (1998) defines a representation of functionality that includes a "task description, shape description, force-shape maps (generated by interacting with the object), and histograms defining the behavior of the system with different materials and functionalities." Piercing and chopping are the two actions tested. The work "proposes a representation and a methodology for recovering functionality of objects for a robotic agent." Therefore, it is an extended version of the functional representation as defined by many others.

Wang et al. (2005) develop a generic ontology of objects. They focus on the context of an indoor environment that contains manufactured objects, and how a robot might interact with such objects. They see the GRUFF functionality-based approach as useful but as needing to be combined with geometric object models: "The Generic Recognition Using Form and Function GRUFF system Stark and Bowyer (1991) performs generic object recognition and context-based scene understanding. Objects are decomposed into functions based on the object's intended usage, where each function describes a minimum set of structural elements, and their geometric properties and relations. . . . GRUFF has instantiated function-based knowledge for everyday objects like furniture, kitchenware, and hand tools, and everyday scenes like office. However, it does not define any formal representation of generic shapes." They develop an ontology that defines functionality in terms of more specific shape and structural information than does GRUFF, and add information about associations between objects and typical interactions with objects. This paper does not present results of any object recognition or classification experiments.

Paletta et al. (2007) propose a multilayered framework for the developmental learning of affordances. This work includes real-world robot experiments to provide a proof of concept, with experiments demonstrating the ability of the system to successfully learn affordance-based cues. In a related line of work, Fritz et al. (2006) provide results from simulated scenarios utilizing this framework. With the thoroughness these researchers have demonstrated in laying the foundation for testing their framework in simulated and real-world scenarios, this line of research will be one to follow closely as new robot control architectures evolve in this area. Also contributing to emerging trends in this area will be new formalisms for affordances to facilitate autonomous robot control, such as those proposed by Sahin et al. (2007). This work is also supported by recent real-world experimental results to examine the strengths and limitations of the proposed formalisms and propose new directions. The "affordances" concepts used here come from the work of Gibson (1979). Gibson's theory of affordances is consistent with function-based vision. An object *affords* support by being flat, horizontal, and positioned at the proper height for sitting, all attributes that can be confirmed visually.

7.3.4 Other Disciplines: Reasoning about Human Perception and Reasoning about Function

Finally, this chapter would not be complete without consideration of related research in human perception and recent implementations applying associated theories. Klatsky et al. (2005) perform experiments to investigate how children reason about whether an object can perform a given function. This area of work in psychology may help to inform the design of algorithms for robotic interaction with objects to reason about their function.

Recent work in the theory of how functional knowledge is represented and processed also includes the HIPE (history, intentional perspective, physical environment, and event sequences) theory of function developed by Barsalou et al. (2005). Although this multimodal system overall may be more complex in terms of the multiple representations of function that are encoded, efficiency is expected to be realized for given events whenever an agent's intentional perspective can be used to determine the functional knowledge that is retrieved.

Researchers such as Raubal and Moratz have expanded on this theory in their redesign of a robot architecture that incorporates the representation of affordance-based attributes associated with tasks (Raubal and Moratz 2007). Raubal and Moratz argue that a robot architecture that can support sensing and action based on functional compounds (rather than properties in isolation) can be more flexibly mapped to human affordance-driven tasks. Moratz (2006) has similarly argued for a function-based representation for tasks to make human-robot interaction and communication more natural and simplified as well as scalable to novel environments.

Along with Worboys, Raubal has also argued for the inclusion of affordances in models for wayfinding to more completely capture the processes of learning and problem-solving in these tasks (Raubal and Worboys 1999). Wayfinding is defined as "the purposeful, directed, and motivated movement from an origin to a specific distant destination that cannot be directly perceived by the traveler" (Raubal 2007). Emphasizing the relevance of ecological psychology (focusing on the information transactions between living systems and their environments), Raubal incorporates three realms of affordances in his model: physical, social-institutional, and mental (Raubal 2001).

7.4 Open Problem Areas

This survey has highlighted both historical and current efforts in using functionality for generic object recognition. Across the subfields of AI, computer vision, and robotics, it is clear that as systems scale up to more complex scenes, reasoning that is functionality-based (as opposed to category-based) holds great promise. The most successful systems described in this chapter were designed with architectures and

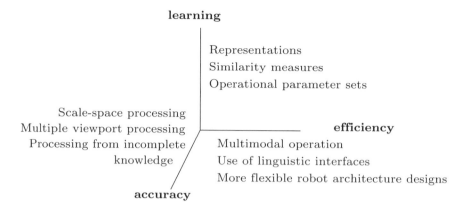

Figure 7.3. Open problem areas impacting future scalability of function-based reasoning approaches in object recognition.

representations supporting multiple sensors and object domains. However, much research is needed to ensure that the systems continue to evolve in ways that demonstrate continued scalability, efficiency, accuracy, and ability to learn, as summarized in Figure 7.3. As we look to the future of this field, in the following sections we examine the strengths and open research areas of GRUFF and a subset of representative systems that address each of these characteristics.

7.4.1 Successes and Limitations of GRUFF

The primary successes of the GRUFF project are as follows: (1) successful functionality-driven recognition of 3-D models of rigid shapes, (2) generalization of the approach to a variety of object categories involving both rigid and articulated shapes, (3) demonstration of functionality-driven analysis of partial object shapes derived from real range images of real objects, and (4) development of an approach for using robotic interaction to confirm actual functionality suggested by interpretation of 3-D shape.

One major limitation of GRUFF is that the shape descriptions that it analyzed were limited to polyhedra. Generalization to handle some broad class of curved shapes would be an important practical advance. This generalization presents some challenges in the implementation of the shape-based reasoning, but it probailly presents even greater challenges in segmenting range images into curved surface patches. Another limitation is that each generalization of GRUFF is essentially hand-crafted. Although some initial work has been done to explore the use of machine learning to speed the implementation of new category definitions, this is an important open area with great future potential.

7.4.2 Scalability and Efficiency

As noted by Raubal and Moratz (2007), the formal incorporation of affordance-based attributes in robot architectures is seen as an approach that will more readily and flexibly map to specified human affordance-based tasks that a robot is given to accomplish. This approach incorporates a hierarchical definition of affordances that is also scale-dependent. Control mechanisms that act at the correct scale for a given task is one open problem in this research as well as in the GRUFF (Stark and Bowyer 1996; Sutton and Stark 2008) work.

Moratz has also noted the impact of perceptual granularity on system performance and observed that additional testing is required to resolve ambiguities (Moratz 2006). However, this is clearly the direction in which service robot scenarios are likely to be headed in order to increase flexibility and reduce training times compared to traditional methods of humans, such as forcing the specification of exact metric locations or use of predefined class IDs that the robot can understand for a subset of predefined tasks (Moratz and Tenbrink 2007). In addition, Moratz and Tenbrink (2007) note that scalable systems will allow multiple modes of spatiotemporal operation, including synchronous and asynchronous instruction that can later lead to problem solving and even learning in novel scenarios. Although their current system is synchronous in nature, the associated representation and model for linguistic interface is to be designed with this level of extensibility to intuitive instruction in mind.

7.4.3 Scalability and Accuracy

The incorporation of physical, social-institutional, and mental affordances in formal models of wayfinding is one approach in this task to create agents that behave like humans; more direct comparisons in this line of work should prove useful as these systems evolve to determine if this improves accuracy (Raubal 2001). The wayfinding model proposed by Raubal (2007) by default involves decisions impacted by multiple viewpoints and scale-space, because the goal cannot be perceived from a single view-point. As this model is applied to more complex tasks, it will be worth examining how readily the architecture handles these forms of data, and how accuracy is impacted by such incomplete knowledge.

7.4.4 Scalability and Learning

The systems just reviewed include sensors ranging from structured light scanners to laser range finders and stereo vision systems. Although stereo systems have some limitations for detecting planar surfaces owing to their lack of scene texture, all three systems will benefit from research on "learning" parameter sets for optimal navigation. Future work in this area includes automatically selecting the parameter sets based on whether the current task requires local (fine) or global (rough) details (Sutton and Stark 2008).

The design of similarity measurements for searches that yield multiple affordances is also a critical area, especially when the end goal is for the system to learn affordances from new environments. It will be worth noting future extensions to recent work with Janowicz, in which Raubal explores context-aware affordance-based similarity measures (Janowicz and Raubal 2007). Clearly future representation systems incorporating function must plan for how affordances can be compared. Janowicz and Raubal support a platform that incorporates weighting based on social-institutional constraints as well as outcomes, with control mechanisms that permit weights to be automatically determined or used as exclusion factors, depending on the task. This approach is important because the types of tasks encountered vary, and systems need to incorporate similarity-based reasoning and planning to "learn" from each task.

As a further example, Maloof et al. (1996) describe a functionality-driven approach to creating a system to recognize blasting caps in x-ray images: "Although blasting caps are manufactured objects, there is enough variability in their manufacture that makes a CAD-based recognition system impractical. What is common to all blasting caps, however, is their functionality. Ultimately, blasting caps are defined by their functionality, not by their shapes." An interesting element of this work is that the AQ15c learning system was used to learn concepts of blasting caps and nonblasting caps from training examples. Although this is a fairly restricted object category to define from its appearance in x-ray images, it was still felt that higher-resolution images that show additional detail would be needed. Nevertheless, this work is important because it illustrates a relatively understudied topic. Very little work has been done on how to learn elements of the representation automatically from examples (Woods et al. 1995). Most research on functionality-driven object recognition has used hand-tailored representations of functionality. The ability to learn, or induce, a functionality-driven representation from a set of labeled examples would also seem to be an important topic for future research.

7.5 Conclusion

The preceding sections provide a window into some of the open areas that remain in function-based reasoning. Two decades ago, systems were limited by hardware and software constraints, but today the impacts of these choices are relatively insignificant. More significant are decisions that must be made early regarding the design of the overall system architecture to ensure scalability for exploring novel environments or completing novel tasks, supporting or deriving multiple function-based interpretations from a single viewpoint, combining function-based details from multiple viewpoints, or learning function-based characteristics from encountered objects or completed tasks. As researchers across the subfields of AI, computer vision, and robotics continue to blend their knowledge and incorporate related progress made in fields such as cognitive psychology, as well as biology and engineering, the systems arising from these efforts in future decades will benefit greatly. New systems evolving from these efforts should also prove to be even more robust, with potentially greater applicability and relevance to human-computer tasks and problem solving.

Bibliography

Barsalou L, Sloman S, Chaigneau S. 2005. The hipe theory of function. In *Representing functional features for language and space: insights from perception, categorization and development*, ed. L Carlson and E van der Zee, 131–147. New York: Oxford University Press.

Baumgartner A, Steger C, Mayer H, Eckstein W. 1997. Multi-resolution, semantic objects and context for road extraction. In *Semantic modeling for the acquisiton of topographic information from images and maps*, 140–156. Basel: Birkhauser Verlag.

Bierderman I. 1987. Recognition-by-components: a theory of human image understanding. *Psychol Rev* 94(2):115–147.

Bogoni L. 1998. More than just shape. *Artif Intell Engineering* 12(4):337–354.

Bogoni L, Bajcsy R. 1995. Interactive recognition and representation of functionality. *Comput Vis Image Und* 62(2):194–214.

Chandrasekaran B. 1994. Functional representation: a brief historical perspective. *Appl Artif Intell* 8(2):173–197.

Chandrasekaran B, Josephson JR. 1997. Representing function as effect. In Proceedings of functional modeling workshop, ed. M. Modarres.

Cooper PR, Birnbaum LA, Brand ME. 1995. Causal scene understanding. *Comput Vis Image Und* 62(2):215–231.

Doermann D, Rivlin E, Rosenfeld A. 1998. The function of documents. *Image Vision Comput* 16(11):799–814.

Duric Z, Fayman JA, Rivlin E. 1996. Function from motion. *IEEE Trans Pattern Anal Mach Intell* 18(6):579–591.

Fritz G, Paletta L, Kumar M, Dorffner G, Breithaupt R, Rome E. 2006. Visual learning of affordance based cues. In Proceedings of the 9th international conference on the simulation of adaptive behavior, SAB 2006, LNAI 4095, 52–64. Berlin: Springer-Verlag.

Froimovich G, Rivlin E, Shimshoni I, Soldea O. 2007. Efficient search and verification for function based classification from real range images. *Comput Vis Image Und* 105:200–217.

Gibson J. 1979. *The ecological approach to visual perception*. Boston: Houghton Mifflin.

Green K, Eggert D, Stark L, Bowyer KW. 1995. Generic recognition of articulated objects through reasoning about potential function. *Comput Vis Image Und* 62(2):177–193.

Gurevich N, Markovitch S, Rivlin E. 2006. Active learning with near misses. In Proceedings of the twenty-first national conference on artificial intellgence.

Hodges J. 1995. Functional and physical object characteristics and object recognition in improvisation. *Comput Vision Image Und* 62(2):147–163.

Hoover AW, Goldgof DB, Bowyer KW. 1995. Extracting a valid boundary representation from a segmented range image. *IEEE Trans Pattern Anal Mach Intell* 17(9):920–924.

Hoover AW, Jean-Baptiste G, Jiang X, Flynn P, Bunke H, Goldgof D, Bowyer KW, Eggert D, Fitzgibbon A, Fisher R. 1996. An experimental comparison of range image segmentation algorithms. *IEEE Trans Pattern Anal Mach Intell* 18(7):673–689.

Janowicz K, Raubal M. 2007. Affordance-based similarity measurement for entity types. In Lecture notes in computer science: spatial information theory – conference on spatial information theory (COSIT'07), ed. S Winter, M Duckham, L Kulik, and B Kuipers. New York: Springer-Verlag.

Kim D, Nevatia R. 1994. A method for recognition and localization of generic objects for indoor navigation. In Proceedings of the DARPA image understanding workshop, II:1069–1076.

Kim D, Nevatia R. 1998. Recognition and localization of generic objects for indoor navigation using functionality. *Image Vision Comput* 16 (11):729–743.

Klatsky RL, Lederman SH, Mankinen JM. 2005. Visual and haptic exploratory procedures in children's judgments about tool function. *Infant Behav Develop* 28:240–249.

Maloof M, Duric Z, Michalski R, Rosenfeld A. 1996. Recognizing blasting caps in x-ray images. In Proceedings of the DARPA image understanding workshop, 1257–1261.

Marr D. 1982. *Vision: a computational investigation into the human representation and processing of visual information*. New York: Holt and Company.

Mayer H. 1999. Automatic object extraction from aerial imagery – a survey focusing on buildings. *Comput Vis Image Und* 74(2):132–149.

Medioni GG, Francois AR. 2000. 3-d structures for generic object recognition. In International conference on pattern recognition, 1030–1037.

Minsky M. 1991. Logical vs. analogical, or symbolic vs. connectionist, or neat vs. scruffy. *AI Magazine* 12(2):34–51.

Mirmehdi M, Palmer PL, Kittler J, Dabis H. 1999. Feedback control strategies for object recognition. *IEEE Trans Image Proc* 8(8):1084–1101.

Moratz R. 2006. Intuitive linguistic joint object reference in human-robot interaction. In Proceedings of the twenty-first national conference on artificial intelligence (AAAI), 1483–1488.

Moratz R, Tenbrink T. 2007. Affordance-based human-robot interaction. In Proceedings of the Dagstuhl seminar 06231 "towards affordance-based robot control," eds. E Rome and J Hertzberg.

Mukerjee A, Gupta K, Nautiyal S et al. 2000. Conceptual description of visual scenes from linguistic models. *Image Vision Comput* 18(2):173–187.

Paletta L, Fritz G, Kintzler F, Irran J, Dorffner G. 2007. Learning to perceive affordances in a framework of developmental embodied cognition. In Proceedings of the 6th IEEE international conference on development and learning (ICDL), 2007.

Peursum P, Venkatesh S, West GA, Bui HH. 2003. Object labelling from human action recognition. In Proceedings of the first IEEE international conference on pervasive computing and communications.

Peursum P, Venkatesh S, West GAW, Bui HH. 2004. Using interaction signatures to find and label chairs and floors. *Pervasive Comput* 3(4):58–65.

Raubal M. 2001. Ontology and epistemology for agent-based wayfinding simulation. *Int J Geog Inf Sci* 15(7):653–665.

Raubal M. 2007. Wayfinding: affordances and agent simulation. In Encyclopedia of GIS, ed. S Shekhar and H Xiong. New York: Springer-Verlag.

Raubal M, Moratz R. 2007. A functional model for affordance-based agents. In Lecture notes in artificial intelligence: affordance-based robot control, ed. J Hertzberg and E Rome. Berlin: Springer-Verlag.

Raubal M, Worboys M. 1999. A formal model of the process of wayfinding in built environments. In Spatial information theory – cognitive and computational foundations of geographic information science. International conference (COSIT), Stade, Germany, 381–399.

Rivlin E, Dickinson SJ, Rosenfeld A. 1995. Recognition by functional parts. *Comput Vis Image Und* 62(2):164–176.

Rivlin E, Rosenfeld A. 1995. Navigational functionalities. *Comput Vis Image Und* 62(2):232–244.

Rosch E, Mervis C, Gray W, Johnson D, Boyes-Braem P. 1976. Basic objects in natural categories. *Cogn Psychol* 8:382–439.

Sahin E, Cakmak M, Dogar M, Ugur E, Ucoluk G. 2007. To afford or not to afford: a new formalization of affordances towards affordance-based robot control. *Adapt Behav* 15(4).

Stark L, Bowyer K. 1996. *Generic object recognition using form and function.* New York: World Scientific.

Stark L, Bowyer KW. 1989. Functional description as a a knowledge representation of 3-d objects. In IASTED international symposium on expert systems theory and applications, 49–54.

Stark L, Bowyer KW. July 1990. Achieving generalized object recognition through reasoning about association of function to structure. In AAAI-90 workshop on qualitative vision, 137–141.

Stark L, Bowyer KW. 1991. Achieving generalized object recognition through reasoning about association of function to structure. *IEEE Trans Pattern Anal Mach Intell* 13(10):1097–1104.

Stark L, Bowyer KW. 1994. Function-based generic recognition for multiple object categories. *CVGIP: Image Understanding* 59(1):1–21.

Stark L, Bowyer KW, Hoover AW, Goldgof DB. 1996. Recognizing object function through reasoning about partial shape descriptions and dynamic physical properties. *Proc IEEE* 84(11):1640–1656.

Stark L, Hoover AW, Goldgof DB, Bowyer KW. July 1993. Function-based object recognition from incomplete knowledge of object shape. In AAAI workshop on reasoning about function, July, 141–148.

Strat TM, Fischler MA. 1990. A context-based recognition system for natural scenes and complex domains. In Proceedings of the DARPA image understanding workshop, September, 456–472.

Sutton M, Stark L, Hughes K. 2002. Exploiting context in function-based reasoning. In Lecture notes in computer science, ed. G Hager, H Christensen, H Bunke, and R Klein, 357–373, Springer.

Sutton MA, Stark L. 2008. Function-based reasoning for goal-oriented image segmentation. In Affordance-based robot control, lectures notes in artificial intelligence 4760, ed. E Rome, 159–172. Berlin: Springer-Verlag.

Sutton MA, Stark L, Bowyer KW. 1994. Gruff-3: generalizing the domain of a function-based recognition system. *Pattern Recog* 27(12):1743–1766.

Sutton MA, Stark L, Bowyer KW. 1998. Function from visual analysis and physical interaction: a methodology for recognition of generic classes of objects. *Image Vision Comput* 16(11):745–764.

Wang E, Kim YS, Kim SA. 2005. An object ontology using form-function reasoning to support robot context understanding. *Comput Aided Des Appl* 2(6):815–824.

Wixson LE. 1992. Exploiting world structure to efficiently search for objects. Technical Report 434, Computer Science Department, University of Rochester.

Woods KS, Cook D, Hall L, Stark L, Bowyer KW. 1995. Learning membership functions in a function-based object recognition system. *J Artif Intell Res* 3:187–222.

Wunstel M, Moratz R. 2004. Automatic object recognition within an office environment. In Proceedings of the first canadian conference on computer and robot vision (CRV), IEEE.

Zerroug M, Medioni G. 1995. The challenge of generic object recognition. In Object representation in computer vision: international NSF-ARPA workshop, 217–232. Springer-Verlag LNCS 994.

CHAPTER 8

The Interface Theory of Perception: Natural Selection Drives True Perception to Swift Extinction

Donald D. Hoffman

8.1 Introduction

The jewel beetle *Julodimorpha bakewelli* is category challenged (Gwynne and Rentz 1983; Gwynne 2003). For the male of the species, spotting instances of the category "desirable female" is a pursuit of enduring interest and, to this end, he scours his environment for telltale signs of a female's shiny, dimpled, yellow-brown elytra (wing cases). Unfortunately for him, many males of the species *Homo sapiens*, who sojourn in his habitats within the Dongara area of Western Australia, are attracted by instances of the category "full beer bottle" but not by instances of the category "empty beer bottle," and are therefore prone to toss their emptied bottles (stubbies) unceremoniously from their cars. As it happens, stubbies are shiny, dimpled, and just the right shade of brown to trigger, in the poor beetle, a category error. Male beetles find stubbies irresistible. Forsaking all normal females, they swarm the stubbies, genitalia everted, and doggedly try to copulate despite repeated glassy rebuffs. Compounding misfortune, ants of the species *Iridomyrmex discors* capitalize on the beetles' category errors; the ants sequester themselves near stubbies, wait for befuddled beetles, and consume them, genitalia first, as they persist in their amorous advances.

Categories have consequences. Conflating beetle and bottle led male *J. bakewelli* into mating mistakes that nudged their species to the brink of extinction. Their perceptual categories worked well in their niche: Males have low parental investment; thus, their fitness is boosted if their category "desirable mate" is more liberal than that of females (as predicted by the theory of sexual selection, e.g., Trivers 1972; Daly and Wilson 1978). But when stubbies invaded their niche, a liberal category transformed stubbies into sirens, 370-ML amazons with matchless allure.

The bamboozled *J. bakewelli* illustrate a central principle of perceptual categorization:

Principle of Satisficing Categories: *Each perceptual category of an organism, to the extent that the category is shaped by natural selection, is a satisficing solution to adaptive problems.*

This principle is key to understanding the provenance and purpose of perceptual categories: They are satisficing solutions to problems such as feeding, mating, and predation that are faced by all organisms in all niches. However, these problems take different forms in different niches and, therefore, require a diverse array of specific solutions. Such solutions are satisficing in that (1) they are, in general, only local maxima of fitness, and (2) the fitness function depends not just on one factor, but on numerous factors, including the costs of classification errors, the time and energy required to compute a category, and the specific properties of predators, prey, and mates in a particular niche. Furthermore (3), the solutions depend critically on what adaptive structures the organism already has. It can be less costly to co-opt an existing structure for a new purpose than to evolve de novo a structure that might better solve the problem. A backward retina, for instance, with photoreceptors hidden behind neurons and blood vessels, is not the "best" solution simpliciter to the problem of transducing light but, at a specific time in the phylogenetic path of *H. sapiens*, it might have been the best solution given the biological structures then available. Satisficing in these three senses is, on evolutionary grounds, central to perception and, therefore, central to theories of perceptual categorization.

According to this principle, a perceptual category is a satisficing solution to adaptive problems only "to the extent that the category is shaped by natural selection." This disclaimer might seem to eviscerate the whole principle, to reduce it to the assertion that perceptual categories are satisficing solutions, except when they're not.

The disclaimer must stand. The issue at stake is the debate in evolutionary theory over adaptationism: To what extent are organisms shaped by natural selection versus other evolutionary factors, such as genetic drift and simple accident? The claim that a specific category is adaptive is an empirical claim, and turns on the details of the case. Thus, this disclaimer does not eviscerate the principle; instead, it entails that, although one expects most categories to be profoundly shaped by natural selection, each specific case of purported shaping must be carefully justified in the normal scientific manner.

8.2 The Conventional View

Most vision experts do not accept the principle of satisficing categories, but instead, tacitly or explicitly, subscribe to the following principle:

Principle of Faithful Depiction: *A primary goal of perception is to recover, or estimate, objective properties of the physical world. A primary goal of perceptual categorization is to recover, or estimate, the objective statistical structure of the physical world.*

For instance, Yuille and Bülthoff (1996) describe the Bayesian approach to perception in terms of faithful depiction: "We define vision as perceptual inference, the estimation of scene properties from an image or sequence of images . . . there is insufficient information in the image to uniquely determine the scene. The brain, or any artificial vision system, must make assumptions about the real world. These assumptions must be sufficiently powerful to ensure that vision is well-posed for those properties in the scene that the visual system needs to estimate." In their view, there is a physical world that has objective properties and statistical structure (objective in the sense that they exist unperceived). Perception uses Bayesian estimation, or suitable approximations, to reconstruct the properties and structure from sensory data. Terms such as "estimate," "recover," and "reconstruct," which appear throughout the literature of computational vision, stem from commitment to the principle of faithful depiction.

Geisler and Diehl (2003) endorse faithful depiction: "In general, it is true that much of human perception is veridical under natural conditions. However, this is generally the result of combining many probabilistic sources of information (optic flow, shading, shadows, texture gradients, binocular disparity, and so on). Bayesian ideal observer theory specifies how, in principle, to combine the different sources of information in an optimal manner in order to achieve an effectively deterministic outcome" (p. 397).

Lehar (2003) endorses faithful depiction: "The perceptual modeling approach reveals the primary function of perception as that of generating a fully spatial virtual-reality replica of the external world in an internal representation" (p. 375).

Hoffman (1983) endorsed faithful depiction, arguing that to understand perception we must ask, "First, why does the visual system need to organize and interpret the images formed on the retinas? Second, how does it remain true to the real world in the process? Third, what rules of inference does it follow?" (p. 154).

Noë and Regan (2002) endorse a version of faithful depiction that is sensitive to issues of attention and embodied perception, proposing that "perceivers are right to take themselves to have access to environmental detail and to learn that the environment is detailed," (p. 576) and that "the environmental detail is present, lodged, as it is, right there before individuals and that they therefore have access to that detail by the mere movement of their eyes or bodies" (p. 578).

Purves and Lotto (2003) endorse a version of faithful depiction that is diachronic rather than synchronic – that is, that includes an appropriate history of the world, contending that "what observers actually experience in response to any visual stimulus is its accumulated statistical meaning (i.e., what the stimulus has turned out to signify in the past) rather than the structure of the stimulus in the image plane or its actual source in the present" (p. 287).

Proponents of faithful depiction will, of course, grant that there are obvious limits. Unaided vision, for instance, sees electromagnetic radiation only through a chink between 400 and 700 nm, and it fails to be veridical for objects that are too large or too small. These proponents maintain that, for middle-sized objects to which vision is adapted, our visual perceptions are in general veridical.

8.3 The Conventional Evolutionary Argument

Proponents of faithful depiction offer an evolutionary argument for their position, albeit an argument different than the one sketched above for the principle of satisficing categories. Their argument is spelled out, for instance, by Palmer (1999, p. 6) in his textbook *Vision Science*, as follows: "Evolutionarily speaking, visual perception is useful only if it is reasonably accurate. . . . Indeed, vision is useful precisely because it is so accurate. By and large, *what you see is what you get*. When this is true, we have what is called *veridical perception . . .* perception that is consistent with the actual state of affairs in the environment. This is almost always the case with vision." [emphases his].

The error in this argument is fundamental: Natural selection optimizes fitness, not veridicality. The two are distinct and, indeed, can be at odds. In evolution, in which the race is often to the swift, a quick and dirty category can easily trump one that is more complex and veridical. The jewel beetle's desirable female is a case in point. Such cases are ubiquitous in nature and central to understanding evolutionary competition between organisms. This competition is predicated, in large part, on exploiting the nonveridical perceptions of predators, prey, and conspecifics, using techniques such as mimicry and camouflage.

Moreover, as noted by Trivers (1976), there are reasons other than greater speed and less complexity for natural selection to spurn the veridical: "If deceit is fundamental to animal communication, then there must be strong selection to spot deception and this ought, in turn, to select for a degree of self-deception, rendering some facts and motives unconscious so as not to betray – by the subtle signs of self-knowledge – the deception being practiced. Thus, the conventional view that natural selection favors nervous systems which produce ever more accurate images of the world must be a very naïve view of mental evolution."

So the claim that "vision is useful precisely because it is so accurate" gets evolution wrong by conflating fitness and accuracy; they are not the same and, as we shall see with simulations and examples, they are not highly correlated. This conflation is not a peripheral error with trivial consequences: Fitness, not accuracy, is the *objective function* optimized by evolution. (This way of saying it doesn't mean that evolution tries to optimize anything. It just means that what matters in evolution is raising more kids, not seeing more truth.) Theories of perception based on optimizing the wrong function can't help but be radically misguided. Rethinking perception with the correct function leads to a theory strikingly different from the conventional. But first, we examine a vicious circle in the conventional theory.

8.4 Bayes' Circle

According to the conventional theory, a great way to estimate true properties of the world is via Bayes' theorem. If one's visual system receives some images, I, and one wishes to estimate the probabilities of various world properties, W, given these images, then one needs to compute the conditional probabilities $P(W|I)$. For instance, I might be a movie of some dots moving in two dimensions, and W might be various rigid and nonrigid interpretations of those dots moving in three dimensions. According to Bayes' theorem, one can compute

$$P(W|I) = P(I|W)P(W)/P(I).$$

$P(W)$ is the *prior probability*. According to the conventional theory, this prior models the assumptions that human vision makes about the world (e.g., that it has three spatial dimensions, one temporal dimension, and contains three-dimensional objects, many of which are rigid.) $P(I|W)$ is the *likelihood*. According to the conventional theory, this likelihood models the assumptions that human vision makes about how the world maps to images; it's like a rendering function of a graphics engine, which maps a prespecified three-dimensional world onto a two-dimensional image using techniques like ray tracing with Gaussian dispersion. $P(I)$ is just a scale factor to normalize the probabilities. $P(W|I)$ is the *posterior*, the estimate human vision computes about the properties of the world given the images I. So the posterior, which determines what we see, depends crucially on the quality of our priors and likelihoods.

How can we check if our priors and likelihoods are correct? According to the conventional theory, we can simply go out and measure the true priors and likelihoods in the world. Geisler and Diehl (2003), for instance, tell us, "In these cases, the prior probability and likelihood distributions are based on measurements of physical and statistical properties of natural environments. For example, if the task in a given environment is to detect edible fruit in background foliage, then the prior probability and likelihood distributions are estimated by measuring representative spectral illumination functions for the environment and spectral reflectance functions for the fruits and foliage" (p. 380).

The conventional procedure, then, is to measure the true values in the world for the priors and likelihoods, and use these to compute, via Bayes, the desired posteriors. What the visual system ends up seeing is a function of these posteriors and its utility functions.

The problem with this conventional approach is that it entails a vicious circle, which we can call

Bayes' Circle: *We can only see the world through our posteriors. When we measure priors and likelihoods in the world, our measurements are necessarily filtered through our posteriors. Using our measurements of priors and likelihoods to justify our posteriors thus leads to a vicious circle.*

Suppose, for instance, that we build a robot with a vision system that computes shape from motion using a prior assumption that the world contains many rigid objects (Ullman 1979). The system takes inputs from a video camera, does some initial processing to find two-dimensional features in the video images, and then uses an algorithm based on rigidity to compute three-dimensional shape. It seems to work well, but we decide to double-check that the prior assumption about rigid objects that we built into the system is in fact true of the world. So we send our robot out into the world to look around. To our relief, it comes back with the good news that it has indeed found numerous rigid objects. Of course it did; that's what we programmed it to do. If, based on the robot's good news, we conclude that our prior on rigid objects is justified, we've just been bagged by Bayes' circle.

This example is a howler, but precisely the same mistake prompts the conventional claim that we can validate our priors by measuring properties of the objective world. The conventionalist can reply that the robot example fails because it ignores the possibility of cross-checking results with other senses, other observers, and scientific instruments. But such a reply hides the same howler, because other senses, other observers, and scientific instruments all have built-in priors. None is a filter-free window on an objective (i.e., observation-independent) world. Consensus among them entails, at most, agreement among their priors; it entails nothing about properties or statistical structures of an objective world.

It is, of course, possible to pursue a Bayesian approach to perception without getting mired in Bayes' circle. Indeed, Bayesian approaches are among the most promising in the field. Conditional probabilities turn up everywhere in perception, because perception is often about determining what is the best description of the world, or the best action to take, given (i.e., conditioned on) the current state of the sensoria. Bayes is simply the right way to compute conditional probabilities using prior beliefs, and Bayesian decision theory, more generally, is a powerful way to model the utilities and actions of an organism in its computation of perceptual descriptions.

It is possible to use the sophisticated tools of Bayesian decision theory, to fully appreciate the importance of utilities and the perception-action loop, and still to fall prey to Bayes' circle – to conclude, as quoted from Palmer, that "evolutionarily speaking, visual perception is useful only if it is reasonably accurate."

8.5 The Interface Theory of Perception

The conventional theory of perception gets evolution fundamentally wrong by conflating fitness and accuracy. This leads the conventional theory to the false claim that a primary goal of perception is faithful depiction of the world. A standard way to state this claim is the

Reconstruction Thesis: *Perception reconstructs certain properties and categories of the objective world.*

This claim is too strong. It must be weakened, on evolutionary grounds, to a less tendentious claim, the

Construction Thesis: *Perception constructs the properties and categories of an organism's perceptual world.*

The construction thesis is clearly much weaker than the reconstruction thesis. One can, for instance, obtain the reconstruction thesis by starting with the construction thesis and adding the claim that the organism's constructs are, at least in certain respects, roughly isomorphic to the properties or categories of the objective world, thus qualifying them to be deemed reconstructions.

But the range of possible relations between perceptual constructs and the objective world is infinite; isomorphism is just one relation out of this infinity and, on evolutionary grounds, an unlikely one. Thus, the reconstruction thesis is a conceptual straightjacket that constrains us to think only of improbable isomorphisms and impedes us from exploring the full range of possible relations between perception and the world. Once we dispense with the straightjacket, we're free to explore all possible relations that are compatible with evolution (Mausfeld 2002).

To this end, we note that, to the extent that perceptual properties and categories are satisficing solutions to adaptive problems, they admit a functional description. Admittedly, a conceivable, although unlikely, function of perception is faithful depiction of the world. That's the function favored by the reconstruction thesis of the conventionalist. Once we repair the conflation of fitness and accuracy, we can consider other perceptual functions with greater evolutionary plausibility. To do so properly requires a serious study of the functional role of perception in various evolutionary settings. Beetles falling for bottles is one instructive example; in the next section, we consider a few more.

Here it is useful to introduce a model of perception that can help us study its function without relapse into conventionalism. The model is the

Interface Theory of Perception: *The perceptions of an organism are a user interface between that organism and the objective world (Hoffman 1998, 2006a, 2008).*

This theory addresses the natural question, "If our perceptions are not accurate, then what good are they?" The answer becomes obvious for user interfaces. The color, for instance, of an icon on a computer screen does not estimate, or reconstruct, the true color of the file that it represents in the computer. If an icon is, say, green, it would be ludicrous to conclude that this green must be an accurate reconstruction of the true color of the file it represents. It would be equally ludicrous to conclude that, if the color of the icon doesn't accurately reconstruct the true color of the file, then the icon's color is useless, or a blatant deception. This is simply a naïve misunderstanding of the point of a user interface. The conventionalist theory that our perceptions are reconstructions is, in precisely the same manner, equally naïve.

Color is, of course, just one example among many: The shape of an icon doesn't reconstruct the true shape of the file; the position of an icon doesn't reconstruct the true position of the file in the computer. A user interface reconstructs nothing. Its predicates and the predicates required for a reconstruction can be entirely disjoint: Files, for instance, have no color.

Yet a user interface is useful despite the fact that it's not a reconstruction. Indeed, it's useful because it's not a reconstruction. We pay good money for user interfaces because we don't want to deal with the overwhelming complexity of software and hardware in a PC. A user interface that slavishly reconstructed all the diodes, resistors, voltages, and magnetic fields in the computer would probably not be a best seller. The user interface is there to facilitate our interactions with the computer by hiding its causal and structural complexity, and by displaying useful information in a format that is tailored to our specific projects, such as painting or writing.

Our perceptions are a species-specific user interface. Space, time, position, and momentum are among the properties and categories of the interface of *H. sapiens* that, in all likelihood, resemble nothing in the objective world. Different species have different interfaces. Because of the variation that is normal in evolution, there are differences in interfaces among humans. To the extent that our perceptions are satisficing solutions to evolutionary problems, our interfaces are designed to guide adaptive behavior in our niche; accuracy of reconstruction is irrelevant. To understand the properties and categories of our interface, we must understand the evolutionary problems, both phylogenetic and ontogenetic, that it solves.

8.6 User Interfaces in Nature

The interface theory of perception predicts the following: (1) each species has its own interface (with some variations among conspecifics and some similarities across phylogenetically related species); (2) almost surely, no interface performs reconstructions; (3) each interface is tailored to guide adaptive behavior in the relevant niche; (4) much of the competition between and within species exploits strengths and limitations of interfaces; and (5) such competition can lead to arms races between interfaces that critically influence their adaptive evolution. In short, the theory predicts that interfaces are essential to understanding the evolution and competition of organisms; the reconstruction theory makes such understanding impossible. Evidence of interfaces should be ubiquitous in nature.

The jewel beetle is a case in point. Its perceptual category "desirable female" works well in its niche. However, its soft spot for stubbies reveals that its perceptions are not reconstructions. They are, instead, quick guides to adaptive behavior in a stubbie-free niche. The stubbie is a so-called supernormal stimulus (i.e., a stimulus that engages the interface and behavior of the organism more forcefully than the normal stimuli to which the organism has been adapted). The bottle is shiny, dimpled, and the right color of brown, but what makes it a supernormal stimulus is apparently its supernormal size. If so, then, contrary to the reconstruction thesis, the jewel beetle's perceptual category "desirable female" does not incorporate a statistical estimate of the true sizes of the most fertile females. Instead its category satisfices with "bigger is better." In its niche this solution is fit enough. A stubbie, however, plunges it into an infinite loop.

Supernormal stimuli have been found for many species, and all such discoveries are evidence against the claim of the reconstruction theory that our perceptual categories estimate the statistical structure of the world; all are evidence for species-specific interfaces that are satisficing solutions to adaptive problems. Herring gulls (*Larus argentatus*) provide a famous example. Chicks peck a red spot near the tip of the lower mandible of an adult to prompt the adult to regurgitate food. Tinbergen and Perdeck (1950) found that an artificial stimulus that is longer and thinner than a normal beak, and whose red spot is more salient than normal, serves as a supernormal stimulus for the chick's pecking behaviors. The color of the artificial beak and head matter little. The chick's perceptual category "food bearer," or perhaps "food-bearing parent," is not a statistical estimate of the true properties of food-bearing parents, but a satisficing solution in which longer and thinner is better and in which greater salience of the red spot is better. Its interface employs simplified symbols that effectively guide behavior in its niche. Only when its niche is invaded by pesky ethologists is this simplification unmasked, and the chick sent seeking what can never satisfy.

Simplified does not mean simple. Every interface of every organism dramatically simplifies the complexity of the world, but not every interface is considered by *H. sapiens* to be simple. Selective sophistication in interfaces is the result, in part, of competition between organisms in which the strengths in the interface of one's nemesis or next meal are avoided and its weaknesses exploited. Dueling between interfaces hones them and the strategies used to exploit them. This is the genesis of mimicry and camouflage, and of complex strategies to defeat them.

Striking examples, despite brains the size of a pinhead, are jumping spiders of the genus *Portia* (Harland and Jackson 2004). *Portia* is araneophagic, preferring to dine on other spiders. Such dining can be dangerous; if the interface of the intended dinner detects *Portia*, dinner could be diner. So *Portia* has evolved countermeasures. Its hair and coloration mimic detritus found in webs and on the forest floor; its gait mimics the flickering of detritus, a stealth technology cleverly adapted to defeat the interfaces of predators and prey. If *Portia* happens on a dragline (a trail of silk) left by the jumping spider *Jacksonoides queenslandicus*, odors from the dragline prompt *Portia* to use its eight eyes to hunt for *J. queenslandicus*. But *J. queenslandicus* is well-camouflaged and, if motionless, invisible to *Portia*. So *Portia* makes a quick vertical leap, tickling the visual motion detectors of *J. queenslandicus* and triggering it to orient to the motion. By the time *J. queenslandicus* has oriented, *Portia* is already down, motionless, and invisible to *J. queenslandicus;* but it has seen the movement of *J. queenslandicus.* Once the eyes of *J. queenslandicus* are safely turned away, *Portia* slowly stalks, leaps, and strikes with its fangs, delivering a paralyzing dose of venom. *Portia's* victory exploits strengths of its interface and weaknesses in that of *J. queenslandicus.*

Jewel beetles, herring gulls, and jumping spiders illustrate the ubiquitous role in evolution of species-specific user interfaces. Perception is not reconstruction; it is construction of a niche-specific, problem-specific, fitness-enhancing interface, which the biologist Jakob von Uexküll (1909, 1934) called an Umwelt, or "self-world" (Schiller 1957). Perceptual categories are endogenous constructs of a subjective Umwelt, not exogenous mirrors of an objective world.

The conventionalist might object that these examples are self-refuting, because they require comparison between the perceptions of an organism and the objective reality that those perceptions get wrong. Only by knowing, for instance, the objective differences between beetle and bottle can we understand a perceptual flaw of *J. backewelli.* So the very examples adduced in support of the interface theory actually support the conclusion that perceptual reconstruction of the objective world in fact occurs, in contradiction to the predictions of that theory.

This objection is misguided. The examples discussed here, and all others that might be unearthed by *H. sapiens*, are necessarily filtered through the interface of *H. sapiens*, an interface whose properties and categories are adapted for fitness, not accuracy. What we observe in these examples is not, therefore, mismatches between perception and a reality to which *H. sapiens* has direct access. Instead, because the interface of *H. sapiens* differs from that of other species, *H. sapiens* can, in some cases, see flaws of others that they miss themselves. In other cases, we can safely assume, *H. sapiens* misses flaws of others due to flaws of its own. In yet other cases, flaws of *H. sapiens* might be obvious to other species.

The conventionalist might further object, saying, "If you think that the wild tiger over there is just a perceptual category of your interface, then why don't you go pet it? When it attacks, you'll find out it's more than an Umwelt category, it's an objective reality."

This objection is also misguided. I don't pet wild tigers for the same reason I don't carelessly drag a file icon to the trash bin. I don't take the icon literally, as though it resembles the real file, but I do take it seriously. My actions on the icon have repercussions for the file. Similarly, I don't take my tiger icon literally but I do take it seriously. Eons of evolution of my interface have shaped it to the point where I had better take its icons seriously or risk harm. So the conventionalist objection fails because it conflates taking icons seriously and taking them literally.

This conventionalist argument is not new. Samuel Johnson famously raised it in 1763 when, in response to the idealism of Berkeley, he kicked a stone and exclaimed "I refute it thus" (Boswell 1791, 1, p. 134). Johnson thus conflated taking a stone seriously and taking it literally. Nevertheless Johnson's argument, one must admit, has strong psychological appeal despite the non sequitur, and it is natural to ask why. Perhaps the answer lies in the evolution of our interface. There was, naturally enough, selective pressure to take its icons seriously; those who didn't take their tiger icons seriously came to early harm. But were there selective pressures not to take its icons literally? Did reproductive advantages accrue to those of our Pleistocene ancestors who happened not to conflate the serious and the literal? Apparently not, given the widespread conflation of the two in the modern population of *H. sapiens*. Hence, the very evolutionary processes that endowed us with our interfaces might also have saddled us with the penchant to mistake their contents for objective reality. This mistake spawned sweeping commitments to a flat earth and a geocentric universe, and prompted the persecution of those who disagreed. Today it spawns reconstructionist theories of perception. Flat earth and geocentrism were difficult for *H. sapiens* to scrap; some unfortunates were tortured or burned in the process. Reconstructionism will, sans the torture, prove even more difficult to scrap; it's not just this or that percept that must be recognized as an icon, but rather perception itself that must be so recognized. The selection pressures on Pleistocene hunter-gatherers clearly didn't do the trick, but social pressures on modern *H. sapiens*, arising in the conduct of science, just might.

The conventionalist might object that death is a counterexample; it should be taken seriously and literally. It is not just shuffling of icons.

This objection is not misguided. In death, one's body icon ceases to function and, in due course, decays. The question this raises can be compared to the following: When a file icon is dragged to the trash and disappears from the screen, is the file itself destroyed, or is it still intact and just inaccessible to the user interface? Knowledge of the interface itself might not license a definitive answer. If not, then to answer the question one must add to the interface a theory of the objective world it hides. How this might proceed is the topic of the next section.

The conventionalist might persist, arguing that agreement between observers entails reconstruction and provides important reality checks on perception. This argument also fails. First, agreement between observers may only be apparent: It is straightforward to prove that two observers can be functionally identical and yet differ in their conscious perceptual experiences (Hoffman 2006b, 2006c); reductive functionalism is false. Second, even if observers agree, this doesn't entail the reconstruction thesis. The observers might simply employ the same constructive (but not reconstructive) perceptual processes. If two PCs have the same icons on their screens, this doesn't entail that the

icons reconstruct their innards. Agreement provides subjective consistency checks –
not objective reality checks – between observers.

8.7 Interface and World

The interface theory claims that perceptual properties and categories no more resemble
the objective world than Windows icons resemble the diodes and resistors of a computer. The conventionalist might object that this makes the world unknowable and is,
therefore, inimical to science.

   This misses a fundamental point in the philosophy of science: Data never determine theories. This under-determination makes the construction of scientific theories
a creative enterprise. The contents of our perceptual interfaces don't determine a true
theory of the objective world, but this in no way precludes us from creating theories and
testing their implications. One such theory, in fact the conventionalist's theory, is that
the relation between interface and world is, on appropriately restricted domains, an isomorphism. This theory is, as we have discussed, improbable on evolutionary grounds
and serves as an intellectual straightjacket, hindering the field from considering more
plausible options.

   What might those options be? That depends on which constraints one postulates
between interface and world. Suppose, for instance, that one wants a minimal constraint
that allows probabilities of interface events to be informative about probabilities of
world events. Then, following standard probability theory, one would represent the
world by a measurable space – that is, by a pair (W, Σ_W), where W is a set and Σ_W is a
σ-algebra of measurable events. One would represent the user interface by a measurable
space (U, Σ_U), and the relation between interface and world by a measurable function
$f : W \to U$. The function f could be many-to-one, and the features represented by
W disjoint from those represented by U. The probabilities of events in the interface
(U, Σ_U) would be distributions of the probabilities in the world (W, Σ_W) – that is, if
the probability of events in the world is μ, then the probability of any interface event
$A \in \Sigma_U$ is $\mu(f^{-1}(A))$. Using this terminology, the problem of Bayes' circle, scouted
previously, can be stated quite simply: It is conflating U with W, and assuming that
$f : W \to U$ is approximately 1 to 1, when in fact it's probably infinite to 1. This
mistake can be made even while using all the sophisticated tools of Bayesian decision
theory and machine learning theory.

   The measurable-space proposal could be weakened if, for instance, one wished to
accommodate quantum systems with noncommuting observables. In this case, the event
structures would not be σ-algebras but instead σ-additive classes, which are closed
under countable disjoint union rather than under countable union (Gudder 1988), and f
would be measurable with respect to these classes. This would still allow probabilities
of events in the interface to be distributions of probabilities of events in the world. It
would explain why science succeeds in uncovering statistical laws governing events
in space-time, even though these events, and space-time itself, in no way resemble
objective reality.

   This proposal could be weakened further. One could give up the measurability of f,
thereby giving up any quantitative relation between probabilities in the interface and

the world. The algebra or class structure of events in the interface would still reflect an isomorphic subalgebra or subclass structure of events in the world. This is a nontrivial constraint: Subset relations in the interface, for instance, would genuinely reflect subset relations of the corresponding events in the world.

Further consideration of the interface might prompt us, in some cases, to weaken the proposal even further. Multistable percepts, for instance, in which the percept switches while the stimulus remains unchanged, may force us to reconsider whether the relation between interface and world is even a *function*: Two or more states of the interface might be associated to a single state of the world.

These proposals all assume that mathematics, which has proved useful in studying the interface, will also prove useful in modeling the world. We shall see.

The discussion here is not intended, of course, to settle the issue of the relation between interface and world, but to sketch how investigation of the relation may proceed in the normal scientific fashion. This investigation is challenging because we see the world through our interface, and it can therefore be difficult to discern the limitations of that interface. We are naturally blind to our own blindness. The best remedy at hand for such blindness is the systematic interplay of theory and experiment that constitutes the scientific method.

The discussion here should, however, help place the interface theory of perception within the philosophical landscape. It is not classical relativism, which claims that there is no objective reality, only metaphor; it claims instead that there is an objective reality that can be explored in the normal scientific manner. It is not naive realism, which claims that we directly see middle-sized objects; nor is it indirect realism, or representationalism, which says that we see sensory representations, or sense data, of real middle-sized objects, and do not directly see the objects themselves. It claims instead that the physicalist ontology underlying both naive realism and indirect realism is almost surely false: A rock is an interface icon, not a constituent of objective reality. Although the interface theory is compatible with idealism, it is not idealism, because it proposes no specific model of objective reality, but it leaves the nature of objective reality as an open scientific problem. It is not a scientific physicalism that rejects the objectivity of middle-sized objects in favor of the objectivity of atomic and subatomic particles; instead it claims that such particles, and the space-time they inhabit, are among the properties and categories of the interface of *H. sapiens*. Finally, it differs from the utilitarian theory of perception (Braunstein 1983; Ramachandran 1985, 1990), which claims that vision uses a bag of tricks (rather than sophisticated general principles) to recover useful information about the physical world. Interface theory (1) rejects the physicalist ontology of the utilitarian theory; (2) asserts instead that space and time, and all objects that reside within them, are properties or icons of our species-specific user interface; and therefore (3) rejects the claim of the utilitarian theory that vision recovers information about preexisting physical objects in space-time. It agrees, however, with the utilitarian theory that evolution is central to understanding perception.

A conventionalist might object, saying, "These proposals about the relation of interface and world are fine as theoretical possibilities. But, in the end, a rock is still a rock." In other words, all the intellectual arguments in the world won't make the physical world – always obstinate and always irrepressible – conveniently disappear. The interface theorist, no less than the physicalist, must take care not to stub a toe on a rock.

Indeed. But in the same sense a trash-can icon is still a trash-can icon. Any file whose icon stubs its frame on the trash will suffer deletion. The trash can is, in this way, as obstinate and irrepressible as a rock. But both are simplifying icons. Both usefully hide a world that is far more complex. Space and time do the same.

The conventionalist might object further, saying, "The proposed dissimilarity between interface and world is contradicted by the user-interface example itself. The icons of a computer interface perhaps don't resemble the innards of a computer, but they do resemble real objects in the physical world. Moreover, when using a computer to manipulate three-dimensional objects, as in computer-aided design, the computer interface is most useful if its symbols really resemble the actual three-dimensional objects to be manipulated."

Certainly. These arguments show that an interface can sometimes resemble what it represents, and that is no surprise at all. But user interfaces can also *not* resemble what they represent, and can be quite effective precisely because they don't resemble what they represent. So the real question is whether the user interface of *H. sapiens* does in fact resemble what it represents. Here, I claim, the smart money says "No."

8.8 Future Research on Perceptual Categorization

So what? So what if perception is a user-interface construction, not an objective-world reconstruction? How will this affect concrete research on perceptual categorization?

Here are some possibilities. First, as discussed already, current attempts to verify priors are misguided. This doesn't mean we must abandon such attempts. It does mean that our attempts must be more sophisticated; at a minimum, they must not founder on Bayes' circle.

But that is at a minimum. Real progress in understanding the relation between perception and the world requires careful theory building. The conventional theory that perception approximates the world is hopelessly simplistic. Once we reject this facile theory, once we recognize that our perceptions are to the world as a user interface is to a computer, we can begin serious work. We must postulate, and then try to justify and confirm, possible structures for the world and possible mappings between world and interface. Clinging to approximate isomorphisms is a natural, but thus far fruitless, response to this daunting task. It's now time to develop more plausible theories. Some elementary considerations toward this end were presented in the previous section.

Our efforts should be informed by relevant advances in modern physics. Experiments by Alain Aspect (1982a,b), building on the work of Bell (1964), persuade most physicists to reject *local realism*, viz., the doctrine that (1) distant objects cannot directly influence each other (*locality*) and (2) all objects have pre-existing values for all possible measurements, before any measurements are made (*realism*). Aspect's experiments demonstrate that distant objects, say two electrons, can be *entangled*, such that measurement of a property of one immediately affects the value of that property of the other. Such entanglement is not just an abstract possibility, it is an empirical fact now being exploited in quantum computation to give substantial improvements over classical computation (Nielsen and Chuang 2000; Kaye et al. 2007). Our untutored categories of space, time, and objects would lead us to expect that two electrons a billion light years apart are separate entities; but in fact, because of entanglement, they are a single entity with a unity that transcends space and time. This is a puzzle for proponents of faithful depiction, but not for interface theory. Space, time, and separate objects are useful fictions of our interface, not faithful depictions of objective reality.

Our theories of perceptual categorization must be informed by explicit dynamical models of perceptual evolution, models such as those studied in evolutionary game theory (Hofbauer and Sigmund 1998; Samuelson 1997; Nowak 2006). Our perceptual categories are shaped inter alia by factors such as predators, prey, sexual selection, distribution of resources, and social interactions. We won't understand categorization until we understand how categories emerge from dynamical systems in which these factors interact. There are promising leads. Geisler and Diehl (2003) simulate interactions between simplified predators and prey, and show how these might shape the spectral sensitivities of both. Komarova, Jameson, and Narens (2007) show how color categories can evolve from a minimal perceptual psychology of discrimination together with simple learning rules and simple constraints on social communication. Some researchers are exploring perceptual evolution in foraging contexts (Sernland et al. 2003; Goldstone et al. 2005; Roberts and Goldstone 2006). These papers are useful pointers to the kind of research required to construct theories of categorization that are evolutionarily plausible. As a concrete example of such research, consider the following class of evolutionary games.

8.9 Interface Games

In the simplest interface game, two animals compete over three territories. Each territory has a food value and a water value, each value ranging from, say, 0 to 100. The first animal to choose a territory obtains its food and water values; the second animal then chooses one of the remaining two territories, and obtains its food and water values. The animals can adopt one of two perceptual strategies. The *truth* interface strategy perceives the exact values of food and of water for each territory. Thus, the total information that *truth* obtains is $I_T = 3$ [territories] $\times$ 2 [resources per territory] $\times$ $\log_2 101$ [bits per resource] ≈ 39.95 bits. The *simple* interface strategy perceives only one bit of information per territory: if the food value of a territory is greater than some fixed value (say 50), *simple* perceives that territory as green; otherwise *simple* perceives that territory as red. Thus, the total information that *simple* obtains is $I_S = 3$ bits.

It costs energy to obtain perceptual information. Let the energy cost per bit be denoted by c_e. Since the *truth* strategy obtains I_T bits, the total energy cost to *truth* is $I_T c_e$, which is subtracted from the sum of food and water values that *truth* obtains from the territory it chooses. Similarly, the total energy cost to *simple* is $I_S c_e$.

It takes t units of time to obtain one bit of perceptual information. If $t > 0$, then *simple* acquires all of its perceptual information before *truth* does, allowing *simple* to be first to choose a territory.

Assuming, for simplicity, that the food and water values are independent, identically distributed random variables with, say, a uniform distribution on the integers from 0 to

100, we can compute a matrix of expected payoffs:

	Truth	Simple
Truth:	a	b
Simple:	c	d

Here a is the expected payoff to *truth* if it competes against *truth*; b is the expected payoff to *truth* if it competes against *simple*; c is the expected payoff to *simple* if it competes against *truth*, and d is the expected payoff to *simple* if it competes against *simple*.

As is standard in evolutionary game theory, we consider a population of *truth* and *simple* players and equate payoff with fitness. Let x_T denote the frequency of *truth* players and x_S the frequency of *simple* players; the population is thus $\vec{x} = (x_T, x_S)$. Then, assuming players meet at random, the expected payoffs for *truth* and *simple* are, respectively, $f_T(\vec{x}) = ax_T + bx_S$ and $f_S(\vec{x}) = cx_T + dx_S$. The selection dynamics is then $x_T' = x_T[f_T(\vec{x}) - F]; x_S' = x_S[f_S(\vec{x}) - F]$, where primes denote temporal derivatives and F is the average fitness, $F = x_T f_T(\vec{x}) + x_S f_S(\vec{x})$.

If $a > c$ and $b > d$, then *truth* drives *simple* to extinction. If $a < c$ and $b < d$, then *simple* drives *truth* to extinction. If $a > c$ and $b < d$, then *truth* and *simple* are bistable; which one goes extinct depends on the initial frequencies, $\vec{x}(0)$, at time 0. If $a < c$ and $b > d$, then *truth* and *simple* stably coexist, with the *truth* frequency given by $(d - b)/(a - b - c + d)$. If $a = c$ and $b = d$, then selection does not change the frequencies of *truth* and *simple*.

The entries in the payoff matrix described above will vary, of course, with the correlation between food and water values, with the specific value of food that is used by *simple* as the boundary between green and red, and with the cost, c_e, per bit of information obtained.

Here is the punchline: *Simple* drives *truth* to extinction for most values of the red-green boundary, even when the cost per bit of information is small and the correlation between food and water is small. This is illustrated in Figure 8.1, which shows the results of Matlab simulations. Evolutionary pressures do not select for veridical perception; instead, they drive it, should it arise, to extinction.

The interface game just described might seem too simple to be useful. One can, however, expand on the simple game just described in several ways, including (1) increasing the number of territories at stake; (2) increasing the number of resources per territory; (3) having dangers as well as resources in the territories; (4) considering distributions other than uniform (e.g., Gaussian) for the resources and dangers; (5) considering two-boundary, three-boundary, n-boundary interface strategies, and more general categorization algorithms that don't rely on such boundaries; (6) considering populations with three or more interface strategies; (7) considering more sophisticated maps from resources to interfaces, including probabilistic maps; (8) considering time and energy costs that vary with architecture (e.g., serial versus parallel) and that are probabilistic functions of the amount of information gleaned; and (9) extending the replicator dynamics – for example, to include communication between players and to include a spatial dimension in which players only interact with nearby players (as has been done with stag hunt and Lewis signaling games; see Skyrms 2002, 2004; Zollman 2005). Interface games, in all these varieties, allow us to explore the complex

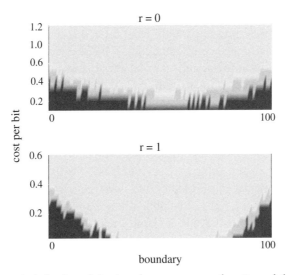

Figure 8.1. Asymptotic behavior of the interface game as a function of the cost per bit of information and the choice of the red-green boundary in the simple strategy. Light gray indicates that *simple* drives *truth* to extinction, intermediate gray, that the two strategies coexist; and dark gray, that *truth* drives *simple* to extinction. The upper plot is for uncorrelated food and water, the lower for perfectly correlated food and water.

evolutionary pressures that shape perception and perceptual categorization, and to do so as realistically as our imaginations and computational resources will allow.

They will also allow us to address a natural question: As an organism's perceptions and behaviors become more complex, shouldn't it be the case that the goal of perception approaches that of recovering the properties of the environment?

Using simulations of interface games, one can ask for what environments (including what kinds of competitors) will the reproductive pressures push an organism to true perceptions of the environment, so that perceptual truth is an evolutionarily stable strategy. My bet: None of interest.

8.10 Conclusion

Most experts assume that perception estimates true properties of an objective world. They justify this assumption with an argument from evolution: Natural selection rewards true perceptions. I propose instead that if true perceptions crop up, then natural selection mows them down; natural selection fosters perceptions that act as simplified user interfaces, expediting adaptive behavior while shrouding the causal and structural complexity of the objective world. In support of this proposal, I discussed mimicry and mating errors in nature, and presented simulations of an evolutionary game.

Old habits die hard. I suspect that few experts will be persuaded by these arguments to adopt the interface theory of perception. Most will still harbor the long-standing conviction that, although we see reality through small portals, nevertheless what we see is, in general, veridical. To such experts I offer one final claim, and one final challenge. I claim that natural selection drives true perception to swift extinction:

Nowhere in evolution, even among the most complex of organisms, will you find that natural selection drives truth to fixation – that is, so that the predicates of perception (e.g., space, time, shape, and color) approximate the predicates of the objective world (whatever they might be). Natural selection rewards fecundity, not factuality, so it shapes interfaces, not telescopes on truth (Pinker 1997, p. 571). The challenge is clear: Provide a compelling counterexample to this claim.

Acknowledgments

Justin Mark collaborated in developing the interface games and wrote the simulations presented in Figure 8.1. For helpful comments on previous drafts, I thank Ori Amir, Mike D'Zmura, Geoff Iverson, Carol Skrenes, Duncan Luce, Larry Maloney, Brian Marion, Justin Mark, Louis Narens, Steve Pinker, Kim Romney, John Serences, Brian Skyrms, and Joyce Wu. For helpful discussions, I thank Mike Braunstein, Larry Maloney, Jon Merzel, Chetan Prakash, Whitman Richards, Rosie Sedghi, and Phat Vu.

Bibliography

Aspect A, Dalibard J, Roger G. 1982b. Experimental test of Bells inequalities using time-varying analyzers. *Phys Rev Lett* 49: 1804–1807.

Aspect A, Grangier P, Roger G. 1982a. Experimental realization of Einstein-Podolsky-Rosen-Bohm gedankenexperiment: a new violation of Bells inequalities. *Phys Rev Lett* 49: 91–94.

Bell JS. 1964. On the Einstein-Podolsky-Rosen paradox. *Physics* 1: 195–200.

Boswell J. 1791. *The life of Samuel Johnson.*

Braunstein ML. 1983. Contrasts between human and machine vision: should technology recapitulate phylogeny? In *Human and machine vision*, eds. J Beck, B Hope, and A Rosenfeld. New York: Academic Press.

Daly M, Wilson M, 1978. *Sex, evolution, and behavior.* Boston: Duxbury Press.

Geisler WS, Diehl RL. 2003. A Bayesian approach to the evolution of perceptual and cognitive systems. *Cognitive Sci* 27: 379–402.

Goldstone RL, Ashpole BC, Roberts ME. 2005. Knowledge of resources and competitors in human foraging. *Psychonomic Bull Rev* 12: 81–87.

Gudder S. 1988. *Quantum probability.* San Diego: Academic Press.

Gwynne DT. 2003. Mating mistakes. In *Encyclopedia of insects*, ed. VH Resh and RT Carde. San Diego: Academic Press.

Gwynne DT, Rentz DCF. 1983. Beetles on the bottle: male buprestids make stubbies for females. *J Austr Entomol Soc* 22: 79–80.

Harland DP, Jackson RR. 2004. *Portia* perceptions: the umwelt of an araneophagic jumping spider. In *Complex worlds from simpler nervous systems*, ed. FR Prete. Cambridge: MIT Press.

Hofbauer J, Sigmund K. 1998. *Evolutionary games and population dynamics.* Cambridge: Cambridge University Press.

Hoffman DD. 1983. The interpretation of visual illusions. *Sci Amer* 249: 154–162.

Hoffman DD. 1998. *Visual intelligence: how we create what we see.* New York: W.W. Norton.

Hoffman DD. 2006a. Mimesis and its perceptual reflections. In *A view in the rear-mirror: romantic aesthetics, culture, and science seen from today. Festschrift for Frederick Burwick on the occasion of his seventieth birthday*, ed. W. Pape (WVT, Wissenschaftlicher Verlag Trier: Trier) (Studien zur Englischen Romantik 3).

Hoffman DD. 2006b. The scrambling theorem: a simple proof of the logical possibility of spectrum inversion. *Conscious Cogn* 15: 31–45.

Hoffman, DD. 2006c. The scrambling theorem unscrambled: A response to commentaries. *Conscious Cogn* 15: 51–53.

Hoffman DD. 2008. Conscious realism and the mind-body problem. In *Mind & Matter* 6: 87–121.

Kaye P, Laflamme R, Mosca M. 2007. *An introduction to quantum computing.* Oxford: Oxford University Press.

Komarova NL, Jameson KA, Narens L. 2007. Evolutionary models of color categorization based on discrimination. *J Math Psychol* 51: 359–382.

Mausfeld R. 2002. The physicalist trap in perception theory. In *Perception and the physical world*, ed. D Heyer and R Mausfeld. New York: Wiley.

Lehar S. 2003. Gestalt isomorphism and the primacy of subjective conscious experience: a Gestalt bubble model. *Behav Brain Sci* 26: 375–444.

Nielsen MA, Chuang IL. 2000. *Quantum computation and quantum information.* Cambridge: Cambridge University Press.

Noë A, Regan JK. 2002. On the brain-basis of visual consciousness: a sensorimotor account. In *Vision and mind: selected readings in the philosophy of perception*, ed. A Noë and E Thompson. Cambridge: MIT Press.

Nowak MA. 2006. *Evolutionary dynamics: exploring the equations of life.* Cambridge: Belknap/ Harvard University Press.

Palmer SE. 1999. *Vision science: photons to phenomenology.* Cambridge: MIT Press.

Pinker S. 1997. *How the mind works.* New York: W.W. Norton.

Purves D, Lotto RB. 2003. *Why we see what we do: an empirical theory of vision.* Sunderland, MA: Sinauer.

Ramachandran VS. 1985. The neurobiology of perception. *Perception* 14: 97–103.

Ramachandran VS. 1990. Interactions between motion, depth, color and form: the utilitarian theory of perception. In *Vision: coding and efficiency*, ed. C Blakemore. Cambridge: Cambridge University Press.

Roberts ME, Goldstone RL. 2006. EPICURE: spatial and knowledge limitations in group foraging. *Adapt Behav* 14: 291–313.

Samuelson L. 1997. *Evolutionary games and equilibrium selection.* Cambridge: MIT Press.

Schiller CH. 1957. *Instinctive behavior: development of a modern concept.* New York: Hallmark Press.

Sernland E, Olsson O, Holmgren NMA. 2003. Does information sharing promote group foraging? *Proc R Soc Lond* 270: 1137–1141.

Skyrms B. 2002. Signals, evolution, and the explanatory power of transient information. *Philos Sci* 69: 407–428.

Skyrms B. 2004. *The stag hunt and the evolution of social structure.* Cambridge: Cambridge University Press.

Tinbergen N, Perdeck AC. 1950. On the stimulus situation releasing the begging response in the newly hatched herring gull chick (*Larus argentatus argentatus Pont.*). *Behaviour* 3: 1–39.

Trivers RL. 1972. Parental investment and sexual selection. In *Sexual selection and the descent of man, 1871–1971*, ed. B Campbell. Chicago: Aldine Press.

Trivers RL. 1976. Foreword. In R Dawkins, *The selfish gene.* New York: Oxford University Press.

Ullman S. 1979. *The interpretation of visual motion.* Cambridge: MIT Press.

Von Uexküll J. 1909. *Umwelt und innenwelt der tiere.* Berlin: Springer-Verlag.

Von Uexküll J. 1934. A stroll through the worlds of animals and men: a picture book of invisible worlds. Reprinted in *Instinctive behavior: Development of a modern concept*, CH Schiller, 1957. New York: Hallmark Press.

Yuille A, Bülthoff, HH. 1996. Bayesian decision theory and psychophysics. In *Perception as Bayesian inference*, ed. D Knill and W Richards. Cambridge: Cambridge University Press.

Zollman K. 2005. Talking to neighbors: the evolution of regional meaning. *Philos Sci* 72: 69–85.

CHAPTER 9

Words and Pictures: Categories, Modifiers, Depiction, and Iconography

D.A. Forsyth, Tamara Berg, Cecilia Ovesdotter Alm,
Ali Farhadi, Julia Hockenmaier, Nicolas Loeff,
and Gang Wang

9.1 Introduction

Collections of digital pictures are now very common. Collections can range from a small set of family pictures, to the entire contents of a picture site like Flickr. Such collections differ from what one might see if one simply attached a camera to a robot and recorded everything, because the pictures have been selected by people. They are not necessarily "good" pictures (say, by standards of photographic aesthetics), but, because they have been chosen, they display quite strong trends. It is common for such pictures to have associated text, which might be keywords or tags but is often in the form of sentences or brief paragraphs. Text could be a *caption* (a set of remarks explicitly bound to the picture, and often typeset in a way that emphasizes this), *region labels* (terms associated with image regions, perhaps identifying what is in that region), *annotations* (terms associated with the whole picture, often identifying objects in the picture), or just *nearby text*. We review a series of ideas about how to exploit associated text to help interpret pictures.

9.2 Word Frequencies, Objects, and Scenes

Most pictures in electronic form seem to have related words nearby (or sound or metadata, and so on; we focus on words), so it is easy to collect word and picture datasets, and there are many examples. Such multimode collections should probably be seen as the usual case, because one usually has to deliberately ignore information to collect only images. It is quite usual to have "noise," which might just mean phenomena we don't want or know how to model, in the words. Issues include words that have nothing to do with image content, a tendency of annotations to ignore some aspects of image content, and a tendency for different annotators to attend to different visual phenomena. Collections that have been used include collections of museum material (Barnard et al. 2001); the Corel collection of images (see Barnard and Forsyth 2001; Duygulu et al. 2002; Chen and Wang 2004; and numerous others); any video with sound or closed captioning (Satoh and Kanade 1997; Satoh et al. 1999; Wang et al. 2002); images collected from the Web with their enclosing Web pages (Berg and Forsyth 2006); captioned news images (Wactlar 1996); and images collected by querying a search engine (one keeps the search terms, or should, e.g. Schroff et al. 2007; Torralba et al. 2007; Wang and Forsyth 2008). In this section, we will discuss what can be done without attending to structure in the text, which might even be reduced to a set of keywords. The literature is very extensive, and we can mention only the most relevant papers here. For a more complete review, we refer readers to (Datta et al. 2005), which has 120 references.

9.2.1 Exploiting Correlations between Words and Pictures

Words can improve image clustering because two images that look the same may have quite different content (which tends to result in different annotations), and because two images that look quite different might have similar content (which tends to result in similar annotations). Belongie and colleagues demonstrate examples of joint image-keyword searches (Carson et al. 2002). Joshi and colleagues (2004) show that one can identify pictures that illustrate a story by searching annotated images for those with relevant keywords, then ranking the pool of images based on similarity of appearance. Barnard and colleagues cluster Corel images and their keywords jointly to produce a browsable representation (Barnard and Forsyth 2001), using a modified version of a clustering method originally due to Hofmann and Puzicha (1998). Each image is represented by a bag of appearance feature vectors for large segments, and a bag of words. The clusterer models joint image-word probabilities as a set of nodes, organized into a tree (which is fixed). Each image is generated by a path from the root to a leaf; each node along the path generates words and feature vectors independently conditioned on the node. The fitting procedure tends to make words and segments that appear over a large range of images be generated by nodes close to the root (which are used by many paths) and more specialized words (respectively, segments) be generated by nodes closer to leaves. As a result, words and segments with roughly similar frequencies that tend to co-occur, tend to be generated by the same node. This clustering gives a joint model of words and image structures. In a following paper, Barnard and colleagues give three applications for such a model: *auto-illustration*, in which one finds pictures with high joint probability with given text (perhaps to suggest illustrations from a collection); *auto-annotation*, in which one finds annotations with high joint probability with given text (perhaps to allow keyword search to find otherwise unannotated images); and *layout*, in which one uses multidimensional scaling to lay out cluster centers in an informative, browsable representation of a collection (Barnard et al. 2001). Coyne and Sproat describe an auto-illustration system that gives naive users a method to produce rendered images from free text descriptions (Wordseye; Coyne and Sproat 2001); http://www.wordseye.com). Auto-illustration and layout are hard to evaluate; auto-annotation can be evaluated by comparing predicted annotations with observed annotations (there is extensive evaluation work in Barnard et al. 2003).

There are now numerous methods for predicting region labels. Predicting region labels is different from predicting annotations, because one must specify which region gets a label. Generally, methods differ by how explicitly they model correspondence

Table 9.1. *Comparison of the performance of various word annotation prediction methods by precision, recall, and F1-measure. We show reported results for the co-occurrence model (Co-occ), translation model (Trans), cross-media relevance model (CMRM), text space to image space (TSIS), maximum entropy model (MaxEnt), continuous relevance model (CRM), 3 × 3 grid of color and texture moments (CT-3 × 3), inference network (InfNet), multiple Bernoulli relevance models (MBRM), mixture hierarchies model (MixHier), PicSOM with global features and the method of section 9.2 (for linear and kernelized classifiers).*

Method	P	R	F1	Ref
Co-occ	0.03	0.02	0.02	Mori et al. 1999
Trans	0.06	0.04	0.05	Duygulu et al. 2002
CMRM	0.10	0.09	0.10	Jeon et al. 2003a
TSIS	0.10	0.09	0.10	Celebi and Alpkocak 2005
MaxEnt	0.09	0.12	0.10	Jeon and Manmatha 2004
CRM	0.16	0.19	0.17	Lavrenko et al. 2003b
CT-3 × 3	0.18	0.21	0.19	Yavlinsky et al. 2005
CRM-rect	0.22	0.23	0.23	Feng et al. 2004
InfNet	0.17	0.24	0.23	Metzler and Manmatha 2004
MBRM	0.24	0.25	0.25	Feng et al. 2004
MixHier	0.23	0.29	0.26	Carneiro and Vasconcelos 2005
(section 9.2)	0.27	0.27	0.27	
(section 9.2, kernel)	0.29	0.29	0.29	
PicSOM	0.35	0.35	0.35	Viitaniemi and Laaksonen 2007

between local image structures and words, and by the specific machinery adopted to manage correspondences. The original work by Barnard and Forsyth (2001) models correspondences implicitly, but is nonetheless capable of predicting region labels quite well. Duygulu and colleagues (2002) build explicit correspondence models between image region representations and individual words (the models mirror standard models in statistical machine translation (Brown et al. 1993). Labeling machinery includes clustering or latent variable methods (Barnard and Forsyth 2001; Barnard et al. 2001; Barnard et al. 2003; Monay and Gatica-Perez 2003) multiple-instance learning (Maron and Ratan 1998; Zhang et al. 2002; Yang et al. 2005) one can attack MIL with a form of smoothing (Maron and Lozano-Pérez 1998; Zhang and Goldman 2001), with an SVM (Andrews et al. 2003; Tao et al. 2004), or with geometric reasoning (Dietterich et al. 1997); comparisons in (Ray and Craven 2005); latent Dirichlet allocation (Blei and Jordan 2003); cross-media relevance models (Jeon et al. 2003b); continuous relevance models (Lavrenko et al. 2003a); and localization reasoning (Carneiro et al. 2007). Barnard and colleagues demonstrate and compare a wide variety of methods to predict keywords, including several strategies for reasoning about correspondence directly (Barnard et al. 2003). Region label prediction is rather more difficult to evaluate on a large scale than word annotation prediction, because one must check to see whether labels have been placed on the right region. One strategy is to drop the correspondence information, evaluate as an auto-annotator, then check whether, if a label has been predicted, it was predicted on the right region (Barnard et al. 2003). We give a summary of performance statistics for current methods in Table 9.1. Generally, methods attempt to predict noun annotations, and are more successful with mass nouns – known in vision circles as "stuff"; examples include sky, cloud, grass, sea – than with count nouns ("things," such as cat, dog, car). Methods are evaluated by comparing predicted annotations with known annotations. Most methods can beat a word prior, but display marked eccentricities. One could then propagate text labels from labelled images to unlabelled images, making keyword-based searches of large image collections possible.

9.2.2 Scenes and Annotations

Image regions seem to be strongly correlated with each other, and word annotations are certainly strongly correlated with each other. This means it can be helpful to cluster words and predict clusters, particularly for annotation (e.g., Chapelle et al. 1999; Wang and Li 2002; Li and Wang 2003; Jin et al. 2004). Exploiting word co-occurrence patterns seems to improve labeling performance, too (Rabinovich 2007). One reasonable source of these correlation patterns is that images are pictures of **scenes**. The term is used loosely, but pictures of a room in a house, of a scenic landscape, and of people on a beach are pictures of different scenes. Human observers can identify scenes astonishingly fast (Fei-Fei et al. 2002; Fei-Fei et al. 2004; Torralba et al. 2006). Scene classification is successful with "gist" features that summarize major coarse-scale properties of the image (e.g., Oliva and Torralba 2006). A second, important cue to the identity of a scene is the objects that are present (Sudderth et al. 2005a,b; in press). Scenes can constrain recognition significantly (Torralba et al. 2003; Crandall and Huttenlocher 2007; Serre et al. 2007). Generative models of relations between activities, scenes, and objects can produce very high-level classification of images (Li and Fei-Fei 2007).

Loeff et al. (2008) give two loose criteria for images to depict the same scene category:

1. Objects that appear in one image could likely appear in the other.
2. The images look similar in an appropriate way.

If we adopt these criteria, then the underlying scene is the source of correlations between words and correlations between regions. This means that we should be able to identify scenes by looking for latent variables that predict these correlations.

Equivalently, if we could estimate a list of all the annotations that could reasonably be attached to the image, we could cluster using that list of annotations. The objects in this list of annotations don't actually have to be present (not all kitchens contain coffee makers, e.g.), but they need to be plausible hypotheses. Predicting all plausible annotations involves predicting elements of a vocabulary of hundreds of words for each of thousands of images. These predictions are correlated with each other, and most likely arise from a subset of the image features, not all of which will be correlated with each other. Loeff et al. (2008) build a set of classifiers that, from a set of image features, can predict a set of word annotations that are like the original annotations. These classifiers are tied by a natural regularization that exploits the tendency of predictions to be correlated and exposes a latent space. Clustering in this latent space is equivalent to clustering on completed annotations, and the clusters are scene types.

Let Y be a matrix of word annotations per image, X the matrix of image features per image, and W a linear classifier matrix; we seek W to minimize

$$J(W) = \text{regularization}(W) + \text{loss}(Y, W^t X) \tag{9.1}$$

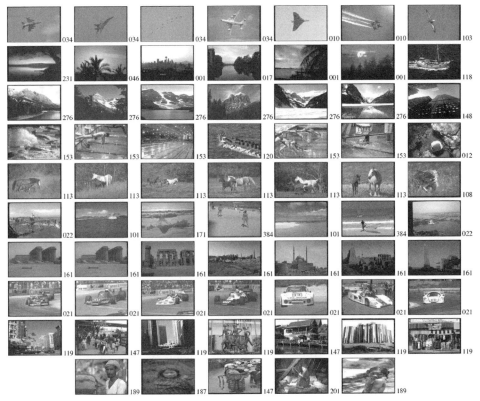

Figure 9.1. Example results on the Corel test set of the method of Loeff et al. (2008). Each row consists of the closest 7 **test** images to each centroid found on the **training set**. The number on the right of each image is the Corel CD label. Rows correspond to scenes, which would be hard to discover with pure visual clustering. Because this method is able to predict word annotations while clustering scenes, it is able to discount large but irrelevant visual differences. Despite this, some mistakes are due to visual similarity (e.g., the bird in the last image of the plane cluster, or the skyscraper in the last image of the mountain cluster). Portrait images have been resized to make the layout more compact.

The regularization term will penalize W with high rank, in order to improve generalization by forcing word classifiers to **share a low dimensional representation**. W can be thought of as the product of two matrices, FG, where the inner dimension is small. This yields a feature mapping (F) that identifies important features, and a mapping from these features to words (G) that encodes correlations in the words. One should notice the relation to multitask learning, which is natural, for the problem of assigning one word to an image is correlated with the other words. In particular, this method reduces dimensionality in the space of classifiers like the work of Ando and Zhang (2005) rather than in the feature space.

It is always difficult to evaluate clustering methods. Loeff et al. (2008) use a subset of the Corel dataset in which CD number is a good proxy for scene type. They apply their method to this subset, and evaluate by checking the purity of clusters. This suggests that, when applied to a dataset containing a clean set of scene types identified by hand, the method produces type clusters that are consistent with human judgement. A more qualitative evaluation involves checking clusters by eye. Figure 9.1 shows scene clusters obtained from a large and complex subset of the Corel dataset. Notice that the clusters form rather natural scene types. This method can also be evaluated as a way to predict word annotations, and it is reassuring that it is rather good at this problem (Table 9.1).

9.2.3 Driving Recognition with Word-Picture Relations

Pure content-based image-retrieval methods do not seem to meet user needs (see Armitage and Enser 1997; Enser 2000; a brief review in (Forsyth 2001), and the major search engines use text-based methods that rely on cues such as file name, alt tags, user labeling, and nearby text. Part of the problem is that visual cues are hard to use, and we don't yet have accurate techniques for exploiting them. Text cues have problems, too; text near an image may not have anything to do with the image's content. We expect errors from misinterpreting text to be uncorrelated with errors from misinterpreting images, and so may consider whether combining image cues with cues from associated text yield higher precision searches for a concept. Some work by Berg and Forsyth (2006) and Wang and Forsyth (2008) suggests that the answer is yes. In this framework, one works with a pool of Web pages, typically collected by querying on an object name (e.g., "frog"), and must then identify images that depict frogs.

Berg and Forsyth obtain a set of word topics relevant to an object name with Latent Dirichlet Allocation (Blei et al. 2003) and use these to obtain images that will serve as exemplars. Test images are then ranked by combining normalized similarity scores (obtained with a voting procedure) obtained for shape, texture, color, and words, independently. This simple procedure allows for the fact that each cue may work well for some images, but poorly for others, because the errors made by each cue seem to be somewhat independent (Fig. 9.2). Detailed results clearly show that combined word and picture cues outperform text-only or image-only approaches. This is confirmed by work of Schroff et al. (2007), who used text features of particular types (image filename, image alt text, and Web site title) and still showed that visual information makes a contribution to the final retrieval results.

Wang and Forsyth (2008) obtain exemplars by identifying **online knowledge sources** that are compiled by humans and likely to be relevant. They then build text and image models separately from these sources. They wish to retrieve object images from noisy Web pages with image and text cues. They have a query q, which is the object class name (e.g., "frog"). They have a collection of Web pages that are collected by inputting q and some extensions to Google. They then build an explicit probabilistic model of the relevance of an image to a query, conditioned on image features and nearby text features. The image model is discriminative, which is unusual; systems for object recognition that are trained on data where location is not known are more typically generative in form (e.g., see Pinz 2006).

Their approach is automatic (i.e., one could build a search engine that took text queries, extracted information from the knowledge sources, and identified relevant images), except for a step in which they identify the sense of the query word (by offering a user a set of senses from Wikipedia). They perform experiments on the same animal data set as Berg et al. (2006), which includes ten animal categories. Their method outperforms reported results (Berg et al. 2006; Schroff et al. 2007) on these

Figure 9.2. Images returned by (*top*) Berg and Forsyth's method, and (*bottom*) Wang and Forsyth's method on a set of test images for the "bear," "dolphin," and "frog" categories. Most of the top classified images for each category are correct and display a wide variety of poses, depictions, and species ("leopard," heads or whole bodies) and even multiple species ("penguins"). Returned "bear" results include "grizzly bears," "pandas," and "polar bears." False-positives are indicated by red squares. (See color plate 9.2.)

data. They collect five new categories: "binoculars," "fern," "laptop," "motorbike," and "rifle," and get high precision over these categories.

9.3 Syntax, Depiction, Modifiers, and Iconography

Images seem to offer information about deeper properties of words than their frequencies; for example, Barnard and Johnson (2005) show one can disambiguate the senses of annotating words using image information, and Yanai and Barnard (2005) use region entropy to identify words that have straightforwardly observed visual properties ("pink" does, "affectionate" does not). Of particular interest is understanding how relations between words constrain our interpretation of the image.

9.3.1 Depiction

Some objects cannot appear in pictures in a concrete way; others can, but aren't in the particular picture described by the sentence, even though the word is in the sentence. Because caption writers assume that readers can see, and are attending to, the image, there is a shared discourse context, and true captions appear to contain numerous phenomena that predict what is **depicted**. At least in part, this is because references to items present in the shared discourse context generally differ from references to items being introduced to a discourse. For example, deictic expressions tend to refer to given items. "A man died in this house" is a caption for a picture in which one expects to see a house, but not the man. "This man died in a house" is a caption for a picture in which one expects to see a man, but most likely not the house. Some such cues (like the deictic example) occur quite close to the surface. Others seem to require full syntactic parsing of the caption. For example, the caption "A man walks past a house that was destroyed by the tsunami" is likely to refer to an image that contains both a man and parts of a house.

Relations between names in captions and faces in images have been studied for a while (space does not permit a full review). In general, one collects captioned images, identifies names in captions and faces in images, and attempts to associate them. This can be complicated, because there may be several names in the caption and several faces in the image. The main variants include association between faces in video and transcripts (Satoh and Kanade 1997; Satoh et al. 1999; Yang and Hauptmann 2004); automatic construction of face datasets from video and transcripts (Houghton 1999); reasoning about explicit relational information in captions (Govindaraju et al. 1989; Srihari 1995); and text-based search for named individuals (Zhang et al. 1999).

It is natural to try to exploit the (rather rough) coherence in different views of the same face to determine which face gets which name. In the simplest case, for each data item, there are single-face, single-name data items somewhere else in the dataset that can disambiguate the correspondence problem. This suggests why depiction analysis could be very helpful: if one can rule out some possible correspondences, because the language suggests a name is not depicted, a data item that appears to be hard may reduce to an easy case. Berg et al. (2004) build methods to tell whether the face of a person, named in a caption, will appear in the image, using a dataset of approximately half a million news pictures and captions collected from Yahoo News over a period of roughly two years. Using Mikolajczyk's face detector (Mikolajczyk) and Cunningham et al.'s (2002) open source named entity recognizer, they obtain a set of faces and names from each captioned picture. In each picture-caption pair, there may be several faces (represented as feature vectors) and several names. Furthermore, some faces may not correspond to any name, and some names may not correspond to any face. The task is to assign one of these names or null (unnamed) to each detected face.

Berg et al. attack depiction by building a generative model, in which a random variable pictured tells whether an individual is depicted or not. This variable is predicted from the linguistic context within which a name appears. Their method seems to

IN Pete Sampras IN of the U.S. celebrates his victory over Denmark's **OUT Kristian Pless OUT** at the **OUT U.S. Open OUT** at Flushing Meadows August 30, 2002. Sampras won the match 6-3 7- 5 6-4. REUTERS/Kevin Lamarque
Germany's **IN Chancellor Gerhard Schroeder IN**, left, in discussion with France's **IN President Jacques Chirac IN** on the second day of the EU summit at the European Council headquarters in Brussels, Friday Oct. 25, 2002. EU leaders are to close a deal Friday on finalizing entry talks with 10 candidate countries after a surprise breakthrough agreement on Thursday between France and Germany regarding farm spending. (AP Photo/European Commission/HO)
'The Right Stuff' cast members **IN Pamela Reed IN**, (L) poses with fellow cast member **IN Veronica Cartwright IN** at the 20th anniversary of the film in Hollywood, June 9, 2003. The women played wives of astronauts in the film about early United States test pilots and the space program. The film directed by **OUT Philip Kaufman OUT**, is celebrating its 20th anniversary and is being released on DVD. REUTERS/Fred Prouser
Kraft Foods Inc., the largest U.S. food company, on July 1, 2003 said it would take steps, like capping portion sizes and providing more nutrition information, as it and other companies face growing concern and even lawsuits due to rising obesity rates. In May of this year, San Francisco attorney **OUT Stephen Joseph OUT**, shown above, sought to ban Oreo cookies in California – a suit that was withdrawn less than two weeks later. Photo by Tim Wimborne/Reuters REUTERS/Tim Wimborne

Figure 9.3. The procedure adopted by Berg et al. (2004) gives a natural language classifier that predicts which name produces a face that appears in the picture. This classifier uses only natural language features, and can be tested on captions alone. Several examples appear above, where names have been labeled with IN (pictured) and OUT (not pictured). Labeling accuracy is high, at 85%. The top 3 labelings are all correct. The last is incorrectly labeling "Stephen Joseph" as not pictured, when in fact he is the subject of the picture.

benefit from three important cues. First, the named entity recognizer occasionally marks phrases like "United Nations" as proper names. One can determine that these names do not refer to depicted people because they appear in quite different linguistic contexts from the names of actual people. Second, caption writers tend to name people who are actually depicted earlier in the caption. Third, caption writers regularly use depiction indicators such as "left," "(R)," "background." For names in captions, depiction can be predicted quite accurately (Fig. 9.3). The language model can be trained while the face model is trained, and each reinforces the other, with depiction information improving the accuracy of face labeling by a substantial margin. (Berg and colleagues give results under several different configurations; typical is to go from 56% to 72% accuracy of labeling a set of test faces (Berg et al., in review).

9.3.2 Modifiers and Attributes

Modifiers are often applied to nouns and suggest **attributes** of objects. Attributes are interesting, because they suggest how categories could be organized internally and perhaps with respect to one another. The way modifiers (such as "blue," "spotted," and so on) are used suggests that some within-class variation of objects is structured and shared between categories. This structure could be exploited, because modifiers refer to properties that many categories of object can share. Crucially, many attributes, particularly those dealing with material or appearance or color, can be observed in images. Yanai and Barnard (2005) have shown that some adjectives can be linked with visual attributes in a fairly straightforward manner, and that doing so can suggest

Figure 9.4. The same object can be depicted in multiple ways. *Left*, Each image can be interpreted as depicting a "crane," but in quite different ways. Appearance based clustering can do a fair job of clustering iconographic senses of an object. *Right*, Some crane images from a cluster built as part of work to understand the notion of iconographic sense (Alm et al. 2006; Loeff et al. 2006).

which image segments make up the object. For example, one might learn the visual consequences of the word "pink" on some data, and by doing so know where in an image a "pink cadillac" lay.

Attributes seem to allow aggressive generalization and possible improvements in training. Two forms of generalization seem to be available. First, if we learn object and attribute models, we may be able to identify new types of known objects; for example, from such data as "glass cup" and "tortoiseshell cat," we might be able to generalize to "glass cat." Second, if we consider the attributes of objects, we may be able to make statements about unknown objects; for example, we may not need to know a model for a "serval" to recognize what we see as a spotted cat of medium size with long legs, and to guess which end has teeth.

9.3.3 Iconography

The different ways in which people choose to depict objects seem to cluster into **iconographic senses** (Fig. 9.4). This idea extends the notion of visual aspect. For example, depicting a "crane" as a chick involves an important variation in appearance not governed by the notion of visual aspect. Iconographic regularities appear to be powerful cues that are exploited by, but not discussed in, the vision literature. For example, the Corel collection is a set of royalty-free images, organized into 100 CDs, and widely used in computer vision research. Chapelle et al. (1999) show that the CD an image came from can be predicted from its color histogram in the Corel collection (this seems to be a result of the tremendous regularity of the way objects are shown in this collection). Iconographic regularities most likely occur because people choose which pictures to take, keep, and display. Although the idea may be less significant for a freely moving visual agent, it is an important and seldom discussed feature of the world of Web images. Iconographic senses seem to be detectable by clustering (Fig. 9.4; Loeff et al. 2006). We expect that the language in captions may constrain the iconographic sense used, and again that discriminative methods applied to parses and surface phenomena may predict which sense will appear. For example, the caption "The glossy ibis is a migratory wading bird in the ibis family" suggests strongly that the picture shows a single glossy ibis prominently (rather than, say, a chick or an egg; more subtle, the caption – unlike the isolated phrase "ibis family" – does not suggest an image of proud ibis parents with eggs or chicks).

The hunt continues (just kidding)

A scene from Tuktoyaktuk: I am not sure why this five-year-old was chasin a dog with a stick.
(Note: Nobody hit the dog, it just looks this way in the picture.)

POSTED BY PHILIPPE MORRI AT MONDAY, MARCH 19, 2007 0 COMMENTS

Chasing a dog with a lobster on Flickr – Photo Sharing!

flickr

Home   The Tour   Sign Up   Explore

Chasing a dog with a lobster

Figure 9.5. The Web is spectacularly rich in labeled images. When one sees the phrase "chasing a dog with a stick," who has the stick? This problem is known as prepositional phrase attachment. One could find a possible answer on the Web if one had a simple object recognizer. At time of writing, there were three sites obtainable on Google using the exact phrase search "chasing a dog with a stick." The figure on the left shows an extract from one site, rendered as a browser would render it. The site is `http://inuvikpm`
`.blogspot.com/2007_03_01_archive.html`. A dog detector and a stick detector, both of which could practically be built, applied to the image would immediately disambiguate this prepositional phrase attachment. One might regard the "stick" as irrelevant and search for "chasing a dog with"; among other items, this yields a single example of a quite bizarre case (`http://www.flickr.com/photos/daveodroid/478332305/`, at flickr). There are fair nonvisualmethods for resolving prepositional phrase attachment, using rules (Kimball 1973; Frazier 1978), or semi-supervised (Volk 2002) or unsupervised data (Pantel and Lin 2000; Nakov and Hearst 2005), but the example indicates just how tightly the underlying meaning can link words and pictures.

9.4 Conclusion

Pictures in collections usually come with words nearby. These words are valuable. They can be used to help cluster images, to train object recognition systems, and to help classify images or image structures. Acknowledging and studying the syntactic structures within which these words appear seems to offer other information about pictures. Language analysis can offer strong constraints on what is present in the image. Language analysis shows how different instances of an object display different appearance phenomena. Language analysis may tell us what an object might look like. Because there are so many annotated images available, one can obtain quite unexpected data (Fig. 9.5). Other important phenomena, which, to our knowledge, have not yet been studied from the perspective of recognition, include how objects are in relations with one another ("The cat sits on the mat"), how objects may be acting on other objects to suggest future outcomes ("The cat is chasing the mouse"), and how one might generate captions for images.

Bibliography

Alm CO, Loeff N, Forsyth DA. 2006. Challenges for annotating images for sense disambiguation. In Proceedings of the workshop on frontiers in linguistically annotated corpora.

Ando RK, Zhang T. 2005. A high-performance semi-supervised learning method for text chunking. In Proceedings of the annual meeting of association for computational linguistic.

Andrews S, Tsochantaridis I, Hofmann T. 2003. Support vector machines for multiple-instance learning. In Proceedings of the NIPS 15, 561–568. Cambridge: MIT Press.

Armitage LH, Enser PGB. 1997. Analysis of user need in image archives. *J Info Sci* 23(4):287–299.

Barnard K, Duygulu P, Forsyth D, de Freitas N, Blei D, Jordan M. 2003. Matching words and pictures. *J Mach Learn Res* 3:1107–1135.

Barnard K, Duygulu P, Forsyth DA. 2001. Clustering art. In IEEE conference on computer vision and pattern recognition, II:434–441.

Barnard K, Forsyth DA. 2001. Learning the semantics of words and pictures. In International conference on computer vision, 408–415.

Barnard K, Johnson M. 2005. Word sense disambiguation with pictures. *Artif Intell* 167(1–2): 13–30.

Berg T, Berg A, Edwards J, Maire M, White R, Teh Y-W, Miller E, Forsyth DA. 2008 (in review). Names and faces.

Berg TL, Berg AC, Edwards J, Forsyth DA. 2004. Who's in the picture. In *Advances in neural information processing*.

Berg TL, Berg A, Forsyth DA. 2006. Animals on the web. In Proceedings of the IEEE conference computer vision and pattern recognition.

Berg TL, Forsyth DA. 2006. Animals on the web. In IEEE conference on computer vision and pattern recognition, vol 2, 1463–1470.

Blei DM, Jordan MI. 2003. Modeling annotated data. In Proceedings of the ACM SIGIR conference on research and development in information retrieval, 127–134.

Blei DM, Ng AY, Jordan MI. 2003. Latent Dirichlet allocation. *J Mach Learn Res* 3:993–1022.

Brown P, Della Pietra SA, Della Pietra VJ, Mercer RL. 1993. The mathematics of statistical machine translation: parameter estimation. *Comput Ling* 32(2):263–311.

Carneiro G, Chan AB, Moreno PJ, Vasconcelos N. 2007. Supervised learning of semantic classes for image annotation and retrieval. *IEEE Trans Pattern Anal Mach Intell* 29(3):394–410.

Carneiro G, Vasconcelos N. 2005. Formulating semantic image annotation as a supervised learning problem. In IEEE conference on computer vision and pattern recognition, 163–168.

Carson C, Belongie S, Greenspan H, Malik J. 2002. Blobworld – image segmentation using expectation-maximization and its application to image querying. *IEEE Trans Pattern Anal Mach Intell* 24(8):1026–1038.

Celebi E, Alpkocak. A. 2005. Combining textual and visual clusters for semantic image retrieval and auto-annotation. Proceedings of the second European workshop on knowledge semantics and digital media technology, 219–225.

Chapelle O, Haffner P, Vapnik V. 1999. Support vector machines for histogrambased image classification. *IEEE Neural Network* 10(5):1055–1064.

Chen Y, Wang JZ. 2004. Image categorization by learning and reasoning with regions. *J Mach Learn Res* 5:913–939.

Coyne B, Sproat R. 2001. Wordseye: an automatic text-to-scene conversion system. In SIGGRAPH: Proceedings of the 28th annual conference on computer graphics and interactive techniques, 487–496.

Crandall D, Huttenlocher D. 2007. Composite models of objects and scenes for category recognition. In IEEE conference on computer vision and pattern recognition.

Cunningham H, Maynard D, Bontcheva K, Tablan V. 2002. Gate: a framework and graphical development environment for robust nlp tools and applications. In 40th anniversary meeting of the association for computational linguistics.

Datta R, Li J, Wang JZ. 2005. Content-based image retrieval: approaches and trends of the new age. In Proceedings of the international workshop on multimedia information retrieval, 253–262.

Dietterich TG, Lathrop RH, Lozano-Pérez T. 1997. Solving the multiple instance problem with axis-parallel rectangles. *Artif Intell* 89(1–2):31–71.

Duygulu P, Barnard K, de Freitas N, Forsyth DA. 2002. Object recognition as machine translation. In European conference computer vision, IV:97–112.

Enser PGB. 2000. Visual image retrieval: seeking the alliance of concept based and content based paradigms. *J Inform Sci* 26(4):199–210.

Fei-Fei L, Koch C, Iyer A, Perona P. 2004. What do we see when we glance at a scene? *J Vision* 4(8):863–863.

Fei-Fei L, VanRullen R, Koch C, Perona P. 2002. Rapid natural scene categorization in the near absence of attention. Proceedings of the national academy of sciences.

Feng SL, Manmatha R, Lavrenko V. 2004. Multiple bernoulli relevance models for image and video annotation. *CVPR* 2:1002–1009.

Forsyth DA. 2001. Benchmarks for storage and retrieval in multimedia databases. In Proceedings of Spie – the international society for optical engineering, vol 4676, 240–247.

Frazier L. 1978. On comprehending sentences: syntactic parsing strategies. PhD diss., University of Connecticut.

Govindaraju V, Sher DB, Srihari RK, Srihari SN. 1989. Locating human faces in newspaper photographs. In IEEE conference on computer vision and pattern recognition, 549–554.

Hofmann T, Puzicha J. 1998. Statistical models for co-occurrence data. A.I. Memo 1635, Massachusetts Institute of Technology.

Houghton R. 1999. Named faces: putting names to faces. *IEEE Intell Syst* 14(5):45–50.

Jeon J, Lavrenko V, Manmatha R. 2003a. Automatic image annotation and retrieval using cross-media relevance models. In Proceedings of the ACM SIGIR conference on research and development in information retrieval, 119–126.

Jeon J, Lavrenko V, Manmatha R. 2003b. Automatic image annotation and retrieval using crossmedia relevance models. In Proceedings of the ACM SIGIR conference on research and development in information retrieval, 119–126.

Jeon J, Manmatha R. 2004. Using maximum entropy for automatic image annotation. In Proceedings of the ACM international conference on image and video retrieval, 24–32.

Jin R, Chai JY, Si L. 2004. Effective automatic image annotation via a coherent language model and active learning. In Multimedia, 892–899.

Joshi D, Wang JZ, Li J. 2004. The story picturing engine: finding elite images to illustrate a story using mutual reinforcement. In Proceedings of the international workshop on multimedia information retrieval.

Kimball J. 1973. Seven principles of surface structure parsing in natural language. *Cognition* 2:15–47.

Lavrenko V, Manmatha R, Jeon J. 2003a. A model for learning the semantics of pictures. In Neural information processing systems.

Lavrenko V, Manmatha R, Jeon J. 2003b. A model for learning the semantics of pictures. In Neural information processing systems.

Li J, Wang JZ. 2003. Automatic linguistic indexing of pictures by a statistical modeling approach. *IEEE Trans Pattern Anal Mach Intell* 25(10).

Li L-J, Fei-Fei L. 2007. What, where and who? Classifying event by scene and object recognition. In International conference on computer vision.

Loeff N, Alm CO, Forsyth DA. 2006. Discriminating image senses by clustering with multimodal features. In Proceedings of the COLING/ACL 2006 main conference poster sessions, 547–554.

Loeff N, Farhadi A, Forsyth D. 2008. Scene discovery by matrix factorization. Technical Report No. UIUCDCS-R-2008-2928.

Maron O, Lozano-Pérez T. 1998. A framework for multiple-instance learning. In NIPS '97: Proceedings of the 1997 conference on advances in neural information processing systems 10, 570–576. Cambridge: MIT Press.

Maron O, Ratan AL. 1998. Multiple-instance learning for natural scene classification. In Fifteenth international conference on machine learning.

Metzler D, Manmatha R. 2004. An inference network approach to image retrieval. In Proceedings of the ACM international conference on image and video retrieval, 42–50.

Mikolajczyk K. Face detector. Technical report, INRIA Rhone-Alpes. Ph.D report.

Monay F, Gatica-Perez D. 2003. On image auto-annotation with latent space models. In Multimedia: Proceedings of the eleventh ACM international conference on multimedia, 275–278. New York: ACM Press.

Mori Y, Takahashi H, Oka R. 1999. Image-to-word transformation based on dividing and vector quantizing images with words. In Proceedings of the first international workshop on multimedia intelligent storage and retrieval management.

Nakov P, Hearst M. 2005. Using the web as an implicit training set: application to structural ambiguity resolution. In Proceedings of the human language technologies, 835–842.

Oliva A, Torralba A. 2006. Building the gist of a scene: the role of global image features in recognition. *Visual Percep, Prog Brain Res* 155.

Pantel P, Lin D. 2000. An unsupervised approach to prepositional phrase attachment using contextually similar words. In Proceedings of the annual meeting of association for computational linguistic, 101–108.

Pinz A. 2006. Object categorization. *Found Trends Comput Graph Vis* 1(4):255–353.

Rabinovich A, Vedaldi A, Galleguillos C, Wiewiora E, Belongie S. 2007. Objects in context. In International conference on computer vision.

Ray S, Craven M. 2005. Supervised versus multiple instance learning: an empirical comparison. In ICML: Proceedings of the 22nd international conference on machine learning, 697–704. New York: ACM Press.

Satoh S, Kanade T. 1997. Name-it: Association of face and name in video. In IEEE conference on computer vision and pattern recognition.

Satoh S, Nakamura Y, Kanade T. 1999. Name-it: naming and detecting faces in news videos. IEEE Multimedia 6(1):22–35.

Schroff F, Criminisi A, Zisserman A. 2007. Harvesting image databases from the web. In International conference on computer vision.

Serre T, Wolf L, Bileschi S, Riesenhuber M, Poggio T. 2007. Object recognition with cortex-like mechanisms. *IEEE Trans Pattern Anal Mach Intell* 29(3):411–426.

Srihari RK. 1995. Automatic indexing and content based retrieval of captioned images. *Computer* 28(9):49–56.

Sudderth E, Torralba A, Freeman WT, Willsky A. In press. Describing visual scenes using transformed objects and parts. *Int J Comput Vis*.

Sudderth EB, Torralba A, Freeman WT, Willsky AS. 2005a. Describing visual scenes using transformed dirichlet processes. In *Advances in neural information processing*.

Sudderth EB, Torralba A, Freeman WT, Willsky AS. 2005b. Learning hierarchical models of scenes, objects and parts. In International conference on computer vision.

Tao Q, Scott S, Vinodchandran NV, Osugi TT. 2004. Svm-based generalized multiple-instance learning via approximate box counting. In ICML.

Torralba A, Fergus R, Freeman WT. 2007. Tiny images. Technical Report MITCSAIL-TR-2007-024, Computer Science and Artificial Intelligence Lab, Massachusetts Institute of Technology.

Torralba A, Murphy K, Freeman W, Rubin, M. 2003. Context-based vision system for place and object recognition. In International conference on computer vision.

Torralba A, Oliva A, Castelhano M, Henderson JM. 2006. Contextual guidance of attention in natural scenes: the role of global features on object search. *Psychol Rev* 113(4):766–786.

Viitaniemi V, Laaksonen J. 2007. Evaluating the performance in automatic image annotation: example case by adaptive fusion of global image features. *Image Commun* 22(6):557–568.

Volk M. 2002. Combining unsupervised and supervised methods for pp attachment disambiguation. In Proceedings of the 19th international conference on computational linguistics, 1–7. Morristown, NJ: Association for Computational Linguistics.

Wactlar H, Kanade T, Smith M, Stevens S. 1996. Intelligent access to digital video: the informedia project. *IEEE Comput* 29(5).

Wang G, Forsyth DA. 2008. Object image retrieval by exploiting online knowledge source (in review).

Wang JZ, Li J. 2002. Learning-based linguistic indexing of pictures with 2-d mhmms. In Proceedings of ACM multimedia. New York: ACM Press.

Wang Y, Liu Z, Huang J-C 2000. Multimedia content analysis-using both audio and visual clues. *IEEE Signal Process Mag* 17(6):12–36.

Yanai K, Barnard K. 2005. Image region entropy: a measure of "visualness" of web images associated with one concept. In Multimedia, 419–422.

Yang C, Dong M, Fotouhi F. 2005. Region based image annotation through multiple-instance learning. In Multimedia, 435–438.

Yang J, Hauptmann AG. 2004. Naming every individual in news video monologues. In Multimedia, 580–587.

Yavlinsky A, Schofield E, Rueger S. 2005. Automated image annotation using global features and robust nonparametric density estimation. In *Automated image annotation using global features and robust nonparametric density estimation*, 507–517.

Zhang Q, Goldman S. 2001. Em-dd: An improvedmultiple-instance learning technique. In Proc NIPS, 1073–1080.

Zhang Q, Goldman SA, Yu W, Fritts J. 2002. Content-based image retrieval using multiple-instance learning. In ICML, 682–689.

Zhang Z, Srihari RK, Rao A. 1999. Face detection and its applications in intelligent and focused image retrieval. In Eleventh IEEE international conference tools with artificial intelligence, 121–128.

CHAPTER 10

Structural Representation of Object Shape in the Brain

Siavash Vaziri, Anitha Pasupathy, Scott L. Brincat, and
Charles E. Connor

10.1 Introduction

In Chapter 1, Dickinson analyzes the complex history of theoretical and computational vision. With some exceptions, the trend in recent decades is away from explicit structural representation and toward direct mapping of image features to semantic categories based on machine learning. The best-known formulations of the older, structural paradigm are those of Marr (Marr and Nishihara 1978) and Biederman (1987), although the central idea that objects are represented as configurations of parts has a long history (Barlow 1972; Binford 1971; Dickinson, Pentland, and Rosenfeld 1992; Hoffman and Richards 1984; Hubel and Wiesel 1959, 1968; Milner 1974; Palmer 1975; Selfridge 1959; Sutherland 1968). A configural representation would be carried by ensembles of processing units or neurons, each encoding the shape and relative position of a constituent part. This coding format is appealing because it solves three major problems in object vision. The first problem is the enormous dimensionality (on the order of 10^6) of retinal activity patterns. A signal of this complexity is too unwieldy to communicate between brain regions (owing to wiring constraints) or store in memory (owing to limited information capacity of synaptic weight patterns). Compression of this signal into a list of part specifications on the order of 10^1 to 10^2 would make communication and storage more practical. The second problem is the extremely variable mapping between retinal images and object identity. The same object can produce an infinity of very different retinal images depending on its position, orientation, lighting, partial occlusion, and other factors. A configural description would be stable across these transformations if the spatial reference frame were defined by the object itself, as in the Marr and Biederman formulations. The third problem is representing the virtual infinity of potential object shapes in our world using a finite number of neurons. A parts-based, configural code would have the combinatorial capacity to span such an enormous domain.

In spite of these hypothetical advantages, structural representation did not take hold as an algorithmic solution for computational image processing. As Dickinson recounts, structural processing was practically successful only when applied to highly abstracted object stimuli. For recognition of objects in real images, problems of segmentation and shape abstraction made it too difficult to identify structural information. As a result, the structural coding paradigm has been replaced by machine learning approaches based directly on appearances of objects or object fragments (Fei-Fei, Fergus, and Perona 2006; Lowe 2004; Moghaddam and Pentland 1997; Murase and Nayar 1995; Riesenhuber and Poggio 1999; Turk and Pentland 1991; Weber, Welling, and Perona 2000). The appearance-based machine learning paradigm avoids segmentation and abstraction problems by forsaking the intermediate goal of representing object structure.

This opportunistic approach, based on gradual learning of natural image statistics across many presentations, has a very biological flavor. The brain is clearly adept at optimizing its use of statistical information in the natural environment to serve perceptual and behavioral goals (Ernst and Banks 2002; Kersten and Yuille 2003; Körding and Wolpert 2006; Mamassian, Landy, and Maloney 2002; Stocker and Simoncelli 2006; Weiss, Simoncelli, and Adelson 2002). Why should the same approach not be applied to the supremely difficult task of object recognition? The ability to recognize objects is perfected over years of exposure, a timeframe compatible with gradual learning of probabilistic relationships between image features and object categories. The brain is massively parallel (each neuron makes on the order of 10^4 synaptic connections) and the total number of such connections is astronomical, providing ample substrate for representing probability relationships. These relationships would be learned and encoded through the multiple intermediate processing stages in ventral pathway visual cortex. In this case, neural sensitivity to visual stimuli at these stages would be essentially uninterpretable. Each neuron would integrate information across diverse image features that are related only by their functional significance in the overall probability mapping. Patterns of feature sensitivity would be free to vary so widely within and between organisms that they would remain experimentally inscrutable. Neural responses with obvious meaning would emerge only at the final stage, with explicit coding for object categories of ecological importance or semantic meaning to the organism.

Through the 1980s, the state of neuroscientific knowledge was compatible with this view. Tuning for local image features had been described at early processing stages (e.g., orientation tuning in V1 and V2 (Baizer, Robinson, and Dow 1977; Burkhalter and Van Essen 1986; Hubel and Livingstone 1987; Hubel and Wiesel 1959, 1965, 1968), and selectivity for natural object categories (e.g., faces and hands) had been described at the highest levels in macaque monkey visual cortex (anterior inferotemporal cortex, or AIT) (Desimone et al. 1984; Gross et al. 1972; Perrett et al. 1982). Neural selectivity at intermediate stages was relatively unexplored. In the early 1990s, however, Tanaka and colleagues began to show that even face and hand responses in AIT could be interpreted in terms of component structure rather than categorical identity (Kobatake and Takana 1994; Tanaka et al. 1991). Later experiments showed that this component structure sensitivity is mapped across the surface of inferotemporal cortex in a columnar fashion (Fujita et al. 1992; Tsunoda et al. 2001). In parallel, experiments at intermediate processing stages in macaque areas V4 and PIT confirmed several basic tenets of the parts-based structural coding paradigm advanced by Marr and Biederman (Brincat and Connor 2004; Pasupathy and Connor 2001; Pasupathy and Connor 2002). Thus, during the same period in which computational vision became nonstructural, biological vision was discovered to be emphatically structural. Some of the critical evidence is reviewed in the following section.

10.2 Is Biological Object Vision Explicitly Structural?

The structural coding theories of Marr and Biederman make a strong prediction that runs directly counter to conventional thinking in neurophysiology over the last half century. The conventional notion is that neurons have one overall response peak in stimulus space. Given this, the basic selectivity of a neuron can be roughly defined by identifying a "best stimulus." This kind of characterization is apt for early stages of visual processing, in which stimulus selectivity is defined by the spatiotopic input structure of the receptive field. At these stages, the best stimulus is a template match to the spatiotopic sensitivity pattern. Thus, the receptive field structure and best stimulus for a retinal ganglion cell is a difference of Gaussians pattern, and for a V1 simple cell it is a 2-D Gabor pattern. The same notion of a single overall response peak in stimulus space has explicitly or implicitly informed almost all research on higher-level ventral pathway visual cortex as well. Most attempts to define response selectivity of higher-level neurons involve identifying, through random search, a maximally effective stimulus. The presence of other pattern information besides the maximally effective stimulus is expected to inhibit the response. Some results suggest that this inhibition amounts to an averaging between response levels across stimuli (Gawne and Martin 2002; Reynolds, Chelazzi, and Desimone 1999; Reynolds and Desimone 2003; Zoccolan, Cox, and DiCarlo 2005).

In contrast, structural coding predicts that neurons will have a virtual infinity of response peaks in stimulus space. This is because neurons must consistently encode the presence of spatially discrete parts within a variety of larger objects. Each neuron must be relatively insensitive to the rest of the global object structure. If responses were strongly inhibited or otherwise altered by that additional structure, the coding scheme would have no value. Thus, the rest of the object can take any number of shapes. As long as the relevant local structure is present, the neuron should respond near its maximum, in effect producing an infinity of response peaks in global shape space. The idea that neurons would respond maximally to an infinity of almost completely different stimulus patterns seems improbable, but it appears to be true at intermediate stages in ventral pathway visual cortex.

Figure 10.1A exemplifies the multipeaked nature of shape response patterns at intermediate stages in the ventral visual pathway. Previous studies had demonstrated that V4 neurons are tuned for the orientation and curvature of contours. The stimulus set for this subsequent experiment was constructed by factorial combination of contour fragments with varying orientation and curvature. Thus, any given fragment appears in a number of very different global shapes. Each stimulus was presented entirely within the V4 neuron's receptive field (RF), and control tests established that responses were consistent across different positions in the RF. This neuron responded to shapes containing a sharp convexity pointing to the lower left, especially when adjacent to a downward facing concavity (see stimuli labeled 1 and 2; either feature alone evoked weaker responses, as in stimuli 3–8). Figure 10.1 shows near maximum responses to

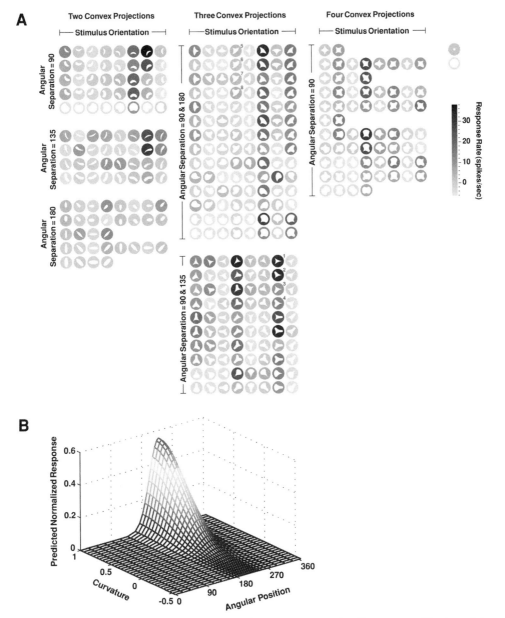

Figure 10.1. V4 shape tuning. *A*, Responses of a V4 neuron to stimuli constructed by factorial combination of boundary fragments. Spike activity of well-isolated individual neurons was recorded from the lower-field V4 representations of rhesus macaque monkeys performing a fixation task to stabilize eye position. Stimuli were flashed in the neuron's RF for 500 ms each in random order. Average responses across five repetitions are indicated by the background color for each stimulus. (The circular background was not part of the display.) This neuron was tuned for boundary fragments defined by sharp convexities facing to the lower left (225°) adjacent to shallow concave curvature facing downward (270°). *B*, Best-fitting Gaussian tuning function captures the neuron's sensitivity to convexity at 225°. Tuning domain axes represent angular position and curvature of boundary elements. Vertical axis and surface color represent normalized response predicted by the tuning function. To determine the best-fitting function, each shape was first decomposed into component boundary elements characterized by their curvatures and angular positions with respect to object center. Curvature runs from –1.0 (for sharp concavities) through 0.0 (for straight edges) to 1.0 for (sharp convexities). Predicted response for each stimulus depended on the value of the tuning function at domain points corresponding to its constituent surface fragments. Nonlinear regression was used to find the 2-D Gaussian function that minimized the sum of squared errors between predicted and observed responses. From Pasupathy and Connor, 2001; used with permission from the *Journal of Neurophysiology*. (See color plate 10.1.)

a wide variety of global shapes containing this local configuration. This strange response pattern makes sense only in terms of the parts-level structure that characterizes all the high-response stimuli. Similar results have been obtained for large samples of V4 neurons (Pasupathy and Connor 2001). Each neuron faithfully encodes some characteristic contour fragment in one part of the stimulus while remaining relatively unaffected by global shape. Such results are highly improbable under any theory besides parts-level structural coding.

The larger prediction of structural coding theories is that ensemble activity patterns across such neurons encode global stimulus shapes. That prediction was tested by reconstructing the V4 population responses to the stimuli used in this experiment. For this purpose, neural contour shape sensitivities were quantified with 2-D Gaussian tuning functions (Fig. 10.1B). The domain represents contour fragment angular position and curvature. The best-fitting Gaussian for this neuron captures its sensitivity to sharp convexity (curvature values near 1.0) at the lower left (225°). (More complex models can be used to capture combined sensitivity to this convexity and the adjacent concavity.) The same kind of function was fit to the responses of 109 V4 neurons. To reconstruct a stimulus (e.g., Fig. 10.2a), each neuron's tuning function was weighted by its response to that stimulus, and the weighted response functions were summed to obtain a pattern like that shown in Figure 10.2b. This pattern contains multiple peaks corresponding to constituent contour fragments. These peaks were used to guide a spline-based shape reconstruction algorithm, which produced a reasonable approximation to the original stimulus shape (Fig. 10.2c). Similar results were obtained for other shapes in the stimulus set (Pasupathy and Connor 2002). Thus, parts-sensitive V4 neurons carry sufficient information to encode the structure of moderately complex object boundaries.

Another prediction of classic structural models is that part position is encoded in a spatial reference frame defined relative to the object itself. This is an important aspect of the theory, because it confers invariance to the image transformations so common in natural vision (translation, rotation, scaling). However, it involves a major transformation of spatial information from the original retinotopic reference frame. Thus, this is another strong prediction that is inconsistent with most other theories and evidence about visual representation.

This prediction, too, turns out to be at least partially supported by neurophysiological evidence from intermediate stages in the macaque monkey ventral pathway. Neural tuning for object-defined position is evident in V4 (Pasupathy and Connor 2001), and even more striking in the next processing stage (PIT), where RFs are larger and provide more scope for testing the effect of position (Brincat and Connor 2004). Figure 10.3 exemplifies PIT tuning for object-centered position of contour fragments. The stimuli shown here are a subset of 500 complex shape stimuli used to probe the selectivity of PIT neurons. Responses across this stimulus set showed that the example neuron in Figure 10.3 was sensitive to opposed concavities associated with a downward projecting limb. The neuron only responded when this configuration occurred to the left of object center, as in the top block of selected stimuli in Figure 10.3. The average response to these stimuli as a function of time following stimulus onset is shown at the right. When the same configuration of two concavities was present to the right of object center (Fig. 10.3, bottom panel), responses were weak or absent. This kind of selectivity for object-centered position was a strong tuning characteristic across a large sample

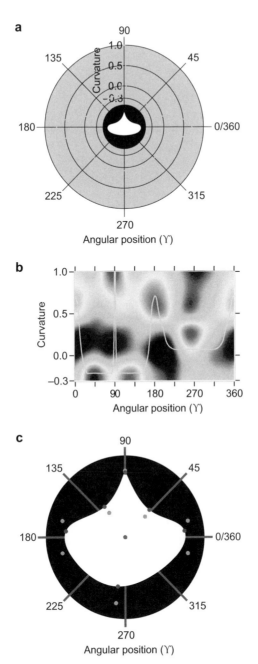

Figure 10.2. Shape reconstruction from V4 neural population response. (**a**) The original stimulus shape is shown at the center of a plot of boundary curvature (radial axis) as a function of angular position (polar axis) (white line). (**b**) Estimated V4 population response across the curvature × position domain (colored surface) with the veridical curvature function superimposed (white line). (**c**) Reconstruction of stimulus shape from the population surface in (b). From Pasupathy and Connor 2002. (See color plate 10.2.)

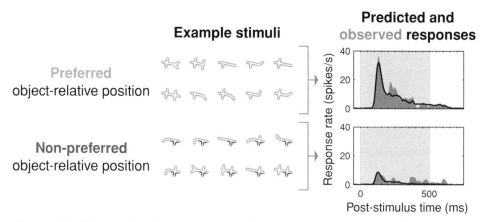

Figure 10.3. PIT tuning for object-centered position. These results are a subset from an experiment in which PIT neural responses were recorded from awake, fixating monkeys. Stimuli were constructed by factorial combination of boundary fragments. This neuron was highly selective for a configuration of opposed concavities positioned to the left of object center, as in the top panel. For these stimuli, the average response is high, as shown by the peristimulus-time response histogram at the right. In the stimuli shown in the bottom panel, the identical double-concavity configuration is positioned to the right of object center, and average response is low. (See color plate 10.3.)

of PIT neurons. Control tests (not shown) established that tuning for object-centered position was consistent across large changes in retinotopic stimulus position. This result confirms another key prediction of structural coding theories and establishes that part-position signals would be invariant to object translation (at least within the span of PIT RFs). Object-relative position signals would provide the configural information required to distinguish different arrangements of the same parts.

The results just described demonstrate structural coding of two-dimensional shape. Object shape is represented in two dimensions on the retina, and two-dimensional shape analysis is bound to be faster and more efficient. However, the classic theories of Marr and Biederman envision structural representation of 3-D shape. If achievable, 3-D shape representation has the advantages of greater stability across views and more direct relationship to inherent object structure. Recent results (Yamane et al. 2008) show that 3-D object structure is encoded by neurons in the final stages of the macaque ventral pathway in central and anterior inferotemporal cortex (CIT/AIT). These neurons are tuned for 3-D spatial configurations of object surface fragments with specific orientations and surface curvatures. This essentially confirms another strong prediction of classic structural coding theories.

In summary, there is clear evidence for parts-based structural coding in the brain. Correlation of V4, PIT, CIT, and AIT neural responses with 2-D and 3-D parts-level shape, decorrelation from global shape, and tuning for object-relative position of parts all fulfill major predictions that are peculiar to structural coding theories. Additional object representation schemes may be implemented at higher levels of visual cortex, in prefrontal cortex (Freedman et al. 2001), or in memory-related limbic structures (Quiroga et al. 2005), especially for behaviorally relevant or unique object categories (Baker, Behrmann, and Olson 2002). Nonstructural processing of image features may underlie extremely rapid, feedforward recognition (Hung et al. 2005; Serre, Oliva, and

Poggio 2007), but it seems clear that, for some purposes, explicit representation of object structure is a major aspect of biological vision.

10.3 Is Computational Vision Secretly Structural?

The gap between biological and computational vision could be at least partly illusory. The fact that object structure is represented so explicitly by neurons suggests that structural information must be useful. If so, perhaps it emerges spontaneously during the process of learning how to identify semantic object categories in images. Careful examination of intermediate representations in machine learning models might reveal such emergent structural information, in the form of correlation between internal activation levels and object structure. Of course, input image features themselves correlate with object structure at specific positions, scales, and orientations. Thus, a critical test would be whether structural correlations generalize across position, scale, and/or orientation. This would demonstrate that the system abstracts structural information from multiple image features as a step toward identification. The alternative would be a highly variable relationship to object structure at different positions and scales, showing that internal structural representation is unnecessary for image-based identification.

As a preliminary approach to this question, we implemented a supervised neural network model to test for spontaneous emergence of internal structural coding. For stimuli, we chose a subset of shapes previously used to study PIT (see Fig. 10.3), because there is evidence that these shapes are represented structurally in visual cortex (Brincat and Connor 2004). For the input layer, we simulated V4-like tuning for contour fragment shape and position (see Figs. 10.1 and 10.2). These V4-like input units connect to hidden-layer units that could be considered analogous to PIT. The PIT units in turn connect to output units that encode shape identity (in a distributed, rather than labeled-line, fashion, for greater biological realism). During training, stimulus shapes were presented at multiple random positions, and the network was required to produce consistent identification across position. This would naturally enhance the utility of consistent sensitivity to structure across position. In this first-pass, highly simplified test, stimulus orientation and scale were constant, so only generalization across position was required.

Explicit structural coding failed to emerge in the hidden (PIT) layer, as evidenced by the inconsistency of fragment shape tuning across position. Figure 10.4 illustrates that typical hidden units accumulated inputs across the entire stimulus position space but did not extract consistent shape structure at those different positions. Results from eight training runs are displayed (columns). For each run, an average hidden unit is presented in the top row. In each case, the 25 input tuning functions for that hidden unit (derived by back-propagation) are represented by 25 colored contour fragment icons. The icons depict Gaussian input tuning function peaks (in the curvature, orientation, and position dimensions), and their colors represent input weight (see scale at right). Visual inspection reveals that there is little or no consistency across input contour structures – they vary widely in curvature and orientation. Thus, these hidden units do not carry consistent signals for stimulus structure.

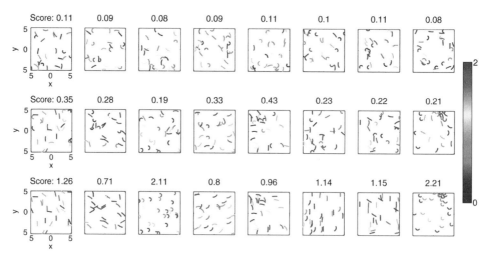

Figure 10.4. Hidden layer tuning in a shape identification network. A three-layer, feedforward neural network was trained using back-propagation to discriminate between 196 2-D shapes (Brincat and Connor 2004) in a position-invariant manner, across 36 random positions spanning 10×10 arbitrary units (average stimulus length = 3 units). Stimuli were described as combinations of contour fragments, with each fragment defined by its curvature, orientation, and x,y-position (Brincat and Connor 2004). Thus, the input corresponding to each stimulus was a set of 4-D vectors representing its contour components. Each V4-like input layer unit was modeled as a product of 4 Gaussian tuning functions, in the curvature, orientation, and x,y-position dimensions (Pasupathy and Connor 2001; Brincat and Connor 2004). The input unit's response to a contour fragment was the amplitude of the 4-D Gaussian at that point in the stimulus domain. The input unit's overall response to a given stimulus was the sum of Gaussian amplitude values for all the contour fragments making up that stimulus.

Each of the 30 hidden units received feedforward connections from 25 input units. (Simulations with fewer hidden units suffered substantial decrements in performance.) Input-layer tuning was not fixed; instead, the tuning parameters for all 25 inputs to each hidden unit were adjusted during training. This made it possible to simulate input from a much larger potential pool of input units. The output layer consisted of eight nodes constrained to represent stimulus identity (regardless of position) with an arbitrary binary code. (Similar results were obtained with other output conditions, including simple maximization of Euclidean distance between output layer activation patterns.) Each hidden unit provided feedforward connections to all eight output nodes. Each connection was modulated by a sigmoidal nonlinearity.

Back-propagation (Rumelhart et al. 1986) was used to adjust input-layer tuning parameters (Gaussian means and standard deviations in the contour curvature, orientation, and position dimensions), connection weights, and sigmoidal output function slopes and offsets. The cost function minimized during training was the mean sum of squared differences between the target and actual responses of the output nodes across all training stimuli (batch algorithm). The cost function included additive penalty terms that constrained the range of network parameters. The training criterion was failure to improve identification performance (nearest neighbor classification) on a validation stimulus set (same shapes at 36 newly generated random positions) across 20 consecutive iterations. Classification accuracy (averaged over 10 separate runs) was $90 +/- 2\%$ on the training stimuli and $84 +/- 3\%$ on the validation stimuli, indicating good generalization to stimulus positions outside the training set

Top row, Typical hidden unit connection patterns for eight training runs (*columns*). In each panel, the curvatures, orientations, and positions of the contour icons represent the 4-D Gaussian tuning peaks for the 25 V4-like inputs to the hidden unit. Color represents input connection strength (see scale at right). Due to the high variability in structural tuning (curvature and orientation) across positions, the structural coding scores (given above each panel; see text) for these hidden units were low (0.08 to 0.11). In each case, the unit chosen for illustration had the structural coding score closest to the mean for that run. *Middle row*, Hidden units with maximum structural coding scores in each run. The structural coding scores for these units ranged from 0.19 to 0.43. *Bottom row*, Idealized hidden units exemplifying robust structural coding. In each case, the observed hidden unit from the middle row was adjusted to produce consistent structural signals across the position domain. This was achieved by identifying input functions in the top quartile of partial structural coding scores, and replacing all other input functions with curvature/orientation values drawn from this top quartile. These hypothetical units exhibit much higher structural coding scores ranging from 0.71 to 2.21. (See color plate 10.4.)

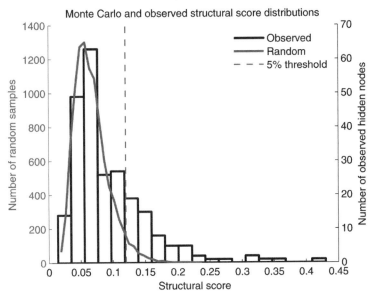

Figure 10.5. Distribution of hidden unit structural coding scores. A distribution of scores expected by chance (red) was generated by randomization (see text). The fifth percentile point on this distribution corresponds to a score of 0.12. Out of 240 hidden unit scores in eight training runs (black), only 60 fell above this threshold.

We quantified hidden unit structural coding with an index based on pairwise relationships between input tuning functions. Structural coding implies that many pairs of inputs should show similar structural tuning (proximity in the curvature and orientation dimensions) even when they are tuned for distant spatial positions. Thus the ratio of structural proximity to spatial proximity should be relatively high. Our structural coding score for each hidden unit was the sum of these pairwise ratios:

$$\text{structural score} = \sum_{\substack{i,j \\ i \neq j}}^{\text{all contour pairs}} w_i w_j \frac{e^{-\frac{1}{2}\left(\frac{\left(\mu_{cr}^i - \mu_{cr}^j\right)^2}{avg\left(\sigma_{i,cr}^2, \sigma_{i,cr}^2\right)} + \frac{\left(\mu_{or}^i - \mu_{or}^j\right)^2}{avg\left(\sigma_{i,or}^2, \sigma_{i,or}^2\right)}\right)}}{1 + e^{-\frac{1}{2}\left(\frac{\left(\mu_{posx}^i - \mu_{posx}^j\right)^2}{avg\left(\sigma_{i,posx}^2, \sigma_{j,posx}^2\right)} + \frac{\left(\mu_{posy}^i - \mu_{posy}^j\right)^2}{avg\left(\sigma_{i,posy}^2, \sigma_{j,posy}^2\right)}\right)}}$$

where μ denotes Gaussian tuning function peak or mean, σ denotes standard deviation, and the subscripts $cr, or, posx,$ and $posy$ denote curvature, orientation, x- and y-position, respectively. The contribution of each tuning function pair is weighted by its connection strengths, w_i and w_j. For hypothetical units with highly consistent curvature/orientation tuning across position, scores ranged from 0.71 to 2.21 (Fig. 10.4, bottom row).

We used a randomization test to assess the statistical significance of structural information in our models. We generated an expected distribution of structural scores by applying the formula to random combinations of 25 V4 input functions selected from the entire set of input functions across all hidden units in all training runs (Fig. 10.5, red). The 5% significance threshold on this distribution is 0.12. Across 8 training runs with 30 hidden units each, the majority of hidden units (180/240,

75%) fell below this threshold. Even among units reaching statistical significance, the maximum structural coding scores ranged from 0.19 to 0.43 (Fig. 10.4, middle row). In contrast, hypothetical units with highly consistent structural tuning had scores ranging from 0.71 to 2.21 (Fig. 10.4, bottom row), an order of magnitude above average observed scores (Fig. 10.4, top row). Thus, some degree of significant structural consistency was observed, but it was not common or substantial enough to explain recognition performance. Similar results were obtained even when object-relative position was included as an input-layer tuning dimension (data not shown). It is difficult to prove a negative, and more realistic recognition problems might lead to spontaneous emergence of structural coding. At a minimum, however, these simulations offer an existence proof that, under highly simplified conditions, networks can learn to map image inputs to object identity without explicit internal representation of object structure.

10.4 Reconciling Biological and Computer Vision

As described in section 10.3, neurons in higher-level primate visual cortex explicitly represent configural object structure. Yet, the current computational vision literature suggests that structural representation is neither sufficient nor necessary for object recognition. Dickinson argues in this volume that the quest for further increases in recognition performance may eventually force computational models back toward structural processing, which would bring computational and biological vision back in line. If, however, the most successful models remain nonstructural, how might that be reconciled with the neurophysiological findings described above? One way would be to conclude that structural representation in visual cortex does not exist to support recognition. In fact, structural representations may evolve too slowly (on the order of 200 ms) to explain the rapidity of human object recognition (Brincat and Connor 2006). On rapid time scales, recognition may depend on the kind of feedforward processing of image features that characterizes recognition based on machine learning (Hung et al. 2005; Serre et al. 2007).

On this view, structural representation in visual cortex must serve other goals. Recognition, in the sense of semantic categorization and associative recall, has been the dominant paradigm for both biological and computational vision science, but recognition-based recall is only one aspect of visual understanding, and it is limited to generalizations across previous experience. Real objects, whether recognized or unfamiliar, present a wealth of unique, continuously evolving, detailed information through their structure and behavior (cf. Gibson 1979). Visual experience of a dog is not limited to recall of generic facts about dogs. It involves detailed appreciation of the particular dog's skeletal and muscular structure, markings and scars, posture and movements, which provides an immediate sense of its strength, speed, ferocity, breeding, age, and history. Physical interaction with a dog depends on accurate perception of its structure to achieve precise contact and physical control and to avoid physical injury. These evaluative and interactive aspects of real-world vision seem likely to depend on the kind of structural information observed in ventral pathway visual cortex. Recognition alone may not require structural representation, but real-world vision may demand it.

As long as computational vision remains focused on recognition only, it may not require structural information. In fact, nonstructural processing in current recognition models may accurately model biological mechanisms for rapid recognition. At some point, however, computer vision systems will be tasked with flexible evaluation of and precise physical interaction with highly variable real-world objects. At that point, computational vision researchers will be facing the same real-world problems that guided the evolution of biological vision. It may then become essential to impose or learn the same solution discovered by the brain – internal representation of object structure.

Bibliography

Baker CI, Behrmann M, Olson CR. 2002. Impact of learning on representation of parts and wholes in monkey inferotemporal cortex. *Nat Neurosci* 5(11): 1210–1216.

Baizer JS, Robinson DL, Dow BM. 1977. Visual responses of area 18 neurons in awake, behaving monkey. *J Neurophysiol* 40: 1024–1037.

Barlow HB. 1972. Single units and sensation: a neuron doctrine for perceptual psychology? *Perception* 1(4): 371–394.

Biederman I. 1987. Recognition-by-components: a theory of human image understanding. *Psychol Rev* 94(2): 115–147.

Binford TO. 1971. Visual perception by computer. In Proceedings of IEEE conference on systems and control, Miami, FL.

Brincat SL, Connor CE. 2004. Underlying principles of visual shape selectivity in posterior inferotemporal cortex. *Nature Neurosci* 7(8): 880–886.

Brincat SL, Connor CE. 2006. Dynamic shape synthesis in posterior inferotemporal cortex. *Neuron* 49(1): 17–24.

Burkhalter A, Van Essen DC. 1986. Processing of color, form and disparity information in visual areas VP and V2 of ventral extrastriate cortex in the macaque monkey. *J Neurosci* 6(8): 2327–2351.

Desimone R, Albright TD, Gross CG, Bruce CJ. 1984. Stimulus-selective properties of inferior temporal neurons in the macaque. *J Neurosci* 4(8): 2051–2062.

Dickinson SJ, Pentland AP, Rosenfeld A. 1992. From volumes to views: an approach to 3-D object recognition. *CVGIP: Image Und* 55: 130–154.

Ernst MO, Banks MS. 2002. Humans integrate visual and haptic information in a statistically optimal fashion. *Nature* 415(6870): 429–433.

Fei-Fei L, Fergus R, Perona P. 2006. One-shot learning of object categories. *IEEE Trans Pattern Anal Mach Intell* 28(4): 594–611.

Freedman DJ, Riesenhuber M, Poggio T, Miller EK. 2001. Categorical representation of visual stimuli in the primate prefrontal cortex. *Science* 291(5502): 312–316.

Fujita I, Tanaka K, Ito M, Cheng K. 1992. Columns for visual features of objects in monkey inferotemporal cortex. *Nature* 360: 343–346.

Gawne TJ, Martin JM. 2002. Responses of primate visual cortical V4 neurons to simultaneously presented stimuli. *J Neurophysiol* 88: 1128–1135.

Gibson JJ. 1979. *The ecological approach to visual perception*. Boston: Houghton Mifflin.

Gross CG, Rocha-Miranda CE, Bender DB. 1972. Visual properties of neurons in inferotemporal cortex of the Macaque. *J Neurophysiol* 35(1): 96–111.

Hoffman DD, Richards WA. 1984. Parts of recognition. *Cognition* 18(1–3): 65–96.

Hubel DH, Livingstone MS. 1987. Segregation of form, color, and stereopsis in primate area 18. *J Neurosci* 7(11): 3378–3415.

Hubel DH, Wiesel TN. 1959. RFs of single neurones in the cat's striate cortex. *J Physiol* 148: 574–591.

Hubel DH, Wiesel TN. 1965. Receptive fields and functional architecture in two nonstriate visual areas (18 and 19) of the cat. *J Neurophysiol* 28(2): 229–289.

Hubel DH, Wiesel TN. 1968. Receptive fields and functional architecture of monkey striate cortex. *J Physiol* 195(1): 215–243.

Hung CP, Kreiman G, Poggio T, DiCarlo JJ. 2005. Fast readout of object identity from macaque inferior temporal cortex. *Science* 310(5749): 863–866.

Kersten D, Yuille A. 2003. Bayesian models of object perception. *Curr Opin Neurobiol* 13: 150–158.

Kobatake E, Tanaka K. 1994. Neuronal selectivities to complex object features in the ventral visual pathway of the macaque cerebral cortex. *J Neurophysiol* 71(3): 856–867.

Körding KP, Wolpert DM. 2006. Bayesian decision theory in sensory motor control. *Trends Cogn Sci* 10(7): 319–326.

Lowe D. 2004. Distinctive image features from scale-invariant keypoints. *Int J Comput Vision* 60(2): 91–110.

Mamassian P, Landy M, Maloney LT. 2002. Bayesian modeling of visual perception. In *Probabilistic models of the brain: perception and neural function*, ed. RPN Rao, BA Olshausen, and MS Lewicki, 13–36. Cambridge: MIT Press.

Marr D, Nishihara HK. 1978. Representation and recognition of the spatial organization of three-dimensional shapes. *Proc R Soc B: Biol Sci* 200(1140): 269–294.

Milner PM. 1974. A model for visual shape recognition. *Psychol Rev* 81(6): 521–535.

Moghaddam B, Pentland A. 1997. Probabilistic visual learning for object representation. *IEEE Trans Pattern Anal Mach Intell* 19(7): 696–710.

Murase H, Nayar SK. 1995. Visual learning and recognition of 3-D objects from appearance. *Int J Comput Vision* 14: 5–24.

Palmer SE. 1975. Visual perception and world knowledge: notes on a model of sensory-cognitive interaction. In *Explorations in cognition*, ed. DA Norman and DE Rumelhart, 279–307. San Francisco: WH Freeman.

Pasupathy A, Connor CE. 2001. Shape representation in area V4: position-specific tuning for boundary conformation. *J Neurophysiol* 86(5): 2505–2519.

Pasupathy A, Connor CE. 2002. Population coding of shape in area V4. *Nat Neurosci* 5(12): 1332–1338.

Perrett DI, Rolls ET, Caan W. 1982. Visual neurones responsive to faces in the monkey temporal cortex. *Exp Brain Res* 47(3): 329–342.

Quiroga RQ, Reddy L, Kreiman G, Koch C, Fried I. 2005. Invariant visual representation by single neurons in the human brain. *Nature* 435(7045): 1102–1107.

Reynolds JH, Chelazzi L, Desimone R. 1999. Competitive mechanisms subserve attention in macaque areas V2 and V4. *J Neurosci* 19(5): 1736–1753.

Reynolds JH, Desimone R. 2003. Interacting roles of attention and visual salience in V4. *Neuron* 37(5): 853–863.

Riesenhuber M, Poggio T. 1999. Hierarchical models of object recognition in cortex. *Nat Neurosci* 2(11): 1019–1025.

Rumelhart DE, Hinton GE, Williams RJ. 1986. Learning internal representations by error propagation. In *Parallel distributed processing*, vol. 1, ed. LJ McClelland and DE Rumelhart, 318–362. Cambridge: MIT Press.

Selfridge OG. 1959. Pandemonium: A paradigm for learning. In *The mechanization of thought process*. London: H.M. Stationary Office.

Serre T, Oliva A, Poggio T. 2007. A feedforward architecture accounts for rapid categorization. *Proc Nat Acad Sci* 104(15): 6424–6429.

Stocker AA, Simoncelli EP. 2006. Noise characteristics and prior expectations in human visual speed perception. *Nat Neurosci* 9: 578–585.

Sutherland NS. 1968. Outlines of a theory of visual pattern recognition in animals and man. *Proc R Soc B: Biol Sci* 171: 297–317.

Tanaka K, Saito H, Fukada Y, Moriya M. 1991. Coding visual images of objects in the inferotemporal cortex of the macaque monkey. *J Neurophysiol* 66(1): 170–189.

Tsunoda K, Yamane Y, Nishizaki M, Tanifuji M. 2001. Complex objects are represented in macaque inferotemporal cortex by the combination of feature columns. *Nat Neurosci* 4(8): 832–838.

Turk M, Pentland A. 1991. Eigenfaces for recognition. *J Cogn Neurosci* 3(1): 71–86.

Weber M, Welling M, Perona P. 2000. Towards automatic discovery of object categories. In Proceedings of the IEEE conference on computer vision and pattern recognition 2101–2108.

Weiss Y, Simoncelli EP, Adelson EH. 2002. Motion illusions as optimal percepts. *Nature Neurosci* 5(6): 598–604.

Yamane Y, Carlson ET, Bowman KC, Wang Z, Connor CE. 2008. A neural code for three-dimensional object shape in macaque inferotemporal cortex. *Nature Neurosci* 11(11): 1352–1360.

Zoccolan D, Cox DD, DiCarlo JJ. 2005. Multiple object response normalization in monkey inferotemporal cortex. *J Neurosci* 25(36): 8150–8164.

CHAPTER 11

Learning Hierarchical Compositional Representations of Object Structure

Sanja Fidler, Marko Boben, and Aleš Leonardis

11.1 Introduction

Visual categorization of objects has captured the attention of the vision community for decades (Dickinson 2008). The increased popularity of the problem witnessed in recent years and the advent of powerful computer hardware have led to a seeming success of categorization approaches on the standard datasets such as Caltech-101 (Fei-Fei et al. 2004). However, the high level of discrepancy between the accuracy of object classification and detection/segmentation (Everingham et al. 2007) suggests that the problem still poses a significant and open challenge. The recent preoccupation with tuning the approaches to specific datasets might have averted attention from the most crucial issue: the representation (Edelman and Intrator 2004).

This chapter focuses on what we believe are two central representational design principles: a hierarchical organization of categorical representations, or, more specifically, the principles of *hierarchical compositionality* and *statistical, bottom-up learning*.

Given images of complex scenes, objects must be inferred from the pixel information through some recognition process. This requires an efficient and robust matching of the internal object representation against the representation produced from the scene. Despite the seemingly effortless performance of human perception, the diversity and the shear number of visual object classes appearing at various scales, 3-D views, and articulations have placed a great obstacle to the task. In fact, it has been shown by Tsotsos (1990) that the unbounded visual search is NP complete; thus, approximate, hierarchical solutions might be the most promising or plausible way to tackle the problem. This line of architecture is also consistent with the findings on biological systems (Rolls and Deco 2002; Connor et al. 2007). A number of authors have further emphasized these computational considerations (Ettinger 1987; Geman et al. 2002; Amit 2002; Shokoufandeh et al. 2006; Hinton 2007), suggesting that matching should be performed at multiple hierarchical stages, in order to gradually and coherently limit the otherwise computationally prohibitive search space (Ettinger 1987; Tsotsos 1990; Califano and Mohan 1994; Amit and Geman 1999; Mel and Fiser 2000; Amit

2002; Geman et al. 2002; Fidler et al. 2006; Shokoufandeh et al. 2006; Fidler and Leonardis 2007). While hierarchies presented a natural way to represent objects in the early vision works (Ettinger 1987; Grimson and Lozano-Perez 1987; Medioni et al. 1989; Dickinson et al. 1992), surprisingly, they have not become an integral part of the modern vision approaches.

Hierarchical representations can derive and organize the features at multiple levels that build on top of each other by exploiting the shareability of features among more complex compositions or objects themselves (Ettinger 1987; Bienenstock and Geman 1995; Fleuret and Geman 2001; Amit 2002; Krempp et al. 2002; Hawkins and Blakeslee 2004; Torralba et al. 2007; Ommer and Buhmann 2007; Ullman 2007). Sharing features, on the one hand, means sharing common computations, which brings about the much desired computational efficiency. Moreover, reusing the commonalities between objects can put their representations in relation, thus possibly leading to high generalization capabilities (Ettinger 1987; Krempp et al. 2002; Torralba et al. 2007). A number of hierarchical recognition systems have been proposed that confirmed the success of such representations in object categorization tasks (Fukushima et al. 1983; Amit and Geman 1999; Fleuret and Geman 2001; Sudderth et al. 2005; Scalzo and Piater 2005; Agarwal and Triggs 2006; Shokoufandeh et al. 2006; Ullman and Epshtein 2006; Mikolajczyk et al. 2006; Nistér and Stewénius 2006; Torralba et al. 2007; Ranzato et al. 2007; Ommer and Buhmann 2007; Fritz and Schiele 2008; Todorovic and Ahuja 2007).

It must be emphasized, however, that hierarchical representations do not necessarily imply computational efficiency and representational plausibility. In this chapter, we will argue for a special form of a multilayered architecture – a *compositional hierarchy*. The nodes in such a hierarchy are formed as compositions that, recursively, model loose spatial relationships between their constituent components. The abundant computational arguments accumulated throughout the history of computational vision speak in favor of its efficiency, robustness to clutter, and flexibility to capture structural variability. Although the classical neural networks have been commonly thought to be a faithful model of the hierarchical processing in the brain, interestingly, ideas of compositional units have also started to emerge in the neuroscience community (Anzai et al. 2007; Connor et al. 2007; Tsunoda et al. 2001).

There have been a number of attempts at compositional categorical representations (Ettinger 1987; Dickinson et al. 1992; Geman et al. 2002; Califano and Mohan 1994; Amit and Geman 1999; Amit 2002); however, the lack of automation might have been a major contributing factor that prevented better realizations of these ideas. It is, in fact, the absence of *unsupervised, bottom-up learning* principles that also seems to be a source of criticism by the neuroscience community targeted at today's computational models of vision (Op de Beeck et al. 2008). By statistically learning the priors to bindings of local features, the representation emerging in this way would be well adjusted to the regularities present in images and could thus reliably, robustly, and quickly form hierarchical groupings, which would facilitate the final recognition of objects.

Based upon the computational considerations of compositional hierarchies and benefits of bottom-up, unsupervised learning, we will summarize our recent approach to representing object categories within a *learnable, hierarchical compositional framework*. The developed *bottom-up, statistical approach* makes use of simple atomic features (i.e., oriented edges) to gradually learn more complex contour compositions that model loose spatial relations between the constituent features. The learned hierarchical vocabulary of features, termed "parts," is organized in accordance with the principle of efficient indexing. This ensures that local retrieval of compositional models during the online object recognition stage runs in a roughly constant time, despite an exponential increase in the number of vocabulary features along the hierarchical layers. An offline grouping stage of part labels brings additional flexibility into the learned representation. The learned contour compositions can be further combined into categorical nodes with minimal human supervision, whereby the hierarchical sharing of features and the efficient indexability constraints could present an important step towards scalable representations of object categories.

The remainder of this chapter is organized as follows. In section 11.2 we argue for the design principles we believe are important to build a plausible representation of object structure. Section 11.3 reviews the work most related to ours. Section 11.4 is more technical and summarizes our recently developed approach to learning hierarchical compositional representations of object structure. The experimental results are presented in section 11.5. The chapter concludes with a summary and discussion in Section 11.6.

11.2 Design Principles for Representing Object Structure

A representation must drive the recognition process from the pixel level through more and more complex interpretations towards object categories themselves. It is thus critical to devote our attention to design principles that would accommodate for scalability and generalizability of the representation and robustness, as well as efficiency, of the subsequent recognition. This section brings forward two issues we believe are crucial for forming plausible representations of object structure.

We will argue for hierarchical compositionality as the line of representational architecture, and the principle of unsupervised, bottom-up learning that statistically extracts the multiple layers of representation from images, making it adjustable to the regularities present in the otherwise highly variable structure of objects.

11.2.1 Hierarchical Compositionality

Compositionality refers to a property of hierarchical representational systems that define their internal nodes in terms of simpler constituent components according to a set of production rules (Bienenstock and Geman 1995). The rules of composition usually take the form of the Gestalt laws of grouping (Ommer and Buhmann 2007; Ferrari et al. 2008) or similar forms of predefined bindings (Ettinger 1987; Amit and Geman 1999; Shokoufandeh et al. 2006; Todorovic and Ahuja 2007; Zhu and Mumford 2006) that in some form or another incorporate spatial relations into the compositional features. Computational benefits of compositionality in terms of storage, processing demands, robustness to clutter, and the exponential expressive power have long been emphasized in the computer vision literature (Bienenstock 1996; Amit and Geman 1999; Geman et al. 2002; Zhu and Yuille 2005; Zhu and Mumford 2006; Fidler and

Leonardis 2007; Califano and Mohan 1994). We elaborate on these issues in the sections that follow.

Storage requirements. In the current state-of-the-art flat representations, millions of distinctive image patches (with dimensions ranging around 25×25 pixels) or local descriptors, such as SIFT or HoG, must be stored to produce good recognition results. In classical hierarchies such as neural networks the number of necessary features to warrant competitive performance is significantly lower (the number ranges from 10–20 in the lowest layer and increases to the order of a few thousand in the topmost layer); however, each hierarchical unit still must encode weights to *all* feature types from a layer below covering a certain spatial neighborhood. Conversely, as the complexity and size or representation grow with the number of layers in compositional hierarchies, each higher-level composition encodes only pointers to a small number of its constituent parts and a modest amount of additional information binding the parts spatially. Furthermore, since all the higher-level compositions are constructed from a smaller common vocabulary from a layer below, it is easier to compare and generalize between them. Consequently, extending the hierarchical library to novel compositions can operate in a more controlled manner, which would lead to more compact and parsimonious hierarchical vocabularies.

Processing complexity. Because each hierarchical unit is shared among many more complex higher-layer compositions, most of the computations performed during an online recognition stage are inherently common and can thus be performed only once. Such sharing of computations greatly reduces the computational cost of matching with respect to searching for each complex interpretation in isolation. Moreover, as processing of images is done by sequential (hierarchical) testing of compositional hypotheses, recognition towards the final categorical nodes proceeds in a more controlled and rapid manner by pruning the object hypothesis space along the hierarchical path.

The important advantage of discrete representations such as the compositional architectures is also the possibility of implementing the *indexing and matching scheme*. Because each internal node of the hierarchical vocabulary participates in only a smaller subset of all compositions from the incident layer above, only this specific subset needs to be matched against the local image neighborhood during the online recognition stage. Consequently, retrieval of permitted composite models can be performed in constant time (the process termed "indexing"), whereas the verification of the retrieved candidates runs in sublinear time with respect to the size of the hierarchical library. This procedure will be described in more detail in section 11.4.2.

Robustness to clutter, repeatability of detection. Each hierarchical node makes inference over a certain size of a local neighborhood, usually referred to as its *receptive field*. The level of hierarchy brings about larger and larger portions of an image that the nodes "cover" and that are likely to contain many structures pertaining to different objects in the scene or rarer structures that the hierarchical units are not essentially tuned to. The classical neural networks that define the units as some nonlinear function of an integrative weighted sum over its entire receptive field, both spatially as well as in all constituent feature types (schematically depicted in Fig. 11.1), are inherently prone to errors because the signal coming from multiple objects is essentially mixed. This can be alleviated by enforcing sparsity on the feature weights to enable a focus on only particular substructures of receptive fields. In turn, compositions are inherently

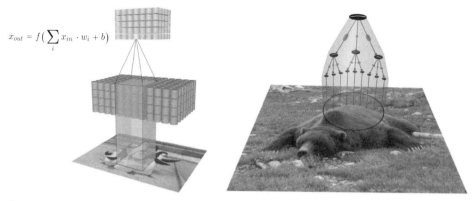

$$x_{out} = f\left(\sum_i x_{in} \cdot w_i + b\right)$$

Figure 11.1. *Left,* A traditional (convolutional) neural network. *Right,* A compositional hierarchy. (See color plate 11.1.)

sparse; they are designed to respond to only small spatial subsets of their receptive fields in which the presence of only a few feature types is accounted for (depicted in Fig. 11.1). This ensures that clutter has little effect on the activity within the hierarchical recognition process and additionally permits faster processing over the traditional neural networks approaches.

Expressive power. Even a small number of feature types defining the outset of the hierarchy can construe a large number of possible combinations that become even more pronounced with the level of hierarchy. Importantly, because the vocabulary is expected to grow exponentially as new layers (compositions of compositions that essentially should converge to objects themselves) are added and the complexity as well as distinctiveness of the representation increase, the principle of indexing ensures tractability of the recognition process.

Feedforward and feedback. There has been a longstanding debate about what can or cannot be achieved in a strictly feedforward manner in vision in general and in hierarchical categorization approaches in particular (Thorpe et al. 1996; Hup et al. 1998; Lee and Mumford 2003; Tsotsos 2008). There is neurophysiological evidence proving good categorization performance in the first feedforward pass by humans (Thorpe et al. 1996; VanRullen 2007), although many authors emphasize the importance of both feedforward and feedback and the iterative process between the two (Hup et al. 1998; Lee and Mumford 2003; Ullman 2007; Tsotsos 2008). The ability to traverse back from the final recognition nodes inferred from the scene back to the original pixels that produced the high-level decision is important for segmentation as well as for looping between bottom-up and top-down inference on ambiguous visual input. This kind of reciprocal inference presents an impediment for the neural network approaches (Huang and LeCun 2006) and their closely related architectures (Riesenhuber and Poggio 1999) because the firing response of a hierarchical unit is too reductive. The information from a cubelike receptive field over lower-layer feature responses is conveyed in only one value – the weighted sum. This makes it difficult to determine and trace back what has in fact caused the response (depicted in Fig. 11.1); it also makes inference less controlled and reliable. Conversely, in compositional architectures the representation inferred from the visual scene is essentially a graph in which each node has only a small number of incident descendants. Such a representation inherently allows for iterative loops between the data (image) and high-level inferences, whereby the segmentation of objects is simply an inverse process of recognition.

A part of the biological evidence could potentially support such a line of compositional architecture (Pasupathy and Connor 1999; Tsunoda et al. 2001; Ito and Komatsu 2004; Anzai et al. 2007; Connor et al. 2007). In addition, attempts have been made to map the mathematical theory of compositionality onto the neuronal structure of the visual cortex (Bienenstock and Geman 1995).

11.2.2 Statistical, Bottom-up Learning

The appealing properties of compositional hierarchies and their advantages over the related hierarchical architectures might prove them to be a suitable form of representing visual information. However, while learning presents an integral part of the neural networks approaches, most compositional approaches have been hindered by the use of predetermined sets of features or grouping rules. Here, we argue for the importance of learning, specifically, we emphasize the critical role of unsupervised, bottom-up learning.

Bottom-up learning. There seems to be a consensus that the higher-level concepts such as selectivity to object categories are learned because, evidently, a genetic predisposition toward mobile phones, for example, and similar ever-evolving technological gadgets would seem far-fetched. Interestingly, there are opposing views on whether the tunings in the early cortical areas are learned or hardwired by evolution. The diverse physiology underlying different brain areas suggests that specific functionalities and computations are performed. This striking systematicity surely is a result of evolution, and it undoubtedly guides and controls what the cells can or cannot become tuned to. However, it is highly improbable that all the low-level sensitivities are instilled genetically; the brain must, after all, adjust its perceptual functioning with respect to its sensory receptors and the input it receives from the environment.

Computationally speaking, the categorical representations are built upon a set of features that must at some point operate on the image data. The design of these features (e.g., corners, T- and L-junctions, etc.) should not rely on our intuition but rather be learned from the data in order to conform well to the local structures of images. The features/models in the lowest level of the hierarchy should thus be brought down close to the images by performing simple operations with little semantic value. The subsequent learning should then be designed in order to statistically build more complex and semantic models in composition.

Once the *visual building blocks* are learned, learning of objects becomes tractable, because only a small number of descriptive structural features are needed to explain them away. Consequently, categorical learning can proceed mainly in the higher hierarchical layers and can thus operate fast and with no or minimal human supervision.

Unsupervised learning. Features and their higher-level combinations should be learned in an unsupervised manner (at least in the first stages of the hierarchy) in order to avoid hand-labeling of massive image data as well as to capture the regularities within the visual data as effectively and compactly as possible (Barlow 1985; Rolls and Deco 2002; Edelman and Intrator 2004; Hawkins and Blakeslee 2004; Fidler et al.

2006; Fidler and Leonardis 2007). Moreover, there are strong implications that the human visual system is driven by these principles as well (Fiser and Aslin 2002).

By learning the compositional binding priors, the representation becomes adjustable to the structural variability of objects. Consequently, it enables a computationally feasible recognition process in which the majority of the exponential number of possible compositional groupings are made unimportant (i.e., unrepeatable) by the statistics of natural images.

Incremental learning. This desirable that the hierarchical vocabulary be extended incrementally as new images/objects are seen by the system. In this way, we avoid batch processing of masses of images (which likely might not even be possible), while ensuring that the representation is open to continuous adaptation to the visual environment.

The issue of incrementality in hierarchical architectures is not completely apparent. If features are changed, removed, or added at any layer exclusive of the top-most one, all the features on the layers above must be adjusted accordingly. This problem is particularly evident in the neural network type of hierarchies, in which adding one feature results in an inefficient restructuring of the weights of the complete representation. In compositional hierarchies this problem concerns only a small subset of higher-level features that compositionally emerge from the point of change. Furthermore, by learning the representation sequentially (i.e., optimally adjusting layer after layer to the regularities present in the natural signals), we guarantee that very little encoded information (if anything at all) will need to be readapted in the lowest layers of the hierarchy as new data are encountered.

11.3 Related Work

The current state-of-the-art categorization methods predominantly build their representations on image patches (Mikolajczyk et al. 2006; Ullman and Epshtein 2006) or other highly discriminative features such as the SIFT (Sudderth et al. 2005). Because the probability of occurrence of such features is rather small, masses of them need to be extracted to represent objects reasonably well. This results in computationally highly inefficient recognition, which demands matching of a large number of image features to enormous amounts of prototypical ones. This drawback has been alleviated within the most recent methods that employ hierarchical clustering in a high-dimensional feature space, yet the resulting representations still demand at least a linear search through the library of stored objects/categories (Mikolajczyk et al. 2006; Sudderth et al. 2005).

To overcome the curse of large-scale recognition, some authors emphasized the need for indexable hierarchical representations (Califano and Mohan 1994; Amit and Geman 1999; Amit 2002). A hierarchy of parts composed of parts that could limit the visual search by means of indexing and matching in each individual layer would enable an efficient way to store and retrieve information.

However, a majority of hierarchical methods perform matching of *all* prototypical units against *all* features found in an image. Mutch and Lowe (2006) employ matching of all 4,000 higher-layer templates against features extracted in each pixel and scale of the resampled pyramid. This is also a drawback in layers of clustered histograms used in Agarwal and Triggs (2006) and hierarchical classifiers in Huang and LeCun (2006).

On the other hand, the success of hierarchical methods that do employ the principles of indexing and matching has been hindered by the use of hand-coded information. Amit and Geman (1999) use hand-crafted local edge features and only learn their global arrangements pertaining to specific object categories. Riesenhuber and Poggio (1999) use predesigned filters and process the visual information in the feed-forward manner, whereas their recent version (Serre et al. 2007) exchanged the intermediate layer with random combinations of local edge arrangements rather than choosing the features in accordance with the natural statistics. Zhu and Mumford (2006) propose a hierarchical stochastic grammar that operates with a number of predetermined grouping rules and learns object representations with supervision upon a number of manually parsed objects. In Zhu et al. (2008), the proposed approach learns a hierarchy of triplets upon a manually determined set of boundary object points.

Approaches that do build the layers by learning and are able to make a sufficient number of them (by starting with simple features) mostly design the parts by histogramming the local neighborhoods of parts of the previous layers (Agarwal and Triggs 2006) or by learning the neural weights based on the responses on previous layers (Huang and LeCun 2006; Fukushima et al. 1983). Besides lacking the means of indexing, another inherent limitation of such methods is the inefficiency in performing incremental learning; as the novel categories arrive, the whole hierarchy has to be re-adapted. Moreover, histograms do not enable robust top-down matching, and convolutional networks would have problems with the objects or features that are supersets/subsets of other features.

Although the concepts of hierarchical representations, indexing and matching, statistical learning, and incrementality have already been explored in the literature, to the best of our knowledge they have not been part of a unifying framework. This chapter summarizes our recent, novel approach to building a hierarchical representation that aims to enable recognition and detection of a large number of object categories. Inspired by the principles of efficient indexing (*bottom-up*), robust matching (*top-down*), and ideas of compositionality, our approach *learns* a hierarchy of spatially flexible compositions (i.e., parts) in a completely unsupervised, statistics-driven manner. As the proposed architecture does not yet perform large-scale recognition, it makes important steps towards scalable representations of visual categories.

The learning algorithm proposed in Fleuret and Geman (2001), which acquires a hierarchy of local edge arrangements by correlation, is conceptually similar to our learning method. However, the approach demands registered training images, employs a fixed grid, and is more concerned with the coarse-to-fine search of a particular category (i.e., faces) than the discovery of features shared by many object classes.

11.4 Learning a Compositional Hierarchy of Parts

This section summarizes our recently proposed framework, which learns a hierarchical compositional representation of object structure from a set of natural images without supervision. The complete architecture addresses three major issues: the representation, learning the representation, and matching the representation against images.

The proposed representation takes the form of a compositional hierarchy with discrete nodes, or compositions (also termed "parts"). Each part in the hierarchical vocabulary models loose spatial relations between its components, which at the lowest level correspond to simple contour fragments. The first layer of the hierarchy is fixed (not learned), and it is also the only layer that operates directly on images. All the higher layers that make inference at subsequent stages are learned without supervision.

The approach is in essence composed of two recursively iterated steps:

- A layer-learning process that extracts the most salient part compositions contained in local image neighborhoods.
- A part matching step that finds the learned compositions in images with an efficient and robust *indexing and matching* scheme.

Layers are learned sequentially, layer after layer, optimally adjusting to the visual data. The advantage of the proposed learned representation lies in its ability to model the exponential variability present in images, yet still retain computational efficiency by keeping the number of indexing links per each part approximately constant across layers.

The compositional representation and its envisioned properties are explained in section 11.4.1. In section 11.4.2 the hierarchical recognition process that matches the representation against images is discussed. We summarize the unsupervised learning procedure that extracts a hierarchy of progressively more complex contour compositions in section 11.4.3. Section 11.4.4 discusses how the learned parts at each layer can be grouped in order to avoid the combinatorial explosion of possible higher level compositions. Finally, section 11.4.5 discusses a potential step towards categorical representations.

11.4.1 The Compositional Library of Parts

We first present the properties of the envisioned hierarchical representation and the information that we would like to be encoded within its discrete nodes – parts/compositions.

To abbreviate the notation, let $\mathcal{L}_n$ denote the n-th Layer of the hierarchical library. We define the parts within the hierarchy recursively in the following way. Each part in $\mathcal{L}_n$ codes spatial relations between its constituent subparts from a layer below. Formally, each composite part $\mathcal{P}_\ell^n$ in $\mathcal{L}_n$ is characterized by a *central subpart* and a list of remaining subparts with their positions relative to the center:

$$\mathcal{P}_\ell^n = \left(\mathcal{P}_{central}^{n-1}, \left\{\left(\mathcal{P}_j^{n-1}, \boldsymbol{\mu}_j, \Sigma_j\right)\right\}_j\right), \tag{11.1}$$

where $\boldsymbol{\mu}_j = (x_j, y_j)$ denotes the relative position of a subpart $\mathcal{P}_j^{n-1}$, while Σ_j denotes the allowed variance of its position around (x_j, y_j). An example of a $\mathcal{L}_3$ composition is depicted in Figure 11.2.

The hierarchy starts with a fixed $\mathcal{L}_1$ composed of a set of arbitrary filters. Here we choose a set of Gabor filters that best respond to oriented edges.

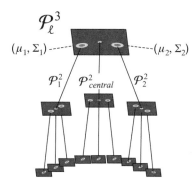

Figure 11.2. Example of an $\mathcal{L}_3$ composition. (See color plate 11.2.)

11.4.2 Hierarchical Recognition: The Indexing
and Matching Scheme

Let us suppose that the representation as described in the previous section has already been acquired (how this is achieved will be explained in the next section). This section discusses how the incoming images are preprocessed and how the hierarchical representation is subsequently matched against the data. The complete procedure can be briefly summarized as follows:

- Each image is first processed with filters comprising $\mathcal{L}_1$ in order to get a (discrete) set of local contour fragments. Each contour segment (i.e., a part) also codes its orientation and position in an image.
- Around each detected part, higher-order compositions are matched within the so-called *indexing and matching scheme*. At each processed layer, a discrete set of parts coding the types of the detected local structures and the corresponding locations is passed onto sequential matching stages. The hierarchical processing steps are all general in their traversal from one layer to the next and will thus be described in their general form. The procedure is illustrated in Figure 11.3.
- To attain robustness with respect to the scale of the objects (or their smaller substructures), the hierarchical recognition procedure is performed at several rescaled versions of the image. This is schematically depicted in Figure 11.4.

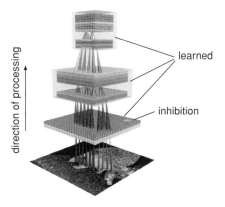

Figure 11.3. The hierarchical recognition architecture. (See color plate 11.3.)

Figure 11.4. The learned hierarchical library of parts is applied in each image point (robustness to position of objects) and several image scales (robustness to objects' size). (See color plate 11.4.)

Processing with Layer 1. For a given image, we first apply a set of $\mathcal{L}_1$ filters, in our current implementation chosen to be the (odd and even) Gabor filters. Next, local maxima of the Gabor energy function (Fidler et al. 2006) that are above a low threshold are located (these pertain to local oriented edges). The set of points (corresponding to the local maxima) together with their locations and labels (types) of filters that locally produced the maximal responses defines the list of $\mathcal{L}_1$ part detections, namely $\{\pi_k^1\}_k$. In general, π_k^n stands for a *realization* of the $\mathcal{L}_n$ part $\mathcal{P}_{\ell_k}^n$ with a corresponding location at which it was detected in an image; $\pi_k^n = \{\mathcal{P}_{\ell_k}^n, x_k, y_k\}$ (here k denotes the successive number of the found part).

This process is repeated at several image scales. However, for simplicity of notation we omit the delineation of part detections into separate scales. The obtained list of binary part detections (i.e., $\{\pi_k^1\}_k$) serves as input to subsequent hierarchical matching stages.

Hierarchical recognition. Let $\{\pi_k^{n-1}\}_k$ denote the list of the binary part detections from layer $\mathcal{L}_{n-1}$. In order to find a higher-level image interpretation, the local neighborhoods around each detected π_k^{n-1} part are compared against the composite $\mathcal{L}_n$

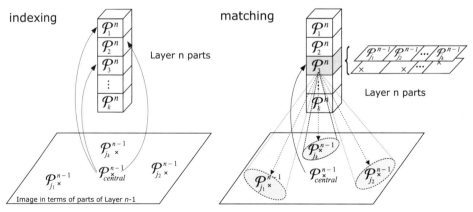

Figure 11.5. *Left,* Indexing – evoking higher-level composite hypotheses. *Right,* Matching – verification of a composite library part. (See color plate 11.5.)

parts stored in the hierarchical library. Each part realization $\pi_k^{n-1} = (\mathcal{P}_{\ell_k}^{n-1}, x_k, y_k)$ in the image under consideration is subjected to the *indexing and matching procedure –* efficient local search for higher level compositions.

The part $\mathcal{P}_{\ell_k}^{n-1}$ encoded in π_k^{n-1} plays the role of the central part in only a subset of all compositions at layer $\mathcal{L}_n$ of the library. This list is an internal part of the library and can be accessed in constant time during the online processing of images – the process referred to as *indexing*. The *matching* step demands comparing the local spatial neighborhood of π_k^{n-1} against the allowable (retrieved in the indexing step) prototypical compositions within the hierarchical library. Matching of one such composition, e.g. $\mathcal{P}_\ell^n = (\mathcal{P}_{central}^{n-1}, \{(\mathcal{P}_j^{n-1}, \boldsymbol{\mu}_j, \Sigma_j)\}_j)$ (where $\mathcal{P}_{central}^{n-1}$ corresponds to the part label $\mathcal{P}_{\ell_k}^{n-1}$), demands checking for the presence of all subparts $\{(\mathcal{P}_j^{n-1}, \boldsymbol{\mu}_j, \Sigma_j)\}_j$ pertaining to the composition $\mathcal{P}_\ell^n$ at their relative locations, $\boldsymbol{\mu}_j = (x_j, y_j)$, and positioned within the allowed variances, Σ_j, with respect to the position of the central part type $\mathcal{P}_{\ell_k}^{n-1}$ coded in π_k^{n-1}. The indexing and matching procedure is schematically depicted in Figure 11.5.

11.4.3 Unsupervised Learning of Part Compositions

The basic idea behind the learning procedure is to extract statistically salient compositions that encode spatial relations between the constituent parts from the layer below. Each modeled relation between components allows also for some displacement (variance) in spatial position.

The learning algorithm is in principle general, proceeding in the same manner when building each additional layer. It will thus be described in its general form.

The learning process consists of three stages – namely, (1) the local inhibition performed around each image feature (part); followed by (2) the statistical updating of the so-called spatial maps that capture pairwise geometric relations between parts; and finally, (3) learning the higher-order compositions by tracking co-occurrence of spatial pairs. We must emphasize that each final composition can have a varying number of subcomponents (the number can be anything from two and higher).

Learning is performed by gathering statistics over a large number of natural images processed up to the last (learned) layer in the hierarchical library (e.g., $\mathcal{L}_{n-1}$). Each image is thus represented by a list of parts with corresponding locations $\{\pi_k^{n-1}\}_k$. A small local neighborhood around each π_k^{n-1} will be inspected in a two-stage process. The first, most crucial step aims to reduce the unnecessary redundancy coded in neighboring parts, referred to as *local inhibition*. Because each π_k^{n-1} is an $(n-1)$-th order composition, it is in fact a set union of a few detected $\mathcal{L}_1$ parts. Within the inhibition step we remove all neighboring parts around π_k^{n-1} that have a large set intersection with respect to the $\mathcal{L}_1$ image parts. This step removes all features that code a large portion of edge structure already coded by π_k^{n-1}. In the next step, learning is performed by tracking frequent co-occurrences of part types and their relative locations.

The learning process commends by forming a set of all allowable pairs of part identities. The list is accompanied by a set of empty matrices, where the dimensions correspond to the spatial extent of the local neighborhoods. The prepared set thus contains information of type: $C^n_{k,j} := (P^{n-1}_k, P^{n-1}_j, V_{k,j})$, where $V_{k,j}$ represents a local spatial voting space for the corresponding combination of pairs of part types P^{n-1}_k and P^{n-1}_j.

Structure of small neighborhoods in terms of part locations is inspected around each part, π^{n-1}_k. The philosophy of local receptive field processing is the following: the location of each part $\pi^{n-1}_j = (P^{n-1}_j, x_j, y_j)$ within the neighborhood of, and relative to, π^{n-1}_k will update the voting space $V_{k,j}$ in $C_{k,j}$ accordingly:

$$x := cx + x_j - x_k, \quad y := cy + y_j - y_k$$
$$V_{k,j}(x, y) = V_{k,j}(x, y) + 1, \tag{11.2}$$

where the vector (cx, cy) denotes the center of the spatial map $V_{k,j}$.

After all images are processed, we detect voting peaks in the learned spatial maps $V_{k,j}$, and for each peak, a spatial surrounding area is formed – modeled by a Gaussian distribution, (μ_j, Σ_j).

In the final step, the local image neighborhoods are checked once again by projecting the learned spatial pairs and repeating the learning process by increasing the number of subparts modeled in a composition (the reader is referred to Fidler and Leonardis (2007) for details) or by tracking the most frequent co-occurrences of the projected spatial pairs.

The final selection of composite parts follows the indexibility constraint – that is, each part of the lower, $(n - 1)$-th Layer must not index into too many higher layer compositions. Thus, the compositions acquired in the learning procedure are sorted according to their decreasing probabilities and only a number of statistically most salient compositions consequently define the next layer. We set the upper bound to the order of 10–20 times the number of parts in the previous, $(n - 1)$-th Layer, meaning that on average each part in $\mathcal{L}_{n-1}$ indexes into 10 to 20 composite parts in $\mathcal{L}_n$. The thresholds used are chosen to comply with the available computational resources and affect only the number of finally selected parts and therefore the efficiency of the representation.

11.4.4 Grouping Part Labels by Similarity and Co-occurrence

The problem with the learned compositions is the fact that they are realized as discrete labels (part types) without a proper geometrical parametrization that would enable a comparison between them. Consequently, two visually similar curvatures are likely to be encoded in two different hierarchical compositions. We deal with this issue in two ways. One approach is grouping by co-occurrence (Fidler and Leonardis 2007), in which parts that frequently co-occur in close spatial proximity to one another are assigned the same label (part type).

However, two visual shapes that are only similar to a certain extent are likely to have a small, random co-occurrence. It is thus crucial to also have the means of comparing two different parts in a geometrical sense. Since each part is formed as a recursive spatially loose composition, a comparison can be performed in a similar manner. We consider two parts to be perceptually similar if both have a similar spatial configuration

Figure 11.6. Examples of natural images used to learn the category-independent layers (most taken from the PASCAL image dataset).

of subparts. For details of such recursive comparison of compositions we refer the reader to our original work (Fidler et al. 2008).

11.4.5 Category-Specific Higher Layers

Learning the lower-layer sharable parts in a category-independent way can only get so far – the overall statistical significance (frequency of parts) drops, whereas the number of parts reaches its critical value for learning. Thus, learning of higher layers proceeds only on a subset of parts, the ones that are the most repeatable for a specific category. Specifically, the learning of higher layers is performed in images of individual categories, whereby the final categorical layer then combines the most repeatable parts through the object center to form the representation of a category (Fidler and Leonardis 2007).

11.5 Experimental Results

The proposed unsupervised part-learning procedure learns the first few layers ($\mathcal{L}1 - \mathcal{L}3$) independent of categorical labels. We applied our approach to a collection of 1500 (unlabeled) natural images that contain a number of diverse categories (cars, faces, mugs, dogs, etc.). A few examples of the images used for learning are presented in Figure 11.6. The complete learning process implemented in C++ took approximately 5 hours on one core of an Intel Core-2 CPU 2.4 Ghz computer. The learning procedure produced a compositional hierarchy consisting of 160 parts on Layer 2 and 553 parts on Layer 3 (a few examples from both layers are depicted in Fig. 11.7). The learned features include corners, end-stopped lines, various curvatures, T- and L-junctions, and so on. Note that a much smaller set of images is in fact needed to result in virtually the same hierarchy. Experiments have shown that learning on approximately 50 images produces almost exactly the same $\mathcal{L}_2$ vocabulary as the larger set of 1500 images, whereas approximately 200 images are required to learn the third layer of the hierarchy. We have also experimented with using different filters at $\mathcal{L}_1$. The learned vocabulary for the Gabor filters that also take into account the polarity of edges is presented in

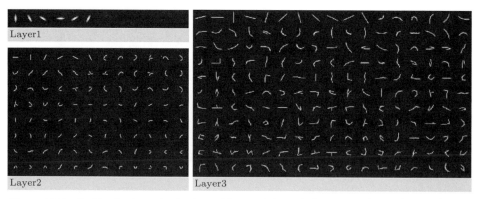

Figure 11.7. $\mathcal{L}_1$ (fixed-oriented edges), and learned $\mathcal{L}_2$ and $\mathcal{L}_3$ parts (only a subset is shown) used in the Caltech-101 experiments.

Figure 11.8. We must emphasize, however, that both Figures 11.7 and 11.8 only show the contours that the parts produce maximal responses to. Each learned part in the vocabulary is in fact a composition (modeling spatial relations among subparts) of the form shown in Figure 11.2.

To put the proposed hierarchical framework in relation to other hierarchical approaches as well as other categorization methods, which focus primarily on shape information, the approach was tested on the Caltech-101 database (Fei-Fei et al. 2004). The Caltech-101 dataset contains images of 101 different object categories with the additional background category. The number of images varies from 31 to 800 per category, with the average image size of roughly 300×300 pixels. Each image was processed on three different scales, spaced apart by $\sqrt{2}$. The average processing times per image per layer (including all three scales) obtained in a C++ implementation are the following: 1.6 seconds for $\mathcal{L}_1$, 0.54 seconds for $\mathcal{L}_2$, and 0.66 seconds for $\mathcal{L}_3$. The features were combined with a linear SVM for multiclass classification. For both, 15 and 30 images for training, we obtained 60.5% and 66.5% classification accuracy, respectively, which is the best result reported by a hierarchical approach so far.

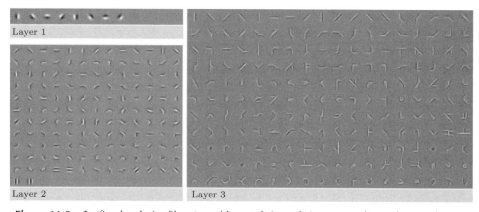

Figure 11.8. $\mathcal{L}_1$ (fixed-polarity filters), and learned $\mathcal{L}_2$ and $\mathcal{L}_3$ parts (only a subset is shown).

Figure 11.9. Examples of images used to learn the categorical layers.

Although we do not believe that SVM classification is the proper form of categorization, the experiments were performed to demonstrate the utility of the learned features with respect to the features used in the current state-of-the-art approaches applied in similar classification settings.

We have also attempted learning higher – categorical layers, using images of specific categories for training. The learning of categorical layers, namely $\mathcal{L}_4$, was run only on images containing faces (6 out of 20 images used for training are shown in the top row of Fig. 11.9), cars (6 out of 20 training images are depicted in the middle row of Fig. 11.9), and mugs (all training images are presented in the bottom row of Fig. 11.9). The obtained parts were then learned relative to centers of faces, cars, and mugs, respectively, to produce $\mathcal{L}_5$-*category layer*. Figure 11.10 shows the learned layers, while Figure 11.11 depicts the learned hierarchical vocabulary for faces with compositional links shown (second image in the top row). It must be noted that the first three layers in the hierarchy are general – the same for faces as for cars and mugs, whereas only layers 4 and 5 are not shareable among the three categories. The recognition and the subsequent segmentation (tracing the recognition nodes down the the image) of parts through the hierarchy on example images are presented in Figure 11.11. In Figure 11.12 several examples of mug detections are presented, showing that the approach is capable of recognizing various class members, hand-drawn objects, as well as peculiar mug-like compositions (a drawn handle plus a basket, a drawn glass plus some handle-like object added accordingly).

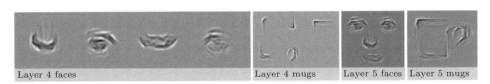

Layer 4 faces   Layer 4 mugs   Layer 5 faces   Layer 5 mugs

Figure 11.10. Learned categorical layers $\mathcal{L}_4$ and $\mathcal{L}_5$ for faces and mugs.

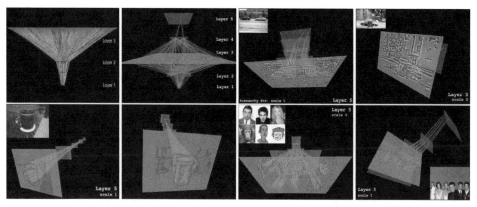

Figure 11.11. Top left two images: learned 3-layer hierarchy for the Caltech experiment; learned hierarchy for faces with compositional links shown. Examples of detections of categories of cars, mugs, and faces, in which the first three layers in the library are common to all three categories. (See color plate 11.11.)

11.6 Conclusion

This chapter summarized our recent approach to building a hierarchical compositional representation of object structure. The method learns a hierarchy of flexible compositions in an unsupervised manner in lower, category-independent layers, while requiring minimal supervision to learn higher, categorical layers.

Furthermore, the design of parts is incremental, where new categories can be continuously added to the hierarchy. Because the hierarchy is built as an efficient indexing machine, the system can computationally handle an exponentially increasing number of parts with each additional layer. The results show that only a small number of higher-layer parts are needed to represent individual categories; thus, the proposed scheme would potentially allow for an efficient representation of a large number of visual categories.

Our ongoing work includes extensions over the current creation of the categorical layers, adding different modalities such as color, texture, and motion, and improving inference by using iterated loops between the bottom-up and top-down information flow.

Figure 11.12. Detections of mugs. (See color plate 11.12.)

Acknowledgments

This research has been supported in part by the following funds: Research program Computer Vision P2-0214 (Slovenian Ministry of Higher Education, Science and Technology), EU FP6-004250-IP project CoSy, EU FP6-511051 project MOBVIS, and EU FP7-215843 project POETICON.

Bibliography

Agarwal A, Triggs B. 2006. Hyperfeatures – multilevel local coding for visual recognition. In *ECCV* (1):30–43.

Amit Y. 2002. *2d object detection and recognition: models, algorithms and networks*. Cambridge: MIT Press.

Amit Y, Geman D. 1999. A computational model for visual selection. *Neural Comp* 11(7):1691–1715.

Anzai A, Peng X, Van Essen DC. 2007. Neurons in monkey visual areaa v2 encode combinations of orientations. *Nat Neurosci* 10(10):1313–1321.

Barlow HB. 1985. Cerebral cortex as a model builder. *Models of the visual cortex*, Chichester: John Wiley & Sons, 37–46.

Bienenstock E. 1996. Composition. In A. Aertsen and V. Braitenberg, ed. *Brain theory: biological basis and computational theory of vision*, 269–300. Philadelphia: Elsevier.

Bienenstock E, Geman S. 1995. Compositionality in neural systems. In *The handbook of brain theory and neural networks*, ed. M. Arbib, 223–226. Cambridge: MIT Press.

Califano A, Mohan R. 1994. Multidimensional indexing for recognizing visual shapes. *IEEE Trans Pattern Anal Mach Intell* 16(4): 373–392.

Connor CE, Brincat SL, Pasupathy A. 2007. Transformation of shape information in the ventral pathway. *Curr Opin Neurobiol* 17(2):140–147.

Dickinson S. 2008. The evolution of object categorization and the challenge of image abstraction. In S. Dickinson, A. Leonardis, B. Schiele, and M.J. Tarr, eds, *Object categorization: computer and human vision perspectives*. Springer-Verlag.

Dickinson S, Pentland A, Rosenfeld A. 1992. 3-D shape recovery using distributed aspect matching. *IEEE Trans Pattern Anal Mach Intell* 14(2): 174–198.

Edelman S, Intrator N. 2004. Unsupervised statistical learning in vision: computational principles, biological evidence. In extended abstract of invited talk at the ECCV-2004 workshop on statistical learning in computer vision.

Ettinger GJ. 1987. Hierarchical object recognition using libraries of parameterized model sub-parts. Technical report, MIT.

Everingham M, Van Gool L, Williams CKI, Winn J, Zisserman A. 2007. The PASCAL visual object classes challenge (VOC2007) Results. http://www.pascal-network.org/challenges/VOC/voc2007/workshop/index.html.

Fei-Fei L, Fergus R, Perona P. 2004. Learning generative visual models from few training examples: an incremental bayesian approach tested on 101 object categories. In IEEE CVPR, workshop on generative-model based vision.

Ferrari V, Fevrier L, Jurie F, Schmid C. 2008. Groups of adjacent contour segments for object detection. *IEEE Trans Pattern Anal Mach Intell* 30(1): 36–51.

Fidler S, Berginc G, Leonardis A. 2006. Hierarchical statistical learning of generic parts of object structure. In CVPR, 182–189.

Fidler S, Boben M, Leonardis A. 2008. Similarity-based cross-layered hierarchical representation for object categorization. In CVPR.

Fidler S, Leonardis A. 2007. Towards scalable representations of visual categories: Learning a hierarchy of parts. In CVPR.

Fiser J, Aslin RN. 2002. Statistical learning of new visual feature combinations by infants. *Proc Natl Acad Sci USA* 99(24):15,822–15,826.

Fleuret F, Geman D. 2001. Coarse-to-fine face detection. *Int J Comput Vision* 41(1/2):85–107.

Fritz M, Schiele B. 2008. Decomposition, discovery and detection of visual categories using topic models. In CVPR.

Fukushima K, Miyake S, Ito T. 1983. Neocognitron: a neural network model for a mechanism of visual pattern recognition. *IEEE Syst Man Cybernetics* 13(3):826–834.

Geman S, Potter D, Chi Z. 2002. Composition systems. *Quart Appl Math* 60(4):707–736.

Grimson WEL, Lozano-Perez T. 1987. Localizing overlapping parts by searching the interpretation tree. *IEEE Trans Pattern Anal Mach Intell* 9(4): 469–482.

Hawkins J, Blakeslee S. 2004. *On intelligence*. New York: Times Books.

Hinton GE. 2007. Learning multiple layers of representation. *Trend Cogn Sci* 11(10):428–434.

Huang F-J, LeCun Y. 2006. Large-scale learning with svm and convolutional nets for generic object categorization. In CVPR, 284–291.

Hup J, James A, Payne B, Lomber S, Girard P, Bullier J. 1998. Cortical feedback improves discrimination between figure and background by v1, v2 and v3 neurons. *Nature* 394:784–787.

Ito M, Komatsu H. 2004. Representation of angles embedded within contour stimuli in area v2 of macaque monkeys. *J Neurosci* 24(13):3313–3324.

Krempp S, Geman D, Amit Y. 2002. Sequential learning of reusable parts for object detection. Technical report.

Lee TS, Mumford D. 2003. Hierarchical bayesian inference in the visual cortex. *J Opt Soc Am A Opt Image Sci Vis* 20(7):1434–1448.

Medioni G, Fan T, Nevatia R. 1989. Recognizing 3-d objects using surface descriptions. *IEEE Trans Pattern Anal Mach Intell* 2(11): 1140–1157.

Mel BW, Fiser J. 2000. Minimizing binding errors using learned conjunctive features. *Neural Comput* 12(4):731–762.

Mikolajczyk K, Leibe B, Schiele B. 2006. Multiple object class detection with a generative model. In CVPR, 26–36.

Mutch J, Lowe DG. 2006. Multiclass object recognition with sparse, localized features. In CVPR, 11–18.

Nistér D, Stewénius H. 2006. Scalable recognition with a vocabulary tree. In CVPR, vol 2, 2161–2168.

Ommer B, Buhmann JM. 2006. Learning compositional categorization models. In ECCV, 316–329.

Ommer B, Buhmann JM. 2007. Learning the compositional nature of visual objects. In CVPR.

Op de Beeck H, Haushofer J, Kanwisher N. 2008. Interpreting fmri data: maps, modules, and dimensions. *Nat Rev Neurosci* 9:123–135.

Pasupathy A, Connor C. 1999. Responses to contour features in macaque area v4. *J Neurophysiol* 82(5):2490–2502.

Pinto N, Cox D, DiCarlo J. 2008. Why is real-world visual object recognition hard? *PLoS Comput Biol* 4(1):151–156.

Ranzato MA, Huang F-J, Boureau Y-L, LeCun Y. 2007. Unsupervised learning of invariant feature hierarchies with applications to object recognition. In CVPR.

Riesenhuber M, Poggio T. 1999. Hierarchical models of object recognition in cortex. *Nature Neurosci* 2(11):1019–1025.

Rolls ET, Deco G. 2002. *Computational neuroscience of vision*. New York: Oxford University Press.

Scalzo F, Piater JH. 2005. Statistical learning of visual feature hierarchies. In *Workshop on learning*, CVPR.

Serre T, Wolf L, Bileschi S, Riesenhuber M, Poggio T. 2007. Object recognition with cortex-like mechanisms. *IEEE Trans Pattern Anal Mach Intell* 29(3): 411–426.

Shokoufandeh A, Bretzner L, Macrini D, Demirci M, Jonsson C, Dickinson S. 2006. The representation and matching of categorical shape. *Comput Vis Image Und* 103:139–154.

Sudderth E, Torralba A, Freeman W, Willsky A. 2005. Learning hierarchical models of scenes, objects, and parts. In ICCV, 1331–1338.

Thorpe SJ, Fize D, Marlot C. 1996. Speed of processing in the human visual system. *Nature* 381:520–522.

Todorovic S, Ahuja N. 2007. Unsupervised category modeling, recognition, and segmentation in images. *IEEE Trans Pattern Anal Mach Intell.*

Torralba A, Murphy KP, Freeman WT. 2007. Sharing visual features for multiclass and multiview object detection. *IEEE Trans Pattern Anal Mach Intell* 29: 854–869.

Tsotsos J. 2008. What roles can attention play in recognition? In 7th international conference on development and learning.

Tsotsos JK. 1990. Analyzing vision at the complexity level. *Behav Brain Sci* 13(3):423–469.

Tsunoda K, Yamane Y, Nishizaki M, Tanifuji M. 2001. Complex objects are represented in macaque inferotemporal cortex by the combination of feature columns. *Nat Neurosci* (4):832–838.

Ullman S. 2007. Object recognition and segmentation by a fragment-based hierarchy. *Trends Cogn Sci* 11:58–64.

Ullman S, Epshtein B. 2006. Visual classification by a hierarchy of extended features. *Towards category-level object recognition*. New York: Springer-Verlag.

VanRullen R. 2007. The power of the feed-forward sweep. *Adv Cogn Psychol* 3(1–2):167–176.

Zhu L, Chen Y, Ye X, Yuille A. 2008. Structure-perceptron learning of a hierarchical log-linear model. In CVPR.

Zhu L, Yuille A. 2005. A hierarchical compositional system for rapid object detection. In NIPS.

Zhu S, Mumford D. 2006. A stochastic grammar of images. *Found Trends Comput Graph Vis* 2(4):259–362.

CHAPTER 12

Object Categorization in Man, Monkey, and Machine*: Some Answers and Some Open Questions

Maximilian Riesenhuber

12.1 Introduction

Understanding how the brain performs object categorization is of significant interest for cognitive neuroscience as well as for machine vision. In the past decade, building on earlier efforts (Fukushima 1980; Perrett and Oram 1993; Wallis and Rolls 1997), there has been significant progress in understanding the neural mechanisms underlying object recognition in the brain (Kourtzi and DiCarlo 2006; Peissig and Tarr 2007; Riesenhuber and Poggio 1999b; Riesenhuber and Poggio 2000; Riesenhuber and Poggio 2002; Serre et al. 2007a). There is now a quantitative computational model of the ventral visual pathway in primates that models rapid object recognition (Riesenhuber and Poggio 1999b; Serre et al. 2007a), putatively based on a single feedforward pass through the visual system (Thorpe and Fabre-Thorpe 2001). The model has been validated through a number of experiments that have confirmed nontrivial qualitative and quantitative predictions of the model (Freedman et al. 2003; Gawne and Martin 2002; Jiang et al. 2007; Jiang et al. 2006; Lampl et al. 2004). In the domain of machine vision, the success of the biological model in accounting for human object recognition performance (see, e.g., (Serre et al. 2007b)) has led to the development of a family of biologically inspired machine vision systems (see, e.g., (Marin-Jimenez and Perez de la Blanca, 2006; Meyers and Wolf, 2008; Mutch and Lowe, 2006; Serre et al. 2007c)).

Key to this progress has been a close and fruitful interaction between machine vision (in the form of providing computationally sound, testable hypotheses and existence proofs) and biological vision (in the form of providing data to test the validity of these hypotheses for biological vision and generating new data to refine and extend the model). Two insights in particular were crucial: Research in machine vision had shown that the competing requirements of invariance (i.e., tolerance to image changes such as object translation, lighting variations, or the presence of clutter) and specificity (i.e., the requirement to be sensitive to small changes in the input) are at the core of

---

* With thanks to Tarr and Bulthoff (1998) for the nice alliteration.

the problem of object recognition. Experiments in neuroscience, on the other hand, had provided evidence that object recognition in primates is mediated by a simple-to-complex hierarchy of brain areas (the so-called ventral visual stream (Ungerleider and Haxby 1994)) in which the complexity of neurons' preferred features as well as their receptive field sizes gradually increased across the hierarchy extending from primary visual cortex (V1) to inferotemporal cortex (IT). In a landmark study, Logothetis and coworkers (Logothetis et al. 1994; Logothetis et al. 1995) showed that some neurons in IT in monkeys trained to recognize novel "paperclip" objects were tuned to the learned objects, responding to particular views of a particular paperclip seen during training (but not to views of other clips), while being tolerant to scale and position changes of the preferred object in the visual field, even though the monkeys had only been exposed to views of the objects at a single position and scale.[1] Finally, electroencephalography (EEG) experiments had established that the visual system is able to perform even complex recognition tasks such as object detection in natural images within 150 ms (Thorpe et al. 1996), which is on the order of the response latency of neurons in prefrontal cortex (PFC), close to the site of the measured effect, suggesting that "rapid" object recognition, even for computationally very hard tasks such as object detection in cluttered natural scenes, could be achieved in basically one feedforward pass through the ventral stream, putting tight constraints on models of object recognition in cortex.

The basic experimental facts led to a "Standard Model" (Riesenhuber and Poggio 2002) of object recognition in cortex that summarized and extended previous proposals (Fukushima 1980; Perrett and Oram 1993; Poggio and Edelman 1990; Riesenhuber and Poggio 1999b; Riesenhuber and Poggio 2000; Wallis and Rolls 1997) (Fig. 12.1). It represents the simplest class of models that reflect the known anatomical and biological constraints. The basic architecture of the model will be discussed in section 12.2. In section 12.3, we will turn to the critical question of how this architecture can support the learning of different object recognition tasks and how the visual system solves the computational challenge of learning in "deep" hierarchies. In particular, for object categorization a crucial question is the interaction of bottom-up versus top-down information (i.e., of stimulus representation and task learning, or unsupervised versus supervised learning, across the hierarchy). Section 12.3 will present a simple algorithm for learning in the visual hierarchy, in which supervised learning (of labels) only occurs at the final stage, with lower levels learning an efficient stimulus representation in an unsupervised fashion. This algorithm can achieve state-of-the-art performance on hard benchmark machine vision tasks, and we will discuss data from human fMRI and monkey electrophysiology showing that the primate brain appears to use this algorithm to perform object categorization, with particular advantages for cognition. However, what if this rapid recognition process fails (e.g., in the presence of heavy clutter)? Of special interest for machine vision, the primate visual system appears to make use of additional computational strategies to improve recognition performance by dynamically modulating feedforward processing, which we will discuss in

---

[1] In addition, a few neurons were shown to respond selectively to particular paperclips in a view-invariant manner, compatible with theories (Poggio and Edelman 1990) describing how neurons tuned to individual views of a particular object can give rise to view-invariant neurons (Fig. 12.1).

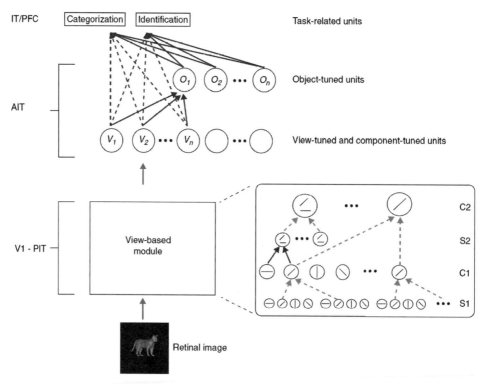

Figure 12.1. The Standard Model of object recognition in cortex (from Riesenhuber and Poggio, 2002). It models the cortical ventral visual stream (Ungerleider and Haxby 1994), running from primary visual cortex (V1) over extrastriate visual areas V2 and V4 to inferotemporal cortex (IT). Starting from V1 simple cells, with small receptive fields that respond preferentially to oriented bars, neurons along the ventral stream (Logothetis and Sheinberg 1996; Perrett and Oram 1993; Tanaka 1996) show an increase in receptive field size as well as in the complexity of their preferred stimuli (Kobatake and Tanaka 1994). At the top of the ventral stream, in anterior IT, cells are tuned to complex stimuli such as faces (Desimone 1991; Desimone et al. 1984; Gross et al. 1972; Perrett et al. 1992). A hallmark of these IT cells is their robust firing to stimulus transformations such as scale and position changes (Logothetis et al. 1995; Logothetis and Sheinberg 1996; Perrett and Oram 1993; Tanaka 1996). The bottom part of the model (inside the *inset*) consists of a view-based module (Riesenhuber and Poggio 1999b), which is an hierarchical extension of the classical paradigm of building complex cells from simple cells. In particular, units in the second layer (C1) pool within a neighborhood defined by their receptive field the activities of the "simple" cells in the first layer (S1) with the same orientation preference. In the model, pooling is through a MAX-like operation (dashed green lines), in which the firing rate of a pooling neuron corresponds to the firing rate of the strongest input, that improves invariance to local changes in position and scale while preserving stimulus selectivity (Riesenhuber and Poggio 1999b) (recent physiological experiments have provided support for the MAX pooling prediction at the level of complex cells in V1 (Lampl et al. 2004) and V4 (Gawne and Martin 2002)). At the next layer (S2), cells pool the activities of earlier neurons with different tuning, yielding selectivity to more complex patterns. The underlying operation is in this case more "traditional": a weighted sum followed by a sigmoidal (or Gaussian) transformation (solid lines). These two operations work together to progressively increase feature complexity and position (and scale) tolerance of units along the hierarchy, in agreement with physiological data (Kobatake and Tanaka 1994). The output of the view-based module is represented by view-tuned model units (VTUs) that exhibit tight tuning to rotation in depth but are tolerant to scaling and translation of their preferred object view, with tuning properties quantitatively similar to those found in IT (Logothetis et al. 1995; Riesenhuber and Poggio 1999b). The second part of the model starts with the VTUs. Invariance to, rotation in depth, for example, is obtained by combining, in a learning module, several VTUs tuned to different views of the same object (Poggio and Edelman 1990), creating view-invariant units (O_n). These, as well as the VTUs, can then serve as inputs to modules that learn to perform different visual tasks such as identification or object categorization. They consist of the same generic learning circuitry (Poggio and Girosi 1990) but are trained with appropriate sets of examples to perform specific tasks. (See color plate 12.1.)

section 12.4. We will close with a discussion of interesting questions for future neuro-science research.

12.2 The Neurocomputational Architecture Underlying Fast, "Feedforward" Object Recognition in Cortex

Figure 12.1 shows a sketch of the aforementioned "Standard Model" of object recognition in cortex. The model is a convenient way to summarize known facts and to ask through quantitative computer simulations a number of questions relevant for experiments; it is very much a working hypothesis rather than a complete and finished explanation. Further information, including source code, is available at http://maxlab.neuro .georgetown.edu/hmax. Note that Figure 12.1 is just a schematic – the actual model has been implemented as a computer program (consisting of several million units and hundreds of millions of connections) simulating neuronal activations along the ventral visual stream in response to the same stimuli and tasks as used in experiments (see, e.g., Freedman et al. 2003; Jiang et al. 2006; Riesenhuber and Poggio 1999b; Serre et al. 2007b).

The model of Figure 12.1 is computationally very simple, consisting of a feedforward processing hierarchy based on just two computational operations – feature combination to increase tuning selectivity and MAX pooling to increase invariance – with mean firing rate units. There is now direct and indirect evidence for both operations from computational as well as monkey and cat electrophysiology studies (Anzai et al. 2007; Cadieu et al. 2007; Finn and Ferster 2007; Gawne and Martin 2002; Ito and Komatsu 2004; Lampl et al. 2004). The computational capabilities of the model derive from the repeated application of these functions across the ventral stream hierarchy, in line with work in machine vision demonstrating the power of composite features and hierarchical architectures for object recognition (Amit and Geman 1999; Bienenstock and Geman 1995).

The feedforward nature of the basic model does not imply that more complex processing, such as recurrent processing, lateral interactions, or temporal dynamics, does not occur in the visual system. Rather, the model provides an existence proof that these are not required for "basic" object recognition (e.g., object detection in briefly presented images (Serre et al. 2007b), and it provides a framework in which to explore the scenarios in which additional feedback signals are needed to enable recognition. Two examples of particular interest in which top-down signals are necessary are during the learning of recognition tasks (to provide information about stimulus labels, see sect. 12.3) and in the case in which feedforward processing "breaks down" during recognition (e.g., in the case of heavy clutter, or when there are multiple possible responses to a particular stimulus) (see sect. 12.4).

12.2.1 One Mechanism Fits All? The Benchmark Test Case of Faces

One provocative prediction of the model of Figure 12.1 is that the same generic computational mechanisms are used by the brain to perform different recognition tasks (e.g., categorization or identification) on any object class (Riesenhuber and Poggio 2000). A particularly good example to test this model prediction is the case of human face discrimination, where "simple-to-complex" feature-based models were widely thought to be insufficient to explain human discrimination performance (Rossion and Gauthier 2002). In particular, the so-called face inversion effect (FIE), which refers to the observation that inversion appears to disproportionately affect the discrimination of faces compared to other objects (Yin 1969), has given rise to theories postulating that face discrimination is based on additional face-specific mechanisms, such as configural coding – positing that face perception proceeds by first recognizing face *parts* such as eyes, mouth, and nose, and then calculating their second-order spatial configuration (i.e., their relative positions) (Carey and Diamond 1986) – and that it is this "configural" coding that makes faces different from non-face objects whose recognition presumably only relies on "feature-based" mechanisms.

To test whether the FIE necessarily required the existence of specific recognition mechanisms separate from the ones of the model in Figure 12.1, we used existing behavioral data (Riesenhuber et al. 2004) to fit tuning parameters of model face units at the VTU level, modeling "face neurons" as found in monkey IT (Desimone 1991), which we hypothesized (Jiang et al. 2006) could underlie selectivity for face stimuli in the human "fusiform face area" (FFA), a brain region shown in many imaging studies to be crucial for human face perception (Kanwisher et al. 1997). Very interestingly, the simulation results showed that the model could indeed quantitatively account for the human behavioral face inversion effect (as well as for "featural" and "configural" effects): A population of face neurons selective for upright faces can support the fine discrimination of novel upright faces but performs rather poorly on inverted faces, which activate the upright face population to a lower degree, leading to smaller activation differences for inverted faces. The simulations led to the prediction that human face neurons in the FFA should show a particular degree of selectivity to support the observed behavioral discrimination performance for upright and inverted faces (Jiang et al. 2006). We then conducted functional magnetic resonance imaging rapid adaptation (fMRI-RA) and behavioral experiments to test the model predictions. fMRI-RA techniques of have been shown to be able to probe neuronal selectivity more directly than conventional fMRI techniques that rely on average BOLD-contrast stimulus responses (Gilaie-Dotan and Malach 2007; Grill-Spector et al. 2001; Jiang et al. 2006; Kourtzi and Kanwisher 2001). The fMRI-RA approach is motivated by findings from IT monkey electrophysiology experiments that showed that when pairs of stimuli were presented sequentially, a smaller neuronal response was observed following presentation of the second stimulus (Lueschow et al. 1994; McMahon and Olson 2007; Miller et al. 1993). It has been suggested that the degree of adaptation depends on stimulus similarity, with repetitions of the same stimulus causing the greatest suppression. In the fMRI version of this paradigm, the BOLD-contrast response to a *pair* of stimuli presented in rapid succession has been measured for pairs differing in specific perceptual aspects (e.g., viewpoint or shape), and the combined response level was assumed to predict stimulus representational dissimilarity at the neural level (Grill-Spector et al. 2006; Murray and Wojciulik 2004). Indeed, we (Jiang et al. 2006) and others (Fang et al. 2007; Gilaie-Dotan and Malach 2007; Murray and Wojciulik 2004) have recently provided evidence that parametric variations in shape, orientation, or viewpoint – stimulus parameters putatively associated with neuronal tuning properties in specific brain areas – are reflected in systematic modulations of the BOLD-contrast response, suggesting that fMRI adaptation can be used as an indirect measure of neuronal population tuning (Grill-Spector and Malach 2001).

Specifically, we used the model of human face neurons to predict how dissimilar two faces would have to be to activate disjoint subpopulations of neurons in the FFA (a prediction that was directly related to the predicted selectivity of human face neurons). Moreover, the model predicted that behavioral performance should likewise asymptote once the two to-be-discriminated stimuli activate disjoint subpopulations. The experimental fMRI and behavioral data provided excellent support for these quantitative predictions (Jiang et al. 2006), demonstrating that even for the "difficult" case of face discrimination, the "Standard Model" could quantitatively and mechanistically link the different experimental levels, from neurons to behavior, and provide nontrivial hypotheses for experiments.

12.3 Learning Different Object Recognition Tasks: Features, Objects, and Labels

The hierarchical nature of visual processing in cortex results in a powerful computational architecture based on simple neural operations. However, this success comes at a price: Learning in deep hierarchical networks is a notoriously difficult computational problem, and the visual system has to solve (and has solved!) this challenge to support the learning of complex visual tasks on a variety of objects. In fact, the ability to learn novel recognition tasks is a crucial feature of the visual system, given that the neural architecture for specific object recognition tasks (such as recognizing my children, recognizing tumors in chest x-rays or suspicious objects in baggage scans) cannot be genetically prespecified. In this section, I will describe recent experimental results on, how the visual system solves the deep learning problem, focusing on two key questions: (1) Which stages of the hierarchy participate in the learning of visual recognition tasks? (2) How do bottom-up, shape-driven, and top-down, label-based information interact in learning across the visual processing hierarchy?

12.3.1 Theories of Perceptual Categorization

Categorization requires learning a mapping of sensory stimuli to category labels. Traditionally, theories of human categorization from psychology have postulated that categorization involves the identification of the relevant stimulus features and the learning of a decision boundary either explicitly or by virtue of storing labeled exemplars or prototypes (Ashby and Maddox 2005). The problem of categorization can thus be broken down into two pieces: (1) The learning of a stimulus representation, and (2) the learning of the stimulus-label association. A question that has been the focus of significant attention in the neuroscience literature (Freedman et al. 2003; Sigala and Logothetis 2002; Thomas et al. 2001) is whether the learning of the stimulus representation proceeds in a bottom-up way (i.e., is driven by the stimuli only) or whether it is biased toward the category-relevant features (i.e., incorporates "top-down" information). Although the latter would at first blush appear preferable for categorization, the former has the appealing computational property that an unbiased high-level shape-based representation can be used more easily in support of other tasks involving the same stimuli (Riesenhuber and Poggio 2000), permitting transfer of learning to novel tasks. For instance, a population of neurons tuned to views of different cats and dogs could provide input to a circuit discriminating cats from dogs, as well as allow either the identification of a specific dog ("my dog Rosie") or its categorization at a different level ("black Labrador retriever").

Indeed, one of the main insights leading to the model of Figure 12.1 was that all object recognition tasks are computationally equivalent in that they involve learning a function that maps stimuli to labels (Riesenhuber and Poggio 2000). Computationally, there is no distinction between, for example, identification versus categorization, and we have shown that the same representation of view-tuned units can support different categorization tasks (see (Riesenhuber and Poggio 2002; Riesenhuber and Poggio 2003)).

For the task of perceptual categorization of visual images in cortex, the model thus predicts (Riesenhuber and Poggio 2000) that neurons in IT (or the lateral occipital complex, or LOC, its putative human homologue) (Grill-Spector et al. 2001; Grill-Spector et al. 1999; Malach et al. 1995; Tanaka 1997) should come to acquire sharper tuning with a concomitant higher degree of selectivity for the training stimuli, without an explicit representation of the category boundary, and that such neurons could provide a computationally efficient representation for neurons in the PFC to learn different tasks, such as categorization with different labels. Thus, the model predicts that learning up to IT/LOC is driven by stimulus signals in a bottom-up fashion and that the connections to PFC are the ones that are shaped by task-specific, top-down information. Recent monkey (Freedman et al. 2003; Op de Beeck et al. 2001; Thomas et al. 2001), as well as fMRI studies by us and others (Gillebert et al. 2008; Jiang et al. 2007), have provided support for such a two-stage model of perceptual category learning (Ashby and Lee 1991; Nosofsky 1986; Op de Beeck et al. 2008; Riesenhuber and Poggio 2000; Sigala 2004; Thomas et al. 2001).[2] The remainder of this section will review these data, showing how the two approaches – fMRI in humans, with its ability to study training effects in humans in a before/after comparison, over the whole extent of the brain, and monkey electrophysiology, with its high spatial and temporal resolution, which makes it possible to resolve tuning and response time courses of single neurons in key brain areas – can be used in complementary ways in the study of the neural bases of object categorization and learning.

12.3.2 Neural Bases of Categorization: Human fMRI Data

Neuroimaging studies of learning commonly compare BOLD-contrast responses to objects before and after training in particular brain voxels of interest. However, given

---

[2] Note that the focus in this chapter is on the perceptual and decision-related neural circuitry set up as a result of feedback-driven learning during training, not on the learning process itself. A number of studies have indicated that a cortical-striatal network is involved during the acquisition of perceptual categories (Ashby and Maddox 2005). The data show that although the basal ganglia appear to play an important role during feedback-driven task learning, little basal ganglia activity is found for well-learned tasks (Boettiger and D'Esposito 2005; Raichle et al. 1994), and frontal circuits appear to be more relevant during the execution of learned tasks (Little et al. 2006; Pasupathy and Miller 2005), and show a closer correlation with behavior (Pasupathy and Miller 2005).

that a voxel typically contains hundreds of thousands of neurons and that total activity in the voxel depends on the number of active neurons as well as their selectivity, learning-induced sharpening of neuronal responses, which by itself would lead to a lower population response as each neuron responds to fewer stimuli (Freedman et al. 2006; Rainer and Miller 2000), could lead to either decreases or increases in neuronal activity, depending on how training affects the number of selective neurons (see the discussion in Jiang et al. 2007). This makes it difficult to use BOLD-contrast amplitude changes as a measure of training-induced neuronal plasticity. Indeed, previous fMRI studies have found that perceptual and category learning can induce BOLD-contrast signal response increases (Gauthier et al. 1999; Op de Beeck et al. 2006; Pollmann and Maertens 2005), decreases (Reber et al. 1998), or both (Aizenstein et al. 2000; Kourtzi et al. 2005; Little et al. 2004).

To more directly probe the changes in neuronal tuning resulting from category acquisition, we trained (Jiang et al. 2007) a group of human participants to categorize stimuli ("cars;" see Fig. 12.2A) generated by a morphing system that was capable of finely and parametrically manipulating stimulus shape (Shelton 2000). This approach allowed us to define precisely the categories and dissociate category selectivity, which requires neurons to respond similarly to dissimilar stimuli from the same category as well as respond differently to similar stimuli belonging to different categories, from mere tuning to physical shape differences, in which neuronal responses are a function of physical shape dissimilarity, without the sharp transition at the category boundary that is a hallmark of perceptual categorization. Importantly, unlike earlier studies, we recorded brain activity before and after training using fMRI-RA techniques. We reasoned (see the discussion of fMRI-RA in the previous section) that if categorization training leads to sharpened neuronal selectivity to car images, then the overlap of neuronal activations caused by two sequentially presented car images differing by a fixed amount of shape change would decrease following training, resulting in an increase of BOLD-contrast response in the car-selective regions.

We provided direct evidence (Jiang et al. 2007) that training on a perceptual categorization task leads to the sharpening of a car-stimulus representation in lateral occipital cortex (LO), a part of LOC (Fig. 12.2C). This LO representation showed no explicit category selectivity, seeming to be selective for physical stimulus shape only, as responses to the $M3_{between}$ and $M3_{within}$ stimulus pairs (see Fig. 12.2B), which were equalized for physical dissimilarity but did or did not belong to different categories, respectively, did not differ significantly. In contrast, an area in the right lateral PFC (rLPFC) exhibited category-selective responses (Fig. 12.2D): When participants were judging the category membership of cars, this area's activity was modulated by explicit changes of category membership, but not by shape differences alone. Note that the ROI was defined by a very selective contrast, $M3_{between} > M3_{within}$, that was specific to categorization without a confound by shape difference.

In addition, as predicted by the model, we found that categorization training also improved subject performance on a *discrimination* task involving the car stimuli, without additional training. Interestingly, there was no effect of categorical perception (CP) (i.e., increased discriminability of stimulus pairs that fall into different categories vs. those belonging to the same category), further supporting that the learned car representation just represented object shape with no bias toward the category boundary.

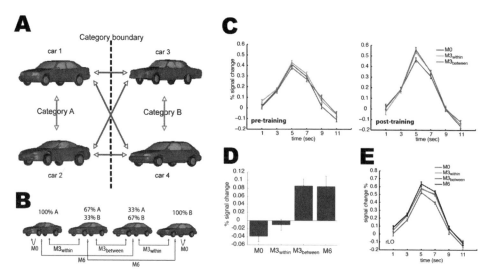

Figure 12.2. Investigating the interactions of bottom-up and top-down information in category learning and categorization using fMRI-RA. *A*, Visual stimuli. Subjects learned to categorize randomly generated morphs from the vast number of possible blends of four prototypes. The placement of the prototypes in this diagram does not reflect their similarity. Red lines show cross-category; green lines show within-category morph lines. *B*, Example morphs for a "cross-category" morph line between the "car 2" and "car 4" prototypes. In the fMRI-RA experiments, pairs of stimuli were shown in each trial, with total BOLD response to each pair indicating how strongly neurons in the area differentiate between the two stimuli. Stimulus pairs were grouped into the following conditions: M0 (0% shape change), M3$_{within}$ (33% shape change, same category), M3$_{between}$ (33% change, different category), and M6 (67% change, different category) *C*, fMRI-RA BOLD activation in right LO pre- (*left*) and post-training (*right*), in which subjects performed a displacement judgment task (for which the trained categories were irrelevant). Category training is shown to increase shape selectivity (M3 > M0 post-, $P < 0.05$, but not pre-training, $P > 0.5$) but not category selectivity (M3$_{within}$ = M3$_{between}$ pre-/post-training, $P > 0.4$). *D*, fMRI-RA activation in a right lateral PFC (rlPFC) ROI defined by the comparison of M3$_{between}$ versus M3$_{within}$ of the morph line on which participants had the best behavioral performance. The activation in the ROI was low for same-category trials, but significantly higher for different-category trials, suggesting that neurons in that area showed category-selective tuning. *E*, Activity in the car-selective rLO region during the categorization experiment: Responses increase with physical shape difference within the cars in a trial, $P < 0.0001$ (ANOVA), with no evidence for category tuning (responses for M3$_{within}$ and M3$_{between}$ not significantly different, $P > 0.9$). Error bars show within-subject SEM. For details, see Jiang et al. 2007). (See color plate 12.2.)

Similar observations of categorization in the absence of CP have been made in other domains – for example, when classifying faces by gender (Bulthoff and Newell 2004) or species (Campbell et al. 1997) – and might point to an automatic recruitment of categorization circuits for discrimination in some situations, but not in others. Importantly, this improvement in fine discrimination ability was not due to a test/retest effect on the discrimination task, but rather depended on the intervening categorization training (see supplementary material to Jiang et al. 2007).

In summary, these observations provide strong support for the "Standard Model," which posits that category learning involves two components: the learning of a shape-sensitive but task-independent representation that provides input to circuits responsible for particular recognition tasks (e.g., categorization). Finally, the results show that fMRI-RA techniques can be used to investigate learning effects at a more direct level

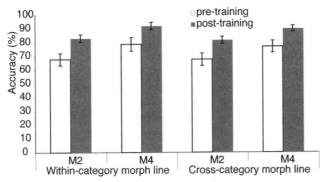

Figure 12.3. Psychophysical performance on the car discrimination task (Jiang et al. 2007). Subjects ($n = 13$) were tested on a 2AFC discrimination task using pairs of car stimuli chosen from all six morph lines, including two within-category morph lines and four cross-category morph lines (see Fig. 12.2). Testing was done both before ("pre-training") and after ("post-training") categorization training. Match and nonmatch stimuli in each trial could either differ by 20% (M2) or 40% shape change (M4). An ANOVA with training (pre- versus post-training), morph lines (within- versus cross-category morph lines), and morph step difference between match and nonmatch choice stimuli (M2 vs. M4) as repeated measures revealed significant effects of category training, $F(1,12) = 7.358$, $P = 0.019$, and morph step difference, $F(1,12) = 172.129$, $P < 0.001$, but not for morph line, $F(1,12) = 2.633$, $P = 0.131$. Importantly, there were no significant interactions, in particular not for training effect versus morph line, demonstrating that category learning improved discrimination of stimuli in general and not just for the category-relevant morph lines. Error bars show SEM.

than conventional approaches based on comparing average BOLD-contrast response amplitude in response to individual stimuli, and providing a powerful tool to study the mechanisms of human cortical plasticity.

12.3.3 Neural Bases of Categorization: Monkey Electrophysiology Data

The human results described above are in excellent agreement with a series of monkey electrophysiology experiments we recently conducted (Freedman et al. 2001; Freedman et al. 2002; Freedman et al. 2003). In those experiments, monkeys were trained to perform a delayed match-to-category task (DMC) on a space of morphed "cats" and "dogs," analogous to the "car" morph space in the human fMRI study, but in this case spanned by three "cat" and three "dog" prototypes. The monkeys viewed two stimuli that were separated by a brief delay (1 s) during which the monkey had to keep the category of the sample stimulus in mind. Monkeys were trained to indicate (by releasing a lever) whether the second (test) stimulus was from the same category as the previously seen (sample) stimulus. Thus, monkeys learned to group a continuous set of stimuli into discrete categories. Note that by using this task design, the monkey's responses (release or hold) indicated match or nonmatch, and neither was uniquely associated with either category. Furthermore, an equal proportion of match and nonmatch trials were presented in a pseudorandom order, and the monkeys could not predict whether a trial would be a match or nonmatch trial until the test stimulus appeared. Therefore, any neuronal signals related to stimulus category must be related to perceptual categorization

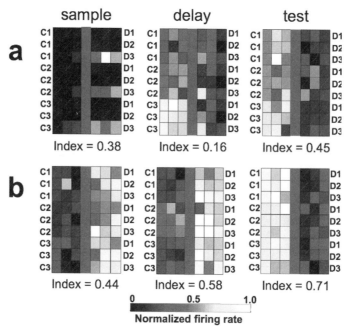

Figure 12.4. Neuronal responses of sample IT and PFC neurons to individual sample stimuli (Freedman et al. 2003), recorded from monkeys trained on a "cat/dog" categorization task over a morph space spanned by six prototypes, three "cats" (C1, C2, C3 in the figure) and three "dogs" (D1, D2, D3) (cf. the car morph space of Fig. 12.2 spanned by four car prototypes). The six color plots show the average activity of three IT (a) and three PFC (b) neurons to stimuli at specific points along each of the nine "between-class" morph lines (from left to right: 100% cat/0% dog, 80% cat/20% dog, . . . , 0% cat/100% dog). Each color plot shows the average activity of one neuron to each of the 42 stimuli along the nine between-class morph lines. The prototypes are represented in the outermost columns, and the blue line in the middle represents the category boundary. Each prototype contributes to three morph lines. A color scale indicates the activity level, normalized for each neuron to its maximum response. The category index of each neuron is indicated below each color plot. The plots are arranged into three columns. The columns, from left to right, show examples of neurons with selective activity during the sample, delay, and test epochs, respectively. These plots show the activity of six different neurons and not the activity of an individual neuron from each area across time. See text. (See color plate 12.4.)

and not the motor responses, because the responses did not differentiate between the categories.

After training, we recorded from a total of 968 neurons during DMC task performance, 525 PFC neurons and 443 IT neurons from three hemispheres of two monkeys (Freedman et al. 2003). To evaluate the strength of neuronal category tuning, a category index was calculated using each neuron's average difference in activity to pairs of stimuli along the morph lines that crossed the category boundary, including pairs of stimuli that were adjacent (within-category differences (WCDs): 100 vs. 80% and 80 vs. 60% cat or dog; between-category differences (BCDs): 60% cat vs. 60% dog), and pairs that differed by two steps (WCD: 100 vs. 60%; BCD: 80% cat vs. 60% dog and vice versa). Thus, the average morph distance between stimuli was identical for BCDs and WCDs. A standard contrast index was computed for each neuron by dividing the difference between BCDs and WCDs by their sum, giving values ranging from -1 to 1. Positive values of the category index indicated larger differences between categories compared to within a category, whereas negative values indicated the opposite. We found that PFC and IT played distinct roles in category-based behaviors (Fig. 12.4): IT seemed more involved in the analysis of currently viewed shapes, whereas the PFC showed stronger category signals, memory effects, and a greater tendency to encode information in terms of its behavioral meaning. In particular, while the average category index values of stimulus-selective IT neurons during the sample presentation (0.025) and during the delay period (0.047) were significantly greater than 0, they were not different from what would be expected from a population of shape-tuned neurons, as estimated with our computational model (see Fig. 12.1) based on the same stimuli as used during training (Freedman et al. 2003; Knoblich et al. 2002). In contrast, the average index value of PFC neurons during all time periods (averages during sample, delay, and test: 0.072, 0.141, and 0.217, respectively) was significantly greater than would be expected as a result of mere shape tuning, indicating that the tuning of these neurons was shaped by top-down category labels (indeed, after being retrained on an orthogonal categorization task, neurons in PFC reflected the new, but not the old, category boundary; Freedman et al. 2001).[3] Interestingly, IT neurons during the *test* period showed significant category selectivity as well, suggesting the intriguing possibility that top-down feedback from PFC may induce category-specific modulations of IT neuron activity under certain task conditions (see Tomita et al. 1999). However, no evidence for such category-related modulations was found in human studies (Gillebert et al. 2008; Jiang et al. 2007). Further strengthening the theory of a split of perceptual and task-based representations, we have recently shown (Roy, Riesenhuber, Poggio, Miller, *Soc Neurosci Abs*, 2006) that in a monkey trained to switch between two categorization schemes on the same morphed stimulus space (spanned by two "cats" and two "dogs," with the boundary in the different categorization schemes placed to group different pairs of prototypes together), the vast majority of PFC neurons strongly preferred one categorization scheme over the other (99 out of 109 PFC neurons), showing category selectivity when their preferred categorization scheme was active but little selectivity when the monkey was categorizing stimuli using the other categorization scheme. In contrast, IT neurons tended to be tuned to individual stimuli rather than to categories (as in our previous studies), and did not show any significant modulation by the currently active categorization scheme. Likewise, recent data from monkey electrophysiology likewise show that IT neuron responses provide a general purpose stimulus representation containing fine-shape information suitable to perform a variety of different recognition tasks efficiently (Hung et al. 2005).

---

[3] Note that this category index is a more selective marker of the presence of top-down category-related information than testing for the presence of "abstract" category information (Meyers et al. 2008), given that members of the different categories differed with respect to certain visual features, such as tail length ("cats" in Freedman et al. 2001) on average tended to have longer tails than "dogs" did). An IT neuron tuned to a long tail would therefore be expected to respond more to "cat" stimuli than to "dog" stimuli, just by virtue of bottom-up shape selectivity. In contrast, the category index tests whether physically similar changes in features cause larger neuronal response changes when crossing a category boundary than when staying within a category, thereby focusing on the key element of categorization, which is increased selectivity at the boundary, and controlling for shape-related effects.

12.3.4 Stimulus-Driven Learning at Lower Levels of the Hierarchy and Its Relevance for Recognition in Clutter

In the initial model simulations, stimulus-driven learning only took place at the LOC/IT/VTU level, and intermediate features in C2/V4 were hard-wired, just corresponding to all possible combinations of (four) different orientations in a 2×2 arrangement of complex cell afferents, for a total of 256 different features (Riesenhuber and Poggio 1999b). Surprisingly, this cartoonish feature set was already sufficient to account for shape selectivity and invariance properties of the experimentally found "paperclip" neurons in monkey IT (Logothetis et al. 1995). This was not an artifact of the impoverished nature of the paperclip stimuli, as the same feature set was able to also account for IT neuron tuning selectivity to cat and dog stimuli in our monkey electrophysiology study (Freedman et al. 2003; Knoblich et al. 2002) as well as for human face discrimination performance and face selectivity in the FFA (Jiang et al. 2006).

The importance of feature selectivity becomes apparent, however, when moving from the recognition of isolated objects to the more natural (and relevant) task of recognizing objects in clutter. To correctly recognize multiple objects in clutter, two problems must be solved (Riesenhuber and Poggio 1999a): (1) features must be extracted robustly, and (2) based on these features, a decision has to be made about which objects are present in the visual scene. The MAX operation can perform robust feature extraction: A MAX pooling cell that receives inputs from cells tuned to the same feature at, for example, different locations, will select the most strongly activated afferent (i.e., its response will be determined by the afferent with the closest match to its preferred feature in its receptive field). Thus, the MAX mechanism effectively isolates the feature of interest from the surrounding clutter. Hence, to achieve robustness to clutter, a VTU should only receive input from cells that are strongly activated by the VTU's preferred stimulus (i.e., those features that are relevant to the definition of the object) and thus less affected by clutter objects (which will tend to activate these afferents less and will therefore be ignored by the MAX response function). The number n of "most strongly active" features providing input to a VTU is a free parameter that can be chosen depending on the desired trade-off between stimulus-specificity and robustness to clutter: Choosing n to be large defines VTU tuning in a high-dimensional feature space, resulting in a high degree of shape selectivity. However, a large n leads to the inclusion of feature detectors among the afferents that are only relatively weakly activated by the preferred object, raising the likelihood that the simultaneous presence of a second object, which might activate the particular features more strongly, will cause interference and thus reduce the VTU's activity in the case of clutter. Conversely, choosing n to be low leads to less-selective VTUs, as their tuning would then be defined in a lower-dimensional feature space. However, the afferents in that case would be the ones that tend to be very strongly activated by the particular preferred object, decreasing the likelihood that a simultaneously presented second object will cause interference. Simulations had shown this predicted trade-off between selectivity and robustness to clutter (Riesenhuber and Poggio 1999a), and recent results from monkey electrophysiology have found evidence for just this trade-off in IT neurons (Zoccolan et al. 2007).

In the model, the selectivity of intermediate features therefore directly impacts how well stimuli can be recognized in clutter: If features are selective enough so that the "most strongly activated" feature sets for two objects are disjoint (or, if there are joint features, the corresponding feature detectors are activated to similar degrees), then these objects can be recognized even when appearing simultaneously. Note that this does not require complete independence of stimulus-specific activation in the feature space, just separation across the "most strongly active" features, whose number can be chosen depending on the desired specificity versus robustness to clutter tradeoff, as outlined previously. Indeed, simulations showed that whereas the model of (Riesenhuber and Poggio 1999b) with the hard-wired S2/C2 features performs poorly on object recognition tasks in clutter, learning more appropriate object class-specific features dramatically improved performance (Serre et al. 2002).

12.3.5 Activation versus Representation

Note that this model of object representation, which is based on strong activations, is in intriguing contrast to other proposals that have posited that both strong *and* weak activations are used in the representation of objects by the brain (Haxby et al. 2001; Tsunoda et al. 2001). It is trivially true that any stimulus causes both weak and strong activations, with a unit's weak response indicating that the stimulus is somewhat dissimilar to that particular unit's preferred stimulus, just as a strong response indicates that the stimulus is similar to the unit's preferred stimulus; thus, it is not surprising that the category of a stimulus can be determined from nonmaximal neural responses (given enough neurons with different tuning), as found in fMRI experiments (Haxby et al. 2001; Spiridon and Kanwisher 2002). However, instead of the question of whether large and small responses carry stimulus information, the more relevant question is whether all responses are involved in the *representation* of the stimulus, which we define to mean the part of the activation pattern that determines a subject's *behavioral response* to the stimulus (e.g., in a discrimination task). It is here where the notion that strong and weak activations are used by the brain to recognize an object runs into conceptual difficulties. Although the idea of including weak activations is attractive, as already discussed, because it provides additional information, the question arises even in the case of a single object on uniform background, which "weakly" activated neurons should be involved in the representation, as it is not feasible to, for instance, memorize the whole activation pattern over ventral temporal cortex caused by a particular stimulus for later comparison to probe stimuli. Even more problematic, as outlined before, the computational model (Riesenhuber and Poggio 1999a) predicts that weak activations are the ones most susceptible to interference from other simultaneously presented objects. Given the widespread and overlapping activation patterns associated with different object classes (Haxby et al. 2001; Spiridon and Kanwisher 2002), it is thus difficult to see how a representational scheme that relies on low activation of non-relevant features could support the visual system's impressive ability to detect objects in rapidly presented cluttered complex natural scenes in parallel (Rousselet et al. 2002) and without the need for attention (Li et al. 2002). Indeed, recent fMRI studies have shown that behavior appears to be driven only by subsets of stimulus-related activation (Grill-Spector et al. 2004; Jiang et al. 2006; Williams et al. 2007), in particular those with optimal tuning for the task (Jiang et al. 2006).

The importance of selective intermediate features for robust object recognition in a hierarchical system immediately raises the question of how these features can be learned. The aforementioned early simulations (Serre et al. 2002) used a form of learning in which features were randomly selected image snippets from the relevant target class. Although feature extraction from the training image set was thus unsupervised, it was still specific for the target class due to the selection of the training images, adding an element of supervised learning. Such a learning scheme has the advantage of high performance even for low numbers of features (see Ullman et al. 2002 for an elegant implementation of this idea), but it raises several issues, such as the challenge of computing and propagating task-related quantities such as mutual information (Ullman et al. 2002) across the hierarchy, or the need to avoid a combinatorial explosion in the number of features if many different object classes are to be recognized. These issues make such algorithms less likely candidates for a biologically plausible learning scheme. However, given that natural objects share many common features (such as edges, surfaces, angles, etc.), the question arises whether it might be possible to extract a set of features from a large set of natural objects that might then be sufficient to support the recognition of arbitrary natural objects. We have recently shown (Serre et al. 2007c) that such a learning scheme is capable of excellent performance on a variety of difficult object recognition tasks: Extracting just 1,000 features out of a large set of natural images (10,000 images downloaded off the Web) was sufficient to support classification on the varied Caltech-101 image set. This completely unsupervised feature learning scheme not only has the virtue of simplicity and biological plausibility (indeed, behavioral experiments have provided support for the idea that the human visual system learns features in an unsupervised way, driven by input statistics; Fiser and Aslin 2001); it is also appealing as a model for biological object recognition, as it allows re-using learned features for novel tasks, in the same way that units at other levels of the hierarchy, such as the VTU level discussed earlier, can be used for a variety of tasks.

12.4 What to Do if Rapid Recognition Breaks: Tweaking Things on the Fly

As outlined in the previous section, a selective feature set is crucial to boosting recognition performance in clutter. Yet, the performance levels of state-of-the-art techniques are still far below human performance levels. The key limiting factor appears to lie in the mechanisms that machines versus those used by human vision systems to deal with large amounts of clutter. Serre and coworkers are used by (2007b) have shown that both humans and the feedforward model of Figure 12.1 show highest (and comparable) performance in the classical "animal/no-animal" detection task (Thorpe et al. 1996) when targets occupy a large portion of the image. Performance in humans (and the feedforward model) drops off precipitously as targets take up progressively less space in the image and the effect of clutter increases (Serre et al. 2007b) for short presentation times (20 ms, followed by a mask after an additional 30 ms). Allowing unlimited viewing time increases human performance to ceiling levels, even if targets only occupy a small part of the image. In contrast, as the model of Figure 12.1 does not include any temporal dynamics, it cannot exploit longer presentation times to boost detection performance of targets in cluttered scenes.

What computational strategies does the visual system use to reduce the effect of clutter for longer presentation times? A computationally very effective strategy is to reduce the effect of clutter by introducing a "spotlight of attention" (Koch and Ullman 1985; Tsotsos et al. 1995) that focuses processing on a particular part of the visual field, suppressing inputs from outside the focus of attention. Note that the role of attention in such a scheme is different from the traditional idea of requiring attention to select which part of the input gets to squeeze through a processing "bottleneck," which results from computational resources insufficient to analyze the whole scene. Rather, attention reduces the interference created by clutter. We have shown previously that this theoretical idea works well in practice to boost recognition performance in clutter (Walther et al. 2002). There is also ample experimental evidence that spatial cues can indeed serve to modulate the extent of receptive fields across the ventral processing stream compatible with the spotlight idea (Moran and Desimone 1985; Rolls et al. 2003; Somers et al. 1999), possibly through a shift of neurons' contrast response function to increase apparent contrast for targets and decrease apparent contrast for nontargets, in line with monkey neurophysiology (Reynolds et al. 2000) and behavior (Carrasco et al. 2004).

Spatial information about target location can thus improve detection performance of the feedforward system of Figure 12.1 by suppressing input from nonrelevant regions. In general, however, a priori information about target location is not available. Rather, there is information about target identity or target features. How to use this "featural" information to reduce the effect of clutter? Numerous experiments have reported task-dependent modulations of responses in visual areas V1 and V2 (Lee et al. 2002) and in particular in V4 (McAdams and Maunsell 1999a; Motter 1993), with neuronal responses to identical visual stimuli being modulated by the stimulus' relevance for a particular task. Specifically, a series of monkey physiology experiments have argued that attention acts by increasing neuronal gain for nonspatial features such as orientation in V4 (McAdams and Maunsell 1999a; Motter 1993) or motion direction in motion-area MT in the dorsal stream (Martinez-Trujillo and Treue 2004).

Discussions of feature-related attentional gain modulation in the literature generally focus on the "labeled line" example case, in which neurons are directly tuned to the feature of interest (e.g., orientation in an orientation discrimination task) (Martinez-Trujillo and Treue 2004; McAdams and Maunsell 1999a). Yet, in a processing hierarchy such as the visual streams, in which neurons in higher levels respond preferentially to specific *distributed* and *graded* activation patterns over their afferents (Haxby et al. 2001; Jiang et al. 2006; Tsunoda et al. 2001), modulating the gain of these afferents (particularly if this is done by varying gain factors depending on the similarity of each afferent's preferred feature to the target feature (Martinez-Trujillo and Treue 2004)) can be highly problematic, because it can change afferents' activation levels in nontrivial ways by differentially scaling the responses of different afferents by different factors, making it difficult for the downstream neuron receiving input from the modulated afferents to recover stimulus identity. Indeed, our computational simulations have shown that gain increases of afferent neurons participating in a distributed representation are generally detrimental to recognition performance (Riesenhuber 2005; Schneider and Riesenhuber 2004). Thus, as in the spatial attention case, a computationally simpler mechanism for feature-based attention to deal with competing stimuli is *to suppress irrelevant information* (Walther et al. 2002) *rather than modulate the relevant information*, compatible with the popular phenomenological "biased-competition" model of attention (Desimone 1998). The question of whether a particular response difference between two attentional conditions is due to enhancement of one or suppression of the other depends on the definition of the baseline. Most studies of attention use an attend-fixation baseline (e.g., (Martinez-Trujillo and Treue 2004; McAdams and Maunsell 1999b)). However, this might lead to a suppression of responses to the unattended object in the baseline condition owing to spatial attention effects. What seems to be "enhancement" in the attended condition might therefore be just the "normal," unmodulated response, and the true effect of attention might be the suppression of interfering distractors, as predicted based on the aforementioned computational considerations. There is intriguing recent support for this idea that attentional modulations predominantly act to increase the inhibition of nonrelevant signals: It has been reported that the strongest attentional modulations in V4 occur in *inhibitory* interneurons (Mitchell et al. 2007), and that top-down, attention-induced response increases in V1 are likewise mostly found in inhibitory interneurons at the focus of attention (Chen et al. 2008), which is compatible with the theory that increasing the activation of these neurons leads to the suppression of activity outside the focus of attention.

What, if these modulations are still insufficient to permit target detection in a feed-forward pass? As visual search experiments have shown, the visual system appears to resort to a divide-and-conquer strategy, sequentially positioning the attentional spotlight at salient locations and attempting to locally detect the target. *Saliency* can be defined either in a task-independent manner through generic low-level features such as color, motion, or orientation contrast, or by incorporation of task-relevant features (e.g., assigning higher salience to red regions when looking for a red soda can) (Itti and Koch 2001). This is an elegant hypothesis that directly leads to the question of where the putative saliency map might be located in the brain. Locating the saliency map outside of the ventral processing stream (e.g., in parietal area LIP) (Gottlieb 2007) has the computational advantage of avoiding interference of saliency and stimulus information, at the expense of duplicating visual processing, once for object recognition and once for saliency computation. Correspondingly, alternative proposals have postulated that a saliency map (or even multiple saliency maps, matching the different feature selectivities in different ventral stream areas) might be located in the ventral visual stream itself, possibly as early as primary visual cortex (Li 2002). Although it is attractive in its efficiency, this option raises the issue of how (unmodulated) object information and (task-modulated) saliency information can be multiplexed in the same pathway with minimal mutual interference (or even in a synergistic way). Again, the earlier proposal of saliency acting by suppressing irrelevant information might provide a suitable computational mechanism, but whether this is in fact the route chosen by the brain is still an open question.

12.5 More Open Questions

Although there is a significant amount of experimental support for the simple-to-complex model of object recognition in cortex shown in Figure 12.1, this, of course, does not mean that the model is necessarily correct in all its details (it certainly will turn out not to be!). Rather, it represents a good current null hypothesis and a computational and conceptual framework in which to ask questions for future research to further help us understand the neural bases of the brain's superior object recognition capabilities. One of those questions, already mentioned in the previous section, is how saliency and object information are multiplexed in the same processing pathway and how the two interact to enable object recognition in clutter. Another question concerns how the visual system leverages prior learning of related tasks during the execution of recognition tasks. In theory, when trying to categorize an object, it can be helpful to incorporate information from other tasks: For example, "The object I am looking at is more likely to be my dog Rosie if I already know that I am looking at a black lab and not a black cat." On the theoretical side, various computational models have been proposed that perform these kinds of image-based inferences (e.g., Hawkins and Blakeslee 2004; Lee and Mumford 2003; Rao 2005). Experimentally, there is ample evidence that signals from different recognition circuits interact in driving behavior, in particular in categorical perception. However, the neural bases of these effects are still unknown. Electrophysiology, fMRI, and MEG experiments have suggested that neurons in ventral temporal cortex can be modulated by top-down signals that likely originate from frontal cortex and can carry information on paired associates (Tomita et al. 1999), category membership (Freedman et al. 2003), or low spatial frequency "gist" information (Bar et al. 2006). What determines whether and which circuits coding for other tasks are activated? How and where are these signals combined? Given that these top-down signals modulate firing in IT, why does this not seem to induce shifts in IT bottom-up selectivities? For instance, normal hebbian learning would predict that if an IT neuron were active to all stimuli from a particular category (see, e.g., the test period response of the IT neuron in Fig. 12.4), then it would learn to acquire category tuning rather than the stimulus-specific tuning found experimentally (see the sample period response in Fig. 12.4 and the discussion in sec. 12.3). Is there a particular temporal window for plasticity or a specific kind of gating signal for plasticity that preferentially acts on the early, bottom-up part of the neuronal response?

The existence of top-down modulations from task-related circuits in prefrontal cortex raises the question of how the source of this modulation is selected. In particular, one could imagine conflicting top-down modulations from interfering task circuits that would have to be suppressed. Indeed, the simple scenario described in the previous sections, focusing on a single task to be performed on a given stimulus, is clearly a special case. Usually, stimulus-response associations are flexible, and a particular stimulus can be acted upon in different ways, raising the need to control which task circuit gets engaged to determine the behavioral response depending on the currently relevant task set. How is this control implemented? As for the attentional modulations of sensory processing, two options appear most viable: Control could amplify the activation of relevant circuits, or suppress the activation of irrelevant circuits. Interestingly, the frontoparietal networks central for attentional modulations of sensory processing have also been implicated in cognitive control (that focuses on the neural mechanisms underlying the selection of the neuronal circuitry coding for the currently relevant task) (Miller and Cohen 2001), suggesting a close link between the two. Similarly to the attentional case, the discussion of whether control acts by suppression or amplification

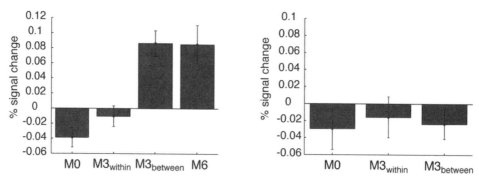

Figure 12.5. Activation in the right lateral PFC ROI of Figure 12.2*D* when subjects were performing a categorization task (*left*), and during a displacement judgment task (for which the stimulus categories were irrelevant) on the same stimuli (*right*; M6 was not included in the displacement judgment scans) (Jiang et al. 2007). ANOVAs with three conditions (M0, M3$_{within}$, and M3$_{between}$) as repeated measures found significant differences when subjects were performing the categorization task (*left*, $P < 0.00001$), but not during the displacement judgment task (*right*, $P > 0.5$). Error bars show within-subject SEM.

is controversial (Aron et al. 2004; Nieuwenhuis and Yeung 2005), and an in-depth treatment of this issue is beyond the scope of this chapter. Briefly, similar considerations as in the sensory case also apply in the case of modulations of task-related activation, arguing for suppression of irrelevant information as a computationally simple way of implementing cognitive control. Indeed, our own fMRI and neurophysiological data are compatible with this idea: In the case of the monkey trained on the category-switching task mentioned earlier (Roy Riesenhuber, Poggio, Miller, *Soc Neurosci Abs*, 2006), we found that the activity of PFC neurons coding for the nonrelevant categorization scheme was suppressed and did not show category selectivity; in the human fMRI study, we likewise found suppression of the categorization circuitry in PFC during the execution of another task (see Fig. 12.5).

Finally, the discussions on learning in the object recognition system in this chapter have focused on the learning of features, objects, and task circuits, and glossed over the important question of how invariances (e.g., tolerance to changes in stimulus position and scale, or possibly even viewpoint) are learned. Early theoretical proposals have shown how temporal context can be utilized to learn invariance by assuming that temporally proximate inputs arise from the same object (Foldiak 1991; see also Wallis and Rolls 1997; Wiskott and Sejnowski 2002). Recent elegant experiments have provided support for such a role of temporal associations in the learning of invariances at the human behavioral (Wallis and Bulthoff 2001) and monkey IT neuron level (Li and DiCarlo 2008), which sets the stage for future studies to establish how neuronal selectivity changes induced through temporal associations can be quantitatively linked to corresponding improvements in invariant object recognition performance.

12.6 Conclusion

The brain performs object categorization exceptionally well and seemingly without effort. We have made significant progress in understanding the underlying neural mechanisms, in particular for rapid feedforward object recognition, thanks to a productive interaction of computational research in machine vision and experimental research in cognitive neuroscience. Given the unrivaled object detection performance of the human brain, continuing this multidisciplinary approach to explore more sophisticated neural mechanisms involved in biological object recognition, in particular those allowing the visual system to deal effectively with heavy clutter, should prove to be fruitful and exciting for everyone involved.

12.7 Acknowledgments

The research described in this chapter was supported in part by an NSF CAREER Award (#0449743), and NIMH grants R01MH076281 and P20MH66239.

Bibliography

Aizenstein HJ, MacDonald AW, Stenger VA, Nebes RD, Larson JK, Ursu S, Carter CS. 2000. Complementary category learning systems identified using event-related functional MRI. *J Cogn Neurosci* 12: 977–987.

Amit Y, Geman D. 1999. A computational model for visual selection. *Neural Comput* 11: 1691–1715.

Anzai A, Peng X, Van Essen DC. 2007. Neurons in monkey visual area V2 encode combinations of orientations. *Nat Neurosci* 10: 1313–1321.

Aron AR, Robbins TW, Poldrack RA. 2004. Inhibition and the right inferior frontal cortex. *Trends Cogn Sci* 8: 170–177.

Ashby FG, Lee WW. 1991. Predicting similarity and categorization from identification. *J Exp Psychol Gen* 120: 150–172.

Ashby FG, Maddox WT. 2005. Human category learning. *Annu Rev Psychol* 56: 149–178.

Bar M, Kassam KS, Ghuman AS, Boshyan J, Schmid AM, Dale AM, Hamalainen MS, Marinkovic K, Schacter DL, Rosen BR, Halgren E. 2006. Top-down facilitation of visual recognition. *Proc Natl Acad Sci USA* 103: 449–454.

Bienenstock E, Geman S. 1995. Compositionality in neural systems. In *The handbook of brain theory and neural networks*, ed. M Arbib, 223–226. Cambridge: MIT/Bradford Books, Elsevier.

Boettiger CA, D'Esposito M. 2005. Frontal networks for learning and executing arbitrary stimulus-response associations. *J Neurosci* 25: 2723–2732.

Bulthoff I, Newell F. 2004. Categorical perception of sex occurs in familiar but not unfamiliar faces. *Vis Cogn* 11: 823–855.

Cadieu C, Kouh M, Pasupathy A, Connor CE, Riesenhuber M, Poggio T. 2007. A model of V4 shape selectivity and invariance. *J Neurophysiol* 98: 1733–1750.

Campbell R, Pascalis O, Coleman M, Wallace SB, Benson PJ. 1997. Are faces of different species perceived categorically by human observers? *Proc Biol Sci* 264: 1429–1434.

Carey S, Diamond R. 1986. Why faces are and are not special: an effect of expertise. *J Exp Psychol Gen* 115: 107–117.

Carrasco M, Ling S, Read S. 2004. Attention alters appearance. *Nat Neurosci* 7: 308–313.

Chen Y, Martinez-Conde S, Macknik SL, Bereshpolova Y, Swadlow HA, Alonso JM. 2008. Task difficulty modulates the activity of specific neuronal populations in primary visual cortex. *Nat Neurosci* 11: 974–982.

Desimone R. 1991. Face-selective cells in the temporal cortex of monkeys. *J Cogn Neurosci* 3: 1–8.

Desimone R. 1998. Visual attention mediated by biased competition in extrastriate visual cortex. *Philos Trans R Soc Lond B Biol Sci* 353: 1245–1255.

Desimone R, Albright TD, Gross CG, Bruce C. 1984. Stimulus-selective properties of inferior temporal neurons in the macaque. *J Neurosci* 4: 2051–2062.

Fang F, Murray SO, He S. 2007. Duration-dependent FMRI adaptation and distributed viewer-centered face representation in human visual cortex. *Cereb Cortex* 17: 1402–1411.

Finn IM, Ferster D. 2007. Computational diversity in complex cells of cat primary visual cortex. *J Neurosci* 27: 9638–9648.

Fiser J, Aslin RN. 2001. Unsupervised statistical learning of higher-order spatial structures from visual scenes. *Psychol Sci* 12: 499–504.

Foldiak P. 1991. Learning invariance from transformation sequences. *Neural Comput* 3: 194–200.

Freedman DJ, Riesenhuber M, Poggio T, Miller EK. 2001. Categorical representation of visual stimuli in the primate prefrontal cortex. *Science* 291: 312–316.

Freedman DJ, Riesenhuber M, Poggio T, Miller EK. 2002. Visual categorization and the primate prefrontal cortex: neurophysiology and behavior. *J Neurophysiol* 88: 929–941.

Freedman DJ, Riesenhuber M, Poggio T, Miller EK. 2003. Comparison of primate prefrontal and inferior temporal cortices during visual categorization. *J Neurosci* 23: 5235–5246.

Freedman DJ, Riesenhuber M, Poggio T, Miller EK. 2006. Experience-dependent sharpening of visual shape selectivity in inferior temporal cortex. *Cereb Cortex* 16: 1631–1644.

Fukushima K. 1980. Neocognitron: a self-organizing neural network model for a mechanism of pattern recognition unaffected by shift in position. *Biol Cybern* 36: 193–202.

Gauthier I, Tarr MJ, Anderson AW, Skudlarski P, Gore JC. 1999. Activation of the middle fusiform 'face area' increases with expertise in recognizing novel objects. *Nat Neurosci* 2: 568–573.

Gawne T, Martin J. 2002. Responses of primate visual cortical V4 neurons to simultaneously presented stimuli. *J Neurophys* 88: 1128–1135.

Gilaie-Dotan S, Malach R. 2007. Sub-exemplar shape tuning in human face-related areas. *Cereb Cortex* 17: 325–338.

Gillebert CR, Op de Beeck HP, Panis S, Wagemans J. 2008. Subordinate categorization enhances the neural selectivity in human object-selective cortex for fine shape differences. *J Cogn Neurosci*.

Gottlieb J. 2007. From thought to action: the parietal cortex as a bridge between perception, action, and cognition. *Neuron* 53: 9–16.

Grill-Spector K, Henson R, Martin A. 2006. Repetition and the brain: neural models of stimulus-specific effects. *Trends Cogn Sci* 10: 14–23.

Grill-Spector K, Knouf N, Kanwisher N. 2004. The fusiform face area subserves face perception, not generic within-category identification. *Nat Neurosci* 7: 555–562.

Grill-Spector K, Kourtzi Z, Kanwisher N. 2001. The lateral occipital complex and its role in object recognition. *Vision Res* 41: 1409–1422.

Grill-Spector K, Kushnir T, Edelman S, Avidan G, Itzchak Y, Malach R. 1999. Differential processing of objects under various viewing conditions in the human lateral occipital complex. *Neuron* 24: 187–203.

Grill-Spector K, Malach R. 2001. fMR-adaptation: a tool for studying the functional properties of human cortical neurons. *Acta Psychol (Amst)* 107: 293–321.

Gross CG, Rocha-Miranda CE, Bender DB. 1972. Visual properties of neurons in inferotemporal cortex of the Macaque. *J Neurophysiol* 35: 96–111.

Hawkins J, Blakeslee S. 2004. *On intelligence*. New York: Macmillan.

Haxby JV, Gobbini MI, Furey ML, Ishai A, Schouten JL, Pietrini P. 2001. Distributed and overlapping representations of faces and objects in ventral temporal cortex. *Science* 293: 2425–2430.

Hung CP, Kreiman G, Poggio T, DiCarlo JJ. 2005. Fast readout of object identity from macaque inferior temporal cortex. *Science* 310: 863–866.

Ito M, Komatsu H. 2004. Representation of angles embedded within contour stimuli in area V2 of macaque monkeys. *J Neurosci* 24: 3313–3324.

Itti L, Koch C. 2001. Computational modelling of visual attention. *Nat Rev Neurosci* 2: 194–203.

Jiang X, Bradley E, Rini RA, Zeffiro T, Vanmeter J, Riesenhuber M. 2007. Categorization training results in shape- and category-selective human neural plasticity. *Neuron* 53: 891–903.

Jiang X, Rosen E, Zeffiro T, Vanmeter J, Blanz V, Riesenhuber M. 2006. Evaluation of a shape-based model of human face discrimination using FMRI and behavioral techniques. *Neuron* 50: 159–172.

Kanwisher N, McDermott J, Chun MM. 1997. The fusiform face area: a module in human extrastriate cortex specialized for face perception. *J Neurosci* 17: 4302–4311.

Knoblich U, Freedman DJ, Riesenhuber M. 2002. Categorization in IT and PFC: model and experiments. CBCL paper 216/AI Memo 2002-007. Massachusetts Institute of Technology, Cambridge, MA.

Kobatake E, Tanaka K. 1994. Neuronal selectivities to complex object features in the ventral visual pathway of the macaque cerebral cortex. *J Neurophysiol* 71: 856–867.

Koch C, Ullman S. 1985. Shifts in selective visual attention: towards the underlying neural circuitry. *Hum Neurobiol* 4: 219–227.

Kourtzi Z, Betts LR, Sarkheil P, Welchman AE. 2005. Distributed neural plasticity for shape learning in the human visual cortex. *PLoS Biol* 3: e204.

Kourtzi Z, DiCarlo JJ. 2006. Learning and neural plasticity in visual object recognition. *Curr Opin Neurobiol* 16: 152–158.

Kourtzi Z, Kanwisher N. 2001. Representation of perceived object shape by the human lateral occipital complex. *Science* 293: 1506–1509.

Lampl I, Ferster D, Poggio T, Riesenhuber M. 2004. Intracellular measurements of spatial integration and the MAX operation in complex cells of the cat primary visual cortex. *J Neurophys* 92: 2704–2713.

Lee TS, Mumford D. 2003. Hierarchical Bayesian inference in the visual cortex. *J Opt Soc Am A Opt Image Sci Vis* 20: 1434–1448.

Lee TS, Yang CF, Romero RD, Mumford D. 2002. Neural activity in early visual cortex reflects behavioral experience and higher-order perceptual saliency. *Nat Neurosci* 5: 589–597.

Li FF, VanRullen R, Koch C, Perona P. 2002. Rapid natural scene categorization in the near absence of attention. *Proc Natl Acad Sci USA* 99: 9596–9601.

Li N, DiCarlo JJ. 2008. Unsupervised natural experience rapidly alters invariant object representation in visual cortex. *Science* 321: 1502–1507.

Li Z. 2002. A saliency map in primary visual cortex. *Trends Cogn Sci* 6: 9–16.

Little DM, Klein R, Shobat DM, McClure ED, Thulborn KR. 2004. Changing patterns of brain activation during category learning revealed by functional MRI. *Brain Res Cogn Brain Res* 22: 84–93.

Little DM, Shi SS, Sisco SM, Thulborn KR. 2006. Event-related fMRI of category learning: differences in classification and feedback networks. *Brain Cogn* 60: 244–252.

Logothetis NK, Pauls J, Bulthoff HH, Poggio T. 1994. View-dependent object recognition by monkeys. *Curr Biol* 4: 401–414.

Logothetis NK, Pauls J, Poggio T. 1995. Shape representation in the inferior temporal cortex of monkeys. *Curr Biol* 5: 552–563.

Logothetis NK, Sheinberg DL. 1996. Visual object recognition. *Annu Rev Neurosci* 19: 577–621.

Lueschow A, Miller EK, Desimone R. 1994. Inferior temporal mechanisms for invariant object recognition. *Cereb Cortex* 4: 523–531.

Malach R, Reppas JB, Benson RR, Kwong KK, Jiang H, Kennedy WA, Ledden PJ, Brady TJ, Rosen BR, Tootell RB. 1995. Object-related activity revealed by functional magnetic resonance imaging in human occipital cortex. *Proc Natl Acad Sci USA* 92: 8135–8139.

Marin-Jimenez M, Perez de la Blanca N. 2006. Empirical study of multi-scale filter banks for object recognition. Paper presented at international conference on pattern recognition.

Martinez-Trujillo JC, Treue S. 2004. Feature-based attention increases the selectivity of population responses in primate visual cortex. *Curr Biol* 14: 744–751.

McAdams CJ, Maunsell JH. 1999a. Effects of attention on orientation-tuning functions of single neurons in macaque cortical area V4. *J Neurosci* 19: 431–441.

McAdams CJ, Maunsell JH. 1999b. Effects of attention on the reliability of individual neurons in monkey visual cortex. *Neuron* 23: 765–773.

McMahon DB, Olson CR. 2007. Repetition suppression in monkey inferotemporal cortex: relation to behavioral priming. *J Neurophysiol* 97: 3532–3543.

Meyers E, Wolf L. 2008. Using biologically inspired features for face processing. *Int J Comp Vis* 76: 93–104.

Meyers EM, Freedman DJ, Kreiman G, Miller EK, Poggio T. 2008. Dynamic population coding of category information in inferior temporal and prefrontal cortex. *J Neurophysiol* 100: 1407–1419.

Miller EK, Cohen JD. 2001. An integrative theory of prefrontal cortex function. *Annu Rev Neurosci* 24: 167–202.

Miller EK, Li L, Desimone R. 1993. Activity of neurons in anterior inferior temporal cortex during a short-term memory task. *J Neurosci* 13: 1460–1478.

Mitchell JF, Sundberg KA, Reynolds JH. 2007. Differential attention-dependent response modulation across cell classes in macaque visual area V4. *Neuron* 55: 131–141.

Moran J, Desimone R. 1985. Selective attention gates visual processing in the extrastriate cortex. *Science* 229: 782–784.

Motter BC. 1993. Focal attention produces spatially selective processing in visual cortical areas V1, V2, and V4 in the presence of competing stimuli. *J Neurophysiol* 70: 909–919.

Murray SO, Wojciulik E. 2004. Attention increases neural selectivity in the human lateral occipital complex. *Nat Neurosci* 7: 70–74.

Mutch J, Lowe D. 2006. Multiclass object recognition using sparse, localized features. Paper presented at IEEE conference on computer vision and pattern recognition.

Nieuwenhuis S, Yeung N. 2005. Neural mechanisms of attention and control: losing our inhibitions? *Nat Neurosci* 8: 1631–1633.

Nosofsky RM. 1986. Attention, similarity, and the identification-categorization relationship. *J Exp Psychol Gen* 115: 39–61.

Op de Beeck H, Wagemans J, Vogels R. 2001. Inferotemporal neurons represent low-dimensional configurations of parameterized shapes. *Nat Neurosci* 4: 1244–1252.

Op de Beeck HP, Baker CI, DiCarlo JJ, Kanwisher NG. 2006. Discrimination training alters object representations in human extrastriate cortex. *J Neurosci* 26: 13025–13036.

Op de Beeck HP, Wagemans J, Vogels R. 2008. The representation of perceived shape similarity and its role for category learning in monkeys: a modeling study. *Vision Res* 48: 598–610.

Pasupathy A, Miller EK. 2005. Different time courses of learning-related activity in the prefrontal cortex and striatum. *Nature* 433: 873–876.

Peissig JJ, Tarr MJ. 2007. Visual object recognition: do we know more now than we did 20 years ago? *Annu Rev Psychol* 58: 75–96.

Perrett D, Oram M. 1993. Neurophysiology of shape processing. *Image Vision Comput* 11: 317–333.

Perrett DI, Hietanen JK, Oram MW, Benson PJ. 1992. Organization and functions of cells responsive to faces in the temporal cortex. *Philos Trans R Soc Lond B Biol Sci* 335: 23–30.

Poggio T, Edelman S. 1990. A network that learns to recognize three-dimensional objects. *Nature* 343: 263–266.

Poggio T, Girosi F. 1990. Networks for approximation and learning. *Proc IEEE* 78: 1481–1497.

Pollmann S, Maertens M. 2005. Shift of activity from attention to motor-related brain areas during visual learning. *Nat Neurosci* 8: 1494–1496.

Raichle ME, Fiez JA, Videen TO, MacLeod AM, Pardo JV, Fox PT, Petersen SE. 1994. Practice-related changes in human brain functional anatomy during nonmotor learning. *Cereb Cortex* 4: 8–26.

Rainer G, Miller EK. 2000. Effects of visual experience on the representation of objects in the prefrontal cortex. *Neuron* 27: 179–189.

Rao RP. 2005. Bayesian inference and attentional modulation in the visual cortex. *Neuroreport* 16: 1843–1848.

Reber PJ, Stark CE, Squire LR. 1998. Cortical areas supporting category learning identified using functional MRI. *Proc Natl Acad Sci USA* 95: 747–750.

Reynolds JH, Pasternak T, Desimone R. 2000. Attention increases sensitivity of V4 neurons. *Neuron* 26: 703–714.

Riesenhuber M. 2005. Object recognition in cortex: Neural mechanisms, and possible roles for attention. In *Neurobiology of attention*, ed. L Itti, G Rees, and J Tsotsos. Cambridge: MIT Press.

Riesenhuber M, Jarudi I, Gilad S, Sinha P. 2004. Face processing in humans is compatible with a simple shape-based model of vision. *Proc R Soc Lond B (Suppl)* 271: S448–S450.

Riesenhuber M, Poggio T. 1999a. Are cortical models really bound by the "binding problem"? *Neuron* 24: 87–93, 111–125.

Riesenhuber M, Poggio T. 1999b. Hierarchical models of object recognition in cortex. *Nat Neurosci* 2: 1019–1025.

Riesenhuber M, Poggio T. 2000. Models of object recognition. *Nat Neurosci Suppl* 3: 1199–1204.

Riesenhuber M, Poggio T. 2002. Neural mechanisms of object recognition. *Curr Opin Neurobiol* 12: 162–168.

Riesenhuber M, Poggio T. 2003. How visual cortex recognizes objects: the tale of the standard model. In *The visual neurosciences*, ed. LM Chalupa and JS Werner, 1640–1653. Cambridge: MIT Press.

Rolls ET, Aggelopoulos NC, Zheng F. 2003. The receptive fields of inferior temporal cortex neurons in natural scenes. *J Neurosci* 23: 339–348.

Rossion B, Gauthier I. 2002. How does the brain process upright and inverted faces? *Behav Cogn Neurosci Rev* 1: 63–75.

Rousselet GA, Fabre-Thorpe M, Thorpe SJ. 2002. Parallel processing in high-level categorization of natural images. *Nat Neurosci* 5: 629–630.

Roy JE, Riesenhuber M, Poggio T, Miller EK. 2006. Activity of monkey inferior temporal cortex neurons compared to prefrontal cortex neurons during shifts in category membership. *Soc Neurosci Abstr* 36.

Schneider R, Riesenhuber M. 2004. On the difficulty of feature-based attentional modulations in visual object recognition: a modeling study. CBCL Paper 235/AI Memo 2004-004. Massachusetts Institute of Technology, Cambridge, MA.

Serre T, Kreiman G, Kouh M, Cadieu C, Knoblich U, Poggio T. 2007a. A quantitative theory of immediate visual recognition. *Prog Brain Res* 165: 33–56.

Serre T, Oliva A, Poggio T. 2007b. A feedforward architecture accounts for rapid categorization. *Proc Natl Acad Sci USA* 104: 6424–6429.

Serre T, Riesenhuber M, Louie J, Poggio T. 2002. On the role of object-specific features for real world object recognition. In Proceedings of BMCV2002, ed. HH Buelthoff, S-W Lee, T Poggio, and C Wallraven. New York: Springer.

Serre T, Wolf L, Bileschi S, Riesenhuber M, Poggio T. 2007c. Robust object recognition with cortex-like mechanisms. *IEEE PAMI* 29: 411–426.

Shelton C. 2000. Morphable surface models. *Int J Comput Vis* 38: 75–91.

Sigala N. 2004. Visual categorization and the inferior temporal cortex. *Behav Brain Res* 149: 1–7.

Sigala N, Logothetis NK. 2002. Visual categorization shapes feature selectivity in the primate temporal cortex. *Nature* 415: 318–320.

Somers DC, Dale AM, Seiffert AE, Tootell RB. 1999. Functional MRI reveals spatially specific attentional modulation in human primary visual cortex. *Proc Natl Acad Sci USA* 96: 1663–1668.

Spiridon M, Kanwisher N. 2002. How distributed is visual category information in human occipito-temporal cortex? An fMRI study. *Neuron* 35: 1157–1165.

Tanaka K. 1996. Inferotemporal cortex and object vision. *Annu Rev Neurosci* 19: 109–139.

Tanaka K. 1997. Mechanisms of visual object recognition: monkey and human studies. *Curr Opin Neurobiol* 7: 523–529.

Tarr MJ, Bulthoff HH. 1998. Image-based object recognition in man, monkey and machine. *Cognition* 67: 1–20.

Thomas E, Van Hulle MM, Vogels R. 2001. Encoding of categories by noncategory-specific neurons in the inferior temporal cortex. *J Cogn Neurosci* 13: 190–200.

Thorpe S, Fize D, Marlot C. 1996. Speed of processing in the human visual system. *Nature* 381: 520–522.

Thorpe SJ, Fabre-Thorpe M. 2001. Neuroscience: seeking categories in the brain. *Science* 291: 260–263.

Tomita H, Ohbayashi M, Nakahara K, Hasegawa I, Miyashita Y. 1999. Top-down signal from pre-frontal cortex in executive control of memory retrieval. *Nature* 401: 699–703.

Tsotsos JK, Culhane SM, Yan Kei Wai W, Lai Y, Davis N, Nuflo F. 1995. Modeling visual attention via selective tuning. *Artif Intell* 78: 507–545.

Tsunoda K, Yamane Y, Nishizaki M, Tanifuji M. 2001. Complex objects are represented in macaque inferotemporal cortex by the combination of feature columns. *Nat Neurosci* 4: 832–838.

Ullman S, Vidal-Naquet M, Sali E. 2002. Visual features of intermediate complexity and their use in classification. *Nat Neurosci* 5: 682–687.

Ungerleider LG, Haxby JV. 1994. 'What' and 'where' in the human brain. *Curr Opin Neurobiol* 4: 157–165.

Wallis G, Bulthoff HH. 2001. Effects of temporal association on recognition memory. *Proc Natl Acad Sci USA* 98: 4800–4804.

Wallis G, Rolls ET. 1997. A model of invariant recognition in the visual system. *Prog Neurobiol* 51: 167–194.

Walther D, Itti L, Riesenhuber M, Poggio T, Koch C. 2002. Attentional selection for object recognition – a gentle way. In Proceedings of BMCV2002, ed. HH Bulthoff, S-W Lee, T Poggio, and C Wallraven. New York: Springer.

Williams MA, Dang S, Kanwisher NG. 2007. Only some spatial patterns of fMRI response are read out in task performance. *Nat Neurosci* 10: 685–686.

Wiskott L, Sejnowski TJ. 2002. Slow feature analysis: unsupervised learning of invariances. *Neural Comput* 14: 715–770.

Yin RK. 1969. Looking at upside-down faces. *J Exp Psychol* 81: 141–145.

Zoccolan D, Kouh M, Poggio T, DiCarlo JJ. 2007. Trade-off between object selectivity and tolerance in monkey inferotemporal cortex. *J Neurosci* 27: 12292–12307.

CHAPTER 13

Learning Compositional Models for Object Categories from Small Sample Sets

Jake Porway, Benjamin Yao, and Song Chun Zhu

13.1 Introduction

Modeling object categories is a challenging task owing to the many structural variations between instances of the same category. There have been many nonhierarchical approaches to modeling object categories, all with limited levels of success. *Appearance-based models*, which represent objects primarily by their photometric properties, such as global PGA, KPCA, fragments, SIFTs, and patches (Lowe 2004; Nayar et al. 1996; Ullman et al. 2001; Weber et al. 2000), tend to disregard geometric information about the position of important keypoints within an object. Thus, they are not well-suited for recognition in scenarios where pose, occlusion, or part reconfiguration are factors. *Structure-based models*, which include information about relative or absolute positions of features, such as the constellation model and pictorial structures (Felzenszwalb and Huttenlocher 2005; Fischler and Elschlager 1973; Weber et al. 2000), are more powerful than appearance-based approaches as they can model relationships between groups of parts and thus improve recognition accuracy, but are rarely hierarchical and, as such, cannot account for radical transformations of the part positions.

Very recently there has been a resurgence in modeling object categories using grammars (Jin and Geman 2006; Todorovic and Ahuja 2006; Zhu and Mumford 2006). Work by Fu (Fu 1981; You and Fu 1980) and Ohta (1985) in the 1970s and 1980s, and later by Dickinson and Siddiqi (Dickinson et al. 1992; Keselman and Dickinson 2001; Siddiqi et al. 199?) introduced these grammars to account for structural variance. Han and Zhu (2005) and Chen et al. (2006) used attributed graph grammars to describe rectilinear scenes and model clothes, but these models were hardcoded for one category of images.

Many of the problems in previous approaches come from lack of a good definition for *object category* that captures what is invariant between instances of the same class. We define an object category as an equivalence class where the object parts and their relations to one another are the invariants that make instances in the same category equivalent. Bikes always have wheels, clocks always have hands, and these parts are always related similarly to one another. We can capture the variation in these commonalities through a constrained compositional model that defines the set of instances for each object category.

From a human vision persepctive, the work we present is similar in concept to the theories put forth by Biederman (1987) about how biological vision systems recognize objects. In his Recognition by Components theory, Biederman postulates that objects are represented by compositions of 3-D objects called "geons." These simple, repeatable geons can be combined under different deformations to form a vast number of complicated objects. Our representation is a similar, though more general, theory of recognizing objects as compositions of parts related by spatial and appearance relationships.

In this chapter we provide a way to generalize the minimax entropy framework to learn such a model for objects with dynamic structure. This model combines a Stochastic Context Free Grammar (SCFG) to capture the variance and hierarchy of object parts with the relational constraints of an Markov Random Process (MRP). This framework accounts for the dynamic structure of the model, in which constraints may not always exist from instance to instance, by pursuing relations according to their frequency of occurrence. The MRP constraints that we add to the SCFG match two main statistics of the model:

1. The frequencies of part ocurrences
2. The statistics on the spatial layouts of parts

We also discuss an inference algorithm called *compositional boosting* that can recursively detect and compose object parts to identify whole objects even in the presence of occlusion or noise.

13.2 Representation

The model we learn for object categories is a combination of a SCFG and an MRP, referred to as an And-Or graph.[1] This model is like a language for an object category in which parts of the object are analogous to words and parts of speech in language, and relational constraints model the context between them (Chen et al. 2006). Figure 13.l(a) shows an example of an And-Or graph. An object is created by starting at the root of the graph and expanding nodes until only terminals remain, as in a SCFG. Node expansions in this structure can be thought of as And nodes, in which one node expands into multiple nodes, and Or nodes, which can only choose one of their child nodes to expand into. For example, node S is an And node, and expands into nodes A and B, which in turn are Or nodes and will only decompose into one child

---

[1] The And-Or graph was previously used by Pearl in (1984) for heuristic searches. In our work, we use it for a very different purpose and should not be confused with Pearl's work.

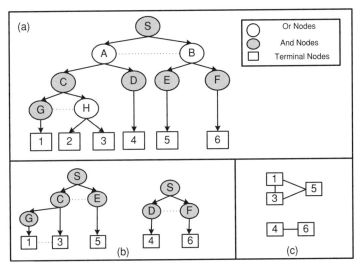

Figure 13.1. (a) An example of an And-Or graph. And nodes must decompose into all of their children, whereas Or nodes can only decompose into one. Constraints are shown as horizontal lines, (b) Parse graphs, which are each one walk of the model. (c) Configurations, which consist only of terminal nodes and any constraints they inherited.

each. Figure 13.l(a) is a visualization of the following grammar:

$$
\begin{aligned}
&S \rightarrow AB && C \rightarrow GH && F \rightarrow 6 \\
&A \rightarrow C \mid D && D \rightarrow 4 && G \rightarrow 1 \\
&B \rightarrow E \mid F && E \rightarrow 5 && H \rightarrow 2 \mid 3
\end{aligned}
$$

The horizontal line between A and B represents a relational constraint. These constraints do not influence the node expansion, but act a posteriori on the selected nodes to constrain their features (e.g. appearance). The constraints are inherited by any children of constrained nodes as well.

We define a *parse graph* (**pg**) as an instance drawn from the model, which is analogous to a sentence diagram in natural language. Figure 13.l(b) shows some parse graphs from our example model. The Or nodes are determined during a walk of the graph, fixing the parts, so only And nodes remain. We also define a *configuration C*, which is simply the constrained parts from the parse graph with hierarchical information removed. This is equivalent to a sentence in natural language, and Figure 13.l(c) shows examples of configurations from our example.

This compositional model can be formalized as the tuple

$$
G_{\text{and-or}} = <V_N, V_T, \mathcal{S}, \mathcal{R}, \mathcal{P}> \tag{13.1}
$$

$V_N = V^{Or} \cup V^{And}$ is the set of all nonterminal nodes, consisting of both the And and Or nodes. We define a switch variable $\omega(v)$ for $v \in V^{\text{or}}$ that takes an integer value to index its child node.

$$
\omega(v) \in \{\emptyset, 1, 2, \ldots, n(v)\} \tag{13.2}
$$

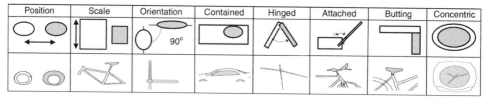

Figure 13.2. Visualization of possible pairwise relationships to be learned in the And-Or graph.

V_T represents a set of terminal nodes producable by the model. S is the root node that all instances start from. Together, these variables form the grammar structure of the model.

$\mathcal{R} = \{r_1, r_2, \ldots, r_{n(R)}\}$ is a dictionary of relationships between nodes. Each relationship can be thought of as a filter that operates on a set of nodes V, producing a response $\Phi_i = r_i(V)$. These responses can be pooled over a number of parse graphs G to create histograms that can be used as node constraints. The type of relationship will likely differ based on whether it is defined for one, two, or more nodes. Figure 13.2 visualizes a set of relationships that could be used to augment an And-Or graph.

Altogether these variables form a language for an object category, $L(G)$, that can produce a combinatorial number of constrained object configurations.

Figure 13.3 shows a parse graph for the bike category. For notational convenience, we denote the following components of a parse graph **pg**:

- $T(\mathbf{pg}) = \{t_1, \ldots, t_{n(\mathbf{pe})}\}$ is the set of leaf nodes in **pg**. For example, $T(\mathbf{pg}) = \{1, 3, 5\}$ for the parse graph shown at the top of Figure 13.l(c).
- $V^{\mathrm{or}}(\mathbf{pg})$ is the set of nonempty Or nodes that are used in **pg**. For instance, the left-hand parse graph in Figure 13.l(b) has $V^{\mathrm{or}}(\mathbf{pg}) = \{A, B, H\}$.
- $E(\mathbf{pg})$ is the set of links in **pg**.

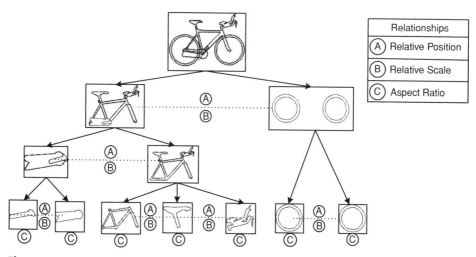

Figure 13.3. A parse graph of a bike. Nodes are composed via certain relations to form the representation of the bike.

The probability for pg takes the following Gibbs form,

$$p(\mathbf{pg}; \ominus, \mathcal{R}, \triangle) = \frac{1}{Z(\ominus)} \exp\{-\mathcal{E}(\mathbf{pg})\} \tag{13.3}$$

where $\mathcal{E}(\mathbf{pg})$ is the total energy,

$$\mathcal{E}(\mathbf{pg}) = \sum_{v \in V^{or}(\mathbf{pg})} \lambda_v(\omega(v)) + \sum_{t \in T(\mathbf{pg}) \cup V^{and}(\mathbf{pg})} \lambda_t(\alpha(t)) + \sum_{(i,j) \in E(\mathbf{pg})} \lambda_{ij}(\alpha(v_i), \alpha(v_j))$$

$$\tag{13.4}$$

The model is specified by a number of parameters $\ominus$, the relations set $\mathcal{R}$ and the vocabulary $\triangle$, where $\mathcal{R} \subseteq \triangle$. The first term in the energy is the same as that of a SCFG. It accounts for how frequently each Or node decomposes a certain way. The second and third terms are typical singleton and pair-clique energy for graphical models. The second term is defined on the geometric and appearance attributes $\alpha()$ of the image primitives, while the third term models the compatibility between the attributes of two related nodes.

This model can be derived using the maximum entropy principle under two types of constraints on the statistics of a training set. One constraint matches the frequency at each Or node, like a SCFG, and the other matches the relation statistics, such as the histograms modeling relative appearance or co-occurrence. $\ominus$ is the set of parameters in the energy,

$$\ominus = \{\lambda_v(), \lambda_t(), \lambda_{ij}(); \ \forall v \in V^{or}, \forall t \in V_T, \forall (i, j) \in \mathcal{R}\}. \tag{13.5}$$

Each $\lambda()$ above is a potential function, not a scalar, and is represented by a vector created by discretizing the function in a nonparametric way, as was done in the FRAME model for texture (Zhu et al. 1997). $\triangle$ is the vocabulary for the generative model. The partition function is summed over all parse graphs in the And-Or graph $G_{and\text{-}or}$

$$Z = Z(\ominus) = \sum_{\mathbf{pg}} \exp\{-\mathcal{E}(\mathbf{pg})\}. \tag{13.6}$$

13.3 Learning and Estimation with the And-Or Graph

Suppose we have a set of observed parse graphs that follow f, the true distribution governing the objects.

$$D^{obs} = \{(\mathbf{I}_i^{obs}, \mathbf{pg}_i^{obs}) : \ i = 1, 2, \ldots, N\} \sim f(\mathbf{I}, \mathbf{pg}). \tag{13.7}$$

The parse graphs $\mathbf{pg}_i^{obs}$ are from a ground truth database or other labeled source. The objective is to learn a model p, which approaches f by minimizing the Kullback-Leibler divergence $KL(f||p)$. This is equivalent to the ML estimate for the optimal vocabulary $\triangle$, relation $\mathcal{R}$, and parameter $\ominus$.

Learning the probability model includes two phases, both of which follow the same principle.

1. Estimating the parameters $\ominus$ from training data D^{obs} for given $\mathcal{R}$ and $\triangle$
2. Learning and pursuing the relation set $\mathcal{R}$ for nodes in G for given $\triangle$.

13.3.1 Maximum Likelihood Learning of Θ

For a given And-Or graph hierarchy and relations, the estimation of Θ follows the MLE learning process. Let $\mathcal{L}(\Theta) = \sum_{i=1}^{N} \log p(\mathbf{I}_i^{\text{obs}}, \mathbf{pg}_i^{\text{obs}}; \Theta, \mathcal{R}, \Delta)$ be the log-likelihood. By setting $\frac{\partial \mathcal{L}(\Theta)}{\partial \Theta} = 0$, we have the following two learning steps.

1. Learning the λ_v at each Or node $v \in V^{\text{or}}$. The switch variable at v has $n(v)$ choices $\omega(v) \in \{\emptyset, 1, 2, \ldots, n(v)\}$ and is $\emptyset$ when v is not included in the $\mathbf{pg}$. We compute the histogram $\mathbf{h}_v^{\text{obs}}(\omega(v))$ in all the parse graphs in $\Omega_{\mathbf{pg}}^{\text{obs}}$. Thus,

$$\lambda_v(\omega(v) = i) = -\log \mathbf{h}_v^{\text{obs}}(\omega(v) = i), \quad \forall v \in V^{\text{or}}. \tag{13.8}$$

This is simply the sample frequency for the Or node decompositions, as shown in Chi and Geman (1998).

2. Learning the potential functions $\lambda_t()$ at the terminal node $t \in V_T$ and $\lambda_{ij}()$ for each pair relation $(i, j) \in \mathcal{R}$. $\frac{\partial \mathcal{L}(\Theta)}{\partial \lambda_t} = 0$ and $\frac{\partial \mathcal{L}(\Theta)}{\partial \lambda_{ij}} = 0$ lead to the statistical constraints,

$$E_{p(\mathbf{pg}; \Theta, \mathcal{R}, \Delta)}[\mathbf{h}(\alpha(t)] = \mathbf{h}_t^{\text{obs}}, \quad \forall t \in V_T \tag{13.9}$$

$$E_{p(\mathbf{pg}; \Theta, \mathcal{R}, \Delta)}[\mathbf{h}(\alpha(v_i), \alpha(v_j))]] = \mathbf{h}_{ij}^{\text{obs}}, \quad \forall (i, j) \in \mathcal{R}. \tag{13.10}$$

In the preceding equation $\mathbf{h}()$ is a statistical measure of the attributes of the nodes in question, such as a histogram pooled over all the occurrences of those nodes in $\Omega_{\mathbf{pg}}^{\text{obs}}$. The λ parameters, when learned, will weight the $\mathbf{h}$ histograms so that $p(\mathbf{pg}; \Theta, \mathcal{R}, \Delta)$ is normalized correctly.

The equations (13.8), (13.9), and (13.10) are the constraints for deriving the Gibbs model $p(\mathbf{pg}; \Theta, \mathcal{R}, \Delta)$ in equation (13.3) through the maximum entropy principle.

Because of the coupling of the energy terms, equations (13.9) and (13.10) are solved iteratively through a gradient method. In a general case, we follow the stochastic gradient method adopted in learning the FRAME model (Zhu et al. 1997), which approximates the expectations $E_p[\mathbf{h}(\alpha(t))]$ and $E_p[\mathbf{h}(\alpha(v_i), \alpha(v_j))]$ by sample means from a set of synthesized examples. This is the method of analysis-by-synthesis adopted in our texture modeling paper (Zhu et al. 1997).

13.3.2 Learning and Pursuing the Relation Set

In addition to learning the parameters Θ, we can also augment the relation set $\mathcal{R}$ in an And-Or graph, thus pursuing the energy terms in $\sum_{(i,j) \in E(\mathbf{pg})} \lambda_{ij}(\alpha(v_i), \alpha(v_j))$ in the same way as filters and statistics were pursued in texture modeling by the minimax entropy principle (Zhu et al. 1997).

Suppose we start with an empty relation set $\mathcal{R} = \emptyset$, creating a parse graph with just its SCFG componenet defined, $p = p(\mathbf{pg}; \lambda, \emptyset, \Delta)$. We define a greedy pursuit where, at each step, we add a relation e_+ to $\mathcal{R}$ and thus augment model $p(\mathbf{pg}; \Theta, \mathcal{R}, \Delta)$ to $p_+(\mathbf{pg}; \Theta, \mathcal{R}_+, \Delta)$, where $\mathcal{R}_+ = \mathcal{R} \cup \{e_+\}$.

e_+ is selected from a large pool $\Delta_{\mathcal{R}}$ so as to maximally reduce KL-divengence,

$$e_+ = \arg\max KL(f\|p) - KL(f\|p_+) = \arg\max KL(p_+\|p), \tag{13.11}$$

Thus, we denote the information gain of e_+ by

$$\delta(e_+) \stackrel{def}{=} KL(p_+||p) \approx f^{\mathrm{obs}}(e_+)d_{\mathrm{manh}}(\mathbf{h}^{\mathrm{obs}}(e_+), \mathbf{h}_p^{\mathrm{syn}}(e_+)). \qquad (13.12)$$

In the preceding formula, $f^{\mathrm{obs}}(e_+)$ is the frequency that relation e_+ is observed in the training data, $\mathbf{h}^{\mathrm{obs}}(e_+)$ is the histogram for relation e_+ over training data D^{obs}, and $\mathbf{h}_p^{\mathrm{syn}}(e_+)$ is the histogram for relation e_+ over the synthesized parse graphs according to the current model p. $d_{\mathrm{manh}}()$ is the Mahalanobis distance between the two histograms.

Intuitively, $\delta(e_+)$ is large if e_+ occurs frequently and creates a large difference between the histograms of the observed and the synthesized parse graphs. Large information gain means e_+ is a significant relationship.

13.4 Experiments on Learning and Sampling

We tested our learned model on 24 categories of objects, shown with representative samples in Figure 13.5. Categories were selected from the Lotus Hill Database (Yao et al. 2007), and between 40 and 60 training instances were collected for each category. The training data for each image consisted of the labeled boundaries of a predetermined set of object parts. The object parts were selected by hand for each category (e.g., a teapot consists of a spout, base, handle, and lid) and outlined by hand. Each part category consists of about 5 to 10 different types (e.g., round handles vs. square handles), which are also selected by hand. Our dictionary of relationships Δ_R consists of the following relations: (aspect ratio, relative position, relative scale, relative orientation, overlap). Aspect ratio is the one singleton relationship, whereas all other relationships are measured over pairs of parts. When initializing the learning algorithm, we measure each relationship across every possible pair of parts. For an object category consisting of k parts and a dictionary of m singleton relationships and n pairwise relations, the algorithm begins with a pool of $m*k + n*(\frac{k(k-1)}{2})$ potential relationships.

Learning by Random Synthesis. Figure 13.4 shows samples drawn from the model at each stage of the relationship pursuit in section 13.3.2. At each stage, a new relationship was added and the parameters were estimated using the process in section 13.3.1. Figure 13.4 shows this process for the clock and bicycle categories. The initial samples are wild and unconstrained, but the objects appear more coherent as relationships are added. Figure 13.5 shows samples from the learned model for 24 different object categories. We can see that the samples are perceptually equivalent to their category examples, even if slightly different on a part-by-part basis.

Figure 13.6 shows the And-Or graph that was learned for the bicycle category and the relationships that were added to pairs and single parts. We can almost see causal chains appearing in the relationships learned (the frame constrains the chain's position and scale, which in turn constrains the pedal's position and scale). Each part decomposes into one of a number of terminals. These terminals could be represented by an appearance model for each part, although in our case we used exemplars from the initial dataset, scaled, oriented, and positioned to create new object configurations.

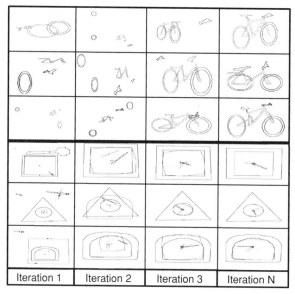

| Iteration 1 | Iteration 2 | Iteration 3 | Iteration N |

Figure 13.4. Samples from p during each stage of the relationship pursuit. Objects become more coherent as new relationships are added. (See color plate 13.4.)

Predicting Missing Parts Using Learned Model. The sampling process can be used to provide top-down proposals for inference. Figure 13.7 shows the results of removing the wheel, frame, and handlebars from a perfect sketch of a bike and predicting the true part positions at each stage of the learning process. The missing parts of the structure are first reintroduced, and then their constraints are sampled for 100 iterations. The model with few constraints does not yield good results, whereas the full model predicts the part locations perfectly, as shown overlaid in the original image. The error is measured as the sum of the thin-plate-spline deformation energy (Bookstein 1989) and affine

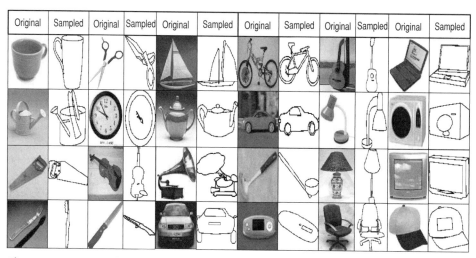

Figure 13.5. Twenty-four object categories with high intraclass variability and their corresponding samples.

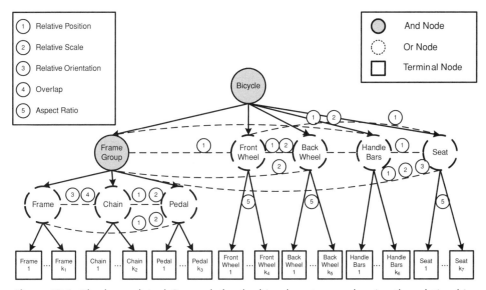

Figure 13.6. The learned And-Or graph for the bicycle category, showing the relationships added between pairs of nodes.

energy needed to move the predicted part to its true location, and is shown in the last column. This shows that the compositional model provides strong top-down cues for part positions and appearances, and can predict the presence of parts that are occluded, missing, or had weak bottom-up cues for recognition and detection tasks.

Small Sample Set Generalization. Because of the consistency of many of the perceptual similarities between objects in the same class (e.g. relative position), we can

Figure 13.7. Top-down prediction of missing parts at each stage of the relationship pursuit. A neighborhood of parts is fixed and the remaining parts are Gibbs sampled. The accuracy of the prediction is measured by the thin-plate-spline + affine transformation needed to move the predicted part to its true position. We can see that this energy decreases drastically as we add more relations to the model. (See color plate 13.7.)

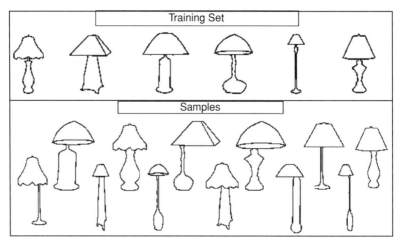

Figure 13.8. Demonstration of the model's generalizability. The model learned from only six training instances can produce the varied samples below.

learn our model from a very small sample set. Figure 13.8 shows samples drawn from the model learned from just six training instances. Despite there being so few training instances, their parts can be reconfigured and adjusted according to the model to produce radically different instances. Note that the part configurations and appearances in the samples differ greatly from those in the training set, yet the objects are still coherent. This is useful for recognition tasks, in which new instances can be recognized despite not appearing in the training data. One can also generate large amounts of training data for discriminative tasks using this model, learned from a small, easily obtained set of images. Such an experiment was done comparing recognition results using two different datasets. The first was fully hand-collected, whereas the second consisted of hand-collected data and samples generated from our model. The latter classifier showed a 15% improvement over solely hand-collected data, likely because there were more varied data samples available in the second dataset (Lin et al. 2007). Further work is being done on this topic.

13.5 Inference with the And-Or Graph

This section contains a brief introduction to our compositional inference algorithm for recognizing objects by parts. We refer readers to Han and Zhu (2005), Lin et al. (2009), and Zhu and Mumford (2006) for a more detailed explanation.

Given an input image $\mathbf{I}$, we would like to compute a parse graph $\mathbf{pg}$ that maximizes the posterior probability

$$\mathbf{pg}^* = \arg \max_{\mathbf{pg}} p(\mathbf{I} \mid \mathbf{pg}; \Delta_{sk}) p(\mathbf{pg}; \Theta, \Delta). \tag{13.13}$$

The likelihood model is based on how well the terminal nodes match the image, and the prior is defined by the grammar model in equation (13.3). In our implementation, our likelihood model follows that of the primal sketch (Guo et al. 2003).

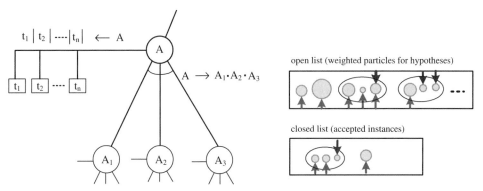

Figure 13.9. Data structure for the recursive inference algorithm on the And-Or graph.

Because the And-Or graph can be defined recursively, so too can the inference algorithm, which largely simplifies the algorithm design and makes it easily scalable to arbitrarily large number of object categories. This algorithm is known as a *compositional boosting* algorithm (Wu et al. 2007).

Consider an arbitrary And node A. Let us assume that A can be decomposed into $n(A) = 3$ parts, or can just terminate at a low-resolution version of itself.

$$A \rightarrow A_1 \cdot A_2 \cdot A_3 \,|\, t_1 \,|\, \cdots \,|\, t_n. \qquad (13.14)$$

This recursive unit is shown in Figure 13.9.

This representation borrows from some common concepts in artificial intelligence (Pearl 1984). An **open list** stores a number of weighted particles (or hypotheses) generated by bottom-up detectors for A. A **closed list** stores a number of instances for A that have been accepted in the top-down process. These instances are nodes in the current parse graph **pg**.

The bottom-up process creates the particles in the Open lists using two methods.

(i) Generating hypotheses for A directly from images using bottom-up processes, such as Adaboosting (Friedman et al. 2000; Viola and Jones 2001) or Hough transforms, to detect various terminals $t_1, \ldots, t_n$. The weight of a detected hypothesis is the logarithm of some local marginal posterior probability ratio given a small image patch Λ^i,

$$\omega_A^i = \log \frac{p(A^i | \mathbf{I}_{\Lambda^i})}{p(\bar{A}^i | \mathbf{I}_{\Lambda^i})} \approx \log \frac{p(A^i | F(\mathbf{I}_{\Lambda^i}))}{p(\bar{A}^i | F(\mathbf{I}_{\Lambda^i}))} = \hat{\omega}_A^i. \qquad (13.15)$$

$\bar{A}$ represents a competing hypothesis. For computational effectiveness, the posterior probability ratio is approximated using local features $F(\mathbf{I}_{\Lambda^i})$ rather than the image $\mathbf{I}_{\Lambda^i}$.

(ii) Generating hypotheses for A by binding k of A's children from the existing Open and Closed lists. The binding process tests the relationships between these child nodes for compatibility and quickly rules out obviously incompatible compositions. The weight of a bound hypothesis is the logarithm of some local conditional posterior probability ratio. Suppose a particle A^i is bound from two existing parts A_1^i and A_2^i

with A_3^i missing, and Λ^i is the domain containing the hypothesized A. Then the weight will be

$$\omega_A^i = \log \frac{p\left(A^i|A_1^i, A_2^i, \mathbf{I}_{\Lambda^i}\right)}{p\left(\bar{A}^i|A_1^i, A_2^i, \mathbf{I}_{\Lambda^i}\right)} = \log \frac{p\left(A_1^i, A_2^i, \mathbf{I}_{\Lambda^i}|A^i\right) p(A^i)}{p\left(A_1^i, A_2^i, \mathbf{I}_{\Lambda^i}|\bar{A}^i\right) p(\bar{A}^i)} \tag{13.16}$$

$$\approx \log \frac{p\left(A_1^i, A_2^i|A^i\right) p(A^i)}{p\left(A_1^i, A_2^i|\bar{A}^i\right) p(\bar{A}^i)} = \hat{\omega}_A^i.$$

where $\bar{A}$ represents a competing hypothesis.

The top-down process validates the bottom-up hypotheses in all the Open lists following the Bayesian posterior probability. During this process it needs to maintain the weights of the Open lists.

(i) Given a hypothesis A^i with weight $\hat{\omega}_A^i$, the top-down process validates it by computing the true posterior probability ratio ω_A^i stated above. If A^i is accepted into the Closed list of A then the current parse graph $\mathbf{pg}$ moves to a new parse graph $\mathbf{pg}_+$. In a reverse process, the top-down process may also select a node A in the Closed list and either delete it (putting it back into the Open list) or disassemble it into independent parts.

(ii) Given two competing hypotheses A and A', which overlap in a domain Λ_o, accepting one hypothesis will lower the weight of the other. Therefore, whenever we add or delete a node A in the parse graph, all the other hypotheses whose domains overlap with that of A will have to update their weights.

The acceptance of a node can be performed using a greedy algorithm that maximizes the posterior probability. At each iteration, the particle whose weight is the largest among all Open lists is accepted. This continues until the largest weight is below a certain threshold.

13.6 Experiments on Object Recognition Using the And-Or Graph

We apply our inference algorithm to five object categories: clock, bike, computer, cup/bowl, and teapot. Figure 13.10 shows an example of inferring a partially occluded bicycle.

In Figure 13.10. The first row shows the input image, an edge map, and bottom-up detection of the two wheels using a Hough transform. The second row shows some top-down predictions of bike frames based on the two wheels, sampled from the learned MRF model. The third row shows the template matching process that matches the predicted frames (in red) to the edges (in blue) in the image. The frame with minimum matching cost is selected. The fourth row shows the top-down hallucinations for the seat and handlebar (in green), which are randomly sampled from the And-Or graph model.

Figure 13.11 shows recognition results for the five categories. For each input image, the image on the right shows the recognized parts from the image in different colors. It should be mentioned that the recognition algorithm is distinct from most of the classification algorithms in the literature. It interprets the image as a parse graph, which includes the classification of categories and parts, matches the leaf templates to images, and hallucinates occluded parts.

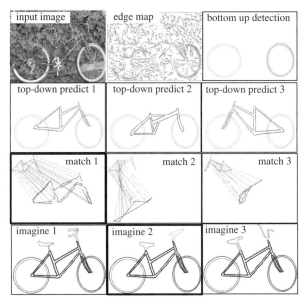

Figure 13.10. The combination of bottom-up and top-down influences for detecting an occluded bicycle (presented in Lin et al. 2009). (See color plate 13.10.)

Figure 13.11. Recognition experiments on five object categories (presented in Lin et al. 2009). (See color plate 13.11.)

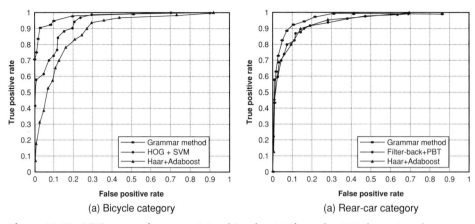

Figure 13.12. ROC curves for recognizing bicycles (a) (from the LHI dataset) and rear-cars (b) (from the Caltech-101 dataset). Our model outperforms a HOG-based SVM and Adaboost on bicycles and PBT and SIFT-based boosting for rear-cars (presented in Lin et al. 2009). (See color plate 13.12.)

Some recent work was done to show the accuracy of our method versus common recognition and classification techniques in Lin et al. (2009). This work uses our methodology for learning but includes additional experimental results for the inference algorithm. In this work, our model was trained on the categories of rear car and bicycle and these models were used to recognize objects in the Lotus Hill Database (Yao et al. 2007) as well as the Caltech-101 dataset (Fei-Fei and Perona 2005). Figure 13.12 shows the results of this experiment. Our model was compared against a HOG-based SVM (Dalal et al. 2006) and a Haar-feature-based Adaboost model (Viola and Jones 2001). One can see that our model performs much better than either of these two methods. For the Caltech-101 dataset, we trained our model and ran it against a Probabilistic Boosting Tree (Tu 2005) as well as a SIFT-based boosting method (Zhang et al. 2005), both of which performed worse than our grammar-based approach.

13.7 Conclusion

In this chapter we have discussed a minimax learning algorithm for a compositional model of object categories. The grammar structure of this model accounts for the variability of part configurations, whereas the relational constraints at each level capture the variability of part appearances. Samples drawn from the model are visually similar to the training data, yet novel instances can be created from even very small training sets. With the use of compositional boosting, objects can be reliably recognized and parsed in new images as well. Our algorithms are similar to theories of recognition in the human-vision system and yield encouraging results for the implementation of part-based recognition theories for biological vision. These are promising results, and we plan to continue studying using grammars for representing visual knowledge.

Acknowledgments

This work was funded by NSF grant IIS 0713652. Projects done at the Lotus Hill Research Institute were supported by an 863 program No. 2006AA012121.

Bibliography

Biederman I. 1987. Recognition-by-components: a theory of human image understanding. *Psychol Rev* 94: 115–147.

Bookstein FL. 1989. Principal warps: thin-plate splines and the decomposition of deformations. *Pattern Anal Mach Intell* 11: 567–585.

Chen H, Xu Z, Liu Z, Zhu SC. 2006 Composite templates for cloth modeling and sketching. In Proceedings of IEEE conference on computer vision and pattern recognition, vol 1, 943–950.

Chi Z, Geman S. 1998. Estimation of probabilistic context-free grammars. *Comput Ling* 24(2).

Dalal N, Triggs B, Schmid C. 2006. Human detection using oriented histograms of flow and appearance. In Proceedings of European conference on computer vision, vol 2, 428–441.

Dickinson S, Pentland A, Rosenfeld A. 1992. From volume to views: an approach to 3D object recognition. *CVGIP: Image Und* 55(2): 130–154.

Fei-Fei L, Perona P. 2005. A Bayesian hierarchical model for learning natural scene categories. In Proceedings of IEEE conference on computer vision and pattern recognition, vol 2, 524–531.

Felzenszwalb P, Huttenlocher D. 2005. Pictorial structures for object recognition. *Int J Comput Vision* 61(1): 55–79.

Fischler M, Elschlager R. 1973. The representation and matching of pictorial structures. *IEEE Trans Comput* 22(1): 67–92.

Friedman J, Hastie T, Tibshirani R. 2000. Additive logistic regression: a statistical view of boosting. *Ann Statistics* 38(2): 337–374.

Fu KS. 1981. *Syntactic pattern recognition and applications*. New York: Prentice Hall.

Guo CE, Zhu SC, Wu YN. 2003. Primal sketch: integrating texture and structure. In Proceedings of the international conference on computer vision 106, 5–19.

Han F, Zhu SC. 2005. Bottom-up/top-down image parsing by attribute graph grammar. In Proceedings of the international conference on computer vision, vol 2.

Jin Y, Geman S. 2006. Context and hierarchy in a probabilistic image model. In Proceedings of IEEE conference on computer vision and pattern recognition, vol 2, 2145–2152.

Keselman Y, Dickinson S. 2001. Generic model abstraction from examples. *Pattern Anal Mach Intell* 27: 1141–1156.

Lin L, Peng S, Porway J, Zhu SC, Wang Y. 2007. An empirical study of object category recognition: sequential testing with generalized samples. In Proceedings of the international conference on computer vision 1–8.

Lin L, Wu T, Porway J, Xu Z. 2009. A stochastic graph grammar for compositional object representation and recognition. Under review for *Pattern Recognition*.

Lowe DG. 2004. Distinctive image features from scale-invariant keypoints. *Int J Comput Vis* 60(2): 91–110.

Nayar SK, Murase H, Nene SA. 1996. Parametric appearance representation. In *Early visual learning*, ed. SK Nayar and T Poggio.

Ohta Y. 1985. *Knowledge-based interpretation of outdoor natural color scenes*. New York: Pitman.

Pearl J. 1984. *Heuristics: intelligent search strategies for computer problem solving*. Boston: Addison-Wesley Longman.

Siddiqi K, Shokoufandeh A, Dickinson SJ, Zucker SW. 1999. Shock graphs and shape matching. *Int J Comput Vis* 35(1): 13–32.

Todorovic S, Ahuja N. 2006. Extracting subimages of an unknown category from a set of images. In Proceedings of IEEE conference on computer vision and pattern recognition, vol 1, 927–934.

Tu Z. 2005. Probabilistic boosting tree: learning discriminative models for classification, recognition, and clustering. In Proceedings of the international conference on computer vision, vol 2, 1589–1596.

Ullman S, Sali E, Vidal-Naquet M. 2001. A fragment-based approach to object representation and classification. In Proceedings of the fourth international workshop on visual form, Capri, Italy.

Viola P, Jones M. 2001. Rapid object detection using a boosted cascade of simple features. In Proceedings of IEEE conference on computer vision and pattern recognition 511–518.

Weber M, Welling M, Perona P. 2000. Towards automatic discovery of object categories. In Proceedings of IEEE conference on computer vision and pattern recognition, vol 2, 101–108.

Wu TF, Xia GS, Zhu SC. 2007. Compositional boosting for computing hierarchical image structures. In Proceedings of IEEE conference on computer vision and pattern recognition 1–8.

Yao B, Yang X, Zhu SC. 2007. Introduction to a large-scale general purpose groundtruth dataset: methodology, annotation tool, and benchmarks. *Energy minimization methods in computer vision and pattern recognition*. Springer LNCS vol 4697: 169–183.

You FC, Fu KS. 1980. Attributed grammar: a tool for combining syntatic and statistical approaches to pattern recognition. *IEEE Trans SMC* 10.

Zhang W, Yu B, Zelinsky GJ, Samaras D. 2005. Object class recognition using multiple layer boosting with multiple features. In Proceedings of IEEE conference on computer vision and pattern recognition, vol 2, 323–330.

Zhu SC, Mumford D. 2006. A stochastic grammar of images. *Found Trends Comput Graph Vision* 2:4: 259–362.

Zhu SC, Wu YN, Mumford D. 1997. Minimax entropy principle and its application to texture modeling. *Neural Comput* 9(9): 1627–1660.

CHAPTER 14

The Neurophysiology and Computational Mechanisms of Object Representation

Edmund T. Rolls

14.1 Introduction

A concise description of the representation of objects and faces provided by inferior temporal cortex neurons in the primate (macaque) brain is followed by new findings about how this representation operates in natural scenes and allows a number of objects and their relative spatial position in a scene to be encoded. Then a computational approach to how the object recognition processes described are performed in the primate brain is discussed as well as the types of strategy that the human brain uses to solve the enormous computational problem of invariant object recognition in complex natural scenes (Rolls 2008b; Rolls and Deco 2002; Rolls and Stringer 2006b). This contribution aims to provide a closely linked neurophysiological and computational approach to object recognition and categorization. Other approaches are represented in this volume and elsewhere (Biederman 1987; Fukushima 1989; Riesenhuber and Poggio 2000; Serre et al. 2007), and are compared with current approaches (Rolls 2008b; Rolls and Deco 2002; Rolls and Stringer 2006b).

14.2 The Neurophysiology of Object Representation in the Inferior Temporal Visual Cortex

Some properties of the hierarchical organization of the primate ventral visual system that lead to the inferior temporal visual cortex (IT), where object representations are present (Rolls 2000; Rolls 2007b, 2008b; Rolls and Deco 2002), are shown in Figure 14.1. The receptive fields of neurons become larger related to the convergence from stage to stage, and the representation develops over the stages from features such as bars and edges, to combinations of features such as combinations of lines or colors in intermediate stages such as V4 (Hegde and Van Essen 2000; Ito and Komatsu 2004) to objects in IT. Neurons in IT provide a sparse distributed representation of objects, in that each neuron has a high firing rate to one or several objects, and gradually decreasing responses to other objects, with little or no response to most objects or faces (see

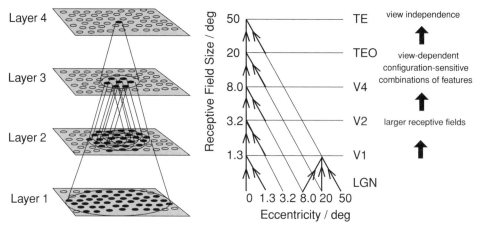

Figure 14.1. *Right*, Schematic diagram showing convergence achieved by the forward projections in the visual system, and the types of representation that may be built by competitive networks operating at each stage of the system from the primary visual cortex (V1) to the inferior temporal visual cortex (area TE) (see text). Lateral geniculate nucleus (LGN). Area TEO forms the posterior inferior temporal cortex. The receptive fields in the inferior temporal visual cortex (e.g., in the TE areas) cross the vertical midline (not shown). *Left*, Hierarchical network structure of VisNet, a feature hierarchy model of the processing in the visual pathways.

example in Fig. 14.2) (Franco et al. 2007; Rolls and Tovee 1995; Treves et al. 1999). Each neuron encodes information about objects that is independent of that carried by other neurons (up to for example 20–40 neurons), corresponding to response profiles to the set of stimuli that are uncorrelated, and providing an exponential increase in the number of objects that can be encoded with the number of neurons in the population (Franco et al. 2007; Rolls et al. 1997). Much of the information can be obtained from a population of neurons by using just a dot product (e.g., synaptically weighted) decoding of the responses (Rolls et al. 1997), which is the simplest type of neuronal decoding (Rolls 2008b). Most of the information from the firing of IT neurons is available if just the first few spikes occurring in a period of 20 or 40 ms after the onset of firing are used, facilitating the rapid transmission of information through the ventral visual system, with just approximately 15 ms per stage being sufficient (Fig. 14.1) (Rolls 2007a; Rolls et al. 1994; Rolls et al. 2006; Tovee and Rolls 1995). Moreover, most of the information is available in the spike counts from each neuron in a short period, rather than in stimulus-dependent correlations between neurons (at least in IT, where this has been examined during natural vision in a top-down attentionally biased search for an object in a complex scene (Aggelopoulos et al. 2005; Rolls 2008b)). This is an indication that stimulus-dependent synchrony (Singer 1999) is not necessary for binding (Rolls 2008b).

The evidence that IT neurons respond to and encode objects (with a sparse distributed representation), and not features, includes the following. Many IT neurons respond only to combinations of complex features, and not to the individual complex features themselves (Perrett et al. 1982; Rolls 2008b; Tanaka et al. 1990). Moreover, for IT neurons, the features need to be in the correct spatial configuration with respect to each other, and do not respond well to scrambled images in which the features have been moved to different positions with respect to each other (Rolls et al. 1994). Further, the

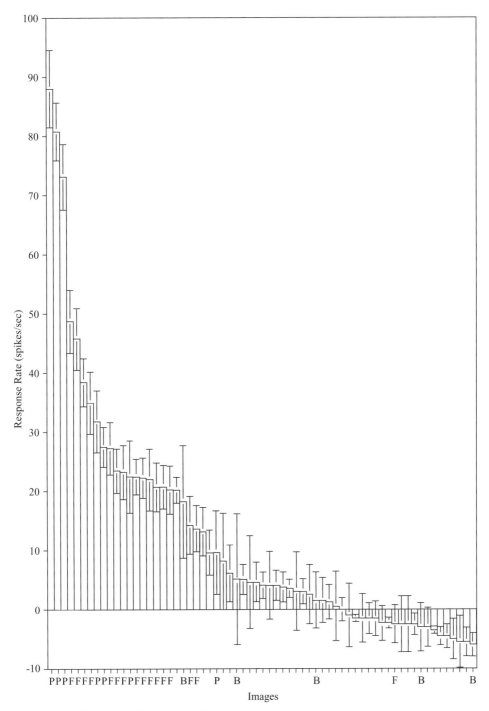

Figure 14.2. Firing-rate distribution of a single neuron in the temporal visual cortex to a set of 23 face (F) and 45 non-face images of natural scenes. The firing rate to each of the 68 stimuli is shown. *P* indicates a face-profile stimulus. *B* indicates a body-part stimulus, such as a hand. After Rolls and Tovee 1995a.

object (and face) representations are useful, in that they are rather invariant with respect to many transforms, including position on the retina, size, spatial frequency, and even view (Rolls 2000; Rolls 2007b, 2008a, b; Rolls and Deco 2002; Rolls and Stringer 2006b). The result is that a small population of neurons can represent which object of a very large number of different real-world objects is being viewed (Rolls 2008b). This is of fundamental importance for later stages of processing that can form memories about that object – for example, about what taste or other reinforcer is associated with the object, where the object is in a spatial scene, whether that object has been seen previously, and whether that object has been seen recently (Rolls 2008b). For this to operate correctly and usefully for objects, the representation in IT must generalize correctly to different transforms and so on of the object, and this is exactly what has been shown (Rolls 2008b).

If we go beyond what is required to represent normal real objects as found in the world with their only partly overlapping sets of features, to stimuli that require the ability to discriminate between stimuli composed of highly overlapping feature combinations in a low-dimensional feature space, then additional processing beyond IT in the perirhinal cortex may contribute to this type of discrimination (Rolls 2008b).

14.3 Outline of a Feature Hierarchy Model of the Computational Mechanisms in the Visual Cortex for Object and Face Recognition

The neurophysiological findings just described, and wider considerations on the possible computational properties of the cerebral cortex (Rolls 1989a, b, 1992, 2008b; Rolls and Treves 1998) lead to the following working hypotheses on object (including face) recognition by visual cortical mechanisms (Rolls 1992, 2008b; Rolls and Deco 2002).

Cortical visual processing for object recognition is considered to be organized as a set of hierarchically connected cortical regions consisting at least of V1, V2, V4, posterior inferior temporal cortex (TEO), and inferior temporal cortex (TE, including TE3, Tea, Tem, TE2, and TE1), as shown schematically in Figure 14.1. There is convergence from each small part of a region to the succeeding region (or layer in the hierarchy) in such a way that the receptive field sizes of neurons (e.g., 1 degree near the fovea in V1) become larger by a factor of approximately 2.5 with each succeeding stage (and the typical parafoveal receptive field sizes found would not be inconsistent with the calculated approximations of, e.g., 8 degrees in V4, 20 degrees in TEO, and 50 degrees in inferior temporal cortex; Boussaoud et al. 1991) (see Fig. 14.1). Such zones of convergence would overlap continuously with each other. This connectivity would be part of the architecture by which translation-invariant representations are computed. Each layer is considered to act partly as a set of local self-organizing competitive neuronal networks with overlapping inputs. (The region within which competition would be implemented would depend on the spatial properties of inhibitory interneurons, and might operate over distances of 1–2 mm in the cortex.) These competitive nets operate by a single set of forward inputs leading to (typically nonlinear, e.g., sigmoid) activation of output neurons; of competition between the output neurons mediated by a set of feedback inhibitory interneurons that receive from many of the principal (in the cortex, pyramidal) cells in the net and project back (via inhibitory interneurons) to many of the principal cells, which serves to decrease the firing rates of the less active neurons relative to the rates of the more active neurons; and then of synaptic modification by a modified Hebb rule, such that synapses to strongly activated output neurons from active input axons strengthen, and from inactive input axons weaken (Rolls 2008b; Rolls and Deco 2002; Rolls and Treves 1998).

Translation, size, and view invariance could be computed in such a system by utilizing competitive learning operating across short time scales to detect regularities in inputs when real objects are transforming in the physical world (Rolls 1992; Rolls 2000; Rolls 2008b; Rolls and Deco 2002; Wallis and Rolls 1997). The hypothesis is that because objects have continuous properties in space and time in the world, an object at one place on the retina might activate feature analyzers at the next stage of cortical processing, and when the object was translated to a nearby position, because this would occur in a short period (e.g., 0.5 s), the membrane of the postsynaptic neuron would still be in its "Hebb-modifiable" state (caused, e.g., by calcium entry as a result of the voltage-dependent activation of NMDA receptors, or by continuing firing of the neuron implemented by recurrent collateral connections forming a short-term memory), and the presynaptic afferents activated with the object in its new position would thus become strengthened on the still-activated postsynaptic neuron. It is suggested that the short temporal window (e.g., 0.5 s) of Hebb-modifiability helps neurons to learn the statistics of objects moving in the physical world, and at the same time to form different representations of different feature combinations or objects, as these are physically discontinuous and present less regular correlations to the visual system. Földiák (1991) has proposed computing an average activation of the postsynaptic neuron to assist with translation invariance. I also suggest that other invariances (e.g., size, spatial frequency, rotation, and view invariance) could be learned by similar mechanisms to those just described (Rolls 1992). It is suggested that the process takes place at each stage of the multiple-layer cortical processing hierarchy, so that invariances are learned first over small regions of space, and then over successively larger regions. This limits the size of the connection space within which correlations must be sought.

Increasing complexity of representations could also be built in such a multiple-layer hierarchy by similar competitive learning mechanisms. In order to avoid a combinatorial explosion, it is proposed that low-order combinations of inputs would be what is learned by each neuron. Evidence consistent with this suggestion that neurons are responding to combinations of a few variables represented at the preceding stage of cortical processing is that some neurons in V2 and V4 respond to end-stopped lines, to tongues flanked by inhibitory subregions, or to combinations of colors (Hegde and Van Essen 2000; Ito and Komatsu 2004); in posterior inferior temporal cortex to stimuli that may require two or more simple features to be present (Tanaka et al. 1990); and in the temporal cortical face-processing areas to images that require the presence of several features in a face (such as eyes, hair, and mouth) in order to respond (Perrett et al. 1982; Rolls 2008b; Tanaka et al. 1990; Yamane et al. 1988). It is an important part of this suggestion that some local spatial information would be inherent in the features that are being combined (Elliffe et al. 2002). For example, cells might not respond to the combination of an edge and a small circle unless they were in the correct spatial relation to each other. This is in fact consistent with the data of Tanaka et al. (1990) and with our data on face neurons (Rolls et al. 1994), in that some face neurons require the face features to be in the correct spatial configuration, and not jumbled. The local spatial information in the features being combined would ensure that the representation at the next level would contain some information about the (local) arrangement of features. Further low-order combinations of such neurons at the next stage would include sufficient local spatial information so that an arbitrary spatial arrangement of the same features would not activate the same neuron, and this is the proposed, and limited, solution that this mechanism would provide for the feature binding problem (Elliffe et al. 2002).

It is suggested that view-independent representations could be formed by the same type of computation, operating to combine a limited set of views of objects. The plausibility of providing view-independent recognition of objects by combining a set of different views of objects has been proposed by a number of investigators (Koenderink and Van Doorn 1979; Logothetis et al. 1994; Poggio and Edelman 1990; Ullman 1996). Consistent with the suggestion that the view-independent representations are formed by combining view-dependent representations in the primate visual system is the fact that in the temporal cortical areas, neurons with view-independent representations of faces are present in the same cortical areas as neurons with view-dependent representations (from which the view-independent neurons could receive inputs) (Booth and Rolls 1998; Hasselmo et al. 1989; Perrett et al. 1987). This solution to "object-based" representations is very different from that traditionally proposed for artificial vision systems, in which the coordinates of objects in 3-D space are stored in a database, and general-purpose algorithms operate on these to perform transforms such as translation, rotation, and scale change in 3-D space (Ullman 1996), or a linked list of feature parts is used (e.g., Marr 1982). In the present, much more limited but more biologically plausible scheme, the representation would be suitable for recognition of an object and for linking associative memories to objects, but would be less good for making actions in 3-D space to particular parts of, or inside, objects, as the 3-D coordinates of each part of the object would not be explicitly available. It is therefore proposed that visual fixation is used to locate in foveal vision part of an object to which movements must be made, and that local disparity and other measurements of depth then provide sufficient information for the dorsal visual system and motor system to make actions relative to the small part of space in which a local, view-dependent representation of depth would be provided (c.f. Ballard 1990; Rolls 2008b; Rolls and Deco 2002).

14.4 A Computational Model of Invariant Visual Object and Face Recognition

To test and clarify the hypotheses just described about how the visual system may operate to learn invariant object recognition, we have performed simulations that implement many of the ideas just described, and that are consistent with, and based on, much of the neurophysiology summarized in the previous sections. The network simulated (VisNet) can perform object, including face, recognition in a biologically plausible way, and after training shows, for example, translation and view invariance (Rolls 2008b; Rolls and Deco 2002; Rolls and Milward 2000; Rolls and Stringer 2006b; Wallis and Rolls 1997; Wallis et al. 1993).

In the four-layer network, the successive layers correspond approximately to V2, V4, the posterior temporal cortex, and the anterior temporal cortex (see Fig. 14.1). The forward connections to a cell in one layer are derived from a topologically corresponding region of the preceding layer, using a Gaussian distribution of connection probabilities to determine the exact neurons in the preceding layer to which connections are made. This schema is constrained to preclude the repeated connection of any cells. Each cell receives 100 connections from the 32×32 cells of the preceding layer, with a 67% probability that a connection comes from within four cells of the distribution center. Figure 14.1 shows the general convergent network architecture used. Within each layer, lateral inhibition between neurons has a radius of effect just greater than the radius of feedforward convergence just defined. The lateral inhibition is simulated via a linear local contrast-enhancing filter active on each neuron. (Note that this differs from the global "winner-take-all" paradigm implemented by Földiák (1991)). The cell activation is then passed through a nonlinear cell activation function, which also produces contrast enhancement of the firing rates (Rolls 2008b; Rolls and Deco 2002; Rolls and Milward 2000; Rolls and Stringer 2006b).

In order that the results of the simulation might be made particularly relevant to understanding processing in higher cortical visual areas, the inputs to layer 1 come from a separate input layer that provides an approximation to the encoding found in visual area 1 (V1) of the primate visual system.

The synaptic learning rule used can be summarized as follows:

$$\delta w_{ij} = k \cdot m_i \cdot r'_j$$

and

$$m_i^t = (1 - \eta)r_i^{(t)} + \eta m_i^{(t-1)}$$

where r'_j is the jth input to the neuron, r_i is the output of the ith neuron, w_{ij} is the jth weight on the ith neuron, η governs the relative influence of the trace and the new input (typically, 0.4–0.6), and $m_i^{(t)}$ represents the value of the ith cell's memory trace at time t. In the simulation the neuronal learning was bounded by normalization of each cell's dendritic weight vector, as in standard competitive learning (see Rolls 2008b; Rolls and Deco 2002; Rolls and Treves 1998).

To train the network to produce a translation invariant representation, one stimulus was placed successively in a sequence of nine positions across the input, then the next stimulus was placed successively in the same sequence of nine positions across the input, and so on through the set of stimuli. The idea was to enable the network to learn whatever was common at each stage of the network about a stimulus shown in different positions. To train on view invariance, different views of the same object were shown in succession, then different views of the next object were shown in succession, and so on. It has been shown that the network can learn to form neurons in the last layer of the network that respond to one of a set of simple shapes (such as "T, L and +") with translation invariance, or to a set of five to eight faces with translation, view, or size invariance, provided that the trace learning rule (not a simple Hebb rule, but see discussion of spatial transformation learning) is used (see Figs. 14.3 and 14.4) (Rolls and Deco 2002; Wallis and Rolls 1997).

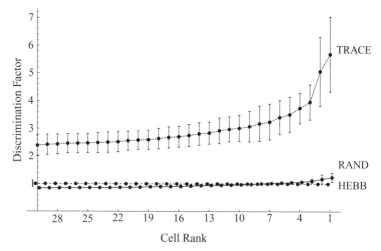

Figure 14.3. Comparison of VisNet network discrimination when trained with the trace learning rule, with a Hebb rule (no trace), and when not trained (Rand) on three stimuli (+, T, and L) at nine different locations. After Wallis and Rolls 1997.

There have been a number of investigations to explore this type of learning further. Rolls and Milward (2000) explored the operation of the trace learning rule used in the VisNet architecture, and showed that the rule operated especially well if the trace incorporated activity from previous presentations of the same object but received no contribution from the current neuronal activity being produced by the current exemplar of the object. The explanation for this is that this temporally asymmetric rule (the presynaptic term from the current exemplar, and the trace from the preceding exemplars) encourages neurons to respond to the current exemplar in the same way as they did to previous exemplars. It is of interest to consider whether intracellular processes related to Long-term potentiation (LTP) might implement an approximation of this rule, given that it is somewhat more powerful than the standard trace learning rule described before. Rolls and Stringer (2001) went on to show that part of the power of this type of trace rule can be related to gradient descent and temporal difference learning (Sutton and Barto 1998).

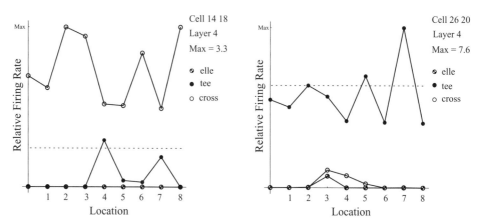

Figure 14.4. Response profiles for two fourth-layer neurons in VisNet (discrimination factors 4.07 and 3.62) in the L, T, and + invariance learning experiment. After Wallis and Rolls 1997.

Elliffe et al. (2002) examined the issue of spatial binding in this general class of hierarchical architecture studied originally by Fukushima (1980, 1989, 1991), and showed how by forming high spatial precision feature combination neurons early in processing, it is possible for later layers to maintain high precision for the relative spatial position of features within an object, yet achieve invariance for the spatial position of the whole object.

These results show that the proposed learning mechanism and neural architecture can produce cells with responses selective for stimulus identity with considerable position or view invariance (Rolls and Deco 2002). This ability to form invariant representations is an important property of the temporal cortical visual areas, for if a reinforcement association leading to an emotional or social response is learned to one view of a face, that learning will automatically generalize to other views of the face. This is a fundamental aspect of the way in which the brain is organized in order to allow this type of capability for emotional and social behavior (Rolls 1999; Rolls 2005). Further developments include operation of the system in a cluttered environment (Stringer and Rolls 2000); generalization from trained to untrained views of objects (Stringer and Rolls 2002); and a unifying theory of how invariant representations of optic flow produced by rotating or looming objects could be produced in the dorsal visual system (Rolls and Stringer 2006a) (sect. 14.10). The approach has also been extended to show that spatial continuity as objects gradually transform during training can be used with a purely associative learning rule to help build invariant representations in what has been termed continuous spatial transformation learning (Perry et al. 2006; Perry et al. 2009; Rolls and Stringer 2006b; Stringer et al. 2006). Further developments are considered after we introduce new neurophysiology on the representation of an object, and even several objects simultaneously, in complex natural scenes.

14.5 Neurophysiology of Object Representations in Complex Natural Scenes

Much of the neurophysiology of ventral stream visual processing has been performed with one feature, set of features, or object presented on a blank background, or in studies of attention two features may be presented on a blank background. How does the visual system operate in more realistic visual conditions when objects are presented in natural scenes? We learn much about computational aspects of natural vision from such investigations.

14.5.1 Object-Based Attention and Object Selection in Complex Natural Scenes

Object-based attention refers to attention to an object. For example, in a visual search task the object might be specified as what should be searched for, and its location must be found. In spatial attention, a particular location in a scene is pre-cued, and the object at that location may need to be identified.

To investigate how attention operates in complex natural scenes, and how information is passed from the IT to other brain regions to enable stimuli to be selected from natural scenes for action, Rolls, Aggelopoulos, and Zheng (2003) analyzed the responses of inferior temporal cortex neurons to stimuli presented in complex natural backgrounds while performing a top-down object-based attentional search task. The monkey had to search for two objects on a screen; a touch of one object was rewarded with juice, and of another object was punished with saline. Neuronal responses to the effective stimuli for the neurons were compared when the objects were presented in the natural scene or on a plain background. It was found that the response of the neuron to objects at the fovea was hardly reduced when they were presented in natural scenes, and the selectivity of the neurons remained (see also Sheinberg and Logothetis 2001). However, the main finding was that the magnitudes of the responses of the neurons typically became much less in the real scene the further the monkey fixated in the scene away from the object – that is, the receptive fields became smaller in complex natural scenes (Fig. 14.5). It is proposed that this reduced translation invariance (i.e., invariance with respect to position on the retina) in natural scenes helps an unambiguous representation of an object that may be the target for action to be passed to the brain regions that receive from the primate IT. It helps with the binding problem, by reducing in natural scenes the effective receptive field of at least some IT neurons to approximately the size of an object in the scene. In a very similar task, in which one of two objects had to be selected against a complex background, it is found that almost all the information (>95% of the total information) is encoded by the firing rates of simultaneously recorded IT neurons, and that very little information is encoded by stimulus-dependent synchronization, which may therefore not be important for implementing feature binding (Aggelopoulos et al. 2005; Rolls 2008b).

It is also found that in natural scenes, the effect of object-based attention on the response properties of IT neurons is relatively small, as illustrated in Figure 14.3 (Rolls et al. 2003). The results summarized in Figure 14.5 for 5-degree stimuli show that the receptive fields were large (77.6 degrees) with a single stimulus in a blank background (top left), and were greatly reduced in size (to 22.0 degrees) when presented in a complex natural scene (top right). The results also show that there was little difference in receptive field size or firing rate in the complex background when the effective stimulus was selected for action (bottom right, 19.2 degrees), and when it was not (middle right, 15.6 degrees) (Rolls et al. 2003). (For comparison, the effects of attention against a blank background were much larger, with the receptive field increasing from 17.2 degrees to 47.0 degrees as a result of object-based attention, as shown in Fig. 14.5.) The computational basis for these relatively minor effects of object-based attention when objects are viewed in natural scenes is considered in section 14.6.

14.5.2 The Interface from Object Representations to Action

These findings on how objects are represented in natural scenes make the interface to memory and action systems simpler, in that what is at the fovea can be interpreted (e.g., by an associative memory in the orbitofrontal cortex or amygdala) partly independently of the surroundings, and choices and actions can be directed if appropriate to what is at the fovea (Ballard 1993; Rolls and Deco 2002). There thus may be no need to have the precise coordinates of objects in space represented in the IT and passed to the

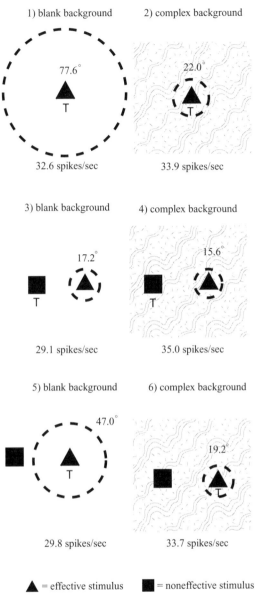

= effective stimulus ■ = noneffective stimulus

Figure 14.5. Summary of the receptive field sizes of inferior IT neurons to a 5-degree effective stimulus presented in either a blank background (blank screen) or in a natural scene (complex background). The stimulus that was a target for action in the different experimental conditions is marked by T. When the target stimulus was touched, a reward was obtained. The mean receptive field diameter of the population of neurons analyzed, and the mean firing rate in spikes/sec, is shown. The stimuli subtended 5 degrees × 3.5 degrees at the retina, and occurred on each trial in a random position in the 70 degrees × 55 degrees screen. The dashed circle is proportional to the receptive field size. *Top row*, Responses with one visual stimulus in a blank (left) or complex (right) background. *Middle row*, Responses with two stimuli, when the effective stimulus was not the target of the visual search. *Bottom row*, Responses with two stimuli, when the effective stimulus was the target of the visual search. After Rolls et al. 2003.

motor system for action to be directed at the target. Instead, given that the output of the IT in complex visual scenes is primarily about an object at the fovea, the dorsal visual system may be able to initiate action to whatever is at the fovea (Rolls 2008b; Rolls and Deco 2006). The condition for an action to be performed is that the ventral visual system must have provided a representation of the object, and this must have been identified as a goal (i.e., as a rewarded object) by, for example, associative reward-based lookup in brain structures such as the orbitofrontal cortex and amygdala, where visual stimuli are interfaced to reward systems (Rolls 2005).

This approach to object representation is very different to that attempted in some artificial vision systems, in which identification of all the objects in a scene, and where they are in the scene, is attempted. The research described here shows that biological systems perform a much simpler task and provide representations in complex natural scenes primarily of objects at or close to the fovea. Consistent with this, much of our perception of the objects in a scene is a memory-based not a perceptual representation, as shown by change blindness. Change blindness refers to our inability to detect a change to objects in a scene that can occur if the scene is changed during, for example, a blink or saccade (Simons and Rensink 2005). (The blink or saccade means that motion, etc., cannot be used to detect the removal of the object.) The small receptive fields of IT neurons in complex scenes provide an explanation for change blindness (Rolls 2008c). Another phenomenon related to the small size of IT neurons in complex natural scenes is inattentional blindness. This is demonstrated, for example, when watching a basketball-passing event in which the instructions were to count the ball passes between the team members with white shirts; the subjects were less likely to report that a black gorilla was walking across the scene compared to participants counting passes between the team members with black shirts (Simons and Chabris 1999). It is proposed here that an important factor that contributes to inattentional and change blindness is the reduced diameter of the receptive fields of IT neurons that occurs in natural scenes. This would result in a failure to activate representations of objects (such as the gorilla that appears in the middle of the basketball-passing event) if they are not close to the fovea, in complex cluttered scenes. If the instructions were to count the number of ball passes between the players with black shirts, this would tend by top-down biassed competition effects to facilitate representations of black stimuli, including the (unexpected) (black) gorilla. This facilitation, the neurophysiology shows (Fig. 14.5) (Rolls et al. 2003), consists of increasing somewhat the receptive field sizes of the neurons that are being biased (in this case, neurons that respond to black features). This, given many eye movements round the scene, would make it more likely that some of the black in the gorilla would activate some IT neurons. Thus, a combination of the reduced receptive field size of neurons in a complex natural scene and the effects of top-down biased competition would help account for inattentional blindness (Rolls 2008c).

The main point here is that these phenomena are related to the small receptive fields of IT neurons in complex natural scenes, and these small receptive fields are fundamental to how the biological visual system operates, for it greatly simplifies the computational problem compared to attempting to analyze the whole scene. It also reduces the binding and segmentation problems. The computational mechanisms that produce this reduction in receptive field size in complex natural scenes are described in section 14.6.

14.5.3 The Representation of Information About the Relative Positions of Multiple Objects in a Scene

These experiments have been extended to address the issue of how several objects are represented in a complex scene. The issue arises because the relative spatial locations of objects in a scene must be encoded (this is possible even in short presentation times without eye movements (Biederman 1972) and has been held to involve some spotlight of attention), and because what is represented in complex natural scenes is primarily about what is at the fovea; however, we can locate more than one object in a scene even without eye movements. Aggelopoulos and Rolls (2005) showed that with five objects simultaneously present in the receptive field of IT neurons, although all the neurons responded to their effective stimulus when it was at the fovea, some could also respond to their effective stimulus when it was in a parafoveal position 10 degrees from the fovea. An example of such a neuron is shown in Figure 14.6. The asymmetry is much more evident in a scene with five images present (Fig. 14.6A) than when only one image is shown on an otherwise blank screen (Fig. 14.6B). Competition between different stimuli in the receptive field thus reveals the asymmetry in the receptive field of IT neurons.

This has been tested computationally in VisNet, and it has been shown that the receptive fields in VisNet become small and asymmetric in scenes in which multiple objects are present, with the underlying mechanism that asymmetries related to the probabilistic nature of the excitatory feedforward connections and lateral inhibitory connections are revealed when the competition is high owing to the presence of multiple objects in a scene (Rolls et al. 2008).

The asymmetry provides a way of encoding the position of multiple objects in a scene. Depending on which asymmetric neurons are firing, the population of neurons provides information (using a distributed representation of the type that a population of receiving neurons with mutual, lateral, inhibition can decode; see Rolls 2008b) to the next processing stage not only about which image is present at or close to the fovea, but where it is with respect to the fovea. This information is provided by neurons that have firing rates that reflect the relevant information, and stimulus-dependent synchrony is not necessary. Top-down attentional biasing input could, by biasing the appropriate neurons, facilitate bottom-up information about objects without any need to alter the time relations between the firing of different neurons. The exact position of the object with respect to the fovea, and effectively its spatial position relative to other objects in the scene, would then be made evident by the subset of asymmetric neurons firing.

This is the solution that these experiments indicate is used for the representation of multiple objects in a scene (Aggelopoulos and Rolls 2005), an issue that has previously been difficult to account for in neural systems with distributed representations (Mozer 1991) and for which "attention" has been a proposed solution.

14.6 Object Representation and Attention in Natural Scenes: A Computational Account

The results described in section 14.5 and summarized in Figure 14.5 show that the receptive fields of IT neurons were large (77.6 degrees) with a single stimulus in a

A   **B**

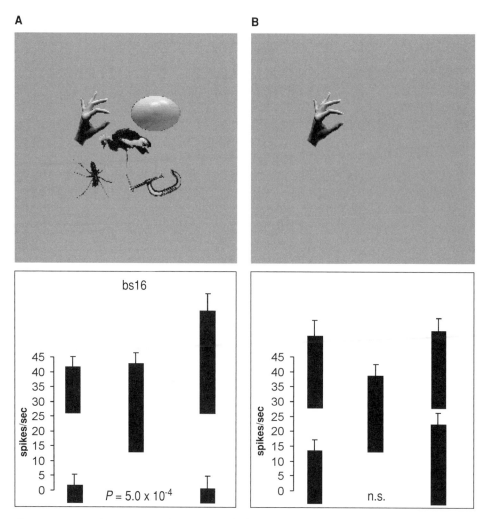

Figure 14.6. *A,* The responses (firing rate with the spontaneous rate subtracted, means ± sem) of one neuron when tested with five stimuli simultaneously present in the close (10-degree) configuration with the parafoveal stimuli located 10 degrees from the fovea. *B,* The responses of the same neuron when only the effective stimulus was presented in each position. The firing rate for each position is that when the effective stimulus for the neuron was in that position. The *P* value is that from the ANOVA calculated over the four parafoveal positions. After Aggelopoulos and Rolls 2005.

blank background (top left), and were greatly reduced in size (to 22 degrees) when presented in a complex natural scene (top right). The results also show that there was little difference in receptive field size or firing rate in the complex background when the effective stimulus was selected for action (bottom right), and when it was not (middle right) (Rolls et al. 2003).

Trappenberg, Rolls, and Stringer (2002) have suggested what underlying mechanisms could account for these findings, and they simulated a model to test the ideas. The model utilizes an attractor network that represents the inferior temporal visual cortex (implemented by the recurrent excitatory connections between IT neurons), and

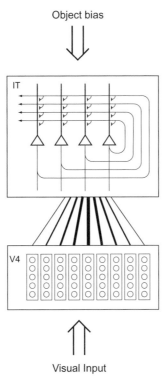

Figure 14.7. The architecture of the inferior temporal cortex (IT) model of Trappenberg et al. (2002) operating as an attractor network with inputs from the fovea given preferential weighting by the greater magnification factor of the fovea. The model also has a top-down, object-selective bias input. The model was used to analyze how object vision and recognition operate in complex natural scenes.

a neural input layer with several retinotopically organized modules representing the visual scene in an earlier visual cortical area such as V4 (Fig. 14.7). An attractor, or autoassociation, network is implemented by associatively modifiable connections between the neurons in the network. Each vector of neuronal firing rates represents a stimulus or memory, and is stored by associative synaptic modification between the neurons representing that stimulus or memory. When even a partial retrieval cue is provided that is similar to one of the patterns stored in the network, the network is attracted into the state with the neurons in the original pattern active and, thus, implements memory retrieval. The neurons continue firing stably with just that set of neurons active, thus implementing short-term memory, too. A description of the operation of these and other networks is provided elsewhere (Rolls 2008b). The attractor network aspect of the model produces the property that the receptive fields of IT neurons can be large in blank scenes by enabling a weak input in the periphery of the visual field to act as a retrieval cue for the object attractor. On the other hand, when the object is shown in a complex background, the object closest to the fovea tends to act as the retrieval cue for the attractor, because the fovea is given increased weight in activating the IT module because the magnitude of the input activity from objects at the fovea is greatest due to the cortical higher magnification factor of the fovea incorporated into the model. (The cortical magnification factor can be expressed as the number of millimeters of cortex representing 1 degree of visual field. The cortical magnification factor decreases rapidly with increasing eccentricity from the fovea (Cowey and Rolls 1975; Rolls and Cowey 1970).) This results in smaller receptive fields of IT neurons in complex scenes, because the object tends to need to be close to the fovea to trigger the attractor into the state representing that object. In other words, if the object is far from the fovea in a cluttered scene, then the object will not trigger neurons in IT that represent it, because neurons in IT are preferentially being activated by another object at the fovea. This may be described as an attractor model in which the competition for which attractor state is retrieved is weighted towards objects at the fovea.

Attentional top-down object-based inputs can bias the competition implemented in this attractor model but have relatively minor effects (e.g., in increasing receptive field size) when they are applied in a complex natural scene, because then the stronger forward inputs dominate the states reached. In this network, the recurrent collateral connections may be thought of as implementing constraints between the different inputs present, to help arrive at firing in the network that best meets the constraints. In this scenario, the preferential weighting of objects close to the fovea because of the increased magnification factor at the fovea is a useful principle in enabling the system to provide useful output. The top-down attentional biasing effect on an object is much more marked in a blank scene, or in a scene with only two objects present at similar distances from the fovea, which are conditions in which attentional effects have frequently been examined. The results of the investigation (Trappenberg et al. 2002) thus suggest that attention may be a much more limited phenomenon in complex, natural scenes than in reduced displays with one or two objects present. The results also suggest that the alternative principle, of providing strong weight to whatever is close to the fovea, is an important principle governing the operation of the IT and, in general, of the output of the ventral visual system in natural environments. This principle of operation is very important in interfacing the visual system to action systems, because the effective stimulus in making IT neurons fire is in natural scenes usually on or close to the fovea. This means that the spatial coordinates of the object in the scene do not have to be represented in the IT, nor passed from it to the action selection system, as the latter can assume that the object making IT neurons fire is close to the fovea in natural scenes (Rolls et al. 2003; Rolls and Deco 2002).

Of course, there may also be a mechanism for object selection that takes into account the locus of covert attention when actions are made to locations that are not being looked at. However, the simulations described in this section suggest that, in any case, covert attention is likely to be a much less significant influence on visual processing in natural scenes than in reduced scenes with one or two objects present.

Given these points, one might question why IT neurons can have such large receptive fields, which show translation invariance (Rolls 2000; Rolls et al. 2003). At least part of the answer to this may be that IT neurons must have the capability for large receptive fields if they are to deal with large objects (Rolls and Deco 2002). A V1 neuron, with its small receptive field, simply could not receive input from all the features necessary to define an object. On the other hand, IT neurons may be able to adjust their size to approximately the size of objects, using in part the interactive attentional effects of bottom-up and top-down effects described elsewhere in this chapter.

In natural scenes, the model is able to account for the neurophysiological data that the IT neuronal responses are larger when the object is close to the fovea, by virtue of the fact that objects close to the fovea are weighted by the cortical magnification factor. The model accounts for the larger receptive field sizes from the fovea of IT neurons in natural backgrounds if the target is the object being selected compared to when it is not selected (Rolls et al. 2003). The model accounts for this by an effect of top-down bias, which simply biases the neurons towards particular objects compensating for their decreasing inputs produced by the decreasing magnification factor modulation with increasing distance from the fovea. Such object-based attention signals could originate in the prefrontal cortex and could provide the object bias for the inferotemporal cortex (Renart et al. 2001; Renart et al. 2000; Rolls and Deco 2002). Important properties of the architecture for obtaining the results just described are the high magnification factor at the fovea and the competition between the effects of different inputs, implemented in the preceding simulation by the competition inherent in an attractor network.

We have also been able to obtain similar results in a hierarchical feedforward network in which each layer operates as a competitive network (Deco and Rolls 2004). This network thus captures many of the properties of our hierarchical model of invariant visual object recognition in the ventral visual stream (Elliffe et al. 2002; Rolls 1992; Rolls and Deco 2002; Rolls and Milward 2000; Rolls and Stringer 2001, 2006a, b; Stringer et al. 2006; Stringer and Rolls 2000, 2002; Wallis and Rolls 1997), but also incorporates a foveal magnification factor and top-down projections with a dorsal visual stream so that attentional effects can be studied, as shown in Figure 14.8.

Deco and Rolls (2004) trained the network described shown in Figure 14.8 with two objects, and used the trace learning rule (Rolls and Milward 2000; Wallis and Rolls 1997) to achieve translation invariance. With this model, we were able to obtain similar effects to those already described, and in addition were able to make predictions about the interaction between stimuli when they were placed in different relative positions with respect to the fovea.

14.7 Learning Invariant Representations of an Object with Multiple Objects in the Scene and with Cluttered Backgrounds

The results of simulations of learning with an object in a cluttered background suggest that in order for a neuron to *learn* invariant responses to different transforms of a stimulus when it is presented during training in a cluttered background, some form of segmentation is required in order to separate the figure (i.e., the stimulus or object) from the background (Stringer and Rolls 2000). This segmentation might be performed using evidence in the visual scene about different depths, motions, colors, and so on of the object from its background. In the visual system, this might mean combining evidence represented in different cortical areas and might be performed by cross-connections between cortical areas to enable such evidence to help separate the representations of objects from their backgrounds in the form-representing cortical areas.

A second way in which training a feature hierarchy network in a cluttered natural scene may be facilitated follows from the finding that the receptive fields of IT neurons shrink from in the order of 70 degrees in diameter when only one object is present in

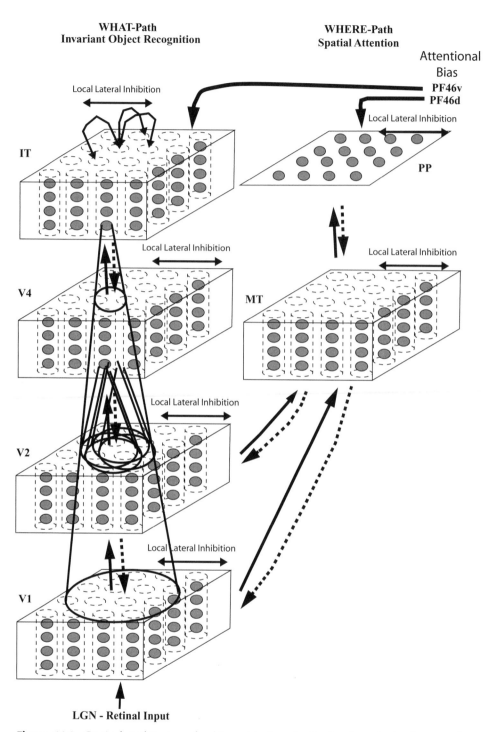

Figure 14.8. Cortical architecture for hierarchical and attention-based visual perception. The system is essentially composed of five modules structured such that they resemble the two known main visual paths of the mammalian visual cortex (MT). Information from the retinogeniculostriate pathway enters the visual cortex through area V1 in the occipital lobe and proceeds into two processing streams. The occipitotemporal stream leads ventrally through V2-V4 and IT (inferior temporal visual cortex), and is mainly concerned with object recognition. The occipitoparietal stream leads dorsally into PP (posterior parietal complex), and is responsible for maintaining a spatial map of an object's location. The solid lines with arrows between levels show the forward connections, and the dashed lines, the top-down backprojections. Short-term memory systems in the prefrontal cortex (PF46) apply top-down attentional bias to the object or spatial processing streams. After Deco and Rolls 2004.

a blank scene to much smaller values of as little as 5–10 degrees close to the fovea in complex natural scenes (Rolls et al. 2003) (see sects. 14.5 and 14.6). This allows primarily the object at the fovea to be represented in the IT and, it is proposed, for learning to be about this object, and not about the other objects in a whole scene.

Third, top-down spatial attention (Deco and Rolls 2004, 2005a; Deco and Rolls 2005b; Rolls and Deco 2002) could bias the competition towards a region of visual space in which the object to be learned is located.

Fourth, if object 1 is presented during training with different objects present on different trials, then the competitive networks that are part of VisNet will learn to represent each object separately, because the features that are part of each object will be much more strongly associated together, than are those features with the other features present in the different objects seen on some trials during training (Stringer and Rolls 2008; Stringer et al. 2007). It is a natural property of competitive networks that input features that co-occur frequently are allocated output neurons to represent the pattern as a result of the learning. Input features that do not co-occur frequently may not have output neurons allocated to them. This principle may help feature hierarchy systems to learn representations of individual objects, even when other objects with some of the same features are present in the visual scene, but with different other objects on different trials. With this fundamental and interesting property of competitive networks, it has now become possible for VisNet to self-organize invariant representations of individual objects, even though each object is always presented during training with at least one other object present in the scene (Stringer and Rolls 2008; Stringer et al. 2007).

14.8 A Biased Competition Model of Object and Spatial Attentional Effects on the Representations in the Visual System

So far, the models have been operating mainly in a feedforward, bottom-up way. In this section, I consider a computational account of how top-down influences of attention operate by biased competition to modulate the representations in the visual system.

Visual attention exerts top-down influences on the processing of sensory information in the visual cortex; therefore, it is intrinsically associated with interactions between cortical areas. Elucidating the neural basis of visual attention is an excellent paradigm for understanding the basic mechanisms of intercortical neurodynamics. Recent developments in cognitive neuroscience allow a more direct study of the neural mechanisms underlying attention in humans and primates. In particular, the work of Chelazzi, Miller, Duncan, and Desimone (1993) has led to a promising account of attention termed the "biased-competition hypothesis" (Desimone and Duncan 1995; Reynolds and Desimone 1999). According to this hypothesis, attentional selection operates in parallel by biasing an underlying competitive interaction between multiple stimuli in the visual field toward one stimulus or another, so that behaviorally relevant stimuli are processed in the cortex while irrelevant stimuli are filtered out. Thus, attending to a stimulus at a particular location or with a particular feature biases the underlying neural competition in a certain brain area in favor of neurons that respond to the location, or the features, of the attended stimulus. As a result of the competition, neurons that represent features without a top-down bias have reduced activity.

Neurodynamical models for biased competition have been proposed and successfully applied in the context of attention and working memory. In the context of attention, Usher and Niebur (1996) introduced an early model of biased competition. Deco and Zihl (2001) extended Usher and Niebur's model to simulate the psychophysics of visual attention by visual search experiments in humans. Their neurodynamical formulation is a large-scale hierarchical model of the visual cortex whose global dynamics is based on biased-competition mechanisms at the neural level. Attention then appears as an emergent effect related to the dynamical evolution of the whole network. This large-scale formulation, using a simplified version of the architecture shown in Figure 14.8, has been able to simulate and explain in a unifying framework, visual attention in a variety of tasks and at different cognitive neuroscience experimental measurement levels (Deco and Rolls 2005a); single-cells (Deco and Lee 2002; Rolls and Deco 2002), fMRI (Corchs and Deco 2002), psychophysics (Deco and Rolls 2005a; Rolls and Deco 2002), and neuropsychology (Deco and Rolls 2002). In the context of working memory, further developments (Deco and Rolls 2003; Rolls 2008b) managed to model in a unifying form attentional and memory effects in the prefrontal cortex, integrating single-cell and fMRI data, and different paradigms in the framework of biased competition.

In particular, Deco and Rolls (2005b) extended previous concepts of the role of biased competition in attention by providing the first analysis at the integrate-and-fire neuronal level, which allows the neuronal nonlinearities in the system to be explicitly modeled, in order to investigate realistically the processes that underlie the apparent gain modulation effect of top-down attentional control. In the integrate-and-fire implementation, the synaptic currents that lead to activation of the neuron, and then the generation of a spike when a threshold is reached, are modeled, producing a system that can model many of the nonlinearities in the system and also the effects of the probabilistic spiking of the neurons in the network on how it operates, as described elsewhere (Rolls 2008b; Rolls and Deco 2002). In the integrate-and-fire model, the competition is implemented realistically by the effects of the excitatory neurons on the inhibitory neurons and their return inhibitory synaptic connections. This was also the first integrate-and-fire analysis of top-down attentional influences in vision that explicitly models the interaction of several different brain areas. Part of the originality of the model is that in the form in which it can account for attentional effects in V2 and V4 in the paradigms of Reynolds, Chelazzi, and Desimone (1999) in the context of biased competition, the model with the same parameters effectively makes predictions that show that the "contrast gain" effects in MT (Martinez-Trujillo and Treue 2002) can be accounted for by the same model. For example, the top-down attentional modulation effects are most evident when the bottom-up input is weak (e.g., has low contrast), because the top-down effects themselves must never be so strong that they dominate perception. In addition, the top-down modulation can appear as a nonlinear multiplication effect with the bottom-up input, although the processes involved include only linear summation within the neurons of bottom-up and top-down synaptic inputs, and the threshold nonlinearity of neurons involved in whether an action potential is generated (Deco and Rolls 2005b). These detailed and quantitative analyses of neuronal dynamical systems are an important step towards understanding the operation of complex processes such as top-down attention, which necessarily involve the interaction of several brain areas.

They are being extended to provide neurally plausible models of decision making and action selection (Deco and Rolls 2003; Deco and Rolls 2005d, 2006; Rolls 2008b).

In relation to representation in the brain, the impact of these findings is that they show details of the mechanisms by which representations can be modulated by attention, and moreover can account for many phenomena in attention using models in which the firing rate of neurons is represented, and in which stimulus-dependent neuronal synchrony is not involved (Rolls 2007b, 2008b).

The top-down back-projection pathways between adjacent cortical areas that implement the attentional effects in this model are weak relative to the forward (bottom-up) inputs. Consistent with this, the back-projection synapses end on the apical dendrites of pyramidal cells in the preceding cortical area, quite far from the cell body, where they might be expected to be sufficient to dominate the cell firing when there is no forward input close to the cell body (i.e., during memory recall, which may be one of the functions of these back-projection pathways, given the very large number of connections and their associative modifiability) (Rolls 1989a, 2008b; Treves and Rolls 1994). In contrast, when there is forward input to the neuron, activating synapses closer to the cell body than the back-projecting inputs, this would tend to electrically shunt the back-projection effects received on the apical dendrites, accounting for their relatively small but useful biasing effect. The associative modifiability is useful for setting up the connectivity required not only for memory recall, but also for top-down attentional effects to influence the correct neurons (Rolls 2008b).

14.9 Decision making in Perception

When the surfaces of a Necker cube flip from back to front, it is as if an internal model of the 3-D structure of the cube is influencing the representation of the depth of the different surfaces of the cube (Gregory 1970, 1998; Helmholtz 1857; Rolls 2008b). When two objects are presented to the visual system in rivalry, first one is seen, and then there is a probabilistic flip to the other object being seen (Maier et al. 2005). Again, an internal representation of each object appears to be influencing visual processing so that first the whole of one object, and then of the other object, is seen, and not a combination of the features of both. A recent model of probabilistic decision making in the brain (Deco and Rolls 2006) contributes to our understanding of these perceptual phenomena, for it is suggested that the underlying computational mechanism may be similar, providing a unifying approach to these aspects of brain processing (Rolls 2008b).

The architecture of the model is that of an attractor network and is within the theoretical framework utilized by Wang (2002), which is based on a neurodynamical model first introduced by Brunel and Wang (2001) and which has been recently extended and successfully applied to explain several experimental paradigms (Deco and Rolls 2002; Deco and Rolls 2003, 2005b; Deco et al. 2004; Deco et al. 2005; Rolls and Deco 2002; Szabo et al. 2004). In this framework, we model probabilistic decision making by an attractor network of interacting integrate-and-fire neurons with spiking activity organized into a discrete set of populations. For a binary decision, there are two populations of neurons, each one corresponding to one of the decisions. Each population has its own biasing input, f1 and f2. The network starts with spontaneous activity, and if the biases are equal, what is effectively a biased competition network eventually falls into one of the attractor states (i.e., with one of the populations of neurons firing with a high rate), with a probability that each attractor wins being 0.5. The probabilistic settling of the network is due to the inherent noise in the finite size network due to the Poisson-like firing of the neurons (Deco and Rolls 2006). The attractor that wins represents the decision. If one of the biases is stronger than the other, then the probability that the network will reach that decision increases. Because the model is a short-term memory network, the system can integrate information over long time periods, of hundreds of milliseconds, before a decision is reached. As the biases become more unequal, the reaction time of the decision made by the network decreases. As the biases are both increased, the magnitude of the difference between them for a decision to be reached must be increased in proportion, that is $\Delta I / I =$ a constant. The network implements Weber's law because as I is increased, the activity of the inhibitory feedback neurons in the integrate-and-fire network increases linearly, and these produce divisive inhibition on the excitatory cells that form the attractor, resulting in a need for ΔI to increase in proportion to the divisive inhibition, resulting in $\Delta I / I =$ a constant (Deco and Rolls 2006; Deco et al. 2009).

The decision-making network was tested (Deco and Rolls 2006) against neurophysiological data on decision making for vibrotactile frequency discrimination. However, it is proposed here that the same type of decision-making network could be implemented in many brain areas, to account for many types of probabilistic decision making. In the context of visual perception, it is proposed that the two attractor states might represent the two alternative interpretations of which side of a Necker cube is closer, or which binocularly presented image is being seen. Then with some adaptation in the excitatory neurons of the synapses between them, which has been modeled (Deco and Rolls 2005c; Deco and Rolls 2005d), the firing rate in the currently active attractor would gradually decrease, allowing the other attractor to spontaneously become active in a probabilistic way that depends on the number of spikes that happen to be generated with Poisson-like statistics by the different neurons in the different attractors. In this way, the higher-level representation of the object (e.g., the cube or the image) would spontaneously and probabilistically flip, and this higher-level representation would bias the lower-level representations by top-down influences so that first one edge and then the other edge of the cube would be biased to appear close, or the features in one image versus the other would be biased by the top-down competitive influence in pattern (Maier et al. 2005) and even binocular rivalry.

It is thus proposed that this model of decision making (Deco and Rolls 2006) might account for many decision-making processes in the brain, including those involved in the interpretation of visual images and the recognition of objects. In this sense, what is seen or emphasized at the lower level is biased or pre-empted by the state of the higher-level representations, themselves determined probabilistically. We may note that in fact the decision may not be taken only in the high-level network but could be distributed throughout the system of interconnected networks, with their feedforward and top-down feedback connections all contributing to the decision making (Deco and Rolls 2006), and all perhaps to the probabilistic change of state according to the extent to which the coupled neurons at different levels of the network show adaptation and by their probabilistic spiking contribute to the noise in the system.

14.10 Invariant Global Object Motion in the Dorsal Visual System

A key issue in understanding the cortical mechanisms that underlie motion perception is how we perceive the motion of objects such as a rotating wheel invariantly with respect to position on the retina and size. For example, we perceive the wheel shown in Figure 14.9a rotating clockwise independently of its position on the retina. This occurs even though the local motion for the wheel in the different positions may be opposite. How could this invariance of the visual motion perception of objects arise in the visual system? Invariant motion representations are known to be developed in the cortical dorsal visual system. Motion-sensitive neurons in V1 have small receptive fields (in the range of 1–2 degrees at the fovea) and can therefore not detect global motion; this is part of the aperture problem (Wurtz and Kandel 2000). Neurons in MT, which receives inputs from V1 and V2, have larger receptive fields (e.g., 5 degrees at the fovea) and are able to respond to planar global motion, such as a field of small dots in which the majority (in practice as little as 55%) move in one direction, or to the overall direction of a moving plaid, the orthogonal grating components of which have motion at 45 degrees to the overall motion (Newsome et al. 1989; Wurtz and Kandel 2000). Further on in the dorsal visual system, some neurons in macaque visual area MST (but not MT) respond to rotating flow fields or looming with considerable translation invariance (Geesaman and Andersen 1996; Graziano et al. 1994).

In a unifying hypothesis with the design of the ventral cortical visual system, Rolls and Stringer (2006a) proposed that the dorsal visual system uses a hierarchical feedforward network architecture (V1, V2, MT, MSTd, parietal cortex) with training of the connections with a short-term memory trace associative synaptic modification rule to capture what is invariant at each stage. The principal difference from VisNet used to the model the ventral visual system is that the input filtering that for the ventral visual system uses difference of Gaussian filtering to produce V1 "oriented bar" simple cell-like receptive fields is replaced for the dorsal visual system by filtering of the image for the local direction and velocity of the optic flow (see Fig. 14.9). Simulations showed that the proposal is computationally feasible, in that invariant representations of the motion flow fields produced by objects self-organize in the later layers of the architecture (see Fig. 14.9). The model produces invariant representations of the motion flow fields produced by global in-plane motion of an object, in-plane rotational motion, looming versus receding of the object, and object-based rotation about a principal axis (Rolls and Stringer 2006a). Thus, the dorsal and ventral visual systems may share some similar computational principles.

14.11 Conclusion

An approach to the computations involved in object recognition that is very closely linked to the neurophysiology of object recognition has been described here and in more detail elsewhere (Rolls 2008b; Rolls and Deco 2002; Rolls and Stringer 2006b). The theory of how different types of invariance are learned is generic, and indeed the

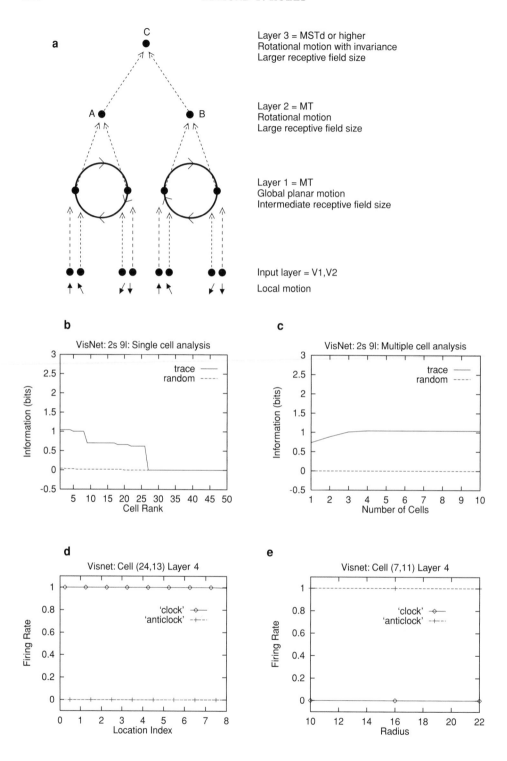

a

C

Layer 3 = MSTd or higher
Rotational motion with invariance
Larger receptive field size

A   B

Layer 2 = MT
Rotational motion
Large receptive field size

Layer 1 = MT
Global planar motion
Intermediate receptive field size

Input layer = V1,V2

Local motion

b

VisNet: 2s 9l: Single cell analysis

Information (bits)

trace ——
random -----

Cell Rank

c

VisNet: 2s 9l: Multiple cell analysis

Information (bits)

trace ——
random -----

Number of Cells

d

Visnet: Cell (24,13) Layer 4

Firing Rate

'clock' ◇
'anticlock' +

Location Index

e

Visnet: Cell (7,11) Layer 4

Firing Rate

'clock' ◇
'anticlock' +

Radius

same architecture and model were used for all the investigations of translation, view, rotation, size, lighting, and object motion invariance described. In all cases, spatial and/or temporal continuity across the different transforms of individual objects was what allowed the architecture to learn invariant representations. The unifying nature of the overall approach is illustrated by the fact that the same architecture was able to form a model of invariant object motion representations in the dorsal visual system just by using local motion inputs instead of the oriented spatial filter inputs normally used for simulations of processing in the ventral visual system (Rolls and Stringer 2006a). Further, by adding top-down biasing inputs to the feedforward architecture, one can model the operation of top-down attentional effects (Deco and Rolls 2004; Rolls 2008b).

Although the architecture is generic, this does not, of course, preclude the local self-organization of topographic maps that provide some segregation of different types of processing. Indeed this is seen to arise from the short-range lateral excitatory and inhibitory connections that are characteristic of the neocortex and to provide the advantage of minimizing the lengths of the connections between neurons that need to exchange information, an important factor in the size of the brain (Rolls 2008b).

An important attribute of the architecture is the inhibitory connections that are important for implementing the competition between neurons. In conjunction with the probabilistic feedforward connectivity, these contribute to making the receptive fields asymmetric in complex scenes when there is increased competition, and thus support representations of multiple objects in a scene and their relative spatial position (Rolls et al. 2008).

The generic nature of the architecture has been further extended by the concept that adding a further layer or layers beyond the fourth layer of VisNet (which corresponds to the anterior inferior temporal visual cortex as shown in Fig. 14.1) and operating by the same principles provides a computational approach to understanding spatial scene representations in areas beyond the ventral visual stream, such as the parahippocampal cortex and hippocampus (Rolls et al. 2008). If such a fifth layer is trained with the same principles, but now with several objects present in a particular spatial arrangement, then the fifth layer learns by the same type of competitive learning to form neurons that respond to spatial views. In other words the fifth-layer neurons respond to the scene

---

Figure 14.9. *a*, Two rotating wheels at different locations rotating in opposite directions. The local flow field is ambiguous. Clockwise or counterclockwise rotation can only be diagnosed by a global flow computation, and it is shown how the network is expected to solve the problem to produce position invariant global motion-sensitive neurons. One rotating wheel is presented at any one time, but the need is to develop a representation of the fact that in the case shown the rotating flow field is always clockwise, independent of the location of the flow field. *b*, Single-cell information measures showing that some layer-4 neurons have perfect performance of 1 bit (clockwise vs. anticlockwise) after training with the trace rule, but not with random initial synaptic weights in the untrained control condition. *c*, The multiple cell information measures show that small groups of neurons have perfect performance. *d*, Position invariance illustrated for a single cell from layer 4, which responded only to the clockwise rotation, and for every one of the nine positions. *e*, Size invariance illustrated for a single cell from layer 4, which after training three different radii of rotating wheel, responded only to anticlockwise rotation, independently of the size of the rotating wheels. After Rolls and Stringer 2006a.

that is a combination of objects, and respond better than when the same objects are shown in a different spatial arrangement (Rolls et al. 2008). This is possible because the neurons in layer 4 become asymmetric in the presence of multiple objects in a scene. The fifth-layer neurons thus have properties like those of spatial view cells in the parahippocampal areas and hippocampus (Rolls 2008b; Rolls and Kesner 2006; Rolls and Xiang 2006).

The general approach is supported by other investigations. It has been shown, for example, that a somewhat comparable feedforward hierarchical feature combination architecture (although with a series of "simple" and "complex" cell layers in which a MAX function is used in the "complex" layers) can learn invariant representations (Riesenhuber and Poggio 2000; Serre et al. 2007). It has also been shown in an architecture trained by gradient descent that temporal continuity is an important principle that can allow invariant representations of objects to be learned from exposure to world-like series of images (Franzius et al. 2007; Wyss et al. 2006).

The overall approach to the computational architecture involved in forming invariant representations of objects is aimed to incorporate what is known about visual object processing in the brain and to provide a way to explore the computational bases of this processing. There are many issues that it would be of interest to explore further; one is training with more real-world–like sequences of images. The simulations performed so far have been with precisely produced image sets that allow particular hypotheses to be investigated and tested, in which typically one parameter is varied, such as spatial position. It would be interesting to extend this to image sequences in which several parameters might be altering simultaneously, such as spatial position and view. Training with images drawn from the natural world would be of interest, and this would allow the matching of the image statistics to the dynamical properties of the real visual system in the brain to be investigated. For example, do the slow times constants of NMDA receptors provide the system with sufficiently slow temporal properties to capture the invariant properties of objects seen in the real world given the rates at which objects transform, or is additional slowness needed, such as that that could be provided by the short-term memory attractor properties instantiated by the cortical recurrent collateral connections (Rolls 2008b)? Another aspect of the architecture that it would be of interest to explore further is its capacity for representing many objects and many transforms of each. The concept is that the capacity should be sufficiently high, given the very large number of neurons in the ventral visual system, and the fact that many stages of processing contribute to the invariant representations, with relatively local invariance of feature combinations in early layers, and object invariance in the final layers. However, the simulations performed have been on a small scale, with 1024 neurons in each of four layers, and it would be interesting to investigate how the system scales up (Rolls 2008b).

Acknowledgments

The author has worked on some of the investigations described here with N. Aggelopoulos, P. Azzopardi, G.C. Baylis, H. Critchley, G. Deco, P. Földiák, L. Franco, M. Hasselmo, J. Hornak, M. Kringelbach, C.M. Leonard, T.J. Milward, D.I. Perrett, S.M.

Stringer, M.J. Tovee, T. Trappenberg, A. Treves, J. Tromans, and G.M. Wallis. Their collaboration is sincerely acknowledged. Discussions on inattentional blindness with Rebekah White were very helpful. Different parts of the research described were supported by the Medical Research Council, PG8513790; by a Human Frontier Science Program grant; by an EC Human Capital and Mobility grant; by the MRC Oxford Interdisciplinary Research Centre in Cognitive Neuroscience; and by the Oxford McDonnell-Pew Centre in Cognitive Neuroscience.

Bibliography

Aggelopoulos NC, Franco L, Rolls ET. 2005. Object perception in natural scenes: encoding by inferior temporal cortex simultaneously recorded neurons. *J Neurophysiol* 93: 1342–1357.

Aggelopoulos NC, Rolls ET. 2005. Natural scene perception: inferior temporal cortex neurons encode the positions of different objects in the scene. *Eur J Neurosci* 22: 2903–2916.

Ballard DH. 1990. Animate vision uses object-centred reference frames. In *Advanced neural computers*, ed. R Eckmiller, 229–236. Amsterdam: North-Holland.

Ballard DH. 1993. Subsymbolic modelling of hand-eye coordination. In *The simulation of human intelligence*, ed. DE Broadbent, 71–102. Oxford: Blackwell.

Biederman I. 1972. Perceiving real-world scenes. *Science* 177: 77–80.

Biederman I. 1987. Recognition-by-components: a theory of human image understanding. *Psychol Rev* 94: 115–147.

Booth MCA, Rolls ET. 1998. View-invariant representations of familiar objects by neurons in the inferior temporal visual cortex. *Cereb Cortex* 8: 510–523.

Boussaoud D, Desimone R, Ungerleider LG. 1991. Visual topography of area TEO in the macaque. *J Comp Neurol* 306: 554–575.

Brunel N, Wang XJ. 2001. Effects of neuromodulation in a cortical network model of object working memory dominated by recurrent inhibition. *J Comput Neurosci* 11: 63–85.

Chelazzi L, Miller E, Duncan J, Desimone R. 1993. A neural basis for visual search in inferior temporal cortex. *Nature* 363: 345–347.

Corchs S, Deco G. 2002. Large-scale neural model for visual attention: integration of experimental single-cell and fMRI data. *Cereb Cortex* 12: 339–348.

Cowey A, Rolls ET. 1975. Human cortical magnification factor and its relation to visual acuity. *Exp Brain Rese* 21: 447–454.

Deco G, Lee TS. 2002. A unified model of spatial and object attention based on inter-cortical biased competition. *Neurocomput* 44–46: 775–781.

Deco G, Rolls ET. 2002. Object-based visual neglect: a computational hypothesis. *Euro J Neurosci* 16: 1994–2000.

Deco G, Rolls ET. 2003. Attention and working memory: a dynamical model of neuronal activity in the prefrontal cortex. *Eur J Neurosci* 18: 2374–2390.

Deco G, Rolls ET. 2004. A neurodynamical cortical model of visual attention and invariant object recognition. *Vision Res* 44: 621–644.

Deco G, Rolls ET. 2005a. Attention, short-term memory, and action selection: a unifying theory. *Prog Neurobiol* 76: 236–256.

Deco G, Rolls ET. 2005b. Neurodynamics of biased competition and co-operation for attention: a model with spiking neurons. *J Neurophysiol* 94: 295–313.

Deco G, Rolls ET. 2005c. Sequential memory: a putative neural and synaptic dynamical mechanism. *J Cognit Neurosci* 17: 294–307.

Deco G, Rolls ET. 2005d. Synaptic and spiking dynamics underlying reward reversal in orbitofrontal cortex. *Cereb Cortex* 15: 15–30.

Deco G, Rolls ET. 2006. Decision-making and Weber's Law: a neurophysiological model. *Eur J Neurosci* 24: 901–916.

Deco G, Rolls ET, Horwitz B. 2004. "What" and "where" in visual working memory: a computational neurodynamical perspective for integrating fMRI and single-neuron data. *J Cognit Neurosci* 16: 683–701.

Deco G, Rolls ET, Romo R. 2009. Stochastic dynamics as a principle of brain function. *Prog Neurobiol* 88: 1–16.

Deco G, Rolls ET, Zihl J. 2005. A neurodynamical model of visual attention. In *Neurobiology of attention*, ed. L Itti, G Rees, and J Tsotos, 593–599. San Diego: Elsevier.

Deco G, Zihl J. 2001. Top-down selective visual attention: a neurodynamical approach. *Vis Cogn* 8: 119–140.

Desimone R, Duncan J. 1995. Neural mechanisms of selective visual attention. *Ann Rev Neurosci* 18: 193–222.

Elliffe MCM, Rolls ET, Stringer SM. 2002. Invariant recognition of feature combinations in the visual system. *Biol Cyber* 86: 59–71.

Földiák P. 1991. Learning invariance from transformation sequences. *Neural Comput* 3: 194–200.

Franco L, Rolls ET, Aggelopoulos NC, Jerez JM. 2007. Neuronal selectivity, population sparseness, and ergodicity in the inferior temporal visual cortex. *Biol Cyber* 96: 547–560.

Franzius M, Sprekeler H, Wiskott L. 2007. Slowness and sparseness lead to place, head-direction, and spatial-view cells. *PLoS Comput Biol* 3: e166.

Fukushima K. 1980. Neocognitron: a self-organizing neural network model for a mechanism of pattern recognition unaffected by shift in position. *Biol Cyber* 36: 193–202.

Fukushima K. 1989. Analysis of the process of visual pattern recognition by the neocognitron. *Neural Netw* 2: 413–420.

Fukushima K. 1991. Neural networks for visual pattern recognition. *IEEE Trans* 74: 179–190.

Geesaman BJ, Andersen RA. 1996. The analysis of complex motion patterns by form/cue invariant MSTd neurons. *J Neurosci* 16: 4716–4732.

Graziano MSA, Andersen RA, Snowden RJ. 1994. Tuning of MST neurons to spiral motions. *J Neurosci* 14: 57–64.

Gregory RL. 1970. *The intelligent eye*. New York: McGraw-Hill.

Gregory RL. 1998. *Eye and brain*. Oxford: Oxford University Press.

Hasselmo ME, Rolls ET, Baylis GC, Nalwa V. 1989. Object-centred encoding by face-selective neurons in the cortex in the superior temporal sulcus of the the monkey. *Exp Brain Res* 75: 417–429.

Hegde J, Van Essen DC. 2000. Selectivity for complex shapes in primate visual area V2. *J Neurosci* 20: RC61.

Helmholtz Hv. 1857. *Handbuch der physiologischen optik*. Leipzig: Voss.

Ito M, Komatsu H. 2004. Representation of angles embedded within contour stimuli in area V2 of macaque monkeys. *J Neurosci* 24: 3313–3324.

Koenderink JJ, Van Doorn AJ. 1979. The internal representation of solid shape with respect to vision. *Biol Cyber* 32: 211–217.

Logothetis NK, Pauls J, Bülthoff HH, Poggio T. 1994. View-dependent object recognition by monkeys. *Curr Biol* 4: 401–414.

Maier A, Logothetis NK, Leopold DA. 2005. Global competition dictates local suppression in pattern rivalry. *J Vision* 5: 668–677.

Marr D. 1982. *Vision*. San Francisco: WH Freeman.

Martinez-Trujillo J, Treue S. 2002. Attentional modulation strength in cortical area MT depends on stimulus contrast. *Neuron* 35: 365–370.

Mozer M. 1991. *The perception of multiple objects: a connectionist approach*. Cambridge: MIT Press.

Newsome WT, Britten KH, Movshon JA. 1989. Neuronal correlates of a perceptual decision. *Nature* 341: 52–54.

Perrett D, Mistlin A, Chitty A. 1987. Visual neurons responsive to faces. *Trends Neurosci* 10: 358–364.

Perrett DI, Rolls ET, Caan W. 1982. Visual neurons responsive to faces in the monkey temporal cortex. *Exp Brain Res* 47: 329–342.

Perry G, Rolls ET, Stringer SM. 2006. Spatial vs. temporal continuity in view invariant visual object recognition learning. *Vision Res* 46: 3994–4006.

Perry G, Rolls ET, Stringer SM. 2009. Continuous transformation learning of translation invariant representations. *Exp Brain Res*.

Poggio T, Edelman S. 1990. A network that learns to recognize three-dimensional objects. *Nature* 343: 263–266.

Renart A, Moreno R, de la Rocha J, Parga N, Rolls ET. 2001. A model of the IT-PF network in object working memory which includes balanced persistent activity and tuned inhibition. *Neurocomputing* 38–40: 1525–1531.

Renart A, Parga N, Rolls ET. 2000. A recurrent model of the interaction between the prefrontal cortex and inferior temporal cortex in delay memory tasks. In *Advances in neural information processing systems*, ed. SA Solla, TK Leen, and K-R Mueller, 171–177. Cambridge: MIT Press.

Reynolds J, Desimone R. 1999. The role of neural mechanisms of attention in solving the binding problem. *Neuron* 24: 19–29.

Reynolds JH, Chelazzi L, Desimone R. 1999. Competitive mechanisms subserve attention in macaque areas V2 and V4. *J Neurosci* 19: 1736–1753.

Riesenhuber M, Poggio T. 2000. Models of object recognition. *Nature Neurosci* 3(Suppl): 1199–1204.

Rolls ET. 1989a. Functions of neuronal networks in the hippocampus and neocortex in memory. In *Neural models of plasticity: experimental and theoretical approaches*, ed. JH Byrne, and WO Berry, 240–265. San Diego: Academic Press.

Rolls ET. 1989b. The representation and storage of information in neuronal networks in the primate cerebral cortex and hippocampus. In *The computing neuron*, ed. R Durbin, C Miall, and G Mitchison, 125–129. Wokingham, England: Addison-Wesley.

Rolls ET. 1992. Neurophysiological mechanisms underlying face processing within and beyond the temporal cortical visual areas. *Philos Trans R Soc Lond B* 335: 11–21.

Rolls ET. 1999. *The brain and emotion*. Oxford: Oxford University Press.

Rolls ET. 2000. Functions of the primate temporal lobe cortical visual areas in invariant visual object and face recognition. *Neuron* 27: 205–218.

Rolls ET. 2005. *Emotion explained*. Oxford: Oxford University Press.

Rolls ET. 2007a. A computational neuroscience approach to consciousness. *Neural Netw* 20: 962–982.

Rolls ET. 2007b. The representation of information about faces in the temporal and frontal lobes. *Neuropsychol* 45: 125–143.

Rolls ET. 2008a. Face processing in different brain areas, and critical band masking. *J Neuropsychol* 2: 325–360.

Rolls ET. 2008b. *Memory, attention, and decision-making: a unifying computational neuroscience approach*. Oxford: Oxford University Press.

Rolls ET. 2008c. Top-down control of visual perception: attention in natural vision. *Perception* 37: 333–354.

Rolls ET, Aggelopoulos NC, Zheng F. 2003. The receptive fields of inferior temporal cortex neurons in natural scenes. *J Neurosci* 23: 339–348.

Rolls ET, Cowey A. 1970. Topography of the retina and striate cortex and its relationship to visual acuity in rhesus monkeys and squirrel monkeys. *Exp Brain Res* 10: 298–310.

Rolls ET, Deco G. 2002. *Computational neuroscience of vision*. Oxford: Oxford University Press.

Rolls ET, Deco G. 2006. Attention in natural scenes: neurophysiological and computational bases. *Neural Netw* 19: 1383–1394.

Rolls ET, Franco L, Aggelopoulos NC, Perez JM. 2006. Information in the first spike, the order of spikes, and the number of spikes provided by neurons in the inferior temporal visual cortex. *Vision Res* 46: 4193–4205.

Rolls ET, Kesner RP. 2006. A computational theory of hippocampal function, and empirical tests of the theory. *Prog Neurobiol* 79: 1–48.

Rolls ET, Milward T. 2000. A model of invariant object recognition in the visual system: learning rules, activation functions, lateral inhibition, and information-based performance measures. *Neural Comput* 12: 2547–2572.

Rolls ET, Stringer SM. 2001. Invariant object recognition in the visual system with error correction and temporal difference learning. *Network: Comput Neural Syst* 12: 111–129.

Rolls ET, Stringer SM. 2006a. Invariant global motion recognition in the dorsal visual system: a unifying theory. *Neural Comput* 19: 139–169.

Rolls ET, Stringer SM. 2006b. Invariant visual object recognition: a model, with lighting invariance. *J Physiol Paris* 100: 43–62.

Rolls ET, Tovee MJ. 1995. Sparseness of the neuronal representation of stimuli in the primate temporal visual cortex. *J Neurophysiol* 73: 713–726.

Rolls ET, Tovee MJ, Purcell DG, Stewart AL, Azzopardi P. 1994. The responses of neurons in the temporal cortex of primates, and face identification and detection. *Exp Brain Res* 101: 473–484.

Rolls ET, Treves A. 1998. *Neural networks and brain function*. Oxford: Oxford University Press.

Rolls ET, Treves A, Tovee MJ. 1997. The representational capacity of the distributed encoding of information provided by populations of neurons in the primate temporal visual cortex. *Exp Brain Res* 114: 177–185.

Rolls ET, Tromans J, Stringer SM. 2008. Spatial scene representations formed by self-organizing learning in a hippocampal extension of the ventral visual system. *Euro J Neurosci* 28: 2116–2127.

Rolls ET, Xiang J-Z. 2006. Spatial view cells in the primate hippocampus, and memory recall. *Rev Neurosci* 17: 175–200.

Serre T, Wolf L, Bileschi S, Riesenhuber M, Poggio T. 2007. Robust object recognition with cortex-like mechanisms. *IEEE Trans Pattern Anal Mach Intell* 29: 411–426.

Sheinberg DL, Logothetis NK. 2001. Noticing familiar objects in real world scenes: the role of temporal cortical neurons in natural vision. *J Neurosci* 21: 1340–1350.

Simons DJ, Chabris CF. 1999. Gorillas in our midst: sustained inattentional blindness for dynamic events. *Perception* 28: 1059–1074.

Simons DJ, Rensink RA. 2005. Change blindness: past, present, and future. *Trends Cogn Sci* 9: 16–20.

Singer W. 1999. Neuronal synchrony: a versatile code for the definition of relations? *Neuron* 24: 49–65.

Stringer SM, Perry G, Rolls ET, Proske JH. 2006. Learning invariant object recognition in the visual system with continuous transformations. *Biol Cyber* 94: 128–142.

Stringer SM, Rolls ET. 2000. Position invariant recognition in the visual system with cluttered environments. *Neural Netw* 13: 305–315.

Stringer SM, Rolls ET. 2002. Invariant object recognition in the visual system with novel views of 3D objects. *Neural Comput* 14: 2585–2596.

Stringer SM, Rolls ET. 2008. Learning transform invariant object recognition in the visual system with multiple stimuli present during training. *Neural Netw* 21: 888–903.

Stringer SM, Rolls ET, Tromans J. 2007. Invariant object recognition with trace learning and multiple stimuli present during training. *Network: Comput Neural Syst* 18: 161–187.

Sutton RS, Barto AG. 1998. *Reinforcement learning*. Cambridge: MIT Press.

Szabo M, Almeida R, Deco G, Stetter M. 2004. Cooperation and biased competition model can explain attentional filtering in the prefrontal cortex. *Euro J Neurosci* 19: 1969–1977.

Tanaka K, Saito C, Fukada Y, Moriya M. 1990. Integration of form, texture, and color information in the inferotemporal cortex of the macaque. In *Vision, memory and the temporal lobe*, ed. E Iwai, and M Mishkin, 101–109. New York: Elsevier.

Tovee MJ, Rolls ET. 1995. Information encoding in short firing rate epochs by single neurons in the primate temporal visual cortex. *Visual Cogn* 2: 35–58.

Trappenberg TP, Rolls ET, Stringer SM. 2002. Effective size of receptive fields of inferior temporal cortex neurons in natural scenes. In *Advances in neural information processing systems 14*, ed. TG Dietterich, S Becker, Z Ghahramani, 293–300. Cambridge: MIT Press.

Treves A, Panzeri S, Rolls ET, Booth M, Wakeman EA. 1999. Firing rate distributions and efficiency of information transmission of inferior temporal cortex neurons to natural visual stimuli. *Neural Comput* 11: 611–641.

Treves A, Rolls ET. 1994. A computational analysis of the role of the hippocampus in memory. *Hippocampus* 4: 374–391.

Ullman S. 1996. *High-level vision: object recognition and visual cognition.* Cambridge: Bradford/MIT Press.

Usher M, Niebur E. 1996. Modelling the temporal dynamics of IT neurons in visual search: a mechanism for top-down selective attention. *J Cogn Neurosci* 8: 311–327.

Wallis G, Rolls ET. 1997. Invariant face and object recognition in the visual system. *Prog Neurobiol* 51: 167–194.

Wallis G, Rolls ET, Földiák P. 1993. Learning invariant responses to the natural transformations of objects. In *International joint conference on neural networks*, vol 2: 1087–1090.

Wang XJ. 2002. Probabilistic decision making by slow reverberation in cortical circuits. *Neuron* 36: 955–968.

Wurtz RH, Kandel ER. 2000. Perception of motion depth and form. In *Principles of neural science*, ed. ER Kandel, JH Schwartz, and TM Jessell, 548–571. New York: McGraw-Hill.

Wyss R, Konig P, Verschure PF. 2006. A model of the ventral visual system based on temporal stability and local memory. *PLoS Biol* 4: e120.

Yamane S, Kaji S, Kawano K. 1988. What facial features activate face neurons in the inferotemporal cortex of the monkey? *Exp Brain Res* 73: 209–214.

CHAPTER 15

From Classification to Full Object Interpretation

Shimon Ullman

15.1 Introduction

In current classification schemes, the goal is usually to identify category instances in an image, together with their corresponding image locations. However, object recognition goes beyond top-level category labeling: when we see a known object, we not only recognize the complete object, but also identify and localize its parts and subparts at multiple levels. Identifying and localizing parts, called "object interpretation," is often necessary for interacting with visible objects in the surrounding environment.

In this chapter I will describe a method for obtaining detailed interpretation of the entire object, by identifying and localizing parts at multiple levels. The approach has two main components. The first is the creation of a hierarchical feature representation that is constructed from informative parts and subparts, that are identified during a learning stage. The second is the detection and localization of objects and parts using a two-pass algorithm that is applied to the feature hierarchy. The resulting scheme has two main advantages. First, the overall recognition performance is improved compared with similar nonhierarchical schemes. Second, and more important, the scheme obtains reliable detection and localization of object parts even when the parts are locally ambiguous and cannot be recognized reliably on their own.

The second part of the chapter will discuss a possible future direction for improving the performance obtained by current classification methods, by the use of a continuous online model update, in an attempt to narrow the so-called performance gap between computational methods and human performance. The method is based on the construction of a nested family of class models of increasing complexity; the class models will be incrementally updated as more data become available. The proposed process starts from a simple class model that will become continuously more complete and complex, when validated by new available data. The initial model family is optimal for the amount of data available at the first training stage, and the training data are used to select the optimal model parameters. At subsequent stages, the goal is to identify when the amount of available data are sufficient to advance to an extended model family and to construct a modified model. At each stage in this incremental process, the model family is appropriate for the available data, and the selected model keeps improving continuously, as the amount of training data increases.

15.2 Beyond Classification

Object classification is an important aspect of high-level vision, but it is not the only goal. In current classification schemes, the main goal is usually limited to the identification of category instances in a novel image. A typical output of such a scheme is a category label, together with a corresponding image location. For example, the final output may indicate that the image contains a car at a specific location, identified by the car center or a bounding box surrounding the car region. But the goal of high-level vision goes well beyond category labeling. For example, object categorization and recognition take place not only at the object level, but also at the sub-object and supra-object levels. At the finer, sub-object scale, we identify not only complete objects, but also their parts and subparts at multiple levels. I will refer to the recognition and localization of object parts at multiple levels as *object interpretation*. Identifying and localizing parts can be important for interacting with visible objects, grasping them, reading an instrument, identifying facial expressions, perceiving the pose of an animal, and the like. At the larger scale, we perceive and interpret object configurations and complete scenes, in a manner that depends on the identity of the objects and the relations among them.

Object recognition should also deal with motion and change, because in natural vision the image is constantly changing over time. There are a number of aspects to such dynamic recognition that need to be incorporated into computational vision system. One, which is already the subject of considerable ongoing work, is the area of recognizing actions, including instantaneous actions as well as prolonged activities. Another, which has not been studied in detail so far, is the process of incremental, continuous recognition. Rather than recognizing each frame in a sequence on its own, it will be advantageous to combine at each time step the analysis of the current input with the existing interpretation from the recent past. The dynamic aspects of recognition provide a rich and important area for future studies in recognition and high-level vision, but they will not be considered further in the current discussion.

In this chapter, I will discuss two directions in which one can extend current object classification schemes. The first has to do with broadening the scope of classification, from providing object labels to supplying a much fuller interpretation of the entire object image. The second has to do with improving the performance obtained by current methods, by a continuous online model update, in an attempt to narrow the so-called performance gap between automatic methods and human performance. I will briefly describe some recent work related to the first problem, and discuss a future direction regarding the second.

15.3 Full Object Interpretation

In this section, I will describe briefly a method for obtaining detailed and reliable recognition of object parts at multiple levels. The approach has two main components. The first is the creation of a hierarchical feature representation constructed from informative parts and subparts, identified automatically during a learning stage. The second is the detection and localization of objects and parts using a two-pass algorithm applied to the feature hierarchy. The resulting scheme has two main advantages. First, the overall recognition performance is improved compared with similar nonhierarchical schemes. The second, and more important, outcome is that the scheme obtains reliable detection and localization of object parts even when the parts are locally ambiguous and cannot be recognized reliably on their own.

15.3.1 Informative Feature Hierarchies

In the next two sections, I will describe briefly a method for automatically constructing an informative feature hierarchy from image examples, and then using the hierarchical representation to obtain a full interpretation of the object image. The main stages of the process are summarized briefly, additional details and extensions are described in Epshtein and Ullman (2005a,b; 2006).

The construction of the feature hierarchy starts from the extraction of top-level informative features. By a repeated application of the same process, the top-level features are broken down into their own informative components. The process continues recursively until it reaches a level of "atomic" features, which cannot be further subdivided without a loss in the delivered information. The top-level features, or object parts, are extracted from image examples by identifying common subregions with high information content (Sali and Ullman 1999; Ullman et al. 2002) by the following procedure. In the first stage, a large pool of candidate patches, or fragments, is considered, at different positions, sizes, and resolutions, extracted from the class images. The information supplied by each candidate feature is estimated by detecting it in the class and nonclass training images, as follows. To detect a given fragment F in an image, the fragment is searched by correlating it with the image. Alternative similarity measures, such as the SIFT measure (Lowe 2004) and affine-invariant measures (Mikolajczyk and Schmid 2004), and incorporation of color, texture, and 3-D cues can also be used. If the similarity at any location exceeds a certain detection threshold θ, then F has been detected in the image ($F = 1$); otherwise, $F = 0$. A binary variable C is used to represent the class – namely, $C(X) = 1$, if the image X contains a class example, and $C = 0$ otherwise. For each candidate fragment, the amount of information it delivers about the class is then estimated based on its detection frequency within and outside the class examples, using the standard definition of mutual information between variables. The delivered information is a function of the detection threshold; the threshold for each fragment is therefore adjusted individually to maximize the delivered information $I(F; C)$ (Ullman et al. 2002). The features are then considered in the order of the information they supply. To avoid redundancy between similar features, fragments are selected successively, where at each stage the fragment that contributes the largest amount of additional information is added to the set of selected fragments (Ullman et al. 2002). This selection process, also called the max-min procedure, was found in theoretical and practical comparisons to be highly effective for feature selection from a large pool of candidates (Fleuret 2004).

The same process used for selecting the initial, top-level features is then repeated to produce a hierarchy of informative parts and subparts (Epshtein and Ullman 2005a).

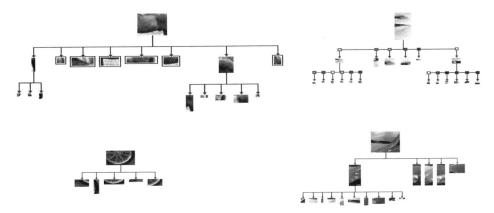

Figure 15.1. Examples of feature hierarchies from several object classes (horses, faces, cars). The feature hierarchies are used to improve recognition performance and to produce a full interpretation of the objects in the scene.

To apply the same process to parts rather than complete objects, the algorithm first identifies for each feature F a set of positive and negative examples. The positive examples are extracted from all the locations in the class images where the fragment F was detected or almost detected (close to detection threshold). A set of negative examples is similarly derived from the nonclass images. Once the positive and negative sets of examples are established, subfragments are selected by exactly the same information maximization procedure used at the first level. If the decomposition of F into simpler features increased the delivered information, the same decomposition is also applied to the subfeatures of F. Otherwise, decomposition is terminated, with F considered an atomic feature in the hierarchy. Examples of informative class features and their hierarchical decomposition are shown in Figure 15.1.

15.3.2 Recognizing Objects and Parts

The feature hierarchy described in the preceding section is used to detect and localize not only the top-level object, but also its parts and subparts at different levels. In this manner, the process provides a detailed interpretation of the object region. The full recognition problem can be described in this setting as inferring the most likely values of the class C and all the parts X_i from the set $\underline{F}$ of all observed features F_i. This goal can be expressed as finding values for C (the class), and $\underline{X}$ (all the parts) to maximize the probability $p(C, \underline{X} \mid \underline{F})$:

$$C, \underline{X} = \text{argmax } p(C, \underline{X} | \underline{F}) \tag{15.1}$$

The variables F_i and X_i can have values in the range 0 to n. $F_i = 0$ means that F_i is not present in the image, and $F_i = k$ means that F_i has been detected at image location k (similarly for the X_i). In the hierarchical representation, the probability $p(C, X, F)$ is approximated in the current model using a factorization into local terms:

$$p(C, X, F) = p(C) \prod p(X_i | X_i^-) p(F_k | X_k) \tag{15.2}$$

In this expression, C is the class variable, F_i stands for image features (fragments), X_k are object parts, and X_k^- is the parent of node X_k in the hierarchy. This decomposition assumes that any part X_i is conditionally independent of its nondescendants, given its parent X_i^-. The decomposition makes a "local context" assumption – namely, that the probability of a part X given all other parts, can be approximated by the probability of X given its parent in the hierarchy. This often holds for object images; for example, the detection of an eyebrow within a local eye region is relatively independent of more remote parts such as ears or chin.

The parameters needed for the computation are $p(C)$, $p(X_i|X_i^-)$, $p(F_k|X_k)$ which are the pair-wise probabilities of each node given its parent. These parameters are estimated from the data during the learning stage (Dempster et al. 1976). In addition, for each fragment, a region of positional tolerance is determined, providing a local search window for the feature. The amount of information that is delivered by a fragment depends on its search window location and size, which are learned adaptively during the construction of the hierarchy (Epshtein and Ullman 2005a).

When the model parameters are known, obtaining the most likely interpretation in equation (15.1) can be obtained efficiently by an application of the so-called factor graph or GDL computation (Kschischang et al. 2001; Aji and McEliece 2000), which will not be discussed here in detail. During the classification of a novel image, only the atomic features are directly correlated with the input image. The detection and localization of all the parts, including the top-level objects, then proceed by the GDL algorithm, which is guaranteed to converge to the global optimum of equation (15.1) after a single phase of message-passing from the low-level features to the class node at the top of the hierarchy, followed by a pass from the top back to the low-level features at the bottom of the hierarchy.

As mentioned previously, the use of the hierarchical scheme has two advantages compared with the use of a similar scheme, based on the nonhierarchical, top-level fea-tures only. The first is improved recognition, which is obtained because the scheme can deal effectively with increased variability compared with the nonhierarchical scheme. The hierarchical scheme learns for each part the allowed local distortion between subparts, and uses this information to cope with the variability in object views. The second, and more important, advantage is that the hierarchical scheme provides a full interpretation by covering the entire object region by a large set of detected parts. Figure 15.2(a) shows examples of parts that are detected and localized accurately by the hierarchical scheme despite local ambiguities and large variability in appearance. Figure 15.2(b) shows an example of the full interpretation obtained by the scheme.

A comparison of hierarchies that are obtained from multiple object classes shows that the lowest-level features are generic in nature, (i.e., they are useful for all natural objects), the highest-level features are specific to a class of visually similar object, and intermediate features are shared by similar classes. The feature sharing between hierarchies is useful because it promotes effective "cross generalization" from one class of objects to related classes (Ullman and Soloviev 1999; Torralba et al. 2004; Fei-Fei et al. 2003; Bart and Ullman 2005). For example, after learning the appearance of a component such as a leg or tail for one class, the resulting representation will be used by other classes that share the same component.

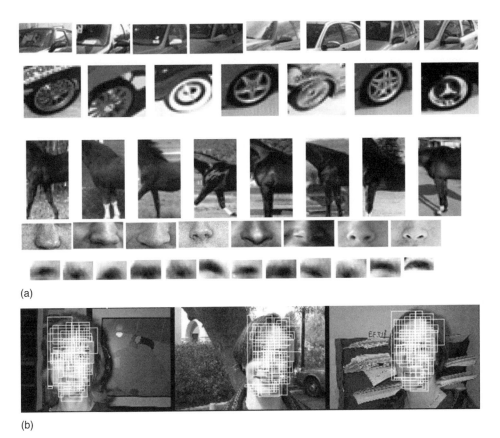

(a)

(b)

Figure 15.2. (a) Part variability. Example of parts from several categories (cars, horses, faces) that are detected and localized accurately by the hierarchical scheme despite local ambiguities and large variability in appearance. (b) Full interpretation. Each detected part is marked by an *enclosing rectangle*. Together, the hierarchical parts produce a full cover of the object, providing an interpretation of the object in terms of parts and subparts.

15.3.3 Semantic Features

The hierarchical representation described in the previous section can compensate effectively for local changes and distortions in the image. However, object components can also have multiple different appearances because of large changes in viewing conditions, such as view direction or shadows, or as a result of transformation of the component, such as an open versus closed mouth in face images. To deal with multiple appearances, the feature hierarchy described is extended by the creation of so-called semantic features. This is obtained by grouping together different appearances of the same component to form a higher-level, more abstract representation. Two plausible mechanisms can be used for identifying equivalent fragments that represent the same object components across changes in appearance. The first abstraction mechanism involves observing objects in motion (Ullman and Soloviev 1999; Stringer and Rolls 2002): Based on spatiotemporal continuity, a fragment can be tracked over time, and different appearances of the changing part can be grouped together. A method for the

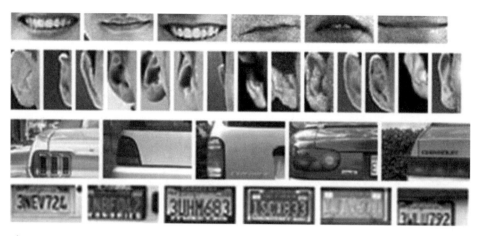

Figure 15.3. Semantic features. Each semantic feature is a set of different appearances representing the same object parts. The sets were extracted automatically based on common context.

extraction and use of motion-grouped fragments for invariant recognition and dealing with changes in viewing directions is described in Ullman and Bart 2004 and Bart et al. 2004. The second abstraction mechanism is based on common context: If two fragments are interchangeable within a common context, they are likely to be semantically equivalent. For example, if multiple instances of the same face are observed, with either a neutral or a smiling mouth, these images provide evidence for the equivalence between the two mouth appearances (Epshtein and Ullman 2005b).

To use semantic features rather than simple object fragments, the feature hierarchy described is extended, to create a so-called semantic hierarchy. Briefly, the construction of the semantic hierarchy proceeds along the following main stages (for details, see Epstein and Ullman 2007). First, a skeleton hierarchy of nonsemantic features is constructed, as described in the previous section. Next, for each training image the optimal location of each feature is determined. The algorithm then extracts new semantic features whenever an object part remains undetected in the training image. For example, if in a new face image one of the eyes, or the mouth, fails to be detected, a new fragment is extracted from the image as a likely new appearance of the missing part. For each missing feature, its optimal position is predicted, using the position of the parent feature and the learned parent-child geometric relationship. From the set of missing features collected from multiple training images, the best representatives are determined and added to the set of semantic appearances of each hierarchy node. Finally, a round of hierarchical decomposition is applied to the newly added appearances in the usual manner, to extract the subparts of the new added features.

Figure 15.3 shows examples of top-level abstract fragments, which are equivalence sets of fragments that depict different appearances of the same object part, obtained automatically using the common-context abstraction process. Following this learning stage, the components in the hierarchy will use abstract features rather than single-appearance fragments. Semantic features improve classification performance because they can handle large variations in appearance, such as nonrigid transformations of parts, or large illumination effects. This ability to deal with large variations will also generalize from a given class to other related classes. The reason is that the hierarchies of related classes share common components in their representation; consequently, the set of equivalent appearances will generalize from a learned class to related classes with shared features. For example, the different appearances of a wheel will generalize from one car to another, and to other wheeled vehicles; eye appearances will generalize from one animal class to another; and so on.

Semantic features are also useful for recognizing individual objects under large changes in the viewing conditions. By using the semantic fragments, each object part is represented by a set of fragments that depict this part under different conditions, such as viewing directions, illumination, and changes in the part itself. A semantic feature is present in an image if one of its fragments is activated by the image. Consequently, the semantic features form a view-invariant representation of objects within a general class. In this approach, invariant recognition at the object level is based on the observed invariance of selected components (Ullman 2006; Ullman and Soloviev 1999). The full semantic hierarchy, therefore, contributes to both classification and individual object recognition. It addition, it is useful for recognizing and localizing parts and subparts regardless of their specific appearance. In this sense, the semantic hierarchy produces what was described as full object interpretation, which is often important for understanding the scene and for interacting with objects in it.

15.3.4 Classifying Configurations

The preceding discussion considered the extension of classification and recognition from the complete object to the subobject level, providing an interpretation of the object in terms of relevant parts and subparts. Another, perhaps more challenging problem is to go in the opposite direction, from the single object to multiple related objects. A number of objects often participate together in meaningful and recognizable configurations, and visual recognition should include the identification of such configuration. For example, in Figure 15.4, both images depict "children feeding a cat." This would be the natural description elicited by a human observer, even a young child, looking at such images. The problem of identifying meaningful configurations is highly challenging, in part because the variability at the configuration level is substantially higher than the variability in the appearance of a single object. Many different configurations will be consistent with the same description of "children feeding a cat." At the same time, images containing the relevant objects, such as a cat, a child, and dish, are not necessarily instances of a child feeding a cat. Dealing with meaningful configurations of this sort remains a challenging problem for future developments in high-level vision, beyond the level of single object classification.

15.4 Incremental Model Selection

15.4.1 The Performance Gap

Current classification methods have reached an impressive level of performance, and they can be used to detect a large variety of object categories in complex scenes. At

Figure 15.4. Classifying configurations. The pictures are very different in appearance, but both depict children feeding a cat. This description depends on a configuration of objects rather than the detection of a single category.

the same time, the performance level of current schemes is still significantly below human-level recognition, and the performance gap seems difficult to close. Existing recognition schemes make more errors than do human observers. It also appears from examining results of different schemes that even state-of-the-art classification schemes can make errors that are unreasonable and unacceptable by human standards, especially when it comes to false detection in nonclass images, as illustrated in Figure 15.5, which shows false detections by two recent classification schemes. The performance gap also appears to widen when existing schemes are applied to multiclass settings that involve a large number of classes.

Will the performance gap be closed by incremental improvements and tuning of current models, or will it require significant changes and additions to existing methods? The answer is difficult to predict, but it should be noted that improvements in performance become increasingly difficult at the high end, when the overall level is already high. In attempting to narrow the performance gap, future improvements are likely to come from different sources, and in the following section I will discuss briefly one new direction that is likely to prove useful when dealing with large and complex object classes.

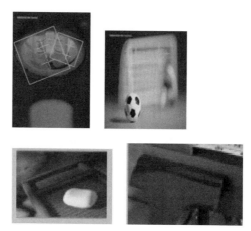

Figure 15.5. Example of false alarms produced by two recent classification schemes. The top images were classified as "faces," the bottom two as "cows." (See color plate 15.5.)

15.4.2 Incremental Model Selection

The overall process of constructing a classifier for a given object category can often be described in the following general terms. The classifier is selected during learning from a general family of possible models, or a parametric model. Examples of successful parametric models for object classification include constellation models, star models, k-fans, feature hierarchies, histograms of visual words, and the like. Each model family has a set of parameters θ that need to be determined during learning. As a concrete example, we may consider a constellation of k image patches, with a spatial configuration determined by a joint Gaussian distribution, similar to Fei-Fei et al. (2003). The patches need to be selected, and the distribution parameters need to be determined during learning. More generally, we start with some model family $M(\theta)$, where θ is a set of model parameters, and select the best value of θ from the training data. In many cases the class model is described by a joint distribution $p(C, F)$ of the class C and the set of features F. The probabilistic setting is not crucial, but it will be convenient for the discussion that follows. The learning process then starts with a parametric family of distributions $p_\theta(C, F)$, and the optimal value of θ is set during leaning. This is typically obtained by minimizing the classification error, or by maximizing the probability of the observed data, for example by the EM algorithm (Dempster et al. 1976) or other statistical methods. There are, in summary, two main stages to the model construction process: specifying the model family $M(\theta)$, and then selecting the optimal θ based on the training data. The selection of a good model family $M(\theta)$ for a given problem is obviously a crucial step. A major consideration used at this selection stage is the complexity of the model family. A full review of the model complexity problem is beyond the scope of the current discussion, but the basic considerations are straightforward. If the family $M(\theta)$ is too restricted, even the best member within the model family may still be a poor approximation to the correct model. On the other hand, the family $M(\theta)$ cannot be too broad either. Mathematical learning theory (e.g., Valiant 1984; Rissanen 1978) has shown that different model families have different sample complexities, and some will require a large number of examples in order to determine, or approximate, the optimal member in the family $M(\theta)$. For a given number of training data, if $M(\theta)$ is too broad, even the best learning algorithms will fail to identify the appropriate model within the family to use for classification.

It appears to me that in current classification schemes, the model family used is often responsible for the performance gap. For example, suppose that $M(\theta)$ is the family of features constellation. A model in this family may consist of, say, five image patches, arranged in a joint Gaussian distribution to classify the category "dog" (Fei-Fei et al. 2003). Training data can be used to efficiently select a good model from this particular family. The resulting performances can be quite good, but they will still be significantly below human level. The reason is that even the best member within the model family is unlikely to capture adequately the full complexity of the "dog" class. The alternative is to try to formulate a more elaborate model family, but this will require adequate training, which may not be immediately available.

A general possible approach to this problem is to combine model selection (the selection of a model family) and learning (of the best model in the family) in a systematic and incremental manner. Future classification schemes, therefore may go beyond specifying a single model family $M(\theta)$, but provide from the start a set of increasingly broader families, $M_1(\theta_1)$, $M_2(\theta_2)$, and so on. Using the index α to indicate the model family, we have a set of parametric model families M_θ^α, where the set of parameters θ depends on the family α, and the models are becoming more complex as α increases. A desired property of the model families is that as α increases, the larger model family includes the previous one (i.e., $M_\alpha < M_{\alpha+1}$). Given a set of training examples, the first goal is to select the appropriate model family α, and then determine θ to select the best model within the family.

Several schemes have been proposed to deal with this combined problem. The two best known ones are the use of minimum description length (MDL) (Rissanen 1978) and structural risk minimization (SRM) (Vapnik 1995). In both of these methods, the model family α and model parameters θ are often determined together, by minimizing a cost function, which combines approximation error together with a measure of model complexity. In MDL the model complexity is measured by the model description length, and in SRM by sample complexity, such as the VC dimension of the model. The combined scheme therefore seeks a model that provides a good approximation of the data and at the same time is as simple as possible.

Other, perhaps better, combination schemes are possible, and the problem remains open for future studies. However, for the purpose of classification, a challenging and relevant related problem is the use of a combined scheme in an incremental manner over a long training period. The general approach is to start from a simple model family and make the model more complete and complex, as more data become available. We start with an initial model family α_1, which is optimal for the amount of data available at the first training stage, and use the training data to select the optimal model parameters θ_1. As the amount of data increases, it will not be possible to improve the classification model substantially without extending the model family. The goal, therefore, is to have a systematic method that will be able to identify when the amount of available data is sufficient to advance to an extended model family α_2 and construct a modified model $M(\alpha_2, \theta_2)$. At each stage in this incremental process, the model family is appropriate for the available data, and the selected model keeps improving as the amount of data increases. In the example of a constellation model, the number of features may increase and their geometric configuration can become more complex, as the amount of training data increases.

Some attempts in this incremental direction have been made in the past (Li et al. 2007; Levi and Ullman 2006), but they were used for improving θ only, with a fixed α. That is, the model family was fixed at the beginning of the training and remained unchanged, and the model parameters were continuously updated as new data became available. An open challenge for the future is to construct a classifier that incrementally updates the model family as well. Unlike current methods, such a classifier will start by not only specifying a particular parametric model family, but a set of nested families with increasing complexity. The method will also provide criteria for updating the selected model family and new model parameters. We can imagine such a method being applied to learn a visual class, such as "dogs," over a long period using a large number of examples, moving during the process from a simple to elaborate class model, as more data warrant the transition to a more complex model. It remains to be seen whether such an approach will lead to a continuous improvement in performance, well beyond the current performance gap.

A comprehensive and detailed model for a complex class will require the use of considerable training data, but two properties of the learning process can simplify the acquisition and use of such data. First, it is desirable for the learning process to be able to update the model incrementally (as in Levi and Ullman 2006; Li et al. 2007) based on recent examples, without storing and using explicitly all past examples. Second, and more important, is the use of cross-generalization. As proposed by a number of recent schemes (Torralba et al. 2004; Fei-Fei et al. 2003; Bart and Ullman 2005), it is possible to learn a set of related classes together, rather than treat each class separately, and in this manner reduce substantially the number of examples required to learn a new class.

Bibliography

Aji SM, McEliece RJ. 2000. The generalized distributive law. *IEEE Trans Info Theory* 46: 325–342.

Bart E, Byvatov E, Ullman S. 2004. View-invariant recognition using corresponding object fragments. In Proceedings of ECCV, vol 8, 152–165.

Bart E, Ullman S. 2005. Learning a novel class from a single example by cross-generalization. In Proceedings of IEEE CVPR, 1063–1069.

Dempster D, Laird N, Rubin D. 1976. Maximum likelihood from incomplete data via the EM algorithm. *R Stat Soc* 39 (Series B): 1–38.

Epshtein B, Ullman S. 2005a. Hierarchical features for object classification. In Proceedings of the IEEE ICCV, 220–227.

Epshtein B, Ullman S. 2005b. Identifying semantically equivalent object parts. In Proceedings of the IEEE CVPR, 2–9.

Epstein B, Ullman S. 2006. Satellite features for the classification of visually similar classes. In Proceedings of the IEEE CVPR, 2079–2086.

Epshtein B, Ullman S. 2007. Semantic hierarchies for recognizing objects and parts. In Proceedings of CVPR, 1–8.

Fei-Fei L, Fergus R, Perona P. 2003. A Bayesian approach to unsupervised one-shot learning of object categories. In Proceedings of ICCV, 1134–1141.

Fleuret F. 2004. Fast binary feature selection with conditional mutual information. *J Mach Learn Res* (5): 1531–1555.

Kschischang FR, Frey BJ, Loeliger HA. 2001. Factor graphs and the sum-product algorithm. *IEEE Proc Info Theory* 47: 498–519.

Levi D, Ullman S. 2006. Learning to classify by ongoing feature selection. In CRV; Candian robotics and vision conference, vol 1.

Li L-J, Wang G, Fei-Fei L. 2007. OPTIMOL: automatic object picture collection via incremental model learning. In Proceedings of IEEE computer vision and pattern recognition CVPR, 1–7.

Lowe D. 2004. Distinctive image features from scale-invariant keypoints. *Int J Comp Vis* 60(2): 91–100.

Mikolajczyk K, Schmid C. 2004. Scale & affine invariant point detectors. *Int J Comp Vis* 60(1): 63–86.

Rissanen J. 1978. Modeling by the shortest data description. *Automatica* 14: 465–471.

Sali E, Ullman S. 1999. Combining class-specific fragments for object classification. In Proceedings of the 10th British machine vision conference, vol 1, 203–213.

Stringer SM, Rolls ET. 2002. Invariant object recognition in the visual system with novel views of 3D objects. *Neural Comput* 14: 2585–2596.

Torralba A, Murphy KP, Freeman WT. 2004. Sharing features: efficient boosting procedures for multiclass object detection. In Proceedings of CVPR, 762–769.

Ullman S. 2006. Object recognition and segmentation by a fragment-based hierarchy. *Trends Cogn Sci* 11(2): 58–64.

Ullman S, Bart E. 2004. Recognition invariance obtained by extended and invariant features. *Neural Netw* 17: 833–848.

Ullman S, Soloviev S. 1999. Computation of pattern invariance in brain-like structures. *Neural Netw* 12: 1021–1036.

Ullman S, Vidal-Naquet M, Sali S. 2002. Visual features of intermediate complexity and their use in classification. *Nat Neurosci* 5(7): 1–6.

Valiant L. 1984. A theory of the learnable. *Commun ACM* 27: 436–445.

Vapnik V. 1995. *The nature of statistical learning theory*. New York: Springer-Verlag.

CHAPTER 16

Visual Object Discovery

Pawan Sinha, Benjamin Balas, Yuri Ostrovsky,
and Jonas Wulff

16.1 The Problem of Object Discovery

It is perhaps not inaccurate to say that much of the brain's machinery is, in essence, devoted to the detection of repetitions in the environment. Knowing that a particular entity is the same as the one seen on a previous occasion allows the organism to put into play a response appropriate to the reward contingencies associated with that entity. This entity can take many forms. It can be a temporally extended event, such as an acoustic phrase or a dance move, a location, such as a living room, or an individual object, such as a peacock or a lamp. Irrespective of what the precise entity is, the basic information-processing problem is the same – to discover how the complex sensory input can be carved into distinct entities and to recognize them on subsequent occasions. In this chapter, we examine different pieces of knowledge regarding visual object discovery and attempt to synthesize them into a coherent framework.

Let us examine the challenges inherent in this problem a little more closely. Consider Figure 16.1(a). This complex landscape appears to be just a random collection of peaks and valleys, with no clearly defined groups. Yet it represents an image that is easily parsed into distinct objects by the human visual system. Figure 16.1(b) shows the image that corresponds exactly to the plot shown in Figure 16.1(a), which simply represents pixel luminance by height. It is now trivial for us to notice that there are three children, and we can accurately delimit their extents as shown in Figure 16.1(c). The exquisite discreteness of this categorization is largely perceptual, because the clean segmentation map that we perceive (Fig. 16.1(c)) is not directly represented in the inherent continuous nature of the sensory input (Fig. 16.1(a)). What is the process responsible for translating experience with complex visual inputs into distinct object representations that can then be used to recognize other instances of the objects in novel inputs?

16.1.1 Object Discovery from the Developmental Perspective

The problem of object discovery is inherently a developmental one. Infants begin to exhibit behaviors indicative of recognition remarkably soon after birth. By two months

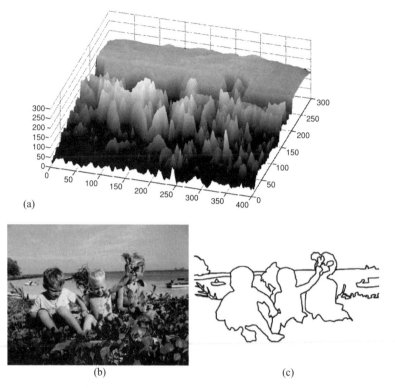

(a)

(b)   (c)

Figure 16.1. (a) A three-dimensional plot of a natural image in which height represents pixel luminance. This plot illustrates the lack of image-level cues for parsing an image into distinct objects. (b) The natural image plotted in (a). (c) Segmentation map generated by a human observer. The clean segmentation of this map contrasts with the complex structure of the underlying image.

of age, they produce voluntary "social smiles" in response to familiar people, show differential responses to various facial expressions, and are able to follow objects. Two more months beyond this, their skill repertoire expands to include food recognition, and by six months, their ability to discriminate between people and between toys is unmistakably evident. These skills continue developing in the months that follow. But, for our discussion here, it is their manifestation within the first half-year of life that is of greatest relevance. This period presents us with an opportunity, not available later in the life span, to study an almost pure form of observational learning. The child's active interaction with the environment is quite circumscribed owing to his or her limited motor proficiency. Complex linguistic constructs for instruction or representation are largely ineffective. Despite these constraints within the first few months of life, the baby brain begins to successfully solve the problem of object discovery, a fundamental challenge that is one of the central, but least understood, aspects of visual neuroscience.

Several aspects of the object learning problem make it computationally challenging. We list a few sources of difficulty:

1. *The objects that need to be discovered occupy only a small portion of the training/test input images*: A face at a distance of six feet constitutes less than 1% of the visual field. The object concept that needs to be learned is thus embedded in a much larger set of potentially irrelevant information.

2. *The inputs are unannotated*: Exacerbating the problem highlighted in point 1, there is typically no "teacher" who can point out where in the training images the object of interest is. The object has to be discovered autonomously, without a priori information about its appearance, location, or extent. Relatedly, there is no feedback signal indicating correctness of classification.

3. *The input image quality is poor*: During the first few months of life, an infant's visual acuity is quite poor relative to that of an adult. Therefore, the learning algorithms are required to work with impoverished images, and do not have access to fine-grained spatial information that might be useful for object recognition. This may actually prove to be an advantage in some circumstances, but whether reduced acuity helps or hinders visual learning in infancy has not been addressed experimentally; existing computational models do not incorporate known attributes of infant vision.

Notwithstanding these difficulties, infants across many different animal species regularly succeed at solving the object learning problem; however, our theoretical understanding of how this might be accomplished is currently very limited. Our goal in this chapter is to review the current computational and experimental literature on object learning and then build upon this to synthesize a theoretical framework that can serve to catalyze further research. We shall argue that empirical data demonstrate the profound significance of dynamic information for organizing early visual experience.

As an aside, it is worth noting that there is evidence to suggest that some objects might not need to be "discovered" through visual experience. Rather, the brain might come pre-equipped with rudimentary representations of these objects. Faces are a prominent example of such a class (Morton and Johnson 1991; Sugita 2008). Even if we assume that faces do not need to be learned from scratch, it is highly likely that most other object categories are not innately specified. They require discovery based on the visual inputs encountered after birth.

The rest of this chapter is organized in three sections: (1) prior work on object discovery; (2) experimental studies of primate visual processing relevant to object discovery; and (3) an experimentally guided framework for object discovery.

16.2 Prior Work on Object Discovery

The development of an "object concept" from a series of images is an instance of the more general problem of learning what structures are common across a diverse set of input instances. In the domain of machine learning, there are many established methods for performing such a task on arbitrary inputs (Duda et al. 2001). Much research on object concept learning has focused on applying variations of these techniques to large collections of images, in the hope that useful representations for object detection and individuation can be "discovered" rather than hard-coded. We discuss the strengths and weaknesses of two broad approaches to this problem. First, we consider supervised models of concept learning that utilize normalized images. Second, we turn our attention to so-called semi-supervised learning models that construct object concepts from unnormalized input without explicit training.

16.2.1 Learning from Normalized Images

A first step toward modeling the learning of an object concept is to determine what features define the object in question. Simply put, what does the object look like most of the time? This question appears simple-minded at first glance, but is in fact quite complex. The key difficulty in obtaining a satisfactory answer is determining aspects of object appearance that are invariant to changes in illumination, scale, or viewing angle. This is a challenge facing models of visual object discovery at all levels. Regardless of whether one wishes to model learning at the basic category level (distinguishing objects at the class level; "face" vs. "car," e.g.) or at the subordinate level (distinguishing faces from one another according to gender or identity), one must learn a robust representation of appearance that supports recognition at the level of interest.

One powerful method for learning such a robust object concept is to employ an external "teacher" who can prenormalize images in the training set. Normalization procedures generally manipulate training images so that they are optimally aligned with one another, are of the same size, and have roughly the same intensity histogram. In effect, normalization explicitly dispenses with much of the variability in object appearance brought about by external factors such as changes in pose or illumination. The transformed images are thus constrained to embody appearance variations due to the intrinsic variability across class instances, meaning that the consistent features observed across the image set are not contaminated by outside variation. Given such a set of normalized images, the most important aspect of any learning procedure is the choice of features that will make up the ultimate representation of an object. Once a set of features has been selected, the strength of the object concept is usually assessed by attempting to detect new examples of the object in a set of cluttered test scenes.

This approach to object learning has been successfully implemented in several domains. Especially prominent is the work on face learning. The training sets comprise scale-normalized and spatially registered face images. A particular choice of image descriptors encodes each of these images as a feature vector, which is then submitted to any of a number of statistical classifiers. In order to learn a robust face concept, researchers have experimented with many different kinds of features, of different degrees of complexity. At the high end of spatial complexity, neural network models have been created to extract a global template that guides the search for faces at multiple scales (Rowley, Baluja, and Kanade 1998). On the other end of the feature-complexity spectrum, simple local analyses of the luminance differences between neighboring face regions has also proven to be a very useful tool for developing a face concept. Wavelet-like features have been shown to provide rapid and accurate face detection in cluttered scenes (Viola and Jones 2001), and we have also observed that a "ratio-template" of ordinal relationships between face regions can be used to build a face concept that is particularly robust to varying illumination (Sinha 2002). Simple relationships between wavelet coefficients have also been shown to be very useful for modeling the detection of pedestrians in cluttered scenes, as well (Oren et al. 1997). Bridging these two extremes of featural complexity, recent results in face detection suggest that features of "intermediate complexity" may constitute an "optimal" set of features to extract from normalized images (Ullman, Vidal-Naquet, and Sali 2002). Such features fall between global templates and wavelet representations on the spectrum of spatial complexity, and as such may represent the best trade-off between generality (the feature present in most exemplars of the class) and specificity (the feature is absent in most nonclass exemplars).

Although quite powerful, these techniques are of limited help for understanding some important issues relevant to the way object concept learning proceeds in the human visual system. In particular, the normalization procedure assumes that the learning algorithm either already knows which sources of variation are external to the class and which are intrinsic, or has access to a "teacher" who can normalize a large number of training instances. Neither of these two possibilities is realistic in the natural learning scenario we outlined in the introduction. In some cases, "dumb" procedures like histogram equalization could be applied to all inputs to factor out some sources of variation, but it is difficult to extend this argument to include all the normalization procedures commonly applied to training images. Secondly, there is a deep difficulty involved with using labeled and normalized training images to develop an object concept. In providing supervision, one assumes that the learning algorithm is already able to locate, segment, and classify objects as class members. If this were already true, one would not need to further develop an object concept. As such, although the use of normalized images provides a means for learning useful features for object detection, it does not provide a satisfactory model of object concept development by infants.

16.2.2 Semi-Supervised Models

One important advance over supervised models of object learning that rely on normalized images is the introduction of what we shall call "semi-supervised" models. Rather than using images of objects in isolation to learn diagnostic features, such models learn object concepts from complex images containing the object of interest as well as substantial background clutter. This gets us one vital step closer to a more realistic model of concept learning in that we do not assume any ability to recognize or pre-segment an object from its surroundings. Features that define the object class must be learned in the presence of distracting features that make up additional object and scene details.

Faced with a multitude of features that could potentially belong to the object of interest, semisupervised models must find a way to isolate some subset of image features for further analysis. Typically, the first step in these models is the application of some form of "interest operator" to an image to extract candidate features that are particularly salient. Such image patches may possess certain low-level properties such as corner/circle structures (Haralick and Shapiro 1993) or high local "entropy" (Fergus, Perona, and Zisserman 2003). Once a vocabulary of "interesting" features has been determined, the model proceeds by learning which of these features are diagnostic of an object's presence, as well as what (if any) consistent spatial relationships exist between diagnostic features. This is usually done by comparing images that contain the object to images that contain no prominent foreground object ("background" images).

These aspects of the object concept can be represented in many ways, including generative object models (Fei-Fei, Fergus, and Perona 2004; Fergus et al. 2003; Weber,

Welling, and Perona 2000) or the construction of sparse feature vectors describing part co-occurrence (Agarwal and Roth 2002). Regardless of the particular implementation, semisupervised models are able to learn object concepts that incorporate image fragments that define an object class, as well as the higher-level organization of those fragments into a coherent object.

The ability to learn both the features that compose an object and the spatial arrangement of those features without presegmentation or normalization is an impressive feat. Clearly, semisupervised models are able to tackle input scenarios that more closely resemble the setting in which the developing human visual system must learn. However, there are also some notable limitations of these models that must be addressed if we wish to align them with human development.

First, although these models do not require images that are normalized in the strongest sense of the word, they have mostly been tested on images of objects in highly consistent poses, illumination conditions, and sizes. In other words, the training data used have been preselected to incorporate a significant amount of normalization. We must assume that the real input to an infant would not be so "nice"; thus, it is unclear to what extent these models could cope with more realistic input. Second, we call these models "semisupervised" because there is still a training stage in which implicit labels are provided to the model. To learn diagnostic features and feature combinations, semisupervised models must be told which images contain the object of interest and which do not. This implicit label represents an external signal that alerts the model to look for consistencies between the current image and other (previously signaled) images. Although this is clearly a step beyond the fully supervised models described previously, it is difficult to reconcile this procedure with developmental reality. We cannot assume that an infant has a reliable external signal that partitions the incoming input into sets of images that contain distinct object classes. Although the infants' multimodal experience of the world might provide an intermittent teaching signal, it is unlikely that there is enough reliable information available to the infant to assume that a fully supervised scenario is an accurate descriptive model of visual object learning. Furthermore, once a set of interesting image fragments is acquired, binding them together to reflect their mutual belongingness to a single object usually requires a costly estimate of a high-dimension probability distribution or a very large number of exemplars. Maintaining such a large set of diverse instances of an object in multiple settings is difficult to reconcile with the limitations on infant memory, a problem that is only exacerbated by the fact that achieving invariance to common sources of appearance variation (pose, illumination) requires still more exemplars. More generally, in order to distinguish object features from irrelevant background features, these models require many training instances, numbering in the hundreds or more. This is not representative of object learning by human infants, who can often acquire an object concept after just one or two exposures to the object. Although the full extent of such "one-shot" visual object learning remains to be specified experimentally, any occurrences of such rapid learning would need to be described by a comprehensive model. A minor concern relates to the very first step of selecting salient image patches. The "interest operators" most commonly used in existing models are generally not founded in what we know about the visual features that guide infant preference. Instead, they are generally designed to locate corners, circles, or areas of high-contrast and, to our knowledge, are rarely modified to reflect the visual limitations of the infant observer. To be fair, the operational goals of most systems designed to accomplish object discovery do not immediately suggest that such a modification would be a valuable strategy, but the extent to which this helps or hinders learning remains an important question.

To summarize, although the current computational visual learning approaches provide a well-defined procedure for discovering objects, they do not seem to capture some of the important features and limitations of the human visual processes. We next examine some of the key experimental results relevant to object learning by primates and in section 16.4 synthesize them into a broad framework for object discovery.

16.3 Experimental Studies of Primate Visual Processing Relevant to Object Discovery

We begin by asking an elementary, but fundamental, question: What is an "object"? In other words, what property is shared by entities as diverse as bicycles, lamps, trees, dolls, rocks, and gummy-bears that makes them all "objects"? Clearly, objectness is not critically dependent on several of the obvious attributes such as colors, sizes, rigidity, or familiarity. Each of these attributes on its own is either too restrictive or too permissive. Is there, then, a simple objective criterion that captures our intuitive notion of what an object is?

Drawing upon recent research on object learning in infancy (Cheries et al. 2008; Huntley-Fennera et al. 2002; Rosenberg and Carey 2006), we suggest that the primary criterion for objecthood is cohesion. An object, in essence, can be defined simply as an entity that remains cohesive across observational epochs. The reader can verify that almost any entity that one would classify as an object fits this membership criterion.

This simple definition of an object has far-reaching implications. Most importantly for our purposes, it highlights a basic cue for discovering objects – common displacement as observed via dynamic visual inputs. Indeed, dynamic information has been shown to play an important (often necessary) role in three aspects of infants' and adults' visual object learning: (1) orientation to "interesting" image regions, (2) grouping of fragments into wholes, and (3) the categorization of multiple object appearances into one object class.

16.3.1 Orienting towards Interesting Regions

The extraction of potential object candidates from a complex visual scene involves two processes – orienting to the approximate location in the scene where the object is likely to be, and then delineating the object from the background (typically referred to as the process of object segmentation). The most effective visual cue for eliciting an orienting response from even very young infants is motion. Infants tend to preferentially look at regions of the visual field that contain motion, over those that do not (Aslin and Shea 1990; Dannemiller and Freedland 1993; Volkman and Dobson 1976). The beneficiary of such attention is believed to be a coarse region comprising a set of patches, rather than a well-delineated object (Pylyshyn et al. 1994). Even though the attentional selection is rather crude, it is effective at markedly reducing the complexity of visual input.

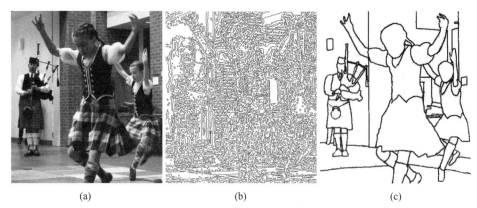

(a)   (b)   (c)

Figure 16.2. Natural images, such as the one shown in (a), are collections of many regions of different hues and luminances, as indicated in (b). The human visual system has to accomplish the task of integrating subsets of these regions into coherent objects, as in (c).

For instance, attending to a 10×10 degree region represents a great simplification of the raw input that has an extent of approximately 170×120 degrees; the area for intensive processing is over two orders of magnitude smaller than the entire visual field. Motion appears to be a primary cue for the required shifts and focusing of attention to specific regions of the visual field. An infant's poorly developed cone photoreceptors and immature cortical mechanisms, which significantly compromise spatial acuity, contrast sensitivity, and color perception, limit the effectiveness of nondynamic cues as orienting signals.

16.3.2 Grouping Regions into Larger Assemblies

Real-world images typically comprise many regions of different colors and luminances (Fig. 16.2). After orienting to a potentially interesting location of the visual field, the next challenge is to integrate subsets of these regions into meaningful entities corresponding to objects. How this is achieved is a fundamental question, and has been researched extensively in the domains of experimental and computational neuroscience. Much of the work has focused on the use of heuristics such as alignment of contours and similarity of texture statistics (Malik et al. 2001). Many of the "heuristics" that allow this to take place were studied by early 20th century Gestaltists such as Koffka (1935) and were compiled by Kanizsa (1979). In circumscribed domains, these heuristics can account rather well for human performance, but using them for analyzing real-world imagery remains an open challenge. The difficulty stems from the fact that it is rare for an entire object to have one uniform attribute. Object parts can be of various textures, colors, luminances, and shapes, and they may even be spatially separated by external occluders. Despite these obstacles, however, observers can segment objects from the background and from other objects quickly and reliably, even with novel objects. Furthermore, although it is clear that a mature visual system makes use of these cues, it is unclear whether these heuristics serve to organize information during the early stages of visual experience. Determining the nature of cues active at this time is important for elucidating the principles of visual learning and bootstrapping. With

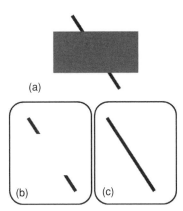

Figure 16.3. The rod-and-frame task. Infants are shown a rod moving back and forth behind an occluding box (a). After habituation, the infants are shown a broken rod (b) and a solid rod (c). Infants will gaze longer at the "novel" display, providing an indicator of whether they perceived the rod as solid or broken. After Kellman and Spelke 1983.

few exceptions (Prodoehl et al. 2003), very little work has been done on how the Gestalt laws themselves develop.

One of the simplest and most revealing behavioral experiments related to region grouping by infants involves the so-called rod-and-frame task (Fig. 16.3) introduced by Kellman and Spelke (1983). The question Kellman and Spelke asked was whether infants saw Figure 16.4(a) as depicting a box and two disconnected pieces of a rod or as a continuous rod behind an occlude. They adopted a habituation paradigm, wherein a child is shown a stimulus long enough to get bored of it. When subsequently shown a pair of stimuli, one similar to the habituation stimulus and the other more novel, children tend to look preferentially at the latter. Using this technique, Kellman and Spelke found that 4-month-old infants perceived Figure 16.4(a) as two disconnected rod pieces. Apparently the cues of collinearity and figural similarity, which to an adult observer indicate the continuity of the rod, are not effective at this young age. However, upon setting the rod in motion behind the occluder, a dramatic change occurred in the infants' percepts. They now began to see the display as depicting a continuous rod. Common motion, apparently, served as a strong cue for grouping disparate regions. Later work has shown that motion is an effective grouping cue even for infants as young as 2 months (Johnson and Aslin 1995), and that static cues begin to be effective significantly later, typically around the age of 6.5 months (Craton 1996).

The rod-and-frame experiments demonstrate the importance of motion for object defragmentation in the very young infant. These results are consistent with the observation that regions that move together typically comprise the same object. It appears that grouping processes in the developing visual system have come to encode this strong environmental regularity. In adults too, the significance of motion-based grouping processes is readily apparent. Studies using camouflaged "embryos" serving as novel objects, have shown that motion on its own can serve as the signal for segmentation when all other image-based cues in any frame of the motion sequence are useless for discerning the borders of an object or its parts (Brady 1999; Brady and Kersten 2003).

Some neurophysiological evidence from primates bears on an important detail related to motion-based grouping. The behavioral evidence reviewed above suggests that estimation of the motion of "parts" may be an important primitive component of object defragmentation in very early visual development. But how does one define the motion of a part? Is a part a collection of local image features, with motion defined independently at each feature location, as in optic-flow analysis? Or is a part more like a "region" or surface, in which motion is defined globally, and the motion of a feature is interpreted based on context, and is not merely the motion of the retinal projection?

Duncan et al. (2000) use an ingenious variation of the barber pole illusion (the barber-diamond stimulus) to decouple surface motion from the motions of visual image features (whose local motion is inconsistent with the overall surface motion, the so-called aperture problem). The authors found that many neurons in the primate middle temporal visual area (area MT) represent the motion of a feature as defined by the global surface motion (the "true" motion direction), not the local retinal motion, suggesting that part motion estimation is more sophisticated than mere feature tracking, at least in adult monkeys. In complementary work, Pack et al. measured adult primate MT neuronal responses to 2-D image-based features (contours and terminators), which could serve as cues to object segmentation (Pack, Gartland, and Born 2004). These neurons responded more strongly when the motion of a feature was consistent with the global motion of the object, whereas features that were incidental to occlusion (and thus, often at odds with the global motion of the object) did not elicit strong responses. These findings suggest that 3-D depth-ordering of regions and surfaces is an implicit signal in part motion estimation.

16.3.3 Grouping Diverse Object Instances within the Same Category

Beyond grouping image regions together based on their common motion, infants also exhibit the ability to track the motion of multiregion constellations by the age of 2 months. The ability to track, coupled with another ability that has been reported quite recently, equips the infants to build rich object representations. This other ability is that of temporal association. Infants have been shown to be able to link together images that consistently appear in temporal proximity (Fiser and Aslin 2002).

Temporal association involves using motion as a kind of "temporal glue," associating disparate views that occur in close temporal proximity of each other. By computing correspondence between object parts in successive frames, motion processing may prompt the visual system to integrate the different views into a coherent 3-D structure, or simply create a richer representation that encodes not just a snapshot appearance frozen in time, but rather how the appearance changes over short time intervals. What makes temporal association plausible is the observation that real-world objects generally exhibit the property of persistence. Thus, linking together spatiotemporally close views makes sense for generating rich object representations.

Evidence in support of temporal association as an important representational process has come from several studies of how subjects learn to recognize novel 3-D objects. Sinha and Poggio (1996) have shown that object representation may be a combination of 2-D images taken from multiple viewpoints, as object and observer rotate relative to each other in a motion sequence. The images taken from multiple viewpoints as the viewer or the object is in motion can then be integrated into a coherent representation, or even a 3-D structure further downstream in processing (Perrett and Oram 1993). Interestingly, the visual system is not bothered if the images are not entirely consistent. Wallis and Bulthoff (2001) showed their subjects' heads rotating in depth where the face morphed into that of another individual as the viewpoint changed. Subjects perceived the views as those of a single person, despite the inconsistency of identity. This "identity blindness" did not occur, however, when the views were presented in random order, showing the importance of the motion signal in viewpoint integration.

Some neurophysiological results have also provided evidence for temporal association processes in object-coding areas of the primate visual cortex. Miyashita trained monkeys on unrelated geometric patterns that were presented consecutively in an arbitrary, but consistent, order (Miyashita 1988). Neurons in anterior ventral temporal cortex that became selective for more than one pattern were far more likely to become selective to the immediate neighbor in the series than to another pattern. This result suggests that temporal contiguity plays a strong role in visual association, suggesting in turn that the temporal contiguity of views while an object is in motion may be responsible for the integration of those views into a coherent object concept.

16.4 Synthesizing the Experimental Data into a Theoretical Framework for Object Discovery

Taken together, the experimental data reviewed in the preceding section provide some guidelines for formulating a tentative model of object discovery. Primarily, the data point to the significance of dynamic cues for this process. Accordingly, we call the model "Dylan," as a loose acronym for a Dynamic Input-based Learner.

The goal of Dylan is to take in unannotated dynamic visual input, extract object representations from it, and then recognize instances of these objects in new inputs, whether static or dynamic. Dylan can be structured as a cascade of four modules.

M1. Orientation to potentially interesting regions of the visual field
M2. Grouping regions into "proto-objects"
M3. Tracking proto-objects and constructing temporally extended appearance models
M4. Matching the appearance models against novel inputs

In what follows, we briefly describe a possible computational instantiation of these modules. Our aim is to keep the design of each of the modules simple and perceptually plausible, so that the overall goal of going from raw visual experience to recognition can be rendered feasible.

It is worth emphasizing that we present Dylan not as a specific implementation, but rather as a general framework. We simply do not yet have enough experimental data to precisely constrain the details of such a model. Furthermore, the issue of exactly how different modules might be best implemented is not of as much importance as Dylan's overall organization. In the following sections, whenever we do describe particular implementations, they should be thought of as replaceable placeholders for any other scheme that can accomplish a similar input-output mapping.

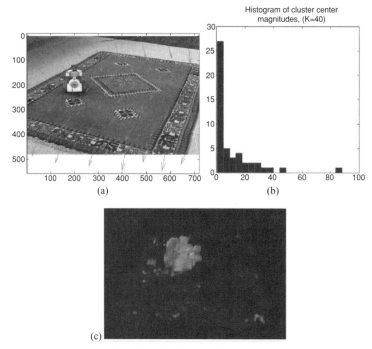

Figure 16.4. Orienting via outlier detection on optic flow maps. (a) An optic flow map. (b) A histogram of optic-flow clusters' magnitudes. A similar histogram can be constructed for flow directions. (c) A region of interest localized based on outlier detection amongst flow clusters. (See color plate 16.4.)

16.4.1 M1: Orienting to Potentially Interesting Regions of the Visual Field

To mimic an infant's ability to orient towards salient patterns in the environment, especially those that are in motion, Dylan computes the optic flow map on the dynamic input and then performs clustering to determine regions of similar flow. The clustering takes in not only the magnitude and direction of the flow vectors, but also their locations, so that the eventual clusters are spatially contiguous, consistent with the spatial coherence of real-world objects. From amongst these clusters, Dylan identifies the one that is the most distinct in its motion properties. This "outlier" constitutes the attention attractor that the system orients to. Figure 16.4 shows sample outputs of these steps on simple input sequences.

16.4.2 M2: Grouping Regions into "Proto-objects"

The region of interest that the first stage yields is not very well defined. It is unclear which of the several subregions belong together and might constitute an "object." In order to make this determination, Dylan uses the similarity of motion trajectories to determine which image regions go together. This is, of course, an instance of the notion of common fate (entities that move together, bind together). In practice, however, the implementation of this idea presents a significant challenge in that motion vectors computed over short time intervals are typically very noisy. The resulting groupings,

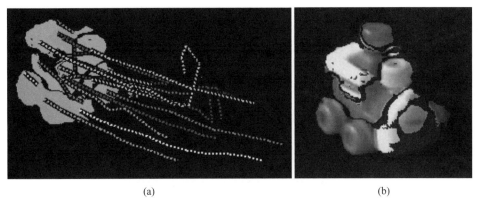

(a)   (b)

Figure 16.5. Motion vectors computed over short durations are typically noisy, and lead to unstable grouping estimates. Computing similarities over extended motion trajectories (a) of regions permits a more stable computation of their mutual grouping relationships (b). (See color plate 16.5.)

therefore, are quite unstable. In order to overcome this challenge, a possible strategy is to integrate trajectory information over more extended periods of time (Fig. 16.5). The problem of computing grouping relations then transforms to one of comparing time series. Although we can get by to a large extent with simple comparison metrics like the Minkowski norms, it is an open problem as to precisely how the different frequency components of the trajectories ought to be weighted to arrive at the overall similarity score.

As Figure 16.6 shows, motion can be used effectively for obtaining grouping relationships among regions. Eventually, a visual system ought to be able to work with static inputs as well. How can this progression from dynamic to static grouping be effected? An important aspect of Dylan is its ability to bootstrap static grouping heuristics, starting with purely motion-based processes. The basic idea here is that even as it performs motion-based grouping, the system learns other attributes that the grouped regions share, such as common hues, textural statistics, and orientations. Over time these correlated attributes come to serve as proxies for common motion and are able to support grouping even in entirely static inputs.

To determine the plausibility of this hypothesis for bootstrapping static grouping heuristics, we took five different video sequences of scenes comparable to what a child is likely to see during the first weeks of life (faces and toys moving and translating in front of a camera; see Fig. 16.6(a) for an example). The motion of these sequences was analyzed using the optical flow algorithm described by Ogale and Aloimonos (2005), resulting in one optical flow map in horizontal (x) and one in vertical (y) direction (see Fig. 16.6(b) for an example).

16.4.2.1 Color Similarity–Based Grouping

To see if common motion correlates with color similarity and can thus bootstrap the latter, the sequences were converted to the perceptually plausible L*A*B* colorspace and subdivided into a grid of squares (here chosen to have a side length of 15 pixels, although the results are valid across a range of values for this parameter). For each

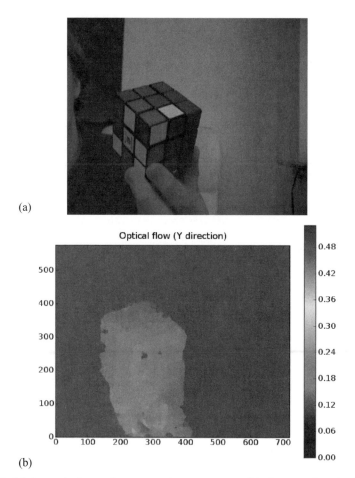

(a)

(b)

Figure 16.6. (a) Example frame from a motion sequence. (b) Computed optical flow in y direction. (See color plate 16.6.)

square we defined the motion vector as a two-component vector consisting of the median of the square's pixels' optical flow in x and y directions, the L value as the mean of all its pixels' L values, and the AB vector as the two-component vector consisting of the mean of all its pixels' A and B values. We then compared each square to its 5×5 neighborhood squares in terms of the absolute difference of the squares' L values, the euclidean norm of their AB vectors, and their motion difference. We defined the motion difference as follows:

$$d_{motion} = \frac{\|\vec{A} - \vec{B}\|}{max(\vec{A}, \vec{B})}$$

We chose this metric because of its perceptual plausibility: two small motion vectors, pointing in opposite directions, can have a very small difference in terms of the euclidean norm, but their motion difference is more perceptually salient than the motion difference of two vectors of different length pointing in roughly the same direction. This is taken into account by our metric.

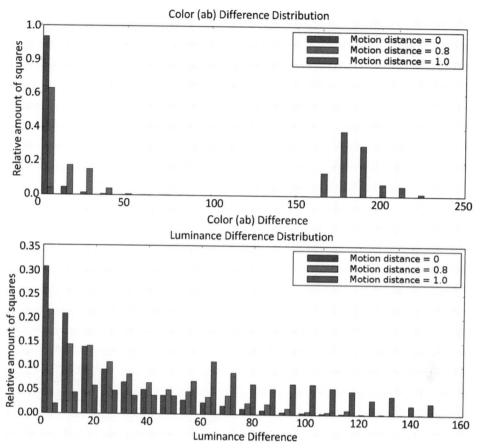

Figure 16.7. Color and luminance distributions. The distributions show that in real world sequences, motion similarity of regions is correlated with their color and luminance similarity. (See color plate 16.7.)

The distributions in Figure 16.7 show that motion similarity between image regions is strongly correlated with their color and luminance similarity. Two regions that have a small motion distance are very likely to also have a small color as well as luminance distance. This correlation can permit color and luminance similarities to be bootstrapped as grouping proxies via initially available motion grouping cues.

16.4.2.2 Collinearity-based Grouping

To see if the Gestalt law of collinearity can also be bootstrapped by motion, we first used the optical flow maps to divide our set of squares into two types: squares along object edges (containing a significant number of pixels with different motion) and squares within objects. To get orientation data from these squares, we used the Sobel operators in x and y directions, resulting in an orientation map like the one shown in Figure 16.8(a). Additionally, the Sobel operators can be used to determine amplitude of orientation (roughly correlating to the contrast across orientation axis). These two pieces of information can then be used to generate a weighted orientation histogram for each squares. We took the difference of the mode (if a "real edge" is contained

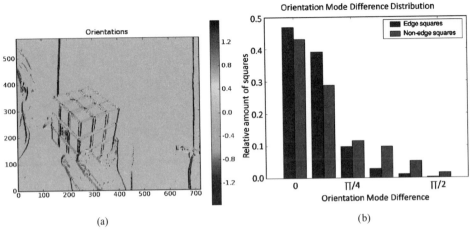

Figure 16.8. (a) Orientation map. (b) Orientation mode difference distribution. (See color plate 16.8.)

within the square, the mode is the most informative value regarding orientation) of the orientations among adjacent squares of the edge square subset and did the same for the nonedge subset. The distributions of the different mode differences are shown in Figure 16.8(b). One can see that among the edge subset the differences are much more concentrated at low values than in the nonedge subset, indicating that along the motion-determined edge of an object the dominant orientation changes much slower than within, a regularity that can be used to learn the heuristic of grouping via collinearity.

In summary, using natural video sequences, we found that the Gestalt laws of grouping via color similarity and collinearity can, in principle, be bootstrapped via a primitive motion-based grouping process. This supports the possibility that those laws might be learned by newborns using a developmentally early sensitivity to motion cues.

Similar analyses remain to be undertaken for more advanced Gestalt laws such as symmetry or colinearity across larger distances or behind occluded objects. By increasing the size of the squares, using more sophisticated metrics to actually describe the contents of the squares, and using a larger corpus of data, it would be interesting to see if not only those laws, but simple shapes and curves common in the world, could be learned.

16.4.3 M3: Tracking Proto-Objects and Constructing Temporally Extended Appearance Models

The set of grouped regions determined by module 2 constitutes an elementary representation of an object. In order to encode how the object transforms over time in the dynamic input sequence, Dylan tracks the region collection via an adaptive procedure, such as the Kalman filter (Ziliani and Moscheni 1997). The different appearances of the object that are revealed over the course of this tracking together constitute its temporally extended appearance model, or TEAM, as illustrated in Figure 16.9. Using the idea of temporal association, these appearances are bound together owing to their spatiotemporal proximity.

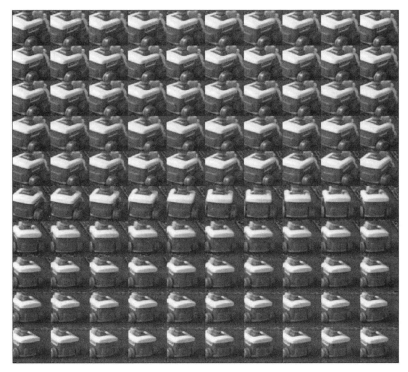

Figure 16.9. We can use motion to segment an object from a cluttered background and then track its appearance over time. The result is a highly redundant "stack" of object images that we refer to as a TEAM, for temporally extended appearance model. How TEAMs should be encoded for recognition is an important open problem.

The resulting spatiotemporal volume of object appearances clearly constitutes a rich data set for constructing a robust object model, but how exactly should we encode it? This apparently simple question has yet to be thoroughly answered either experimentally or computationally.

The simplest thing we could do with such a volume is store it in its entirety for future reference. Individual images or new spatiotemporal inputs could be compared to the stored volume using any set of features we wish. The storage requirements of this strategy are obviously prohibitive, though. If we are to remember every spatiotemporal object volume we encounter, we will be overwhelmed with data very quickly. Even discarding the temporal contingencies between frames and maintaining only newly encountered static images does not do much to mitigate this very expensive encoding strategy. To learn anything useful from dynamic data, the visual system must represent spatiotemporal volumes efficiently and with enough information for recognition to proceed.

There is a great deal of redundancy in the data depicted in Figure 16.9, and finding encodings that reduce it can help guide the search for an efficient representation. However, we must be mindful of two issues as we consider possible methods of redundancy reduction in this setting: First, does a particular representation support robust recognition? Second, is the proposed representation consistent with human psychophysical performance?

To consider the first issue, there are existing methods for recovering a "sparse" encoding of natural image data (van Hateran and Ruderman 1998; Olshausen 1996, 2003). Implementing these methods on local image patches or spatiotemporal sub-volumes tends to produce basis functions that resemble edge-finding filters, which translate over time. These provide a useful vocabulary for describing an image or an image sequence using a small set of active units, but these features are often not ideal for recognition tasks (Balas and Sinha 2006).

In terms of our second issue, building representations that are consistent with human performance, there are many computations we could carry out on our volume that are "too strong" in some sense to be relatable to human performance. For example, we could potentially use our image sequence to reconstruct a 3-D volumetric model of our object using structure-from-motion algorithms (Ullman 1979). The smoothness of appearance change across the images in Figure 16.9 could reduce the usual difficulty of solving the correspondence problem, and we can easily obtain far more object views than strictly necessary to solve for a rigid form. However, it seems unlikely that human observers actually recognize objects based on view-invariant volumetric models of shape (Ullman 1996). View-based models currently seem more commensurate with the psychophysical data (Tarr and Pinker 1989; Bulthoff and Edelman 1992). To revisit a point raised earlier, however, there are also good psychophysical reasons against storing all the views of an object within some spatiotemporal volume. Specifically, observers trained to recognize novel dynamic objects do not behave as though they have stored all the views they are trained with. For example, they find novel dynamic objects harder to recognize if the stimulus presented at test is the time-reversed version of the training sequence (Stone 1998, 1999; Vuong and Tarr 2004). An ideal observer that maintains a representation of each image should not be impaired by this manipulation, suggesting human observers do not simply store copies of all object views encountered during training. Instead, the order of appearances is maintained and becomes a critical part of the representation.

Learning purely local features in space and time is useful within particular domains (Ullman and Bart 2004), but potentially difficult to "scale up" to natural settings. Also, maintaining fully volumetric object models or large libraries of static object views is both inefficient and inconsistent with human data. The challenge we are faced with then is to develop a compact and expressive representation of a dynamic object that is consistent with human performance.

We suggest that recent results describing the effects of temporal association between object images are a good foundation for developing new models of dynamic object encoding. Temporal proximity between images is a strong binding cue for the human visual system, which works under the assumption that object properties (including identity) are stable over short intervals of time. Multiple computational experiments have demonstrated that temporal smoothness assumptions are a simple and powerful means for learning shift-invariance and disparity from image sequences (Stone and Harper 1999; Foldiak 1991). Moreover, both physiological and psychophysical experiments have demonstrated that the primate and human visual systems use temporal proximity to bind distinct images together into a common representation (Cox et al. 2005; Miyashita 1988; Miyashita and Chang 1988; Wallis and Bulthoff 2001). These results indicate that a key role of object motion during object concept learning is to provide a set of appearances that a consistent object label should be propagated over.

Recent work from our lab also suggests that dynamic training also enhances sensitivity to subtle appearance changes at the same time as increased generalization is learned (Balas and Sinha 2006b).

A model of object concept learning built on temporal association offers an attractive alternative to existing proposals. Instead of storing an intractably large number of ordered static views of an object, it should be possible to store only a few prototypical images and use dynamic input to learn a valid generalization function around each prototype. Redundancy reduction within a spatiotemporal volume is thus accomplished at the level of global appearance (however we choose to represent it), and the ultimate encoding of the object is view-based with a learned "tuning width" in appearance space around each prototype view. The result is a strategy for efficiently storing dynamic object data that is consistent with human performance in several tasks.

There are multiple aspects of this model that have yet to be thoroughly explored psychophysically. For example, how are prototypical views of an object selected within a volume? There is very little work on how such views (or "keyframes"; Wallraven and Bulthoff 2001) might be determined computationally or the extent to which they are psychologically real. Likewise, we do not yet have a detailed picture of how generalization around an image evolves following dynamic exposure. We have recently suggested that distributed representations of object appearance follow from dynamic experience with a novel object, but as yet we have not investigated the long-term consequences of dynamic training. These two issues constitute key parameters in what is essentially a statistical model of dynamic object appearance. Finding "keyframes" is analogous to identifying multiple modes in the data, whereas understanding patterns of generalization around those keyframes is analogous to identifying the variance of data around some mode. In this framework, motion is not a new feature for recognition, but rather a principled way to establish a sort of "mixture model" for object appearance.

The advantage of this strategy is that it makes explicit the fact that while observers probably have access to global appearance data, temporal data is only available locally. Thus, we do not try to build an object representation that covers the whole viewing sphere of possible appearances (Murase and Nayar 1995). Instead, we limit ourselves to learning what changes an object is likely to undergo in a short time interval. This basic proposal leads to many interesting questions for psychophysical research and makes easy contact with several physiological studies of object representation in high-level cortical areas.

To summarize, the question of TEAM representation has not yet been adequately explored in the experimental domain. In the absence of human data to guide computational strategies, current proposals are necessarily speculative. One idea that seems perceptually plausible and computationally attractive is to encode a TEAM via "keyframes" and some specification of the transformation linking these keyframes. Keyframes can be computed via a cluster analysis. They would correspond to the frames that minimize the sum of distances between themselves and all other frames of the TEAM, under the constraint of minimizing the number of keyframes. Of course, the error metric will keep decreasing monotonically as more and more keyframes are selected. However, as is the case with principal components analysis, the decrease in error obtained by adding a new keyframe diminishes as the number of key frames increases. The knee of the corresponding scree plot would indicate the number of keyframes to be included. As for encoding the transformation linking these keyframes, a manifold in a low-dimensional space – for instance, one corresponding to the principal components of object appearances seen – might be adequate. The computational choices here await experimental validation.

16.4.4 M4: Matching the Appearance Models against Novel Inputs

Although not technically a part of the object discovery process, the ability to match internal object representations against new inputs is crucial for demonstrating the success or failure of the previous steps. The challenge is to localize instances of previously seen objects in novel inputs, which may be static or dynamic. The conventional approach to this problem is to scan the new input exhaustively and determine whether the previously seen object appears at any of the locations. This is clearly a computationally expensive and highly inefficient strategy. However, human observers are able to scan a scene much more efficiently, even when there are no constraints on where in the image the object might appear. What underlies this efficient search ability? In other words, what guides the sequence of fixations that eventually leads to foveation of the target object? An important clue comes from observations of search behavior in patients with tunnel vision. Such individuals are much less efficient than normal observers at detecting targets in larger images (Luo and Peli 2006). It appears, therefore, that visual information from the periphery, although limited in its acuity, color, and contrast sensitivity, provides valuable guidance for scan-path generation. Indeed, in computational simulations, the inclusion of peripheral information to augment foveal matching significantly enhances search efficiency. Tentatively, then, the last module of Dylan can be conceptualized as an image search process that implicitly adopts a coarse-to-fine matching approach, implemented via the acuity distribution of the primate eye. Other cues to image salience, such as color, luminance, and motion, would further facilitate this search, as has been demonstrated compellingly by Itti and colleagues (Itti and Koch 2000).

Through these four modules, Dylan can accomplish the input-output mapping we had stated at the outset: given unannotated dynamic visual experience, such a system is able to extract, represent, and match objects in the input. Motion information plays a crucial role in this process, consistent with the experimental results reviewed in section 16.3.

16.5 Conclusion

Although not complete, the Dylan model constitutes a simple high-level modular framework that enables the formulation and testing of computational theories of key aspects of object discovery and recognition. We have presented a possible instantiation of each module, informed by evidence from human visual performance and development. Elements of Dylan's architecture that remain to be specified include the encoding of TEAMS, be it through an extraction of representative "keyframes" and/or a "spatiotemporal signature" (Stone 1993) of object appearance, and explicit mechanisms for comparing objects efficiently during learning and recognition. An analysis of behavioral and neurophysiological evidence within the context of the Dylan framework

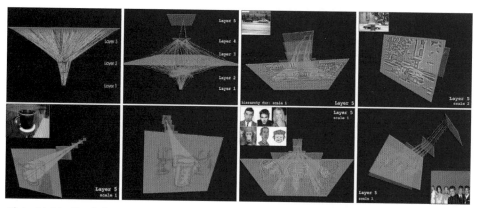

Plate 11.11. Top left two images: learned 3-layer hierarchy for the Caltech experiment; learned hierarchy for faces with compositional links shown. Examples of detections of categories of cars, mugs, and faces, in which the first three layers in the library are common to all three categories.

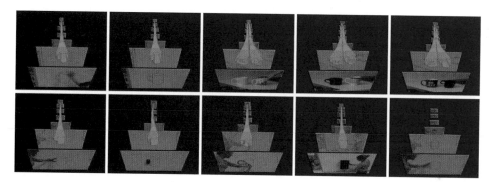

Plate 11.12. Detections of mugs.

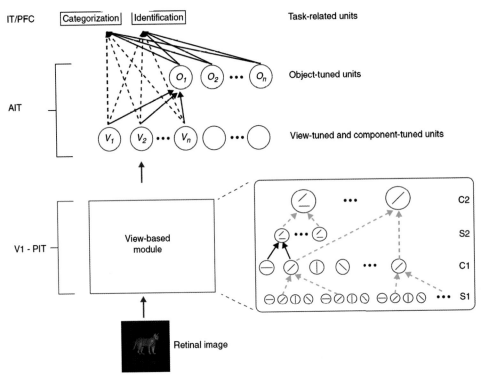

Plate 12.1. The Standard Model of object recognition in cortex (from Riesenhuber and Poggio 2002). It models the cortical ventral visual stream (Ungerleider and Haxby 1994), running from primary visual cortex (V1) over extrastriate visual areas V2 and V4 to inferotemporal cortex (IT). Starting from V1 simple cells, with small receptive fields that respond preferentially to oriented bars, neurons along the ventral stream (Logothetis and Sheinberg 1996; Perrett and Oram 1993; Tanaka 1996) show an increase in receptive field size as well as in the complexity of their preferred stimuli (Kobatake and Tanaka 1994). At the top of the ventral stream, in anterior IT, cells are tuned to complex stimuli such as faces (Desimone 1991; Desimone et al. 1984; Gross et al. 1972; Perrett et al. 1992). A hallmark of these IT cells is their robust firing to stimulus transformations such as scale and position changes (Logothetis et al. 1995; Logothetis and Sheinberg 1996; Perrett and Oram 1993; Tanaka 1996). The bottom part of the model (inside the *inset*) consists of a view-based module (Riesenhuber and Poggio 1999b), which is an hierarchical extension of the classical paradigm of building complex cells from simple cells. In particular, units in the second layer (C1) pool within a neighborhood defined by their receptive field the activities of the "simple" cells in the first layer (S1) with the same orientation preference. In the model, pooling is through a MAX-like operation (dashed green lines), in which the firing rate of a pooling neuron corresponds to the firing rate of the strongest input, that improves invariance to local changes in position and scale while preserving stimulus selectivity (Riesenhuber and Poggio 1999b) (recent physiological experiments have provided support for the MAX pooling prediction at the level of complex cells in V1 (Lampl et al. 2004) and V4 (Gawne and Martin 2002)). At the next layer (S2), cells pool the activities of earlier neurons with different tuning, yielding selectivity to more complex patterns. The underlying operation is in this case more "traditional": a weighted sum followed by a sigmoidal (or Gaussian) transformation (solid lines). These two operations work together to progressively increase feature complexity and position (and scale) tolerance of units along the hierarchy, in agreement with physiological data (Kobatake and Tanaka 1994). The output of the view-based module is represented by view-tuned model units (VTUs) that exhibit tight tuning to rotation in depth but are tolerant to scaling and translation of their preferred object view, with tuning properties quantitatively similar to those found in IT (Logothetis et al. 1995; Riesenhuber and Poggio 1999b). The second part of the model starts with the VTUs. Invariance to, rotation in depth, for example, is obtained by combining, in a learning module, several VTUs tuned to different views of the same object (Poggio and Edelman 1990), creating view-invariant units (O_n). These, as well as the VTUs, can then serve as inputs to modules that learn to perform different visual tasks such as identification or object categorization. They consist of the same generic learning circuitry (Poggio and Girosi 1990) but are trained with appropriate sets of examples to perform specific tasks.

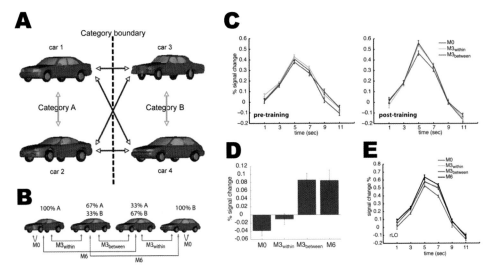

Plate 12.2. Investigating the interactions of bottom-up and top-down information in category learning and categorization using fMRI-RA. *A*, Visual stimuli. Subjects learned to categorize randomly generated morphs from the vast number of possible blends of four prototypes. The placement of the prototypes in this diagram does not reflect their similarity. Red lines show cross-category; green lines show within-category morph lines. *B*, Example morphs for a "cross-category" morph line between the "car 2" and "car 4" prototypes. In the fMRI-RA experiments, pairs of stimuli were shown in each trial, with total BOLD response to each pair indicating how strongly neurons in the area differentiate between the two stimuli. Stimulus pairs were grouped into the following conditions: M0 (0% shape change), M3$_{within}$ (33% shape change, same category), M3$_{between}$ (33% change, different category), and M6 (67% change, different category) *C*, fMRI-RA BOLD activation in right LO pre- (*left*) and post-training (*right*), in which subjects performed a displacement judgment task (for which the trained categories were irrelevant). Category training is shown to increase shape selectivity (M3 > M0 post-, $P < 0.05$, but not pre-training, $P > 0.5$) but not category selectivity (M3$_{within}$ = M3$_{between}$ pre-/post-training, $P > 0.4$). *D*, fMRI-RA activation in a right lateral PFC (rlPFC) ROI defined by the comparison of M3$_{between}$ versus M3$_{within}$ of the morph line on which participants had the best behavioral performance. The activation in the ROI was low for same-category trials, but significantly higher for different-category trials, suggesting that neurons in that area showed category-selective tuning. *E*, Activity in the car-selective rLO region during the categorization experiment: Responses increase with physical shape difference within the cars in a trial, $P < 0.0001$ (ANOVA), with no evidence for category tuning (responses for M3$_{within}$ and M3$_{between}$ not significantly different, $P > 0.9$). Error bars show within-subject SEM. For details, see Jiang et al. 2007).

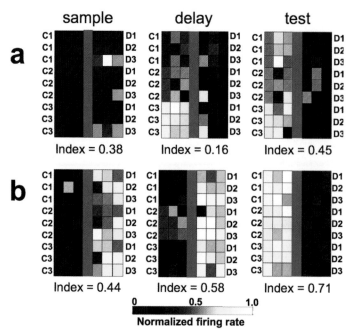

Plate 12.4. Neuronal responses of sample IT and PFC neurons to individual sample stimuli (Freedman et al. 2003), recorded from monkeys trained on a "cat/dog" categorization task over a morph space spanned by six prototypes, three "cats" (C1, C2, C3 in the figure) and three "dogs" (D1, D2, D3) (cf. the car morph space of Fig. 12.2 spanned by four car prototypes). The six color plots show the average activity of three IT (a) and three PFC (b) neurons to stimuli at specific points along each of the nine "between-class" morph lines (from left to right: 100% cat/0% dog, 80% cat/20% dog, . . . , 0% cat/100% dog). Each color plot shows the average activity of one neuron to each of the 42 stimuli along the nine between-class morph lines. The prototypes are represented in the outermost columns, and the blue line in the middle represents the category boundary. Each prototype contributes to three morph lines. A color scale indicates the activity level, normalized for each neuron to its maximum response. The category index of each neuron is indicated below each color plot. The plots are arranged into three columns. The columns, from left to right, show examples of neurons with selective activity during the sample, delay, and test epochs, respectively. These plots show the activity of six different neurons and not the activity of an individual neuron from each area across time. See text.

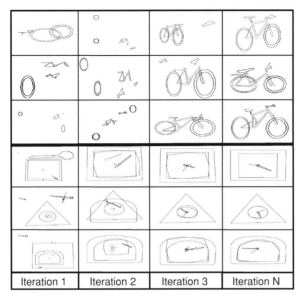

Iteration 1	Iteration 2	Iteration 3	Iteration N

Plate 13.4. Samples from p during each stage of the relationship pursuit. Objects become more coherent as new relationships are added.

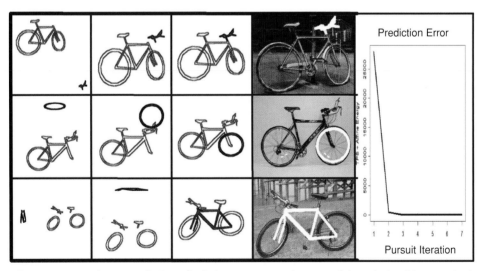

Plate 13.7. Top-down prediction of missing parts at each stage of the relationship pursuit. A neighborhood of parts is fixed and the remaining parts are Gibbs sampled. The accuracy of the prediction is measured by the thin-plate-spline + affine transformation needed to move the predicted part to its true position. We can see that this energy decreases drastically as we add more relations to the model.

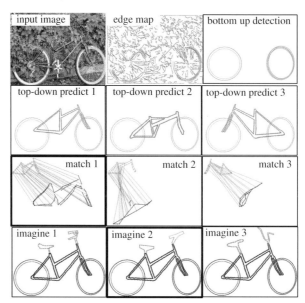

Plate 13.10. The combination of bottom-up and top-down influences for detecting an occluded bicycle (presented in Lin et al. 2009).

Plate 13.11. Recognition experiments on five object categories (presented in Lin et al. 2009).

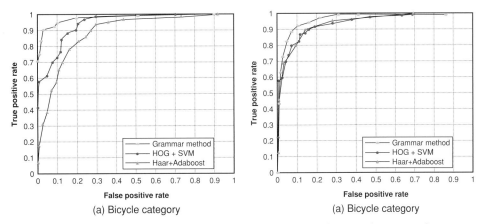

(a) Bicycle category

(a) Bicycle category

Plate 13.12. ROC curves for recognizing bicycles (a) (from the LHI dataset) and rear-cars (b) (from the Caltech-101 dataset). Our model outperforms a HOG-based SVM and Adaboost on bicycles and PBT and SIFT-based boosting for rear-cars (presented in Lin et al. 2009).

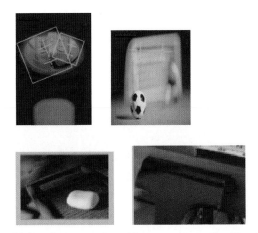

Plate 15.5. Example of false alarms produced by two recent classification schemes. The top images were classified as "faces," the bottom two as "cows."

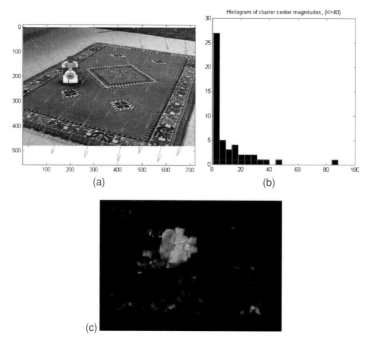

(a)

(b)

(c)

Plate 16.4. Orienting via outlier detection on optic flow maps. (a) An optic flow map. (b) A histogram of optic-flow clusters' magnitudes. A similar histogram can be constructed for flow directions. (c) A region of interest localized based on outlier detection amongst flow clusters.

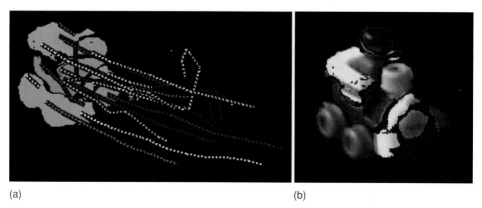

(a)

(b)

Plate 16.5. Motion vectors computed over short durations are typically noisy, and lead to unstable grouping estimates. Computing similarities over extended motion trajectories (a) of regions permits a more stable computation of their mutual grouping relationships (b).

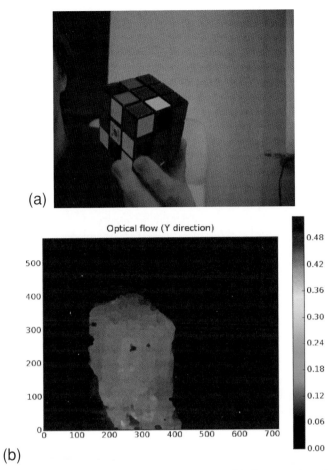

Plate 16.6. (a) Example frame from a motion sequence. (b) Computed optical flow in *y* direction.

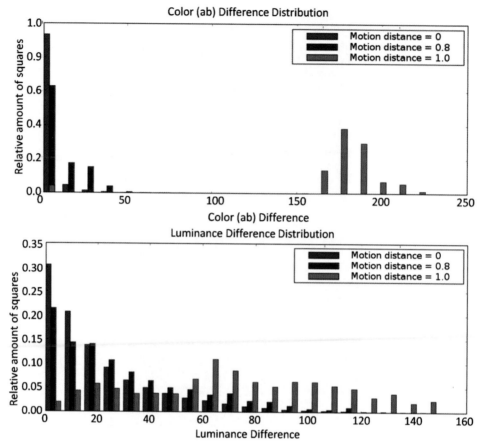

Plate 16.7. Color and luminance distributions. The distributions show that in real world sequences, motion similarity of regions is correlated with their color and luminance similarity.

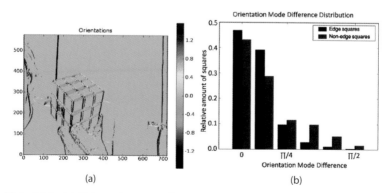

(a)

(b)

Plate 16.8. (a) Orientation map. (b) Orientation mode difference distribution.

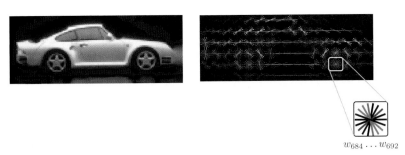

Plate 17.1. Dense gradient histogram representation. The loupe shows the nine possible edge orientations of the histogram bins that are interpreted as words.

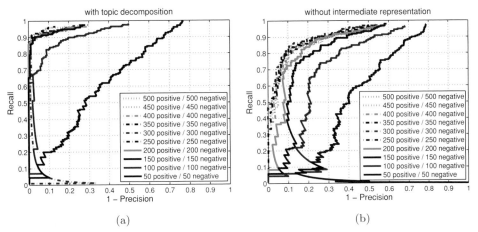

Plate 17.7. (a) and (b), Comparison of learning curve for proposed intermediate representation versus SVM on pure features on UIUC single-scale database.

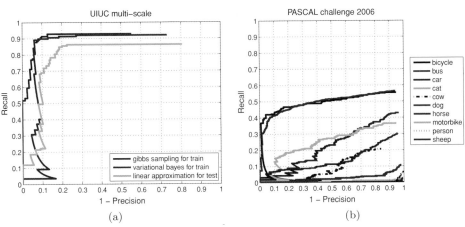

Plate 17.8. (a) Performance on UIUC multiscale dataset using topic model estimated via Gibbs sampling versus variational Bayes approach compared to using pseudotopic activations. (b) Precision-recall curves on the PASCAL VOC challenge 2006. Precision-recall curves and example detections.

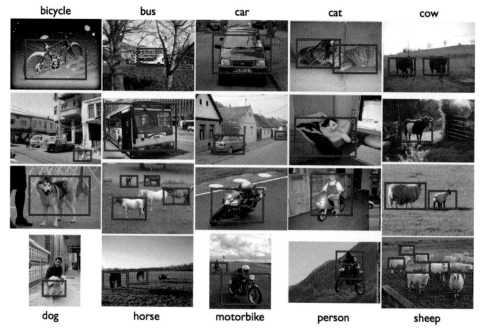

Plate 17.9. Example detections on the PASCAL VOC challenge 2006.

Plate 17.10. Example detections on the ETH shape database.

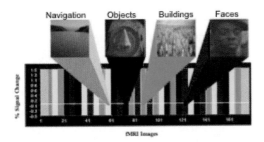

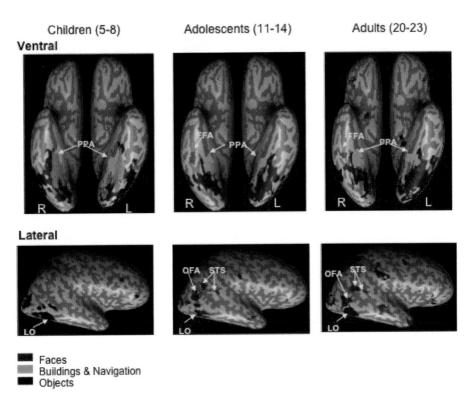

Faces
Buildings & Navigation
Objects

Plate 18.1. Ventral stream category-specific topography within each age group. Contrast maps for each object category ($p < .05$ corrected) from the group-level random-effects (GLM) mapped onto the ventral projection, and the lateral right hemisphere of a single representative inflated brain in order to show consistency, or lack thereof, across the age groups in category-selective activation. *FFA*, fusiform face area; *OFA*, occipital face area; *STS*, superior temporal sulcus; *LO*, lateral occipital object area; *PPA*, parahippocampal place area.

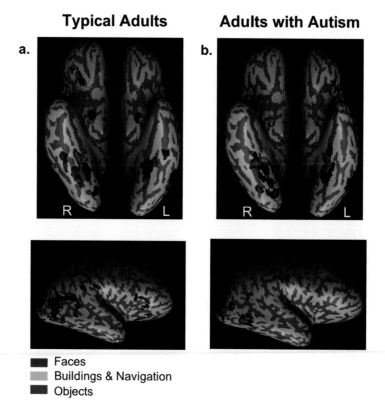

Faces
Buildings & Navigation
Objects

Plate 18.2. Group map reflecting average activation for faces, buildings, scenes, and objects for (a) typical adults and (b) adults with autism. Maps are inflated and shown from the ventral view (upper panel) and the lateral view of the right hemisphere (lower panel). For both groups, the maps were computed using a random effects general linear model and are thresholded at $P = .006$.

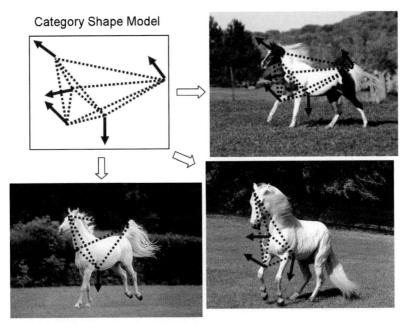

Plate 19.1. The model is a graph whose edges are abstract pairwise geometric relationships. It integrates generic configurations common to most objects from a category as well as more specific configurations that capture different poses and aspects.

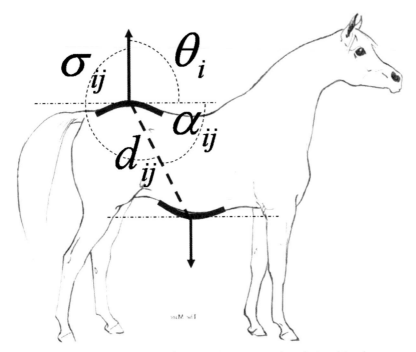

Plate 19.2. Parameters that capture the pairwise geometric relationships between object parts.

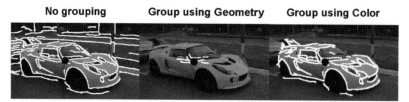

No grouping **Group using Geometry** **Group using Color**

Plate 19.5. The grouping stage enforces pairwise constraints that could significantly prune our matching/recognition search space. The contours in white (for second and third image) are the ones likely to be on the same object as the red circle, given the geometric or color cues.

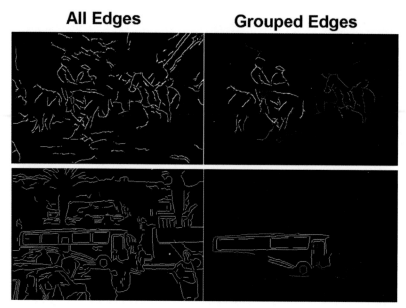

All Edges **Grouped Edges**

Plate 19.6. If grouping is not used, it is very hard to distinguish the separate objects (*left column*). After grouping (*right column*), it is perceptually easier to distinguish them (the bus and the horse).

has pointed to a likely role for common motion in bootstrapping object recognition processes. Further evidence is required before such a hypothesis is to be accepted. However, infants' early sensitivity to visual motion and the consistent developmental timeline that follows is likely no accident, and at the very least indicates a substantive source of visual information that has been underutilized in computational object discovery modeling. The model we have described permits exploration and elaboration of this possibility, and points the way towards a truly developmentally informed model of object concept learning.

Bibliography

Agarwal S, Roth D. 2002. Learning a sparse representation for object detection. In Proceedings of ECCV.

Aslin RN, Shea SL. 1990. Velocity thresholds in human infants: implications for the perception of motion. *Dev Psychol* 26: 589–598.

Balas B, Sinha P. 2006. Receptive field structures for recognition. *Neural Comput* 18: 497–520.

Balas B, Sinha P. 2006b. Learning about objects in motion: better generalization and sensitivity through temporal association. *J Vision* 6: 318a.

Brady MJ. 1999. Psychophysical investigations of incomplete forms and forms with background, PhD diss, University of Minnesota.

Brady MJ, Kersten D. 2003. Bootstrapped learning of novel objects. *J Vision* 3(6): 413–422.

Bulthoff HH, Edelman S. 1992. Psychophysical support for a 2-dimensional view interpolation theory of object recognition. *Proc Nat Acad Sci USA* 89(1): 60–64.

Cheries E, Mitroff S, Wynn K, Scholl B. 2008. The critical role of cohesion: how splitting disrupts infants' object representations. *Dev Sci* 11: 427–432.

Cox DD, Meier P, Oertelt N, DiCarlo JJ. 2005. 'Breaking' position-invariant object recognition. *Nat Neurosci* 8: 1145–1147.

Craton LG. 1996. The development of perceptual completion abilities: infants' perception of stationary, partially occluded objects. *Child Dev* 67(3): 890–904.

Dannemiller JL, Freedland RL. 1993. Motion-based detection by 14-week-old infants. *Vis Res* 33: 657–64.

Duda RO, Hart PE, Stork DG. 2000. *Pattern classification*. Baltimore: Wiley Interscience.

Duncan RO, Albright TD, Stoner GR. 2000. Occlusion and the interpretation of visual motion: perceptual and neuronal effects of context. *J Neurosci* 20(15): 5885–5897.

Fei-Fei L, Fergus R, Perona P. 2004. Learning generative visual models from few training examples: an incremental Bayesian approach tested on 101 object categories. In IEEE CVPR workshop of generative model based vision.

Fergus R, Perona P, Zisserman A. 2003. Object class recognition by unsupervised scale-invariant learning. In Proceedings of CVPR.

Fiser J, Aslin RN. 2002. Statistical learning of higher-order temporal structure from visual shape-sequences. *J Exp Psychol Learn Mem Cogn* 28(3): 458–467.

Foldiak P. 1991. Learning invariance from transformation sequences. *Neural Comput* 3: 194–200.

Haralick RM, Shapiro LG. 1993. *Computer and robot vision II*, 323. Reading, MA: Addison-Wesley.

Huntley-Fennera G, Carey S, Solimando A. 2002. Objects are individuals but stuff doesn't count: perceived rigidity and cohesiveness influence infants' representations of small groups of discrete entities. *Cognition* 85(3): 203–221.

Itti L, Koch C. 2000. A saliency-based search mechanism for overt and covert shifts of visual attention. *Vision Res* 40: 1489–1506.

Johnson SP, Aslin RN. 1995. Perception of object unity in 2-month-old infants. *Dev Psychol* 31: 739–745.

Kanizsa G. 1979. *Organization in vision : essays on Gestalt perception*. New York: Praeger.

Luo G, Peli E. 2006. Use of an augmented-vision device for visual search by patients with tunnel vision. *Invest Ophthal Vis Sci* 47: 4152–4159.

Kellman PJ, Spelke ES. 1983. Perception of partly occluded objects in infancy. *Cogn Psychol* 15(4): 483–524.

Koffka K. 1935. *Principles of Gestalt psychology*. New York: Harcourt.

Malik J, Belongie S, Leung T, Shi J. 2001. Contour and texture analysis for image segmentation. *Int J Comput Vis* 43: 7–27.

Miyashita Y. 1988. Neuronal correlate of visual associative long-term-memory in the primate temporal cortex. *Nature* 335(6193): 817–820.

Miyashita Y, Chang HS. 1988. Neuronal correlate of pictorial short-term memory in the primate temporal cortex. *Nature* 331: 307–311.

Morton J, Johnson MH. 1991. CONSPEC and CONLERN: a two-process theory of infant face recognition. *Psychol Rev*. 98(2): 164–181.

Murase H, Nayar SK. 1995. Visual learning and recognition of 3-D objects from appearance. *Int J Comput Vis* 14: 5–24.

Ogale AS, Aloimonos Y. 2005. Shape and the stereo correspondence problem. *Int J Comput Vis* 65(1).

Olshausen BA. 1996. Emergence of simple-cell receptive field properties by learning a sparse code for natural images. *Nature* 381.

Olshausen BA. 2003. Principles of image representation in visual cortex. In *The visual neurosciences*, ed. LM Chalupa and JS Werner, 1603–1615. Cambridge: MIT Press.

Oren M, Papageorgiou C, Sinha P, Osuna E, Poggio T. 1997. Pedestrian detection using wavelet templates. In Proceedings of the IEEE computer society conference on computer vision and pattern recognition.

Pack CC, Gartland AJ, Born RT. 2004. Integration of contour and terminator signals in visual area MT of alert macaque. *J Neurosci* 24(13): 3268–3280.

Perrett DI, Oram MW. 1993. Neurophysiology of shape processing. *Image Vis Comput* 11(6): 317–333.

Prodoehl C, Wuertz R, von der Malsburg C. 2003. Learning the gestalt rule collinearity from object motion. *Neural Comput* 15: 1865–1896.

Pylyshyn Z, Burkell J, Fisher B, Sears C, Schmidt W, Trick L. 1994. Multiple parallel access in visual attention. *Can J Exp Psychol* 48: 60–83.

Rosenberg RD, Carey S. 2006. Infants' indexing of objects vs. non-cohesive substances [abstract]. *J Vis* 6(6): 611, 611a.

Rowley HA, Baluja S, Kanade T. 1998. Neural network-based face detection. *Pattern Anal Mach Intell* 20: 23–38.

Sinha P. 2002. Qualitative representations for recognition. Lecture notes in computer science, vol LNCS 2525, 249–262. Springer-Verlag.

Sinha P, Poggio T. 1996. Role of learning in three-dimensional form perception. *Nature* 384(6608): 460–463.

Stone JV. 1993. Computer vision: what is the object? In Proceedings of the AISB, Birmingham, AL.

Stone JV. 1998. Object recognition using spatiotemporal signatures. *Vision Res* 38: 947–951.

Stone JV. 1999. Object recognition: view-specificity and motion-specificity. *Vision Res* 39: 4032–4044.

Stone JV, Harper N. 1999. Temporal constraints on visual learning: a computational model. *Perception* 28: 1089–1104.

Sugita Y. 2008. Face perception in monkeys reared with no exposure to faces. *Proc Natl Acad Sci USA* 105: 394–398.

Tarr MJ, Pinker S. 1989. Mental rotation and orientation-dependence in shape recognition. *Cogn Psychol* 21(2): 233–282.

Ullman S. 1979. The interpretation of structure from motion. *Proc R Soc Lond B* 203: 405–426.

Ullman S. 1996. *High-level vision*. Cambridge: MIT Press.

Ullman S, Bart E. 2004. Recognition invariance obtained by extended and invariant features. *Neural Netw* 17: 833–848.

Ullman S, Vidal-Naquet M, Sali E. 2002. Visual features of intermediate complexity and their use in classification. *Nat Neurosci* 5: 682–687.

van Hateran JH, Ruderman DL. 1998. Independent component analysis of natural image sequences yields spatio-temporal filters similar to simple cells in primary visual cortex. *Proc R Soc Lond B* 265: 2315–2320.

Viola P, Jones M. 2001. Rapid object detection using a boosted cascade of simple features. Paper presented at the accepted conference on computer vision and pattern recognition.

Volkmann FE, Dobson MV. 1976. Infant responses of ocular fixation to moving visual stimuli. *J Exp Child Psychol* 22: 86–99.

Vuong QC, Tarr MJ. 2004. Rotation direction affects object recognition. *Vision Res* 44: 1717–1730.

Wallis G, Bulthoff HH. 2001. Effects of temporal association on recognition memory. *Proc Nat Acad Sci USA* 98(8): 4800–4804.

Wallraven C, Bulthoff HH. 2001. Automatic acquisition of exemplar-based representations for recognition from image sequences. In Proceedings of CVPR.

Weber M, Welling M, Perona P. 2000. Unsupervised learning of models for recognition. In Proceedings of ECCV, 18–32.

Ziliani F, Moscheni F. 1997. Kalman filtering motion prediction for recursive spatio-temporal segmentation and object tracking. In Proceedings of IEEE workshop on image analysis for multimedia interactive services, 63–68.

CHAPTER 17

Towards Integration of Different Paradigms in Modeling, Representation, and Learning of Visual Categories

Mario Fritz and Bernt Schiele

17.1 Introduction

Object representations for categorization tasks should be applicable for a wide range of objects, scalable to handle large numbers of object classes, and at the same time learnable from a few training samples. While such a scalable representation is still illusive today, it has been argued that such a representation should have at least the following properties: it should enable sharing of features (Torralba et al. 2007), it should combine generative models with discriminative models (Fritz et al. 2005; Jaakkola and Haussler 1999), and it should combine both local and global as well as appearance- and shape-based features (Leibe et al. 2005). Additionally, we argue that such object representations should be applicable both for unsupervised learning (e.g., visual object discovery) as well as supervised training (e.g., object detection). Therefore, we extend our previous efforts of hybrid modeling (Fritz et al. 2005) with ideas of unsupervised learning of generative decompositions to obtain an approach that integrates across different paradigms of modeling, representing, and learning of visual categories.

We present a novel method for the discovery and detection of visual object categories based on decompositions using topic models. The approach is capable of learning a compact and low-dimensional representation for multiple visual categories from multiple viewpoints without labeling of training instances. The learnt object components range from local structures over line segments to global silhouette-like descriptions. This representation can be used to discover object categories in a totally unsupervised fashion. Furthermore we employ the representation as the basis for building a supervised multicategory detection system making efficient use of training examples and outperforming pure features-based representations. Experiments on three databases show that the approach improves the state-of-the-art in unsupervised learning as well as supervised detection. In particular we improve the state-of-the-art on the challenging PASCAL'06 multiclass detection tasks for several categories.

Outline Existing approaches to visual categorization reveal a surprising diversity in the way they model, represent, and learn visual categories. In section 17.1.1 we will categorize previous work along these three axes. As described in section 17.1.2, this particular view on related work motivates us to develop a new approach that combines these different paradigms in a single model. We implement this idea in section 17.2 by deriving generative decompositions of visual categories that we use for unsupervised discovery of visual categories in section 17.3 and discriminative detection of visual categories in section 17.4. Finally, we show the merits of this approach on supervised as well as unsupervised task with respect to the state-of-the-art in section 17.5.

17.1.1 Approaches to Visual Categorization

This section sketches three main axes along which we categorize methods for visual categorization proposed in the literature. We are inspired by this topology of related approaches to derive methods that integrate different paradigms along the described axes. We argue in section 17.1.2 that it is important to integrate these paradigms to obtain adaptive and flexible approaches that lead to more robust and scalable systems for visual categorization.

17.1.1.1 Model Paradigm

There is a fundamental difference in models whether they describe what all category instances have in common (*generative model*) or what distinguishes them from other categories (*discriminative model*). In technical terms this boils down to the design decision if the data X associated with a training example is explicitly modeled or if the approaches focus on the class label y given the data. Often generative models are also associated with probabilistic models, as they allow for sampling from the model that exploits the generative nature. Equally, several discriminative models can be also associated with a probabilistic model as the class posterior trained in a discriminative fashion can be modeled by a probability density function $p(y|X)$. These models are often termed *conditional models*. Following common practice, we will refer to them also as *discriminative models*. More frequently people retreat to a statistical machine learning framework and seek just a discriminant function $y = f(X)$, which performs best on the prediction task without worrying about probabilistic modeling. These kind of models are commonly called *discriminative models*. For a more detailed discussion on the spectrum between generative and discriminative and the associated terminology, we refer to Jebara (2002).

Because of the many implications of choosing one of these two learning paradigms, various approaches for visual category recognition and detection have been proposed, ranging from generative, probabilistic models like Burl and Perona (1996), Fergus et al. (2003), and Leibe et al. (2004) to discriminative ones like Torralba et al. (2004), Viola and Jones (2004), and Dalal and Triggs (2005).

Benefits of Generative Models Generative models are quite appealing for various reasons in the context of object categorization. For example, those models can be learned incrementally (e.g., Skočaj and Leonardis 2003), they can deal with missing data in a principled way, and they allow for modular construction of composed solutions to complex problems and, therefore, lend themselves to hierarchical design (e.g., Fidler and Leonardis 2007). Also, prior knowledge can be easily taken into account (e.g., Fei-Fei et al. 2003). In practice generative models show considerable robustness with respect to partial occlusion and viewpoint changes and can tolerate significant intraclass variation of object appearance (Burl and Perona 1996; Fergus et al. 2003; Leibe et al. 2004). However, the price for this robustness typically is that they tend to produce a significant number of false-positives. This is particularly true for object classes that are visually similar.

Benefits of Discriminative Models Discriminative methods enable the construction of flexible decision boundaries, resulting in classification performances that are often superior to those obtained by purely probabilistic or generative models (Jaakkola and Haussler 1999; Ng and Jordan 2002; Friedman 1997). This allows for example to explicitly learn the discriminant features of one particular class versus background (Viola et al. 2003) or between multiple classes (Torralba et al. 2004; Nilsback and Caputo 2004). Object categorization algorithms that use discriminative methods combined with global and/or local representations have been shown to perform well in the presence of clutter, viewpoint changes, partial occlusion, and scale variations. Also, recent work has shown the suitability of discriminative methods for recognition of large numbers of categories Torralba et al. (2004) via the concept of sharing features across classes.

Hybrid Methods Combining Generative and Discriminative Approaches Although so far the object recognition community has in most cases chosen one of these two modeling approaches, there has been an increasing interest in the machine learning community in developing algorithms that combine the advantages of discriminative methods with those of probabilistic generative models (e.g., Jaakkola and Haussler 1999). Some prominent examples include the models of Hillel et al. (2005), Holub et al. (2005), and Fritz et al. (2005), which add a discriminative aspect on top of a generative model. Typically, these model expose the good generalization capabilities of the generative approach that lead to high recall, whereas the discriminant part leads to increased precision of the model. In sections 17.2 we will build on those ideas and add an unsupervised learning aspect to the generative part of our model.

17.1.1.2 Representation Paradigm

Feature representations based on gradient histograms have been popular and highly successful. The proposed features range from local statistics like SIFT (Lowe 2004) to global representations of entire objects (Gavrila 1998) and from sparse interest points Mikolajczyk and Schmid (2005) to dense feature responses (Dalal and Triggs 2005). In the following sections, we will outline the different choices and the associated benefits and drawbacks:

Local Representation Local feature representations are very popular and lead to a series of successful approaches for visual categorization like Burl and Perona (1996),

Leibe et al. (2008), Fergus et al. (2003), and Mikolajczyk et al. (2006). In particular the combination with probabilistic models leads to approaches with high recall due to robustness with respect to occlusion and the ability to capture the variance of visual categories well. The drawback of breaking down the images into jigsaw puzzles is that the models that describe the possible constellations are often weakly structured (e.g., bag-of-words, as in Csurka et al. 2004), simplifying (e.g., ISM model with star topology in Leibe et al. 2008; the missing interdependencies between parts can lead to hallucination of superfluous parts that correspond to fake evidence), or expensive to evaluate (e.g., constellation model in Fergus et al. 2003).

Global Representation A prominent example for global approaches are chamfer matching of silhouettes (Gavrila 1998) or the HOG representation by Dalal and Triggs (2005). In contrast to the local representation, global consistency is implicitly modeled. On the other hand, these approaches typically lose recall because of the inflexible structure and the missing capability of sharing information across object instances. Often these kinds of models have to pay for their rigid approach with large amounts of training data to capture object variations in a more explicit fashion.

Semilocal Representation Mohan et al. (2001) proposed to detect part structures by local histograms first, which are combined to object detections afterward. In order to not define the subparts manually, Laptev (2006) constructs a representation on random subcrops. This is an extension of the method of Levi and Weiss (2004). A boosting method is used to select a representation most suited for the task.

Shape-based approaches also have recently received a lot of attention, as they provide a first abstraction level from the image gradients and are capable of representing elongated structures as edges as well as more localized features like corners. In particular, progress in the edge-detection procedure (Martin et al. 2004) and description of edge structures (Ferrari et al. 2008) revived the discussion.

Sparse Features Sparse feature representations like SIFT (Lowe 2004) have been very successful. They are based on methods to select distinctive points in the image. Only these selected points are represented and considered for further processing. Typically, the selection is based on local maxima detection of an interest function that responds to edge- or corner-like structures (Mikolajczyk and Schmid 2005). Besides achieving data reduction, the development of scale-invariant interest points (Lindeberg 1998), invariance w.r.t. rotation, and affine deformations (Mikolajczyk and Schmid 2002), as well as robustness to partial object occlusion, spurred the success of these approaches.

Dense Representation Studies have shown that sparse representations are inferior to a denser sampling in terms of system performance (Nowak et al. 2006). Although the difference might by less pronounced for some categories, objects in which the interest point detector fails to capture a sufficient statistic are better captured by random sampling or sampling on a regular grid.

In particular as machine learning methods made good progress in handling large amounts of data, dealing with noise, and extracting the relevant information, combination with dense feature representation has led to state-of-the-art recognition and detection approaches like Dalal and Triggs (2005).

17.1.1.3 Learning Paradigm

Over the last years, various approaches have been proposed for learning of object categories by gathering statistics from training data. The approaches, however, vary greatly in the amount of supervision that has to be provided for training. The types of annotation varies from pixel-level segmentations (e.g., Leibe et al. 2008), bounding-box annotations (e.g., Viola and Jones 2001), and image level annotation (e.g., Fergus et al. 2003; Winn and Jojic 2005) to unsupervised methods (e.g., Weber et al. 2000; Sivic et al. 2005; Fergus et al. 2005) that do not even require information about which category is presented in which image. Although approaches that use more supervision tend to require fewer training data, there is a clear desire to use less supervision, typically at the price of more unlabeled training data.

Supervised Learning Traditionally, providing more annotation information results in better performance given the same amount of training data. Besides bounding-box information (Viola and Jones 2001), approaches have shown to successfully exploit pixel-wise segmentations (Leibe et al. 2008) or viewpoint annotations (Chum and Zisserman 2007) to increase performance.

Weakly Supervised Learning Weakly supervised learning typically denotes learning from an image-level annotation of the presence or absence of the object category. Learning object models in this fashion may be formulated in one EM-loop as in Weber et al. 2000, for example. In this method, appearance and structure are learned simultaneously, making the learning computationally expensive and thus restricting the complexity of the model. More recently, weakly supervised approaches were derived by finding frequent item sets (Quack et al. 2007), substructure mining (Nowozin et al. 2007), or discovery of recurring patterns (Fritz and Schiele 2006), leading to more computational efficiency.

Unsupervised Learning Unsupervised learning is very attractive, as the annotation effort and biases introduced by the human labeling process become increasingly problematic for large training sets with many classes (Ponce et al. 2006). As today's internet-based services provide image data in abundance, learning in an unsupervised fashion provides a promising alternative to these problems. As those data sources typically return lots of unrelated images (Fergus et al. 2005) and images of poor quality, these method have to be robust against outliers and a large variety of image degradations (e.g., Fergus et al. 2005; Li et al. 2007; Schroff et al. 2007). Recently, a variety of approaches have been proposed that are based on topic models such as pLSA (Hofmann 2001) or LDA (Blei et al. 2003). Since the underlying model is a bag-of-word representation, the object discovery is based on local appearance alone, and neglects structural information (Sivic et al. 2005). Fergus et al. (2005), Russell et al. (2006), and Cao and Fei-Fei (2007) extend the initial approach to also include some structural information on top of the pLSA model.

Semi-Supervised Learning Semi-supervised learning has recently gained a lot of interest in the machine learning literature, as it combines the unsupervised approach with supervised information to overcome the inherent limitation of fully data-driven approaches. For an overview, we refer to Zhu (2005) and Chapelle et al. (2006). In the vision community, the impact of these approaches has been less prominent up to now. But approaches like Holub et al. (2008) and, in particular, extension toward active learning, as in Kapoor et al. (2007), seem promising.

17.1.2 Towards Integration Across Paradigms

The previous section has spanned a space of design choices that represent a particular view on previous work. Many approaches make very particular design choices in how they address the modeling, representation, and learning challenges in visual categorization. As we have discussed, each paradigm has its particular pros and cons. Understanding the merits and drawbacks inherent to these paradigms leads us to the conclusion that committing to a single paradigm in any of these three axes won't be sufficient to cope with the overwhelming variety encountered in visual categorization. We therefore promote approaches that integrate different paradigms along these three axes. Having scalability in the number of categories in mind, we address this challenge in a learning-based manner that results in approaches that are more flexible and can adapt to the particularities of the individual object classes.

Combining Generative and Discriminative Section 17.2 derives a generative decomposition of visual category instances based on a representation of localized gradients. The latent space implied by the learned components builds the foundation of our approach to unsupervised discovery as well as supervised detection. For the supervised detection task, we complement the generative decomposition by a discriminative classifier to leverage the intermediate representation. The experiments underline the benefit of combining these two views on the data.

Combining Local and Global A closer examination of the components learned by the generative decomposition will reveal an interesting result. By not enforcing any spatial constraints and only relying on the co-occurrence statistic in the data, we are able to learn components that range from local structures over line segments to global silhouette-like descriptions. As our model interprets each observation in terms of these components, we have indeed attained a learning-based approach that covers the whole range from local to global paradigms.

Combining Unsupervised and Supervised As we do not provide any supervision in terms of the category label while learning the generative decomposition, we can address unsupervised as well as supervised settings equally. The representation builds a common ground for both tasks. Even in the supervised detection task, we leverage the unsupervised learning aspect that allows for sharing of information across classes that results in improved learning as well as benefits in terms of scalability (see also Torralba et al. 2007).

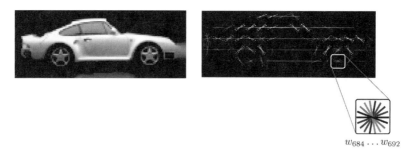

$w_{684} \cdots w_{692}$

Figure 17.1. Dense gradient histogram representation. The loupe shows the nine possible edge orientations of the histogram bins that are interpreted as words. (See color plate 17.1.)

17.2 Generative Decomposition of Visual Categories

In this section, we describe our approach to decomposition of multiple visual categories by combining dense localized gradient representations and probabilistic topic models. Starting from the image, we first present our data representation. Then we describe how we apply the topic model to this representation and provide visualizations and insights for the obtained model.

17.2.1 Data Representation

Inspired by Dalal and Triggs (2005), we compute gradients on each color channel of the images and use the maximum response to obtain a grid of histograms that overlays the image. Each histogram in the grid has nine orientation bins equally spaced from $0°$ to $180°$ to represent the unsigned gradient orientation. An example of such an encoding is visualized in Figure 17.1. In each cell, the nine possible edge orientations associated with the orientation bins are displayed by short lines. The grayscale value encodes the accumulated gradient magnitude in each bin. The size of the cells in the grid is 8×8 pixels.

As the following topic models operate on discrete word counts, we normalize the histograms to have a constant sum of discrete entries. We decided not to compute a redundant coding like the blocks in the HOG descriptor of Dalal and Triggs (2005), as we believe that the introduced nonlinearities by local normalization would hinder the fitting of the probabilistic model.

17.2.2 Probabilistic Topic Models of Localized Gradients

Figure 17.2 visualizes the kind of decompositions we are aiming at. On the left, a bicycle example is depicted with its representation in localized gradients. On the right, we have decomposed the object into activations θ of subcomponents depicted in the rectangles. As we do not know either activations or components, we face a challenging learning problem. To relax this rather ill-conditioned learning problem and to obtain a more robust estimate, we consider a sparsity prior on the coefficients as well as on the components themselves.

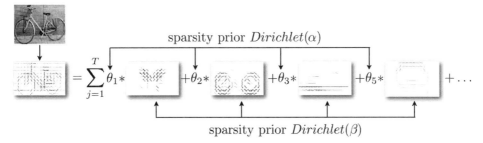

Figure 17.2. Localized, oriented gradient distributions of object instances are represented by a mixture model of latent components. The model is learnt in an LDA framework with sparsity priors on the components as well as the corresponding activation coefficients.

For the coefficients we seek sparsity, as our component set will encode multiple categories that share only a certain subset of components with each other; therefore, we expect each instance to activate only a subset of the available components. For example, we do not expect the bicycle instance to activate the component 5 in Figure 17.2, which is highly activated for car back views.

For the components, we also seek sparsity, as we are interested in a decomposition in substructures. Dense components do not facilitate sharing of compact substructures and are likely to degenerate to a simple clustering approach. However, as we are only setting a prior, our learning setting can still extract larger structures, if the data and the associated co-occurrence statistic advocates it.

To define a generative process for our data that fits these needs, we employ probabilistic topic models from Hofmann (2001), Blei et al. (2003), and Griffiths and Steyvers (2004) that were originally motivated in the context of text analysis. As it is common habit, we adopt the terminology of this domain. In the following, a document d refers to a sequence of words $(w_1, w_2, \ldots, w_{N_d})$, where each w_i is one word occurrence. The underlying idea of these models is to regard each document as a mixture of topics. This means that each word w_i of the total N_d words in document d is generated by first sampling a topic z_i from a multinomial topic distribution $P(z)$ and then sampling a word from a multinomial topic-word distribution $P(w|z)$. Therefore, the word probabilities for the combined model are:

$$P(w_i) = \sum_{j=1}^{T} P(w_i|z_i = j)P(z_i = j), \qquad (17.1)$$

where T is the number of topics and $P(w_i|z_i = j)$ as well as $P(z_i = j)$ are unobserved. According to the notation of Griffiths and Steyvers (2004), we will abbreviate

$$\theta^{(d)}\text{: topic distribution } P(z) \text{ for document } d$$
$$\phi^{(j)}\text{: topic-word distribution } P(w_i|z = j) \text{ for topic } j$$

The particular topic models differ in which additional hyperparameters/priors they introduce and in how inference and parameter estimation is performed. We will discuss the *Latent Dirichlet Allocation* model of Blei et al. (2003) in some more detail, focusing on the version presented in Griffiths and Steyvers (2004) that uses Gibbs sampling for inference and estimation. The graphical representation of this model is depicted in

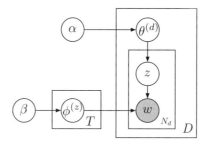

Figure 17.3. Latent Dirichlet Allocation model. Adapted from Griffiths and Steyvers 2004.

Figure 17.3. It visualizes the process that generates a total of D documents d, where each document has N_d words. We already described how each word w_i of a particular document is generated. In the full model, there are two additional hyperparameters, α and β, which place symmetric dirichlet priors on the topic distribution of each document $\theta^{(d)}$ and the topic-word distributions $\phi^{(j)}$, respectively. As the setting for α and β is common to all documents, these act as forces that impose global tendencies on these distributions. Intuitively, the prior α for the topic distribution θ favors co-activation (sharing) of multiple topics for each document for values larger than 1, whereas smaller values result in sparser topic distribution, ultimately having single topics explaining whole documents (clustering). Consequently, the sparseness of the topic-word distribution $\phi^{(j)}$ is affected by this choice. The second parameter β has a direct smoothing effect on the topic distributions.

For more details on the models, inference, and estimation, we refer to Blei et al. (2003) and Steyvers and Griffiths (2007). The idea behind the employed Gibbs sampling procedure is that all topic assignments z_i are initialized (typically randomly) and then iteratively updated in a random order. To perform such a single update, a topic is drawn from the conditional distribution $P(z_i | \Omega \setminus z_i)$ and assigned to z_i, where $\Omega \setminus z_i$ denotes all observed and unobserved variables but z_i. This is repeated for a fixed number of iterations.

17.3 Unsupervised Discovery of Visual Categories

In this section we describe how the representation from section 17.2.1 is linked to the generative model from section 17.2.2 and perform a quantitative evaluation on an unsupervised learning task.

We use the orientation bins of the histograms described in section 17.2.1 as word vocabulary in section 17.2.2. For histograms computed on a m by n grid with b bins for each orientation histogram, our vocabulary is of size $|V| = m \cdot n \cdot b$. As each word is associated with a gradient orientation at a grid location, this representation preserves quantized spatial information of the original gradients. The topic model is trained on the documents given the encoded training examples. The representations that we promote are given by the topic activations of the document in the latent space.

Table 17.1. *Comparison to other approaches on re-ranking task of Google images. Performance is measured in precision at 15% recall. In contrast to the other methods, our approach does not use any validation set*

	Airplane	Cars Rear	Face	Guitar	Leopard	Motorbike	Wrist Watch	Average
Out method	100%	83%	100%	91%	65%	97%	100%	91%
Fergus Fergus et al. (2005)	57%	77%	82%	50%	59%	72%	88%	69%
Schroff Schroff et al. (2007)	35%	–	–	29%	50%	63%	93%	54%

To prove the effectiveness of our representations and to compare our work with previous approaches, we first present quantitative results on the unsupervised ranking task of Fergus et al. (2005) and then provide further insights connected to the multiclass data we use in section 17.5.3.

17.3.1 Google Re-ranking Task

Previously, Sivic et al. (2005) used topic models on local feature representations for unsupervised learning. Fergus et al. (2005) extended their approach to encode spatial information. As the latter can be seen as the sparse counterpart to our dense representation, we compare on the unsupervised image re-ranking task specified in Fergus et al. (2005). The provided datasets are results of image Google queries. The task is to re-rank the images so that relevant ones appear first. The main challenge is to extract the relevant information that is hidden in an image set containing up to 70% junk images in an unsupervised fashion. Given that our representation effectively encodes the object structures, we expect our data to live in compact subspaces of the latent space. Therefore, we perform k-means clustering on the activations and consecutively accept the clusters with the most samples. The precision we obtain in this manner at 15% recall is shown in Table 17.1 and compared to our competitors. The average precision of 69% obtained by Fergus et al. (2005) and 54% obtained by Schroff et al. (2007) is surpassed by our approach, which obtains an average precision of 91%. This performance is obtained without using the provided validation set that the other two approaches use. Although our method performs worst on the leopard data, we still improve over Fergus et al. (2005). This is surprising, as one would have suspected that the local feature-based approach is more suited to encode the spotted texture of these animals. We attribute the success of our method to the added expressiveness by enabling the discovery of reoccurring contour fragments and edge segment-like structures. Because of the dense and localized nature of our input features, we are more flexible to adapt to the object outline and to neglect background information. Figure 17.4 shows some topics from the presented experiment that expose these characteristics. Furthermore, in contrast to local feature-based methods, our representation can easily be visualized (Fig. 17.4), which lends itself to interaction and inspection by a user.

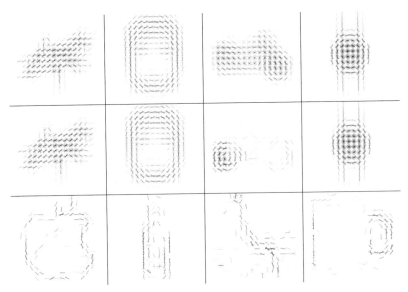

Figure 17.4. *First row*, Example topics of 8-topic model for classes airplane, face, motorbike, watch. *Second row*, Example topics of 50-topic model for the same classes. *Third row*, Example topics of 100-topic model jointly learned on apple-logos, bottles, giraffes, mugs, and swans.

17.3.2 Object Class Discovery

To extend our findings to the detection task that we are aiming for in section 17.5.3, we extract our representation on the multicategory, multiview PASCAL'06 dataset (Everingham et al. 2006), in order to obtain a decomposition that is shared across categories.

In the first row of Figure 17.5, 13 of 100 topic distributions are visualized that were trained on the bounding-box annotations of the training and validation data of the PASCAL'06 challenge. The rows below display the examples that most activated this particular topic. We observe that the topics capture different levels of objects, ranging from global silhouettes (car rear in column 10 and side view in column 13) over localized parts (legs in column 3, bicycle frame in column 8, and bicycle wheels in column 12) to line segments and corners (corner in column 1, and line segments in column 2 and 4). The model discovers distinctive parts that even separate several examples of different categories and their viewpoints, although no such information was available to the system during training. Importantly, we can see that other topics like those that got activated on legs are shared across several categories, which is a desirable property of a compact decomposition in order to be scalable Torralba et al. (2007).

To illustrate that this is indeed an appropriate and effective approach to capture the variety of the data and to stress the power of modeling combinations of these discovered topics, we cluster the topic distributions as proposed in the last paragraph. Figure 17.6 shows in each row the 10 cluster members that are closest to the cluster center of all of the 50 cluster centers. Keeping in mind that they are obtained in an entirely unsupervised fashion, the clusters turn out to be surprisingly clean.

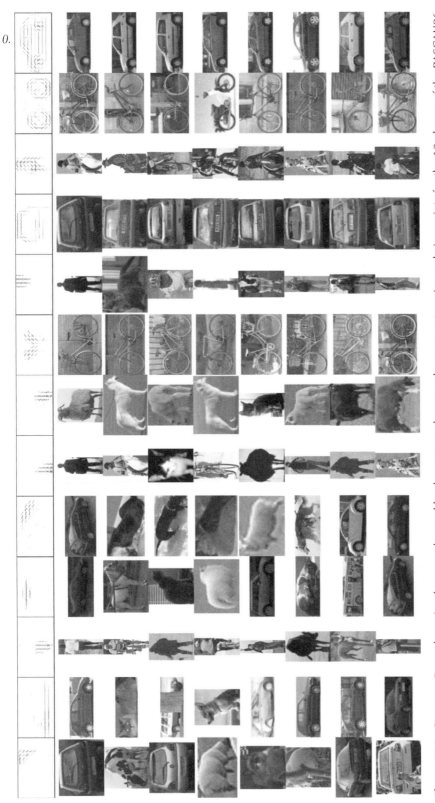

Figure 17.5. *First row,* Example topics that were learned by the proposed approach across categories and viewpoints for the 10 classes of the PASCAL'06 data. *Below first row,* Training images that activated the topic above most. The topics model local structures, line segments, and silhouette-like structures. The topics are distinctive enough to separate several category members and even viewpoints. On the other hand, they are general enough to be shared across categories and viewpoints.

335

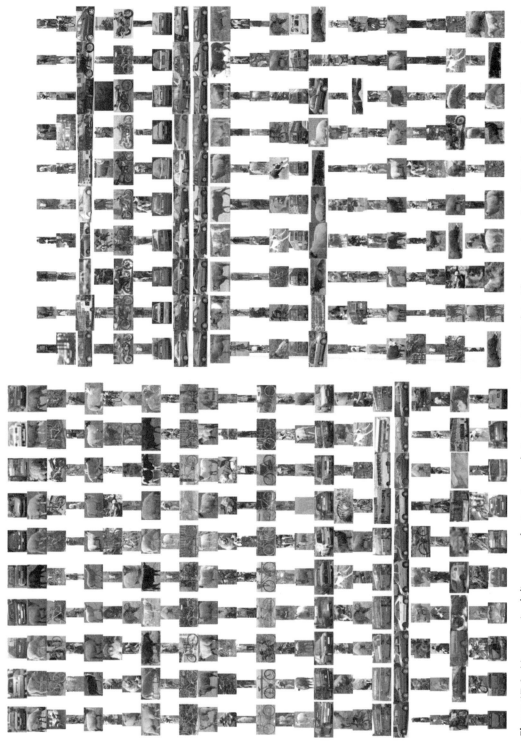

Figure 17.6. Unsupervised discovery of categories and viewpoints in PASCAL'06 data. The rows show for all 50 clusters those 10 examples that are closest to the cluster center. The *left block* visualizes the clusters 1 to 25, and the *right block* visualizes the clusters 26 to 50.

We interpret these findings as strong evidence that our model indeed captures an effective and low-dimensional representation for this difficult multicategory detection task.

17.4 Discriminative Detection of Visual Categories

Based on the promising results on unsupervised learning in the last section, this section describes a complete system for supervised multicategory detection that leverages the learned representation.

17.4.1 Generative/Discriminative Training

Recently, the combination of generative approaches with discriminative ones has shown to be very effective (Jaakkola and Haussler 1999; Fritz et al. 2005). The idea is that generative models can easily incorporate prior information to support learning from small samples, have increased robustness to noise, and generally have more principled ways of dealing with missing data. Discriminative models, on the other hand, have shown to give superior performance for well-posed learning tasks and a sufficient number of training examples. We also follow this idea and complement the generative model described in section 17.2.2 by a discriminative SVM classifier with an RBF kernel (Chang and Lin 2001). In particular, we train an SVM to discriminate between the topic distributions $\theta^{(d)}$, which are inferred for images containing the category of interest and others that do not contain these. By doing so, we seek to profit from the aforementioned benefits of the generative model combined with the discriminative classifier.

17.4.2 Sliding-Window Approach to Detection

As proposed in Dalal and Triggs (2005), a sliding-window approach can be done efficiently in this setting if the sliding window is always shifted by exactly one cell in x or y direction. In this case, the gradient histograms of the cell grid are computed once, and for each sliding window, the relevant subgrid is used.

Typically, sliding-window techniques not only assign a high score for the correct location and scale in an image, but also for test windows that have a small offset in space and scale. We use a simple greedy scheme to cope with this issue: Although there are unprocessed windows in an image, we accept the one with the highest score and reject all other windows that fulfill the symmetric overlap criterion

$$\max\left(\frac{A_i \cap A_j}{A_i}, \frac{A_i \cap A_j}{A_j}\right) > 0.3 \qquad (17.2)$$

where A_i and A_j are the areas covered by the two windows. As the bounding-box scores from our approach turn out to be surprisingly consistent over different scales, this basic scheme has proven to work well in our setting.

Of course a multiscale detection task ranging over multiple octaves requires the investigation of large number of test windows typically more than 10,000 per image.

While feature extraction and SVM classification are fast, our approach requires inference in the topic model for each test window, rendering the method computationally infeasible for applications of interest. Therefore, we dedicate the following section to describe speed-ups that make our approach applicable to large databases.

17.4.3 Speed-ups: Linear Topic Response and Early Rejection

Although we use the Gibbs sampling method of Griffiths and Steyvers (2004) to estimate the model, we use the variational inference method described in Blei et al. (2003) for testing, for it turns out to be computationally more efficient given our setting. For more substantial improvements, we propose to compute a linear topic response to get an initial estimate on the topic activations. The aim is to avoid the more expensive inference scheme by performing an early rejection of the test windows. Unlike to linear methods like PCA, in which there is linear dependency between the feature space and the coefficient space, the mixture coefficients of the topic distribution have to be fitted to the observation. This means that each word/feature can be associated to different topics depending on its context (presence of other features) and, therefore, can also lead to strengthening or inhibition of other topic activations. This requires an iterative technique to find the best reconstruction. Therefore, we ask how important is this iterative fitting and how much performance do we lose by reverting to the following simple, linear approximation of the dependency between observed feature histogram x and topic activations $\theta^{(d)}$:

$$\tilde{\theta}^{(d)} = \left(\phi^{(1)} \ldots \phi^{(T)}\right)^t x, \qquad (17.3)$$

In fact, our results on the UIUC single-scale database show that there is a significant loss of about 8% in equal error rate performance (see section 17.5.2), but a more detailed analysis on the UIUC multiscale database reveals interesting results. Although the linear approximation might be quite coarse, it can still be used for early rejection of test windows. It turns out that full recall is achieved for the 2500 highest scored windows of a total of 2.826.783. Consequently, more than 99.9% of the test windows can be handled by the linear computation that we measured to be 166 times faster than the proper inference. Taking all optimizations together, we can cut down the computation time by a factor of 180 which corresponds to an reduction from 1 hour to around 20 seconds per image (AMD Opteron 270 (Dual-Core), 2.0 GHz).

17.5 Experiments

This section is divided into four parts. First, we show that our approach makes efficient use of the provided training examples by comparing to a baseline experiment on the UIUC single-scale car database. Second, we evaluate different methods for estimation of the topic model on the UIUC multiscale database and compare the obtained performance to previous work. Third, we present results on the PASCAL Challenge 2006 data that outperform the state-of-the-art on three of the ten categories. Fourth, we compare to a shape-based approach on the ETH-shape database to underline the versatility and adaptivity of our approach.

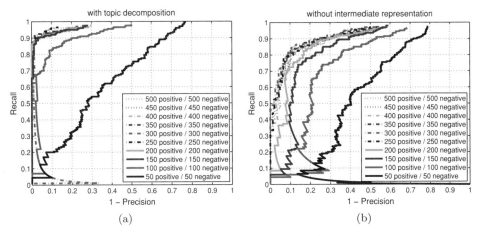

Figure 17.7. (a) and (b), Comparison of learning curve for proposed intermediate representation versus SVM on pure features on UIUC single-scale database. (See color plate 17.7.)

17.5.1 Efficient Use of Training Examples and Parameter Selection

To select parameters appropriate to our problem domain, we run detection experiments on the UIUC single-scale car database, which consists of a training set of 550 car and 500 background images of small size, and a test set that has 170 images showing side views of cars in street scenes at a fixed scale. It turns out that the heuristic specified in Steyvers and Griffiths (2007) for selecting the hyperparameters α and β works very well for our setting. Therefore, we use $\alpha = 50/\#topics$ and $\beta = 0.01$. We obtain best performance using 30 topics and a grid size of 16×6 for the gradient histograms.

To show that our approach makes efficient use of the provided training examples, we compare to a baseline experiment that does not use the proposed representation. Figures 17.7(a) and 17.7(b) show the precision-recall curves of our system, when trained on different numbers of positive and negative examples. We start with 50 car and 50 background images and increase by 50 until we use the full training dataset. The maximum performance is reached rapidly using only 150 positive and 150 negative examples. In contrast, the linear SVM trained on the same data representation but without our representation has a much slower learning curve. In fact the performance is 9.5% below the equal error rate of our new approach using 250 positive and 250 negative examples. We also tried RBF kernels, but obtained similar, inferior results.

We attribute this significant improvement to the generative properties of our model inferring a generative decomposition of the presented data. We conclude that this low-dimensional representation simplifies the learning problem for the discriminative SVM classifier, which leads to more efficient use of training examples.

17.5.2 Comparison of Methods for Estimation and Evaluation of Approximate Inference

In this section we test the model that we trained for the UIUC single-scale database on the multiscale version and compare different estimation schemes for the topic model during training (Blei et al. 2003; Griffiths and Steyvers 2004). We also evaluate the

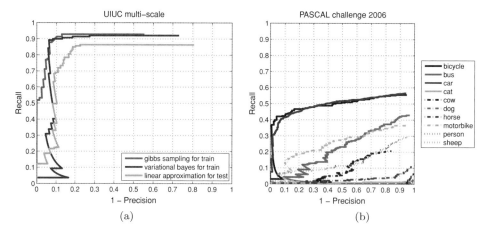

Figure 17.8. (a) Performance on UIUC multiscale dataset using topic model estimated via Gibbs sampling versus variational Bayes approach compared to using pseudotopic activations. (b) Precision-recall curves on the PASCAL VOC challenge 2006. Precision-recall curves and example detections. (See color plate 17.8.)

linear topic activations for testing that we proposed in section 17.4.3. The results are reported in Figure 17.8(a). The estimation method based on Gibbs sampling Griffiths and Steyvers (2004) leads to a performance similar to that of the variational inference method of Blei et al. (2003) when evaluated in the whole system, but shows better precision. We notice that the automatic selection of α that we use for the variational approach converged to a value of 0.373, which enforces less co-activation and therefore less sharing of topics. By visual inspection of the topic-distributions, we confirmed that the method of Blei et al. (2003) learned more global topics, whereas the ones obtained by the Gibbs sampling method tend to be a little sparser. We believe that for detection tasks, the second is to be preferred, because global representations can be mislead more easily by effects like occlusion, as it is also supported by our results.

Replacing the proper inference with the linear approximation (section 17.4.3) results in the third curve which is displayed in Figure 17.8(a). This confirms the importance and superiority of the proper inference in comparison to linear topic activations. For this comparison we use nonmaxima suppression in combination with the linear approximation scheme while it is switched off when used for early rejection to achieve maximum recall.

The best results obtained by the Gibbs sampling approach with an equal error performance of 90.6% outperform Fritz et al. (2005) and are on par with the results in Mutch and Lowe (2006). The best performances on this dataset have been reported by Wu and Nevatia (2007), with 93.5%, and Mikolajczyk et al. (2006), with 94.7, in which the latter used a different training set.

17.5.3 Comparison to State-of-the-Art on PASCAL'06 VOC Detection Challenge

We evaluate our approach on the third competition of the PASCAL challenge 2006 (Everingham et al. 2006) that poses a much harder detection problem, as 10 visual categories are to be detected from multiple viewpoints over a large scale range.

Table 17.2. *Average Precision Achieved on the PASCAL'06 Database*

Bicycle	Bus	Car	Cat	Cow	Dog	Horse	Motorbike	Person	Sheep
49.75%	25.83%	50.07%	9.09%	15.63%	4.55%	9.40%	27.43%	0.98%	17.22%

We leave the hyperparameters untouched but increase the number of topics to 100 and adapt the aspect ratio of the grid to 16×10. To reduce confusion between categories and the number of false-positives, we adapt a bootstrapping strategy. First we train an initial model for each category versus the other categories. This model is then used to generate false-positives on the training set (see also Osuna et al. 1997; Fritz et al. 2005; Dalal and Triggs 2005). Up to 500 of the strongest false detection are added for each detector to its training set, and the model is retrained. The average precisions of the final detector of all 10 categories on the test set are shown in Table 17.2, and the corresponding precision-recall curves are plotted in Figure 17.8(b). Figure 17.9 shows some example detections of the system.

We outperform all other competitors in the three categories bicycle, bus, and car by improving the state-of-the-art (Everingham et al. 2006) on this dataset by 5.75%, 9.14%, and 5.67% in average precision, respectively. In particular we surpass the fully global approach of Dalal and Triggs (2005) that our method was motivated by. Compared to Chum and Zisserman (2007), we improve on bicycles and bus only by 0.65% and 0.93%, but again significantly on cars with 8.87%. However, in contrast to Chum and Zisserman (2007) we do not use the viewpoint annotations to train our approach. For the other categories, we perform about average, but also showed some inferior results

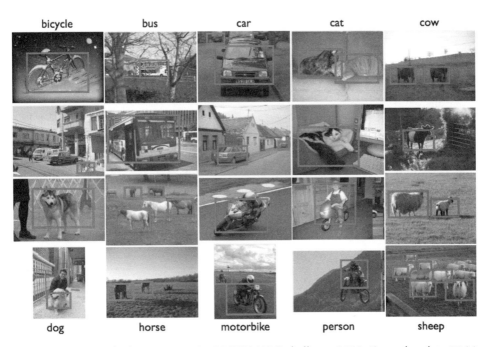

Figure 17.9. Example detections on the PASCAL VOC challenge 2006. (See color plate 17.9.)

Table 17.3. *Comparison against shape-based approach of Ferrari et al. (2007) on ETH shape database. Average detection-rate at 0.4 false-positives per image averaged over five-fold. Standard deviation is specified in brackets*

	Applelogos	Bottles	Giraffes	Mugs	Swans	Average
Our method	89.9% (4.5)	76.8% (6.1)	90.5% (5.4)	82.7% (5.1)	84.0% (8.4)	84.8%
Ferrari et al. (2007)	83.2% (1.7)	83.2% (7.5)	58.6% (14.6)	83.6% (8.6)	75.4% (13.4)	76.8%

on the highly articulated categories. We are currently investigating means to make the approach less rigid and carry over the good results from the first three categories to the other ones.

17.5.4 Comparison to Shape Features on ETH Shape Database

As pointed out in the previous experiments, our representation learns features with different characteristics, from local to global, and is also particularly capable of modeling contours. Therefore, we ask how our representation compares to shape-based approaches. We compare to Ferrari et al. (2007) on the ETH shape database using the same detection system with the same settings as described in the last section. Example topics that were learned across the five classes are depicted in Figure 17.4. Using fivefold cross-validation, as proposed in Ferrari et al. (2007), we obtain the results presented in Table 17.3. Averaged over all classes we improve the performance of Ferrari et al. (2007) by 8.0% to 84.8%. On apple logos, giraffes, and swans, we improve the performance by 6.7%, 31.9%, and 8.6%, respectively. On mugs our approach performs comparable and on bottles it looses 6.4%. We attribute the worst performance on the bottles to the shape, which is less discriminative with respect to the background. Some example detections are shown in Figure 17.10. Note how the objects are well localized and the approach even detects a half visible mug that is not annotated (third image, top row). As the database was designed to test shape-based approaches, the improvements obtained by our approach underline the versatility and adaptivity of the learned representation.

Figure 17.10. Example detections on the ETH shape database. (See color plate 17.10.)

17.6 Conclusion

We present a novel method that leverages the combination of different paradigms of modeling, representing, and learning visual categories. We showed that the approach is capable of representing multiple categories from multiple viewpoints and successfully employs it in various settings, ranging from unsupervised learning to supervised detection tasks. In various experiments, our approach shows superior performance with respect to purely local, shape-based, or global approaches. In particular, we outperformed hand-crafted approaches like the one for shape-based representation. Our method has proven effective and efficient in showing an increased learning curve in the detection setting. Beyond the modeling aspects, we pay particular attention to computational feasibility, which enables scalability to large databases. Lastly, we want to highlight the results on the challenging PASCAL'06 dataset, where we improve the state-of-the-art on three categories, to underline our contribution to category modeling in the context of a complete detection system.

Despite our progress, we see the need to make our approaches even more flexible and look for a tighter integration. Because scalability is one of the main challenges in a number of categories, the following issues seem to be some of the most pressing:

Modeling Outlook In terms of modeling there is a clear need to structure information on visual categories in some hierarchical or at least sparse graph-based structure. Otherwise, sustainable scalability is hardly imaginable. While promising methods to learn such structures have been proposed (Fidler and Leonardis 2007; Sivic et al. 2008), lots of computational as well as conceptual challenges remain. How to advance the combination of generative and discriminative approaches to these hierarchical structures has yet to be investigated.

Representation Outlook Although in this chapter the range between local and global representation was only covered in terms of features derived from image gradient histogram, there are clearly many more ways of encoding image information. In accordance with our argumentation, recent results (Varma and Ray 2007) underline the importance of drawing from a large pool of features so that cues can be selected to best describe what constitutes a certain category. Although approaches typically leverage discriminative information to determine cue importances, this leads to approaches that do not scale well. How to draw from a rich feature set and still maintain scalability is an open challenge.

Learning Outlook Although we managed to incorporate some unsupervised learning in our discriminative detection process, we want to aim for methods that are capable of tapping into all sorts of supervision. Active learning approaches (Kapoor et al. 2007; Holub et al. 2008) seem to be particularly promising for overcoming the inherent limitation of fully unsupervised approaches, while maintaining high effectiveness in the labeling process. Besides the conceptual challenges, we also face difficulties in evaluation and comparison of different approaches, because these greatly diverge from the traditional batch processing.

Bibliography

Blei D, Ng A, Jordan M. 2003. Latent dirichlet allocation. *J Mach Learn Res* 3.

Burl MC, Perona P. 1996. Recognition of planar object classes. In IEEE conference on computer vision and pattern recognition (CVPR'96), 223, San Francisco, CA, USA. IEEE Computer Society.

Cao L, Fei-Fei L. 2007. Spatially coherent latent topic model for concurrent object segmentation and classification. In IEEE international conference on computer vision (ICCV'07), Rio de Janeiro, Brazil, IEEE Computer Society.

Chang CC, Lin CJ. 2001. LIBSVM: a library for support vector machines. Software available at http://www.csie.ntu.edu.tw/~cjlin/libsvm.

Chapelle O, Schölkopf B, Zien A. 2006. *Semi-supervised learning*. Cambridge: MIT Press.

Chum O, Zisserman A. 2007. An exemplar model for learning object classes. In IEEE conference on computer vision and pattern recognition (CVPR'07), Minneapolis, Minnesota, USA. IEEE Computer Society.

Csurka G, Dance C, Fan L, Willarnowski J, Bray C. 2004. Visual categorization with bags of keypoints. In SLCV'04, 59–74, Prague, Czech Republic.

Dalal N, Triggs B. 2005. Histograms of oriented gradients for human detection. In IEEE international conference on computer vision (ICCV'05), Beijing, China. IEEE Computer Society.

Everingham M, Zisserman A, Williams CKI, Van Gool L. 2006. The PASCAL Visual Object Classes Challenge 2006 (VOC2006) Results. http://www.pascal-network.org/challenges/VOC/voc2006/results.pdf.

Fei-Fei L, Fergus R, Perona P. 2003. A Bayesian approach to unsupervised one-shot learning of object categories. In IEEE international conference on computer vision (ICCV'03), 1134–1141, Nice, France. IEEE Computer Society.

Fergus R, Zisserman A, Perona P. 2003. Object class recognition by unsupervised scale-invariant learning. In IEEE conference on computer vision and pattern recognition (CVPR'03), Madison, WI, USA. IEEE Computer Society.

Fergus R, Fei-Fei L, Perona P, Zisserman A. 2005. Learning object categories from google's image search. In IEEE international conference on computer vision (ICCV'05), Beijing, China. IEEE Computer Society.

Ferrari V, Fevrier L, Jurie F, Schmid C. 2007. Accurate object detection with deformable shape models learnt from images. In IEEE conference on computer vision and pattern recognition (CVPR'07), Minneapolis, Minnesota, USA. IEEE Computer Society.

Ferrari V, Fevrier L, Jurie F, Schmid C. 2008. Groups of adjacent contour segments for object detection. *IEEE Trans Pattern Anal Mach Intell* (in press).

Fidler S, Leonardis A. 2007. Towards scalable representations of object categories: learning a hierarchy of parts. In IEEE conference on computer vision and pattern recognition (CVPR'07), Minneapolis, Minnesota, USA. IEEE Computer Society.

Friedman JH. 1997. On bias, variance, 0/1–loss, and the curse-of-dimensionality. *Data Min Knowl Discov* 1(1): 55–77.

Fritz M, Leibe B, Caputo B, Schiele B. 2005. Integrating representative and discriminant models for object category detection. In IEEE international conference on computer vision (ICCV'05), Beijing, China. IEEE Computer Society.

Fritz M, Schiele B. 2006. Towards unsupervised discovery of visual categories. In DAGM symposium for pattern recognition (DAGM'06), Berlin, Germany.

Gavrila D. 1998. Multi-feature hierarchical template matching using distance transforms. In International conference on pattern recognition (ICPR'98), vol 1, 439–444.

Griffiths TL, Steyvers M. 2004. Finding scientific topics. PNAS USA.

Hillel AB, Hertz T, Weinshall D. 2005. Efficient learning of relational object class models. In IEEE international conference on computer vision (ICCV'05), Beijing, China. IEEE Computer Society.

Hofmann T. 2001. Unsupervised learning by probabilistic latent semantic analysis. *Mach Learn* 42.

Holub AD, Wellling M, Perona P. 2005. Combining generative models and fisher kernels for object recognition. In IEEE international conference on computer vision (ICCV'05), Beijing, China. IEEE Computer Society.

Holub AD, Welling M, Perona P. 2008. Hybrid generative-discriminative visual categorization. *Int J Comput Vis,* 77(1–3): 239–258.

Jaakkola TS, Haussler D. 1999. Exploiting generative models in discriminative classifiers. In Proceedings of the 1998 conference on advances in neural information processing systems II, 487–493. Cambridge: MIT Press.

Jebara T. 2002. Discriminative, generative and imitative learning. PhD diss, MIT, 2002. Supervisor, AP Pentland.

Kapoor A, Grauman K, Urtasun R, Darrell T. 2007. Active learning with gaussian processes for object categorization. In IEEE international conference on computer vision (ICCV'07), Rio de Janeiro, Brazil. IEEE Computer Society.

Laptev I. 2006. Improvements of object detection using boosted histograms. In British machine vision conference (BMVC'06), Edinburgh, UK. British Machine Vision Association.

Leibe B, Leonardis A, Schiele B. 2004. Combined object categorization and segmentation with an implicit shape model. In SLCV'04, 17–32, Prague, Czech Republic.

Leibe B, Leonardis A, Schiele B. 2008. Robust object detection with interleaved categorization and segmentation. *Int J Comput Vis* 77(1–3): 259–289.

Leibe B, Seemann E, Schiele B. 2005. Pedestrian detection in crowded scenes. In IEEE conference on computer vision and pattern recognition (CVPR'05), San Diego, CA, USA. IEEE Computer Society.

Levi K, Weiss Y. 2004. Learning object detection from a small number of examples: the importance of good features. In IEEE conference on computer vision and pattern recognition (CVPR'04), Washington, DC, USA. IEEE Computer Society.

Li LJ, Wang G, Fei-Fei L. 2007. Optimol: automatic online picture collection via incremental model learning. In IEEE conference on computer vision and pattern recognition (CVPR'07), Minneapolis, Minnesota, USA. IEEE Computer Society.

Lindeberg T. 1998. Feature detection with automatic scale selection. *Int J Comput Vis* 30(2): 79–116, 1998.

Lowe D. 2004. Distinctive image features from scale-invariant keypoints. *Int J Comput Vis* 60(2): 91–110.

Martin DR, Fowlkes CC, Malik J. 2004. Learning to detect natural image boundaries using local brightness, color, and texture cues. *IEEE Trans Pattern Anal Mach Intell* 26(5): 530–549.

Mikolajczyk K, Leibe B, Schiele B. 2006. Multiple object class detection with a generative model. In IEEE conference on computer vision and pattern recognition (CVPR'06), New York, NY, USA. IEEE Computer Society.

Mikolajczyk K, Schmid C. 2002. An affine invariant interest point detector. In European conference on computer vision (ECCV'02), vol 2350, Lecture notes in computer science, 128–142, Copenhagen, Denmark, Springer.

Mikolajczyk K, Schmid C. 2005. A performance evaluation of local descriptors. *IEEE Trans Pattern Anal Mach Intell* 27(10): 1615–1630.

Mohan A, Papageorgiou C, Poggio T. 2001. Example-based object detection in images by components. *IEEE Trans Pattern Anal Mach Intell* 23(4): 349–361.

Mutch J, Lowe DG. 2006. Multiclass object recognition with sparse, localized features. In IEEE conference on computer vision and pattern recognition (CVPR'06), New York, NY, USA. IEEE Computer Society.

Ng AY, Jordan MI. 2002. On discriminative vs. generative classifiers: a comparison of logistic regression and naive bayes. In *Advances in neural information processing systems (NIPS'01)*, 841–848, Cambridge: MIT Press.

Nilsback M, Caputo B. 2004. Cue integration through discriminative accumulation. In IEEE conference on computer vision and pattern recognition (CVPR'04), Washington, DC, USA. IEEE Computer Society.

Nowak E, Jurie F, Triggs B. 2006. Sampling strategies for bag-of-features image classification. In European conference on computer vision (ECCV'06), vol 3951, Lecture notes in computer science, Graz, Austria, Springer.

Nowozin S, Tsuda K, Uno T, Kudo T, Bakir G. 2007. Weighted substructure mining for image analysis. In IEEE conference on computer vision and pattern recognition (CVPR'07), Minneapolis, Minnesota, USA. IEEE Computer Society.

Osuna E, Freund R, Girosi F. 1997. Training support vector machines: an application to face detection. In IEEE conference on computer vision and pattern recognition (CVPR'97), San Juan, Puerto Rico. IEEE Computer Society.

Ponce J, Berg TL, Everingham M, Forsyth D, Hebert M, Lazebnik S, Marszałek M, Schmid C, Russell C, Torralba A, Williams C, Zhang J, Zisserman A. 2006. Dataset issues in object recognition. In *Towards category-level object recognition*, 29–48. New York: Springer.

Quack T, Ferrari V, Leibe B, Gool LV. 2007. Efficient mining of frequent and distinctive feature configurations. In IEEE international conference on computer vision (ICCV'07), Rio de Janeiro, Brazil. IEEE Computer Society.

Russell BC, Freeman WT, Efros AA, Sivic J, Zisserman A. 2006. Using multiple segmentations to discover objects and their extent in image collections. In IEEE conference on computer vision and pattern recognition (CVPR'06), 1605–1614, New York, NY, USA. IEEE Computer Society.

Schroff F, Criminisi A, Zisserman A. 2007. Harvesting image databases from the web. In IEEE international conference on computer vision (ICCV'07), Rio de Janeiro, Brazil. IEEE Computer Society.

Sivic J, Russell BC, Efros AA, Zisserman A, Freeman WT. 2005. Discovering objects and their locations in images. In IEEE international conference on computer vision (ICCV'05), Beijing, China. IEEE Computer Society.

Sivic J, Russell BC, Zisserman A, Freeman WT, Efros AA. 2008. Unsupervised discovery of visual object class hierarchies. In IEEE conference on computer vision and pattern recognition (CVPR'08), Anchorage, Alaska, USA. IEEE Computer Society.

Skočaj D, Leonardis A. 2003. Weighted and robust incremental method for subspace learning. In IEEE international conference on computer vision (ICCV'03), 1494–1501, Nice, France. IEEE Computer Society.

Steyvers M, Griffiths TL. 2007. Probabilistic topic models. In *Handbook of latent semantic analysis*. Lawrence Erlbaum Associates.

Torralba A, Murphy K, Freeman W. 2004. Sharing features: efficient boosting procedures for multiclass object detection. In IEEE conference on computer vision and pattern recognition (CVPR'04), Washington, DC, USA. IEEE Computer Society.

Torralba A, Murphy KP, Freeman WT. 2007. Sharing visual features for multiclass and multiview object detection. *IEEE Trans Pattern Anal Mach Intell* 29(5).

Varma M, Ray D. 2007. Learning the discriminative power-invariance trade-off. In IEEE international conference on computer vision (ICCV'07), Rio de Janeiro, Brazil. IEEE Computer Society.

Viola P, Jones M. 2001. Rapid object detection using a boosted cascade of simple features. In IEEE conference on computer vision and pattern recognition (CVPR'01), 511–518, Kauai, HI, USA. IEEE Computer Society.

Viola P, Jones M. 2004. Robust real-time face detection. *Int J Comput Vis* 57(2): 137–154.

Viola P, Jones M, Snow D. 2003. Detecting pedestrians using patterns of motion and appearance. In IEEE international conference on computer vision (ICCV'03), 734–741, Nice, France. IEEE Computer Society.

Weber M, Welling M, Perona P. 2000. Unsupervised learning of object models for recognition. In European conference on computer vision (ECCV'00), vol 1843, Lecture notes in computer science, Dublin, Ireland, Springer.

Winn JM, Jojic N. 2005. Locus: learning object classes with unsupervised segmentation. In IEEE international conference on computer vision (ICCV'05), 756–763, Beijing, China. IEEE Computer Society.

Wu B, Nevatia R. 2007. Cluster boosted tree classifier for multi-view, multi-pose object detection. In IEEE international conference on computer vision (ICCV'07), Rio de Janeiro, Brazil. IEEE Computer Society.

Zhu X. 2005. Semi-supervised learning literature survey. Technical Report 1530, Computer Sciences, University of Wisconsin-Madison. http://www.cs.wisc.edu/~jerryzhu/pub/ssl_survey.pdf.

CHAPTER 18

Acquisition and Disruption of Category Specificity in the Ventral Visual Stream: The Case of Late Developing and Vulnerable Face-Related Cortex

K. Suzanne Scherf, Marlene Behrmann, and Kate Humphreys

18.1 Introduction

The discrimination and recognition of individual visual objects, including faces, words, and common objects, are among the most taxing perceptual challenges confronting observers in their day-to-day life. Not only does the observer need to derive precise information about the various objects under dramatically differing lighting conditions, scales, and vantage points, but the object must also be perceptually individuated from all other instances of that object so that identity can be assigned and the appropriate semantics (and phonology, where relevant) activated. Moreover, all of these processes must be executed accurately and rapidly, notwithstanding the ambiguity of the input arising from the commonality of input features (e.g., all faces have two eyes, a nose, and a mouth in the same spatial arrangement, and all words are made from the same relatively small set of letters). Despite the clear computational challenge associated with object recognition, human observers are remarkably efficient at assigning identity effortlessly and accurately, particularly for faces.

Much recent research has suggested that one way in which this efficiency is achieved is through a division of labor, that is, different classes of input are assigned to different underlying neural systems to mediate the representation of that object type (Downing et al. 2006). At present, there is clear consensus that segregated regions of human ventral cortex are activated differentially in response to different stimulus classes, although the extent to which these regional distinctions are truly domain-specific and exclusive is highly debated. Also, elucidating the nature of the underlying computations in these differing regions is highly challenging, and much remains to be done to understand the mechanisms supporting recognition. Controversial, too, is the means by which this segregated topography and coherent organization emerges in human cortex. This latter point is the focus of this chapter. We also consider the consequences for object perception when this selectivity pattern is disrupted, either in the course of development or as a consequence of brain damage in premorbidly normal individuals.

18.2 Category-Specific Topography of the Ventral
Visual Pathway

In adults, the functional topography of the ventral cortex reflects an organized category-selective map with particular stimulus classes eliciting distinct patterns of cortical activation (Downing et al. 2006; Grill-Spector, Chap. 6; Grill-Spector and Malach 2004; Hasson et al. 2003). Converging neuropsychological and neuroimaging studies indicate that common objects activate medial portions of the posterior fusiform gyrus and a region of the lateral occipital cortex (LO) (Grill-Spector et al. 1999), whereas buildings and landscapes activate the collateral sulcus (CoS) (Aguirre, Zarahn, and D'Esposito 1998) and the parahippocampal gyrus ("parahippocampal place area" (PPA); Epstein and Kanwisher 1998). Faces consistently engage a lateral portion of the posterior fusiform gyrus ("fusiform face area" (FFA); Kanwisher, McDermott, and Chun 1997), a lateral region in the inferior occipital cortex separable from the object-related region ("occipital face area" (OFA); Gauthier et al. 2000), and the superior temporal sulcus (STS) (Hoffman and Haxby 2000). Much recent evidence suggests that these areas are not necessarily fully independent and, at least for face processing, a distributed network of these nodes make up a core network that then interfaces with other relevant areas of cortex (Ishai 2007; Fairhall and Ishai 2007; Gobbini and Haxby 2007; Thomas et al. 2009).

Recently, researchers have begun to employ high-resolution neuroimaging techniques to evaluate how this functional topography develops in children's brains. Some progress has been made in elucidating the developmental trajectory by which this cortical organization emerges. We already know from decades of behavioral studies that there is a differential maturational trajectory associated with different visual stimulus classes. For example, children's recognition skills for face identity and expression do not mature until late childhood and lag behind recognition skills for other categories of visual objects. Specifically, children do not exhibit mature recognition skills for facial identity (Carey and Diamond 1977; Carey, Diamond, and Woods 1980; Ellis, Sheppard, and Bruce 1973; Flin 1985; Mondloch et al. 2003, 2004) or facial expressions (Herba and Phillips 2004; Thomas et al. 2007) until early adolescence, although their recognition skills for houses and objects appears to mature much earlier (Carey and Diamond 1977; Golarai et al. 2007; Teunisse and de Gelder 2003). Indeed, children continue to show improvements in their abilities to recognize unfamiliar faces until 12 years of age, and this delayed developmental trajectory may be related to changes in the neural substrate for face processing (Diamond, Carey, and Black 1983).

Given the different developmental trajectories for recognition skills across different object categories, one might expect that the functional specialization of face-, object-, and place-selective patterns of brain activation also follows different developmental trajectories that coincide with the ages at which recognition skills become adult-like. This pattern of functional brain development is consistent with the "interactive specialization" model, which suggests that specialization is dependent on learning processes and interrelations among brain regions (Johnson 2001; Johnson and Munakata 2005). Alternatively, given the importance of object recognition, and face recognition in particular, one might expect that this category-specific organization is architecturally innate and functionally organized from an early age (Farah et al. 2000). In this case, one would expect to see adult-like patterns of face-selective activation even in very young children. Because the functional topography in the adult ventral visual pathway is so well characterized, studying the development of this system and the consequences for object perception that ensue when this selectivity pattern is disrupted provides a unique opportunity to evaluate models of the neural basis of object perception and of functional brain development more broadly.

18.3 Typical Development of Face-Related Cortex

Several neuroimaging studies have begun to explore the emergence of face-related activation in the developing brain, particularly in the fusiform gyrus. Although a PET study with infants suggested that face-related activation may be present in 2-month-old infants (Tzourio-Mazoyer et al. 2002), fMRI studies, which have better spatial resolution, are providing converging results that children less than 8 years of age, as a group, do not consistently activate the FFA and that FFA activation continues to mature through early adolescence (Aylward et al. 2005; Gathers et al. 2004; Golarai et al. 2007; Passarotti et al. 2003; Passarotti et al. 2007).

As an example of one such a study, Figure 18.1 presents data from a recent fMRI experiment conducted with observers aged 5 to 8, 11 to 14, and 20 to 23 years of age (Scherf et al. 2007). Participants viewed naturalistic, real-time movies of unfamiliar faces, buildings, navigation through open fields, and objects in a blocked fMRI paradigm (Fig. 18.1(a)). The movie clips were organized into 32 blocks of 15-s duration, each containing a single stimulus category. This task has been used successfully to map category-selective activation in the ventral visual cortex in adults (Hasson et al. 2004; Avidan et al. 2005). There were no specific task demands associated with this paradigm (by design), so performance differences between the different age groups could not account for different levels of functional activation. Also, the groups did not differ in the amount of motion throughout the scan, which was limited to 2 mm in any direction. Figure 18.1(b) shows the average activation maps for the different age groups in this experiment. Note that we group together the building and scene-related activation, as both typically activate the PPA in the collateral sulcus (CoS) (Avidan et al. 2005).

A number of important findings emerge from this study. As is evident in the group map for the adults shown in Figure 18.1(b), there is clear topographic organization in ventral visual cortex, replicating the numerous studies of this sort conducted with adults. Of greater interest for the present work is the apparent adult-like cortical profile in adolescents and the absence of face-related activation in the youngest age group. Statistically, there were no age differences in activation profiles for areas PPA or LO, which are building- and object-selective regions, respectively. However, children show significantly less face-selective activation than adolescents or adults, and this was true for both the right and left hemispheres. That face-selectivity emerges late and after the selectivity associated with other classes is interesting and has been taken to suggest that there is a protracted neural trajectory underlying the maturation of face processing. Note that the failure to observe face-related activation in the young children cannot be attributed to differences in motion or a lack of statistical power

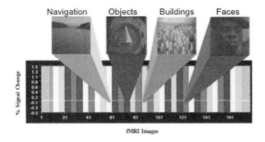

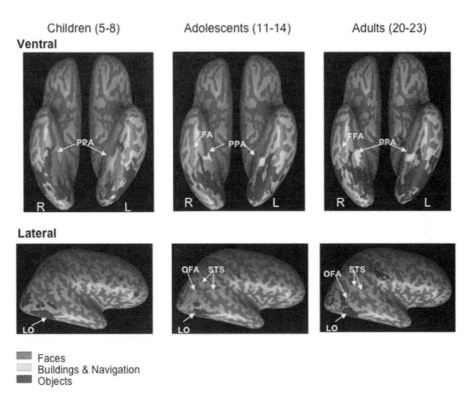

Figure 18.1. Ventral stream category-specific topography within each age group. Contrast maps for each object category ($p < .05$ corrected) from the group-level random-effects (GLM) mapped onto the ventral projection, and the lateral right hemisphere of a single representative inflated brain in order to show consistency, or lack thereof, across the age groups in category-selective activation. *FFA*, fusiform face area; *OFA*, occipital face area; *STS*, superior temporal sulcus; *LO*, lateral occipital object area; *PPA*, parahippocampal place area. (See color plate 18.1.)

given the robust and comparable activation for the other stimulus classes across the age groups.

18.3.1 Mechanisms of Functional Brain Development in Fusiform Gyrus

Although this study and others like it have provided some indication about when face-related activation in the fusiform gyrus begins to mature, there is little consensus on how this occurs. There are several candidate mechanisms for the maturation of face-related activation in the fusiform gyrus. They are not mutually exclusive and may occur along different developmental timelines, which may help explain the discrepancy in findings among the existing studies. For example, several reports suggest that the fusiform face area matures via an increase in the amount of face-selective activation within the gyrus, particularly in the right hemisphere (Aylward et al. 2005; Gathers et al. 2004; Golarai et al. 2007) but perhaps also bilaterally (Scherf et al. 2007). In one study, the size of children's (ages 7–11) right FFA was one-third the size of the adult's FFA (Golarai et al. 2007). Other findings reveal a shift in the locus of the face-selective activation from a more posterior portion of the ventral visual pathway to the more anterior region of the fusiform (Aylward et al. 2005; Gathers et al. 2004) and/or from a distributed to a more localized pattern of activation within the fusiform gyrus (Passarotti et al. 2003). Additionally, the emergence of the location of face-related activation in a group of individuals might arise via an increase in the consistency of the location of activation across individuals in these regions of cortex. It has been reported that there is more variability in the individually defined locus of face-related activation in young children, preventing the ability to detect group-level regions in a whole-brain analysis (Scherf et al. 2007). Finally, two studies reported a developmental increase in the magnitude of face-selectivity in the classic adult FFA region, particularly in the transition from childhood to early adolescence (Golarai et al. 2007; Scherf et al. 2007). In other words, during development there appears to be an increase in the number of neurons in the fusiform gyrus, particularly those near the classical FFA region, that are becoming selectively tuned for faces over other visual categories.

Importantly, these findings converge to indicate that face-related cortex is clearly immature in young children, which is not consistent with the strong version of the innately specified model of functional brain development in the ventral visual pathway. Furthermore, the consistency in findings that the transition from childhood to early adolescence appears to represent an important time for the development of face speci-ficity, particularly in the fusiform gyrus, overlaps a great deal with that observed in behavioral performance on face-processing tasks. This suggests that experience plays an important role in influencing the course of functional specialization in the ventral visual pathway, which is consistent with the predictions of the interactive specialization model (Cohen Kadosh and Johnson 2007).

A large literature supports the notion that the ability to encode and recognize un-familiar faces (Carey and Diamond 1977; Carey, Diamond, and Woods 1980; Ellis, Shepard, and Bruce 1973; Diamond and Carey 1986; Mondloch et al. 2004) and facial expressions (Herba and Phillips 2004) continues to improve into late childhood, and, in some cases, into adolescence. Many of these groups have argued that the ability to recognize individual faces continues to improve as children develop expertise in configural encoding. This involves recognizing faces on the basis of subtle metric vari-ations between their constituent features, and is thought to reflect the acquisition of expertise. Several neuroimaging studies with adults have shown that both the FFA and the OFA are involved in recognizing individual faces (e.g., Gauthier et al. 2000). Also, expertise for classes of perceptually homogenous novel objects and objects of exper-tise produces increased activation in the classically defined FFA region (e.g., Gauthier et al. 1999). Thus, the apparent transition in the development of face-selective activation may be related to the acquisition of expertise for individual face recognition and the subsequent fine-tuning of large populations of neurons in the adult face-related regions.

18.3.2 Relating Developmental Changes in Face-Processing Behavior and Face-Related Activation

A prerequisite in determining how experience influences the development of functional specialization in the brain is evidence of a relation between improvements in face-processing behavior and changes in the functional organization of the ventral visual pathway. Unfortunately, very few studies have been able to report developmental changes in such brain-behavior correspondences. Golarai and colleagues (2007) found a relation between the size of the right FFA and the accuracy of recognition memory for faces, but not places or objects, in children (ages 7–11) and adolescents (ages 12–16), but not in adults. They did not report whether a developmental increase in *face selectivity* in the right FFA was related to recognition memory performance.

Two studies employed the classic *face inversion* task as a means of evaluating the relation between changes in brain function and face-processing ability. Children and adults are slower and less accurate in their ability to recognize an inverted face (Yin 1969; Gilchrist & McKone 2003; Sangrigoli and de Schonen 2004), and developmental increases in the magnitude of the face-inversion effect have been interpreted to reflect more sophisticated use of face-recognition strategies, particularly in terms of improved configural processing (Carey and Diamond 1977). Aylward and colleagues (2005) found that the magnitude and extent of activation in both the right and left fusiform gyri correlated significantly with the magnitude of the face inversion effect (tested after the scanning session) in children (ages 8–10) and adolescents (ages 12–14). However, the authors did not report whether there was a developmental increase in the face inversion effect from childhood to adolescence, so it is possible that the brain-behavior correlations could have been mediated by individual differences, regardless of age. Finally, Passarotti and colleagues (2007) engaged children, adolescents, and adults in an emotion expression detection task while viewing upright and inverted faces during an fMRI scan. These authors did report a developmental increase in the magnitude of the behavioral face inversion effect. They further found that in the right lateral fusiform gyrus, there were significant positive correlations between age and the magnitude of the neural face inversion effect (e.g., activation upright > inverted faces) and between the magnitudes of the behavioral and neural face inversion effects. However, the relation between the behavioral and neural face inversion effects was present across the age groups. In other words, the correspondence between face-related activation and face-processing behavior did not change with age.

These findings are a promising first step toward understanding the relation between developmental changes in face-related cortex and face-processing skills, but they also reflect the difficulty in evaluating such brain-behavior correspondences. Part of the difficulty may be related to the focus on the fusiform gyrus, the use of face inversion as a measure of face-processing behavior, and the need to understand potential developmental changes in the computational properties of cortical regions comprising the face-processing network. We also note that, to date, there is no longitudinal study that directly assesses functional changes in brain organization and its relationship to behavior.

First, in order to truly understand how changes in brain function are related to children's emerging abilities to represent and recognize faces, developmental changes in face-related activation *throughout the face network*, which includes a widely distributed set of cortical and subcortical regions that extends beyond the ventral temporal lobe, will need to be evaluated in the context of children's performance on tests of face processing. Only two of the previously described fMRI studies investigated developmental changes in other face-selective regions within the ventral visual processing stream (e.g., OFA or STS). Scherf and colleagues (2007) found developmental increases in the size and selectivity of both of these regions bilaterally through adolescence; however, Golarai and colleagues (2007) did not observe similar developmental changes in the right STS in their study, and they did not evaluate changes in the OFA.

In addition to understanding how the maturation of individual regions within the face-processing network is related to changes in behavior, it will be important to evaluate how *dynamic interactions* among these distributed regions changes developmentally and how these interactions relate to improvements in face-processing behavior. Recent evidence suggests that in adults there is a hierarchical feedforward flow of information from the OFA to the FFA and separately to the STS supporting face perception (Fairhall and Ishai 2007). To date, there are no investigations of developmental changes in functional and/or structural connectivity between these "core" face-processing regions (Ishai 2007). One possible prediction is that the flow of information, or the functional coupling of activation, between the OFA and FFA, is weak in children, and this might significantly reduce the quality of face representations in this distributed network. Similar predictions might also be made with respect to the structural circuitry; the structural connections between cortical face-processing regions may be less organized in children, degrading the quality of the face representations. We have obtained preliminary evidence to this effect using diffusion tensor imaging studies with individuals of the same ages as those in the fMRI study shown in Figure 18.1 (Doyle et al. 2008). Understanding functional and structural specialization for faces in ventral visual cortex, and brain development more broadly, will require that all three of these potential mechanisms of change be investigated.

In addition to the "core" ventral temporal face-related regions, limbic regions including the amygdala, insula, and medial prefrontal cortex and regions in the anterior paracingulate cortex make up the "extended" face-processing network and process more changeable aspects of faces (Ishai 2007), such as facial expressions (for review, see Phan et al. 2002; Phillips et al. 2003) and associating "person knowledge" with faces, including personal traits, attitudes, mental states, and intentions (see Gobbini and Haxby 2007 for review). Although, to our knowledge there are no existing developmental studies investigating changes in the medial prefrontal or paracingulate cortices related to face processing, there are reports of developmental changes in amygdala function related to face processing. Researchers investigating developmental changes in the neural basis of affect regulation often use fearful faces as stimuli and have found (1) increasing amygdala responses during facial recognition tasks through adolescence (Baird et al. 1999), (2) a transition from late childhood to adulthood in amygdala function (i.e., children show more amygdala activation to neutral faces and adults show more amygdala activation to fearful faces; Thomas et al. 2001), and (3) a pattern of increasing right lateralization in amygdala activation to fearful faces in females but not males during adolescence (Killgore, Oki, and Yurgelun-Todd 2001).

These findings are especially interesting in light of the evidence in adults that the amygdala is part of a subcortical system that receives rapid (<100 ms) low-spatial-frequency information about faces (and potentially other visual objects) that is sufficient to develop a course or "quick and dirty" representation of a face and that can modulate face processing in the fusiform gyrus through direct feedback connections (for review, see Vuilleumier and Pourtois 2007). By some accounts, this subcortical component of face processing is primary in development and ultimately bootstraps the development of cortical face processing (Johnson 2005). In future studies, it will be critical to understand whether and how developmental changes in amygdala function are related to developmental changes in other parts of the face-processing network (e.g., the more posterior fusiform, OFA, and STS) and to developmental changes in face-processing behavior. Ultimately, the ability to understand how developmental changes in face identification, recognition, and expression recognition are related to changes in functional organization in the developing brain may require a broader systems-level approach that evaluates both the "core" and the "extended" regions in the face-processing network.

Relating developmental changes in face-processing behavior and functional brain organization may also require the use of more fine-grained tests of face-processing behavior that are sensitive enough to observe differences through adolescence, when face-related activation continues to change. Most of the existing studies attempting to relate behavior and brain activation have relied on the face inversion effect (Aylward et al. 2005; Passarotti et al. 2007). Although several groups have reported that the behavioral face inversion effect increases from ages 6 to 12 as children's representations of upright faces improve (Carey and Diamond 1977; Schwarzer 2000), many studies have also found adult-like sensitivity to inversion effects in children of the same age (e.g., Gilchrist and McKone 2003; Lewis 2003; Tanaka et al. 1998). Furthermore, there is great debate about what mechanisms of face processing are being measured and, therefore, evaluated for developmental change in face inversion (see Maurer et al. 2002; Ashworth et al. 2008).

Another, potentially more fruitful approach for studying the relation between changes in face-processing behavior and face-related brain activation is to employ behavioral tasks that tax the visuoperceptual and emotional components of face processing simultaneously, which may be more sensitive to developmental changes across a broader age range and may activate both the core and extended regions in the face-processing network more successfully. Previous work has shown that recognition memory for emotional expressions improves from late childhood through adolescence (Herba and Phillips 2006; Thomas et al. 2007), particularly for fear and disgust (Herba and Phillips 2004; Herba et al. 2006). Employing behavioral tasks that require participants to discriminate and/or recognize perceptually homogenous faces (e.g., similar-looking females) across changes in facial expressions may be more sensitive for measuring developmental changes in face-processing behavior that continue through adolescence and that could be linked with specific changes in brain function.

To date, the existing studies have implicated several potential mechanisms of developmental change in face-selective activation that could be related to changes in face-processing behavior. However, an additional possibility is that the specific nature of the computations being performed within individual face-related regions may change through the course of development, and these may be highly correlated with changes in face-recognition performance. For example, there is a growing consensus that face recognition can be divided up into different subprocesses such as those required to detect the presence of a face and those required to categorize or identify the face (Bowers and Jones 2008; Mack et al. 2008). Similarly, the adult face-processing network can be parcellated into regions that detect a face (i.e., posterior FFA, OFA) versus regions that identify an individual face (i.e., anterior FFA and posterior STS) versus regions that link semantic and biographic information with the perception of a face (i.e., inferior temporal gyrus). There are no existing studies evaluating whether these kinds of computations change developmentally in the face-processing network. Given that children are less accurate at unfamiliar face recognition, one might predict that the identity computations in the anterior FFA may be much weaker than in adults and may be highly correlated with accuracy in face recognition tasks (Scherf et al., under review).

As is evident, much remains to be done to elucidate, in detail, the developmental manifestations of face selectivity both at a neural and at a psychological level, as well as the interrelations between these two levels. In parallel, there is much to be done on the developmental emergence of category specificity for other non-face objects, too, in order to uncover fully the topographic organization of ventral visual cortex and its functionality. This work will be critical for evaluating the predictions of the interactive specialization model of functional brain development in the ventral visual pathway and will provide the basis for beginning to understand the computations supporting efficient object perception.

18.4 Atypical Development of Category-Specific Topography in Ventral Visual Cortex

As reviewed in the preceding section, it takes many years to attain the adult profile of category-selective face activation in ventral visual cortex, and this protracted development is likely correlated with the difficulties children experience in face processing. Another way of understanding how experience with visual objects influences functional brain organization in the ventral visual pathway is to study individuals who experience lifelong difficulties in face processing. Identifying the atypicalities in the face-processing behavior and structural and functional organization in such individuals can cast light on how the system might normally emerge.

One group of individuals who meet this criterion includes those with autism specturm disorder (ASD). Autism spectrum disorder is a neurodevelopmental disorder in which individuals exhibit marked deficits in social interaction, verbal, and nonverbal communication and have restricted or stereotyped patterns of behaviors (Baron-Cohen and Belmonte 2005; Frith and Happe 2005; Behrmann, Thomas, and Humphreys 2006b). Impairments in face processing are a relatively recent discovery in ASD, but have quickly become a widely accepted aspect of the behavioral profile (Behrmann et al. 2006b) and undoubtedly are related to the social difficulties experienced by these individuals, even in adulthood. The impairment in these individuals goes beyond face recognition, and involves difficulty in remembering faces (Boucher and Lewis 1992), processing facial expressions (Ashwin et al. 2007; Humphreys et al. 2007), and knowing which components of faces convey especially important communicative information (Joseph and Tanaka 2003). Despite the growing empirical evidence, the origin of the face-processing deficits in autism remains unknown.

One view suggests that individuals with autism have decreased motivation to attend to social stimuli, which limits the ability to gain expertise in face processing (Dawson et al. 2002; Grelotti, Gauthier, and Schultz 2002). In support of this hypothesis, several groups have reported that individuals with autism spend less time looking at the eye region of faces (Klin et al. 2002; Adolphs et al. 2008; Spezio et al. 2007), which is critical for identity recognition in typically developing individuals. Furthermore, this atypical fixation pattern may be related to aberrant activation in the fusiform gyrus (Dalton et al. 2005). This social motivation impairment is not predicted to affect the recognition of nonsocial objects.

An alternative hypothesis is that the face-processing deficits result from atypical perceptual processing (e.g., enhanced processing of local features; Happé and Frith 2006; Mottron et al. 2006). On the basis of a fundamental perceptual difficulty (and/or bias to process features preferentially), individuals with ASD may be limited in the ability to develop expertise with *any class* of visual objects (Behrmann et al. 2006a; Behrmann et al. 2006b) that are perceptually homogeneous, like faces. This is because fine-grained discrimination and representation of the configural properties of these stimuli (Diamond and Carey 1986) is required to differentiate these similar objects. In this framework, the limited time spent fixating the eye region has been interpreted in a different way. The eye region of a face is especially laden with configural information. Additional evidence for atypical visuoperceptual processing in ASD is the finding that children with autism are not sensitive to configural properties in the eye region of faces (Joseph and Tanaka 2003), perhaps because of increased reliance on local features (Klin et al. 2002; Lahie et al. 2006). This failure to encode the face in a typical fashion may hamper their ability to master visuoperceptual expertise that is critical for face recognition.

A recent study evaluated whether individuals with autism have difficulty developing perceptual expertise and whether any such decrement is specific to faces or extends to other objects, too (Scherf et al. 2008). Children (ages 8–13) and adults with high-functioning autism (FSIQ > 80) and age- and IQ-matched control participants performed perceptual discrimination tasks, including a face inversion task and a classification-level task, which requires especially fine-grained discriminations between individual exemplars, on three classes of stimuli: faces, perceptually homogeneous novel objects, Greebles, and perceptually heterogeneous common objects. They found that by late childhood, individuals with autism do reveal some visuoperceptual expertise for faces (as indicated by similar magnitude face inversion effect and similar success at exemplar-level discriminations as controls) but are, in general, less skilled at discriminating and recognizing faces than are typically developing individuals. Interestingly, children and adults with autism also evince poorer recognition for novel perceptually homogeneous objects (see also Ashworth et al. 2008), especially at the exemplar level, suggesting that they have a generalized deficit in visuoperceptual processing that may interfere with their ability to develop expert configural processing, which adversely impacts their recognition of any within-class perceptually homogenous objects, and especially faces. These results suggest that even if a social aversion to faces contributes to limitations in the development of face expertise in autism, it may not be the primary factor, because processing of other nonsocial objects, specifically perceptually homogeneous objects, is also affected. These findings of limited development of visuoperceptual expertise for faces in autism lead to clear predictions about disruptions in the development of functional specialization in the ventral visual pathway, particularly for face-related activation.

These predictions have begun to be tested in some recent studies. In one of these, children and adolescents with autism (ages 6–12) performed a 1-back task on faces of an adult stranger, their mother, a familiar child, an unknown child, and objects while in the scanner. A significant reduction in the number of active voxels was noted in the right and left fusiform for the autism group, specifically when they were observing an unfamiliar adult face, relative to the controls, although a similar reduction was noted during the object condition in the right fusiform, too. A whole brain voxelwise analysis revealed a similar finding. These findings led the authors to conclude that there is a selective hypoactivation of the fusiform region in response to unfamiliar adults. Of particular interest is whether there are any differences in the autism (and control) group as a function of age. Given that there is growing consensus that younger typical children are unlikely to evince normal fusiform activation, one wonders whether the major group difference emerges in the children in the higher age range in the autism group.

Several recent studies have begun to elucidate the category selectivity in ventral visual cortex in adults with autism, although there still remain inconsistencies between the findings. Using fMRI, many studies (Critchley et al. 2000; Schultz et al. 2000; Pierce et al. 2001; Hall, Szechtman, and Nahmais 2003; Hubl et al. 2003; Ogai et al. 2003; Piggot et al. 2004; Wang et al. 2004; Dalton et al. 2005; Grelotti et al. 2005; Deeley et al. 2007; Humphreys et al. 2008) have found reduced face selectivity in the fusiform face area (FFA), but five studies have failed to replicate this finding (Hadjikhani et al. 2004, 2007; Pierce et al. 2004; Bird et al. 2006; Kleinhans et al. 2008). It has also been proposed that FFA activation is normalized when people with autism look at the face stimuli (Hadjikhani et al. 2004), specifically the eye region (Dalton et al. 2005, 2007), although this does not always seem to be entirely the case (Hasson et al., submitted). The findings from the fMRI studies are also supported by a recent study using magnetoencephalography (MEG). In this study, the neural responses to images of faces, observed in right extrastriate cortices at approximately 145 ms after stimulus onset, were significantly weaker, less lateralized, and less affected by stimulus repetition than in control subjects (Bailey et al. 2005). Additionally, early latency (30–60 ms) responses to face images over right anterior temporal regions also differed significantly between the two subject groups in an image identification task. Interestingly, no such difference was observed for images of mugs or meaningless geometrical patterns, again pointing to a specific or more severe difficulty with face stimuli.

Far fewer studies have paid attention to other face-selective regions such as the superior temporal sulcus (STS) and the occipital face area (OFA). The existing results indicate that there is also weaker face-related activation in these regions (Pierce et al. 2001; Hadjikhani et al. 2007) and in the extended face-processing regions, including the amygdala, inferior frontal cortex, and face-related somatosensory and premotor cortex (Hadjikhani et al. 2007). There are also reports of increased face-related activation in individuals with autism bilaterally in the inferior temporal gyrus (Schultz et al. 2000) and atypical activation in the frontal and primary visual cortices (Pierce et al. 2001).

The inconsistency among these findings also applies to cortical responses to other visual object classes, although rather few studies have been conducted in this domain. One study found no consistent differences in cortical object activation in individuals with autism (Schultz et al. 2000), and another found no differences in activation for houses (Bird et al. 2006). In a MEG study, however, the sources of object-related signals were more variable in the autism group than in the typical group (Bailey et al. 2005). Finally, the LO object-related region apparently responds to both face and pattern processing in individuals with autism, and the superior parietal lobule, usually associated with visuospatial processing (Gitelman et al. 2000; Gitelman et al. 2002), is also more active.

In an attempt to map out the large-scale organization of ventral visual cortex in adults with autism, we used the movie localizer paradigm (Fig. 18.1) to contrast face-, place-, and object-selective activation in ASD adults, and age- and IQ-matched controls (Humphreys et al. 2008). Figure 18.2 shows the group maps averaged over ten typical individuals (Fig. 18.2(a)) and ten individuals with autism (Fig. 18.2(b)). The autism group consisted of individuals who were in the high functioning range (FSIQ < 75), with a group mean in the average range (VIQ=103, PIQ=106). The diagnosis of autism was established using the Autism Diagnostic Interview Revised (ADI-R) (Lord et al. 1994), the Autism Diagnostic Observation Schedule (ADOS) (Lord et al. 2000), and expert clinical diagnosis. Potential participants were excluded if they had an associated neuropsychiatric disorder or a history of birth asphyxia, head injury, or seizure disorder. Exclusions were based on neurological history and examination, chromosomal analysis, and, if indicated, metabolic testing.

The findings from the typical group largely replicate the adults maps in Figure 18.1 (and other similar studies in the literature), except that building/scene-related activation (green) in PPA appears somewhat reduced, especially in the left hemisphere. Others have observed similar PPA variability in the left hemisphere, too (Avidan et al. 2005). The most marked feature in the maps for the autism participants is the clear reduction in face-related activity. In fact, the only face-related activity at this threshold for the autism group is in the right OFA. In contrast, object-related activity in object-related LO appears more extensive for the autism group than the comparison group, a pattern that has been noted previously as well.

In common with many previous studies, in this study, there is a reduction in FFA activity in response to faces in adults with autism. In contrast to the group differences in face-related regions, there were no consistent BOLD differences between the groups in place-related (building- and scene-related) activation, across any of the dependent measures or analyses. This replicates the absence of a group difference for activation to house stimuli (Bird et al. 2006). The selective activity in place-related cortex was fairly

Typical Adults   Adults with Autism

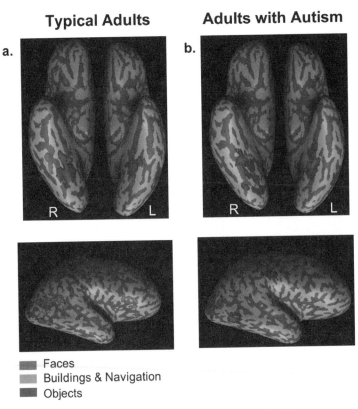

- ■ Faces
- ■ Buildings & Navigation
- ■ Objects

Figure 18.2. Group map reflecting average activation for faces, buildings, scenes, and objects for (a) typical adults and (b) adults with autism. Maps are inflated and shown from the ventral view (upper panel) and the lateral view of the right hemisphere (lower panel). For both groups, the maps were computed using a random effects general linear model and are thresholded at $P = .006$. (See color plate 18.2.)

low for both groups relative to other regions sampled, so it is possible that this result represents a floor effect. If any atypicalities exist for place-related activation in autism, they are much more subtle than those affecting face-related activation. It does not, however, seem that differences in functional organization of the ventral visual pathway in autism are limited to face-related regions, as there was evidence of differences, albeit subtle, affecting the representation of common objects as well.

How should we interpret the broad pattern of results, of markedly reduced activation and selectivity in face-related cortex in the group of adults with autism, but with fairly typical levels of activation in object and place areas? Notably, as we discussed, studies with typically developing children have shown that activation in place and object areas is adult-like even in early childhood, whereas the development of the face-related regions (FFA, OFA, STS) is much more protracted, becoming more selective and responsive to faces with age, but not reaching adult-like activation until early adulthood (Golarai et al. 2007; Scherf et al. 2007). One rather obvious possibility, then, is that visual category-selective organization in autism reflects an early plateau in development, rather than deviance, with the category selectivity resembling that of younger, typically developing children. Studies comparing individuals with autism and typically developing children of different ages would be useful to evaluate this possibility.

Alternatively, a number of authors propose abnormalities of neural connectivity in autism (Belmonte et al. 2004; Frith 2003; Courchesne and Pierce 2005a,b; Rippon et al. 2007), specifically underconnectivity between different functional regions (long-range) and over-connectivity at a more local level (short-range) (Markram, Rinaldi, and Markram 2007). These findings are evident even intrinsically when the brain is at rest (Kennedy and Courchesne 2008). Along with previous authors (e.g., Johnson et al. 2002), we speculate that the longer a particular function takes to mature, the greater the cascading effects of differences in the development of neurons and synapses. This may explain how differences in face-related cortex are much more pronounced in autism than are those affecting the earlier maturing place- or object-related cortices. The refinement in selectivity of later-developing cortex may be impeded as a result of overconnectivity at a local level, giving rise to a face-processing system prone to crosstalk and noise, resulting in reduced functional specificity (see Rippon et al. 2007). This framework would also predict that greater typical/autism group differences would be evident in other, later-developing brain functions. For example, we would expect to find greater differences on tasks that engage secondary and tertiary visual cortex compared to those relying on primary visual cortices (Hasson et al. submitted). These predictions are consistent with findings of greater divergence between the groups on tasks tapping frontal functions (e.g., Luna et al. 2002; Takarae et al. 2007).

18.5 Conclusion

Object perception, and face perception more specifically, is a highly complicated process at both the visuoperceptual/cognitive and neural levels. Recent neuroimaging work indicates that children exhibit adult-like patterns of activation for the perception of places and objects, but that face-related activation continues to develop into adolescence and early adulthood. These findings converge with behavioral reports of early maturation of house and object recognition skills compared to later-developing face recognition skills.

An important question to consider is why different object categories develop at different rates, with specialization for faces developing particularly late. Given their social significance, one might have expected faces to be amongst the very first visual classes mastered by young children, but it turns out that faces are an especially difficult stimulus for the visual system. First, compared to other classes of objects, faces are remarkably perceptually homogeneous and are typically distinguished at the individual level (e.g., Jane's versus Sally's face). This requires sensitivity to differences in facial features and in the subtle metric differences in spacing or configuration among the features, which are especially difficult to detect. Objects, on the other hand, are typically identified at the basic level (e.g., pencil versus paper), and it may well be the case that there are sufficient featural differences to support identification without having to engage the more difficult configural processing to converge on the identity of the object. In fact, despite all the experience with faces, typically developing adults and young adolescents (ages 10–13) are both less accurate with faces than common objects when performing a simple forced choice recognition task (Scherf et al. 2008). Furthermore, to a far greater extent than is true for any other visual class, faces are dynamic stimuli from which we typically extract many different kinds of information simultaneously (e.g., identity, expression, eye gaze). It is the case, though, that the dynamic information in faces is probably highly salient to young infants and may initiate the long developmental process of acquiring the neural and behavioral foundation for sophisticated face processing. However, learning to perform many computations (e.g., extracting invariant qualities of a face for individual recognition versus abstracting categories of emotional expressions across individual faces) on the same dynamically changing input may contribute to the late trajectory for sophisticated face processing skills.[1] It has been argued previously that extracting these different kinds of computations on a single source of input may give rise to interference effects (Cohen Kadosh and Johnson 2007) and, we would like to argue, may make the system more vulnerable to disruption (as is seen in adults with autism).

On the other hand, visuoperceptual and neural specialization for objects and place cortex may consolidate earlier in development as a result of the perceptual heterogeneity, and therefore ease of identification/recognition, and relatively more limited kinds of invariances that need to be extracted from such stimuli. The consequence of this earlier specialization may be that these mechanisms/specialized regions of cortex are less likely to be disrupted in developmental disorders. One caveat to this notion is that we still know very little about the computational properties of all of these regions and how they change developmentally.

Another important point that emerges from this work is that the transition from late childhood to early adolescence is especially important for the development of visuoperceptual and neural specialization for faces. This transition appears to represent a sensitive developmental window in which a convergence of sufficient visual experience and experience-dependent influences on the plasticity of the developing brain lead to increasing visuoperceptual and neural specialization for faces. The outcome of this developmental transition is computationally efficient and spatially organized regions of cortex that support fast and efficient face and object recognition processes. This may also represent a particularly vulnerable time for developmental disruptions to the functional organization of the ventral visual pathway, particularly for face-related cortex. Future studies investigating changing relations in brain-behavior correspondences in both typically developing children and those with developmental disorders that affect object recognition skills, including autism, congenital prosopagnosia, and developmental visual agnosia, will be critical for understanding more about early adolescence as a sensitive period for functional brain development.

Finally, there appear to be several mechanisms by which the neural specialization emerges within this sensitive period. One possibility is that there is a contingent progression among these mechanisms that ultimately leads to adult-like selectivity and computational properties within a particular region. For example, in the fusiform gyrus, it may be the case that initially some neurons must learn to respond preferentially to faces, particularly in the anterior part of the gyrus. Experience-dependent strengthening of the local connections among these neurons may then lead to a sufficiently large

---

[1] There is an alternative possibility that the dynamic nature of the faces may make it easier to extract identity information and facilitate individuation rather than contributing additional difficulty/variance to the problem.

number of such neurons that are in close enough proximity to collaboratively represent the complexity of faces, which ultimately allows the neurons to settle on the most efficient computations to represent faces in a fine enough grain to accomplish the task or tasks at hand (e.g., detection, recognition, categorization). Disruption to the more primary mechanisms earlier in the course of development may have catastrophic down-stream effects, preventing the development of adult-like specialization. For example, one possible explanation for the hypoactivation in the FFA in adults with autism is that there are face-selective groups of neurons, but that intrinsic disruptions in the local connections among these neurons prevent a sufficiently large number of such neurons from working together to collaboratively represent the complexity of faces.

Taking all these findings into account, we suggest that the face- and object-perception systems are ideal for testing broad theories of functional brain development, including understanding the relation between experience-dependent learning and experience-dependent brain plasticity, and elucidating the consequences when development is disrupted as in cases like autism. Engaging computational models of vision will be enormously helpful in working through the different possible scenarios and in thinking about issues such as category specificity and its emergence and the mechanistic processes that drive the organization of ventral visual cortex. Understanding whether fine-tuning of category-selective organization emerges from tuning of initially non-selective neurons and/or through some competitive interaction between neurons across the entire ventral visual cortex will assist in elucidating the typical developmental trajectory as well as the mechanisms that are adversely impacted during altered neuro-development.

Bibliography

Adolphs R, Spezio ML, Parlier M, Piven J. 2008. Distinct face processing strategies in parents of autistic children. *Curr Biol* 18(14): 1090–1093.

Aguirre GK, Zarahn E, D'Esposito M. 1998. An area within human ventral cortex sensitive to "building" stimuli: evidence and implications. *Neuron* 21: 373–83.

Ashwin C, Baron-Cohen S, Wheelwright S, O'Riordan M, Bullmore ET. 2007. Differential activation of the amygdala and the 'social brain' during fearful face-processing in Asperger syndrome. *Neuropsychologia* 45(1): 2–14.

Ashworth ARS, Vuong QC, Rossion B, Tarr MJ. 2008. Recognizing rotated faces and greebles: what properties drive the face inversion effect? *Visual Cogn* 16(6): 754–784.

Avidan G, Hasson U, Malach R, Behrmann M. 2005. Detailed exploration of face-related processing in congenital prosopagnosia: 2. Functional neuroimaging findings. *J Cogn Neurosci* 17: 1150–67.

Aylward EH, Park JE, Field KM, Parsons AC, Richards TL, Cramer SC, Meltzoff AN. 2005. Brain activation during face perception: evidence of a developmental change. *J Cogn Neurosci* 17: 308–19.

Bailey AJ, Braeutigam S, Jousmaki V, and Swithenby SJ. 2005. Abnormal activation of face processing systems at early and intermediate latency in individuals with autism spectrum disorder: a magnetoencephalographic study. *Eur J Neurosci* 21(9): 2575–85.

Baird AA, Gruber SA, Fein DA, Maas LC, Steingard RJ, Renshaw PE, Cohen BM, Yurgelun-Todd DA. 1999. Functional magnetic resonance imaging of facial affect recognition in children and adolescents. *J Am Acad Child Adolesc Psych* 38: 195–199.

Baron-Cohen S, Belmonte MK. 2005. Autism: a window onto the development of the social and analytic brain. *Ann Rev Neurosci* 28: 109–126.

Behrmann M, Avidan G, Leonard GL, Kimchi R, Luna B, Humphreys K, et al. 2006a. Configural processing in autism and its relationship to face processing. *Neuropsychologia* 44(1): 110–129.

Behrmann M, Thomas C,Humphreys K. 2006b. Seeing it differently: visual processing in autism. *Trends Cogn Sci* 10(6): 258–264.

Belmonte M, Cook Jr, EH, Anderson G, Rubenstein J, Greenough W, Beckel-Mitchener A, Courchesne E, et al. 2004. Autism as a disorder of neural information processing: directions for research and targets for therapy. *Mol Psych* 9: 646–663.

Bird G, Catmur C, Silani G, Frith C, Frith U. 2006. Attention does not modulate neural responses to social stimuli in autism spectrum disorders. *NeuroImage* 31: 1614–1624.

Boucher J, Lewis V. 1992. Unfamiliar face recognition in relatively able autistic children. *J Child Psychol Psychiatry* 33(5): 843–859.

Bowers JS, Jones KW. 2008. Detecting objects is easier than categorizing them. *Quart J Exp Psych (Colchester)* 61(4): 552–557.

Carey S, Diamond R. 1977. From piecemeal to configurational representation of faces. *Science* 195(4275): 312–314.

Carey S, Diamond R, Woods B. 1980. Development of face recognition: A maturational component? *Dev Psychol* 16: 257–269.

Cohen Kadosh K, Johnson MH. 2007. Developing a cortex specialized for face perception. *Trends Cogn Sci* 11(9): 367–369.

Courchesne E, Pierce K. 2005a. Brain overgrowth in autism during a critical time in development: implications for frontal pyramidal neuro and interneuron development and connectivity. *Int J Dev Neurosci* 23: 153–170.

Courchesne E, Pierce K. 2005b. Why the frontal cortex in autism might be talling only to itself: local over-connectivity but long-distance disconnection. *Curr Opin in Neurobiol* 15: 225–230.

Critchley HD, Daly EM, Bullmore ET, Williams SC, Van Amelsvoort T, Robertson DM, et al. 2000. The functional neuroanatomy of social behaviour: changes in cerebral blood flow when people with autistic disorder process facial expressions. *Brain* 123 (Pt 11): 2203–2212.

Dalton KM, Nacewicz BM, Alexander AL, Davidson RJ. 2007. Gaze-fixation, brain activation and amygdala volume in unaffected siblings of individuals with autism. *Biol Psychiatry* 61: 512–520.

Dalton KM, Nacewicz BM, Johnstone T, Shaefer HS, Gernsbacher MA, Goldsmith HH, et al. 2005. Gaze fixation and the neural circuitry of face processing in autism. *Nat Neurosci.* 8: 519–526.

Dawson G, Carver L, Meltzoff AN, Panagiotides H, McPartland J, Webb SJ. 2002. Neural correlates of face and object recognition in young children with autism spectrum disorder, developmental delay, typical development. *Child Dev* 73(3): 700–717.

Deeley Q, Daly EM, Surguladze S, Page L, Toal F, Robertson D, et al. 2007. An event-related functional magnetic resonance imaging study of facial emotion processing in Asperger syndrome. *Biol Psychiatry* 62: 207–217.

Diamond R, Carey S. 1986. Why faces are and are not special. *J Exp Psychol Gen* 115(2): 107–117.

Diamond R, Carey S, Black KJ. 1983. Genetic influences on the development of spatial skills during adolescence. *Cognition* 13: 167–185.

Downing PE, Chan AW, Peelen MV, Dodds CM, Kanwisher N. 2006. Domain specificity in visual cortex. *Cereb Cortex* 16(10): 1453–1461.

Doyle JL, Scherf KS, Thomas C, Behrmann M. 2008. The age-related emergence of cortical connectivity underlying face processing revealed by diffusion tensor imaging. Poster presented at the annual cognitive neuroscience society meeting, San Francisco, CA.

Ellis HD, Shepard J, Bruce A. 1973. The effects of age and sex on adolescents' recognition of faces. *J Genet Psychol* 123: 173–174.

Epstein R, Kanwisher N. 1998. A cortical representation of the local visual environment. *Nature* 392(6676): 598–601.

Farah MJ, Rabinowitz C, Quinn GE, Lui GT. 2000. Early comittment of neural substrates for face recognition. *Cogn Neuropsychol* 17: 117–123.

Fairhall SL, Ishai A. 2007. Effective connectivity within the distributed cortical network for face perception. *Cereb Cortex* 17(10): 2400–2406.

Flin RH. 1985. Development of face recognition: an encoding switch? *Br J Psychol* 76 (Pt 1): 123–134.

Frith U. 2003. *Autism: explaining the enigma*. UK: Blackwell Publishers.

Frith U, Happé R. 2005. Autism spectrum disorder. *Curr Bioll* 15(19): R786–90.

Gathers AD, Bhatt R, Corbly CR, Farley AB, Joseph JE. 2004. Developmental shifts in cortical loci for face and object recognition. *Neuroreport* 15(10): 1549–1553.

Gauthier I, Tarr MJ, Anderson AW, Skudlarski P, Gore JC. 1999. Activation of the middle fusiform 'face area' increases with expertise in recognizing novel objects. *Nature Neurosci* 2(6): 568–573.

Gauthier I, Tarr MJ, Moylan J, Skudlarski P, Gore JC, Anderson AW. 2000. The fusiform "face area" is part of a network that processes faces at the individual level. *J Cogn Neurosci* 12: 495–504.

Gilchrist A, McKone, E. 2003. Early maturity of face processing in children: local and relational distinctiveness effects in 7-year-olds. *Visual Cogn* 10(7): 769–793.

Gitelman DR, Parrish TB, Friston KJ, Mesulam MM. 2002. Functional anatomy of visual search: regional segregations within the frontal eye fields and effective connectivity of the superior colliculus. *Neuroimage* 15: 970–982.

Gitelman DR, Parrish TB, LaBar KS, Mesulam MM. 2000. Real-time monitoring of eye movements using infrared video-oculography during functional magnetic resonance imaging of the frontal eye fields. *Neuroimage* 11: 58–65.

Gobbini MI, Haxby JV. 2007. Neural systems for recognition of familiar faces. *Neuropsychologia* 45: 32–41.

Golarai G, Ghahremani DG, Whitfield-Gabrieli S, Reiss A, Eberhardt JL, Gabrieli JDE, Grill-Spector K. 2007. Differential development of high-level cortex correlates with category-specific recognition memory. *Nat Neurosci* 10(4): 512–22.

Grelotti DJ, Gauthier I, Schultz RT. 2002. Social interest and the development of cortical face specialization: what autism teaches us about face processing. *Dev Psychobiol* 40(3): 213–225.

Grelotti DJ, Klin AJ, Gauthier I, Skudlarski P, Cohen DJ, Gore JC, et al. 2005. fMRI activation of the fusiform gyrus and amygdala to cartoon characters but not to faces in a boy with autism. *Neuropsychologia* 43: 373–385.

Grill-Spector K, Kushnir T, Edelman S, Avidan G, Itzchak Y, Malach R. 1999. Differential processing of objects under various viewing conditions in the human lateral occipital complex. *Neuron* 24(1): 187–203.

Grill-Spector K, Malach R. 2004. The human visual cortex. *Ann Rev Neurosci* 27: 649–677.

Hadjikhani N, Joseph RM, Snyder J, Chabris CF, Clark J, Steele S, et al. 2004. Activation of the fusiform gyrus when individuals with autism spectrum disorder view faces. *Neuroimage* 22: 1141–1150.

Hadjikhani N, Joseph RM, Snyder J, Tager-Flusberg H. 2007. Abnormal activation of the social brain during face perception in autism. *Hum Brain Mapping* 28: 441–449.

Hall GB, Szechtman H, Nahmias C. 2003. Enhanced salience and emotion recognition in autism: a PET study. *Am J Psych* 160: 1439–1441.

Happé F, Frith U. 2006. The weak central coherence account: Detail-focused cognitive style in autism spectrum disorders. *J Aut Dev Disord* 36(1): 5–25.

Hasson U, Avidan G, Gelbard H, Vallines I, Harel M, Minshew N, et al. Submitted. Extrinsic and intrinsic cortical activation patterns in autism revealed under continuous real-life viewing conditions.

Hasson U, Nir Y, Levy I, Fuhrmann G, Malach R. 2004. Intersubject synchronization of cortical activity during natural vision. *Science* 303(5664): 1634–1640.

Haxby JV, Hoffman E, Gobbini MI. 2000. The distributed human neural system for face perception. *Trends Cogn Sci* 4(6): 223–232.

Herba CM, Landau S, Russell T, Ecker C, Phillips M. 2006. The development of emotion-processing in children: effects of age, emotion, an intensity. *J Child Psychol Psych* 47(11): 1098–1106.

Herba C, Phillips M. 2004. Annotation: Development of facial expression recognition from childhood to adolescence: behavioral and neurological perspectives. *J Child Psychol Psych* 45: 1185–1198.

Hoffman EA, Haxby JV. 2000. Distinct representations of eye gaze and identity in the distributed human neural system for face perception. *Nat Neurosci* 3(1): 80–84.

Hubl D, Bolte S, Feineis-Matthews S, Lanfermann H, Federspeil A, Strik W, et al. 2003. Functional imbalance of visual pathways indicates alternative face processing strategies in autism. *Neurology* 61: 1232–1237.

Humphreys K, Hasson U, Avidan G, Minshew N, Behrmann M. 2008. Cortical patterns of category-selective activation for faces, places, and objects in adults with autism. *Autism Res* 1: 52–63.

Humphreys K, Minshew N, Lee Leonard G, Behrmann M. 2007. A fine-grained analysis of facial expression processing in autism. *Neuropsychologia* 45: 685–695.

Ishai A. 2008. Let's face it: It's a cortical network. *Neuroimage* 40(2): 415–419.

Johnson MH. 2001. Functional brain development in humans. *Nate Rev Neurosci* 2(7): 475–483.

Johnson MH. 2005. Subcortical face processing. *Nat Rev Neurosci* 6: 766–774.

Johnson MH, Halit H, Grice SJ, Karmiloff-Smith A. 2002. Neuroimaging of typical and atypical development: a perspective from multiple levels of analysis. *Dev Psychopathol* 14(3): 521–36.

Johnson MH, Munakata Y. 2005. Processes of change in brain and cognitive development. *Trends Cogn Sci* 9(3): 152–158.

Joseph JE, Gathers AD, Liu X, Corbly CR, Whitaker SK, Bhatt RS. 2006. Neural developmental changes in processing inverted faces. *Cogn Affec Behav Neurosci* 6(3): 223–235.

Joseph RM, Tanaka, J. 2003. Holistic and part-based face recognition in children with autism. *J Child Psychol Psych* 44(4): 529–542.

Kanwisher N, McDermott J, Chun MM. 1997. The fusiform face area: a module in human extrastriate cortex specialized for face perception. *J Neurosci* 17(11): 4302–4311.

Kennedy DP, Courchesne E. 2008. The intrinsic functional organization of the brain is altered in autism. *Neuroimage* 39(4): 1877–85.

Kilgore WDS, Oki M, Yurgelun-Todd DA. 2001. Sex-specific developmental changes in amygdala responses to affective faces. *Neuroreport* 12: 427–433.

Kleinhas NM, Richards T, Sterling L, Stregbauer KC, Mahurin R, Johnson LC, Greenson J, Dawson G, Aylward E. 2008. Abnormal functional connectivity in autism spectrum disorders during face processing. *Brain* 131: 1000–1012.

Klin A, Jones W, Schultz R, Volkmar F, Cohen D. 2002. Visual fixation patterns during viewing of naturalistic social situations as predictors of social competence in individuals with autism. *Arch Gen Psych* 59(9): 809–816.

Lahaie A, Mottron L, Arguin M, Berthiaume C, Jemel B, Saumier D. 2006. Face perception in high-functioning autistic adults: evidence for superior processing of face parts, not for a configural face-processing deficit. *Neuropsychology* 20(1): 30–41.

Lewis MB. 2003. Thatcher's children: Development and the Thatcher illusion. *Perception* 32: 1415–1421.

Lord C, Risi S, Lambrecht L, Cook EH Jr., Leventhal BL, DiLavore, PC, Pickles A. 2000. The autism diagnostic observation schedule – generic: a standard measure of social and communication deficits associated with the spectrum of autism. *J Aut Dev Disord* 30: 205–223.

Lord C, Rutter M, Le Couteur A. 1994. Autism diagnostic interview-revised: a revised version of a diagnostic interview for caregivers of individuals with possible pervasive developmental disorders. *J Aut Dev Disord* 24(5): 659–685.

Luna B, Minshew NJ, Garver KE, Lazar NA, Thulborn KR, Eddy WF, Sweeney JA. 2002. Neorcortical system abnormalities in autism: an fMRI study of spatial working memory. *Neurology* 59(6): 834–40.

Mack MM, Gauthier I, Sadr J, Palmeri, T. 2008. Object detection and basic-level categorization: sometimes you know it is there before you know what it is. *Psychol Bull Rev* 15(1): 28–35.

Markram H, Rinaldi T, Markram K. 2007. The intense world syndrome – an alternative hypothesis for autism. *Front Neurosci* 1: 77–96.

Maurer D, Le Grand R, Mondloch CJ. 2002. The many faces of configural processing. *Trends Cogn Sci* 6(6): 255–260.

Maurer D, Salapatek, P. 1976. Developmental changes in the scanning of faces by young infants. *Child Dev* 47: 523–527.

Mondloch CJ, Dobson KS, Parsons J, Mauer D. 2004. Why 8-year-olds cannot tell the difference between Steve Martin and Paul Newman: factors contributing to the slow development of sensitivity to the spacing of facial features. *J Exp Child Psychol* 89: 159–181.

Mondloch CJ, Geldart S, Maurer D, Le Grand R. 2003. Developmental changes in face processing skills. *J Exp Child Psychol* 86(1): 67–84.

Mottron L, Dawson M, Soulieres I, Hubert B, Burack J. 2006. Enhanced perceptual functioning in autism: an update, and eight principles of autistic perception. *J Aut Dev Disord* 36(1): 27–43.

Murphy KM, Beston BR, Boley PM, Jones DG. 2005. Development of human visual cortex: a balance between excitatory and inhibitory plasticity mechanisms. *Dev Psychobiol* 46: 209–221.

Ogai M, Matsumoto H, Suzuki K, Ozawa F, Fukada R, Ichiyama I, et al. 2003. fMRI study of recognition of facial expressions in high-functioning autistic patients. *Neuroreport* 14: 559–563.

Passarotti AM, Paul BM, Bussiere JR, Buxton RB, Wong E, Stiles J. 2003. The development of face and location processing: an fMRI study. *Dev Sci* 6(1): 100–117.

Passarotti AM, Smith J, DeLano M, Huang J. 2007. Developmental differences in the neural bases of the face inversion effect show progressive tuning of face-selective regions to the upright orientation. *Neuroimage* 34: 1708–1722.

Phan KK, Wager T, Taylor SF, Liberzon I. 2002. Review: functional neuroanatomy of emotion: A meta-analysis of emotion activation studies in PET and fMRI. *Neuroimage* 16: 331–348.

Phillips ML, Drevets WC, Rauch SL, Lane R. 2003. Neurobiology of emotion perception I: The neural basis of normal emotion perception. *Biolo Psychi* 54: 504–514.

Pierce K, Haist F, Sedaghat F, Courchesne E. 2004. The brain response to personally familiar faces in autism: findings of fusiform activity and beyond. *Brain* 127: 2703–2716.

Pierce K, Muller RA, Ambrose J, Allen G, Courchesne E. 2001. Face processing occurs outside the fusiform 'face area' in autism: evidence from functional MRI. *Brain* 124: 2059–2073.

Pierce K, Redcay E. 2008. Fusiform function in children with an autism spectrum disorder is a matter of "who." *Biol Psych* 64(7): 552–560.

Piggot J, Kwon H, Mobbs D, Blasey C, Lotspeich L, Menon V, et al. 2004. Emotional attribution in high-functioning individuals with autistic spectrum disorder: a functional imaging study. *J Am Acad Child Adol Psych* 43: 473–480.

Rippon G, Brock J, Brown C, Boucher J. 2007. Disordered connectivity in the autistic brain: challenges for the "new psychophysiology." *Int J Psychophysiol* 63: 164–172.

Sangrigoli S, De Schonen, S. 2004. Recognition of own-race and other-race faces by three-month-old infants. *J Child Psychol Psych* 45(7): 1219–1227.

Scherf KS, Behrmann M, Humphreys K, Luna B. 2007. Visual category-selectivity for faces, places, and objects emerges along different developmental trajectories. *Dev Sci* 10(4): F15–F30.

Scherf KS, Behrmann M, Minshew N, Luna B. 2008. Atypical Development of Face and Greeble Recognition in Autism. *J Child Psychol Psych* 49(8): 838–847.

Scherf KS, Luna, B, Avidan G, Behrmann M. under review. What preceds which: developmental neural tuning inface- and place-related cortex: an fMRI-Adaptation study.

Schultz RT, Gauthier I, Klin A, Fulbright RK, Anderson AW, Volkmar F, et al. 2000. Abnormal ventral temporal cortical activity during face discrimination among individuals with autism and Asperger syndrome. *Arch Gen Psych* 57: 331–340.

Schwarzer G. 2000. Development of face processing: the effect of face inversion. *Child Dev* 71(2): 391–401.

Spezio ML, Adolphs R, Hurley RS, Piven J. 2007. Abnormal use of facial information in high-functioning autism. *J Aut Dev Disord* 37(5): 929–939.

Takarae Y, Minshew NJ, Luna B, Sweeney JA. 2007. Atypical involvement of frontostriatal systems during sensorimotor control in autism. *Psychi Res* 156(2): 117–127.

Tanaka JW, Kay JB, Grinnell E, Stansfield B, Szechter L. 1998. Race recognition in young children: when the whole is greater than the sum of its parts. *Visual Cogn* 5(4): 479–496.

Teunisse JP, de Gelder B. 2003. Face processing in adolescents with autistic disorder: the inversion and composite effects. *Brain Cogn* 52: 285–294.

Thomas C, Avidan G, Humphreys K, Jung KJ, Gao F, Behrmann M. 2008. Reduced structural connectivity in ventral visual cortex in congenital prosopagnosia. *Nature Neurosci* 12(1): 29–31.

Thomas KM, Drevets WC, Whalen PJ, Eccard CH, Dahl RE, Ryan ND, Casey BJ. 2001. Amygdala response to facial expressions in children and adults. *Biol Psychi* 49: 309–316.

Thomas LA, De Bellis MD, Graham R, Kevin S. 2007. Development of emotional face recognition in late childhood and adolescence. *Dev Sci* 10(5): 547–558.

Tzourio-Mazoyer N, De Schonen S, Crivello F, Reutter B, Aujard Y, Mazoyer, B. 2002. Neural correlates of woman face processing by 2-month-old infants. *Neuroimage* 15: 454–461.

Vuilleumier P, Pourtois G. 2007. Distributed and interactive brain mechanisms during emotion face perception: evidence from functional neuroimaging. *Neuropsychologia* 45: 174–194.

Wang AT, Dapretto M, Hariri AR, Sigman M, Bookheimer SY. 2004. Neural correlates of facial affect processing in children and adolescents with autism spectrum disorder. *J Am Acad Child Adol Psych* 43: 481–490.

Yin RK. 1969. Looking at upside-down faces. *J Exp Psychol* 81: 141–145.

CHAPTER 19

Using Simple Features
and Relations

Marius Leordeanu, Martial Hebert, and Rahul Sukthankar

19.1 Introduction[†]

One possible approach to category recognition is to model object categories as graphs
of features, and to focus mainly on the second-order (pairwise) relationships between
them: category-dependent as well as perceptual grouping constraints. This differs from
the popular bag-of-words model (Csurka et al. 2004), which concentrates exclusively
on local features, ignoring the higher-order interactions between them. The main observation is that higher-order relationships between model features are more important
for category recognition than local, first-order features. Earlier studies support the
view that simple, unary features, without higher-order relationships (such as geometric
constraints or conjunctions of properties), are not sufficient at higher cognitive levels
where object category recognition takes place (Treisman 1986; Hummel 2000). The
importance of using pairwise relationships between features was recognized early on,
starting with Ullman's theory of the correspondence process, which introduced the
notion of *correspondence strength* that takes into consideration both the local/unary
affinities, but also pairwise interactions between features (Marr 1982).

  More generally, using pairwise or global geometric constraints between contour
fragments was explored extensively in early work. For example, interpretation trees
were used to find correspondences between contour fragments, aligning an object model
and the object instance in a novel image of a cluttered scene (Grimson and Lozano-Pérez
1987; Grimson 1990a). Other approaches relied on more global techniques based on
transformation voting alignment (Lowe 1985), as well as geometric reasoning on groups
of fragments (Goad 1983; Brooks 1981). Another approach for finding correspondences
between a model and observed data is by generating initial hypotheses (i.e., candidate
transformations between the observed scene and recorded aspects of the reference
object) and by pruning these hypotheses based on pairwise geometric constraints

---

[†] Portions reprinted, with permission, from "Beyond Local Appearance: Category Recognition from Pairwise
Interactions of Simple Features", M. Leordeanu, M. Hebert, and R. Sukthankar, Proceedings of International
Conference on Computer Vision and Pattern Recognition. © 2007 IEEE.

and by global alignment (Chen and Stockman 1998). A good survey of the early work on recognition based on geometric matching of contour fragments can be found in (Grimson 1990b). All of these approaches were limited by an explicit parametric model of the global transformation between the input and the model, and although they could be used for specific object recognition, they could not easily represent the variation of geometric configurations of contour fragments across a category. Early approaches based on graphical models did capture the variation in shape in a more flexible way (Li 1995) using higher-order constraints. After a period of limited activity in this area, the importance of shape for object recognition was re-emphasized by Belongie et al. (Belongie et al. 2000) and later by Berg et al. (Berg et al. 2005). The shape context descriptor introduced in (Belongie et al. 2000) is a local, unary (one per feature) descriptor that loosely captures global shape transformations but, by nature, is also sensitive to background clutter. Later, Berg et al. used second-order geometric relationships between features, emphasizing the local geometric information (using the geometric blur descriptor).

This body of work suggests that is possible to take advantage more effectively of the second-order geometric relationships between shape fragments. In this chapter, we summarize one possible approach to a matching approach that uses pairwise geometric constraints and that can be used for category modeling from training data. We represent these models as cliques of very simple features (sparse points and their normals), and focus only on the pairwise geometric relationships between them. We demonstrate that simple geometric relationships with no local appearance features can be used successfully for semi-supervised object class recognition. Of course, it is clear that simple features based on the local configuration of contour fragments are limited in their representative power and that larger groups should be used in addition to the local features. We show how to develop a feature grouping mechanism that can be incorporated with our overall approach based on spectral matching.

The use of second-order geometric relationships enables the algorithm to successfully overcome problems often encountered by previous methods from the literature. Specifically, we integrate several training images into a single abstract shape model that captures both common information shared by several training images as well as useful information that is unique to each training image. We also automatically discover and remove the irrelevant clutter from training images, keeping only the features that are indeed useful for recognition. This gives us a more compact representation, which reduces the computational and memory cost, and improves generalization. During training, the algorithm is translation invariant, robust to clutter, and does not require aligned training images, which is often a limitation (Berg et al. 2005; Opelt et al. 2006a; Mikolajczyk et al. 2006; Ferrari et al. 2006). We efficiently learn models consisting of hundreds of fully interconnected parts. Most previous work handles models only up to 30 sparsely interconnected parts, such as the star-shaped (Fergus et al. 2005; Crandall et al. 2005), k-fan (Crandall and Huttenlocher 2006), or hierarchical models (Felzenszwalb and Huttenlocher 2004; Bouchard and Triggs 2005). There has been work in handling hundreds of parts (Carneiro and Lowe 2006), but each object part is connected only to its k-nearest neighbors. We select features based on how well they work together as a team rather than individually. This gives us a larger pool of very useful features, which are discriminative together, albeit not necessarily on an individual basis. This differs from previous work that first selects the features based on how well they work individually before considering their pairwise geometric relationships (Crandall and Huttenlocher 2006; Opelt et al. 2006a).

19.2 Recognition Using Simple Contour Features

19.2.1 Model Representation and Recognition Algorithm

In this section, we describe an algorithm for object category recognition (not using grouping cues) (Leordeanu et al. 2007) that is based on the observation that for a wide variety of common object categories, the shape matters more than local appearance. Although shape alone was previously used for category recognition (Opelt et al. 2006b; Ferrari et al. 2008), we demonstrate that simple geometric relationships with no local appearance features can be used successfully in a semi-supervised setting.

Our approach combines two popular classes of approaches in recognition. The first one formulates the problem as a matching problem, and uses either a nearest-neighbor approach (Berg et al. 2005) or a SVM classifier (Grauman and Darrell 2005). The second one formulates the problem as an inference problem and use the machinery of graphical models (Fergus et al. 2003; Fergus et al. 2005; Carneiro and Lowe 2006; Crandall and Huttenlocher 2006). We use ideas from matching using second-order geometric relationships (Berg et al. 2005), but, unlike current approaches in matching, we build a category model that is a compact representation of the training set (Leordeanu and Hebert 2005).

We formulate the problem as follows: given a set of negative images (not containing the object) and weakly labeled positive images (containing an object of a given category somewhere in the image), the task is to learn a category shape model that can be used both for the *localization* and *recognition* of objects from the same category in novel images. This problem is challenging because we do not have any prior knowledge about the object's location in the training images. Also, these images can contain a substantial amount of clutter that is irrelevant to the category we want to model. All we know at training time is that the object is somewhere in the positive training images and nowhere in the negative ones.

The category shape model is represented as a graph of interconnected parts (nodes) whose geometric interactions are modeled using pairwise potentials. The nodes in this graph are fully interconnected (they form a clique) with a single exception: there is no link between two parts that have not occurred together in the training images. These model parts have a very simple representation: they consist of sparse, abstract points together with their associated normals. Of course, we could add local information in addition to their normals, but our objective is to assess the power of the geometric relationships between these simple features. We represent the pairwise relationships by an overcomplete set of parameters. The parts as well as their geometric relationships are learned from actual boundary fragments extracted from training images, as described in (Leordeanu et al. 2007).

Our model is a graph whose edges are abstract pairwise geometric relationships. It is a compact representation of a category shape, achieved by sharing generic geometric configurations common to most objects from a category and also by integrating specific configurations that capture different aspects or poses (Fig. 19.1).

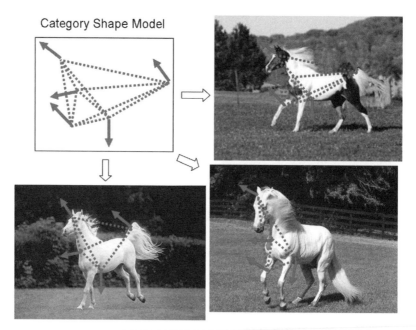

Category Shape Model

Figure 19.1. The model is a graph whose edges are abstract pairwise geometric relationships. It integrates generic configurations common to most objects from a category as well as more specific configurations that capture different poses and aspects. (See color plate 19.1.)

We define the object localization problem as finding which feature in the image best matches each model part. We formulate it as a quadratic assignment problem (QAP) in which the matching score E is written as:

$$E = \sum_{ia;jb} x_{ia} x_{ib} G_{ia;jb}. \tag{19.1}$$

Here x is an indicator vector with an entry for each pair (i, a) such that $x_{ia} = 1$ if model part i is matched to image feature a and 0 otherwise. With a slight abuse of notation we consider ia to be a unique index for the pair (i, a). We also enforce the mapping constraints that one model part can match only one model feature and vice versa: $\sum_i x_{ia} = 1$ and $\sum_a x_{ia} = 1$.

The *pairwise potential* $G_{ia;jb}$ (terminology borrowed from graphical models) reflects how well the parts i and j preserve their geometric relationship when being matched to features a, b in the image. Similar to previous approaches taken in the context of CRFs (Lafferty et al. 2001; Kumar 2005), we model these potentials using logistic classifiers:

$$G_{ia;jb} = \frac{1}{1 + exp(-\mathbf{w}^T \mathbf{g}_{ij}(a, b))}. \tag{19.2}$$

Here $\mathbf{g}_{ij}(a, b)$ is a vector describing the geometric deformations between the parts (i, j) and their matched features (a, b). We now explain in greater detail the type of features used and their pairwise relationships. Each object part can be seen as an abstract point and its associated normal (with no absolute location). For a pair

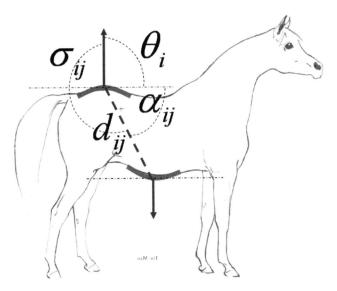

Figure 19.2. Parameters that capture the pairwise geometric relationships between object parts. (See color plate 19.2.)

of model parts (i, j) we capture their translation-invariant relationship in the vector $e_{ij} = \{\theta_i, \theta_j, \sigma_{ij}, \sigma_{ji}, \alpha_{ij}, \beta_{ij}, d_{ij}\}$, where d_{ij} represents the distance between them, β_{ij} is the angle between their normals and the rest are angles described in Figure 19.2.

The same type of information is extracted from input images, each image feature corresponding to a point sampled from some boundary fragment extracted from that image. We consider a similar pairwise relationship e_{ab} for the pair (a, b) of image features that were matched to (i, j). Then we express the pairwise geometric deformation vector as $g_{ij}(a, b) = [1, \epsilon_1^2, \ldots, \epsilon_7^2]$, where $\epsilon = e_{ij} - e_{ab}$. The geometric parameters e_{ij} form an overcomplete set of values, some highly dependent on each other. Considering all of them becomes very useful for geometric matching and recognition because it makes $G_{ia;jb}$ more robust to changes in the individual elements of $g_{ij}(a, b)$.

In order to localize the object in the image, we find the assignment x^* that maximizes the matching score E (written in matrix notation by setting $G(ia; jb) = G_{ia;jb}$):

$$x^* = argmax(x^T G x) \tag{19.3}$$

For one-to-one constraints (each model part can match only one image feature and vice-versa), this combinatorial optimization problem is known as the QAP. For many-to-one constraints it is also known in the graphical models literature as MAP inference for pairwise Markov networks. In general, both problems are intractable. We enforce the one-to-one constraints, and use the spectral matching algorithm presented earlier (Leordeanu and Hebert 2005).

A key parameter in this algorithm is the vector of relative weights between features, w. This parameter can be learned independently of the specific categories used in recognition from training data that contain correct correspondences between features (positive exemples) and random correspondences (negative examples). Different learning strategies have been used for estimating w, as described in Leordeanu and Hebert (2008), Leordeanu et al. (2007), and Caetano et al. (2007). For brevity, we assume that w has been estimated already by using one of these techniques.

In the previous section, we presented how we localize the object by efficiently solving a quadratic assignment problem. However, this does not solve the recognition problem, because the matching algorithm will return an assignment even if the input image does not contain the object. In order to decide whether the object is present at the specific location x^* given by our localization step, we need to model the posterior $P(C|x^*, D)$ (where the class $C = 1$ if the object is present at location x^* and $C = 0$ otherwise). Modeling the true posterior would require modeling the likelihood of the data D given the background category, which is infeasible in practice. Instead, we take a discriminative approach and try to model this posterior directly.

$P(C|x^*, D)$ should take into account two important requirements. First, it should depend on the quality of the match (localization) as given by the pairwise potentials $G_{ia;jb}$ for the optimal solution x^* (we denote by G_o the submatrix of G containing only the assignments in x^*.) Second, it should depend only on those model parts that indeed belong to the category of interest and are discriminative against the negative class. It is not obvious which are those parts, because we learn the model in a semi-supervised fashion. The first consideration suggests that $P(C|x^*, D)$ can be approximated by passing $\mathbf{1}^T G_o \mathbf{1}$ through a logistic transformation. The second remark motivates the use of a *relevance* parameter r_i for each part i (in section 19.2.2 we explain how the relevance weights are learned), which has high value if part i is discriminative against the background, and low value otherwise. In practice, the relevance parameter is used for each correspondence, thus capturing the relative importance of different features.

19.2.2 Learning

The model parameters to be learned consist of the pairwise geometric relationships e_{ij} between all pairs of parts, the sensitivity to deformations w (which defines the pairwise potentials), the relevance parameters r and the parameters used for computing $P(C|x^*, D)$. The learning steps are described next.

We first initialize the pairwise geometric parameters (e_{ij}) for each pair of model parts by simply copying them from a positive training image. Thus, our initial model will have as many parts as the first training image used and the same pairwise relationships. We initialize the rest of the parameters to a set of default values. For each part i we set the default value of its relevance r_i to 0. The default parameters of the pairwise potentials (w) are learned independently.

Starting from the previous values, we update the parameters by minimizing the familiar sum-of-squares error function using gradient descent. The objective function is differentiable with respect to r and the other parameters because they do not affect the optimum x^* (for the other parameters we differentiate assuming fixed x^*):

$$J = \sum_{n=1}^{N} b_n (S(G_o^{(n)}, r) - t^{(n)})^2 \tag{19.4}$$

Here $t^{(n)}$ represents the ground truth for the nth image (1 if the object is present in the image, 0 otherwise). The weights b_n are fixed to m_N/m_P if $t^{(n)} = 1$ and 0 otherwise, where m_N and m_P are the number of negative and positive images, respectively. These

Figure 19.3. Training images (*left*) and the contours on which the relevant features were found during training (*right*).

weights balance the relative contributions to the error function between positive and negative examples. The matrix $G_0^{(n)}$ contains the pairwise potentials for the optimal localization for the nth image.

We update the parameters using gradient descent, looping over all training images for a fixed number of iterations. Using a general rule we can easily write the update rules for all of the model parameters. The pairwise potentials (G_0) do not depend on the parameters $r, \ldots$. It follows that the optimal labeling x^* of the localization problem remains constant if we update only $r, \ldots$. In practice we update only $r, \ldots$ and the pairwise distances d_{ij}, while assuming that x^* does not change, thus avoiding the computationally expensive step of matching after each gradient descent update.

As mentioned earlier, in general the relevance values r_i for each part i tend to converge toward either 1 or 0, with very few parts staying in between. This is due to the fact that the derivative of J with respect to the free relevance parameters r_i is zero only when the output $S(G_0^{(n)}, r)$ is either 0 or 1, or the relevance r_i is either 0 or 1, the latter being much easier to achieve. This is the key factor that allows us to discard irrelevant parts without significantly affecting the output $S(G_0^{(n)}, r)$. Therefore, all parts with $r_i \approx 0$ are discarded. In our experiments we have observed that the relevant features found were most of the time belonging to the true object of interest (Fig. 19.3).

We proceed by merging the current model with a newly selected training image (randomly selected from the ones on which the recognition output was not close enough to 1): we first localize the current model in the new image, thus finding the subset of features in the image that shares similar pairwise geometric relationships with the current model. Next, we add to the model new parts corresponding to all the image features that did not match the current model parts. As before, we initialize all

Table 19.1. *Confusion Matrix for PASCAL Dataset (Using Bounding Boxes)*

Category	Bikes	Cars	Motorbikes	People
Bikes	80.7%	0%	7%	12.3%
Cars	5.7%	88.6%	5.7%	0%
Motorbikes	4.7%	0%	95.3%	0%
People	7.1%	0%	0%	92.9%

the corresponding parameters involving newly added parts, by copying the geometric relationships between the corresponding features and using default values for the rest. At this stage, different viewpoints or shapes of our category can be merged together.

19.2.3 Examples

We compare the performance of our method with the one by Winn et al. (2005) on the PASCAL challenge training dataset (Table 19.4). This is an interesting experiment because our method focuses only on geometry and ignores the local appearance, while, Winn et al. (2005) in contrast, focus on local texture information and ignore the geometry. We followed the same experimental setup, splitting the dataset randomly into two equal training and testing sets. In the first set of experiments we used the bounding box provided (also used by Winn et al. 2005). We outperform the texture-based classifier (Winn et al. 2005) by more than 10%, which confirms our intuition that shape is a stronger cue than local appearance for these types of object categories. Surprisingly, bikes and motorcycles were not confused as much as we expected, given that they have similar shapes. In the second set of experiments, we did not use the bounding boxes (in both training and testing) in order to demonstrate that our algorithm can learn in a weakly supervised fashion. The performance dropped by approximately 5%, which is significant, but relatively low considering that in this experiment the objects of interest sometimes occupy less than 25% of the training and testing images.

The models we learn are compact representations of the relevant features present in the positive training set. The algorithm is able to discover relevant parts that, in our experiments, belong in a large majority to the true object of interest, despite the background clutter present sometimes in large amounts in the training images (Fig. 19.3). At run-time, the algorithm locates the parts that best match the model by using the global spectral matching criterion. For example, Figure 19.4 shows the contour fragments matched in a few test images from the ETHZ database for five different categories.

Table 19.2. *Average Multiclass Recognition Rates on the PASCAL Dataset*

Algorithm	Ours (bbox)	Ours (no bbox)	Winn (Winn et al., 2005) (bbox)
PASCAL Dataset	89.4%	84.8%	76.9%

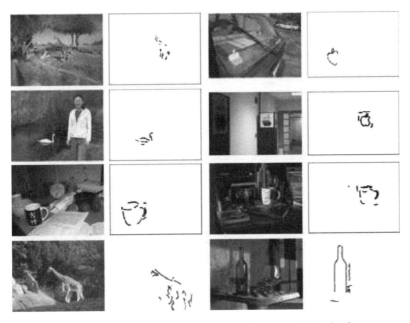

Figure 19.4. Sample results on test image from the ETHZ database.

19.3 Grouping

In section 19.2 we presented an object category recognition algorithm that did not use any grouping cues to help the matching and recognition of specific categories. The matching part of the algorithm considered all pairs of features (pieces of contours) from an image, as if all pairs were equally likely to belong to the same object. Grouping is a way of constraining the matching/recognition search space by considering only pairs of features that are likely to come from the same object. Grouping is essential in improving the recognition rate because it uses general, category-independent information to prune the search space and guide the recognition process on the right path. Figure 19.6 shows two examples that intuitively explain this idea. The images in the left column contain edges extracted from a scene. We notice that without grouping, the objects are not easily distinguished (e.g., the bus, or the horse). However, after using color information for perceptual grouping, we are able to retain only the edges that are likely to belong to the same object as the edge pointed out by the red circle (right column). Perceptual

Figure 19.5. The grouping stage enforces pairwise constraints that could significantly prune our matching/recognition search space. The contours in white (for second and third image) are the ones likely to be on the same object as the red circle, given the geometric or color cues. (See color plate 19.5.)

All Edges   **Grouped Edges**

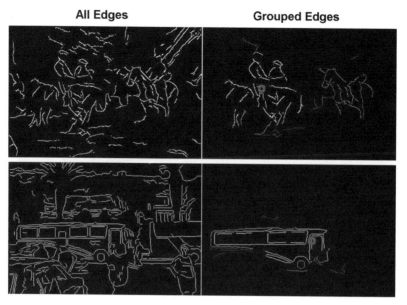

Figure 19.6. If grouping is not used, it is very hard to distinguish the separate objects (*left column*). After grouping (*right column*), it is perceptually easier to distinguish them (the bus and the horse). (See color plate 19.6.)

grouping could also bring a second benefit to the recognition process, because without it, matching could be very expensive, especially when the image contains a lot of background features/clutter. As Grimson (1990b) has shown, the complexity of the matching process is reduced from an exponential to a low-order polynomial when the search is constrained. Therefore, it is important to be able to establish a priori which pairs of features are likely to be part of the same object and discard all the other pairs.

19.3.1 Pairwise Grouping of Features

Earlier work in geometric matching was limited by the fact that it relied on deterministic matching techniques, which commit to hard assignments. Similarly, prior approaches to using grouping were limited by making hard decisions about which features belong together (Mahamud et al. 2003; Sarkar and Soundararajan 2000; Lowe 1985; Etemadi et al. 1991; Roth and Levine 1994; Mohan and Nevatia 1994; Jacobs 1996). There is an important motivation for avoiding hard assigments: it is sometimes impossible to divide features into their correct groups without the knowledge of the specific category (or the desired level of detail). For example, is the wheel of a car a separate object or is it part of the whole car? Both answers can be correct at the same time, depending on what we are looking for. If we are looking for whole cars, then the wheel is definitely a part of it. If we are looking just for wheels then (at least conceptually) it is not. Although perceptual grouping alone should most of the time separate correctly most objects (the ones that are clearly at different depths, such as a flying plane from a close car), it does not have access to enough information to make the correct hard decisions. We immediately see why it is important to keep most of the grouping information around and transmit it

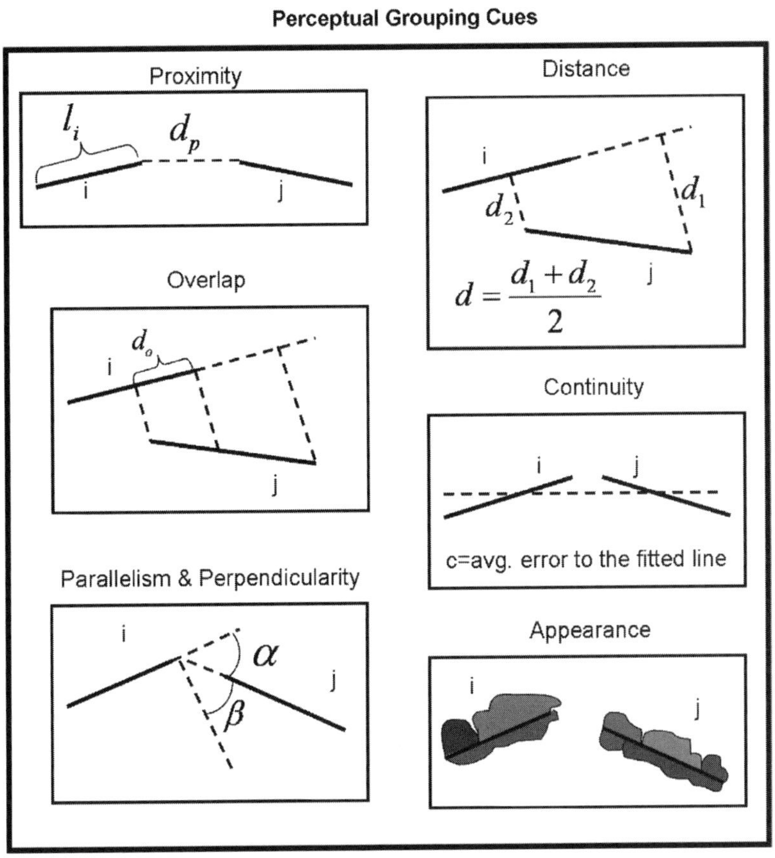

Perceptual Grouping Cues

Figure 19.7. Geometric perceptual cues used for grouping pairs of line features. (See color plate 19.7.)

to the higher recognition processes without making hard decisions, except for pruning the cases when the pairwise grouping relationship is extremely weak. Instead of being interested in forming exact feature groups based on perceptual information alone, we focus on the quality of pairwise grouping relationships and how to integrate them into the recognition algorithm. Because we use pairwise relationships at both the grouping and the recognition levels, the two could be naturally integrated.

By contrast, our pairwise grouping relationships are soft weights that should reflect the likelihood that the two features belong together (prior to recognition – i.e., before using any category-specific knowledge). We focus on perceptual, pairwise grouping based on the classical geometric cues such as proximity, good continuation, parallelism/ perpendicularity (Fig. 19.7), although the approach can be easily extended to color cues, capturing the fact that objects tend to have unique and relatively homogenous color distributions.

Geometric perceptual cues are particularly important for grouping because of their connection to important studies in human vision. Our main features for object recognition are pieces of contours extracted from the image. In the grouping stage, we approximate these contours by fitted line segments. The geometric grouping cues that we propose to use include specific relationships between pairs of line segments:

Table 19.3. *Perceptual Cues Used to Describe the Relationship between Pairs of Lines. Based on these cues, we estimate the likelihood that pairs of lines belong to the same object or not*

Cue	Description
Proximity	$\frac{d_p}{l_i+l_j}$
Distance	$\frac{d_i+d_j}{l_i+l_j}$
Overlap	$\frac{d_{oi}+d_{oj}}{l_i+l_j}$
Continuity	c
Parallelism	α
Perpendicularity	β
$Color_1$	difference in mean colors
$Color_2$	difference in color histograms
$Color_3$	difference in color entropies

proximity, distance, overlap, continuity, parallelism, and perpendicularity, as shown in Figure 19.7. We also use some local appearance cues, which are computed over the superpixels adjacent to the pair of lines, such as difference between the mean colors of the superpixels belonging to each line, as well as the differences in color histogram and color entropy. All these cues, both geometric and appearance-based, form a *relation* vector $r(i, j)$ for any pair of lines (i, j) whose elements are described in Table 19.3 (each row of the table corresponds to an element of $r(i, j)$). Figure 19.8 shows example results from an experiment in which we have manually collected about 300 positive pairs of lines (lines that belong to the same object) and 1000 negative ones

Figure 19.8. Pairwise grouping constraints based on geometry. The contours in white are the ones that establish a pairwise grouping relationship with the contour pointed out by the red circle. (See color plate 19.8.)

(pairs of lines that do not belong to the same object), and learned a binary classifier on the corresponding relation vectors r, using the logistic regression version of Adaboost (Collins et al. 2002) with weak learners based on decision trees (Friedman et al. 2000). We use the soft output of this classifier (the likelihood that a pair of lines belongs to the same object) later in the object recognition approach described previously.

The contours shown in red belong to line segments that were classified as being part of the same object as the line segment pointed by the white circle. We notice that in general only lines that are relatively close to the white circle are positively classified. This is due to the fact that in general, geometric perceptual grouping is a local process and is not able to link directly pairs of faraway lines. Such pairs could be ultimately connected indirectly through intermediate lines.

A key feature of this approach is that the the grouping constraints can be combined with the category-specific constraints in the same spectral matching framework as before, by augmenting the initial pairwise scores $M(ia; jb)$ as follows:

$$M(ia; jb) = M_o(ia; jb)P(a, b). \qquad (19.5)$$

Here $M_o(ia; jb)$ is the score previously defined in section 19.2, which measures how well the geometry (and possibly the local appearances) of model features (i, j) agree with the geometry of image features (a, b). Using the grouping cues we include the perceptual grouping score $P(a, b)$ that uses a priori pairwise grouping information to quantify how likely the image features (a, b) are to be part of the same object:

$$P(a, b) = \mathbf{exp}(w_0 + w_1 g(a, b)). \qquad (19.6)$$

$P(a, b)$ includes all of the grouping cues. Here we limit ourselves to the geometric cues obtained as just described, so that $P(a, b)$ is the output of the classifier trained on the geometric cues above. In Figure 19.5 we present the potential advantage of using grouping. On the left we show all the pieces of contours (in white) that are likely to be part of the same object as the contour indicated by the red circle, as considered by the previous equation (19.2). Because no grouping information was used, all contours are considered. In the middle we show the contours likely to be grouped with the circle if we use the current implementation of the geometrically driven grouping method. On the right, we show the same type of results if we are using the color histogram – based grouping. As already discussed, it is clear that grouping could significantly improve the performance of our recognition algorithm, because most pairs that should not be considered can be automatically discarded, as shown in Figure 19.5. Although the precise way of optimally combining pairwise grouping with feature matching is not known, it is clear that even a straight forward, natural solution, such as the one we presented in this section, should improve the recognition performance.

19.4 Conclusion

We have shown that by exploiting the second-order interactions between very simple features (edge points and their normals), we can match the performance of state-of-the-art algorithms that use more complex, but local descriptors. Our results confirm the intuition that shape is a powerful cue for object category recognition. In this chapter we demonstrated that by capturing shape through second-order relationships (as opposed to local, first order descriptors), we can build flexible models that can accommodate significant deformations, while still being discriminative against the background clutter. Although this study focused solely on geometry in order to stress its importance, future extensions involve integrating local appearance information.

Bibliography

Belongie S, Malik J, Puzicha J. 2000. Shape context: a new descriptor for shape matching and object recognition. In NIPS.

Berg A, Berg T, Malik J. 2005. Shape matching and object recognition using low distortion correspondences. In Proceedings of CVPR.

Bouchard G, Triggs B. 2005. Hierarchical part-based visual object categorization. In Proceedings of CVPR.

Brooks R. 1981. Symbolic reasoning among 3-D models and 2-D images. PhD diss, Stanford University Computer Science Dept.

Caetano T, Cheng L, Le Q, Smola AJ. 2007. Learning graph matching. In ICCV.

Carneiro G, Lowe D. 2006. Sparse flexible models of local features. In ECCV.

Chen J, Stockman GC. 1998. 3d free-form object recognition using indexing by contour features. *Comput Vis Image Und* 71: 334–335.

Collins M, Schapire R, Singer Y. 2002. Logistic regression, adaboost and bregman distances. In *Machine learning*.

Crandall D, Felzenszwalb P, Huttenlocher D. 2005. Spatial priors for part-based recognition using statistical models. In Proceedings of CVPR.

Crandall D, Huttenlocher D. 2006. Weakly supervised learning of part-based spatial models for visual object recognition. In ECCV.

Csurka G, Bray C, Dance C, Fan L. 2004. Visual categorization with bags of keypoints. In ECCV workshop on statistical learning in computer vision.

Etemadi A, Schmidt J-P, Matas G, Illingworth J, Kittler J. 1991. Low-level grouping of straight line segments. In BMVC.

Felzenszwalb P, Huttenlocher D. 2004. Pictorial structures for object recognition. IJCV. (in press).

Fergus R, Perona P, Zisserman A. 2003. Object class recognition by unsupervised scale-invariant learning. In Proceedings of CVPR, vol II, 264–270.

Fergus R, Perona P, Zisserman A. 2005. A sparse object category model for efficient learning and exhaustive recognition. In Proceedings of CVPR.

Ferrari V, Fevrier L, Jurie F, Schmid C. 2008. Groups of adjacent contour segments for object detection. *IEEE Trans Pattern and Mach Intell*.

Ferrari V, Tuytelaars T, Gool LV. 2006. Object detection by contour segment networks. In ECCV.

Friedman J, Hastie T, Tibshirani R. 2000. Additive logistic regression: a statistical view of boosting. In *Annals of Statistics*.

Goad C. 1983. Special purpose automatic programming for 3D model-based vision. In Proceedings DARPA image understanding workshop, 94–104.

Grauman K, Darrell T. 2005. Pyramid match kernels: discriminative classification with sets of image features. In ICCV.

Grimson W. 1990a. The combinatorics of object recognition in cluttered environments using constrained search. *Arti Intell* 44(1–2): 121–166.

Grimson W, Lozano-Pérez T. 1987. Localizing overlapping parts by searching the interpretation tree. *IEEE Trans Pattern Anal Mach Intell* 9(4): 469–482.

Grimson WEL. 1990b. *Object recognition by computer: the role of geometric constraints*. Cambridge: MIT Press.

Hummel JE. 2000. Where view-based theories break down: The role of structure in shape perception and object recognition. In *Cognitive dynamics: conceptual change in humans and machines*. Erlbaum.

Jacobs D. 1996. Robust and efficient detection of salient convex groups. *IEEE Trans Pattern Anal Mach Intell*.

Kumar S. 2005. Models for learning spatial interactions in natural images for context-based classification. PhD diss, The Robotics Institute, Carnegie Mellon University.

Lafferty JD, McCallum A, Pereira FCN. 2001. Conditional random fields: probabilistic models for segmenting and labeling sequence data. In ICML. Morgan Kaufmann.

Leordeanu M, Hebert M. 2005. A spectral technique for correspondence problems using pairwise constraints. In ICCV.

Leordeanu M, Hebert M. 2008. Smoothing-based optimization. In Proceedings of CVPR.

Leordeanu M, Hebert M, Shukthankar R. 2007. Beyond local appearance: category recognition from pairwise interactions of simple features. In Proceedings of CVPR.

Li SZ. 1995. *Markov random field modeling in computer vision*. New York: Springer.

Lowe D. 1985. *Perceptual organization and visual recognition*. Boston: Kluwer Academic.

Mahamud S, Williams L, Thornber K, Xu K. 2003. Segmentation of multiple salient closed contours from real images. *IEEE Trans Pattern Anal Mach Intell*.

Marr D. 1982. *Vision*. San Francisco: WH Freeman.

Mikolajczyk K, Leibe B, Schiele B. 2006. Multiple object class detection with a generative model. In Proceedings of CVPR.

Mohan R, Nevatia R. 1994. Using perceptual organization to extract 3-d structures. *IEEE Trans Pattern Anal Mach Intell*.

Opelt A, Pinz A, Fussenegger M, Auer P. 2006a. Generic object recognition with boosting. *IEEE Trans Pattern Anal Mach Intell*.

Opelt A, Pinz A, Zisserman A. 2006b. A boundary-fragment-model for object detection. In ECCV.

Roth G, Levine M. 1994. Geometric primitive extraction using a genetic algorithm. *IEEE Trans Pattern Anal Mach Intell*.

Sarkar S, Soundararajan P. 2000. Supervised learning of large perceptual organization: graph spectral partitioning and learning automata. *IEEE Trans Pattern Anal Mach Intell*.

Treisman A. 1986. Features and objects in visual processing. *Sci Am*.

Winn J, Criminisi A, Minka T. 2005. Object categorization by learned universal visual dictionary. In ICCV.

CHAPTER 20

The Proactive Brain: Using Memory-Based Predictions in Visual Recognition

Kestutis Kveraga, Jasmine Boshyan, and Moshe Bar

20.1 Introduction

You are speeding along an empty stretch of highway in the southwestern Nevada desert on a clear, starlit night. It is very late, and you have been driving for many hours, fighting boredom and encroaching sleepiness. Suddenly you notice a strange, dark shape near the road, a few hundred yards away. What is this thing? Your mind is racing through the possibilities: Is it a police cruiser parked at an odd angle? An unusual rock formation? Some top-secret weapons system that the U.S. military is testing in the desert? As whatever-that-thing-is fades in the rearview mirror, you still have no idea what it was. Perhaps it was just a harmless piece of highway maintenance equipment that became unrecognizable at night?

The hypothetical example just described demonstrates a failure of the visual system to map input to any stored memory of an object. It is remarkable because of its rarity – most of our conscious visual recognition experience consists of recognizing things in our environment seemingly without effort. Recognition, by definition, relies on matching input to representations already stored in the brain. However, given that any real visual stimulus can be seen literally in an infinite number of views, determined by its orientation, lighting, distance, visual "noise," and occlusion, it is highly improbable that the brain performs recognition by matching detailed input to a representation of every possible view of an object. Even with fully visible objects, such detailed matching would require an impossibly large number of stored representations, incur tremendous neurometabolic costs, and result in an intractable search space. Furthermore, partial or fragmentary occlusion by other objects or by noise presents additional problems for a purely bottom-up recognition, in which a stimulus is first fully reconstructed before it is recognized.

Contrary to this view, we propose that the brain does not reactively process input in bottom-up fashion, but rather is proactively generating predictions for proximate events, including the interpretation of visual stimuli it is trying to perceive. Specifically, we propose that recognition first occurs by matching a coarse form of the input to a most similar memory representation, which also has coarse or prototypical form. The brain

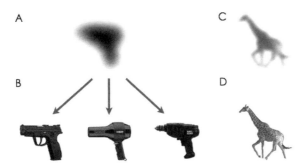

Figure 20.1. The predictions activated by coarse, global properties of two stimuli. The identities of the blurred items in *A* and *C* can be guessed within close proximity, in spite of the lack of detail. Such blurred representations contain primarily low spatial frequencies, which are available in the brain early and rapidly.

is essentially trying to answer a "what is this like?" question about visual input. If the coarse representation of the input is quite specific, it might give rise to a small and manageable set of predictions (Fig. 20.1). When one or more templates match the initial input sufficiently well, they can exert top-down biasing of bottom-up visual analysis toward the most likely alternatives, which quickly completes the recognition process with matching fine details. However, if no good matches are found at this early stage (as in our hypothetical example), recognition can take several seconds or longer, because of the absence of top-down guidance. In the rare cases when the stimulus is truly novel, we eventually may realize that we have never seen something like this before.

How might this recognition process be implemented in the brain? Before we describe the evidence supporting this view, let us quickly review some relevant properties of the human visual system. It has been known for quite some time that the human visual system processes visual information in parallel "channels" encompassing a particular range of spatial frequencies (DeValois and DeValois 1988). The two major physiological divisions in the visual system are the magnocellular (M) and parvocellular (P) pathways, which may be further subdivided into specific channels with differing spatial frequency and differing luminance/color sensitivity (the specific role and characteristics of the third, koniocellular, pathway are at present poorly understood). Anatomically, the M pathway is associated with the action-oriented dorsal stream, which projects to the parietal lobe and extends to the frontal regions, whereas the identity-oriented ventral stream, projecting from the occipital through the ventral temporal cortex, is thought to be predominantly, though not exclusively, parvocellular. The M pathway comprises several types of neurons that are tuned to low and middle spatial frequency range (Kaplan and Shapley 1982), have little sensitivity to wavelength (i.e., cannot distinguish color); high, nonlinear gain at low light levels (i.e., can respond strongly to visual information, even at very low levels of illumination); high temporal sensitivity (i.e., can distinguish visual information that is changing rapidly); and fast conduction velocity (i.e., information propagates very quickly from the retina to the cortex). The P cells, in contrast, are tuned to a somewhat higher spatial frequency range, are sensitive to color, have lower conduction velocity and temporal sensitivity, and low, linear gain. Although the overall spatial frequency tuning curves overlap for the M and P cells

(Kaplan and Shapley 1982), the higher sensitivity of M neurons to low-contrast stimuli, and their higher conduction speeds, effectively mean that M information arrives in the higher cortical areas before P-mediated information. This speed advantage is enhanced for very low luminance contrast and high temporal frequency stimuli, to which the P cells are poorly responsive or nonresponsive.

The high-contrast gain and fast conduction of the M pathway are not the only factors that affect rapid processing of low-resolution visual information. Natural stimuli tend to contain most spectral power in the low spatial frequencies (LSF), which convey global shape information (Field 1987; Hughes et al. 1996). Furthermore, global properties of a stimulus interfere asymmetrically with the processing of local stimulus properties, indicating global inhibition of local processing (Hughes et al. 1996). The combination of these factors results in a global primacy effect observed in many psychophysical studies, manifested as faster recognition of global patterns, low-frequency gratings, and hierarchical letter shapes over high-frequency gratings and local components (Navon 1977; Hughes 1986; Lamb and Robertson 1989; Hughes et al. 1996). These findings in visual psychophysics suggest that we indeed see the forest before the trees.

Despite these findings, object recognition has been traditionally associated with feedforward, hierarchical processing along the ventral visual stream in which visual forms are synthesized from the bottom-up (i.e., retinotopic, point-by-point representations). This process propagates from the retina to the lateral geniculate nucleus of the thalamus, the primary visual cortex (V1), and the increasingly more complex and less retinotopic areas in the ventral temporal lobe, terminating in the anterior inferior temporal cortex. Recognition is thought to occur when the input is fully analyzed and matched to a memory representation. However, early work by Potter (1975) showed that coarse top-down information (knowing only the gist (semantic description) of a visual stimulus) could facilitate its rapid recognition nearly as well as being primed with the image itself, indicating a significant role of top-down information in facilitating recognition. The discovery of certain anatomical and functional properties of the primate visual system also have led to the realization that, under real-world viewing conditions, a purely bottom-up process is unlikely and usually insufficient for successful recognition (Bullier 2001a; Bullier 2001b; Ullman et al. 2002; Sharon et al. 2006). For example, connections between visual regions are not purely feedforward (top-down), but rather most often bidirectional, with the number of feedback projections exceeding the number of feedforward (bottom-up) projections according to some estimates (Pandya 1995; Salin and Bullier 1995; Rockland and Drash 1996). Moreover, receptive fields of visual cortical neurons change their properties depending on high-level influences, such as attention, experience with the stimulus, and context, which can only be explained by top-down modulation provided by the feedback connections (Rao and Ballard 1997; Angelucci et al. 2002a; Angelucci et al. 2002b).

20.2 The Role of Orbitofrontal Cortex in the Activation of Top-Down Predictions

In an early study examining the neural correlates of explicit object recognition, Bar et al. (2001) employed a paradigm that allowed the comparison of brain activation for stimuli that initially could not be recognized, but became recognizable with multiple exposures. To accomplish this, line drawings of common objects were shown very briefly (26 ms), and masked before and after the exposure. This made the stimuli very difficult to recognize at first exposure, but after up to four more exposures of the same stimuli, it became possible to recognize some of the drawings. Comparing the functional magnetic resonance imaging (fMRI) signal elicited by stimuli that were successfully recognized with the activation elicited by the same stimuli that could not be recognized earlier, Bar et al. (2001) observed activation in the orbital prefrontal cortex, in addition to the expected modulation of activity in the occipitotemporal visual regions. Further analyses showed that this activity was modulated by recognition success. Because the orbitofrontal cortex (OFC) had been known primarily for processing affective and reward-related information, this activation could be reflecting a post-recognition processing of associations evoked by the recognized stimuli. On the other hand, earlier electrophysiological work in monkeys had shown that neurons in OFC are sensitive to visual stimuli very early, at around 100 ms (Thorpe et al. 1983), so it was also possible that OFC was involved in object recognition per se.

To determine whether OFC was activated early or late in the process, and to compare it with the ventral temporal object recognition regions, we employed the same paradigm while recording brain activity at a high temporal resolution with magnetoencephalography (MEG). The MEG results revealed that when recognition was successful, left OFC was activated early, at around 130 ms, and this activation preceded activation in the object recognition areas, located in the fusiform gyrus in the ventral temporal cortex, by at least 50 ms (Fig. 20.2). These findings indicated that OFC had an early role in object recognition, rather than in post-recognition processes (Bar et al. 2006).

20.3 Top-Down Facilitation Model of Object Recognition

Drawing on many of the findings summarized in the preceding section Bar (2003) proposed the following model describing the process of object recognition. Low spatial frequencies are quickly extracted from visual input after minimal processing, and are rapidly projected to OFC, possibly using fast magnocellular projections, so that predictions about the identity of the input can be generated. This low-resolution input is compared against similarly coarse visual memory representations. The best matches in the richly associative OFC are activated and exert top-down influence on object representations in the ventral temporal cortex (Fig. 20.3). These top-down predictions facilitate the upstream processing of slower-arriving stimulus details by enhancing only the neural representations of known stimuli that have the same gross shape, eliminating the need for an exhaustive search.

This model gives rise to several testable predictions. One prediction is that low spatial frequencies should activate OFC more than high spatial frequencies. Another prediction is that projections to OFC should be predominantly magnocellular, given the early activation of OFC during recognition. A third prediction is that if OFC indeed receives information from early visual regions and sends top-down information to object recognition regions in the fusiform cortex, there should be corresponding

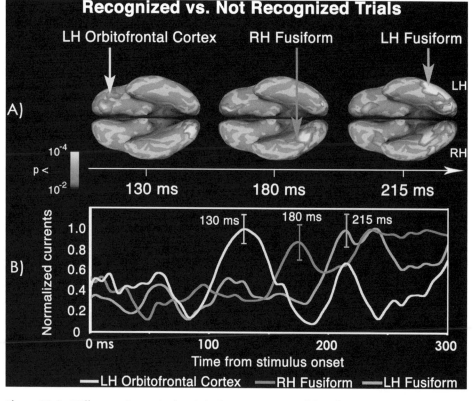

Figure 20.2. Difference in cortical activity between successful and unsuccessful recognition attempts. Differential OFC activity (yellow) occurred approximately 50 ms before activity in recognition-related inferior temporal areas. Right fusiform cortex elicited differential activity (*magenta*) 35 ms before left fusiform cortex (green). From Bar et al. (2006) with permission from the *Proceedings of the National Academy of Sciences*. (See color plate 20.2.)

evidence of neural communication between early visual areas, OFC, and the fusiform cortex.

20.4 The Contribution of Low Spatial Frequencies

We tested the first prediction with a paradigm that employed pictures of objects that were low-pass-filtered, high-pass-filtered, or unfiltered. Thus, intact and low-pass-filtered stimuli would contain low spatial frequencies, whereas the high-pass-filtered stimuli would contain only high spatial frequencies (HSF). This experiment was performed both in fMRI and MEG. As predicted, LSF-containing stimuli activated OFC early (at around 110 ms), but HSF-only stimuli did not (Fig. 20.4).

We also performed a phase-locking analysis of the MEG data. Phase-locking analysis is a technique that relies on isolating the phase of the activation in each region of interest (ROI) and then comparing the phase variability in one ROI versus that in another ROI. High phase correlation between two regions signifies phase locking, an indicator of

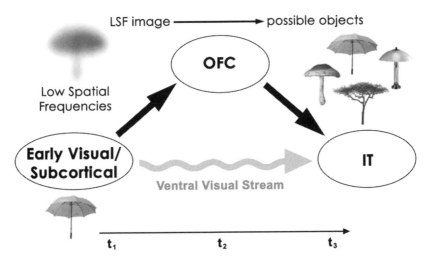

Figure 20.3. A schematic description of the top-down facilitation model of object recognition. According to this model, a coarse, low spatial frequency representation of the input image is rapidly extracted and projected to OFC from early visual and/or subcortical regions. OFC uses this low spatial frequency, "gist," information to generate a set of predictions regarding the possible identity of the object. In parallel, detailed, systematic processing proceeds along the ventral visual stream culminating in IT. The initial guesses produced by OFC facilitate recognition by sensitizing IT to the most likely candidate objects, thereby reducing the search space that the visual system needs to consider to identify the object. From Kveraga, Boshyan, and Bar (2007) with permission from *Journal of Neuroscience*.

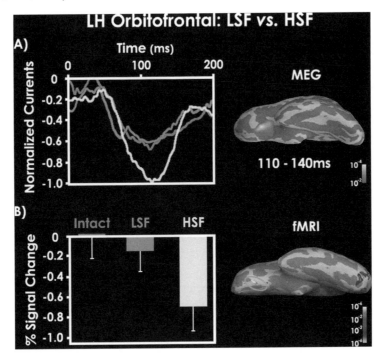

Figure 20.4. Orbitofrontal cortex activations in MEG and fMRI. *A*, The noise-normalized currents for unfiltered (blue), LSF (pink), and HSF (yellow) stimuli in OFC (*left*) and the region in OFC activated in MEG by comparing LSF versus HSF stimuli (*right*). *B*, The blood oxygen level-dependent (BOLD) signal averages for the intact, LSF, and HSF stimulus conditions (*left*) and the region in OFC activated by an LSF versus HSF contrast in fMRI (*right*). From Bar et al. (2006) with permission from the *Proceedings of the National Academy of Sciences*. (See color plate 20.4.)

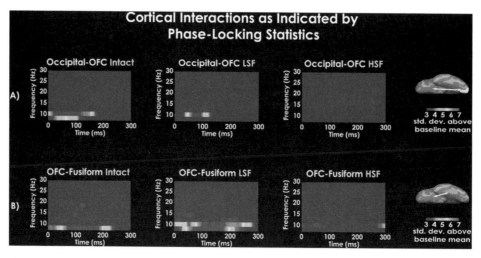

Figure 20.5. Phase-locking analysis showing significant trial-by-trial phase covariance between occipital visual areas and OFC, and, later, between OFC and the fusiform gyrus for intact (*first column*) and LSF (*second column*) images. Little significant phase-locking was seen for HSF images (*third column*). The images in the right-most column show the brain regions from which data were extracted for phase-locking analyses and the *color bars* indicating the phase-locking in terms of standard deviations above the mean. From Bar et al. (2006) with permission from the *Proceedings of the National Academy of Sciences*. (See color plate 20.5.)

communication (although not enough to demonstrate causality) between these regions (Lachaux et al. 1999; Lin et al. 2004). Analysis of MEG signal in the early visual areas in the occipital lobe and in OFC (Fig. 20.5A, rightmost panel) revealed significant phase-locking between OFC and the early visual regions for intact and LSF stimuli, but not for HSF-only stimuli. When comparing activity in OFC and the object recognition regions in the ventral temporal lobe (Fig. 20.5B, rightmost panel), we again found strong phase-locking, occurring about 50 to 80 ms later for LSF-containing stimuli, but not for the stimuli in which low spatial frequencies were filtered out (Fig. 20.5B).

20.5 The Magnocellular Pathway Mediates Top-Down Facilitation

We next tested another prediction of the top-down facilitation model – that top-down predictions are activated early because the critical shape information is projected via the fast M pathway. To accomplish this, we needed a way to minimize the P pathway processing while allowing the M pathway processing, and vice versa. Because M cells have high contrast gain and can readily resolve low luminance contrast, we created M-biased line drawings with a grayscale luminance contrast of <5%, which cannot be resolved by parvocellular neurons (Tootell et al. 1988). Conversely, because M cells are not sensitive to the wavelength of light, we made P-biased line drawings that were defined only chromatically, by setting the foreground and background to isoluminant red and green (the color intensities and luminance thresholds for the stimuli were

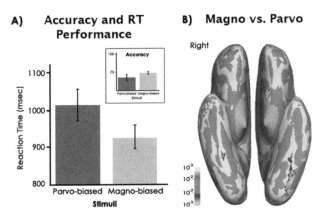

Figure 20.6. Comparison of M and P conditions. *A*, The reaction time (large graph) and response accuracy (small graph) results for M (red, 1010 ms) and P (gray, 905 ms) reveal that observers were both faster and slightly more accurate in recognizing *M*-biased line drawings. Only the correct responses, without outliers ($> \pm 2$ SD) are included, although the M-P relationship does not change qualitatively when all trials are included. *B*, Statistical parametric map ($P < 0.01$) of fMRI activations in the M versus P contrast. The M activations are in red-yellow color map, the P activations are in blue-cyan color map. From Kveraga, Boshyan, and Bar (2007) with permission from *Journal of Neuroscience*. (See color plate 20.6.)

individually determined for each observer). The P-biased stimuli were set to higher light intensities than the M-biased stimuli, but despite being brighter and subjectively more visible, they were recognized more slowly than M-biased stimuli (Fig. 20.6A). The M-biased stimuli activated OFC significantly more than the P-biased stimuli, whereas the opposite was the case for the object recognition regions in the fusiform cortex in the ventral temporal lobe (Fig. 20.6B). Moreover, the fMRI signal in OFC predicted the recognition advantage of M-biased versus P-biased stimuli; the fusiform cortex activity was inversely correlated with this measure. In other words, greater OFC activity was correlated with the speed of recognition of the M-biased stimuli, whereas greater ventral temporal activity predicted *slower* responses for the P-biased stimuli.

To explore how the M- and P-biasing affected connectivity between our regions of interest, we employed Dynamic Causal Modeling (DCM). Dynamic Causal Modeling is a recently developed method of inferring directional connectivity between two or more neural regions based on fMRI signal time series from those regions (Friston et al. 2003; Penny et al. 2004a; Friston 2006; Stephan and Penny 2006). We examined the connections between three ROIs: OFC, fusiform gyrus (FG), and the early object form region in the middle occipital gyrus (MOG), which served as the input region to OFC and FG. A set of six DCMs was constructed, specifying feedforward, feedback, or both feedforward and feedback connections between MOG, OFC, and FG (Fig. 20.7A). The model identified via the Bayesian Model Selection procedure (Stephan and Penny 2006) as the most probable model in the majority of subjects was model no. 4, which specified feedforward connections from MOG to both OFC and FG, and a feedback connection from OFC to FG. Critically, making the line drawings M-biased increased the effective connectivity in the feedforward connection from MOG to OFC and the feedback connection from OFC to FG. Conversely, when the

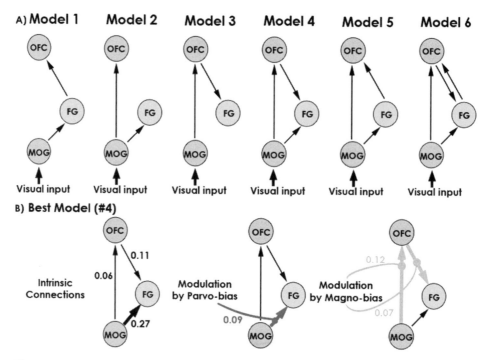

Figure 20.7. Dynamic causal modeling of brain connectivity with fMRI data. *A*, The six intrinsic connectivity patterns of dynamic causal models tested in our functional connectivity analyses. Model 4 was estimated to be the best fit for the data. *B*, (*left*), Intrinsic connection weights; (*middle and right*), modulatory connections activated by P and M bias in the stimuli. The thick arrows indicate significant effects at the $P < 0.05$ level. From Kveraga, Boshyan, and Bar (2007) with permission from *Journal of Neuroscience*. (See color plate 20.7.)

stimuli were made P-biased, the effective connectivity increased only in the feedforward connection from MOG to FG (Fig. 20.7B). Thus, these findings confirm both the critical role of OFC in mediating top-down predictions to the fusiform object recognition regions, and that the projections through which these predictions are conveyed are indeed magnocellular.

The studies just described tested and confirmed several predictions of the top-down facilitation model proposed by Bar (2003): (1) that if OFC were to facilitate bottom-up recognition processes, it should be activated early in the recognition process; (2) that given the importance of LSFs in global shape representation, LSFs should activate OFC more than HSFs; (3) that the rapid projections to OFC should be predominantly magnocellular; and (4) that OFC should be involved in receiving and interpreting coarse information from the early visual regions, and sending top-down predictions to object recognition regions in the ventral temporal cortex, as demonstrated by evidence from phase-locking analyses and Dynamic Causal Modeling (Bar et al. 2006; Kveraga et al. 2007). However, in these studies we addressed how objects are recognized in isolation. The more ecological, and more difficult, problem in both human and machine vision is recognizing objects embedded in their natural context and segmenting objects from their background (Sharon et al. 2006). In the next section we discuss how the knowledge of contextual associations can help facilitate the recognition of objects and scenes, and how this process may be implemented in the brain.

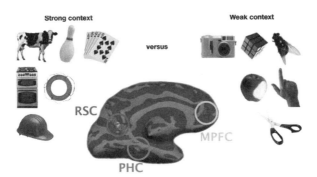

Figure 20.8. Neural activity evoked by contextual processing. Experimental conditions and a statistical activation map representing the difference between perceiving strongly contextual objects and weakly contextual objects. This is a medial view of activity in the left hemisphere averaged across all participants. Figure adapted from Bar (2004) with permission from *Nature Reviews Neuroscience*. (See color plate 20.8.)

20.6 Contextual Predictions for Object Recognition

Objects and events in our environment tend to be associated with other objects and events co-occurring closely in space and/or time. For example, after a flash of lightning or a rumble of thunder, we expect to see rain clouds; in the supermarket we know to look for salsa next to corn chips; and at the beach we are not surprised to see beach umbrellas next to beach chairs. Our brain encodes these statistical regularities and later uses them to predict proximate objects and events under similar circumstances in our environment. Both individual objects and particular environments can predict objects and events strongly associated with them. How contextual associations are represented in the brain and employed in facilitating recognition until recently has been studied primarily behaviorally. Early studies showed that the gist of a scene can be extracted rapidly from LSF information (Biederman et al. 1974; Schyns and Oliva 1994; Sanocki and Epstein 1997; Oliva and Torralba 2001). This information can be used to facilitate the recognition of contextually congruent objects in the scene (Biederman 1972; Palmer 1975; Biederman, Mezzanotte et al. 1982; Lopez and Leekam 2003; Davenport and Potter 2004). Key contextual objects can also activate contextual associations, which can then be used to recognize other contextually related objects (Bar and Ullman 1996).

To determine where contextual processes occur in the brain, Bar and Aminoff (2003) used fMRI to compare hemodynamic (fMRI) responses evoked by objects that differed in the strength of their contextual associations. Some objects were strongly related to a specific context (e.g., a construction hat), while others were weakly related to many contexts (e.g., a pen). Compared with objects weakly associated with many different contexts, images of objects with strong contextual associations evoked greater neural activity in the parahippocampal cortex (PHC), the retrosplenial complex (RSC), and, for some subjects, in the medial prefrontal cortex (MPFC), displayed in Figure 20.8. While PHC was more sensitive to the specific instantiation of contextual information in the stimulus, being modulated by the amount of background in the stimulus, RSC appeared to be more responsive to the strength of contextual associations of a stimulus per se.

The PHC activations overlapped with the region that had been previously reported to be activated by images of places, such as houses and indoor scenes (Aguirre et al. 1996; Aguirre et al. 1998; Epstein and Kanwisher 1998; O'Craven and Kanwisher 2000). Moreover, both PHC and RSC had been previously implicated in mediating episodic memory (Maguire 2001a; Maguire 2001b; Ranganath and D'Esposito 2001) and are known to be reciprocally connected (Suzuki and Amaral 1994). The seemingly disparate functions for the same set of neural regions make sense only when one considers that contextual associations are central to binding together both spatial information and episodic memories. This question was further explored in a study by Aminoff, Gronau, and Bar (2007), in which subjects had to form de novo contextual associations between novel shapes. The associations were either spatial (the shapes appeared together in a particular spatial order) or nonspatial (the shapes appeared together, but their spatial relationship varied randomly). After training, the spatial contexts activated the posterior part of PHC, whereas the nonspatial contexts evoked activity in the anterior part of PHC. Both the spatial and nonspatial contextual stimuli activated PHC more strongly than control, noncontextual, stimuli. The area activated by spatial contexts also overlapped with the region in PHC activated by pictures of places and houses in previous studies (Epstein and Kanwisher 1998). Thus, PHC appears to mediate instances of both spatial and nonspatial context, whereas RSC may be representing more abstract aspects of a context. The idea that the PHC does not subserve places and scenes exclusively, but rather is more broadly used for general associations has recently gained further support (Bar et al., 2008).

Bar and Ullman (1996) have proposed that contextual knowledge may be organized in memory structures termed context frames, which bind together information about the objects likely to co-appear in a scene and the spatial relations between them. Such context frames are reminiscent of *schemata* (Mandler and Johnson 1976; Hock et al. 1978), *scripts* (Schank 1975), and *frames* (Minsky 1975), which have been proposed in the 1970s. We have since elaborated the concept of context frames to distinguish specific types of contextual frames in the brain: *prototypical context frames*, which provide a spatial template for the global structure of familiar contexts; and *episodic context frames*, which represent more detailed information about the specific instantiation of a given context. These two types of context frames are not independent subtypes but rather representations of a context at different levels of specificity: a coarse type of representation (*prototypical frame*) is gradually filled in with details and becomes an *episodic* representation of a particular instance of a context.

What is the role of a prototypical context frame? Instances of a context (e.g., a city street) can vary widely in their particular details but tend to share basic global properties. These shared properties are represented by the LSF of a scene, which conveys instance-invariant, or prototypical, features and omit details that differ from one instance to another. Prototypical context frames likely develop through experience with instances of a particular context. The representation of the common features of a contextual scene is gradually strengthened with each new instance, whereas varying details are "averaged out," such as in Figure 20.9, in which the street prototype in the left panel is the result of averaging over a 100 images of a street (Torralba and Oliva 2003). This forming of a prototype resembles the result of LSF filtering. An LSF image of the input scene can be conveyed more quickly and guide attention to the regions of

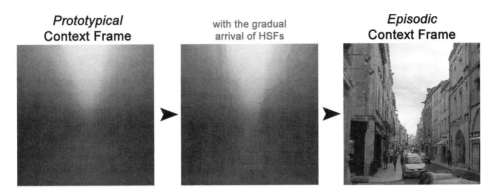

Prototypical Context Frame — with the gradual arrival of HSFs — **Episodic Context Frame**

Figure 20.9. In parallel to the bottom-up systematic progression of the image details along the visual pathways, there are quick projections of LSF information, possibly via the magnocellular pathway. This coarse but rapid information is sufficient for generating an "initial guess." Image on the left courtesy of A. Torralba.

the image that should be explored further. Moreover, matching an LSF representation of a scene with a prototypical context frame in memory should be faster and more robust because of the filtering out of instance-specific (and thus, likely category-irrelevant) details. Indeed, such averaging recently has been shown to improve substantially the recognition success of automatic face recognition software (Jenkins and Burton 2008). Faces are, in a sense, highly structured contexts, in that their key constituent parts (eyes, nose, and mouth) are always present in roughly the same spatial arrangement. In fact, famous faces, which by virtue of their fame tend to have more contextual associations, have been shown recently to activate PHC more than unfamiliar faces (Bar et al. 2008a). Like contextual scenes, faces share global properties but vary widely in local details and viewpoints, which gives rise to a large number of errors in automatic face recognition systems (Zhao et al. 2003). These errors can be reduced or even eliminated by averaging a greater number of instances of a face (Jenkins and Burton 2008), with the end result resembling an LSF representation.

While the LSF of a scene are usually sufficient to generate rapid predictions guiding biologically important goals, such as navigation of one's immediate environment and threat avoidance, the slower arrival of HSF information enables the gradual generation of episodic context frames containing instance-specific details. Episodic context frames enable us to bind together information, which can facilitate the formation and retrieval of episodic memories. Episodic memories weave together spatial and self-referencing information and concatenate it temporally. The usefulness of episodic context frames can be easily demonstrated by an old memory "trick" in which memorization of a large list of unrelated items is facilitated by placing the items in contextually related spatial and temporal frames.

Our studies of contextual processing thus far have shown that contextual associations primarily engage a medial network of brain regions comprising PHC, RSC, and MPFC. The role of PHC may be to process specific visual instances of contextual stimuli, whereas RSC may handle the more abstract aspects of coordinating the contextual associations across different context frames. The role of MPFC with respect to contextual processing is currently less clear, but seems to be most directly related to

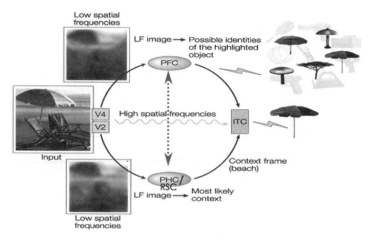

Figure 20.10. A schematic description of the combined top-down and contextual facilitation model. When seeing a novel image of a scene, its LSF version rapidly activates a prototypical context frame (*left*) in memory. The relatively slower and gradual arrival of detail in the HSFs (*middle*) results in a more episodic context frame (*right*), with scene-specific information. Figure adapted from Bar (2004) with permission from *Nature Reviews Neuroscience*.

the activation of predictions. Figure 20.10 depicts our evolving model of how context frames interact with the visual system to facilitate the recognition of an object in a scene, which is then updated with detailed (HSF) episodic information. According to this model, LSF information is projected from the early visual regions to OFC and PHC/RSC. Salient objects, or other objects of interest segmented from the scene, are evaluated in OFC, whereas the gist of the scene as a whole may be interpreted in PHC and RSC. The object-based and scene-based information can then exert top-down influence on the bottom-up processes in the ventral temporal cortex, speeding up visual processing by biasing object-based, as well as scene context-based, representations. Indeed, it has been demonstrated that ambiguous objects can be interpreted differently depending on the scene context (Oliva and Torralba 2001; Bar 2004), and although it remains to be tested, it is possible that the reverse also holds.

20.7 Conclusion

We have proposed that visual recognition depends as much on acquired knowledge as it does on incoming visual information. The early, coarse version of the input information is compared to what we already know and may proactively expect, given the particular viewing circumstances. In essence, we propose that the brain is continuously asking a "what is this like?" question during the process of recognition (Bar 2007). If the early-arriving afferent information matches sufficiently well with the "initial guess" predictions, the higher regions can exert top-down biasing influence on bottom-up processing, which saves time and energy.

Important outstanding questions are concerned with what form these top-down representations take, how they are formed, and to what extent they are malleable. As alluded to in the beginning of this chapter, it is unlikely that the brain contains detailed representations of objects and scenes. Such representations would be far too numerous to compare to and match efficiently, and would not be robust enough to deal with the variability in the retinal image that even the same exact object can generate, depending on environmental conditions and viewpoint. It is possible that these representations reflect a compilation of all experiences with an object, in which the most frequent features of the objects in a particular category overlap. These "fuzzy" templates are essentially object prototypes shaped by many different views of objects during years of development (or scene prototypes, as in Fig. 20.9). Think of parents repeatedly showing babies and toddlers various objects and naming them, or the toddlers exploring the function, structure, and feel of objects. The same process continues somewhat more formally in later childhood and adulthood, and enables the formation of robust object categories. The process of the formation and use of categories in visual recognition was recently examined by Freedman and Miller (2003), while recording from the inferior temporal and prefrontal cortices of monkeys. Freedman et al. (2003) employed artificial "dog" and "cat" category prototypes that were morphed in various proportions to produce a set of stimuli with a specific degree of "dogness" or "catness." While the inferior temporal neurons were primarily sensitive to specific instances of stimuli, the dorsal prefrontal neurons were responsive to the category membership and meaning of the stimuli. Early arriving coarse visual information is similar to prototypical category representations in that most of the spectral power is in the most common features, which become the global features of a category with sufficient exposure to category exemplars. Matching the LSF of an image to prototypical representations of a particular category via a fast projection from OFC to the dorsal prefrontal cortex could account for efficient categorization of the input, as well as viewpoint and size invariance in object recognition.

Visual representations are associated with other types of information that may be stored for a given object – texture, heft, sound, smell, taste. Tightly linked with the perceptual associations may be emotional and reward information, as well as the context in which the object most frequently occurs. Associations may evoke images, sounds, and smells of contextually linked objects. For example, a long, thin shape may activate the image of a cigarette in a smoker, with accompanying smell of smoke, the texture and feel of a cigarette, feelings of pleasure and perhaps guilt, the sound of a match lighting the cigarette, the surroundings in which one usually smokes, and so forth. The seemingly automatic activation of these associations should enable effective cross-modal priming for associatively linked objects or concepts. We expect that a whiff of cigarette smoke would facilitate visual recognition of a cigarette and association objects (e.g., a pack or a matchbox), or that briefly flashed elongated object would enable faster recognition of a flick of a cigarette lighter or the smell of tobacco. Indeed, cross-modal priming with visual objects and associated sounds has been recently demonstrated behaviorally (Schneider et al. 2008), and in electroencephalography recordings was marked by enhanced electrical signal (Molholm et al. 2007) and gamma-band (>30 Hz) oscillations in the middle and inferior temporal cortex regions known for cross-modal processing (Schneider et al., in press).

It is obvious that vision is certainly not the only modality that benefits from the use of predictions in facilitating the perception of incoming information. For example, we can recognize and understand callers over a poor mobile phone connection with its severely compressed audio-frequency range and line crackling, and do it in the middle of a loud party, something that audio-recording and amplification devices can not handle very well. The reason we are able to accomplish this difficult feat is surely due to our ability to activate and amplify in a top-down fashion only the informative aspects of the incoming auditory information, and screen out the rest. Knowing what is informative, and filling in what is missing due to noise or audio compression, can only be possible because of top-down predictions formed by previous exposures to the speaker's voice, speech patterns, syntax of the language being spoken, and sentence context. Top-down predictions also have been shown to play an important role in studies of music perception (Huron 2006; Marmel et al. 2008), in which the perception of pitch was influenced by the expectations activated by the harmonic structure of the preceding measures. Current proposals that predictions provide a universal principle for the operation of the brain (e.g., Engel et al. 2001; Bar 2007), and future experiments that will test these proposals, promise to open exciting new doors for our understanding of the human brain, as well as for developing better computer-based implementations of human faculties.

Acknowledgment

Supported by NINDS R01-NS044319 and NS050615.

Bibliography

Aguirre GK, Detre JA et al. 1996. The parahippocampus subserves topographical learning in man. *Cereb Cortex* 6(6): 823–829.

Aguirre GK, Zarahn E et al. 1998. An area within human ventral cortex sensitive to building stimuli: evidence and implications. *Neuron* 21(2): 373–383.

Angelucci A, Levitt JB et al. 2002a. Anatomical origins of the classical receptive field and modulatory surround field of single neurons in macaque visual cortical area V1. *Prog Brain Res* 136: 373–388.

Angelucci, A, Levitt JB et al. 2002b. Circuits for local and global signal integration in primary visual cortex. *J Neurosci* 22(19): 8633–8646.

Bar, M. 2004. Visual objects in context. *Nat Rev Neurosci* 5(8): 617–629.

Bar, M. 2007. The proactive brain: using analogies and associations to generate predictions. *Trends Cogn Sci* 11(7): 280–289.

Bar M, Aminoff E et al. 2008a. Famous faces activate contextual associations in the parahippocampal cortex. *Cereb Cortex* 18(6): 1233–1238.

Bar M, Aminoff E et al. 2008b. Scenes unseen: the parahippocampal cortex intrinsically subserves contextual associations, not scenes or places per se. *J Neurosci* 28: 8539–8544.

Bar M, Kassam KS et al. 2006. Top-down facilitation of visual recognition. *Proc Nat Acad Sci* 103(2): 449–454.

Bar M, Tootell R et al. 2001. Cortical mechanisms of explicit visual object recognition. *Neuron* 29(2): 529–535.

Bar M, Ullman S. 1996. Spatial context in recognition. *Perception* 25(3): 343–352.

Biederman I. 1972. Perceiving real-world scenes. *Science* 177(43): 77–80.

Biederman I, Mezzanotte RJ et al. 1982. Scene perception: detecting and judging objects undergoing relational violations. *Cogn Psychol* 14(2): 143–177.

Biederman I, Rabinowitz JC et al. 1974. On the information extracted from a glance at a scene. *J Exp Psychol* 103: 597–600.

Bullier J. 2001a. Feedback connections and conscious vision. *Trends Cogn Sci* 5(9): 369–370.

Bullier J. 2001b. Integrated model of visual processing. *Brain Res Rev* 36: 96–107.

Davenport JL, Potter MC. 2004. Scene consistency in object and background perception. *Psychol Sci* 15(8): 559–564.

DeValois RL, DeValois KK. 1988. *Spatial vision*. New York: Oxford Science Publications.

Engel AK, Fries P et al. 2001. Dynamic predictions: oscillations and synchrony in top-down processing. *Nat Rev Neurosci* 2(10): 704–716.

Epstein R, Kanwisher N. 1998. A cortical representation of the local visual environment. *Nature* 392(6676): 598–601.

Field DJ. 1987. Relations between the statistics of natural images and the response properties of cortical cells. *J Opt Soc Am A* 4(12): 2379–2394.

Friston KJ. 2006. Dynamic causal models for fMRI. In *Statistical parametric mapping: the analysis of functional brain images*, ed. KJ Friston, 541–560. Amsterdam: Elsevier.

Friston KJ, Harrison L et al. 2003. Dynamic causal modelling. *NeuroImage* 19: 1273–1302.

Hock HS, Romanski L et al. 1978. Real-world schemata and scene recognition in adults and children. *Memory Cogn* 6: 423–431.

Hughes HC. 1986. Asymmetric interference between components of suprathreshold compound gratings. *Percep Pyschophys* 40: 241–250.

Hughes HC, Nozawa G et al. 1996. Global precedence, spatial frequency channels, and the statistics of natural images. *J Cogn Neurosci* 8(3): 197–230.

Huron D. 2006. *Sweet anticipation: music and the psychology of expectation*. Cambridge: MIT Press.

Jenkins R, Burton AM. 2008. 100% accuracy in automatic face recognition. *Science* 319(5862): 435.

Kaplan E, Shapley RM. 1982. X and Y cells in the lateral geniculate nucleus of macaque monkeys. *J Physiol* 330: 125–143.

Kveraga K, Boshyan J et al. 2007. Magnocellular projections as the trigger of top-down facilitation in recognition. *J Neurosci* 27: 13232–13240.

Lachaux JP, Rodriguez E et al. 1999. Measuring phase synchrony in brain signals. *Hum Brain Mapp* 8(4): 194–208.

Lamb MR, Robertson LC. 1989. Do response time advantage and interference reflect the order of processing of global- and local-level information? *Percept Psychophys* 46(3): 254–258.

Lin FH, Witzel T et al. 2004. Spectral spatiotemporal imaging of cortical oscillations and interactions in the human brain. *NeuroImage* 23(2): 582–595.

Lopez B, Leekam S. 2003. The use of context in children with autism. *J Child Psychol Psychiatr* 44(2): 285–300.

Maguire EA. 2001a. Neuroimaging studies of autobiographical event memory. *Philos trans R Soc Lond B: Biol Sci* 356(1413): 1441–1451.

Maguire EA. 2001b. Neuroimaging, memory and the human hippocampus. *Rev Neurol* 157(8–9): 791–794.

Mandler JM, Johnson NS. 1976. Some of the thousand words a picture is worth. *J Exp Psychol Hum Learn Mem* 2(5): 529–540.

Marmel F, Tillmann B et al. 2008. Tonal expectations influence pitch perception. *Percept Pyschophys* 70(5): 841–852.

Minsky M. 1975. A framework for representing knowledge. In *the psychology of computer vision*, ed. PH Winston. New York: McGraw-Hill.

Molholm S, Martinez A et al. 2007. Object-based attention is multisensory: co-activation of an object's representations in ignored sensory modalities. *Eur J Neurosci* 26(2): 499–509.

Navon D. 1977. Forest before trees: the precedence of global features in visual perception. *Cogn Psychol* 9: 1–32.

O'Craven KM, Kanwisher N. 2000. Mental imagery of faces and places activates corresponding stimulus-specific brain regions. *J Cogn Neurosci* 12(6): 1013–1023.

Oliva A, Torralba A. 2001. Modeling the shape of a scene: a holistic representation of the spatial envelope. *Int J Comput Vis* 42(3): 145–175.

Palmer SE. 1975. The effects of contextual scenes on the identification of objects. *Mem Cogn* 3: 519–526.

Pandya DN. 1995. Anatomy of the auditory cortex. *Rev Neurol* 151(8–9): 486–494.

Penny WD, Stephan KE et al. 2004a. Comparing dynamic causal models. *NeuroImage* 22: 1157–1172.

Ranganath C, D'Esposito M. 2001. Medial temporal lobe activity associated with active maintenance of novel information. *Neuron* 31(5): 865–873.

Rao RP, Ballard DH. 1997. Dynamic model of visual recognition predicts neural response properties in the visual cortex. *Neural Comput* 9(4): 721–763.

Rockland KS, Drash GW. 1996. Collateralized divergent feedback connections that target multiple cortical areas. *J Comp Neurol* 373(4): 529–548.

Salin PA, Bullier J. 1995. Corticocortical connections in the visual system: Structure and function. *Physiol Rev* 75(1): 107–154.

Sanocki T, Epstein W. 1997. Priming spatial layout of scenes. *Psychol Sci* 8(5): 374–378.

Schank, RC. 1975. *Conceptual information processing*. New York: Elsevier Science.

Schneider TR, Debener S. et al. 2008. Enhanced EEG gamma-band activity reflects multisensory semantic matching in visual-to-auditory object priming. *NeuroImage* 42(3): 1244–1254.

Schneider TR, Engel AK. et al. 2008. Multisensory identification of natural objects in a two-way crossmodal priming paradigm. *Exp Psychol* 55: 121–131.

Schyns PG, Oliva A. 1994. From blobs to boundary edges: evidence for time– and spatial–dependent scene recognition. *Psychol Sci* 5(4): 195–200.

Sharon E, Galun M. et al. 2006. Hierarchy and adaptivity in segmenting visual scenes. *Nature* 442(7104): 810–813.

Stephan KE, Penny WD. 2006. Dynamic causal models and Bayesian selection. In *Statistical parametric mapping: the analysis of functional brain images*, ed. KJ Friston, 577–585. Amsterdam: Elsevier.

Suzuki WA, Amaral DG. 1994. Topographic organization of the reciprocal connections between the monkey entorhinal cortex and the perirhinal and parahippocampal cortices. *J Neurosci* 14(3): 1856–1877.

Thorpe SJ, Rolls ET et al. 1983. The orbitofrontal cortex: neuronal activity in the behaving monkey. *Exp Brain Res* 49(1): 93–115.

Tootell RB, Hamilton SL et al. 1988. Functional anatomy of macaque striate cortex. IV. Contrast and magno-parvo streams. *J Neurosci* 8(5): 1594–1609.

Torralba A, Oliva A. 2003. Statistics of natural image categories. *Network* 14(3): 391–412.

Ullman S, Vidal-Naquet M et al. 2002. Visual features of intermediate complexity and their use in classification. *Nat Neurosci* 5(7): 682–687.

Zhao W, Chellappa R et al. 2003. Face recognition: a literature survey. *ACM Comput Surv* 35(4): 400–459.

CHAPTER 21

Spatial Pyramid Matching

Svetlana Lazebnik, Cordelia Schmid, and Jean Ponce

21.1 Introduction

This chapter deals with the problem of whole-image categorization. We may want to classify a photograph based on a high-level semantic attribute (e.g., indoor or outdoor), scene type (forest, street, office, etc.), or object category (car, face, etc.). Our philosophy is that such global image tasks can be approached in a *holistic* fashion: It should be possible to develop image representations that use low-level features to directly infer high-level semantic information about the scene without going through the intermediate step of segmenting the image into more "basic" semantic entities. For example, we should be able to recognize that an image contains a beach scene without first segmenting and identifying its separate components, such as sand, water, sky, or bathers. This philosophy is inspired by psychophysical and psychological evidence that people can recognize scenes by considering them in a "holistic" manner, while overlooking most of the details of the constituent objects (Oliva and Torralba 2001). It has been shown that human subjects can perform high-level categorization tasks extremely rapidly and in the near absence of attention (Thorpe et al. 1996; Fei-Fei et al. 2002), which would most likely preclude any feedback or detailed analysis of individual parts of the scene.

Renninger and Malik (2004) have proposed an orderless texture histogram model to replicate human performance on "pre-attentive" classification tasks. In the computer vision literature, more advanced orderless methods based on *bags of features* (Csurka et al. 2004) have recently demonstrated impressive levels of performance for image classification. These methods are simple and efficient, and they can be made robust to clutter, occlusion, viewpoint change, and even nonrigid deformations. Unfortunately, they completely disregard the spatial layout of the features in the image, and thus cannot take advantage of the regularities in image composition and the spatial arrangement of the features, which can make very powerful cues for scene classification tasks. Therefore, an important research direction is to augment bags of features with global spatial relations in a way that significantly improves classification performance, yet

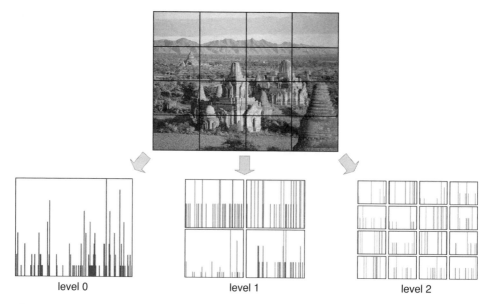

level 0   level 1   level 2

Figure 21.1. A schematic illustration of the spatial pyramid representation. A spatial pyramid is a collection of orderless feature histograms computed over cells defined by a multi-level recursive image decomposition. At level 0, the decomposition consists of just a single cell, and the representation is equivalent to a standard bag of features. At level 1, the image is subdivided into four quadrants, yielding four feature histograms, and so on. Spatial pyramids can be matched using the pyramid kernel, which weights features at higher levels more highly, reflecting the fact that higher levels localize the features more precisely (see section 21.3). (See color plate 21.1.)

does not compromise the simplicity and computational efficiency that makes them so attractive for real-world applications.

In Lazebnik et al. (2006), we have proposed to extend bags of features to *spatial pyramids* by partitioning the image into increasingly fine subregions and concatenating histograms of local features found inside each subregion (Fig. 21.1). This representation is combined with a kernel-based *pyramid matching* scheme (Grauman and Darrell 2005) that efficiently computes approximate global geometric correspondence between sets of features in two images. Although the spatial pyramid representation sacrifices the geometric invariance properties of bags of features, it more than compensates for this loss with increased discriminative power derived from the global spatial information. This has allowed the spatial pyramid method to significantly outperform bags of features on challenging image categorization tasks, in our original experiments (Lazebnik et al. 2006), as well as in several subsequent publications (Bosch et al. 2007a,b; Chum and Zisserman 2007; Liu et al. 2007; Marszalek et al. 2007; Varma and Ray 2007).

The rest of this chapter is organized as follows. In section 21.2, we discuss relevant previous work on global image representations and scene recognition. In section 21.3, we review pyramid matching as introduced by Grauman and Darrell (2005) and then describe our adaptation of this framework to the spatial domain. Section 21.4 presents our original experimental results on a fifteen-category scene dataset and on the standard Caltech-101 benchmark. Finally, section 21.5 surveys recent extensions and applications of the technique that have appeared in the literature since our original publication.

21.2 Survey of Related Work

The origin of many of today's image classification systems can be traced to empirical *appearance-based methods* for recognition, including subspace methods (Turk and Pentland 1991; Murase and Nayar 1995) and histograms (Swain and Ballard 1991; Schiele and Crowley 2000). Many of the early appearance-based approaches required registered training images, and did not tolerate unmodeled photometric or geometric transformations. For these reasons, global appearance-based representations were superceded by *local invariant features* (see Schmid and Mohr (1997); Lowe (2004) for two important examples), which have much better tolerance to clutter, occlusion, lighting changes, and geometric deformations. In the last few years, local features have been successfully incorporated into many state-of-the-art recognition systems (Csurka et al. 2004; Opelt et al. 2004; Grauman and Darrell 2005; Lazebnik et al. 2005; Sivic et al. 2005; Zhang et al. 2007).

Today, local features continue to enjoy a great degree of success, but at the same time there is a notable resurgence of interest in global appearance-based methods (Oliva and Torralba 2001; Hays and Efros 2007; Russell et al. 2007; Torralba et al. 2007, 2008). There are two reasons for this revival. One is the availability of large-scale training datasets gathered from the Web (Ponce et al. 2006). Instead of having to factor out geometric and photometric variations with local invariant features, we can essentially use large datasets to sample all possible variations by brute force. The second reason is an improved understanding of *context* (Hoiem et al. 2005; Oliva and Torralba 2007), or the way that global image appearance and geometry influence the perception of individual objects in the scene. A good contextual description of an image may be used to inform the subsequent search for specific objects. For example, if the image, based on its context, is likely to be a highway, we have a high probability of finding a car, but not a toaster, and we should adjust the prior probabilities of the different types of objects accordingly.

The spatial pyramid method can be viewed as an updated version of a global appearance-based method, or as a hybrid of local and global representations. In any case, it can prove useful for efficient scene recognition in large datasets, as well as for capturing contextual information. It follows the strategy of "subdivide and disorder" – that is, partition the image into subblocks and compute orderless statistics of low-level image features in these subblocks. This strategy has been practiced numerous times in computer vision, for global image description (Gorkani and Picard 1994; Szummer and Picard 1998; Vailaya et al. 1998; Squire et al. 1999; Torralba et al. 2003), as well as for description of image subwindows (Dalal and Triggs 2005) and keypoints (Lowe 2004). Existing methods have used a variety of different features (raw pixel values, gradient orientations, or filter bank outputs), orderless statistics (means or histograms), and different spatial subdivision schemes (including regular grids, quadtrees, as well as "soft" windows). The spatial pyramid method attempts to replace ad-hoc implementation choices by a clean overarching framework. The framework itself is independent of the choice of features (as long as the features can be quantized to a discrete vocabulary), and the spatial decomposition is determined by the goal of approximate geometric matching. In this way, it is not necessary to find the single "best" level of spatial subdivision, and the different levels are combined in a principled way to improve performance over any single level.

A possible unifying theory underlying the seemingly disparate variety of subdivide-and-disorder techniques in the literature is offered by the concept of *locally orderless images* of Koenderink and Van Doorn (1999). This concept generalizes histograms to histogram-valued scale spaces. For each Gaussian aperture at a given location and scale, the locally orderless image returns the histogram of image features aggregated over that aperture. Our spatial pyramid approach can be thought of as a more restricted kind of a locally orderless image, in which instead of a Gaussian scale space of apertures, we define a fixed hierarchy of rectangular windows. Koenderink and Van Doorn (1999) have argued persuasively that locally orderless images play an important role in visual perception. The practical success of spatial pyramids observed in our experiments as well as subsequent work suggests that locally orderless matching may be a powerful mechanism for estimating overall perceptual similarity between images.

Additional hints as to the importance of locally orderless representations may be gleaned from a few recent publications in the machine learning literature. For example, Lebanon et al. (2007) have proposed *locally weighted bags of words* for document analysis. This is essentially a locally orderless representation for text documents, although it does not include any explicit multiscale structure. Cuturi and Fukumizu (2006) have described a very general and abstract framework for kernel-based matching of nested histograms, which is potentially applicable to many different data types. An important direction for future work is extending the insights from these publications into the domain of visual learning, and unifying them with existing image-based theories of locally orderless representations.

21.3 Spatial Pyramid Matching

In this section, we describe the general pyramid matching framework of Grauman and Darrell (2005), and then introduce our application of this framework to create a *spatial pyramid* image representation.

21.3.1 Pyramid Match Kernels

Let X and Y be two sets of vectors in a d-dimensional feature space. Grauman and Darrell (Grauman and Darrell 2005) propose *pyramid matching* to find an approximate correspondence between these two sets. Informally, pyramid matching works by placing a sequence of increasingly coarser grids over the feature space and taking a weighted sum of the number of matches that occur at each level of resolution. At any fixed resolution, two points are said to match if they fall into the same cell of the grid; matches found at finer resolutions are weighted more highly than matches found at coarser resolutions. More specifically, let us construct a sequence of grids at resolutions $0, \ldots, L$, such that the grid at level ℓ has 2^ℓ cells along each dimension, for a total of $D = 2^{d\ell}$ cells. Let H_X^ℓ and H_Y^ℓ denote the histograms of X and Y at this resolution, so that $H_X^\ell(i)$ and $H_Y^\ell(i)$ are the numbers of points from X and Y that fall into the ith cell of the grid. Then the number of matches at level ℓ is given by the *histogram intersection* function (Swain and Ballard 1991):

$$\mathcal{I}\left(H_X^\ell, H_Y^\ell\right) = \sum_{i=1}^{D} \min\left(H_X^\ell(i), H_Y^\ell(i)\right). \tag{21.1}$$

In the following, we will abbreviate $\mathcal{I}(H_X^\ell, H_Y^\ell)$ to $\mathcal{I}^\ell$.

Note that the number of matches found at level ℓ also includes all the matches found at the finer level $\ell + 1$. Therefore, the number of *new* matches found at level ℓ is given by $\mathcal{I}^\ell - \mathcal{I}^{\ell+1}$ for $\ell = 0, \ldots, L - 1$. The weight associated with level ℓ is set to $\frac{1}{2^{L-\ell}}$, which is inversely proportional to cell width at that level. Intuitively, we want to penalize matches found in larger cells because they involve increasingly dissimilar features. Putting all the pieces together, we get the following definition of a *pyramid match kernel*:

$$k^L(X, Y) = \mathcal{I}^L + \sum_{\ell=0}^{L-1} \frac{1}{2^{L-\ell}} \left(\mathcal{I}^\ell - \mathcal{I}^{\ell+1}\right) \tag{21.2}$$

$$= \frac{1}{2^L} \mathcal{I}^0 + \sum_{\ell=1}^{L} \frac{1}{2^{L-\ell+1}} \mathcal{I}^\ell. \tag{21.3}$$

Both the histogram intersection and the pyramid match kernel are Mercer kernels (Grauman and Darrell, 2005).

21.3.2 Spatial Matching Scheme

As introduced in Grauman and Darrell (2005), a pyramid match kernel works with an orderless image representation. It allows for multiresolution matching of two collections of features in a high-dimensional appearance space, but discards all spatial information. Another problem with this approach is that the quality of the approximation to the optimal partial match provided by the pyramid kernel degrades linearly with the dimension of the feature space (Grauman and Darrell 2007), which means that the kernel is not effective for matching high-dimensional features such as SIFT descriptors. To overcome these shortcomings, we propose instead to perform pyramid matching in the two-dimensional image space, and use standard vector quantization techniques in the feature space. Specifically, we quantize all feature vectors into M discrete types, and make the simplifying assumption that only features of the same type can be matched to one another. Each channel m gives us two sets of two-dimensional vectors, X_m and Y_m, representing the coordinates of features of type

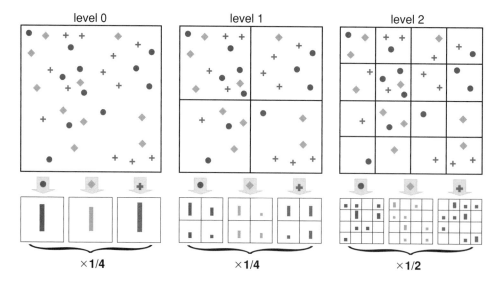

Figure 21.2. Toy example of constructing a pyramid for $L = 2$. The image has three feature types, indicated by circles, diamonds, and crosses. At the top, we subdivide the image at three different levels of resolution. Next, for each level of resolution and each channel, we count the features that fall in each spatial bin. Finally, we weight each spatial histogram according to equation (21.3). (See color plate 21.2.)

m found in the respective images. The final kernel is then the sum of the separate channel kernels:

$$K^L(X, Y) = \sum_{m=1}^{M} k^L(X_m, Y_m). \tag{21.4}$$

This approach has the advantage of maintaining continuity with the popular "visual vocabulary" paradigm; in fact, it reduces to a standard bag of features when $L = 0$.

Because the pyramid match kernel (21.3) is simply a weighted sum of histogram intersections, and because $c \min(a, b) = \min(ca, cb)$ for positive numbers, we can implement K^L as a single histogram intersection of "long" vectors formed by concatenating the appropriately weighted histograms of all channels at all resolutions (Fig. 21.2). For L levels and M channels, the resulting vector has dimensionality $M \sum_{\ell=0}^{L} 4^\ell = M \frac{1}{3}(4^{L+1} - 1)$. Several experiments reported in section 21.3 use the settings of $M = 400$ and $L = 3$, resulting in 34,000-dimensional histogram intersections. However, these operations are efficient because the histogram vectors are very sparse. In fact, just as in Grauman and Darrell (2005), the computational complexity of the kernel is linear in the number of features (more recently, Maji et al. (2008) have shown that the histogram intersection kernel is amenable to further optimizations, leading to extremely fast support vector classifiers).

The final issue is normalization, which is necessary to account for images with different numbers of local features. In our own work, we follow a very simple strategy: we normalize all histograms by the total weight of all features in the image, in effect forcing the total number of features in all images to be the same. Because we use a dense feature representation (see section 21.4.1), and thus do not need to worry about spurious feature detections resulting from clutter, this practice is sufficient to deal with the effects of variable image size.

21.4 Experiments

21.4.1 Experimental Setup

We have conducted experiments with two types of features: "weak features," which have very small spatial support (a single pixel) and take on just a few possible discrete values; and "strong features," which are computed over larger image patches and quantized using a large vocabulary to capture more distinctive and complex patterns of local appearance. More specifically, the weak features are oriented edge points (i.e., points whose gradient magnitude in a given direction exceeds a minimum threshold). We extract edge points at two scales and eight orientations, for a total of $M = 16$ channels. We designed these features to obtain a representation similar to the "gist" (Oliva and Torralba 2001) or to a global SIFT descriptor (Lowe 2004) of the image. The strong features are SIFT descriptors of 16×16 pixel patches computed over a grid with spacing of 8 pixels. Our decision to use a dense regular grid instead of interest points was based on the comparative evaluation of Fei-Fei and Perona (2005), who have shown that dense features work better for scene classification. Intuitively, a dense image description is necessary to capture uniform regions such as sky, calm water, or road surface (to deal with low-contrast regions, we skip the usual SIFT normalization procedure when the overall gradient magnitude of the patch is too weak). We perform k-means clustering of a random subset of patches from the training set to form a visual vocabulary. Typical vocabulary sizes for our experiments are $M = 200$ and $M = 400$.

Next, we report results on a fifteen-category scene dataset and the standard Caltech-101 benchmark (Fei-Fei et al. 2004). We perform all processing in grayscale, even when color images are available. All experiments are repeated ten times with different randomly selected training and test images, and the average of per-class recognition rates is recorded for each run. The final result is reported as the mean and standard deviation of the results from the individual runs. Multiclass classification is done with a support vector machine (SVM) trained using the one-versus-all rule: a classifier is learned to separate each class from the rest, and a test image is assigned the label of the classifier with the highest response.

21.4.2 Scene Category Recognition

Our first dataset (Fig. 21.3) is composed of fifteen scene categories: thirteen were provided by Fei-Fei and Perona (2005) (eight of these were originally collected by Oliva and Torralba (2001)), and two (industrial and store) were collected by ourselves. Each category has 200 to 400 images, and average image size is 300×250 pixels.

Table 21.1 shows detailed results of classification experiments using 100 images per class for training and the rest for testing, which is the same setup as Fei-Fei and Perona (2005). The table lists the performance achieved using just the highest level of the pyramid (the "single-level" columns), as well as the performance of the complete

Table 21.1. *Classification results for the scene category database (see text). The highest results for each kind of feature are shown in* bold

L	Weak features ($M = 16$)		Strong features ($M = 200$)		Strong features ($M = 400$)	
	Single-level	Pyramid	Single-level	Pyramid	Single-level	Pyramid
0 (1×1)	45.3 ± 0.5		72.2 ± 0.6		74.8 ± 0.3	
1 (2×2)	53.6 ± 0.3	56.2 ± 0.6	77.9 ± 0.6	79.0 ± 0.5	78.8 ± 0.4	80.1 ± 0.5
2 (4×4)	61.7 ± 0.6	64.7 ± 0.7	79.4 ± 0.3	81.1 ± 0.3	79.7 ± 0.5	81.4 ± 0.5
3 (8×8)	63.3 ± 0.8	66.8 ± 0.6	77.2 ± 0.4	80.7 ± 0.3	77.2 ± 0.5	81.1 ± 0.6

matching scheme using multiple levels (the "pyramid" columns). First, let us examine the performance of strong features for $L = 0$ and $M = 200$, corresponding to a standard bag of features. Our classification rate is 72 .2%. For the thirteen classes inherited from Fei-Fei and Perona (2005), it is 74.7%, which is much higher than their best results of 65.2%, achieved with an orderless method and a feature set comparable to ours. With the spatial pyramid at $L = 2$, the performance of our method goes up to 81.1% – an almost 10% improvement over a bag of features.

More generally, for all three kinds of features (weak features and strong features with $M = 200$ and $M = 400$), results improve dramatically as we go from $L = 0$ to a multilevel setup. Though matching at the highest pyramid level seems to account for most of the improvement, using all the levels together confers a statistically significant benefit. For strong features, single-level performance actually drops as we go from $L = 2$ to $L = 3$. This means that the highest level of the $L = 3$ pyramid is too finely subdivided, with individual bins yielding too few matches. Despite the diminished discriminative power of the highest level, the performance of the

Figure 21.3. Example images from the scene category database. The database is publicly available at http://www-cvr.ai.uiuc.edu/ponce_grp/data.

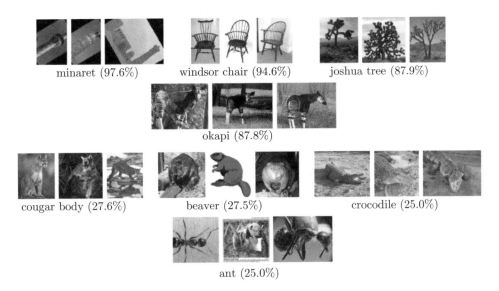

minaret (97.6%)   windsor chair (94.6%)   joshua tree (87.9%)

okapi (87.8%)

cougar body (27.6%)   beaver (27.5%)   crocodile (25.0%)

ant (25.0%)

Figure 21.4. *Top two rows,* Some classes on which our method ($L = 2$, $M = 200$) achieved high performance. *Bottom two rows,* Classes on which our method performed poorly.

entire $L = 3$ pyramid remains essentially identical to that of the $L = 2$ pyramid. This, then, is the main advantage of the spatial pyramid representation: because it combines multiple resolutions in a principled fashion, it is robust to failures at individual levels.

It is also interesting to compare performance of different feature sets. As expected, weak features do not perform as well as strong features, although in combination with the spatial pyramid, they can also achieve acceptable levels of accuracy (note that because weak features have a much higher density and much smaller spatial extent than strong features, their performance continues to improve as we go from $L = 2$ to $L = 3$). Increasing the visual vocabulary size from $M = 200$ to $M = 400$ results in a small performance increase at $L = 0$, but this difference is all but eliminated at higher pyramid levels. Thus, we can conclude that the coarse-grained geometric cues provided by the pyramid have more discriminative power than an enlarged visual vocabulary. Of course, the optimal way to exploit structure both in the image and in the feature space may be to combine them in a unified multiresolution framework; Liu et al. (2007) is a recent example of work in this direction.

21.4.3 Caltech-101

Our second set of experiments is on the Caltech-101 database (Fei-Fei et al. 2004) (Fig. 21.4). This database contains from 31 to 800 images per category. Most images are medium resolution (i.e., about 300×300 pixels). Caltech-101 is one of the most diverse object database available today, although it is not without shortcomings. Namely, most images feature relatively little clutter, and the objects are centered and occupy most of the image. In addition, a number of categories, such as minaret (see Fig. 21.4), are affected by "corner" artifacts resulting from artificial image rotation. Although

Table 21.2. *Classification results for the Caltech-101 database*

L	Weak features		Strong features (200)	
	Single-level	Pyramid	Single-level	Pyramid
0	15.5 ± 0.9		41.2 ± 1.2	
1	31.4 ± 1.2	32.8 ± 1.3	55.9 ± 0.9	57.0 ± 0.8
2	47.2 ± 1.1	49.3 ± 1.4	63.6 ± 0.9	64.6 ± 0.8
3	52.2 ± 0.8	54.0 ± 1.1	60.3 ± 0.9	64.6 ± 0.7

these artifacts are semantically irrelevant, they can provide stable cues resulting in misleadingly high recognition rates.

We follow the standard experimental setup of training on 30 images per class and testing on the rest. For efficiency, we limit the number of test images to 50 per class. Note that because some categories are very small, we may end up with just a single test image per class. Table 21.2 gives a breakdown of classification rates for different pyramid levels for weak features and strong features with $M = 200$. The results for $M = 400$ are not shown, because just as for the scene category database, they do not bring any significant improvement. For $L = 0$, strong features give 41.2%, which is slightly below the 43% reported by Grauman and Darrell (2005). Our best result is 64.6%, achieved with strong features at $L = 2$. Thus, the spatial pyramid improves over the bag of features by over 20%. The behavior of weak features on this database is also noteworthy: for $L = 0$, they give a classification rate of 15.5%, which is consistent with a naive gray-level correlation baseline Berg et al. (2005), but in conjunction with a four-level spatial pyramid, their performance rises to a much more respectable 54%.

Figure 21.4 shows a few of the "easiest" and "hardest" object classes for our method. The successful classes are either dominated by rotation artifacts (like minaret), have very little clutter (like windsor chair), or represent coherent natural "scenes" (like joshua tree and okapi). The least successful classes are either textureless animals (like beaver and cougar), animals that camouflage well in their environment (like crocodile), or "thin" objects (like ant).

At the time of its initial publication, the results of our method have exceeded previously published state-of-the-art orderless methods (Grauman and Darrell 2005; Zhang et al. 2007) and methods based on precise geometric correspondence (Berg et al. 2005). Concurrently, two other methods (Wang et al. 2006; Zhang et al. 2006) were published reporting classification rates similar to ours. Since then, a few more approaches have established new records on the Caltech-101 dataset, and these will be discussed in section 21.5. Finally, it must also be noted that a re-implementation of the spatial pyramid method has received good baseline performance for the Caltech-256 dataset (Griffin et al. 2007), which is the "next generation" version of Caltech-101.

21.4.4 Discussion

In summary, our experiments have shown that the spatial pyramid method does very well on global scene classification tasks, or on object recognition tasks in the absence of clutter with most of the objects assuming "canonical" poses, as in the Caltech-101 dataset. However, because the spatial pyramid method relies on a noninvariant spatial decomposition of an image, it may seem susceptible to heavy clutter and geometric deformations. In practice, however, this is not the case. As discussed in section 21.4.2, spatial pyramid matching tends to "zero in" on the scale that contains the most discriminative spatial information. If a dataset happens to be so highly variable that global position of features yields no useful cues at all, the matching scheme will simply "fall back" on level 0, which is equivalent to an orderless bag of features. To test how well spatial pyramid matching performs under highly variable conditions, we have performed another set of experiments on the Graz dataset (Opelt et al. 2004), which features people and bikes in varying positions and at varying scales, against heavily cluttered backgrounds. Even in this relatively adverse setting, the spatial pyramid was still able to achieve about a 4% improvement over an orderless bag of features (see Lazebnik et al. (2006) for details). These results underscore the surprising and ubiquitous power of global scene statistics: even in highly variable datasets like the Graz, they can still provide useful discriminative information.

21.5 Applications and Extensions

This section surveys the extensions and applications of spatial pyramid matching that have appeared since its original publication (Lazebnik et al. 2006). Major themes and areas of improvement include (1) learning adaptive weights for different levels of the spatial pyramid; (2) extending the weighted kernel framework to combine multiple feature "channels"; (3) applying the spatial pyramid within an image subwindow for more precise object localization; and (4) extending pyramid matching to video.

Bosch et al. (2007a) have generalized the spatial pyramid kernel in two ways. First, they do not restrict themselves to the histogram intersection kernel for single-level comparisions, but consider other kinds of kernels for comparing bags of features, including kernels based on χ^2 distance. Second, instead of using fixed weights determined by the approximate geometric matching formulation, they select class-specific weights for each level using a validation set. Moreover, this adaptive weighting scheme extends not only across different pyramid levels, but also across different feature types. Specifically, Bosch et al. (2007a) use histograms of gradient orientations (Dalal and Triggs 2005), as well as SIFT descriptors computed either on the grayscale image or the three color channels. In Bosch et al. (2007b), spatial pyramid matching is further generalized to find a region of interest containing the object. This work also introduces a *random forest* classification approach that achieves slightly lower classification accuracy than support vector machines, but is much more computationally efficient for the task. Varma and Ray (2007) use the spatial pyramid kernel with the same features as (Bosch et al. 2007a,b), as well as geometric blur descriptors (Berg and Malik 2001). Instead of selecting the adaptive kernel weights by cross-validation, they introduce a convex optimization framework to learn them automatically.

Besides Caltech-101, another major benchmark in the recognition community is the PASCAL Visual Object Classes Challenge (Everingham et al. 2006). One of the top-performing methods for this challenge is by Chum and Zisserman (2007), who use a spatial pyramid inside an image subwindow to automatically learn regions of interest containing instances of a given object class, without requiring training data annotated with bounding boxes. Marszalek et al. (2007) present another high-performing method on the PASCAL challenge. Like Bosch et al. (2007a,b); Varma and Ray (2007), this method learns adaptive weights to combine different feature "channels," but it uses a genetic algorithm to accomplish this task.

Finally, a few recent methods apply the spatial pyramid kernel to video. Liu et al. (2007) have combined spatial pyramid kernels with feature space pyramid kernels, for an approach that performs simultaneous multiscale partitioning of the high-dimensional feature space and the two-dimensional image space. The resulting *feature and space covariant kernel* has been shown to perform better than either the methods of Grauman and Darrell (2005) or Lazebnik et al. (2006). While this work has been successfully applied to video indexing on the TRECVID dataset, it does not include any explicit matching over the temporal domain. By contrast, Xu and Chang (2007) develop a scheme for *temporally aligned pyramid matching* to explicitly capture multiscale temporal structure in establishing correspondence between video clips. Laptev et al. (2008) also generalize pyramid matching to the spatiotemporal domain for the application of human action recognition in movies.

21.6 Conclusion

This chapter has discussed a "holistic" approach for image categorization based on a modification of pyramid match kernels (Grauman and Darrell 2005). This method, which works by repeatedly subdividing an image and computing histograms of image features over the resulting subregions, has shown promising results in the initial experiments (Lazebnik et al. 2006), and has since been extended in multiple ways by multiple researchers, as discussed in section 21.5. Despite its simplicity and its reliance on global spatial information, spatial pyramid matching consistently achieves an improvement over orderless bag-of-features image representations. This is not a trivial accomplishment, given that a well-designed bag-of-features method can outperform more sophisticated approaches based on parts and relations (Zhang et al. 2007). The computational efficiency of spatial pyramid matching, together with its tendency to yield unexpectedly high recognition rates on challenging data, make it a good baseline for calibrating new datasets, such as Caltech-256 (Griffin et al. 2007), as well as a highly effective "trick" for boosting the performance of any method that combines kernel-based classification and local features.

Despite the above practical advantages, we must emphasize that by itself, the spatial pyramid method is not meant as a sufficient or definitive solution to the general problem of scene recognition or understanding. After all, global scene statistics are not capable of localizing objects or making fine-scale semantic distinctions necessary to discriminate between subtly different scenes. For example, to correctly determine whether a given scene is a living room or bedroom, it may be necessary to locate and recognize individual objects, such as beds, sofas, coffee tables, and so on. Qualitatively, the spatial pyramid method seems to capture something akin to "pre-attentive" perceptual similarity, but extensive psychophysical studies are required to validate and quantify this conjecture (see Oliva and Torralba (2007) for some initial insights on the relationship between context models in human and computer vision). In the future, in addition to pursuing connections to computational models of human vision, we are also interested in developing a broad theoretical framework that encompasses spatial pyramid matching and other locally orderless representations in the visual and textual domains (Koenderink and Van Doorn 1999; Lebanon et al. 2007).

Acknowledgments

The majority of the research presented in this chapter was done while S. Lazebnik and J. Ponce were with the Department of Computer Science and the Beckman Institute at the University of Illinois at Urbana-Champaign, USA. This research was supported in part by the National Science Foundation under grant IIS-0535152 and the INRIA associated team Thetys.

Bibliography

Berg A, Berg T, Malik J. 2005. Shape matching and object recognition using low distortion correspondences. In Proceedings of CVPR, vol 1, 26–33.

Berg A, Malik J. 2001. Geometric blur for template matching. In Proceedings of CVPR, vol 1, 607–614.

Bosch A, Zisserman A, Muñoz X. 2007a. Representing shape with a spatial pyramid kernel. In CIVR '07: Proceedings of the 6th ACM international conference on image and video retrieval, 401–108.

Bosch A, Zisserman A, Muñoz X. 2007b. Image classification using random forests and ferns. In Proceedings of ICCV.

Chum O, Zisserman A. 2007. An exemplar model for learning object classes. In Proceedings of CVPR.

Csurka G, Dance C, Fan L, Willamowski J, Bray C. 2004. Visual categorization with bags of keypoints. In ECCV workshop on statistical learning in computer vision.

Cuturi M, Fukumizu K. 2006. Kernels on structured objects through nested histograms. In *Advances in neural information processing systems*.

Dalal N, Triggs B. 2005. Histograms of oriented gradients for human detection. In Proceedings of CVPR, vol II, 886–893.

Everingham M, Zisserman A, Williams CKI, Van Gool L. 2006. The PASCAL Visual Object Classes Challenge 2006 (VOC2006) results. http://www.pascal-network.org/challenges/VOC/voc2006/results.pdf.

Fei-Fei L, Fergus R, Perona P. 2004. Learning generative visual models from few training examples: an incremental Bayesian approach tested on 101 object categories. In IEEE CVPR workshop on generative-model based vision. http://www.vision.caltech.edu/Image_Datasets/Caltech101.

Fei-Fei L, Perona P. 2005. A Bayesian hierarchical model for learning natural scene categories. In Proceedings of CVPR.

Fei-Fei L, VanRullen R, Koch C, Perona P. 2002. Natural scene categorization in the near absense of attention. *Proc Natl Acad Sci USA* 99(14): 9596–9601.

Gorkani M, Picard R. 1994. Texture orientation for sorting photos "at a glance." In Proceedings of ICPR, vol 1, 459–464.

Grauman K, Darrell T. 2005. Pyramid match kernels: Discriminative classification with sets of image features. In Proceedings of ICCV.

Grauman K, Darrell T. 2007. The pyramid match kernel: Efficient learning with sets of features. *J Mach Learn Res* 8: 725–760.

Griffin G, Holub A, Perona P. 2007. Caltech-256 object category dataset. Technical Report 7694, California Institute of Technology. URL http://authors.library.caltech.edu/7694.

Hays J, Efros A. 2007. Scene completion using millions of photographs. In SIGGRAPH.

Hoiem D, Efros A, Hebert M. 2005. Geometric context from a single image. In Proceedings of ICCV.

Koenderink J, Van Doorn A. 1999. The structure of locally orderless images. *Int J Comput Vis* 31(2/3): 159–168.

Laptev I, Marszalek M, Schmid C, Rozenfeld B. 2008. Learning realistic human actions from movies. In Proceedings of CVPR.

Lazebnik S, Schmid C, Ponce J. 2005. A sparse texture representation using local affine regions. *IEEE Trans Pattern and Mach Intell* 27(8): 1265–1278.

Lazebnik S, Schmid C, Ponce J. 2006. Beyond bags of features: Spatial pyramid matching for recognizing natural scene categories. In Proceedings of CVPR.

Lebanon G, Mao Y, Dillon J. 2007. The locally weighted bag of words framework for document representation. *J Mach Learn Res* 8: 2405–2441.

Liu X, Wang D, Li J, Zhang B. 2007. The feature and spatial covariant kernel: adding implicit spatial constraints to histogram. In CIVR '07: Proceedings of the 6th ACM international conference on image and video retrieval, 565–572.

Lowe D. 2004. Distinctive image features from scale-invariant keypoints. *Int J Comput Vis* 60(2): 91–110.

Maji S, Berg A, Malik J. 2008. Classification using intersection kernel support vector machines is efficient. In Proceedings of CVPR.

Marszalek M, Schmid C, Harzallah H, van de Weijer J. 2007. Learning object representations for visual object class recognition. In ICCV 2007 visual recognition challenge workshop.

Murase H, Nayar SK. 1995. Visual learning and recognition of 3D objects from appearance. *Int J Comput Vis* 14(1): 5–24.

Oliva A, Torralba A. 2001. Modeling the shape of the scene: a holistic representation of the spatial envelope. *Int J Comput Vis* 42(3): 145–175.

Oliva A, Torralba A. 2007. The role of context in object recognition. *Trends Cognit Sci* 11(12): 520–527.

Opelt A, Fussenegger M, Pinz A, Auer P. 2004. Weak hypotheses and boosting for generic object detection and recognition. In Proceedings of ECCV, vol 2, 71–84. http://www.emt.tugraz.at/~pinz/data.

Ponce J, Berg TL, Everingham M, Forsyth DA, Hebert M, Lazebnik S, Marszałek M, Schmid C, Russell BC, Torralba A, Williams CKI, Zhang J, Zisserman A. 2006. Dataset issues in object recognition. In *Toward Category-level object recognition*, ed. J Ponce, M Hebert, C Schmid, A Zisserman. Springer-Verlag Lecture Notes in Computer Science 4170.

Renninger L, Malik J. 2004. When is scene identification just texture recognition? *Vision Res* 44: 2301–2311.

Russell BC, Torralba A, Liu C, Fergus R, Freeman WT. 2007. Object recognition by scene alignment. In *Advances in neural information processing systems*.

Schiele B, Crowley J. 2000. Recognition without correspondence using multidimensional receptive field histograms. *Int J Comput Vis* 36(1): 31–50.

Schmid C, Mohr R. 1997. Local greyvalue invariants for image retrieval. *IEEE Trans Pattern and Mach Intell* 19(5): 530–535.

Sivic J, Russell B, Efros A, Zisserman A, Freeman W. 2005. Discovering objects and their location in images. In Proceedings of ICCV.

Squire D, Muller W, Muller H, Raki J. 1999. Content-based query of of image databases, inspirations from text retrieval: inverted fles, frequency-based weights and relevance feedback. In Proceedings of the 11th scandinavian conference on image analysis, 143–149.

Swain M, Ballard D. 1991. Color indexing. *Int J Comput Vis* 7(1): 11–32.

Szummer M, Picard R. 1998. Indoor-outdoor image classification. In IEEE international workshop on content-based access of image and video databases, 42–51.

Thorpe S, Fize D, Marlot C. 1996. Speed of processing in the human visual system. *Nature* 381: 520–522.

Torralba A, Fergus R, Freeman WT. 2007. 80 million tiny images: a large dataset for non-parametric object and scene recognition. Technical report, Massachusetts Institute of Technology.

Torralba A, Fergus R, Weiss Y. 2008. Small codes and large databases for recognition. In Proceedings of CVPR.

Torralba A, Murphy KP, Freeman WT, Rubin MA. 2003. Context-based vision system for place and object recognition. In Proceedings of ICCV.

Turk M, Pentland A. 1991. Face recognition using eigenfaces. In Proceedings of CVPR, 586–591.

Vailaya A, Jain A, Zhang H-J. 1998. On image classification: city vs. landscape. In Proceedings of the IEEE workshop on content-based access of image and video libraries, 3–8.

Varma M, Ray D. 2007. Learning the discriminative power-invariance trade-off. In Proceedings of ICCV.

Wang G, Zhang Y, Fei-Fei L. 2006. Using dependent regions for object categorization in a generative framework. In Proceedings of CVPR.

Xu D, Chang S-F. 2007. Visual event recognition in news video using kernel methods with multi-level temporal alignment. In Proceedings of CVPR.

Zhang H, Berg A, Maire M, Malik J. 2006. SVM-KNN: discriminative nearest neighbor classification for visual category recognition. In Proceedings of CVPR.

Zhang J, Marszałek M, Lazebnik S, Schmid C. 2007. Local features and kernels for classification of texture and object categories: a comprehensive study. *Int J Comput Vis* 73(2): 213–238.

CHAPTER 22

Visual Learning for Optimal Decisions in the Human Brain

Zoe Kourtzi

22.1 Introduction

In our everyday interactions we encounter a plethora of novel experiences in different contexts that require prompt decisions for successful actions and social interactions. Despite the seeming ease with which we perform these interactions, extracting the key information from the highly complex input of the natural world and deciding how to classify and interpret it is a computationally demanding task for the primate visual system. Accumulating evidence suggests that the brain's solution to this problem relies on the combination of sensory information and previous knowledge about the environment. Although evolution and development have been suggested to shape the structure and organization of the visual system (Gilbert et al. 2001a; Simoncelli and Olshausen 2001), learning through everyday experiences has been proposed to play an important role in the adaptive optimization of visual functions. In particular, numerous behavioral studies have shown experience-dependent changes in visual recognition using stimuli ranging from simple features, such as oriented lines and gratings (Fahle 2004), to complex objects (Fine and Jacobs 2002). Recent neurophysiological (Logothetis et al. 1995; Rolls 1995; Kobatake et al. 1998; Rainer and Miller 2000; Jagadeesh et al. 2001; Schoups et al. 2001b; Baker et al. 2002; Ghose et al. 2002; Lee et al. 2002; Sigala and Logothetis 2002; Freedman et al. 2003; Miyashita 2004; Rainer et al. 2004; Yang and Maunsell 2004) and functional magnetic resonance imaging (fMRI) investigations (Dolan et al. 1997; Gauthier et al. 1999; Schiltz et al. 1999; Grill-Spector et al. 2000; van Turennout et al. 2000; Furmanski et al. 2004; Kourtzi et al. 2005b) have focused on elucidating the loci of brain plasticity and changes in neuronal responses that underlie this visual learning. In this chapter we focus on the role of learning in perceptual decisions that relate to the detection of objects in cluttered scenes and their assignment to meaningful categories that is critical for recognition and interactions in the complex environments we inhabit. We propose that the brain learns to exploit flexibly the statistics of the environment, extract the image features relevant for perceptual decisions, and assign objects into meaningful categories in an adaptive manner.

22.2 Perceptual Decisions and Learning

Detecting and recognizing meaningful objects in complex environments are critical skills that underlie a range of behaviors, from identifying predators and prey and recognizing edible and poisonous foods, to diagnosing tumors on medical images and finding familiar faces in a crowd. Despite the ease and speed with which we recognize objects, the computational challenges of visual recognition are far from trivial. In particular, the recognition of coherent, meaningful objects entails integration at different levels of visual complexity, from local contours to complex objects independent of image changes (e.g., changes in position, size, pose, or background clutter). As with many skills, learning has been shown to be a key facilitator in the detection and recognition of targets in cluttered scenes (Dosher and Lu 1998; Goldstone 1998; Schyns et al. 1998; Gold et al. 1999; Kovacs et al. 1999; Sigman and Gilbert 2000; Gilbert et al. 2001b; Brady and Kersten 2003) by enhancing the integration of relevant object features and their segmentation from clutter. Recent studies suggest that regularities (e.g., orientation similarity for neighboring elements) are characteristic of natural scenes, and the primate brain has developed a network of connections that mediate integration of features based on these correlations (Gilbert 1992; Geisler et al. 2001; Sigman et al. 2001). During the course of training, observers have been shown to learn distinctive target features by using these image regularities in natural scenes more efficiently and by suppressing the background noise (Dosher and Lu 1998; Gold et al. 1999; Brady and Kersten 2003; Eckstein et al. 2004; Li et al. 2004a). In particular, learning has been suggested to enhance the correlations between neurons responding to the features of target patterns while de-correlating neural responses to target and background patterns. As a result, redundancy in the physical input is reduced and target salience is enhanced (Jagadeesh et al. 2001), supporting efficient detection and identification of objects in cluttered scenes (Barlow 1990).

What is the neural signature of this visual learning in the primate brain? Numerous neurophysiological (Sakai and Miyashita 1991; Logothetis et al. 1995; Rolls 1995; Baker et al. 2002; Sigala and Logothetis 2002; Freedman et al. 2003; Op de Beeck et al. 2003; Sheinberg and Logothetis 2001; Rolls et al. 2003) and imaging (Dolan et al. 1997; Gauthier et al. 1999; Grill-Spector et al. 2000; Chao et al. 2002) studies on object learning have concentrated on the higher stages of visual (inferior temporal cortex) and cognitive processing (prefrontal cortex), providing evidence that the representations of shape features in these areas are modulated by learning. In contrast, computational approaches have proposed that associations between features that mediate the recognition of familiar objects may occur across different stages of visual analysis, from orientation detectors in the primary visual cortex to occipitotemporal neurons tuned to object parts and views (Poggio and Edelman 1990; Wallis and Rolls 1997; Riesenhuber and Poggio 2000). In particular, perceptual learning of basic visual features (e.g., orientation) has been suggested to result in experience-dependent changes at early stages of visual analysis, as this learning is somewhat confined to the trained retinal location (Schoups et al. 1995; Crist et al. 2001a; Fahle 2004); that is, changes in the receptive field tuning properties of neurons in the primary visual cortex (V1) might account for the specificity of learning effects for the stimulus position in the visual field and the trained stimulus attribute. Recent imaging studies (Schiltz et al. 1999; Schwartz et al. 2002; Furmanski et al. 2004) provide evidence for the involvement of V1 in object feature learning. However, neurophysiological evidence for the contribution of V1 in behavioral improvement after training on visual discrimination, remains controversial (Schoups et al. 2001b; Ghose et al. 2002). There is some evidence for sharpening of orientation tuning after training (Schoups et al. 2001b), but no evidence for changes in the size of the cortical representation or the receptive field properties of neurons in V1 (Crist et al. 2001b; Ghose et al. 2002). One possibility is that V1 learning effects observed in imaging studies reflect changes over large numbers of neurons that are very small at the level of individual neurons. Interestingly, a recent study (Li et al. 2008) showing enhanced delayed V1 responses in a contour detection rather than a fixation task, suggest that learning may reflect task-dependent plasticity in V1 that involves changes at both the level of local connections and inter-area connectivity.

Recent fMRI studies (Kourtzi et al. 2005b; Sigman et al. 2005) that examine the relationship between shape learning and experience-dependent reorganization across stages of visual analysis provide evidence for recurrent mechanisms of visual learning that tune processing in early visual areas through feedback from higher cortical circuits (Roelfsema and van Ooyen 2005; Roelfsema 2006). Sigman et al. (2005) suggest that shape representation may shift from higher to early visual areas that support rapid and automatic search and detection in visual cluttered scenes independent of attentional control. These findings are consistent with the suggestion that learning shapes object representations not only by enhancing the processing of feature detectors with increasing complexity along the stages of visual analysis in a bottom-up manner, but also in a top-down manner that takes into account the relevant task dimensions and demands. These results are consistent with the proposal that learning begins at higher visual areas for easy tasks and proceeds to early retinotopic areas that have higher resolution for finer and more difficult discriminations (Ahissar and Hochstein 2004).

Further, Kourtzi et al. (2005b) provide evidence that distributed plasticity mechanisms are adaptable to natural image regularities which determine the salience of targets in cluttered scenes (Fig. 22.1). In particular, their results suggest that opportunistic learning (Brady and Kersten 2003) of salient targets in natural scenes may be mediated by sparser feature coding at higher stages of visual analysis, whereas learning of low-salience camouflaged targets is implemented by bootstrapped mechanisms (Brady and Kersten 2003) that enhance the segmentation and recognition of ambiguous targets in both early and higher visual areas. Specifically, observers were instructed to discriminate between two shapes that were presented simultaneously and consisted of contours defined by aligned Gabor elements and embedded in a field of Gabors. Before training, no significant differences were observed in the performance and fMRI responses for a set of shapes on which the observers were to be trained and a set of shapes that were to remain untrained. In contrast, after training, when the shapes appeared camouflaged in a background of randomly oriented and positioned Gabors (low-salience shapes), fMRI responses were higher for trained than untrained shapes, suggesting enhanced representations of the trained shapes. However, when shapes popped-out from the background of a uniformly oriented Gabors (high-salience shapes), decreased fMRI responses were observed for trained shapes. Interestingly, this learning-dependent plasticity was distributed across early and higher visual areas for

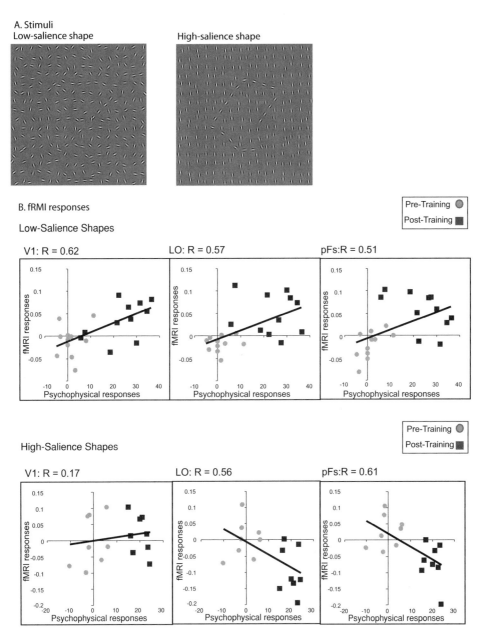

Figure 22.1. Learning to detect targets in cluttered scenes. *A*, Examples of low- and high-salience shapes defined by collinear Gabor elements and embedded in a background of randomly oriented and positioned elements (low salience) or a homogeneous background of elements of the same orientation (high salience). *B*, Relationship between psychophysical and fMRI learning effects: fMRI data and the corresponding psychophysical response for low-salience and high-salience shapes. For each individual subject, we plotted a behavioral learning index (percent correct for trained minus percent correct for untrained stimuli) and an fMRI learning index (percent signal change for trained minus percent signal change for untrained stimuli) after training. Positive values indicate stronger responses for trained than untrained shapes, whereas negative values indicate lower responses for trained than untrained shapes. For low-salience shapes, the regression analysis showed that responses across early (e.g., V1) and higher (LO, pFs) visual areas were higher for trained than untrained shapes. In contrast, for high-salience shapes the regression was significant only in the LOC subregions (LO, pFs) but not in the early visual areas (e.g., V1). Interestingly, decreased fMRI responses were observed in the LOC for trained than untrained high-salience shapes.

low-salience shapes, but restricted to higher occipitotemporal areas for high-salience shapes.

Enhanced fMRI responses have been associated with increased neural recruitment when the sensory input is ambiguous and the task difficult, in contrast decreased responses have been observed when learning has been consolidated, the sensory input has become more salient, and the task easier (Schwartz et al. 2002; Kourtzi et al. 2005a; Sigman et al. 2005; Op de Beeck et al. 2006; Mukai et al. 2007; Yotsumoto et al. 2008). Enhanced neuronal sensitivity during perceptual learning (Sakai and Miyashita 1991; Logothetis et al. 1995; Kobatake et al. 1998; Vaina et al. 1998) has been suggested to involve increased recruitment of neurons with enhanced responses to similar features of the trained stimuli. As a result, the signal-to-noise ratio in the neural responses is increased for trained shapes as compared to untrained shapes. This process may enhance the salience of the target features, facilitating their segmentation from the background and enhancing the global integration that is important for the detection and recognition of visual targets in noise. In contrast, when targets appear in uniform backgrounds, they are easily segmented and can be searched more efficiently (Wolfe et al. 1989; Treisman et al. 1992). Decreased fMRI responses may relate to gain changes (i.e., lower firing rates or shorter duration of firing) or changes in neuronal tuning that result in enhanced selectivity for the relevant stimulus features in a smaller neural population and a decrease of the average fMRI signal across populations within a given region. The decreased fMRI responses observed for high-salience shapes but not low-salience shapes, (despite the fact that the same training protocol involving the same amount of exposure to both types of stimuli was used) are consistent with the idea that training with pop-out targets engages smaller neural ensembles that increase their selectivity for features unique to the stimulus but most relevant for its discrimination in the context of a task. This mechanism results in sparser, but more efficient, representations (Altmann et al. 2004) of the trained stimuli or features that are important for prompt and successful object categorization and recognition. Supporting evidence for such a mechanism comes from learning effects in the primary visual cortex after training on orientation discrimination tasks (Schiltz et al. 1999; Schoups et al. 2001a), and in the prefrontal cortex (Rainer and Miller 2000), where fewer neurons respond selectively to familiar objects than novel objects, but are more narrowly tuned.

Interestingly, fMRI studies show similar effects for long-term and rapid learning that depend on the nature of the stimulus representation. In particular, enhanced responses have been observed when learning engages processes that are necessary for the formation of new representations, as in the case of unfamiliar (Schacter et al. 1995; Gauthier et al. 1999; Henson et al. 2000), degraded (Tovee et al. 1996; Dolan et al. 1997; George et al. 1999), masked unrecognizable (Grill-Spector et al. 2000; James et al. 2000), or noise-embedded (Vaina et al. 1998; Schwartz et al. 2002; Rainer et al. 2004) targets. However, when the stimulus perception is unambiguous (e.g., familiar, undegraded, recognizable targets presented in isolation), training results in more efficient processing of the stimulus features indicated by attenuated neural responses (Schiltz et al. 1999; Henson et al. 2000; James et al. 2000; Jiang et al. 2000; van Turennout et al. 2000; Koutstaal et al. 2001; Chao et al. 2002). Importantly, these effects are evident in areas that encode the relevant stimulus features selectively, whereas opposite activation patterns may occur in other cortical areas implicated in the task performed by the observers (Vaina et al. 1998; Jiang et al. 2000; Rainer and Miller 2000; van Turennout et al. 2000; Rainer et al. 2004).

One of the main advantages of fMRI is that it provides global brain coverage and thus is a highly suitable method for studying learning-dependent changes across stages of analysis in the visual system. However, experience-dependent activation changes in fMRI studies could be the result of changes in the number, gain, or tuning of neurons recruited for processing of a stimulus in the context of a task. As imaging studies measure activation at the large scale of neural populations rather than the single neuron, it is difficult to discern these different neural plasticity mechanisms. Recent neurophysiological studies (Rainer and Miller 2000; Rainer et al. 2004) shed light on cortical reorganization mechanisms at the level of the single neuron when monkeys learn to discriminate images of natural scenes presented in noise. These studies show that learning enhances the selective processing of critical features for the detection of object targets in early occipitotemporal areas, while the efficiency of their processing is independent of background noise in the prefrontal cortex. These findings suggest that learning in different cortical areas bolsters functions that are important for different tasks ranging from the bottom-up detection and integration of target features in clutter scenes across visual occipitotemporal areas to the top-down selection of familiar objects in the prefrontal cortex. Consistent with top-down approaches to visual processing, recent neuroimaging studies suggest that learning may enhance the functional interactions between occipitotemporal areas that encode physical stimulus experiences and parietofrontal circuits that represent our perceptual interpretations of the world (Dolan et al. 1997; Buchel et al. 1999; McIntosh et al. 1999). Future studies combining fMRI and simultaneous chronic recordings from these areas will provide novel insights for understanding both bottom-up and top-down mechanisms for experience-dependent reorganization at the level of inter- and intra-area networks.

In sum, the current experimental evidence suggests that brain plasticity underlying visual learning is distributed across cortical circuits rather than confined to a single locus. These findings are consistent with computational approaches that propose that associations between features that mediate the recognition of familiar objects may occur across stages of visual analysis from orientation detectors in the primary visual cortex to occipitotemporal neurons tuned to object parts and views (Poggio 1990; Wallis and Rolls 1997; Riesenhuber and Poggio 1999). At the neuronal level, learning could be implemented by changes in core feedforward neuronal processing (Li 2001), especially at higher visual stages (Yang and Maunsell 2004), or by changes in the interactions between object analysis centers in temporal and frontal cortical areas and local connections in the primary visual cortex based on top-down feedback mechanisms. Recent computational models suggest that such recurrent processing across cortical circuits is key for the development of biologically plausible systems (Roelfsema and van Ooyen 2005; Schafer et al. 2007). For example, learning has been suggested to modulate neuronal sensitivity in the early visual areas by modulating networks of lateral interactions and, via feedback connections, from higher visual areas (Sagi and Tanne 1994; Sigman and Gilbert 2000; Crist et al. 2001b; Gilbert et al. 2001b; Schwartz et al. 2002; Li et al. 2004b). Such changes in the connectivity of visual analysis circuits may be adaptive and efficient compared to changes in core feedforward visual processing (e.g. receptive fields) that may have catastrophic consequences for the visual processing of the trained stimuli in another context or task.

22.3 Categorical Decisions and Learning

Our ability to group diverse sensory events and assign novel input into meaningful categories is a cognitive skill that is critical for adaptive behavior and survival in a dynamic, complex world (Miller and Cohen 2001). Extensive behavioral work on visual categorization (Nosofsky 1986; Schyns et al. 1998; Goldstone et al. 2001) suggests that the brain solves this challenging task by representing the relevance of visual features for categorical decisions rather than their physical similarity.

Converging evidence from neurophysiology suggests that the prefrontal cortex plays a fundamental role in adaptive neural coding and learning (Duncan and Owen 2000; Duncan 2001; Miller and Cohen 2001; Moore et al. 2006). In particular, the prefrontal cortex has been suggested to resolve the competition for processing of the plethora of input features in complex scenes by guiding visual attention to behaviorally relevant information (Desimone and Duncan 1995; Desimone 1998; Reynolds and Chelazzi 2004; Maunsell and Treue 2006), representing the task-relevant features and shaping selectivity in sensory areas according to task demands (for reviews, see Miller (2000); Duncan (2001); and Miller and D'Esposito (2005)). In contrast, the role of temporal cortex in categorization remains controversial. Some neurophysiological studies propose that the temporal cortex represents primarily the visual similarity between stimuli and their identity (Op de Beeck et al. 2001; Thomas et al. 2001; Freedman et al. 2003), whereas others show that it represents diagnostic dimensions for categorization (Sigala and Logothetis 2002; Mirabella et al. 2007) and is modulated by task demands (Koida and Komatsu 2007) and experience (e.g., see Miyashita and Chang (1988); Logothetis et al. (1995); Gauthier et al. (1997); Booth and Rolls (1998); Kobatake et al. (1998); Baker et al. (2002); Kourtzi et al. (2005b); and Op de Beeck et al. (2006)).

Neuroimaging studies have identified a large network of cortical and subcortical areas in the human brain that are involved in visual categorization (Keri 2003; Ashby and Maddox 2005) and have revealed a distributed pattern of activations for object categories in the temporal cortex (Haxby et al. 2001; Hanson et al. 2004; O'Toole et al. 2005; Williams et al. 2007). However, isolating this flexible code for sensory information in the human brain is limited at the typical fMRI resolution, which does not allow us to discern selectivity for features represented by overlapping neural populations. A recent imaging study (Li et al. 2007) provides evidence that by using multivariate methods for the analysis of neuroimaging data (Cox and Savoy 2003; Haynes and Rees 2006; Norman et al. 2006), we can determine human brain regions that carry information about the diagnostic stimulus features for the different categorization tasks (Nosofsky 1986; Schyns et al. 1998; Goldstone et al. 2001; Sigala et al. 2002; Palmeri and Gauthier 2004; Smith et al. 2004). That is, we can decode selectivity for visual features that is shaped by task context and feature-based attention (i.e., whether the observers attend and categorize the stimuli based on single or combined stimulus dimensions) rather than features fixed by low-level processes (i.e., similarity in the physical input). In particular, observers were presented with a space of dynamic displays comprising synthetic movements rendered with dots placed in a skeleton; the structure of these movements was unfamiliar, but their trajectories followed biological constraints. This stimulus space was generated by linear morphing between protoypical movement configurations (spatial dimension) and temporal warping of their speed profile (temporal dimension). Observers were instructed to categorize these stimuli based on the spatial or temporal dimension. Further, observers were trained to learn an abstract rule of classifying these stimuli that required taking into account both stimulus dimensions. The results showed that fMRI signals in brain areas encoding behaviorally relevant information are decoded more reliably when brain responses for stimulus categories were classified based on the categorization rule used by the observers rather than on a rule that does not match the perceived stimulus categories (Fig. 22.2). These findings demonstrate that adaptive coding is implemented in the human brain by shaping neural representations in a network of areas with dissociable roles in visual categorization. Although activation patterns in the network of human brain areas involved in categorization contain information about visual categories, only in prefrontal, lateral occipitotemporal, inferior-parietal areas, and the striatum do these distributed representations mediate categorical decisions. That is, neural representations in these areas are shaped by the behavioral relevance of sensory features and previous experience to reflect the perceptual (categorical) rather than the physical similarity between stimuli. Specifically, temporal and parietal areas were shown to encode the perceived form and motion similarity, respectively. In contrast, frontal areas and the striatum were shown to represent task-relevant conjunctions of spatiotemporal features that are critical for complex and adaptive categorization tasks and potentially modulate selectivity in temporal and parietal areas.

These findings are consistent with neurophysiological evidence for recurrent processes in visual categorization. It is possible that information about spatial and temporal stimulus properties in temporal and parietal cortex is combined with motor responses to form associations and representations of meaningful categories in the striatum and frontal cortex (Toni et al. 2001; Muhammad et al. 2006). In turn, these category-formation and decision processes modulate selectivity for perceptual categories along the behaviorally relevant stimulus dimensions in a top-down manner (Freedman et al. 2003; Smith et al. 2004; Rotshtein et al. 2005; Mirabella et al. 2007), resulting in enhanced selectivity for form similarity in temporal areas, and for temporal similarity in parietal areas.

22.4 Conclusion

Visual object perception and recognition in cluttered, natural scenes pose a series of computational challenges to the adult visual system – detecting image regularities, binding contours, parts, and features into coherent objects, recognizing them independent of image changes (e.g., position, scale, pose, clutter), and assigning them to abstract categories. Learning and experience play a fundamental role in the functional optimization of the adult visual system for solving these challenges. In particular, the adult human brain appears to capitalize on natural image correlations that determine the target distinctiveness in a scene and learn to detect, categorize, and identify novel objects

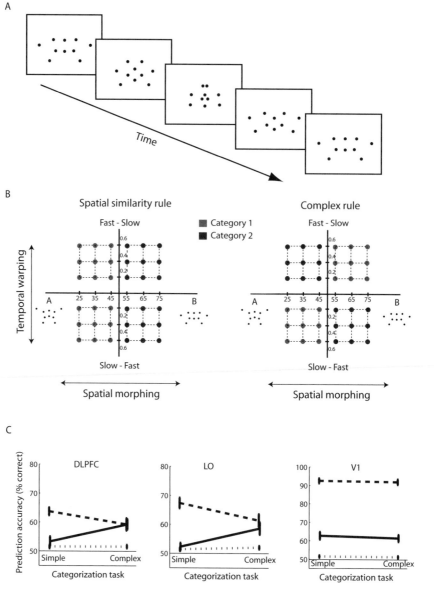

Figure 22.2. Learning to categorize novel patterns. *A*, Stimuli: Five sample frames of a prototypical stimulus depicting a dynamic figure. Each stimulus comprised ten dots that were configured in a skeleton arrangement and moved in a biologically plausible manner (i.e., sinusoidal motion trajectories). *B*, Stimulus space and categorization tasks: Stimuli were generated by applying spatial morphing (steps of percent stimulus B) between prototypical trajectories (e.g., A-B) and temporal warping (steps of time warping constant). Stimuli were assigned to one of four groups: A fast-slow (AFS), A slow-fast (ASF), B fast-slow (BFS), and B slow-fast (BSF). For the simple categorization task (*left panel*), the stimuli were categorized according to their spatial similarity: category 1 (red dots) consisted of AFS, ASF, and category 2 (blue dots), of BFS, BSF. For the complex task (*right panel*) the stimuli were categorized based on their spatial and temporal similarity: category 1 (red dots), consisted of ASF, BFS, and category 2 (blue dots), of AFS, BSF. *C*, Multivariate pattern analysis of fMRI data: Prediction accuracy (i.e., probability with which we correctly predict the presented and perceived stimuli from brain activation patterns) for the spatial similarity and complex classification schemes across categorization tasks (simple, complex task). Prediction accuracies for these MVPA rules are compared to accuracy for the shuffling rule (baseline prediction accuracy, dotted line). Interactions of prediction accuracy across tasks in DLPFC and LO indicate that the categories perceived by the observers are reliably decoded from fMRI responses in these areas. In contrast, the lack of interaction in V1 shows that the stimuli are represented based on their physical similarity rather than the rule used by the observers for categorization. (See color plate 22.2.)

in a flexible manner. This adaptive behavior is implemented by experience-dependent plasticity mechanisms that reorganize processing across multiple cortical areas; that is, there is no exclusive locus of plasticity in the visual system that underlies object learning. On the contrary, learning is implemented through recurrent mechanisms that support adaptive processing of object features based on the task context and demands. Such processing allows the brain to combine noisy and ambiguous sensory input with previous knowledge that is critical for optimal decisions and actions. An important goal for future work is to understand how learning through everyday experiences relates to long-term optimization of the visual system through evolution and development. Investigating the commonalities and/or differences between the long-term optimization of the visual system's neural architecture (hardware) and the adaptive processes (software) that it supports is critical for understanding the key principles that underlie our ability for robust object recognition and designing artificial, but biologically plausible, vision systems for automatic recognition and neural prosthesis.

Bibliography

Ahissar M, Hochstein S. 2004. The reverse hierarchy theory of visual perceptual learning. *Trends Cogn Sci* 8:457–464.

Altmann CF, Deubelius A, Kourtzi Z. 2004. Shape saliency modulates contextual processing in the human lateral occipital complex. *J Cogn Neurosci* 16:794.

Ashby FG, Maddox WT. 2005. Human category learning. *Annu Rev Psychol* 56:149.

Baker CI, Behrmann M, Olson CR. 2002. Impact of learning on representation of parts and wholes in monkey inferotemporal cortex. *Nat Neurosci* 5:1210–1216.

Barlow H. 1990. Conditions for versatile learning, Helmholtz's unconscious inference, and the task of perception. *Vision Res* 30:1561–1571.

Booth MCA, Rolls ET. 1998. View-invariant representations of familiar objects by neurons in the inferior temporal visual cortex. *Cereb Cortex* 8:510–523.

Brady MJ, Kersten D. 2003. Bootstrapped learning of novel objects. *J Vision* 3:413–422.

Buchel C, Coull JT, Friston KJ. 1999. The predictive value of changes in effective connectivity for human learning. *Science* 283:1538–1541.

Chao LL, Weisberg J, Martin A. 2002. Experience-dependent modulation of category-related cortical activity. *Cereb Cortex* 12:545–551.

Cox DD, Savoy RL. 2003. Functional magnetic resonance imaging (fMRI) "brain reading": detecting and classifying distributed patterns of fMRI activity in human visual cortex. *Neuroimage* 19:261.

Crist RE, Li W, Gilbert CD. 2001a. Learning to see: experience and attention in primary visual cortex. *Nat Neurosci* 4:519–525.

Crist RE, Li W, Gilbert CD. 2001b. Learning to see: experience and attention in primary visual cortex. *Nat Neurosci* 4:519–525.

Desimone R. 1998. Visual attention mediated by biased competition in extrastriate visual cortex. *Philos Trans R Soc Lond B Biol Sci* 353:1245–1255.

Desimone R, Duncan J. 1995. Neural mechanisms of selective visual attention. *Annu Rev Neurosci* 18:193–222.

Dolan RJ, Fink GR, Rolls E, Booth M, Holmes A, Frackowiak RS, Friston KJ. 1997. How the brain learns to see objects and faces in an impoverished context. *Nature* 389:596–599.

Dosher BA, Lu ZL. 1998. Perceptual learning reflects external noise filtering and internal noise reduction through channel reweighting. *Proc Natl Acad Sci USA* 95:13988–13993.

Duncan J. 2001. An adaptive coding model of neural function in prefrontal cortex. *Nat Rev Neurosci* 2:820–829.

Duncan J, Owen AM. 2000. Common regions of the human frontal lobe recruited by diverse cognitive demands. *Trends Neurosci* 23:475–483.

Eckstein MP, Abbey CK, Pham BT, Shimozaki SS. 2004. Perceptual learning through optimization of attentional weighting: human versus optimal Bayesian learner. *J Vision* 4:1006–1019.

Fahle M. 2004. Perceptual learning: a case for early selection. *J Vision* 4:879–890.

Fine I, Jacobs RA. 2002. Comparing perceptual learning tasks: a review. *J Vision* 2:190–203.

Freedman DJ, Riesenhuber M, Poggio T, Miller EK. 2003. A comparison of primate prefrontal and inferior temporal cortices during visual categorization. *J Neurosci* 23:5235–5246.

Furmanski CS, Schluppeck D, Engel SA. 2004. Learning strengthens the response of primary visual cortex to simple patterns. *Curr Biol* 14:573–578.

Gauthier I, Anderson AW, Tarr MJ, Skudlarski P, Gore JC. 1997. Levels of categorization in visual recognition studied using functional magnetic resonance imaging. *Curr Biol* 7:645–651.

Gauthier I, Tarr MJ, Anderson AW, Skudlarski P, Gore JC. 1999. Activation of the middle fusiform 'face area' increases with expertise in recognizing novel objects. *Nat Neurosci* 2:568–573.

Geisler WS, Perry JS, Super BJ, Gallogly DP. 2001. Edge co-occurrence in natural images predicts contour grouping performance. *Vision Res* 41:711–724.

George N, Dolan RJ, Fink GR, Baylis GC, Russell C, Driver J. 1999. Contrast polarity and face recognition in the human fusiform gyrus. *Nat Neurosci* 2:574–580.

Ghose GM, Yang T, Maunsell JH. 2002. Physiological correlates of perceptual learning in monkey V1 and V2. *J Neurophysiol* 87:1867–1888.

Gilbert CD. 1992. Horizontal integration and cortical dynamics. *Neuron* 9:1–13.

Gilbert CD, Sigman M, Crist RE. 2001a. The neural basis of perceptual learning. *Neuron* 31:681.

Gilbert CD, Sigman M, Crist RE. 2001b. The neural basis of perceptual learning. *Neuron* 31:681–697.

Gold J, Bennett PJ, Sekuler AB. 1999. Signal but not noise changes with perceptual learning. *Nature* 402:176–178.

Goldstone RL. 1998. Perceptual learning. *Annu Rev Psychol* 49:585–612.

Goldstone RL, Lippa Y, Shiffrin RM. 2001. Altering object representations through category learning. *Cognition* 78:27–43.

Grill-Spector K, Kushnir T, Hendler T, Malach R. 2000. The dynamics of object-selective activation correlate with recognition performance in humans. *Nat Neurosci* 3:837–843.

Hanson SJ, Matsuka T, Haxby JV. 2004. Combinatorial codes in ventral temporal lobe for object recognition: Haxby (2001) revisited: is there a "face" area? 23:156.

Haxby JV, Gobbini MI, Furey ML, Ishai A, Schouten JL, Pietrini P. 2001. Distributed and overlapping representations of faces and objects in ventral temporal cortex. *Science* 293:2425–2430.

Haynes JD, Rees G. 2006. Decoding mental states from brain activity in humans. *Nat Rev Neurosci* 7:523.

Henson R, Shallice T, Dolan R. 2000. Neuroimaging evidence for dissociable forms of repetition priming. *Science* 287:1269–1272.

Jagadeesh B, Chelazzi L, Mishkin M, Desimone R. 2001. Learning increases stimulus salience in anterior inferior temporal cortex of the macaque. *J Neurophysiol* 86:290–303.

James TW, Humphrey GK, Gati JS, Menon RS, Goodale MA. 2000. The effects of visual object priming on brain activation before and after recognition. *Curr Biol* 10:1017–1024.

Jiang Y, Haxby JV, Martin A, Ungerleider LG, Parasuraman R. 2000. Complementary neural mechanisms for tracking items in human working memory. *Science* 287:643–646.

Keri S. 2003. The cognitive neuroscience of category learning. *Brain Res Brain Res Rev* 43:85.

Kobatake E, Wang G, Tanaka K. 1998. Effects of shape-discrimination training on the selectivity of inferotemporal cells in adult monkeys. *J Neurophysiol* 80:324–330.

Koida K, Komatsu H. 2007. Effects of task demands on the responses of color-selective neurons in the inferior temporal cortex. *Nat Neurosci* 10:108–116.

Kourtzi Z, Betts LR, Sarkheil P, Welchman AE. 2005a. Distributed neural plasticity for shape learning in the human visual cortex. *PLoS Biol* 3:e204.

Kourtzi Z, Betts LR, Sarkheil P, Welchman AE. 2005b. Distributed neural plasticity for shape learning in the human visual cortex. *PLoS Biol* 3:e204.

Koutstaal W, Wagner AD, Rotte M, Maril A, Buckner RL, Schacter DL. 2001. Perceptual specificity in visual object priming: functional magnetic resonance imaging evidence for a laterality difference in fusiform cortex. *Neuropsychologia* 39:184–199.

Kovacs I, Kozma P, Feher A, Benedek G. 1999. Late maturation of visual spatial integration in humans. *Proc Natl Acad Sci USA* 96:12204–12209.

Lee TS, Yang CF, Romero RD, Mumford D. 2002. Neural activity in early visual cortex reflects behavioral experience and higher-order perceptual saliency. *Nat Neurosci* 5:589–597.

Li RW, Levi DM, Klein SA. 2004a. Perceptual learning improves efficiency by re-tuning the decision 'template' for position discrimination. *Nat Neurosci* 7:178–183.

Li S, Ostwald D, Giese M, Kourtzi Z. 2007. Flexible coding for categorical decisions in the human brain. *J Neurosci* 27:12321–12330.

Li W, Piech V, Gilbert CD. 2004b. Perceptual learning and top-down influences in primary visual cortex. *Nat Neurosci* 7:651–657.

Li W, Piech V, Gilbert CD. 2008. Learning to link visual contours. *Neuron* 57:442–451.

Li Z. 2001. Computational design and nonlinear dynamics of a recurrent network model of the primary visual cortex. *Neural Comput* 13:1749–1780.

Logothetis NK, Pauls J, Poggio T. 1995. Shape representation in the inferior temporal cortex of monkeys. *Curr Biol* 5:552–563.

Maunsell JH, Treue S. 2006. Feature-based attention in visual cortex. *Trends Neurosci* 29:317–322.

McIntosh AR, Rajah MN, Lobaugh NJ. 1999. Interactions of prefrontal cortex in relation to awareness in sensory learning. *Science* 284:1531–1533.

Miller BT, D'Esposito M. 2005. Searching for "the top" in top-down control. *Neuron* 48:535–538.

Miller EK. 2000. The prefrontal cortex and cognitive control. *Nat Rev Neurosci* 1:59–65.

Miller EK, Cohen JD. 2001. An integrative theory of prefrontal cortex function. *Annu Rev Neurosci* 24:167–202.

Mirabella G, Bertini G, Samengo I, Kilavik BE, Frilli D, Della Libera C, Chelazzi L. 2007. Neurons in Area V4 of the Macaque Translate Attended Visual Features into Behaviorally Relevant Categories. *Neuron* 54:303–318.

Miyashita Y. 2004. Cognitive memory: cellular and network machineries and their top-down control. *Science* 306:435–440.

Miyashita Y, Chang HS. 1988. Neuronal correlate of pictorial short-term memory in the primate temporal cortex. *Nature* 331:68–70.

Moore CD, Cohen MX, Ranganath C. 2006. Neural mechanisms of expert skills in visual working memory. *J Neurosci* 26:11187–11196.

Muhammad R, Wallis JD, Miller EK. 2006. A comparison of abstract rules in the prefrontal cortex, premotor cortex, inferior temporal cortex, and striatum. *J Cogn Neurosci* 18:974.

Mukai I, Kim D, Fukunaga M, Japee S, Marrett S, Ungerleider LG. 2007. Activations in visual and attention-related areas predict and correlate with the degree of perceptual learning. *J Neurosci* 27:11401–11411.

Norman KA, Polyn SM, Detre GJ, Haxby JV. 2006. Beyond mind-reading: multi-voxel pattern analysis of fMRI data. *Trends Cogn Sci* 10:424–430.

Nosofsky RM. 1986. Attention, similarity, and the identification-categorization relationship. *J Exp Psychol Gen* 115:39–61.

O'Toole AJ, Jiang F, Abdi H, Haxby JV. 2005. Partially distributed representations of objects and faces in ventral temporal cortex. *J Cogn Neurosci* 17:580–590.

Op de Beeck H, Wagemans J, Vogels R. 2001. Inferotemporal neurons represent low-dimensional configurations of parameterized shapes. *Nature Neurosci* 4:1244.

Op de Beeck H, Wagemans J, Vogels R. 2003. The effect of category learning on the representation of shape: dimensions can be biased but not differentiated. *J Exp Psychol Gen* 132:491–511.

Op de Beeck HP, Baker CI, DiCarlo JJ, Kanwisher NG. 2006. Discrimination training alters object representations in human extrastriate cortex. *J Neurosci* 26:13025–13036.

Palmeri TJ, Gauthier I. 2004. Visual object understanding. *Nat Neurosci* 5:291.

Poggio T. 1990. A theory of how the brain might work. *Cold Spring Harb Symp Quant Biol* 55:899–910.

Poggio T, Edelman S. 1990. A network that learns to recognize three-dimensional objects. *Nature* 343:263–266.

Rainer G, Lee H, Logothetis NK. 2004. The effect of learning on the function of monkey extrastriate visual cortex. *PLoS Biol* 2:E44.

Rainer G, Miller EK. 2000. Effects of visual experience on the representation of objects in the prefrontal cortex. *Neuron* 27:179–189.

Reynolds JH, Chelazzi L. 2004. Attentional modulation of visual processing. *Annu Rev Neurosci* 27:611–647.

Riesenhuber M, Poggio T. 1999. Hierarchical models of object recognition in cortex. *Nat Neurosci* 2:1019–1025.

Riesenhuber M, Poggio T. 2000. Models of object recognition. *Nat Neurosci* 3 *Suppl:*1199–1204.

Roelfsema PR. 2006. Cortical algorithms for perceptual grouping. *Annu Rev Neurosci* 29:203–227.

Roelfsema PR, van Ooyen A. 2005. Attention-gated reinforcement learning of internal representations for classification. *Neural Comput* 17:2176–2214.

Rolls ET. 1995. Learning mechanisms in the temporal lobe visual cortex. *Behav Brain Res* 66:177–185.

Rolls ET, Aggelopoulos NC, Zheng F. 2003. The receptive fields of inferior temporal cortex neurons in natural scenes. *J Neurosci* 23:339–348.

Rotshtein P, Henson RN, Treves A, Driver J, Dolan RJ. 2005. Morphing Marilyn into Maggie dissociates physical and identity face representations in the brain. *Nat Neurosci* 8:107.

Sagi D, Tanne D. 1994. Perceptual learning: learning to see. *Curr Opin Neurobiol* 4:195–199.

Sakai K, Miyashita Y. 1991. Neural organization for the long-term memory of paired associates. *Nature* 354:152–155.

Schacter DL, Reiman E, Uecker A, Polster MR, Yun LS, Cooper LA. 1995. Brain regions associated with retrieval of structurally coherent visual information. *Nature* 376:587–590.

Schafer R, Vasilaki E, Senn W. 2007. Perceptual learning via modification of cortical top-down signals. *PLoS Comput Biol* 3:e165.

Schiltz C, Bodart JM, Dubois S, Dejardin S, Michel C, Roucoux A, Crommelinck M, Orban GA. 1999. Neuronal mechanisms of perceptual learning: changes in human brain activity with training in orientation discrimination. *Neuroimage* 9:46–62.

Schoups A, Vogels R, Qian N, Orban G. 2001a. Practising orientation identification improves orientation coding in V1 neurons. *Nature* 412:549–553.

Schoups AA, Vogels R, Orban GA. 1995. Human perceptual learning in identifying the oblique orientation: retinotopy, orientation specificity and monocularity. *J Physiol (Lond)* 483:797–810.

Schoups AA, Vogels R, Qian N, Orban GA. 2001b. Practising orientation identification improves orientation coding in V1 neurons. *Nature* 412:549–553.

Schwartz S, Maquet P, Frith C. 2002. Neural correlates of perceptual learning: a functional MRI study of visual texture discrimination. *Proc Natl Acad Sci USA* 99:17137–17142.

Schyns PG, Goldstone RL, Thibaut JP. 1998. The development of features in object concepts. *Behav Brain Sci* 21:1–17; discussion 17–54.

Sheinberg DL, Logothetis NK. 2001. Noticing familiar objects in real world scenes: the role of temporal cortical neurons in natural vision. *J Neurosci* 21:1340–1350.

Sigala N, Gabbiani F, Logothetis NK. 2002. Visual categorization and object representation in monkeys and humans. *J Cogn Neurosci* 14:187–198.

Sigala N, Logothetis NK. 2002. Visual categorization shapes feature selectivity in the primate temporal cortex. *Nature* 415:318–320.

Sigman M, Cecchi GA, Gilbert CD, Magnasco MO. 2001. On a common circle: natural scenes and Gestalt rules. *Proc Natl Acad Sci USA* 98:1935–1940.

Sigman M, Gilbert CD. 2000. Learning to find a shape. *Nat Neurosci* 3:264–269.

Sigman M, Pan H, Yang Y, Stern E, Silbersweig D, Gilbert CD. 2005. Top-down reorganization of activity in the visual pathway after learning a shape identification task. *Neuron* 46:823–835.

Simoncelli EP, Olshausen BA. 2001. Natural image statistics and neural representation. *Annu Rev Neurosci* 24:1193–1216.

Smith ML, Gosselin F, Schyns PG. 2004. Receptive fields for flexible face categorizations. *Psychol Sci* 15:753–761.

Thomas E, Van Hulle MM, Vogels R. 2001. Encoding of categories by noncategory-specific neurons in the inferior temporal cortex. *J Cognit Neurosci* 13:190.

Toni I, Rushworth MF, Passingham RE. 2001. Neural correlates of visuomotor associations. Spatial rules compared with arbitrary rules. *Exp Brain Res* 141:359–369.

Tovee MJ, Rolls ET, Ramachandran VS. 1996. Rapid visual learning in neurones of the primate temporal visual cortex. *Neuroreport* 7:2757–2760.

Treisman A, Vieira A, Hayes A. 1992. Automaticity and preattentive processing. *Am J Psychol* 105:341–362.

Vaina LM, Belliveau JW, des Roziers EB, Zeffiro TA. 1998. Neural systems underlying learning and representation of global motion. *Proc Natl Acad Sci USA* 95:12657–12662.

van Turennout M, Ellmore T, Martin A. 2000. Long-lasting cortical plasticity in the object naming system. *Nat Neurosci* 3:1329–1334.

Wallis G, Rolls ET. 1997. Invariant face and object recognition in the visual system. *Prog Neurobiol* 51:167–194.

Williams MA, Dang S, Kanwisher NG. 2007. Only some spatial patterns of fMRI response are read out in task performance. *Nat Neurosci* 10:685–686.

Wolfe JM, Cave KR, Franzel SL. 1989. Guided search: an alternative to the feature integration model for visual search. *J Exp Psychol Hum Percept Perform* 15:419–433.

Yang T, Maunsell JH. 2004. The effect of perceptual learning on neuronal responses in monkey visual area V4. *J Neurosci* 24:1617–1626.

Yotsumoto Y, Watanabe T, Sasaki Y. 2008. Different dynamics of performance and brain activation in the time course of perceptual learning. *Neuron* 57:827–833.

CHAPTER 23

Shapes and Shock Graphs: From Segmented Shapes to Shapes Embedded in Images

Benjamin B. Kimia

23.1 Introduction

The recognition of objects in images is a central task in computer vision. It is particularly challenging because the *form* and *appearance* of 3-D objects projected onto 2-D images undergo significant variation owing to the numerous dimensions of visual transformations, such as changes in viewing distance and direction, illumination conditions, occlusion, articulation, and, perhaps most significantly, within-category type variation. The challenge is how to encode the collection of these forms and appearances (Fig. 23.1), which are high-dimensional manifolds embedded in even higher-dimensional spaces, such that the topology induced by such variations is preserved. We believe this is the key to the successful differentiation of various categories.

Form and appearance play separate, and distinct, but perhaps interacting roles in recognition. The early exploration of the form-only role assumed that figures can be successfully segregated from image. This assumption was justified by the vast platform of "segmentation" research going on at the same time. Currently, it is generally accepted that segmentation as a stand-alone approach is ill-posed and that segmentation must be approached together with recognition or other high-level tasks. Nevertheless, research on form-only representation and recognition remains immensely valuable in that it has identified key issues in shape representation and key challenges in recognition such as those in the presence of occlusion, articulation, and other unwieldy visual transformations, which are present even in such a highly oversimplified domain. Section 23.2 reviews some of the lessons learned and captured in the context of the shock-graph approach to recognition.

In a parallel stream to recognition based on form, the lack of success in producing a perfect segmentation led to a paradigm shift in the past decade towards the use of appearance, moving away from relying on fully segmented images for recognition and other visual tasks, to one using a collection of features that captures appearance and shape in a small area, as driven by the availability of a new generation of feature detectors such as Harris-Affine, Harris-Laplace, and others (Mikolajczyk et al. 2005) and a new generation of feature descriptors such as SIFT (Lowe 2004) and others

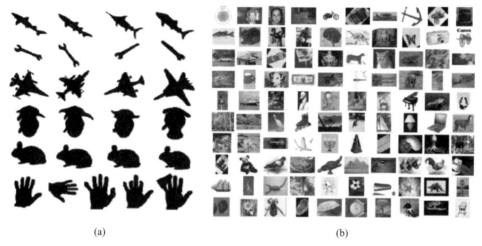

Figure 23.1. (a) The shapes in the Brown Dataset I (Sharvit et al. 1998) can be differentiated by their form. (b) Sample images from the Caltech-101 database (Fei-Fei et al. 2004) can be differentiated mainly by their appearance.

(Mikolajczyk and Schmid 2005) that are more stable to viewpoint variation, lighting change, and so on. The main idea is that although these features may not remain present under all variations, given the sheer number of features, the common presence of a few discriminative features can discriminate between the presence or absence of a particular, previously observed object in an image.

In contrast to object instance recognition, however, generic object recognition, in which the intra-category type variations must also be accounted for, has proven to be more challenging. Approaches to generic object recognition, which are based on key-point descriptors, span a continuum between two extremes of part-based models, where the spatial relationship between parts is represented, such as in the constellation model (Fergus et al. 2003; Fei-Fei et al. 2006) and the k-fan model (Crandall et al. 2005), and the bag-of-words approach, which completely discards the spatial relationship and instead relies on an unorganized collection of codeword-encoded appearance parts. The part-based approach is faced with a combinatorial search arising from an exponential number of correspondences, whereas the bag-of-words approach avoids the combinatorial difficulties (e.g., see Csurka et al. 2004; Zhang et al. 2007), but is more brittle to situations when some of the features have been removed (e.g., due to partial occlusion).

The success of the aforementioned approaches indicates the significance of *appearance* in discriminating the presence or absence of objects in typical scenes (Csurka et al. 2004) and in object localization (Berg et al. 2005; Leibe and Schiele 2004), where bottom-up segmentation could not conceivably segment figure from ground. However, appearance-based approaches are also limited in several significant ways. Stable key features are not always abundantly available (e.g., in low lighting conditions; in bright backgrounds; objects with large homogeneous patches, especially manmade objects; cartoons; sketches; line drawings; objects in low-resolution imagery, e.g., aerial video images of vehicles, where the total extent of the object is of the same order as that required for feature descriptors (Ozcanli et al. 2006)). A more fundamental shortcoming is that the role of appearance may become severely diminished as the intra-category variation increases the range of appearances that an object category captures (e.g., in recognizing bottles and cups, the surface markings are simply too varied to be useful) (Opelt et al. 2006). In these cases, the edge content of the silhouette and of the internal markings consistent across the category become the primary source of information for recognition.

In general, it can be argued that *function* is more dependent on object *form* than on its appearance (Leordeanu et al. 2007; Siddiqi et al. 1996; Siddiqi and Kimia 1995; Siddiqi et al. 2001), and can be critically valuable in augmenting the role of appearance for object recognition. Thus, a range of recent shape-based models have been developed (Selinger and Nelson, 1999; Berg et al. 2005; Jurie and Schmid 2004; Belongie et al. 2002; Fergus et al. 2004; Kumar et al. 2004; Opelt et al. 2006; Shotton et al. 2005; Kelly and Levine 1995; Leordeanu et al. 2007; Yu et al. 2007; Ferrari et al. 2006, 2007, 2008; Felzenszwalb and Schwartz 2007) that use simple oriented *edges* (Belongie et al. 2002; Berg et al. 2005; Leordeanu et al. 2007; Jurie and Schmid 2004), *curve bundles* (Tamrakar and Kimia 2007), contour fragments (Nelson and Selinger 1998; Kumar et al. 2004; Opelt et al. 2006; Shotton et al. 2005; Felzenszwalb and Schwartz 2007; Fergus et al. 2005; Tamrakar and Kimia 2007), pairs of contour segments in a common annular region (Kelly and Levine 1995; Jurie and Schmid 2004), and others, as described later in context. In addition to *keypoint-based* and *contour-based* representations, *region-based* features (Ahuja 1996; Tao et al. 2001; Shi and Malik 2000; Sharon et al. 2001; Tu and Zhu 2002; Comaniciu and Meer 2002), used in the form of *superpixels* (Ren et al. 2006; Stein et al. 2007; Mori 2005; Mori et al. 2004) or as a *segmentation hierarchy* (Russell et al. 2006; Todorovic and Ahuja 2006; Liu et al. 2007; Tu et al. 2005), and class-specific features (Vidal-Naquet and Ullman 2003; Borenstein and Ullman 2002; Borenstein and Malik 2006; Cour and Shi 2007; Leibe et al. 2004; Yuille and Hallinan 1993) have been used in recognition. The drawback of using regions is that they cannot represent open contours, which frequently occur on objects (Koenderink and van Doorn 1982; Huggins et al. 2001). Also, in some cases no combination of regions may result in the object due to overgrouping. Class-specific fragments require training for each model.

What is significant here is that each of these types of representations captures an important aspect of the image that should ideally be merged. Even more significant than the choice of representation is how topographic information, be it among isolated features, contour fragments, and region fragments, is represented. We submit that this topographical information is the essence of shape. The choice of a *mid-level representation* depends on which type of feature to use and how the spatial relationship is represented. The choice is critical because intermediate-level representation forms the bottleneck in communicating information from pixels to objects and back. We describe in section 23.3 our choice, which is the influence zone of shock-graph segments, the regions bounded by two adjacent contour fragments, (what we refer to as a visual fragment or, more descriptively, a shock-patch image fragment) (Fig. 23.10 and 23.3). It represents partial shape information as well as the appearance for this fragment; as such, it allows for perceptual reasoning beyond good continuation of contours in the form (both contours) as well as good continuation of appearance (sect. 23.3). We show how these perceptually organized and grouped fragments can be used for bottom-up

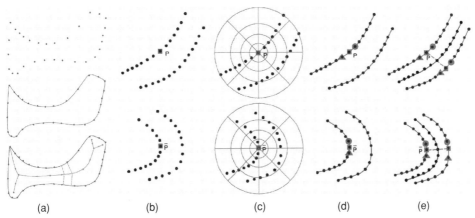

Figure 23.2. (a) A schematic comparison of shape representation using unorganized points, outline curve, and shock graph. (b) The point-based representation uses a local or global similarity measure. (c) Shape context adds a form signature and extrinsic regularization of spatial deformation. (d) The curve representation induces an ordering of points. (e) The shock-graph representation introduces an additional constraint by the pairing two boundary segments (shown by dotted lines) to represent the interior of the shape. From Sebastian et al. (2004). (See color plate 23.2.)

object recognition (sect. 23.4) as well as for top-down model-based recognition (sect. 23.5).

23.2 Shock-Graph Representation of Figure-Ground Segregated Shape

Why should the medial axis/shock-graph representations be favored over other point-based or curve-based representation? Figure 23.2(a) illustrates that when using an unorganized cloud of points, a point P can be matched to a corresponding point $\bar{P}$ only based on the merit of some attribute such as appearance (Fig. 23.2(b)). The "shape context" approach introduces a form signature to favor correspondences whose spatial form context is similar, and whose extrinsic spatial deformation of the neighborhood is regular (Fig. 23.2(c)). The use of curves is significantly more discriminative than points in that order along the curve restricts the number of viable correspondences. Dynamic programming-type algorithms have been used to take advantage of order along curves to efficiently find the optimal correspondence between two curves (Fig. 23.2(d)).

The use of medial axis/shock graph is another step in increasing the distinctiveness of a point in the matching process. Now, in addition to order along the curve, the point P has a "mate" on an adjacent curve so that there is a "joint" representation of a boundary neighborhood of P with a boundary neighborhood of its mate. This joint representation is extremely powerful in that it survives many variations (e.g., articulation, partial occlusion, etc.) (Fig. 23.7). The medial axis (MA) is also motivated along additional lines in (Leymarie and Kimia 2007).

The MA as the loci of centers of maximal inscribed circles is itself an unorganized set of points. The shock graph (SG) is a re-interpretation of the medial axis as a refined classification. A traditional view of the MA by Blum is based on the notions of a grassfire: the shape is considered a field of grass whose boundary is ignited;

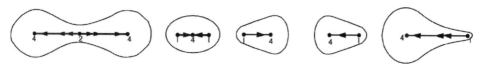

Figure 23.3. The geometric locus and graph topology of the medical-axis graph, a single segment between two nodes, cannot tell these shapes apart, but the directed shock graph, which has a richer structure, can. From Giblin and Kimia (1999).

the resulting fire propagates with uniform speed to quench itself at the MA. This characterization of the MA is static. Alternatively, the Eikonal equation governing the propagation can be viewed as creating shock waves. *Shocks* are discontinuous points of propagation front whose velocity direction points into the discontinuity, thus irreversibly losing parts of the front. *Rarefaction waves* have velocity direction pointing outward from the discontinuity, thus requiring a gap to be filled. *Contact shocks* are front discontinuities with matching velocities on both sides. Observe that each curvature maximum gets sharper in curvature in the course of propagation and eventually becomes infinite (Kimia et al. 1992, 1995), thus forming a shock, unless, of course, the waves from another boundary quench it first. When the latter happens, the shock that is formed travels along the MA, thus providing a dynamic view of the MA. This dynamic view differentiates qualitatively distinct shapes that have similar MA (Fig. 23.3). Specifically, there is a distinction between sources of flows (necks) from sinks of flows (blobs).

The dynamic view allows for an explicit connectivity between shock points, so that the "topology" of the shock set can naturally be captured in a graph where *links* represent continuous flow along *shock curve segments* and where *nodes* are shock points at which flow is interrupted. A medial-axis graph can also be derived from this by ignoring the prior differentiation of types of nodes, but this also reduces the *categorical sensitivity* of the representation: The set of possible shapes corresponding to a given shock graph of a shape and its exterior all appear perceptually equivalent, but this not true of the medial-axis graph (Fig. 23.3).

Formally, the preceding intuitive discussion of the types of medial axis/shock graph points can be cast as a formal classification based on the degree of contact (Giblin and Kimia 1999). Let A_k^n describe k-fold tangency at n distinct points so that A_1 denotes regular two-point tangency of a circle with a curve, while A_2 describes three-point tangency, and A_3 describes four-point tangency, and so on. Generally, only A_1 and A_3 points appear on the MA; A_2 points do not appear (Fig. 23.4). Similarly, A_1^2, and A_1^3 describe tangency at two and three district points, respectively. Generically, the MA points can only be A_1^3 (branch points), A_3 (end points), and A_1^2 (remaining points), with A_1^3 and A_3 forming nodes and A_1^2 forming links in the MA graph. A_1^4 (tangency at four distinct points) and $A_1 A_3$ (simultaneous A_1 and A_3 tangency at two distinct points; i.e., one is a regular tangency and one is tangency at a curvature maximum) points can also appear, but a slight perturbation removes these, so they are viable, and important, only in a one-parameter family of deformations. Similarly, shock points are classified into six types: A_3 (end points), $A_1^3 - 1$ (saddle branch point), $A_1^3 - 4$ (sink branch point), $A_1^2 - 4$ (sink), $A_1^2 - 2$ (source), and $A_1^2 - 1$ (continuous flow points) (Giblin and Kimia 1999) (Fig. 23.4).

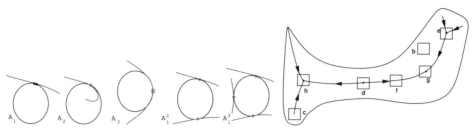

Figure 23.4. This figure from Giblin and Kimia (1999) and Tek and Kimia (1999) illustrates the A_k^n notation in the context of the order of contact of the curves (*thick blue*) with circles (*thin brown*), which leads to a classification of generic possibilities for shock formation and propagation on the left, and in the context of a shape on the right: b is A_1 while f, d, g are A_1^2 (source, regular, and sink types, respectively), h is an A_1^3 sink, e is an A_1^3 with one branch outflowing, and c is an A_3. (See color plate 23.4.)

The shock points A_3, $A_1^3 - 1$, $A_1^3 - 4$, $A_1^2 - 4$, and $A_1^2 - 2$ have isolated topology, while $A_1^2 - 1$ forms continuous curve segments. This motivates the definition of a shock graph as the directed graph connecting the first five types of shock points through links defined by the sixth type of shock curve. An alternate definition, *rooted shock tree* is used by Siddiqi et al. (1999b) who define nodes and links differently. See Sebastian et al. (2004) for a comparison of these definitions. Shock graphs have been used in Sharvit et al. (1998), Sebastian et al. (2004, 2001, 2002), Sebastian and Kimia (2002), Ozcanli and Kimia (2007), and Trinh and Kimia (2007). Rooted shock trees have been used in Siddiqi et al. (1999b), Pelillo et al. (1999), Siddiqi et al. (2005), Dimitrov et al. (2000), Siddiqi et al. (1999a, 2002), Torsello and Hancock (2006), and Pearce et al. (1994).

Another important consideration in representing shape is the *dynamic versus static representation*, especially in regard to shape matching. In one approach to shape matching, a representation of shape maps each shape to a point in some space and the distance between two shapes is the inherited distance between the representations in the embedding space. In this static view no attention is paid to any other "intermediate" shapes. In contrast, in a dynamic view, a shape is mapped to point in some space and the distance between the two shapes is the geodesic distance of the optimal path between them. In other words, the focus is on generating the sequence of shapes to morph one shape to another. This geodesic distance is defined based on generating a local neighborhood of shapes for each point and a deformation cost for each, as in defining a Riemannian metric. The distinction between static and dynamic views is of utmost significance in that a highly variable space of observable shapes is mirrored in the representation in a dynamic view, but not necessarily in a static view.

Formally, slightly deforming a shape generally results in slightly deforming its shock graph, except at certain configurations, shown in the central columns of Figure 23.5. Giblin and Kimia (2007) classified the six types of instability, or transition, a shock graph can experience. For example, Figure 23.5(a) is the classic instability of the medial axis, which in the past had been universally acknowledged as the main reason that MA cannot be used in practice. In our work, these instabilities are the fundamental building blocks of the representation. Figure 23.6 illustrates a schematic of a shape A deforming to the shape B, experiencing transitions indicated as solid dots along the

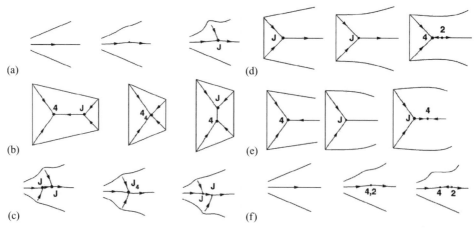

Figure 23.5. The central column in each group represents the transition point in the deformation from left to right, or right to left columns. In the notation of Giblin and Kimia (1999) (a) is the $A_1 A_3$ transition; (b) and (c) are the two types of A_1^4, (d) and (e) are the two types of A_1^3 with infinite velocity, and (f) is the A_1^2 point with infinite velocity and zero acceleration. The graph operations to make the right and left columns equivalent are splice, contract (two types), and merge (three types). From Giblin and Kimia (1999).

path. These transitions are stable, as a small perturbation of this one-parameter family of deformations generally does not affect the transition, except at certain higher-order transitions, where new transitions are experienced (Fig. 23.6(b)). Thus, deformation paths between two shapes can be characterized and represented by the sequence of transitions (instabilities) between the two shapes!

Similarity between two shapes is defined as the cost of the optimal path. The representation of infinite-dimensional deformation paths through defining an equivalence class based on the sequence of transitions is essentially a discretization of the space of deformations. The search for the optimal path in this space is further narrowed down by avoiding all paths that initially make the shape complex and then reduce the complexity. This is done by breaking the deformation path into two simplifying deformation

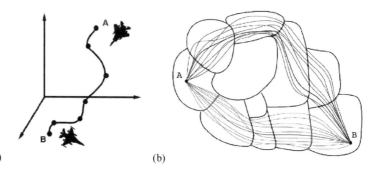

Figure 23.6. Every pair of shapes in the shape space is related by an infinite number of deformation paths, few of which are shown here. Each deformation path can be effectively characterized by the sequence of transitions (dots represent the transition from one shape cell to another) the shape experiences in the morphing process. From Sebastian et al. (2004).

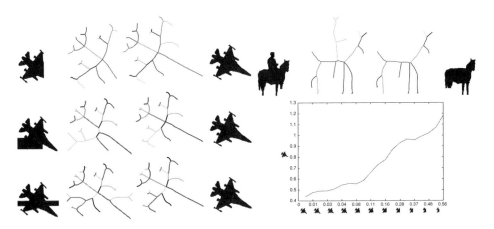

Figure 23.7. Partial occlusion. This figure illustrates that shock-graph matching gives intuitive correspondence in the presence of partial occlusion, both when the occluder blends with the background (*top row*) and with the object (*middle* and *bottom left*). Observe in particular how the optimal edit sequence between a horse and a rider with the horse by itself involves pruning the shock edges corresponding to the rider. The plot shows that normalized edit cost (*y*-axis) increases as the fraction of the plane occluded (*x*-axis) increases. (See color plate 23.7.)

paths, one from each shape meeting at a common shape. A tree edit distance algorithm was developed for matching shock graphs (Klein et al. 2001, 2000) where the edits are the shock transitions (Sebastian et al. 2004). Object recognition results were reported on several datasets in Sebastian et al. (2004, 2002): the 99 shapes, 216 shapes, 1032 shapes. Figure 23.8 shows the first database, and results that have since appeared in comparison are reporting a modest improvement. However, no comparison results have been reported on the 216-shape and 1032-shape databases. Our results for the 1032-shape database are a 97% recognition rate. We have no reported results on the MPEG7 database because it includes shapes with holes.

23.3 Perceptional Grouping: A Case for Intermediate-Level Representation

The failure of segmentation algorithms to reliably produce whole objects is indicative of the vast degree of variability inherent in the visual projection of objects arising from pose, illumination, articulation, and so on. While these algorithms mostly succeed in grouping *small patches* of similar regions and grouping edges into small *contour fragments* whenever evidence is significant, as the granularity of the expected grouping becomes coarser (i.e., larger regions and longer contours) ambiguities increase exponentially and so does the failure rate. The task of segmenting entire objects in one shot is therefore ill-posed. This has motivated an intermediate-level of representation, when only highly reliable organizations are accepted, leaving the rest of the data to be organized by a higher-level module. Partial organization in the form of contour fragment representations cannot represent spatial relationships among contours while those in the form of region fragments are essentially "regions without boundaries" (i.e., a group of pixels whose affinity has led to a grouping, but the grouping is not

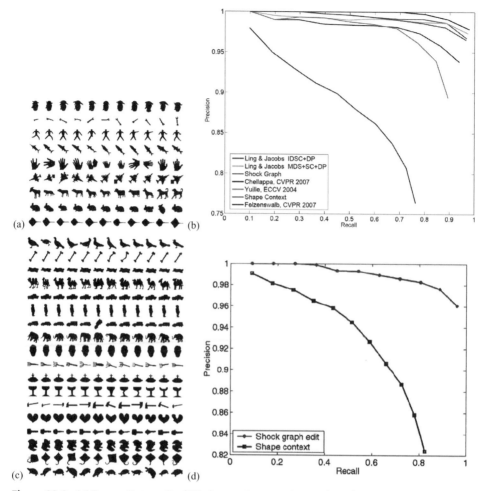

Figure 23.8. (a) Brown Dataset II of 99 shapes, 9 categories, and 11 shapes each. (b) The PRC of various algorithms (Biswas et al. 2007; Ling and Jacobs 2007; Tu and Yuille 2004). (c) Brown Dataset III of 216 shapes, 18 categories and 12 shapes each. (d) Fewer results are available on the more challenging dataset III and the dataset IV containing 1032 shapes, where our recognition rate is 97%. (See color plate 23.8.)

exclusive of adjacent pixels, and its boundaries are not always meaningful). Rather, what is needed is a partial organization of the form of the object, a "shapelet" that includes both contour- and region-based aspects (Fig. 23.9).

A representation for object fragments was introduced in Kimia (2003) and Tamrakar and Kimia (2004) under the name "visual fragment" but which can more accurately be called a "shock-patch image fragment," where an image with an associated contour map (a set of curve segments) is partitioned into a set of regional fragments curve of length L, γ_k is parameterized by arclength $s \in [0, L]$ with a local coordinate system of axis tangent/normal $(\vec{T}(s), \vec{N}(s))$ and shock velocity $v(s)$. Observe in Figure 23.10(a) that the shock graph divides a shape into regions, each of which is the "influence zone" of a shock segment. These regions make the overall representations immune to such

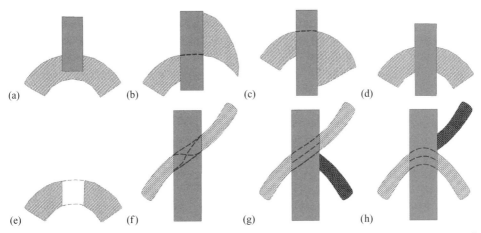

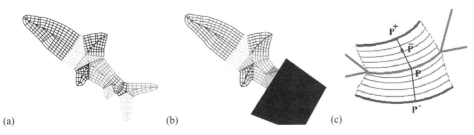

Figure 23.9. The Gestalt notion of good continuation of contours leaves a high degree of ambiguity in reasoning about real images. What is needed is a notion of "fragment continuity," which involves (1) "silhouette continuity" in the form of joint continuity of a pair of silhouettes (d-e) as well as (2) "surface cue continuity," as in (g-h).

changes as occlusion (Fig. 23.10(b)); specifically, each point $\bar{P}(x, y)$ in the image "belongs" to a shock segment k where

$$(x, y) = \gamma_k(s) + t\left(-\frac{1}{v}\vec{T} \pm \frac{\sqrt{v^2 - 1}}{|v|}\vec{N}\right), \ s \in [0, L], \ t \in [0, r(s)].$$

The shock-patch image fragment in assigning each point to a group also assigns its appearance (Fig. 23.3). This allows for grouping well beyond traditional contour grouping in perceptual organization as not only the contours, but their spatial relationship and the appearance of the region between contours are also represented (Fig. 23.9). The operations to transform these image fragments are derived from shock transitions that are now not only the ones listed in section 23.2 but also new ones arising from *gaps* (removing a single point from a contour breaks it into the segments) and *spurious edges* (introduction of a single point introduces a loop in the shock graph). We have called these operation the *gap transform* (Fig. 23.12), and the *loop transform* (Fig. 23.13).

Figure 23.10. (a) The shock-induced coordinate system defines shock-patch image fragments, which are immune to occlusion (b). (c) Each image point $\bar{P}$ belongs to a region claimed by a pair of contour segments: waveforms P^+ and P^- quench at P and claim points on the way, such as $\bar{P}$, as their own. (See color plate 23.10.)

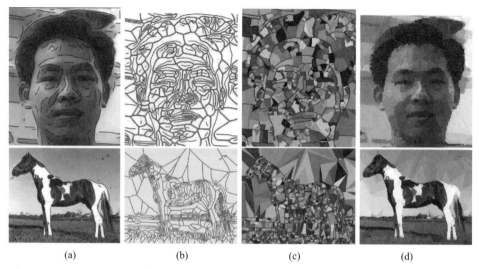

Figure 23.11. (a) Image with contour fragments superimposed in blue. (b) The shock graph is shown in red with contour in blue. (c) The shock patch image fragments colored randomly. (d) A reconstruction of each patch with the average intensity shows a remarkable reconstruction of the image. (See color plate 23.11.)

In what sequence should these transforms be applied to organize the image? Recall that when two objects are to be related we search for the optimal path of deformation between them and use its cost as an indicator of similarity. These deformation paths were restricted to those consisting of a pair of paths of simplification of each shape to reach a common shape. Now, when organizing the form of an object without having a second shape to relate to, the lack of availability of a second shape only allows us to prepare all reasonable paths of simplification in anticipation of a future match. In other words, in this view perceptual grouping is half the recognition problem (Johannes et al.

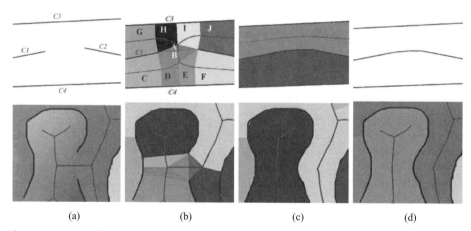

Figure 23.12. (a) The good continuation of contour c_1 onto contour c_2 can be augmented by the continuity of c_3 and c_4 in the form of fragment continuity G onto J and C onto F (b). (c) Applying the gap transform merges fragments (G, H, I, J, A) and (C, D, E, F, B) and fills the gap between c_1 and c_2, as shown in isolation in (d). The bottom rows shows this on a real image. (See color plate 23.12.)

Perceptual Grouping Cues

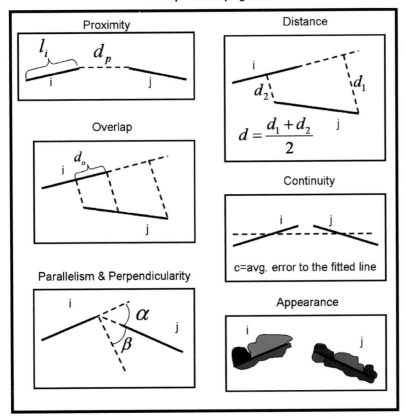

Plate 19.7. Geometric perceptual cues used for grouping pairs of line features.

Plate 19.8. Pairwise grouping constraints based on geometry. The contours in white are the ones that establish a pairwise grouping relationship with the contour pointed out by the red circle.

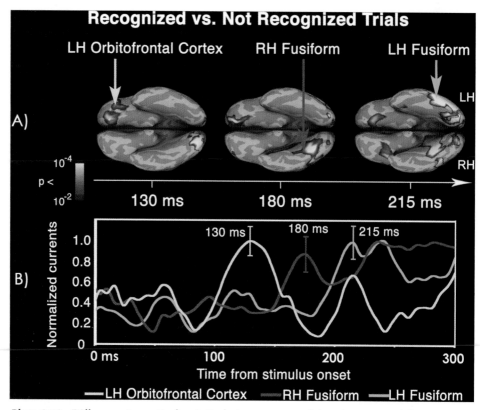

Plate 20.2. Difference in cortical activity between successful and unsuccessful recognition attempts. Differential OFC activity (yellow) occurred approximately 50 ms before activity in recognition-related inferior temporal areas. Right fusiform cortex elicited differential activity (*magenta*) 35 ms before left fusiform cortex (green). From Bar et al. (2006) with permission from the *Proceedings of the National Academy of Sciences*.

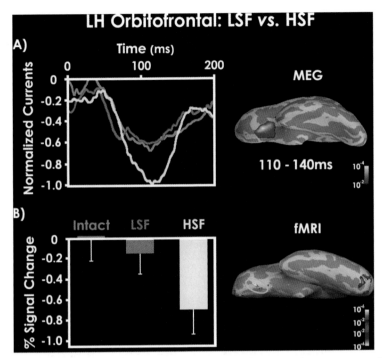

Plate 20.4. Orbitofrontal cortex activations in MEG and fMRI. *A*, The noise-normalized currents for unfiltered (blue), LSF (pink), and HSF (yellow) stimuli in OFC (*left*) and the region in OFC activated in MEG by comparing LSF versus HSF stimuli (*right*). *B*, The blood oxygen level-dependent (BOLD) signal averages for the intact, LSF, and HSF stimulus conditions (*left*) and the region in OFC activated by an LSF versus HSF contrast in fMRI (*right*). From Bar et al. (2006) with permission from the *Proceedings of the National Academy of Sciences*.

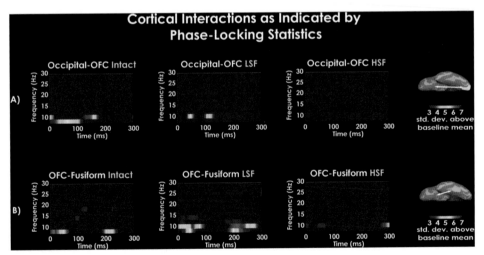

Plate 20.5. Phase-locking analysis showing significant trial-by-trial phase covariance between occipital visual areas and OFC, and, later, between OFC and the fusiform gyrus for intact (*first column*) and LSF (*second column*) images. Little significant phase-locking was seen for HSF images (*third column*). The images in the right-most column show the brain regions from which data were extracted for phase-locking analyses and the *color bars* indicating the phase-locking in terms of standard deviations above the mean. From Bar et al. (2006) with permission from the *Proceedings of the National Academy of Sciences*.

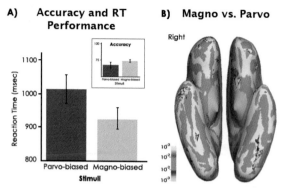

Plate 20.6. Comparison of M and P conditions. *A,* The reaction time (large graph) and response accuracy (small graph) results for M (red, 1010 ms) and P (gray, 905 ms) reveal that observers were both faster and slightly more accurate in recognizing *M*-biased line drawings. Only the correct responses, without outliers ($> \pm 2$ SD) are included, although the M-P relationship does not change qualitatively when all trials are included. *B,* Statistical parametric map ($P < 0.01$) of fMRI activations in the M versus P contrast. The M activations are in red-yellow color map, the P activations are in blue-cyan color map. From Kveraga, Boshyan, and Bar (2007) with permission from *Journal of Neuroscience.*

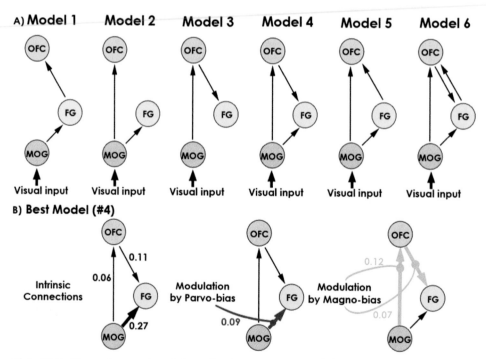

Plate 20.7. Dynamic causal modeling of brain connectivity with fMRI data. *A,* The six intrinsic connectivity patterns of dynamic causal models tested in our functional connectivity analyses. Model 4 was estimated to be the best fit for the data. *B, (left),* Intrinsic connection weights; *(middle and right),* modulatory connections activated by P and M bias in the stimuli. The thick arrows indicate significant effects at the $P < 0.05$ level. From Kveraga, Boshyan, and Bar (2007) with permission from *Journal of Neuroscience.*

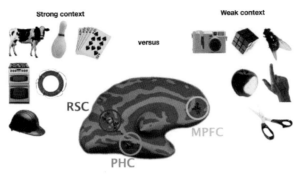

Plate 20.8. Neural activity evoked by contextual processing. Experimental conditions and a statistical activation map representing the difference between perceiving strongly contextual objects and weakly contextual objects. This is a medial view of activity in the left hemisphere averaged across all participants. Figure adapted from Bar (2004) with permission from *Nature Reviews Neuroscience*.

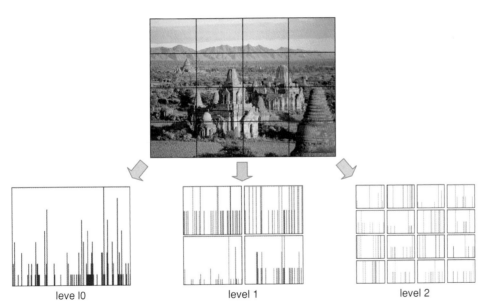

Plate 21.1. A schematic illustration of the spatial pyramid representation. A spatial pyramid is a collection of orderless feature histograms computed over cells defined by a multi-level recursive image decomposition. At level 0, the decomposition consists of just a single cell, and the representation is equivalent to a standard bag of features. At level 1, the image is subdivided into four quadrants, yielding four feature histograms, and so on. Spatial pyramids can be matched using the pyramid kernel, which weights features at higher levels more highly, reflecting the fact that higher levels localize the features more precisely (see section 21.3).

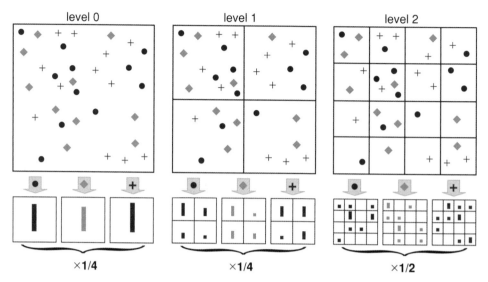

Plate 21.2. Toy example of constructing a pyramid for $L = 2$. The image has three feature types, indicated by circles, diamonds, and crosses. At the top, we subdivide the image at three different levels of resolution. Next, for each level of resolution and each channel, we count the features that fall in each spatial bin. Finally, we weight each spatial histogram according to equation (21.3).

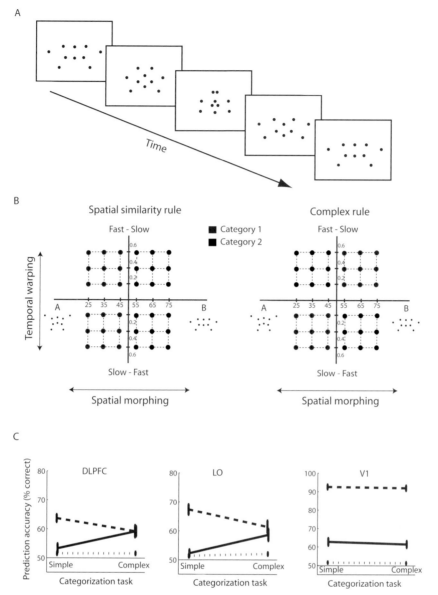

Plate 22.2. Learning to categorize novel patterns. *A,* Stimuli: Five sample frames of a prototypical stimulus depicting a dynamic figure. Each stimulus comprised ten dots that were configured in a skeleton arrangement and moved in a biologically plausible manner (i.e., sinusoidal motion trajectories). *B,* Stimulus space and categorization tasks: Stimuli were generated by applying spatial morphing (steps of percent stimulus B) between prototypical trajectories (e.g., A-B) and temporal warping (steps of time warping constant). Stimuli were assigned to one of four groups: A fast-slow (AFS), A slow-fast (ASF), B fast-slow (BFS), and B slow-fast (BSF). For the simple categorization task (*left panel*), the stimuli were categorized according to their spatial similarity: category 1 (red dots) consisted of AFS, ASF, and category 2 (blue dots), of BFS, BSF. For the complex task (*right panel*) the stimuli were categorized based on their spatial and temporal similarity: category 1 (red dots), consisted of ASF, BFS, and category 2 (blue dots), of AFS, BSF. *C,* Multivariate pattern analysis of fMRI data: Prediction accuracy (i.e., probability with which we correctly predict the presented and perceived stimuli from brain activation patterns) for the spatial similarity and complex classification schemes across categorization tasks (simple, complex task). Prediction accuracies for these MVPA rules are compared to accuracy for the shuffling rule (baseline prediction accuracy, dotted line). Interactions of prediction accuracy across tasks in DLPFC and LO indicate that the categories perceived by the observers are reliably decoded from fMRI responses in these areas. In contrast, the lack of interaction in V1 shows that the stimuli are represented based on their physical similarity rather than the rule used by the observers for categorization.

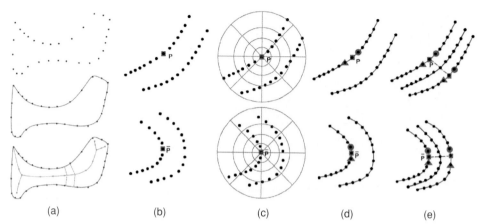

(a)   (b)   (c)   (d)   (e)

Plate 23.2. (a) A schematic comparison of shape representation using unorganized points, outline curve, and shock graph. (b) The point-based representation uses a local or global similarity measure. (c) Shape context adds a form signature and extrinsic regularization of spatial deformation. (d) The curve representation induces an ordering of points. (e) The shock-graph representation introduces an additional constraint by the pairing two boundary segments (shown by dotted lines) to represent the interior of the shape. From Sebastian et al. (2004).

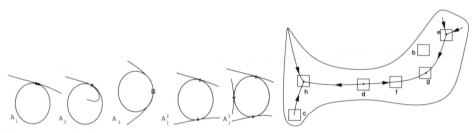

Plate 23.4. This figure from Giblin and Kimia (1999) and Tek and Kimia (1999) illustrates the A_k^n notation in the context of the order of contact of the curves (*thick blue*) with circles (*thin brown*), which leads to a classification of generic possibilities for shock formation and propagation on the left, and in the context of a shape on the right: b is A_1 while f, d, g are A_1^2 (source, regular, and sink types, respectively), h is an A_1^3 sink, e is an A_1^3 with one branch outflowing, and c is an A_3.

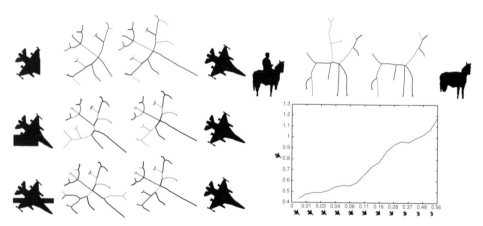

Plate 23.7. Partial occlusion. This figure illustrates that shock-graph matching gives intuitive correspondence in the presence of partial occlusion, both when the occluder blends with the background (*top row*) and with the object (*middle* and *bottom left*). Observe in particular how the optimal edit sequence between a horse and a rider with the horse by itself involves pruning the shock edges corresponding to the rider. The plot shows that normalized edit cost (*y*-axis) increases as the fraction of the plane occluded (*x*-axis) increases.

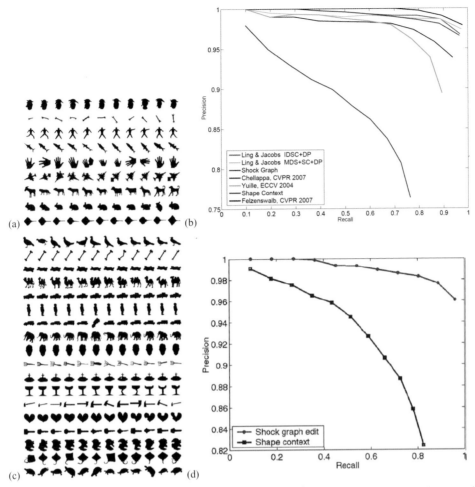

(a) (b)

(c) (d)

Plate 23.8. (a) Brown Dataset II of 99 shapes, 9 categories, and 11 shapes each. (b) The PRC of various algorithms (Biswas et al. 2007; Ling and Jacobs 2007; Tu and Yuille 2004). (c) Brown Dataset III of 216 shapes, 18 categories and 12 shapes each. (d) Fewer results are available on the more challenging dataset III and the dataset IV containing 1032 shapes, where our recognition rate is 97%.

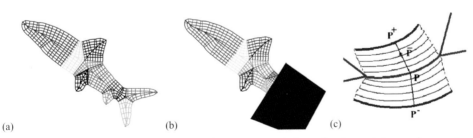

(a) (b) (c)

Plate 23.10. (a) The shock-induced coordinate system defines shock-patch image fragments, which are immune to occlusion (b). (c) Each image point $\bar{P}$ belongs to a region claimed by a pair of contour segments: waveforms P^+ and P^- quench at P and claim points on the way, such as $\bar{P}$, as their own

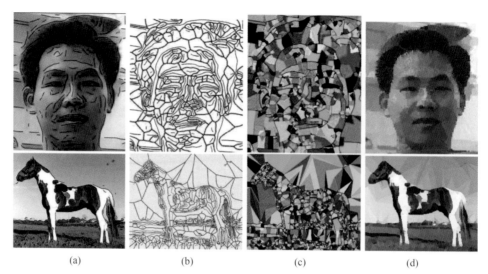

(a)   (b)   (c)   (d)

Plate 23.11. (a) Image with contour fragments superimposed in blue. (b) The shock graph is shown in red with contour in blue. (c) The shock patch image fragments colored randomly. (d) A reconstruction of each patch with the average intensity shows a remarkable reconstruction of the image.

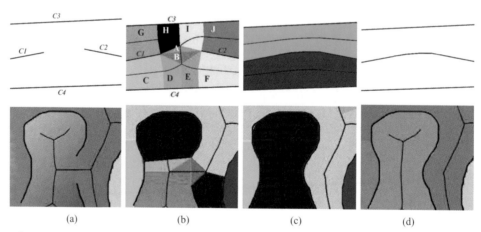

(a)   (b)   (c)   (d)

Plate 23.12. (a) The good continuation of contour c_1 onto contour c_2 can be augmented by the continuity of c_3 and c_4 in the form of fragment continuity G onto J and C onto F (b). (c) Applying the gap transform merges fragments (G, H, I, J, A) and (C, D, E, F, B) and fills the gap between c_1 and c_2, as shown in isolation in (d). The bottom rows shows this on a real image.

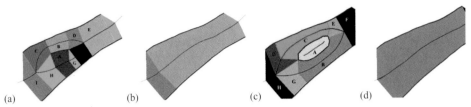

(a) (b) (c) (d)

Plate 23.13. The shock graph loops that form around internal contours in three different ways – (a) around a open contour, (c) around a closed contour, and (c) around a boundary between two fragments (not shown) – define shock-patch image fragment, which allows for reasoning using appearance, whether they can be safely merged to remove the spurious element, as in (b, d).

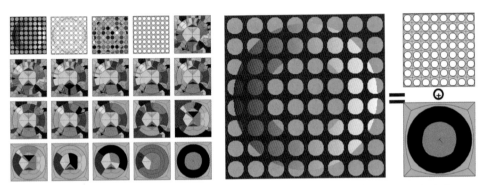

Plate 23.14. A sequence of visual fragment transforms are illustrated on an occluded torus image. The occluder is "recognized" and removed onto another "layer" by a loop disocclusion transform. The removal of an occluder to a different layer is currently done manually but the remaining steps (i.e., gaps transforms to link the individual visual fragments into a coherent whole) are automatic. Because there is more evidence to link up the outer edges of the torus, this will happen first. The grouping of the contour fragments of the outer edge will produce a grouping of the visual fragments into larger ones, as illustrated. After the outer edges are grouped, there is more evidence for the inner contour fragments to link up, thus producing a pair of closed contours. This defines the fragment into the shape of torus, as illustrated. As a result of this organization, the image is organized into two layers, a torus that is occluded by the mesh of holes. This cannot easily be acclaimed by a contour-based representation.

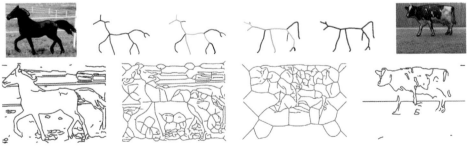

Plate 23.15. *Top row* observes how the shock graph of a segmented horse is optimally transformed to the shock graph of a segmented cow (colored edges are matching and the thinner black edges are edited out). This approach works equally well for shock graphs of edge maps of real images (bottom up). Although this can be done segmented images with a polynomial time algorithm, the algorithm for matching the shock graphs in the bottom row is NP-complete (blue: boundaries; red: shock graphs).

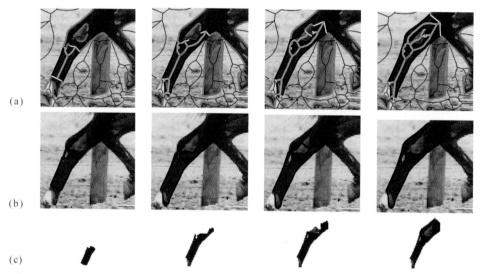

(a)

(b)

(c)

Plate 23.16. (a) Shock subgraphs at depths 1, 2, 3, and 4, respectively. The shock graph is shown in red, and the subgraph in light green. Image boundaries are shown in green, shock patch boundaries in blue. (b) The simple closed boundary in blue traced from the outer face of the subgraph. (c) The four fragments in isolation.

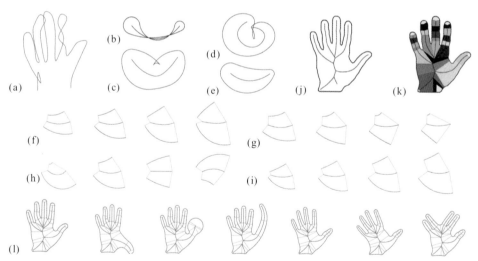

Plate 23.18. (a) Generative models of shape need to avoid generating invalid or "illegal" shapes, with problematic cases of intersection, swallowtail shown in (b-d), and a legal shape example in (e). (f-i) The effect of variations in the four parameters of an A_1^2 fragment. (j) The shock graph of a hand, and (k) its fragmentation based on a piecewise circular approximation giving a low-dimensional space (58) that generates all possible shapes, (l) seven of which are shown here. We emphasize that the use of a shape prior will significantly further constrain the number of parameters (e.g., the length of one finger is specified as a function of another).

Plate 23.19. (*a-b*) Segmenting an object from the binary image of a noisy contour while keeping its qualitative shape (its skeletal topology). (*c*) Segmenting a giraffe using a generative shock-graph model (with branches) constructed from a hand-drawn model of a giraffe. (*d-i*) Examples of correct segmentation of bottles: the model is robust to partial occlusion, clutters, and low contrast. (*j-l*) Examples of false-positives in bottle segmentation. We expect appearance information and training on model parameters will help avoid these cases. All images are from the ETHZ Shape Classes dataset (Ferrari et al. 2006).

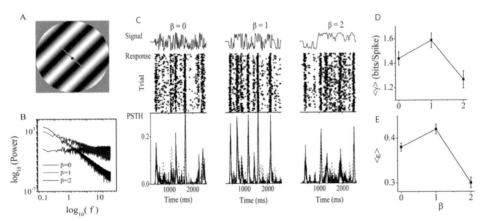

Plate 24.1. Neuronal preference for 1/f correlational structures in natural scenes. *A*, An example of the sine-wave grating stimulus input. The arrow indicates the direction of motion of the grating. *B*; The power spectra for the three classes of $1/f^\beta$ signals with $\beta = 0$ (white), $\beta = 1$ (pink), and $\beta = 2$ (brown), respectively. *C*, The top row depicts the phase of the motion of the input grating. The second row is the raster plot of a V1 neuron's response to the three sequences of input. The third row is the PSTH of the neuron's response. The $\beta = 1$ signal evokes the most robust response in the neuron, as indicated by the tall peaks, which reflect repeatability of the response when the same stimulus was presented. The solid lines represent the actual neural responses, and the dotted lines represent the predicted responses based on the models recovered respectively from each class of signals. The reliability of the neuronal responses for 1/f signal also lead to better predictability of its recovered kernel. Coding efficiency (*D*) and information transmission rate (*E*) both exhibit a preference for the 1/f correlational structure. Adapted from Yu, Romero, and Lee (2005).

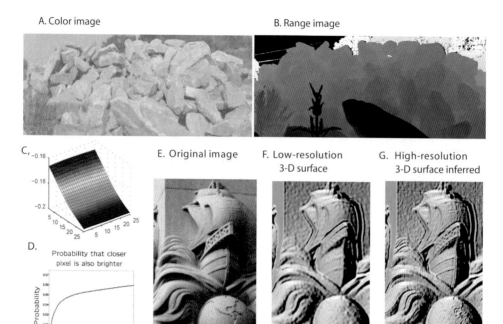

Plate 24.2. *A*, An example color image from our database. *B*, The corresponding range image. In this image, owing to the shadowing in the rocky cliff face, the correlation between depth and pixel intensity is −0.37. *C*, Typical correlation between an intensity pixel and the surrounding range pixels across patches centered at intensity pixel's location. On average, the correlation between image intensity and range value at the same location is $r = -0.18$ – as shown by (13,13) in the graph. *D*, Given two pixels, the brighter pixel is usually closer to the observer. *E*, An example image from our database. *F*, The corresponding range image was subsampled to produce a low-resolution depth map, and then (for illustration purposes) rendered to create an artificial, computer-generated image. Next, a computer algorithm was used to learn the statistical relationship between the low-resolution 3-D shape of (*F*) and the 2-D image of (*E*). This includes both shading and shadow (nearness/brightness correlation) cues. In this example, shadow cues were stronger. This learned statistical relationship was then extrapolated into higher spatial frequencies to estimate the high-resolution 3-D shape, shown in (*G*). Some high-resolution depth features are "hallucinated" by the algorithm correctly, such as the cross on the sail and the details on the globe. Adapted from Potetz and Lee (2003) and Potetz and Lee (2005).

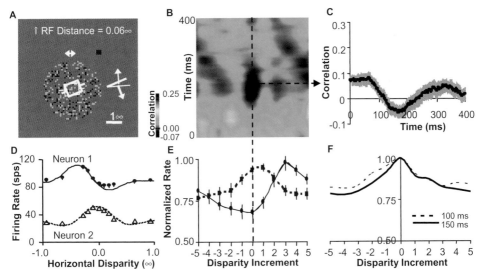

Plate 24.4. Local competitive interaction. *A*, Receptive fields, preferred orientation, and direction of motion (white) overlaying the RDS stimuli for an example competitive pair of neurons (red square is fixation point). *B*, Population summary of interaction strength (correlation) versus time and disparity for 17 neuronal pairs with antagonistic disparity tuning. *C*, A section of *B* noted by the dashed line. *D*, Disparity tuning for neuronal pair described in *A*. *E*, Population summary of disparity tuning for same pairs described in *B*. *F*, Population summary of sharpened disparity tuning after competitive interaction described in *B*. Adapted from Samonds et al. (2009).

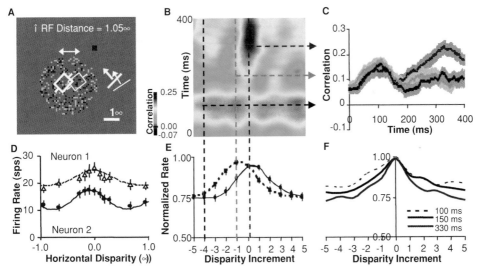

Plate 24.6. Cooperative interaction. *A*, Receptive fields, preferred orientation, and direction of motion (white) overlaying the RDS stimuli for an example cooperative pair of neurons. *B*, Population summary of interaction strength (correlation) versus time and disparity for 41 neuronal pairs with similar disparity tuning. *C*, Sections of *B* noted by the corresponding dashed lines. *D*, Disparity tuning for neuronal pair described in *A*. *E*, Population summary of disparity tuning for same pairs described in *B*. *F*, Population summary of sharpened disparity tuning after competitive interaction described in Figure 24.4B (blue) and cooperative interaction described in *B* (red). Adapted from Samonds et al. (2009).

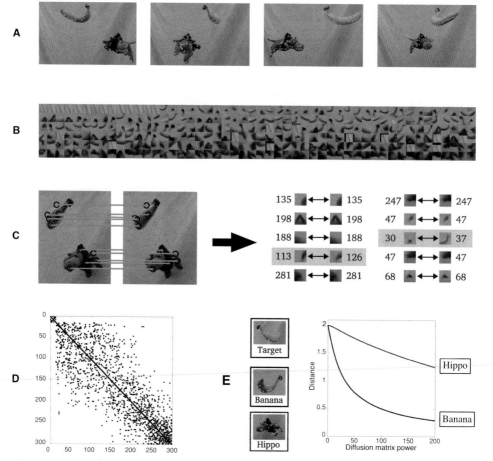

Plate 24.8. A demonstration example of the method for learning the appearance dynamics of low-level image features. *A*, The input video contains a banana and a toy hippo rotating in space. Sparse, local image features of various scales are detected in each frame. Descriptors for those features are simply the 15 × 15 pixel, three color image patches themselves. Next, *K*-means is run on a random assortment of extracted descriptor patches to yield a 300-bin discretization of the feature descriptor space; cluster centers appear in *B*. *C*, Features are tracked between video frames (*left*). Discretized descriptors of tracked features yield the appearance transitions at *right*, which then inform the Markov transition matrix whose sparsity structure appears in *D*. *E*, L1 diffusion distance comparison of one image feature bag-of-words histogram (target) with two others. The banana histogram becomes similar after a few diffusion steps; the hippo histogram remains distinct.

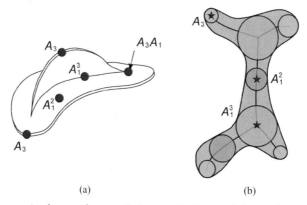

(a)   (b)

Plate 25.2. The generic classes of points that comprise the medial locus in 3-D (a) and 2-D (b). Adapted from Siddiqi and Pizer (2008).

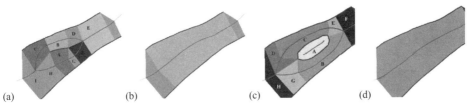

(a) (b) (c) (d)

Figure 23.13. The shock graph loops that form around internal contours in three different ways – (a) around a open contour, (c) around a closed contour, and (c) around a boundary between two fragments (not shown) – define shock-patch image fragment, which allows for reasoning using appearance, whether they can be safely merged to remove the spurious element, as in (b, d). (See color plate 23.13.)

2001). We then iteratively apply the shock transform with the lowest cost at each step, thus moving in a gradient descent fashion in the space of all transforms (Fig. 23.14). Observe that we have not so far used appearances as a cost, but it will be used in the future as the technique matures (Ozcanli et al. 2006).

23.4 Bottom-Up Recognition of Shapes Embedded in Figures

The shock-graph approach to recognition described in section 23.2 is equally applicable to a set of contour fragments that may not necessarily form a closed shape, but the matching complexity is no longer polynomial (Fig. 23.15). This motivates a partial match in the form of matching fragments consisting of a few shock-patch image fragments (Fig. 23.16) (Ozcanli and Kimia 2007). The presence of numerous gaps and spurious edges prevents the formation of fragments that are meaningful. Thus, we first

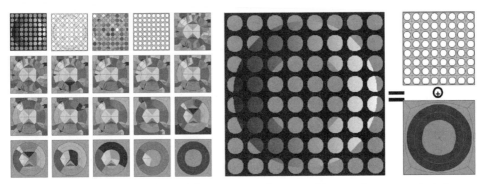

Figure 23.14. A sequence of visual fragment transforms are illustrated on an occluded torus image. The occluder is "recognized" and removed onto another "layer" by a loop disocclusion transform. The removal of an occluder to a different layer is currently done manually but the remaining steps (i.e., gaps transforms to link the individual visual fragments into a coherent whole) are automatic. Because there is more evidence to link up the outer edges of the torus, this will happen first. The grouping of the contour fragments of the outer edge will produce a grouping of the visual fragments into larger ones, as illustrated. After the outer edges are grouped, there is more evidence for the inner contour fragments to link up, thus producing a pair of closed contours. This defines the fragment into the shape of torus, as illustrated. As a result of this organization, the image is organized into two layers, a torus that is occluded by the mesh of holes. This cannot easily be acclaimed by a contour-based representation. (See color plate 23.14.)

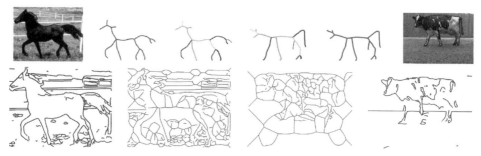

Figure 23.15. *Top row* observes how the shock graph of a segmented horse is optimally transformed to the shock graph of a segmented cow (colored edges are matching and the thinner black edges are edited out). This approach works equally well for shock graphs of edge maps of real images (bottom up). Although this can be done segmented images with a polynomial time algorithm, the algorithm for matching the shock graphs in the bottom row is NP-complete (blue: boundaries; red: shock graphs). (See color plate 23.15.)

apply the transforms discussed in section 23.3 and then form fragments, as shown in Figure 23.16. Many of these fragments are meaningful parts of the object, whereas others are either from the background or a combination of figure-ground. The shape-based similarity of these fragments to those of stored models is ambiguous. Therefore, multiple fragments with consistent spatial relationships are needed. An experiment relying on evidence from only two fragments yielded 92% recall at 85% precision with a *single training model and no training*. This compares favorably with Opelt et al. (2006), who, with 30 training models and extrusive training, get 92% recall at 92% precision. We are currently extending this model.

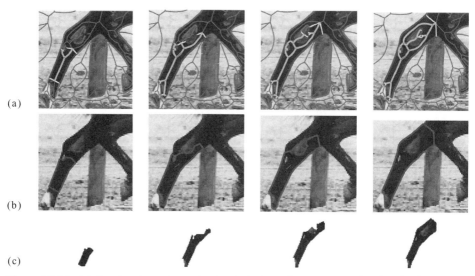

Figure 23.16. (a) Shock subgraphs at depths 1, 2, 3, and 4, respectively. The shock graph is shown in red, and the subgraph in light green. Image boundaries are shown in green, shock patch boundaries in blue. (b) The simple closed boundary in blue traced from the outer face of the subgraph. (c) The four fragments in isolation. (See color plate 23.16.)

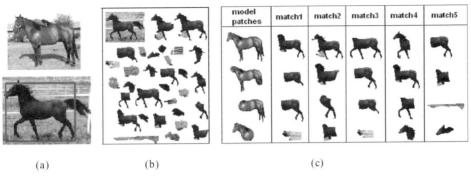

		model patches	match1	match2	match3	match4	match5

Figure 23.17. (a) Two horses to be matched. (b) Fragments of one horse. (c) The result of matching.

23.5 Model-Based Segmentation: Top-Down Organization Using the Shock Graph

The previous sections outlined a bottom-up approach when the image is organized as much as possible and its fragments are matched into the fragments of a database of stored examples. When the bottom-up organization is not sufficiently powerful to uniquely identify the object category or when context is available, or when the object is identified but its outline is ambiguous, top-down processes need to be used in the form of generative models for each category.

Generative models of shape face challenges that are not experienced by nongenerative models. First, a given representation must generate a "legal" shape, a member in good standing (i.e., without self-intersections, swallowtails, with valid topology; Fig. 23.18(a–e). Second, the model has to be capable of generating a comprehensive and *complete* variety of shapes, approximated to the desired level of accuracy. Indeed some of the existing shape models may leave out big chunks of the shape space (e.g., active shape models generate shapes only for the classes learnt) (Cootes et al. 1995).

Third, a generative model needs to balance *expressiveness* of the model with its *dimensionality*. The challenge, given the extremely high-dimensional shape space, is to capture the essential variations in shape while ignoring the irrelevant ones. While free-form models (e.g., "snakes" (Kass et al. 1988) and its level-set counterpart (Malladi et al. 1995; Han et al. 2003)) generate a wide variety of shapes, they are high-dimensional, which is problematic even when shape is restricted to certain models by knowledge (Leventon et al. 2000; Cremers et al. 2006). In contrast, parametric models such as superquadrics (Terzopoulos and Metaxas 1991) or Fourier models (Staib and Duncan 1992), and PCA-based modeling of deformations from a known prototype or template/atlas restrict the dimensionality of the model, but this is at the expense of discarding large chunks of the shape space.

Graph-based representations, initially used by Yuille et al. (1992) and later for hand (Triesch and von der Malsburg 2002), for body (Balan and Black 2006; Zhang et al. 2004), and for general shape via the symmetry medial axis (Pizer et al. 2003; Joshi et al. 2002), are effective because they are able to model parts and thus model

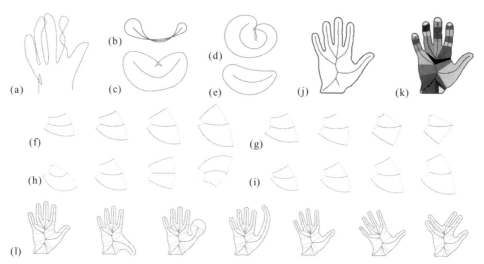

Figure 23.18. (a) Generative models of shape need to avoid generating invalid or "illegal" shapes, with problematic cases of intersection, swallowtail shown in (b-d), and a legal shape example in (e). (f-i) The effect of variations in the four parameters of an A_1^2 fragment. (j) The shock graph of a hand, and (k) its fragmentation based on a piecewise circular approximation giving a low-dimensional space (58) that generates all possible shapes, (l) seven of which are shown here. We emphasize that the use of a shape prior will significantly further constrain the number of parameters (e.g., the length of one finger is specified as a function of another). (See color plate 23.18.)

articulated shapes effectively. Pizer (2003) and Joshi et al. (2002) pioneered the use of a predetermined and fixed topology skeleton to model limited anatomic variations in medical applications. Their *m-rep* representation is a discrete sampling of the medial axis and its local geometry. Due to its discrete nature, continuous interpolation can fail to generate valid shapes. A continuous function representation of the medial geometry and the radius field was explored in Yushkevich et al. (2003) and improved in Yushkevich et al. (2005), which modeled a medial axis branch by a Poisson PDE with a nonlinear boundary condition. Although this was significant progress that allowed for statistical shape comparison, the problem of shape synthesis from a medial axis of arbitrary topology remained unsolved.

We have solved the problem of generating a dense sampling of the shape space for arbitrary shock graph topologies. Since all boundary curves can be approximated to any degree of accuracy by a circular arc spline (Yang 2002), we show that a small portion of a shock-graph segment, an A_1^2 fragment, can be fully modeled by four extrinsic (position, orientation, and scale) and four intrinsic parameters, as shown in Figure 23.18(f-i). Constraints of joining A_1^2 fragments smoothly, either in pairs or among junctions, are completely derived, leading to a highly reduced parameter set for a fairly complex shape (e.g., a hand; Fig. 23.18(j-l) (Trinh and Kimia 2007). This model avoids all local self-intersections/swallowtail as well as global intersections from inside (Fig. 23.18(b)). However, outer intersections (Fig. 23.18(d)) can only be avoided when the outer shocks are also represented.

We have begun using this model in top-down image segmentation using dynamic programming on the shock-graph representation (Fig. 23.19).

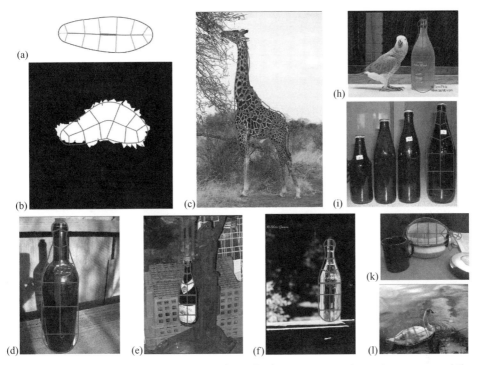

Figure 23.19. (*a-b*) Segmenting an object from the binary image of a noisy contour while keeping its qualitative shape (its skeletal topology). (*c*) Segmenting a giraffe using a generative shock-graph model (with branches) constructed from a hand-drawn model of a giraffe. (*d-i*) Examples of correct segmentation of bottles: the model is robust to partial occlusion, clutters, and low contrast. (*j-l*) Examples of false-positives in bottle segmentation. We expect appearance information and training on model parameters will help avoid these cases. All images are from the ETHZ Shape Classes dataset (Ferrari et al. 2006). (See color plate 23.19.)

23.6 Conclusion

The essence of shape is in the topographic representation of spatial relationships. The shock-graph topology captures this, while the specific information at shock nodes and shock links capture the details of form. This is supported by its excellent performance in delimiting categories. The shock-patch image fragment provides an intermediate-level representation of pieces of the image that then allows for perceptual reasoning and grouping, object recognition, and model-based segmentation.

Bibliography

Ahuja N. 1996. A transform for multiscale image segmentation by integrated edgeand region detection. *IEEE Trans Pattern Anal Mach Intell* 18(12): 1211–1235.

Balan AO, Black, MJ. 2006. An adaptive appearance model approach for model-based articulated object tracking. In CVPR, 758–765. IEEE Computer Society.

Belongie S, Malik J, Puzicha J. 2002. Shape matching and object recognition using shape contexts. *IEEE Trans Pattern Anal Mach Intell* 24(4): 509–522.

Berg AC, Berg TL, Malik J. 2005. Shape matching and object recognition using low distortion correspondences. In CVPR, 26–33. IEEE Computer Society.

Biswas S, Aggarwal G, Chellappa R. 2007. Efficient indexing for articulation invariant shape matching and retrieval. In CVPR. IEEE Computer Society.

Borenstein E, Malik J. 2006. Shape guided object segmentation. In CVPR, 969–976. IEEE Computer Society.

Borenstein E, Ullman S. 2002. Class-specific, top-down segmentation. In Proceedings of the European conference on computer vision, 109–124.

Comaniciu D, Meer P. 2002. Mean shift: a robust approach toward feature space analysis. *IEEE Trans Pattern Anal Mach Intell* 24(5): 603–619.

Cootes T, Taylor C, Cooper D, Graham J. 1995. Active shape models – their training and applications. *Comput Vis Image Und* 61(2).

Cour T, Shi J. 2007. Recognizing objects by piecing together the segmentation puzzle. In CVPR. IEEE Computer Society.

Crandall D, Felzenszwalb P, Huttenlocher D. 2005. Spatial priors for part-based recognition using statistical models. In CVPR, 10–17. IEEE Computer Society.

Cremers D, Osher S, Soatto S. 2006. Kernel density estimation and intrinsic alignment for shape priors in level set segmentation. *Int J Comput Vis* 69(3): 335–351.

Csurka G, Dance CR, Fan L, Willamowski J, Bray C. 2004. Visual categorization with bags of keypoints. In ECCV international workshop on statistical learning in computer vision.

Dimitrov P, Phillips C, Siddiqi K. 2000. Robust and efficient skeletal graphs. In CVPR, 1417–1423. Hilton Head Island, South Carolina, USA. IEEE Computer Society.

Fei-Fei L, Fergus R, Perona P. 2004. Learning generative visual models from few training examples: an incremental Bayesian approach tested on 101 object categories. In Proceedings of IEEE CVPR workshop on generative model based vision.

Fei-Fei L, Fergus R, Perona P. 2006. One-shot learning of object categories. *IEEE Trans Pattern and Mach Intell* 28(4): 594–611.

Felzenszwalb PF. Schwartz JD. 2007. Hierarchical matching of deformable shapes. In CVPR. IEEE Computer Society.

Fergus R, Perona P, Zisserman A. 2003. Object class recognition by unsupervised scale-invariant learning. In Proceedings of the IEEE computer society conference on computer vision and pattern recognition, 264–271. Madison, Wisconsin. IEEE Computer Society Press.

Fergus R, Perona P, Zisserman A. 2004. A visual category filter for google images. In ECCV, vol 3021, 242–256. *Lecture notes in computer science*. Springer.

Fergus R, Perona P, Zisserman A. 2005. A sparse object category model for efficient learning and exhaustive recognition, 380–397. In CVPR, IEEE Computer Society.

Ferrari V, Fevrier L, Jurie F, Schmid C. 2008. Groups of adjacent contour segments for object detection. *IEEE Trans Pattern Anal Mach Intell* 30(1): 36–51.

Ferrari V, Jurie F, Schmid C. 2007. Accurate object detection with deformable shape models learnt from images, 1–8. In CVPR. IEEE Computer Society.

Ferrari V, Tuytelaars T, Gool LV. 2006. Object detection by contour segment networks. In ECCV, vol 3951, 14–28. *Lecture notes in computer science*. Springer.

Giblin PJ, Kimia BB. 1999. On the local form and transitions of symmetry sets, and medial axes, and shocks in 2D. In Proceedings of the fifth international conference on computer vision, 385–391. KerKyra, Greece. IEEE Computer Society Press.

Giblin PJ, Kimia BB. 2007. Local forms and transitions of the medial axis. In *Medial representations: mathematics, algorithms and applications* ed. K Siddiqi and S Pizer. Kluwer Academic.

Han X, Xu C, Prince JL. 2003. A topology preserving level set method for geometric deformable models. *IEEE Trans Pattern Anal Mach Intell* 25(6): 755–768.

Huggins P, Chen H, Belhumeur P, Zucker, S. 2001. Finding folds: on the appearance and identification of occlusion. In Proceedings of the IEEE computer society conference on computer vision and pattern recognition, II:718–725. Kauai, Hawaii, USA. IEEE Computer Society Press.

Johannes MS, Sebastian TB, Tek H, Kimia BB. 2001. Perceptual organization as object recognition divided by two. In Workshop on perceptual organization in computer vision, 41–46.

Joshi S, Pizer S, Fletcher P, Yushkevich P, Thall A, Marron J. 2002. Multiscale deformable model segmentation and statistical shape analysis using medial descriptions. *Med Imag* 21(5): 538–550.

Jurie F, Schmid C. 2004. Scale-invariant shape features for recognition of object categories, II: 90–96. In CVPR.

Kass M, Witkin A, Terzopoulos D. 1988. Snakes: active contour models. *Int J Comput Vis* 1(4): 321–331.

Kelly MF, Levine MD. 1995. Annular symmetry operators: a method for locating and describing objects. In ICCV.

Kimia BB. 2003. On the role of medial geometry in human vision. *J Physiol-Paris* 97(2–3): 155–190.

Kimia BB, Tannenbaum AR, Zucker SW. 1992. On the evolution of curves via a function of curvature, I: the classical case. JMAA 163(2): 438–458.

Kimia BB, Tannenbaum AR, Zucker SW. 1995. Shapes, shocks, and deformations, I: The components of shape and the reaction-diffusion space. *Int J Comput Vis* 15(3): 189–224.

Klein P, Sebastian T, Kimia B. 2001. Shape matching using edit-distance: an implementation. In Twelfth annual ACM-SIAM symposium on discrete algorithms (SODA), 781–790. Washington, D.C.

Klein P, Tirthapura S, Sharvit D, Kimia B. 2000. A tree-edit distance algorithm for comparing simple, closed shapes. In Tenth annual ACM-SIAM symposium on discrete algorithms (SODA), 696–704. San Francisco, California.

Koenderink J, van Doorn A. 1982. The shape of smooth objects and the way contours end. *Perception* 11(2): 129–137.

Kumar MP, Torr PHS, Zisserman A. 2004. Extending pictorial structures for object recognition, 789–798. In BMVC'04: British Machine Vision Association.

Leibe B, Leonardis A, Schiele B. 2004. Combined object categorization and segmentation with an implicit shape model. In ECCV'04 workshop on statistical learning in computer vision.

Leibe B, Schiele B. 2004. Scale-invariant object categorization using a scale-adaptive mean-shift search, 145–153. In DAGM symposium.

Leordeanu M, Hebert M, Sukthankar R. 2007. Beyond local appearance: category recognition from pairwise interactions of simple features. In CVPR. IEEE Computer Society.

Leventon ME, Grimson WEL, Faugeras, OD. 2000. Statistical shape influence in geodesic active contours. In Proceedings of the IEEE computer society conference on computer vision and pattern recognition, 1316–1323. Hilton Head Island, South Carolina, USA. IEEE Computer Society Press.

Leymarie FF, Kimia BB. 2007. From the infinitely large to the infinitely small: Applications of medial symmetry representations of shape. In *Medial representations: mathematics, algorithms and applications* ed. K Siddiqi and S Pizer. Kluwer Academic (in press).

Ling H, Jacobs DW. 2007. Shape classification using the inner-distance. *IEEE Trans Pattern Anal Mach Intell* 29(2): 286–299.

Liu G, Lin Z, Tang X, Yu Y. 2007. A hybrid graph model for unsupervised object segmentation. In ICCV'07 Proceedings of the eleventh IEEE international conference on computer vision: IEEE Computer Society.

Lowe D. 2004. Distinctive image features from scale-invariant keypoints. *Int J Comput Vis* 60(2): 91–110.

Malladi R, Sethian JA, Vemuri BC. 1995. Shape modelling with front propagation: A level set approach. *IEEE Trans Pattern Anal Mach Intell* 17.

Mikolajczyk K, Schmid C. 2005. A performance evaluation of local descriptors. *IEEE Trans Pattern Anal Mach Intell* 27(10): 1615–1630.

Mikolajczyk K, Tuytelaars T, Schmid C, Zisserman A, Matas J, Schaffalitzky F, Kadir T, and Gool LJV. 2005. A comparison of affine region detectors. *Int J Comput Vis* 65(1-2): 43–72.

Mori G. 2005. Guiding model search using segmentation. In ICCV: Proceedings of the tenth IEEE international conference on computer vision, 1417–1423. IEEE Computer Society.

Mori G, Ren X, Efros AA, Malik J. 2004. Recovering human body configurations: Combining segmentation and recognition. In CVPR'04 326–333. IEEE Computer Society.

Nelson RC, Selinger A. 1998. A cubist approach to object recognition. In Proceedings of the sixth international conference on computer vision, 614–621. Bombay, India. IEEE Computer Society Press.

Opelt A, Pinz A, Zisserman A. 2006. A boundary-fragment-model for object detection. In ECCV'06, vol 3951, 575–588. *Lecture notes in computer science*. Springer.

Ozcanli OC, Kimia BB. 2007. Generic object recognition via shock patch fragments. In *Proceedings of the British machine vision conference*, ed. NM Rajpoot and A Bhalerao, 1030–1039. Coventry, USA: Warwick Print.

Ozcanli OC, Tamrakar A, Kimia BB, Mundy JL. 2006. Augmenting shape with appearance in vehicle category recognition. In CVPR'06, 935–942. IEEE Computer Society.

Pearce A, Caelli T, Bischof WF. 1994. Rulegraphs for graph matching in pattern recognition. *Pattern Recog* 27: 1231–1247.

Pelillo M, Siddiqi K, Zucker SW. 1999. Matching hierarchical structures using association graphs. *IEEE Trans Pattern Anal Mach Intell* 21(11): 1105–1120.

Pizer SM, Fletcher PT, Joshi S, Thall A, Chen JZ., Fridman Y, Fritsch DS, Gash AG, Glotzer JM, Jiroutek MR, Lu C, Muller KE, Tracton G, Yushkevich P, Chaney EL. 2003. Deformable m-reps for 3d medical image segmentation. *Int J Comput Vis* 55(2-3): 85–106.

Ren X, Fowlkes C, Malik J. 2006. Figure/ground assignment in natural images. In ECCV'06, vol 3951, 614–627. *Lecture notes in computer science*. Springer.

Russell BC, Efros AA, Sivic J, Freeman WT, Zisserman A. 2006. Using multiple segmentations to discover objects and their extent in image collections. In CVPR'06, 1605–1614. IEEE Computer Society.

Sebastian T, Klein P, Kimia B. 2004. Recognition of shapes by editing their shock graphs. *IEEE Trans Pattern Anal Mach Intell* 26: 551–571.

Sebastian TB, Kimia BB. 2002. Metric-based shape retrieval in large databases. In Proceedings of international conference on pattern recognition, vol 3, 30291–30296. Quebec City, Quebec, Canada: Computer Society Press.

Sebastian TB, Klein PN, Kimia BB 2001. Recognition of shapes by editing shock graphs. In Proceedings of the eighth international conference on computer vision, 755–762. Vancouver, Canada. IEEE Computer Society Press.

Sebastian TB, Klein PN, Kimia BB. 2002. Shock-based indexing into large shape databases. In ECCV'02, vol 2350. *Lecture notes in computer science* (Part III:731–746). Springer.

Selinger A, Nelson RC. 1999. A perceptual grouping hierarchy for appearance-based 3d object recognition. *Comput Vis Image Und* 76(1): 83–92.

Sharon E, Brandt A, Basri R. 2001. Segmentation and Boundary Detection Using Multiscale Intensity Measurements. In Proceedings IEEE conference on computer vision and pattern recognition, 469–476.

Sharvit D, Chan J, Tek H, Kimia BB. 1998. Symmetry-based indexing of image databases. *J Vis Commun Image Rep* 9(4): 366–380.

Shi J, Malik J. 2000. Normalized cuts and image segmentation. *IEEE Trans Pattern Anal Mach Intell* 22(8): 888–905.

Shotton J, Blake A, Cipolla R. 2005. Contour-based learning for object detection. In ICCV, 281–288.

Siddiqi K, Bouix S, Tannenbaum A, Zucker SW. 1999a. The hamilton-jacobi skeleton. In ICCV: Proceedings of the international conference on computer vision, vol 2, 828. Washington, DC, USA: IEEE Computer Society.

Siddiqi K, Bouix S, Tannenbaum A, Zucker SW. 2002. Hamilton-jacobi skeletons. *Int J Comput Vision* 48(3): 215–231.

Siddiqi K, Kimia BB. 1995. Parts of visual form: computational aspects. *IEEE Trans Pattern Anal Mach Intell* 17(3): 239–251.

Siddiqi K, Kimia BB, Tannenbaunm AR, Zucker SW. 2001. On the psychophysics of the shape triangle. *Vision Res* 41(9): 1153–1178.

Siddiqi K, Shokoufandeh A, Dickinson SJ, Zucker SW. 1999b. Shock graphs and shape matching. *Int J Comput Vis* 35(1): 13–32.

Siddiqi K, Shokoufandeh A, Macrini D, Dickinson S, Zucker SW. 2005. Indexing hierarchical structures using graph spectra. *IEEE Trans Pattern Anal Mach Intell* 27(7): 1125–1140.

Siddiqi K, Tresness KJ, Kimia BB. 1996. Parts of visual form: ecological and psychophysical aspects. *Perception* 25, 399–424.

Staib L, Duncan J. 1992. Boundary finding with parametrically deformable models. *IEEE Trans Pattern Anal Mach Intell* 14(11): 1061–1075.

Stein A, Hoiem D, Hebert M. 2007. Learning to find object boundaries using motion cues. In ICCV: Proceedings of the eleventh IEEE international conference on computer vision. IEEE Computer Society.

Tamrakar A, Kimia BB. 2004. Medial visual fragments as an intermediate image representation for segmentation and perceptual grouping. In Proceedings of CVPR workshop on perceptual organization in computer vision, 47.

Tamrakar A, Kimia BB. 2007. No grouping left behind: From edges to curve fragments. In ICCV'07 Proceedings of the eleventh IEEE international conference on computer vision. Rio de Janeiro. Brazil. IEEE Computer Society.

Tao H, Sawhney HS, Kumar R. 2001. A global matching framework for stereo computation. In Proceedings of the eighth international conference on computer vision, 532–539. Vancouver, Canada. IEEE Computer Society Press.

Tek H, Kimia BB. 1999. Symmetry maps of free-form curve segments via wave propagation. In ICCV.

Terzopoulos D, Metaxas DN. 1991. Dynamic 3D models with local and global deformations: Deformable superquadrics. *IEEE Trans Pattern Anal Mach Intell* 13(7): 703–714.

Todorovic S, Ahuja N. 2006. Extracting subimages of an unknown category from a set of images. In CVPR, 927–934). IEEE Computer Society.

Torsello A, Hancock ER. 2006. Learning shape-classes using a mixture of tree-unions. *IEEE Trans Pattern Anal Mach Intell*, 28(6): 954–967.

Triesch J, von der Malsburg C. 2002. Classification of hand postures against complex backgrounds using elastic graph matching. *Image Vis Comput* 20(13-14): 937–943.

Trinh N, Kimia BB. 2007. A symmetry-based generative model for shape. In ICCV: Proceedings of the eleventh IEEE international conference on computer vision. Rio de Janeiro, Brazil. IEEE Computer Society.

Tu Z, Chen X, Yuille AL, Zhu SC. 2005. Image parsing: unifying segmentation, detection, and recognition. *Int J Comput Vis* 63(2): 113–140.

Tu Z, Yuille AL. 2004. Shape matching and recognition – using generative models and informative features. In *ECCV'04*, vol 3021, 195–209. *Lecture notes in computer science*. Springer.

Tu ZW, Zhu SC. 2002. Image segmentation by data-driven markov chain monte carlo. *IEEE Trans Pattern Anal Mach Intell* 24(5): 657–673.

Vidal-Naquet M, Ullman S. 2003. Object recognition with informative features and linear classification. In ICCV, 281–288. Nice, France.

Yang X. 2002. Efficient circular arc interpolation based on active tolerance control. *Comput-Aid Design* 34(13): 1037–1046.

Yu X, Yi L, Fermuller C, Doermann D. 2007. Object detection using a shape codebook. In Proceedings of the British machine vision conference ed. NM Rajpoot and A Bhalerao, 1020–1029. Coventry, USA: Warwick Print.

Yuille A, Hallinan P. 1993. Deformable templates. In *Active vision*, 21–38. Cambridge: MIT Press.

Yuille AL, Hallinan PW, Cohen DS. 1992. Feature extraction from faces using deformable templates. *Int J Comput Vis* 8(2): 99–111.

Yushkevich P, Fletcher PT, Joshi S, Thall A, Pizer SM. 2003. Continuous medial representations for geometric object modeling in 2d and 3d. *Image Vis Comput* 21(1): 17–28.

Yushkevich PA, Zhang H, Gee JC. 2005. Parametric medial shape representation in 3-d via the poisson partial differential equation with non-linear boundary conditions. In IPMI, 162–173.

Zhang J, Collins RT, Liu Y. 2004. Representation and matching of articulated shapes. In CVPR'04, 342–349. IEEE Computer Society.

Zhang J, Marszalek M, Lazebnik S, Schmid C. 2007. Local features and kernels for classification of texture and object categories: a comprehensive study. *Int J Comput Vis* 73(2): 213–238.

CHAPTER 24

Neural Encoding of Scene Statistics for Surface and Object Inference

Tai Sing Lee, Tom Stepleton, Brian Potetz, and Jason Samonds

24.1 Introduction

Visual scenes are often complex and ambiguous to interpret because of the myriad causes that generate them. To understand visual scenes, our visual systems have to rely on our prior experience and assumptions about the world. These priors are rooted in the statistical correlation structures of visual events in our experience. They can be learned and exploited for probabilistic inference in a Bayesian framework using graphical models. Thus, we believe that understanding the statistics of natural scenes and developing graphical models with these priors for inference are crucial for gaining theoretical and computational insights to guide neurophysiological experiments. In this chapter, we will provide our perspective based on our work on scene statistics, graphical models, and neurophysiological experiments.

An important source of statistical priors for inference is the statistical correlation of visual events in our natural experience. In fact, it has long been suggested in the psychology community that learning due to coherent covariation of visual events is crucial for the development of Gestalt rules (Koffka 1935) as well as models of objects and object categories in the brain (Gibson 1979; Roger and McClelland 2004). Nevertheless, there has been relatively little research on how correlation structures in natural scenes are encoded by neurons. Here, we will first describe experimental results obtained from multielectrode neuronal recording in the primary visual cortex of awake-behaving monkeys. Each study was conducted on at least two animals. These results reveal mechanisms at the neuronal level for the encoding and influence of scene priors in visual processing. Insofar as these mechanisms likely emerge from Hebbian learning (Hebb 1949) or its variant, which is sensitive to the timing of the events (Markram et al. 1997), we conjecture that the same basic principles and mechanisms are universal, repeating themselves throughout the visual cortex. We argue that extending these principles to the inferotemporal cortex could provide a new perspective on object representation.

451

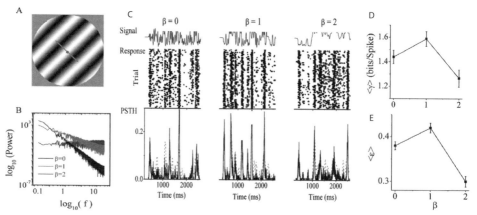

Figure 24.1. Neuronal preference for $1/f$ correlational structures in natural scenes. *A,* An example of the sine-wave grating stimulus input. The arrow indicates the direction of motion of the grating. *B,* The power spectra for the three classes of $1/f^{\beta}$ signals with $\beta = 0$ (white), $\beta = 1$ (pink), and $\beta = 2$ (brown), respectively. *C,* The top row depicts the phase of the motion of the input grating. The second row is the raster plot of a V1 neuron's response to the three sequences of input. The third row is the PSTH of the neuron's response. The $\beta = 1$ signal evokes the most robust response in the neuron, as indicated by the tall peaks, which reflect repeatability of the response when the same stimulus was presented. The solid lines represent the actual neural responses, and the dotted lines represent the predicted responses based on the models recovered respectively from each class of signals. The reliability of the neuronal responses for $1/f$ signal also lead to better predictability of its recovered kernel. Coding efficiency (D) and information transmission rate (E) both exhibit a preference for the $1/f$ correlational structure. Adapted from Yu, Romero, and Lee (2005). (See color plate 24.1.)

24.2 Neural Coding of Statistical Correlations in Natural Scenes

In natural scenes, there are a variety of correlation structures. First, at a single point in space, a visual signal is correlated over time. Second, different aspects of the visual signal, such as luminance and binocular disparity, can be correlated due to interaction of luminance and depth in 3-D scenes. Third, visual signals are correlated across space when they arise from a single surface. How are these correlations encoded in the nervous system? We found two potential mechanisms: (1) tuning properties of individual neurons, and (2) connectivity among neurons. Neurons develop tuning properties that can capture correlation structures in the feedforward input at the earliest stages of processing, and correlation in the input signals will likely exhibit correlation in the tuning properties in the different feature dimensions. Spatially and temporally correlated visual events are likely encoded in recurrent (horizontal and feedback) connections between neurons. On a conceptual level, it might be meaningful to consider the former process as extracting unified information from earlier areas and the latter process as unifying associated representations in the same visual area.

24.2.1 Encoding Correlation Structures in Tuning Properties

Neurons are often characterized by tuning properties (i.e. whether they exhibit preferences for certain stimulus parameters along a certain feature dimension). To explore

whether and how a correlation structure in visual features is encoded in the tuning properties of neurons, we have performed two neurophysiological experiments in primary
visual cortex (V1). The first experiment concerns correlation structures with respect
to time, and the second experiment concerns a correlation structure between depth
and luminance cues at a single point in space. In these experiments, as well as all
other physiological experiments presented in this chapter, the recordings were done on
awake-behaving monkeys performing a simple fixation task using multiple electrodes,
each isolating single-unit activity of individual neurons.

Natural signals often exhibit similar statistical properties at all scales, and are thus
described as having self-similar, or fractal, structure. One consequence of this scale-
invariance property is that natural signals typically have a power spectrum that obeys
a power-law, of the form $1/f^\beta$ (Ruderman and Bialek 1996; Potetz and Lee 2006). In
the time domain, natural signals are characterized by a $1/f$ power spectrum, meaning
that the total amount of power in each octave of frequency is the same for every octave.
We evaluated how V1 neurons respond to noise signals with different power spectra –
that is, white noise ($\beta = 0$), pink or natural noise ($\beta = 1$), and brown noise ($\beta = 2$),
as shown in Figure 24.1A and B. We found that signals with $\beta = 1$ were preferred
over white and brown noise in the robustness and reliability of the response and in the
amount of information about the stimulus transmitted in each spike (Yu et al. 2005).
Figure 24.1C shows that $\beta = 1$ signals generated more repeatable responses (higher
peaks in the peri-stimulus time histograms PSTH). Figures 24.1D and 24.1E show that
the coding efficiency and information transmission rate are highest for $\beta = 1$ signals.
In a related experiment in the auditory system, Garcia-Lazaro et al. (2006) discovered
that auditory neurons are also sensitive to this correlational structure. These findings
suggest that neurons in early sensory areas are adapted for this important temporal
correlation in natural signals, which might be a key factor underlying why neurons
prefer natural stimuli over other stimuli as some studies have earlier observed.

In a second experiment, we tested a prediction generated by the discovery of an
inverse correlation between depth and Luminance in 3-D natural scenes. Using co-
registered 2-D color images and laser-acquired 3-D range data, Potetz and Lee (2003)
found that there is an inverse correlation ($r = -0.18$) between values of luminance
and the depth of the camera from the point of observation; that is, brighter regions in
an image tend to be nearer. Centuries ago, Leonardo da Vinci observed a perceptual
phenomenon whereby brighter surfaces are perceived to be nearer, all other things being
equal. This observation has been exploited by artists in paintings. This study therefore
provides an ecological reason for such perception, demonstrating that correlational
structures in natural scenes might be explicitly encoded as priors in our visual system.
These correlational structures, we found, arise primarily from shadows in natural scenes
(e.g., farther surfaces are more likely to lie within shadow) and turns out to be especially
useful information for inferring depth from images (Potetz and Lee 2006) (Fig. 24.2).

How are correlation structures between visual cues encoded in neurons? We know
that neurons in V1 are tuned to binocular disparity (Cumming and DeAngelis 2001);
for example, some neurons prefer near surfaces, whereas other neurons prefer far
surfaces relative to the fixation plane. Do neurons tuned to nearer surfaces also tend
to prefer brighter surfaces? Indeed, we found this tendency to be the case at the
population level in V1 (Potetz et al. 2006). Many neurons exhibit sensitivity (tunings)

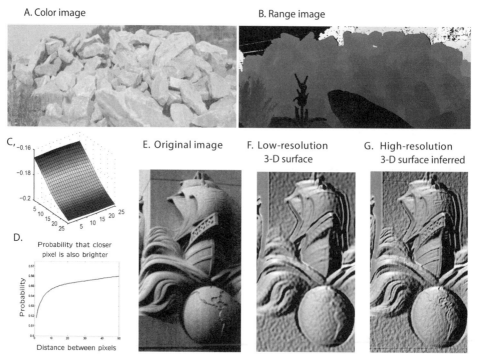

A. Color image

B. Range image

C.

D. Probability that closer pixel is also brighter

Probability

Distance between pixels

E. Original image

F. Low-resolution 3-D surface

G. High-resolution 3-D surface inferred

Figure 24.2. *A,* An example color image from our database. *B,* The corresponding range image. In this image, owing to the shadowing in the rocky cliff face, the correlation between depth and pixel intensity is −0.37. *C,* Typical correlation between an intensity pixel and the surrounding range pixels across patches centered at intensity pixel's location. On average, the correlation between image intensity and range value at the same location is $r = -0.18$ – as shown by (13,13) in the graph. *D,* Given two pixels, the brighter pixel is usually closer to the observer. *E,* An example image from our database. *F,* The corresponding range image was subsampled to produce a low-resolution depth map, and then (for illustration purposes) rendered to create an artificial, computer-generated image. Next, a computer algorithm was used to learn the statistical relationship between the low-resolution 3-D shape of (*F*) and the 2-D image of (*E*). This includes both shading and shadow (nearness/brightness correlation) cues. In this example, shadow cues were stronger. This learned statistical relationship was then extrapolated into higher spatial frequencies to estimate the high-resolution 3-D shape, shown in (*G*). Some high-resolution depth features are "hallucinated" by the algorithm correctly, such as the cross on the sail and the details on the globe. Adapted from Potetz and Lee (2003) and Potetz and Lee (2005). (See color plate 24.2.)

to both visual cues simultaneously. Among a population of 47 neurons, there is a strong trend for near-tuned cells to prefer a bright surface versus a dark surface with a statistically significant correlation between the disparity and brightness preference of $r = -0.39$ with $p = 0.01$ (Fig. 24.3). Thus, correlation between the two cues in natural scenes is reflected in the joint tunings to the two cues at the population level. This is the first physiological finding relating the tuning curves of individual neurons across two different depth-defining cues, and might be the physiological underpinning of psychophysical studies that revealed the interaction of different visual cues on depth perception (Moreno-Bote et al. 2008).

The idea that the tuning properties of neurons are capable of capturing correlation structures in natural scenes is by no means new and is in fact the fundamental

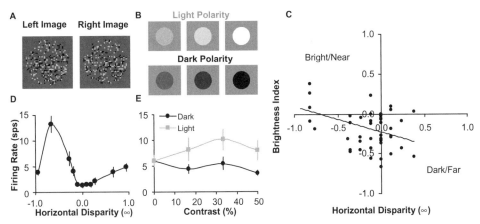

Figure 24.3. Testing for a correlation between disparity and luminance preference in V1. *A*, Random dot stereogram (RDS) stimulus. *B*, Light and dark spot stimuli. *C*, Scatter plot of brightness preference (light response – dark response)/(light response – dark response) versus disparity preference (disparity with peak response). *D*, Sample disparity tuning curve. *E*, Sample contrast response curve for light and dark polarity. From Potetz, Samonds, and Lee (2006).

assumption for a number of seminal theoretical studies on the emergence of simple cell receptive fields (Olshausen and Field 1996) and of tuning properties of retinal ganglian neurons (Atick and Redlich 1992). However, all these theoretical studies are ad-hoc, primarily providing explanations on well known existing physiological findings on the tuning properties of neurons. Our neurophysiological experiments are motivated and predicted by scene statistics' results and, for the first time, yielded brand new neurophysiological evidence that is consistent with the theoretical assumption/prediction on neural encoding of correlational structures.

24.2.2 Encoding Competitive Constraints in Neuronal Interaction

Although visual features or visual cues co-occurring at the same spatial regions can be encoded in the tuning properties of the neurons, as in the case of simple cells encoding the correlated activities of LGN neurons aligned in a particular orientation, some visual entities cannot occur simultaneously or are mutually exclusive. For example, given an observed surface, the hypothesis that it is at a particular depth is incompatible with the hypothesis it is at a different depth. This scenario requires neurons representing different hypotheses to compete with each other in explaining the observed image patch. The early computational model for stereopsis proposed by Marr and Poggio (1976) required a uniqueness constraint that stipulates that neurons coding for different disparities at the same location should inhibit one another. The independent component (sparse coding) explanation for the emergence of of simple cells' receptive fields (Olshausen and Field 1996) also requires similar competitive interaction. Later on, we will discuss how this uniqueness constraint is also relevant to object representations. Curiously, little is known about the competition between neurons in a cortical hypercolumn that are analyzing information within the same spatial window. To understand the neural implementation of mutual exclusion or the uniqueness constraint, we have carried out an experiment to study the interaction of neurons of different disparity tunings with spatially overlapping receptive fields.

In this experiment, while the monkeys fixate at a spot on a computer monitor, different depth planes rendered in dynamic random dot stereograms were presented in a 5-degree–diameter aperture for 1.2 seconds, one at a time. These are the stimuli typically used to measure the disparity tuning of a neuron. The novel component of our study was that we recorded from multiple neurons simultaneously, using multiple electrodes or a single electrode, and studied their interaction. The separated spikes from single electrodes or from two different electrodes recording from neurons with overlapping receptive fields were subject to cross-correlation analysis. Interaction strength between neurons is typically measured by cross-correlating spike trains, a measurement that can be positive or negative, reflecting the likelihood of a spike from one neuron coinciding with a spike from the other neuron. Correlation between two neurons' spike trains is first computed, and then the part of the the cross-correlation that can be attributed to the response firing rates of both neurons is discounted, and finally the estimate is normalized by the firing rates or variation in firing rates. That is, if the interaction strength between a pair of neurons is fixed, this measurement will remain constant irrespective of the stimulus being presented and how the neurons respond to the stimulus. In the end, a strong positive or negative cross-correlation suggests that the neurons are connected in some manner within the cortical network.

We found that neurons with very different disparity tunings exhibited negative correlation (competitive interaction) in their spiking activity (Samonds et al. 2007; Samonds et al. 2009). Figures 24.4A and D show the receptive-field locations and tuning relationships of a typical pair of neurons that exhibit competitive interaction. Figures 24.4B and C show the temporal evolution of neuronal interaction over time as a function of the depth as defined by the disparity of the presented random dot stereograms. These graphs are population results, averaged across all competitive pairs in the population, aligned by the negative correlation peaks. Figure 24.4B shows a significant early negative correlation component (competitive interaction), superimposed on the baseline correlation, between the two neurons. This is most severe where their disparity tunings diverge the most (Figs. 24.4E, C). This interaction is accompanied by the emergence of the disparity tuning and the sharpening of disparity tuning over time (Fig. 24.4F) (i.e., an improved estimate of the image depth). The neurons that exhibit competitive interaction are different not only in their disparity tunings, but also in motion direction tuning as well. It remains to be resolved whether neurons common in some cue dimension but different in other cue dimensions would still engage in competitive interaction exclusively, or whether the interactions between these neurons are cue-dependent.

This is the first piece of evidence that neurons analyzing the same spatial location engage in competitive interaction that is consistent with the uniqueness constraint during stereopsis computation (Marr 1981; Marr and Poggio 1976). It is well known that inhibitory connections and suppressive interactions are restricted to be local (Lund et al. 2003), but earlier studies tend to suggest that these inhibitions are not specific to stimulus or the cells' tuning properties (Das and Gilbert 1999; Bosking et al. 1997; Shapley et al. 2003). Our results suggest that the competitive interaction does depend on the tuning properties of the neurons. A uniqueness constraint, however, implies a winner-take-all scenario among the neurons, which might not be a desirable property

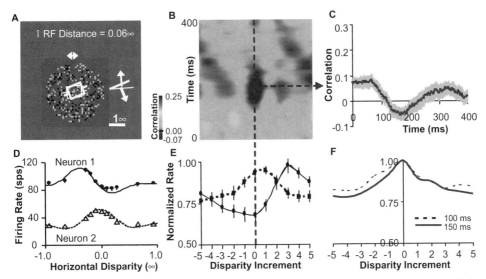

Figure 24.4. Local competitive interaction. *A*, Receptive fields, preferred orientation, and direction of motion (white) overlaying the RDS stimuli for an example competitive pair of neurons (red square is fixation point). *B*, Population summary of interaction strength (correlation) versus time and disparity for 17 neuronal pairs with antagonistic disparity tuning. *C*, A section of *B* noted by the dashed line. *D*, Disparity tuning for neuronal pair described in *A*. *E*, Population summary of disparity tuning for same pairs described in *B*. *F*, Population summary of sharpened disparity tuning after competitive interaction described in *B*. Adapted from Samonds et al. (2009). (See color plate 24.4.)

in most cases. It is more desirable to encode a posterior probability distribution of the different hypotheses using the neuronal population at each location to enable a more robust inference and representation. This is analogous to beliefs at a node in a graphical model of a Bayes net (Rao 2004; Potetz and Lee 2008; see also Knill and Pouget 2004). The fact that neurons will continue to respond to suboptimal features also suggests that the uniqueness constraint is probably a soft one. We will discuss the role of such constraint in object representations in a later section.

24.2.3 Encoding Spatial Correlations in Neuronal Connectivity

Our next question concerns the neural encoding of correlated events across space, such as the co-occurrence of features belonging to a surface or parts belonging to an object at different spatial locations. The standard argument is that neurons coding for events that occur together simultaneously across space can lead to the formation of specific neurons downstream that encode this joint event. Recursively repeating this principle along the visual hierarchy can conceptually allow the formation of codes for features, subparts, parts, and objects in a compositional architecture. In order to avoid a combinatorial explosion in the number of codes required at the higher level, Geman (2006) proposed that higher-order structures or representations can be dynamically constructed by composing reusable parts at each level along the visual hierarchy. The parts themselves are meaningful entities, learned from natural scene statistics, and are reusable in an enormous assortment of meaningful combinations. Such compositional hierarchies provide structured representations over which a probability distribution may be defined and used as prior models in scene interpretation. The key concept is that frequently co-occurring features are encoded explicitly by neurons, whereas occasionally co-occurring features are encoded transiently through the correlated activities or synchrony of the existing neurons.

There is indeed some evidence that the correlated activity or functional connectivity between V1 neurons across space is dynamic and stimulus-dependent. A number of multielectrode neurophysiological studies have shown that the interaction between a pair of neurons is dynamic (Singer 1999; Samonds et al. 2006; Samonds et al. 2007; Kohn and Smith 2005). The main finding emerging from these studies is that the interaction strength (also termed effective or functional connectivity, spike correlation, and synchrony) between a pair of neurons is not fixed but varies as a function of the stimuli and stimulus context presented to the neurons in relation to the tuning properties of these neurons, and is typically greatest at the peak of the product of the two tuning curves. Furthermore, the vast majority of measurements of interaction between neurons has been positive or facilitatory in nature. Thus, these findings on stimulus-dependent correlated activities of V1 neurons can reflect such dynamic functional connectivity suggested by Geman.

Although Geman's composition machine is mediated primarily by bottom-up feed-forward connections, in the visual cortex, besides these, there are vast numbers of horizontal and feedback connections. What are the functional roles of these recurrent connections, particularly the horizontal connections? Most of the extra-classical surround effects that neurophysiologists have observed are suppressive in nature. Thus, lateral inhibition or surround suppression is thought to be the dominant action of the horizontal connections, notwithstanding the fact that 80 percent of the synapses on the horizontal collaterals are excitatory in nature. We propose that the horizontal connections are implementing the constraints on how the different parts across space can vary relative to one another when the parts are being dynamically composed into a larger entity. In computer vision, this is modeled in terms of Markov random-field models, which allow information from a node's surrounding region to influence its interpretation of of the stimulus in its analyzing window. A node here can be represented by a population of neurons analyzing the same spatial location. The connections define the statistical distribution of the relationship between different features or parts across space – how the distance and relative orientation between the different parts tend to vary in natural scenes, and what range of variation is permitted when higher-order structures are composed and interpreted.

The simplest constraint used in computer vision for surface inference and segmentation is the ubiquitous *surface smoothness* constraint (i.e., surfaces tend to be smooth locally). More precisely, the variation in the surface orientations might follow a statistical distribution, such as a Gaussian or a Laplacian distribution. This constraint arises naturally from natural scene statistics. In our study of co-registered range and color images, we have examined the nature of this smoothness constraint (Potetz and Lee 2003). Figure 24.5A shows the correlation between pixels in range data as a function of distance, and Figure 24.5B shows the correlation between pixels in the image data as a function of distance. Both show some kind of exponential decay in correlation as a function of distance that can be fitted well with Laplacian distributions. The decay

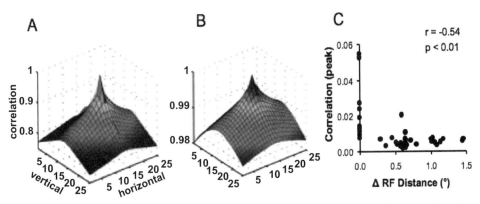

Figure 24.5. *A*, Correlation between intensity at a center pixel (13,13) and all the pixels in the same intensity patch, over all image patches (e.g., Fig. 24.2A). *B*, Correlation between range at a center pixel (13,13) and all the pixels in the same range patch, over all image patches (e.g., Fig. 24.2B). *C*, Peak in the correlogram of the activities of a pair of neurons that exhibit positive correlation as a function of distance between the receptive fields of the two neurons in visual space in degree visual angle.

in correlation is significantly slower in the range data than in the luminance data, reflecting the fact that surfaces tend to be smooth and that variation in surface depth was less than the variation in the luminance patterns or markings on the surface. This predicts that neurons with similar disparity tunings or other feature tunings should interact cooperatively, and their interaction strength should drop off exponentially as a function of distance according to scene statistics.

To test this hypothesis, we carried out an experiment to measure how V1 disparity-tuned neurons interact across space when presented with different depth planes as rendered by dynamic random dot stereogram, one depth at a time. This is, in fact, the same experiment described in our earlier discussion on the uniqueness constraint, except now we are considering the interaction between neurons with spatially distinct receptive fields. We observed significant positive cross-correlation of the spike trains for a variety of neuronal pairs, but most noticeably for neurons with similar disparity tunings. Excitatory interaction, as indicated by positive correlation in neural activities, extends a greater distance (a few millimeters in cortical distance) than the more local inhibitory interaction discussed earlier.

Figures 24.6A and D show the receptive field locations and disparity tuning curves of a typical pair of neurons exhibiting excitatory interaction. The neurons typically have spatially distinct receptive fields and very similar disparity tuning. The rest of Figure 24.6B shows a population average of the interaction between 41 similar pairs of neurons, aligned by their peaks of strongest positive correlation, revealing that the strongest interaction occurred at the disparity where the two tuning curves intersect (i.e., shared the most in common). There appeared to be temporal dynamics in the neuronal interaction: the earlier phase (the first 100 ms) is nonstimulus-specific, whereas the later phase (150–400 ms) is stimulus-specific. The early phase in the correlated responses is likely because of the simultaneous burst in neuronal responses due to stimulus onset. That this early correlation tends to be strongest for stimuli that both neurons prefer the least also suggests that this correlation might arise from a common suppressive input

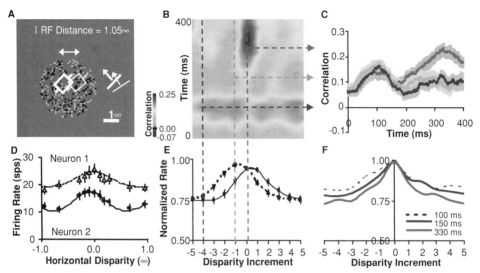

Figure 24.6. Cooperative interaction. *A*, Receptive fields, preferred orientation, and direction of motion (white) overlaying the RDS stimuli for an example cooperative pair of neurons. *B*, Population summary of interaction strength (correlation) versus time and disparity for 41 neuronal pairs with similar disparity tuning. *C*, Sections of *B* noted by the corresponding dashed lines. *D*, Disparity tuning for neuronal pair described in *A*. *E*, Population summary of disparity tuning for same pairs described in *B*. *F*, Population summary of sharpened disparity tuning after competitive interaction described in Figure 24.4B (blue) and cooperative interaction described in *B* (red). Adapted from Samonds et al. (2009). (See color plate 24.6.)

shared by the both neurons, presumably from neurons which prefer that disparity, as a manifestation of the uniqueness constraint (see also Fig. 24.4). The second phase of strong and positive interaction likely reflects mutual facilitation, as it occurred only when the stimulus is precisely of their shared preferred disparity (Figs. 24.6B, C, and E), potentially reflecting the implementation of the smoothness constraint. The initial competitive interaction is accompanied by a development of disparity tuning, whereas the later interaction is accompanied by further sharpening of the disparity tuning curves (Fig. 24.6F). Figure 24.5C shows preliminary results that indicate the strength of positive correlation between neurons with similar disparity tunings dropped off with distance rather rapidly. More data, however, are required to allow a quantitative comparison with the prediction of the scene statistics.

The observation that correlation in neuronal activities is a function of disparity tunings of neurons (Samonds et al. 2007) extends the earlier observation based on orientation tunings (Ts'o et al. 1986; Singer 1999; Samonds et al. 2006) to the depth domain. It is worth noting that the correlation of neural activities discussed here is a measure computed within a 25- to 50-ms window, distinct from the so-called fast-time synchrony (correlation within a 1-5 msec window) or slow-time spike count correlation (correlation within a temporal window ranging from 500 ms to seconds). Slow spike count correlation might arise from fluctuation of the states of the system such as attention, arousal, or other mechanisms. Fast-time synchrony is important for understanding one-to-one neuronal connectivity, and might be important for von der Malsburgh's "binding by synchrony" concept. It is, however, not certain whether fast-time correlation is necessary for Geman's compositional hierarchy. The intermediate time correlation we observe is informative of the dynamics of neuronal interaction during computation and might be sufficient for generating the higher-order codes. This hypothesis, however, needs to be confirmed by computational and neurophysiological experiments.

The surface smoothness constraint arises from the fact that visual cues (texture, disparity, color) tend to be smooth and continuous when they belong to the same surface. The co-occurrence and correlation of these visual cue events can lead to the formation of connections between neurons with similar tuning properties across space by classical Hebbian learning mechanisms. The contour version of this constraint is the contour smoothness constraint, or the association field, which has been demonstrated in both psychophysical experiments (Field et al. 1993) and scene statistics studies on the statistical distribution of luminance edge signals across space (Geisler et al. 2001; Sigman et al. 2001; Elder and Goldberg 2002). Such an association field has been shown to be useful for contour completion (Grossberg and Mingolla 1985; Williams and Jacobs 1997) and might be part of the underlying mechanisms for illusory contour representation in the early visual cortex (Lee and Nguyen 2001). Von der Malsburg and colleagues have shown that such facilitatory connectivity patterns can be learned by Hebbian learning based on the moving edges of objects in video in an unsupervised manner (Prodohl et al. 2003). Our evidence (Samonds et al. 2007; Samonds et al. 2009) on a neural substrate for a smoothness constraint in depth suggests that the association field concept might generalize beyond contours to statistical priors and Gestalt rules for organizing surfaces and, furthermore, to statistical constraints for organizing configural parts of objects in object representation. In summary, our conjecture is that horizontal connectivity is not simply for mediating surround inhibition. Rather, it can enforce statistical constraints on the spatial and possibly temporal relationships between parts of surfaces and objects to facilitate the elimination of improbable solutions in generating the higher-order representations, and to resolve ambiguity during perceptual inference.

24.3 Computational Implications on Cortical Object Representation

In the preceding section, we discussed evidence for three major neural mechanisms for encoding statistical priors in the natural scenes: (1) feedforward convergent connections for encoding correlational or conjunctive structures between different visual cues/features occurring at the same spatial location in neuronal tuning properties; (2) competitive interaction among neurons at the same spatial location for encoding the uniqueness constraint or enforcing mutual exclusiveness of hypotheses; and (3) cooperative recurrent (lateral and feedback) connections to encode spatial correlations of features or the distribution of the variations among their parameters. As anatomical architecture is fairly uniform across the different visual areas in the hierarchical visual cortex, these three fundamental mechanisms are likely repeated in each visual area to generate a hierarchy of priors to bring about hierarchical Bayesian learning and inference (Lee and Mumford 2003).

Even though our neurophysiological experiments, as discussed, have focused on the early visual cortex and issues of surface and depth inference, the lessons we learned should be relevant to understanding computational architecture in the higher visual areas such as inferotemporal cortex (IT) for object representation and analysis. The main question we asked is this: What is the functional role of the horizontal connections in higher visual areas such as V4 and IT, particularly in the context of object representation and inference? Interestingly, almost all of the popular neural models on object representation construct a hierarchy primarily based on convergent feedforward connections (Fukushima 1980; Foldiak 1991; Riesenhuber and Poggio 1999; Wallis and Rolls 1997; Wiskott 2002; Geman 2006). Lateral connections, if considered at all in these models, are used to implement competition or inhibition within each level based on the prevalent neurophysiological reports on surround suppression. We have provided evidence in the last section that lateral connections in the early visual areas could be encoding spatial constraints such as the smoothness prior seen in popular models in computer vision like Markov random fields. In higher visual areas, receptive fields become larger and larger as one traverses up the visual hierarchy, four times wider at V4 relative to V1 at the same eccentricity, and covering much of the visual field at the level of IT. Inferotemporal cortex neurons have been shown to be selective to specific views of objects but by and large invariant to their positions and scale. The cortical layout of IT is no longer retinotopic, as in early visual areas, but exhibits some clustering among represented objects. Thus, the horizontal connections of IT must be encoding some relationships between objects that are no longer defined in terms of space. What could these relationships be?

24.3.1 IT Horizontal Connections for Encoding Temporal Association of Views

Our conjecture is that horizontal connections between IT neurons can be used to encode temporal association of different views of objects in our visual experience. These connections can serve two purposes: (1) achieving invariance with flexibility; and (2) generating predictions during imagination and inference.

Learning features that are invariant within each class while maintaining enough specificity to allow discrimination between different classes is the central issue in object representation. An object's appearance can change dramatically in different poses, perspectives, and lighting conditions. How does the visual system learn to recognize an object as the same despite its multitude of possible views?

In our visual experience, the world is dynamic because of changing illumination, deformation, and the relative motions of the objects in the scene. Under these conditions, the temporal contiguity of visual events offers a powerful cue for our visual systems to link the different appearances of an individual object together as its appearance changes; that is, most objects present in one instant will likely be present in the near future. Any visual pattern that can be measured for specific object will likely exhibit relatively smooth changes within small-to-medium time intervals. A dining couple in a restaurant scene might tilt their heads, smile, and speak, but neither is likely to disappear or spontaneously transform into another object. This principle of persistence or smooth variation is either implicit or explicit in a wide variety of computer vision tasks, especially tracking. Thus, by observing the dynamic behavior of objects in a visual scene over time, one can develop a set of dynamically linked observations of the objects themselves, which in turn can inform the construction of equivalence classes of visual patterns representing the same object.

The idea that temporal correlation of visual events can promote invariance learning has been explored by a number of earlier neural models (Foldiak 1991; Wallis and Rolls 1997; Wiskott 2002), even though learning from video is still in its infancy in computer vision. The earlier neural models, however, used a feedforward network to learn the invariance based on gradual convergence of inputs from neurons coding different views onto the downstream neuron. Typically, a downstream neuron learns to associate two visual stimuli appearing in rapid succession as same based on the trace-learning rule, which stipulates that lingering activity of a downstream neuron responding to a first stimulus will potentiate its synapses to respond to a second stimulus as well, provided it arrives within a short time window (300–500 ms). A Hebbian-like mechanism will eventually cause the cell to respond equally well to both stimuli after repeated viewings. The disadvantages of such feedforward networks are threefold: first, specificity of a particular view (pose) of an object is lost when multiple views are converged into a single entity, so that a neuron coding an object in an invariant manner will necessarily have no idea of the pose being seen; second, a hierarchy with many layers is required, as invariance has to be achieved gradually by combining a few views at a time at each level; third, these feedforward networks cannot be used to predict what views will be seen next for the purpose of furnishing prediction to facilitate inference.

Although the trace-learning rule might be useful for associating events based on convergent input, we argue here that the spike-timing dependent plasticity learning rule (Markram et al. 1997) might be useful for learning a lateral association network in each visual area based on temporal contiguity of visual events: as the synapses between a presynaptic neuron representing one view and a postsynaptic neuron representing a subsequent view will be reinforced during visual experience. The lateral connections in such a network link the different views of an object in a graph, which is disconnected from members or nodes of the graphs representing other objects.

Figure 24.7A illustrates the essence of these ideas. Here, views of two distinct objects (persons) are arranged in a simulated perceptual space, where distances between views reflect a measure of low-level perceptual similarity. There is considerable overlap between these two objects within the space: frontal views of the two different persons' faces are more similar to each other than the frontal view and the profile view of the same person. The horizontal connections, which can be considered as transition edges in a hidden Markov model, offer new ways to measure similarity based on the temporal correlations of the views observed in our experience. For example, we might propose that the similarity between two different views is the marginal probability of making transition from one view to the other in a fixed number of steps. The similarity between views (e.g., frontal views) that are weakly connected or not connected by any path is thereby zero or nearly zero, even though they resemble each other in low-level image space.

We have implemented an unsupervised learning system that takes many short clips of videos with objects exhibiting a variety of pose changes and learns the horizontal connections based on the temporal contiguity and the perceptual similarity of the visual

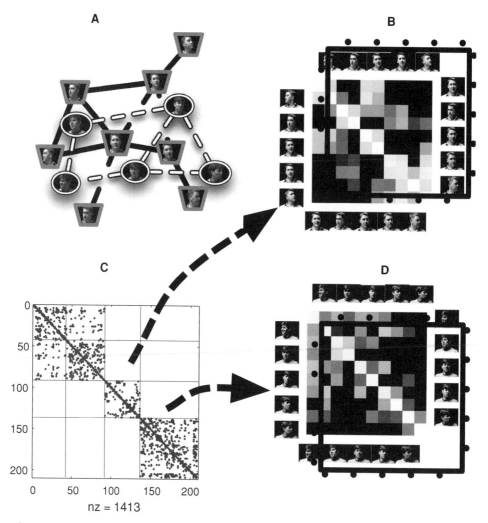

Figure 24.7. *A,* Diagrammatic depiction of linking together object views into view-based object models with probabilistic transitions between views (see text for details). *C,* Sparsity structure of a Markov transition matrix over a collection of object views: blocks along the diagonal correspond to different objects. *B, D,* Connectivity between some views of two learned objects. Transitions in matrices are created by marginalizing out other object views; the intensity map is nonlinearly compressed to show detail.

events. Figure 24.7 presents the horizontal connection matrix among 209 views learned from four different objects the system observed. This is essentially a transition matrix of a hidden Markov model with each state representing a particular view. The sparsity structure of the transition matrix for the learned graph connecting these views appears in Figure 24.7*C*; it exhibits a mostly block-diagonal structure corresponding to the four objects, which indicates that transitions between two different objects are unlikely (top left two blocks) or impossible (bottom right). For two of the objects, we have selected ten-member subsets of the learned views (indicated by the frames from which the view models were trained) and created probabilistic transition matrices for these subsets by marginalizing out other views from the Figure 24.7*C* matrix. The results appear in

Figures 24.7*B* and *D* and exhibit a sensible connectivity structure for the chosen views (elements further from the diagonal, corresponding to transitions between nonadjacent views, are darker).

These networks might offer some advantages over the earlier models based purely on feedforward convergence in invariance learning. First, when the node coding for one view is activated by bottom-up input, the activation will spread across the network along the horizontal connections. The activation of the entire network in the next moment represents a probability distribution over what the input might become in the future. This activation spreading with its probabilistic interpretation can facilitate inference by potentiating the sensitivity of neuronal detectors to particular incoming stimuli. The IT neurons related by such a graph preserve the specificity of the "view" they are coding but can also spread predictions about the incoming visual stimulus. These predictions specify potential appearances of whole objects and salvaging the interpretation of ambiguous and obscured stimuli. Second, these networks of facilitative, lateral connections offer a more efficient, one-layer mechanism for invariance learning: rather than gradually building invariance within a hierarchy, strongly connected components give rise to patterns of propagated co-activation within ensembles of views that together, collectively, represent an object. A view-invariant neuron need only "tap" a few locations in this network of view-selective neurons with sparse, long-range connections to detect this co-activation. In addition to the improved efficiency of this method when compared to models with gradually converging layers, this account may also draw support from the fact that few intermediate view-invariant neurons have been found.

These lateral association networks are similar to an aspect graph in computer vision, with some differences. In a traditional aspect graph, nodes reflect topologically identical configurations of image components; here, a node represents a range of appearance for which the model associated with the node, which characterizes an object view as configurations of component parts, is sufficiently accurate. In the lateral association network we envisioned, each node is a view of a face, and other nodes are different views of the face of the same person that this view is likely to evolve to. The lateral connectivity describes edges in the graph whose strengths reflect the probability of the transitions between the different views of a person. Interestingly, Tanifuji and colleagues (Wang et al. 1996) found that neurons coding different views of a face are arranged in spatially adjacent cortical locations in the IT cortex.

From a statistical learning perspective, the hidden Markov model (HMM) characterization of object representation just described presents several interesting challenges. Like the mammalian visual system, we would like a computational mechanism for learning such dynamically linked view-based object models to flexibly infer both how many objects exist in its visual world and how many views are necessary to model the objects. The latter problem, which is equivalent to inferring how many states an HMM needs to model data, has been addressed by recent "infinite HMM" techniques based on the hierarchical Dirichlet process from nonparametric Bayesian statistics (Beal et al. 2002; Teh et al. 2006). To tackle the first issue, we are developing an extension of these models embodying the notion that views of the same object are temporally clustered in our visual experience. The key to this model is a prior that favors a nearly block-diagonal structure in the transition matrix describing the HMM's dynamic behavior.

Each object's ensemble of views thus corresponds to a block of states within the model, and transitions between views in the same block are generally much more likely than transitions between views in different blocks. A particular view is assigned to one and only one block, and as such visually similar views of separate objects will be modeled with two distinct, object-specific states – a joint representation of appearance and identity that permits finer predictions of future appearance through conditioning on the knowledge of what the viewed object actually is. Finally, as with the views, the model flexibly accommodates varying numbers of objects using similar nonparametric Bayesian machinery.

24.3.2 V4 Horizontal Connections Encoding Spatial Relationships between Parts

In the preceding discussion, we have assumed that IT neurons encode specific views of objects for simplicity in exposition. Such a view-based scheme might require explicitly storing a huge number of views of an almost infinite number of objects and their parts. Geman (2006) suggested that one can have a hierarchy of composable and reusable parts to construct object representation dynamically to avoid this combinatorial explosion problem. Each view neuron, rather than encoding an image, should really be encoding an ensemble of parts, with specific spatial configural relationship constrained by the horizontal connections one visual area below. Each of these parts in turn represents a cluster or distribution of appearances of that part, computed by some invariance transforms. The parts themselves are meaningful entities, learned from natural scene statistics, and are reusable in different combinations for representing the multitude of objects.

Again, as in IT, the temporal association of the parts of objects can be learned from our dynamic visual experience and represented explicitly in intra-areal (within-area) connections in the intermediate visual areas such as V4 in the form of a Markov transition matrix. This matrix will produce predictions on how a given appearance of a part will evolve over time to produce a more invariant object representation using "fuzzier parts."

Figure 24.8 illustrates these ideas. Let us assume V4 neurons encode fragments and corners with some positional slack within relatively large receptive fields. The Markov transition matrix is learned by first tracking the parts over time based on feature similarity and spatiotemporal proximity, then quantizing the stimulus space into clusters of distinct part appearances, and finally building links between corresponding parts that are sufficiently different in appearance. In this demonstration example, our system analyzed a video of a banana and a hippo moving around in a baby mobile (Fig. 24.8A). The part-features of the moving objects are automatically learned and partitioned into 300 discrete part feature clusters using K-means (Fig. 24.8B). These part-features are tracked over time based on spatial and temporal contiguity of the parts, as shown in Fig. 24.8C. This allows a Markov transition matrix between the features to be built (as shown in Figure 24.8D). Note that this matrix is much less block diagonal than the transition matrix for the object-view representation just discussed, since parts are more local and less object-specific.

Multiplying the transition matrix with the input observation (a delta function in the 300-tuple vector or, more generally, a data likelihood function) gives you the predicted

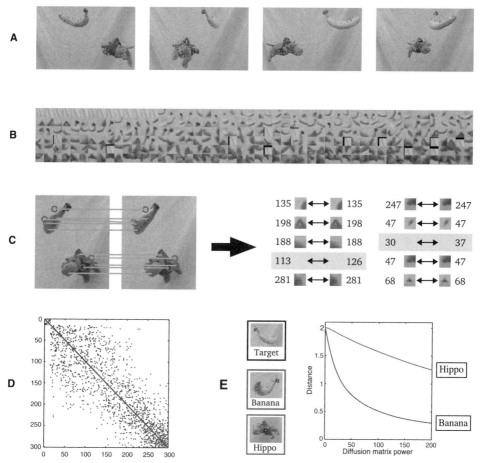

Figure 24.8. A demonstration example of the method for learning the appearance dynamics of low-level image features. *A,* The input video contains a banana and a toy hippo rotating in space. Sparse, local image features of various scales are detected in each frame. Descriptors for those features are simply the 15 × 15 pixel, three color image patches themselves. Next, *K*-means is run on a random assortment of extracted descriptor patches to yield a 300-bin discretization of the feature descriptor space; cluster centers appear in *B. C,* Features are tracked between video frames (*left*). Discretized descriptors of tracked features yield the appearance transitions at *right*, which then inform the Markov transition matrix whose sparsity structure appears in *D. E,* L1 diffusion distance comparison of one image feature bag-of-words histogram (target) with two others. The banana histogram becomes similar after a few diffusion steps; the hippo histogram remains distinct. (See color plate 24.8.)

distribution of hypotheses of part appearances in the next time step. This prediction serves as a prior distribution for visual interpretation of the incoming image. Successive multiplication of the observation by the matrix simulates an experience-based diffusion process that predicts distribution of the possible appearance at different time points in the future. The diffused representation is more robust when matching the input representation to the stored representation for the following reason. For simplicity, let us consider that an object's view is represented by a histogram of the occurrence frequency of a certain set of features. Without diffusion, only identical views will have identical feature count histograms. A slight change of view on an object will produce a drastically different histogram. Blurring the histogram using this temporal association matrix will create a histogram that is more tolerant against variations in the appearance of the object, so that the incoming view does not have to be exactly the same as any of the stored views in order to be recognized. Figure 24.8*E* shows the L1 distance (sum of the absolute difference between each bin for two histograms) comparison of one image feature histogram (target) with two others, after some blurring with the Markov transition matrix. The banana histograms become more similar to each other after a few diffusion steps, while remaining distinct from the hippo histogram. This illustrates how such association of parts derived from observed dynamics can increase invariance for object recognition by integrating information about the temporal association of part appearance through the relatively local facilitatory connections between the parts.

The mathematics behind such an experience-based metric for data similarity has recently been studied by Lafon and Lee (2006), among others. Conceptually, the idea is also related to Ullman's features of intermediate complexity (Ullman et al. 2002), in which fuzzy intermediate representation is shown to promote a certain degree of invariance and slack that can promote object recognition. However, our proposed blurring with HMM is more general and might be more sensible, as it reflects the invariance that is learned based on temporal association of visual events in natural scenes.

Although we envision that the horizontal connections in IT encode temporally associated views, we expect the horizontal connections in the earlier retinotopic visual areas such as V4 and V1 to encode constraints about spatial relationships between the configural parts for representing objects, as in the compositional AND/OR graphs in computer vision (Zhu and Mumford 2006; Zhu et al. 2008). The temporal association matrix of the HMM model described will likely be represented by the connections within a local cortical neighborhood such as hypercolumn. Interestingly, that would mean that within a hypercolumn in the early visual areas, there will be inhibitory connections to enforce the uniqueness constraint as well as facilitatory connections to enforce the temporal association prior.

In a recent hierarchical composition model proposed by Yuille and colleagues (Zhu et al. 2008), features and the spatial configural relationship between the features in a hierarchy can be learned in an unsupervised manner from a set of unlabeled images that contain the object to be learned based on the principle of *suspicious coincidence* and the principle of *competitive exclusion*. The first principle dictates that proposals based on frequent cooccurrence of a set of features, subject to some invariant transformation, across all the images in the training set, will be learned as higher-order features whereas proposals based on spurious co-occurrence of features that do not recur often enough will be considered suspicious and eliminated. When co-occurring features come together to generate a higher-order proposal, these conjunctive features will undergo an invariant transform to map a class of conjunctive features to one higher-order proposal according to some rules. The invariant transformation is important, as it is rather unlikely that identical image fragments will be seen across a significant number of the images in the training set. The Markov transition network that we discussed can be one way to implement this "invariant transform" by blurring each of the observed image fragments in an experience- dependent manner, but other clustering mechanisms, such as *K*-means clustering in our first example (Fig. 24.7) or Zhu and colleagues' (2008) clustering method, are also reasonable. The competitive exclusion principle suggests that multiple proposed higher-order concepts will compete to explain an image fragment represented to that level, and that only the one that provides the best explanation across the entire training set will be chosen and remembered over the others. Thus proposed, higher-order features engage in the same competition as the disparity neurons in V1 engaged in during depth inference under the "uniqueness constraint." This is also similar to the competition among the representations of the different objects (the graphs or webs of views) for explaining each observed view during learning and inference, as enforced by the block-diagonal prior in our extended infinite HMM machine, which we discussed previously. It is important to understand that the competition interaction takes place during both learning and inference, because learning requires inference at each level.

24.4 Conclusion

In this chapter, we present some of our neurophysiological evidence for how spatial and temporal correlational structures in natural scenes could be encoded in neurons in terms of their tuning properties and in terms of their connectivity. Some of these structures, such as correlation between luminance and depth, and the spatial correlation of visual cues within a surface, can serve as surface priors useful for robust probabilistic 3-D surface inference. The evidence on neuronal tuning to temporal correlation reflects neurons' sensitivity to temporal events and is partly the inspiration for our conjecture on temporal association networks in the visual cortex. While theories on the importance of correlation structures in shaping the nervous system are longstanding, there has been almost no direct physiological evidence demonstrating neural encoding of correlations of natural scenes, particularly those resulting from theoretical predictions, except for the work of Dan et al. (1996) on LGN. The findings discussed here serve to strengthen those theoretical claims, as well as to reveal the diversity of strategies for encoding correlation structures in natural scenes.

We found neural evidence in support of three basic mechanisms for learning and encoding priors: (1) individual neurons' basic tuning properties, likely based on feedforward connections, are sensitive to correlation structures in natural scenes (the principle of coincidence conjunction); (2) neurons representing different hypotheses compete with one another to explain the input from the same visual window of analysis (the principle of competitive exclusion); and (3) neurons with similar tunings tend to exhibit excitatory interaction with neurons with similar tunings at the same spatial location or across spatial location, possibly encoding temporal association and spatial co-occurrence of features respectively (the principle of spatiotemporal association). These mechanisms or principles, to a first approximation, have direct correspondence with the necessary and maybe sufficient computational mechanisms deployed in models that perform unsupervised learning of object representation in a hierarchical composition system (Zhu et al. 2008).

The general principle underlying all these mechanisms and principles is redundancy reduction or minimum-length description codes (MDL). Mumford (1992) had argued that visual cortex encodes a hierarchy of efficient codes that minimize the redundancy in image description (necessary for behavior) as a whole. During learning and inference, the representations in a higher-order area produce "hallucinations" or "image hypotheses" to earlier visual areas to explain away the bottom-up proposals they provide. Given the relative uniformity in anatomical structures and computational architecture across the different visual areas, we expect the mechanisms we observed in V1 for encoding spatiotemporal correlations are relevant to understanding the strategies of the higher visual areas such as IT and beyond for object and category representations.

However, while the three mechanisms just discussed are general, the functional roles of horizontal connections in different visual areas might be different because of the difference between neurons in these areas in terms of spatial and temporal tuning properties. We conjecture that the horizontal connections in early visual areas are enforcing spatial constraints among features and parts, whereas those in IT are enforcing temporal constraints among views. We envision the competitive interactions mediated by the vertical interactions within each hypercolumn in each visual area to be enforcing the uniqueness or competitive exclusion constraint, but the facilitatory interactions mediated by the vertical connections within each area are enforcing the temporal association constraint to generate prediction and invariance. It is worth noting that both the vertical connections and horizontal connections in IT might be shaped by temporal association, with vertical connections linking local clusters of views that are similar to one another – views separated by a short time span during learning, and horizontal connections linking views that are more distinct. Diffusion among neurons in the vertical column makes representation more fuzzy and robust, but competition among these neurons will make view or pose interpretation more precise. This suggests that the interaction between groups of neurons might be dynamic in nature, exhibiting facilitatory or inhibitory interactions at different points in time. In our experiments, we did find the interaction or the effective connectivity between neurons evolve and change over time with an intermediate time scale of 30 to 50 ms. This dynamic possibly reflects the evolution of neuronal interaction associated with the progression of perceptual computation. It also provides some possible constraints on the time scale of interaction as well as the permissible time frame of spike integration or coincidence for learning the higher-order structures by downstream neurons.

Two new elements in our proposal for object representation are worth emphasizing. First, lateral connections in IT can serve to encode the temporal association of visual events (e.g., views). This organization allows the generation of predictions about how an object would look over time to facilitate object recognition. We have argued that this organization might be more efficient in terms of implementation in IT for achieving invariance without losing specificity. Second, the implication of similar temporal association networks in intermediate visual areas is that these can provide *invariance transforms* on the parts or an experience-dependent measure for evaluating data similarity, which also provides a more robust object representation for learning and inference. Although many of these ideas are still in the realm of speculation, they are nevertheless precise enough to be tested experimentally.

The research described here represents only baby steps in our understanding of how scene statistical priors might be encoded in the brain. Many questions and challenges along this line of research remain unanswered. First, after demonstrating that neurons are sensitive to these correlational structures, a logical next step is to understand whether and how these sensitivities can be used effectively for learning and inference. In our opinion, developing computational models that actually work is critically important for guiding neurophysiological experimental research for understanding the neural representations and mechanisms underlying the solution of a problem. To this end, we have developed a computational framework based on graphical models with efficient belief propagation algorithms that can flexibly learn and incorporate a variety of priors, including higher-order cliques in Markov random field, for depth inference (Potetz 2007; Lee and Potetz 2008). With this framework, we have already produced state-of-the-art techniques for inference of 3-D shape from shading in Lambertian surfaces. It would be important to explore how the correlational structures between depth and luminance images in natural scenes can be harnessed to improve shape inference on non-Lambertian surfaces. However, incorporating too many priors or loops in the model will cause efficiency, stability, and convergence issues. Neurophysiological and psychophysical investigation can help us select the appropriate priors and representations, which could be useful for overcoming these obstacles.

The AND/OR graph, or hierarchical composition model, of Geman (2006), Zhu and Mumford (2006), and Zhu et al. (2008) provides an elegant computational framework for conceptualizing feedforward and feedback connections in the visual cortex. Coming up with experiments to test this class of models is an important challenge in neuroscience because this framework offers an interesting perspective on how the visual system might operate that is fundamentally different from the current feedforward hierarchical model (Fukushima 1980; Riesenhuber and Poggio 1999) or the popular conceptualization of feedback in terms of attention mediated by biased competition (Desimone and Duncan 1995). In this chapter, we have advocated the important role of encoding temporal association of visual events at different levels of the cortical hierarchy for constructing invariant object representation. Although neural modelers have long recognized the importance of coherent covariation and temporal association in concept learning and invariant object representation learning, this is a relatively unexplored territory in computer vision. As discussed earlier, we are developing a computational framework based on hierarchical dirichelet processes that can organize video data into coherent view-based object classes based on temporal correlation of these visual events (Stepleton et al. 2009). This effort might provide new insights into the amazing cortical organization of visual information during learning and development.

Bibliography

Angelucci A, Bressloff PC. 2006. The contribution of feedforward, lateral and feedback connections to the classical receptive field and extra-classical receptive field surround of primate V1 neurons. *Prog Brain Res* 154: 93–121.

Atick JJ, Redlich AN. 1992. What does the retina know about natural scenes? *Neural Comput* 4: 196–210.

Beal M, Ghahramani Z, Rasmussen CE. 2002. The infinite hidden Markov model. *Neural information processing systems*, ed. TG Dietterich, S Becker, and Z Ghahramani, 577–585, Vol. 14. Cambridge: MIT Press.

Blake A, Zisserman A. 1987. *Visual reconstruction*. Cambridge: MIT Press.

Bosking WH, Zhang Y, Schofield B, Fitzpatrick D. 1997. Orientation selectivity and the arrangement of horizontal connections in tree shrew striate cortex. *J Neurosci* 17: 2112–2127.

Cumming BG, DeAngelis GC. 2001. The physiology of stereopsis. *Annu Rev Neurosci* 24: 203–238.

Dan Y, Atick JJ, Reid RC. 1996. Efficient coding of natural scenes in the lateral geniculate nucleus: experimental test of a computational theory. *J Neurosci* 16(10): 3351–3362.

Das A, Gilbert CD. 1999. Topography of contextual modulations mediated by short-range interactions in primary visual cortex. *Nature* 399: 655–661.

Desimone R, Duncan J. 1995. Neural mechanisms of selective visual attention. *Annu Rev Neurosci* 18: 193–222.

Elder JH, Goldberg RM. 2002. Ecological statistics of Gestalt laws for the perceptual organization of contours. *J Vision* 2: 324–353.

Field DJ, Hayes A, Hess RF. 1993. Contour integration by the human visual system: evidence for a local association field. *Vision Res* 33: 173–193.

Foldiak P. 1991. Learning invariance from transformation sequences. *Neural Comput* 3: 194–200.

Fukushima K. 1980. Neocognitron: a self-organizing neural network model for a mechanism of pattern recognition unaffected by shift in position. *Biol Cyber* 36(4): 93–202.

Garcia-Lazaro J, Ahmed B, Schnupp J. 2006. Tuning to natural stimulus dynamics in primary auditory cortex. *Curr Biol* 16(3): 264–271.

Geisler WS, Perry JS, Super BJ, Gallogly DP. 2001. Edge co-occurrence in natural images predicts contour grouping performance. *Vision Res* 41: 711–724.

Geman S. 2006. Invariance and selectivity in the ventral visual pathway. *J Physiol Paris* 100: 212–224.

Gibson J. 1979. *The ecological approach to visual perception*. New Jersey: Lawrence Erlbaum Associates.

Grossberg S, Mingolla E. 1985. Neural dynamics of form perception: boundary completion, illusory figures, and neon color spreading. *Psychol Rev* 92(2): 173–211.

Hebb DO. 1949. *The organization of behavior: a neuropsychological theory*. New York: Wiley.

Kapadia MK, Ito M, Gilbert CD, Westheimer G. 1995. Improvement in visual sensitivity by changes in local context: parallel studies in human observers and in V1 of alert monkeys. *Neuron* 15: 843–856.

Knill DC, Pouget A. 2004. The Bayesian brain: the role of uncertainty in neural coding and computation. *Trends Neurosci* 27(12): 712–719.

Koffka K. 1935. *Principles of Gestalt psychology*. London: Lund Humphries.

Kohn A, Smith MA. 2005. Stimulus dependence of neuronal correlation in primary visual cortex of the macaque. *J Neurosci* 25: 3661–3673.

Lafon S, Lee AB. 2006. Diffusion maps and coarse-graining: a unified framework for dimensionality reduction, graph partitioning, and data set parameterization. *IEEE Trans Pattern Anal Mach Intell* 28(9): 1393–1403.

Lee TS, Mumford D. 2003. Hierarchical Bayesian inference in the visual cortex. *J Optic Soc Am A* 20(7): 1434–1448.

Lee TS, Nguyen M. 2001. Dynamics of subjective contour formation in early visual cortex. *Proc Natl Acad Sci USA* 98(4): 1907–1911.

Lund JS, Angelucci A, Bressloff PC. 2003. Anatomical substrates for functional columns in macaque monkey primary visual cortex. *Cereb Cortex* 13: 15–24.

Markram H, Lubke J, Frotscher M, Sakmann B. 1997. Regulation of synaptic efficacy by coincidence of postsynaptic APs and EPSPs. *Science* 275: 213–215.

Marr D. 1982. *Vision*. San Francisco: WH Freeman.

Marr D, Poggio T. 1976. Cooperative computation of stereo disparity. *Science* 194(4262): 283–287.

Moreno-Bote R, Shpiro A, Rinzel J, Rubin N. 2008. Bi-stable depth ordering of superimposed moving gratings. *J Vision* 8(7):20, 1–13.

Olshausen BA, Field DJ. 1996. Emergence of simple-cell receptive field properties by learning a sparse code for natural images. *Nature* 381: 607–609.

Potetz B. 2007. Efficient belief propagation for vision using linear constraint nodes. In Proceedings of IEEE conference on computer vision and pattern recognition.

Potetz B, Lee TS. 2003. Statistical correlations between 2D images and 3D structures in natural scenes. *J Optic Soc Am A* 20(7): 1292–1303.

Potetz B, Lee TS. 2006. Scaling laws in natural scenes and the inference of 3D shape. *Advances in neural information processing Systems*, Vol. 18, 1089–1096. Cambridge: MIT Press.

Potetz B, Lee TS. 2008. Belief propagation for higher order cliques using linear constraint nodes. *Comput Vis Image Und* (in press).

Potetz BR, Samonds JM, Lee TS. 2006. Disparity and luminance preference are correlated in macaque V1, matching natural scene statistics. *Soc Neurosci* abstract.

Prodhl C, Wurtz RP, von der Malsburg C. 2003. Learning the Gestalt rule of collinearity from object motion. *Neural Comput* 15: 1865–1896.

Rao R. 2004. Bayesian computation in recurrent neural circuits. *Neural Comput* 16(1): 1–38.

Riesenhuber M, Poggio T. 1999. Hierarchical models of object recognition in cortex. *Nat Neurosci* 2: 1019–1025.

Rogers TT, McClelland JL. 2004. *Semantic cognition: a parallel distributed processing approach*. Cambridge: MIT Press.

Ruderman DL, Bialek W. 1994. Statistics of natural images: scaling in the woods. *Phys Rev Lett* 73: 814–817.

Samonds JM, Potetz BR, Lee TS. 2007. Neurophysiological evidence of cooperative mechanisms for stereo computation. In *Advances in neural information processing systems*, Vol. 19, ed., 1201–1208. A McCallum Cambridge: MIT Press.

Samonds JM, Potetz BR, Lee TS. 2009. Cooperative and competitive interactions facilitate stereo computations in macaque primary visual cortex (submitted).

Samonds JM, Zhou Z, Bernard MR, Bonds AB. 2006. Synchronous activity in cat visual cortex encodes collinear and cocircular contours. *J Neurophysiol* 95: 2602–2616.

Sigman M, Cecchi GA, Gilbert CD, Magnasco MO. 2001. On a common circle: natural scenes and Gestalt rules. *Proc Natl Acad Sci USA* 98: 1935–1940.

Singer W. 1999. Neuronal synchrony: a versatile code for the definition of relations? *Neuron* 24: 11–125.

Stepleton T, Ghahramani Z, Gordon G, Lee TS. 2009. The block diagonal infinite hidden Markov model. In Proceedings of the twelfth international conference on artificial intelligence and statistics. *J Mach Learn Res* 5: 552–559.

Tappen MF, Freeman WT. 2003. Comparison of graph cuts with belief propagation for stereo using identical MRF parameters. In Proceedings of IEEE international conference on computer vision.

Teh YW, Jordan MI, Beal MJ, Blei DM. 2006. Hierarchical dirichlet processes. *J Am Stat Assoc* 101(476): 1566–1581.

Ts'o DY, Gilbert CD, Wiesel TN. 1986. Relationships between horizontal interactions and functional architecture in cat striate cortex as revealed by cross-correlation analysis. *J Neurosci* 6: 1160–1170.

von der Malsburg C. 1995. Binding in models of perception and brain function. *Curr Opin Neurobiol* 5: 520–526.

Wallis G, Rolls E. 1997. Invariant face and object recognition in the visual system. *Prog Neurobiol* 51: 167–194.

Wang G, Tanaka K, Tanifuji M. 1996. Optical imaging of functional organization in the monkey inferotemporal cortex. *Science* 272(5268): 1665–1668.

Williams LR, Jacobs DW. 1997. Stochastic completion fields: a neural model of illusory contour shape and salience. *Neural Comput* 9(4): 837–858.

Wiskott L. 2002. Slow feature analysis: unsupervised learning of invariances. *Neural Comput* 14: 715–770.

Yu Y, Romero R, Lee TS. 2005. Preference of sensory neural coding for 1/f signals. *Phys Rev Lett* 94: 108103, 1–4.

Zhu L, Lin C, Huang H, Chen Y, Yuille A. 2008. Unsupervised structure learning: hierarchical recursive composition, suspicious coincidence and competitive exclusion. In Proceedings of ECCV.

Zhu SC, Mumford D. 2006. A stochastic grammar of images. *Found T Comput Graph Vis* 2(4): 259–362.

CHAPTER 25

Medial Models for Vision

Kaleem Siddiqi* and Stephen Pizer

25.1 Medial Representations of Objects

A medial representation of an object describes a locus midway between (at the center of a sphere bitangent to) two sections of the boundary, and gives the distance to the boundary, called the medial radius. The object is obtained as the union of overlapping bitangent spheres. This results in a locus of $(\mathbf{p}, r)$, where $\mathbf{p}$ gives the sphere center and r gives the radius of the sphere. In some representations, the vectors from the medial point to the two or more corresponding boundary points are included; in others they are derived.

The Blum medial axis is a transformation of an object boundary that has the same topology as the object; thus, the boundary can generate the medial locus $(\mathbf{p}, r)$, and the latter can also generate the object boundary. In the first direction the transformation is a function, but in the second direction it is one-to-many, because a medial point describes more than one boundary point. One of the strengths of using the medial representation as a primitive is that any unbranching, connected subset of the medial locus generates intrinsic space coordinates for the part of the object interior corresponding to it. These coordinates include positional location in the medial sheet, a choice of spoke (left or right) and length along that spoke.

There are related representations in the literature that are based on bitangent spheres, such as Leyton's Process Induced Symmetric Axis (PISA) (Leyton 1992). This representation is obtained by connecting the two points of bitangency along the geodesic path on the bitangent sphere and taking the associated medial point to be the center of this path. Leyton proposed that more complex objects are formed by protrusion or indentation processes acting on the boundary of simpler ones (Leyton 1988, 1989). A formal justification for this view is a symmetry-curvature duality principle whereby the

---

* Much of the material on which this chapter is based is presented in expanded form in Siddiqi and Pizer (2008). We are grateful to all the contributors to this book.

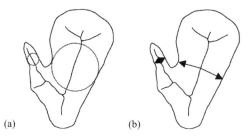

(a)   (b)

Figure 25.1. The figure on the left (a) depicts a continuous locus of medial spheres (disks in 2-D). On the right (b), the spoke vectors associated with two selected medial points are shown. Adapted from Siddiqi and Pizer (2008).

endpoints of this construction are related to curvature extrema on the object's boundary (Leyton 1987; Yuille and Leyton 1990).

The use of medial models for object categorization in computer vision has been discussed in some detail by Sven J. Dickinson in the Chapter 1 of this book. Recent approaches to applying medial models for recognition directly from image data are presented in Chapter 23 by Ben Kimia. This chapter is complementary to this material. We develop a connection to human vision and suggest the role of a type of flux calculation to both locate medial points as well as recover their associated boundary points. In the remainder of this section, we define the medial locus and then discuss its local geometry as well as its topological properties.

Definition 25.1   Let S be a connected closed set in $\mathbb{R}^n$. A closed ball $B \subset \mathbb{R}^n$ is called a *maximal inscribed ball* in S if $B \subset S$ and there does not exist another ball $B' \neq B$ such that $B \subset B' \subset S$.

Let Ω denote an n-dimensional object and let $\partial\Omega$ denote its boundary.

Definition 25.2   The *internal medial locus* of Ω is the set of centers and radii of all the maximal inscribed balls in Ω.

Definition 25.3   The *external medial locus* of Ω is the set of centers and radii of all the maximal inscribed balls in the closure of $\mathbb{R}^n / \Omega$.

Definition 25.4   The *Blum medial locus* of Ω is the union of its internal and external medial loci.

Definition 25.5   The tuple $\{\mathbf{p}, r\}$ that belongs to the Blum medial locus of an object Ω is called a *medial point* of Ω.

The medial locus is thus a subset of the space $\mathbb{R}^n \times [0, +\infty]$. The terms *skeleton*, *medial axis*, and *symmetric axis* have been used in the literature to describe both the internal medial locus as well as the entire medial locus as a whole. The medial locus of a 2-D object consists of a number of curves and isolated points, and the medial locus of a 3-D object consists of surface patches, curves, and isolated points. The manifolds composing the internal medial locus lie inside the object and are bounded, whereas the manifolds in the external medial locus lie outside of the object and extend to infinity.

The medial locus can also be obtained using Blum's *grassfire analogy* (Blum 1973). The boundary of an object is lit on fire and as its interior burns the fire fronts propagate towards one another. Mathematically, this can be described by the following differential equation:

$$\frac{\partial \mathscr{C}(t, p)}{\partial t} = -\alpha \mathbf{n}(p). \tag{25.1}$$

Here $\mathscr{C}(t, p)$ denotes the fire front at time t, parameterized by p, $\mathbf{n}(p)$ is the unit outward normal to the fire front, and α is a constant, positive for inward propagation and negative for outward propagation. As the propagation progresses, segments of fire fronts that originate from disjoint parts of the boundary collide and quench themselves at points that are called *shocks* in the computer vision literature (Kimia et al. 1995). The medial locus is then defined as the set of all the shocks, along with associated values of time t (corresponding to the radius function) at which each shock is formed.

25.1.1 Topological Properties of Medial Loci

A rigorous description of the structural composition and local geometric properties of Blum medial loci of 3-D objects is given in Chapters 2 and 3 of Siddiqi and Pizer (2008). This description classifies medial points based on the multiplicity and order of contact that occurs between the boundary of an object and the maximal inscribed ball centered at a medial point.

Each medial point $P = \{\mathbf{p}, r\}$ in the object Ω is assigned a label of form A_k^m. The superscript m indicates the number of distinct points at which a ball of radius r centered at $\mathbf{p}$ has contact with the boundary $\partial\Omega$. The subscript k indicates the order of contact between the ball and the boundary. The order of tangent contact is a number that indicates how tightly a ball B fits a surface S at a point of contact P.

The following theorem, proved in Giblin and Kimia (2000), specifies all the possible types of contact that can generically occur between the boundary of a 3-D object and the maximal inscribed balls that form its medial locus.

Theorem 25.1 (Giblin and Kimia) *The internal medial locus of a 3-D object Ω generically consists of*

1. *sheets (manifolds with boundary) of A_1^2 medial points;*

2. *curves of A_1^3 points, along which these sheets join, three at a time;*

3. *curves of A_3 points, which bound the free (unconnected) edges of the sheets and for which the corresponding boundary points fall on a crest;*

4. *points of type A_1^4, which occur when four A_1^3 curves meet;*

5. *points of type $A_1 A_3$ (i.e., A_1 contact and A_3 contact at a distinct pair of points) which occur when an A_3 curve meets an A_1^3 curve.*

In two dimensions, a similar classification of medial points is possible. The internal medial locus of a 2-D object generically consists of (i) curves of bitangent A_1^2 points,

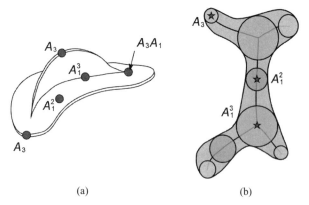

Figure 25.2. The generic classes of points that comprise the medial locus in 3-D (a) and 2-D (b). Adapted from Siddiqi and Pizer (2008). (See color plate 25.2.)

(ii) points of type A_1^3 at which these curves meet, three at a time, and (iii) points of type A_3 which form the free ends of the curves. These classes of contact in 3-D and 2-D are illustrated in Figure 25.2.

The medial locus is in fact a subset of a more general construct called the *symmetry set*, defined as the closure of the locus of centers and radii of all balls bitangent to the boundary of an object (Giblin and Brassett 1985). The relationship between the structure of symmetry sets and the extrema of boundary curvature of 2-D objects is central to Leyton's theory of symmetry (Leyton 1987). In this theory the curves composing the symmetry set of an object represent the history of events that have formed the object. Extrema of curvature are interpreted as the places where the boundary has been pushed in from the outside or pushed out from the inside, indicating a growth or deformation process. Thus, the symmetry set is interpreted as a diagram of protrusion and indentation operations that have been applied to the object (Leyton 1992).

25.1.2 Local Geometry of Medial Loci

Blum investigated the geometric relationships between medial points and the associated points of contact of the maximal inscribed disc with the boundary – that is, the boundary pre-image (Blum 1967; Blum and Nagel 1978). He showed that the points in the boundary pre-image can be expressed in terms of the position and radius of the medial point and from derivatives along the medial locus. In addition to the position of a medial point $\mathbf{p}$ and the radius r, two first-order properties are used. The first property is the slope of the medial curve at the medial point, which can be expressed as a unit-length tangent vector $\mathbf{U}^0$. The second is called the *object angle* and is given by

$$\theta = \arccos\left(-\frac{dr}{ds}\right), \tag{25.2}$$

where s is the arc length along the medial curve.

Figure 25.3 describes the local geometry of a medial point, characterized by $\mathbf{p}$, r, $\mathbf{U}^0$, and θ, along with its associated boundary pre-image points $\mathbf{b}^{-1}$ and $\mathbf{b}^{+1}$. The angle formed by the points $\mathbf{b}^{-1}$, $\mathbf{p}$, and $\mathbf{b}^{+1}$ is bisected by the vector $\mathbf{U}^0$, the unit tangent

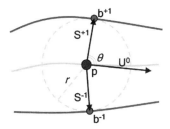

Figure 25.3. Local geometric properties of a medial point and its boundary pre-image points. Adapted from Siddiqi and Pizer (2008)

vector of the medial curve at **p**. The values of **p**, r, and their derivatives can be used to qualitatively describe the local bending and thickness of an object, as first shown by Blum and Nagel (1978). The measurements **p** and $\mathbf{U}^0$ along with the curvature of the medial curve describe the local shape of the medial locus. The measurement r describes how thick the figure is locally, while $\cos\theta$ describes how quickly the object is narrowing with respect to movement along the medial curve. Free ends of medial curves, where the maximal inscribed disk and the boundary osculate and the boundary pre-image contains only a single point, are a limiting case of the bitangent disk situation. The object angle θ is zero at such end points.

Having reviewed the geometric and topological properties of medial loci, we point the reader to Chapters 1 and 23, parts of which develop the application of medial models to object recognition in computer vision. There are several success stories in the computer vision literature. These include the development of matching algorithms for 2-D shapes using skeletal graphs, the view-based recognition of 3-D objects from 2-D views, each described by a skeletal graph, and the more recent use of medial models for object segmentation and recognition directly from grayscale images. Less has been said about the relevance of medial models in human vision, which is the focus of the next section.

25.2 Medial Loci in Human Vision

Medial representations have not only found many applications in computer vision but have also been found to be relevant components of human vision models. In this section we review some of the findings that point to a role for medial loci in shape perception.

Among the first reported psychophysical data is that of Frome (1972), who examined the role of medial axes in predicting human performance in shape alignment tasks. In these experiments subjects were required to position an ellipse so as to be parallel to a reference line. It was found that for this task, the acuity with which the stimulus was placed could be explained by the length of the medial axis within the ellipse (i.e., the straight line connecting the centers of curvatures corresponding to the end points of the major axis of the ellipse).

Later, Psotka (1978) examined the role of medial loci in representing the perceived form of more complex outlines. Subjects were given outline forms (a square, a circle, a humanoid form, and various rectangles) and were asked to draw a dot within each outline in the first place that came to mind. The superimposed dots for each outline were found to coincide well, for the most part, with the locations predicted by Blum's grassfire flow.

Adopting a different experimental procedure, the effect of closure on figure-ground segmentation along with a possible role for medial loci was examined by Kovács and Julesz (1993, 1994) and Kovács et al. (1998). In the experiments reported in Kovács and Julesz (1993), subjects viewed a display of Gabor patches (GPs) aligned along a sampled curve presented in a background of randomly oriented Gabor patches playing the role of distractors. Using a two-alternative forced-choice paradigm, subjects were required to decide whether the display included an open curve or a closed one. The percentage of correct responses were recorded as a function of the separation distance between successive GPs. A significant advantage was found for the correct detection of configurations of closed (roughly circular) targets. In a second series of experiments, subjects were required to detect a target GP of varying contrast placed either inside or outside a circular arrangement of GPs in a field of distractors. It was found that the contrast threshold at which the target could be detected was decreased by a factor of 2 when it was located at the center of the circle, as opposed to the periphery, suggesting a special role for a medial location.

This second finding of increased contrast sensitivity at the center was later examined more carefully in Kovács and Julesz (1994). For an elliptical configuration of GPs it was found that the peak locations of increased contrast sensitivity were in fact predicted by a type of medial model. Specifically, these locations coincided with the local maxima of a D_ε distance function, representing at each location the percentage of boundary locations over the entire outline that were equidistant within a tolerance of ε. Examples of the D_ε function for more complex forms were presented in Kovács et al. (1998) (see Fig. 25.4) along with the proposal that its maxima could play an important role in form perception tasks such as the processing of motion.

Whereas the preceding notion of an ε parameter is fixed as a global quantity, a different notion of scale provides the key motivation for medially subserved perceptual models based on *cores* (Burbeck and Pizer 1995). Underlying this model is the hypothesis that the scale at which the visual system integrates local boundary information is proportional to object width at medial loci. This view is corroborated by the findings of Burbeck et al. (1996), where the core model was shown to explain human performance in bisection tasks on shapes. In these experiments elongated stimuli were created by placing two sinusoidal waves in phase, side by side, and then filling in the region in between. An example of such a "wiggle" stimulus is shown in Figure 25.5. The amount that it is perceived to bend depends on the frequency and amplitude of the sinusoids. For any given stimulus a subject was asked to judge whether a probe dot, placed between two sinusoidal peaks, appeared to the left or right of the object's center. By varying the position of the probe dot, the perceived center was chosen to be the point about which a subject was equally likely to choose left or right in the task. The perceived central modulation was then defined as the horizontal distance between the centers for a successive left and right peak. The experiments revealed that for a fixed width the central modulation increased with increasing amplitude but decreased with increasing frequency. Furthermore, the modulation effects were greater for a narrow

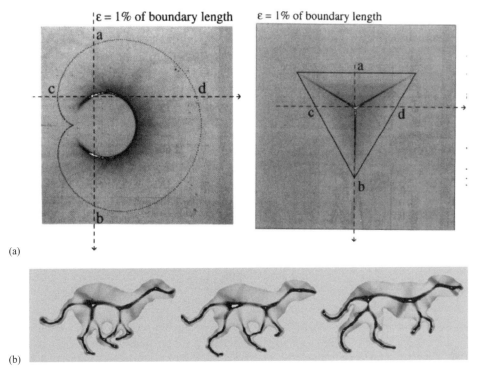

(a)

(b)

Figure 25.4. The function D_ε for various objects. Dark shading corresponds to increasing values of D_ε, and the "white spot" denotes its maximum. (a) D_ε for a cardioid on the left and a triangle on the right; cross-sections through maximum loci are indicated as dotted lines a-b and c-d. (b) D_ε for a few frames in a sequence depicting the movement of an animal. Adapted from Kovács et al. 1998, Figs. 2, 8, 9, and 10; with permission from Ilona Kovács.

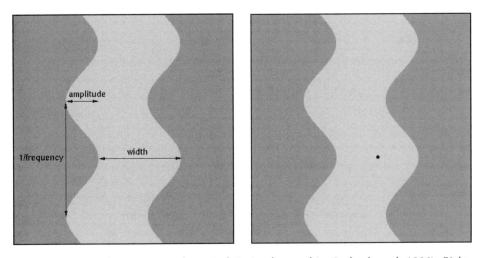

Figure 25.5. *Left,* The geometry of a "wiggle" stimulus used in (Burbeck et al. 1996). *Right,* The task is for the subject to judge whether the probe dot is to the left or to the right of the object's center. Adapted from Siddiqi et al. (2001).

object, in a manner that was adequately explained by the linking of object boundaries at a scale determined by object width, as predicted by the core model.

These wiggle stimuli were revisited by Siddiqi et al. (2001), who showed that in fact the perceived centers in the study of Burbeck et al. (1996) were located precisely on the Blum medial axis, at locations that coincided with local maxima of the radius function. In several experiments using similar stimuli, but with varying degrees of translation between the sinusoidal boundaries, properties of medial loci were shown to account for human performance in shape discrimination tasks using a visual search paradigm.

Taken together, the body of work just discussed provides a wealth of support for the role of medial loci in shape perception. Unfortunately, far less research has been carried out to provide neurophysiological support for medial axes. The one exception is the work of Lee (1995) and Lee et al. (1998), in which neurons were isolated in the primary visual cortices of awake rhesus monkeys and their response to a set of texture images was examined. In the first study (Lee 1995) the input images consisted of either a linear boundary with two regions of contrasting texture, or a rectangular strip or a square on a background of contrasting texture. In each case the texture was comprised of scattered bars in a vertical or horizontal orientation. The findings revealed a subset of neurons that had a peak response when their receptive fields were centered at the texture boundaries. Some of these neurons also had a sharp response when centered at the center of the rectangular strip or square (i.e., at locations predicted by the Blum medial axis). The subsequent, more comprehensive results reported in Lee et al. (1998) revealed that the neurons with interior response peaks appeared to focus in the vicinity of the center of mass of compact shapes (squares and diamonds) but along the entire medial axis for elongated shapes (rectangles). This finding is consistent with the special status attributed to a local maximum of the radius function (e.g., in the context of the wiggle bisection experiments and the contrast sensitivity enhancement experiments discussed earlier). However, this neurophysiological data has not yet been corroborated in the literature by other researchers.

25.3 Grassfire Flow, Average Outward Flux, and Object Angle

The human vision models described in section 25.2 suggest that medial information is somehow extracted from the contrast available at boundaries or from the boundaries themselves. How do we get a computer to extract medial loci? There are a variety of approaches in the literature, many of which are reviewed in Siddiqi and Pizer (2008). Here we concentrate on an approach that locates medial points via a type of flux calculation, and as a byproduct reveals the object angle θ (see Fig. 25.3).

25.3.1 Grassfire Flow

The skeletonization method in Siddiqi et al. (1999, 2002) and Dimitrov et al. (2003) is based on a characterization of singularities of the grassfire flow. The key insight is that in the limit as the area (2-D) or volume (3-D) within which average outward flux is computed shrinks to zero, the average outward flux of the gradient of the

Euclidean distance function has different limiting behaviors at nonmedial and medial points. This allows for a uniform treatment in 2-D and 3-D, and the development of associated skeletonization algorithms. It turns out that for the case of shrinking circular neighborhoods, the limiting values of the average outward flux reveal the object angle and hence allow for the explicit recovery of their boundary pre-image (Dimitrov et al. 2003; Dimitrov 2003).

25.3.2 Average Outward Flux and Object Angle

As explained by Jim Damon in Chapter 3, section 4.5, in Siddiqi and Pizer (2008), it is possible to extend the standard divergence theorem to the case of a vector field defined on a region Ω in $\mathbb{R}^n$ with smooth boundary $\mathcal{B}$ defined by a skeletal structure $(M, \mathbf{S})$. Let ϕ be the signed Euclidean distance function to the boundary of the object. Then $G = \nabla \phi$ denotes the unit vector field generating the grassfire flow for the region Ω with Blum medial axis M. For a piecewise smooth region $\Gamma \subset \Omega$

$$\int_\Gamma \text{div}\, G\, dV \;=\; \int_{\partial \Gamma} G \cdot \mathbf{n}_\Gamma\, dS \;+\; \int_{\tilde{\Gamma}} dM. \qquad (25.3)$$

Here $\mathbf{n}_\Gamma$ is the unit outward normal to Γ and $\tilde{\Gamma}$ consists of those $x \in \tilde{M}$ with smooth value $\mathbf{S}$ such that the radial line determined by $\mathbf{S}$ has nonempty intersection with Γ.

The first term on the right-hand side of equation (25.3) is the outward flux of the grassfire flow across $\partial \Gamma$. It differs from the divergence integral of G over Γ by the "medial volume of $\tilde{\Gamma}$". Chapter 3 of Siddiqi and Pizer (2008) by Jim Damon discusses the role of this medial volume term in the discrimination of medial points from nonmedial ones. The key idea is to consider the limiting behavior of the average outward flux (the outward flux normalized by the volume of $\partial \Gamma$) as Γ shrinks to a point $\mathbf{x}$. For points not on the medial locus the standard divergence theorem applies and it can be shown that the limiting value of the average outward flux is 0. However, for points on the medial axis the limiting average outward flux is nonvanishing, with the exception of edge points.

In the absence of any prior assumptions about boundary shape, for the purposes of computation it is appropriate to choose Γ to be a n-disk. In this case a tighter bound can be obtained for the limiting values of the average outward flux. These calculations are presented in (Dimitrov et al. 2003) and (Dimitrov 2003) for the case $n = 2$; very similar results hold for $n = 3$. The remarkable fact is that for Γ a disk the limiting values actually provide a function of the object angle θ at all generic points of M. The results are summarized in Table 25.1 for $n = 2$. For the case of the junction points the formula must be interpreted by considering the sum of the object angles for each of the three incoming branches at $\mathbf{x}$. Thus, an average outward flux computation not only allows medial points to be distinguished from nonmedial ones, but also yields the object angle θ (and hence $\mathbf{S}$) as a byproduct for each skeletal point $\mathbf{p}$.

Returning now to the local geometry of medial loci, discussed in section 25.1.2, this in turn allows for boundary reconstruction of the bi-tangent points $\mathbf{b}^{\pm 1}$ associated with each skeletal point, with the radius values obtained from the Euclidean distance

Table 25.1. A summary of results from Dimitrov et al. (2003) relating the limiting values of the average outward flux of $\nabla\phi$ through a shrinking disk to the object angle θ for the case of $n = 2$. Here $\mathcal{F}_\varepsilon(\mathbf{x})$ denotes the outward flux at a point x of $\nabla\phi$ through $\partial\Gamma$, with Γ a disk of radius ε. Adapted from Dimitrov et al. 2003

Point type	$\displaystyle\lim_{\varepsilon\to 0}\frac{\overline{\mathcal{F}_\varepsilon(\mathbf{x})}}{2\pi\varepsilon}$
Regular points	$-\frac{2}{\pi}\sin\theta$
End points	$-\frac{1}{\pi}(\sin\theta - \theta)$
Junction points	$-\frac{1}{\pi}\sum_{i=1}^{n}\sin\theta_i$
Nonskeletal points	0

function. In this sense the average outward flux of $\nabla\phi$ through a shrinking disk may be viewed as a type of flux invariant for detecting medial loci as well as characterizing the geometry of the implied boundary (Dimitrov 2003; Dimitrov et al. 2003). Using these ideas, algorithms for computing medial axes have been developed for voxelized objects (Siddiqi et al. 2002) as well as for objects with boundary given as a polyhedral mesh (Stolpner and Siddiqi 2006).

Figure 25.7 shows several examples of medial loci detected using the limiting average outward flux through a shrinking disk, and also shows the boundary pre-image points (dark circles) estimated directly from this flux invariant. In other words, the boundary pre-image points are obtained by using the relationship between the limiting flux value and the object angle θ (Table 25.1) and then extending the spoke vectors on either side of each medial point a distance given by the radius function. A connection can now be made to the special medial points implicated in the psychophysical tasks in Figures 25.4 and 25.5. We hypothesize that

Hypothesis 25.2 *The special medial points implicated in the shape-bisection experiments of Burbeck et al. (1996) and the contrast-sensitivity experiments of Kovács and Julesz (1994) are locations of nonzero limiting average outward flux through a shrinking disk of the Euclidean distance gradient vector field which are also simulatenously maxima of the radius function.*

It turns out that when discretized, the average outward flux results in the summation of a number of terms. Each term measures the angle between the outward normal to the disk and the gradient of the Euclidean distance function at that location, computed as a simple inner product (the first term on the right hand side of equation. (25.3) divided by the perimeter of the disk). One can therefore envision a biological implementation of this quantity, which involves a summation of weighted orientations of the Euclidean distance function gradient vector field, along the perimeter of a shrinking disk. This

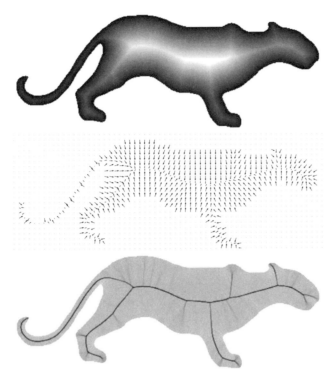

Figure 25.6. The Euclidean distance function ϕ to the boundary of a panther shape (*top*) with brightness proportional to increasing distance, its gradient vector field $\nabla\phi$ (*center*), and the associated average outward flux (*bottom*). Whereas the smooth regime of the vector field gives zero flux (medium grey), strong singularities give large negative values (dark grey) in the interior of the object. Adapted from Dimitrov et al. 2000.

idea of a flux invariant can be developed further, due to the relationship with the object angle θ (see Fig. 25.7). For example, given a parametrization of a medial curve, it is possible to write down explicit formulae for the boundary curvature on either side in terms of the flux invariant and the medial radius.

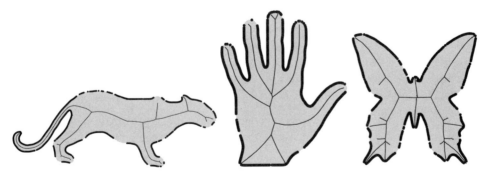

Figure 25.7. For each shape the original is shown in gray, the skeleton obtained using the average outward flux is shown with curves and the boundary points estimated from the skeleton using the relationship between the average outward flux and the object angle θ are shown with black circles. Adapted from Dimitrov et al. 2003.

25.4 Conclusion

This chapter has argued that there is an intimate connection between medial representations used in computer and human vision. A working hypothesis is that certain special medial points can be obtained by an average outward flux calculation, combined with a local extremum of the radius function. The chapter also reviews the topologial and local geometry of medial loci, providing useful background material for Chapters 1 and 23 in this book in which the role of medial models for object recognition in computer vision is discussed.

Bibliography

Blum H. 1967. A transformation for extracting new descriptors of shape. In *Models for the perception of speech and visual form*, ed. W Wathen-Dunn. Cambridge: MIT Press.

Blum H. 1973. Biological shape and visual science. *J Theoret Biol* 38: 205–287.

Blum H, Nagel R. 1978. Shape description using weighted symmetric axis features. *Pattern Recogn* 10(3): 167–180.

Burbeck CA, Pizer SM. 1995. Object representation by cores: identifying and representing primitive spatial regions. *Vision Res* 35(13): 1917–1930.

Burbeck CA, Pizer SM, Morse BS, Ariely D, Zauberman GS, Rolland J. 1996. Linking object boundaries at scale: a common mechanism for size and shape judgements. *Vision Res* 36(3): 361–372.

Dimitrov P. 2003. Flux invariants for shape. MSc thesis, School of Computer Science, McGill University.

Dimitrov P, Jamon JN, Siddiqi K. 2003. Flux invariants for shape. In Proceedings of the IEEE conference on computer vision and pattern recognition, vol 1, 835–841, Madison, WI.

Dimitrov P, Phillips C, Siddiqi K. 2000. Robust and efficient skeletal graphs. In Proceedings of the IEEE conference on computer vision and pattern recognition. 417–423, Hilton Head, South Carolina.

Frome FS. 1972. A psychophysical study of shape alignment. Technical Report TR-198, University of Maryland, Computer Science Center.

Giblin PJ, Brassett SA. 1985. Local symmetry of plane curves. *Am Math Mon* 92: 689–707.

Giblin PJ, Kimia BB. 2000. A formal classification of 3D medial axis points and their local geometry. In Proceedings of the IEEE conference on computer vision and pattern recognition, vol 1, 566–573.

Kimia BB, Tannenbaum AR, Zucker SW. 1995. Shapes, shocks, and deformations, I: the components of shape and the reaction-diffusion space. *Int J Comput Vis* 15(3): 189–224.

Kovács I, Feher A, Julesz B. 1998. Medial-point description of shape: a representation for action coding and its psychophysical correlates. *Vision Res* 38: 2323–2333.

Kovács I, and Julesz B. 1993. A closed curve is much more than an incomplete one: effect of closure in figure-ground segmentation. *Proc Nat Acad Sci USA* 90(16): 7495–7497.

Kovács I, Julesz B. 1994. Perceptual sensitivity maps within globally defined visual shapes. *Nature* 370: 644–646.

Lee TS. 1995. Neurophysiological evidence for image segmentation and medial axis computation in primate V1. In Fourth annual computational neuroscience meeting, ed. J Bower, 373–378. New York: Academic Press.

Lee TS, Mumford D, Romero R, Lamme VAF. 1998. The role of the primary visual cortex in higher level vision. *Vision Res* 38: 2429–2454.

Leyton M. 1987. Symmetry-curvature duality. *Comput Vis Graph Image Proc* 38(3): 327–341.

Leyton M. 1988. A process grammar for shape. *Artif Intell* 34: 213–247.

Leyton M. 1989. Inferring causal history from shape. *Cognit Sci* 13: 357–387.

Leyton M. 1992. *Symmetry, causality, mind*. Cambridge: MIT Press.

Psotka J. 1978. Perceptual processes that may create stick figures and balance. *J Exp Psychol Hum Percept Perform* 4(1): 101–111.

Siddiqi K, Bouix S, Tannenbaum A, Zucker SW. 1999. The Hamilton-Jacobi skeleton. In Proceedings of the IEEE international conference on computer vision, 828–834, Kerkyra, Greece.

Siddiqi K, Bouix S, Tannenbaum A, Zucker SW. 2002. Hamilton-Jacobi skeletons. *Int J Comput Vision* 48(3): 215–231.

Siddiqi K, Kimia BB, Tannenbaum AR, Zucker SW. 2001. On the Psychophysics of the Shape Triangle. *Vision Res* 41: 1153–1178.

Siddiqi K, Pizer SM, eds. 2008. *Medial representations: mathematics, algorithms and applications*. Springer.

Stolpner S, Siddiqi K. 2006. Revealing significant medial structure in polyhedral meshes. In 3DPVT: Proceedings of the third international symposium on 3D data processing, visualization, and transmission, 365–372, Washington, DC, USA. IEEE Computer Society.

Yuille A, Leyton M. 1990. 3D symmetry-curvature duality theorems. *Comput Vis Graph Image Proc* 52: 124–140.

CHAPTER 26

Multimodal Categorization

Christian Wallraven and Heinrich H. Bülthoff

26.1 Introduction

Imagine entering a room for the very first time (Fig. 26.1) and then being asked to look around and to see what is in it. The first glance already tells you what kind of room it is (in our case it clearly is a scene set in a museum); immediately afterwards you begin to notice objects in the room (the prominent statue in the foreground, several other statues on pedestals, paintings on the walls, etc.). Your attention might be drawn more towards certain objects first and then wander around taking in the remaining objects. Very rarely will your visual system need to pause and take more time to investigate what a particular object is – even more rarely will it not be able to interpret it at all (perhaps the four-horned statue in the back of the room will be confusing at first, but it still can be interpreted as a type of four-legged, hoofed animal). The remarkable ability of the (human) visual system to *quickly* and *robustly* assign labels to objects (and events) is called categorization.

The question of how we learn to categorize objects and events has been at the heart of cognitive and neuroscience research for the last decades. At the same time, advances in the field of computational vision – both in terms of the algorithms involved as well as in the capabilites of today's computers – have made it possible to begin to look at how computers might solve the difficult problem of categorization. In this chapter, we will therefore address some of the key challenges in categorization from a combined cognitive and computational perspective. We will focus on issues that so far have only started to be addressed but that are crucial for a deeper understanding of categorization in biological and artificial systems.

Historically, psychophysics has sought to investigate a functional relationship between a mathematically defined input and an observed behavioral response. Several very refined experimental methods have been developed to measure and describe this relationship very precisely. Early experiments in psychophysics dealt mostly with very simple, easily describable stimuli such as sine-wave gratings or lines and measured thresholds for contrast sensitivity or line orientation. The question, however, remains to what degree these results can be extrapolated to real-world situations in which

Figure 26.1. Example scene. Even though you probably have never seen this picture before, the type of scene as well as the objects contained in the scene are immediately apparent.

much richer statistical properties exist that need to be processed efficiently by the visual system. In order to answer this question using psychophysical methodology one would need to create mathematically defined stimuli that accurately capture real-world statistics.

Recent developments in computer graphics have made it possible to both produce highly realistic stimulus material for controlled experiments in lifelike environments as well as to enable highly detailed analyses of the physical properties of real-world stimuli. Results from these experiments have shed light on specific processing strategies that the human visual system employs to solve fundamental problems in categorization.

This chapter, therefore, is set in a fusion of perceptual research, computer graphics, and computer vision. As shown in Figure 26.2, this fusion has the possibility of opening up synergies for all three research areas:

- Highly controllable, yet realistic computer-generated stimuli offer novel possibilities for advanced psychophysical experiments. The results from those experiments can be used to derive perceptual "shortcuts" to more efficient rendering approaches.

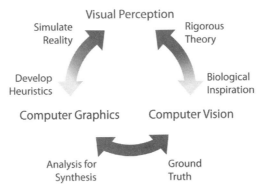

Figure 26.2. Illustration of the synergies inherent in the fusion of perceptual research, computer graphics, and computer vision.

- Algorithms from computer vision and machine learning can be used to model human performance. Conversely, the results from perceptual experiments can inform computer scientists about how the human brain solves "vision."
- Generating virtual worlds with computer graphics also helps computer vision researchers, as "ground truth" is available for testing of recognition algorithms, for example. Such algorithms can, on the other hand, be used to generate and model highly complex scenes more quickly.

In the following, we will try to illustrate such an integrated approach using the topic of categorization. Based on evidence from several psychophysical experiments, we will discuss issues such as the need for spatiotemporal object representations, perception of material properties, as well as multimodal/multisensory aspects of object processing. For each of those issues, we will mention possible implications and applications for computational/cognitive modeling.

26.2 Spatiotemporal Object Representations

26.2.1 Exemplar-Based Versus Structural Object Representations

One of the core topics in cognitive psychophysics that has been at the centre of a hot debate over the last two decades is the question about the nature of visual object representations (Tarr and Bülthoff 1999; Hayward 2003). The two extreme positions on this topic are given by the structural description model and exemplar-based model. The most prominent structural description model, the Recognition-by-Components model (RBC) (Biederman 1987), states that objects are represented in the brain as 3-D entities that are made up of an alphabet of basic, geometric shapes called "geons." Given an input image, the brain matches its alphabet of geons to individual object parts and tries to combine the reconstructed geons into a whole. The other extreme is given by the exemplar-based model (Bülthoff and Edelman 1992), which is based on the assumption that no 3-D reconstruction is necessary for recognition or categorization. Instead, the input image is directly compared to a viewer-centred, appearance-based representation that is more "image-like" in nature. Experimental evidence so far has favored the exemplar-based account in recognition over the predictions made by the RBC model (Tarr and Bülthoff 1999). Interestingly, the historical development of recognition and categorization approaches in computer vision has also paralleled this trend away from vision as 3-D reconstruction towards more data-driven, appearance-based algorithms.

Because most of the debate in cognitive psychophysics has concerned the issue of view-invariance versus view-dependent performance, a recent development has been to connect core ideas of the two approaches into a hybrid model that contains both view-invariant and view-dependent processing. Experimental evidence for such hybrid models has started to appear. In a set of recent psychophysical experiments (Foster and Gilson 2002), for example, it was investigated to what extent a *combination* of view-dependent and view-invariant processing might explain object recognition. Their experiments employed the same paradigm (recognition of objects across rotations in depth) using novel paper-clip–like stimuli as in the original study by Bülthoff and Edelman (1992). The stimulus parameters that were varied, however, now were metric properties (thickness or size of the paper-clips) or nonaccidental structural properties (the number of limbs/parts of a paper-clip). Results for *both parameters* showed strong viewpoint dependency for an angular range of 90° around the learned viewpoint, whereas for the remaining angular range, the viewpoint dependency was much less pronounced. The only difference between the two conditions were that nonaccidental changes were faster and more accurately recognized (in accordance with the aforementioned findings) with an otherwise completely identical angular dependence pattern. The authors interpreted their findings as the result of two processes that are additively combined in order to yield the final recognition result across depth rotations: the first process is independent of viewpoint but dependent on structure, whereas the second process is dependent on viewpoint but dependent on structure. Note that this means a departure from the traditional view of view-dependent and view-invariant processing towards a new combination of view-invariant processing. Whereas this study has led to some important impulses in the psychophysical community, it remains to be seen, however, how such ideas could be implemented in computational systems (for some ideas in this direction, see, e.g., Hoiem et al. 2007).

26.2.2 Temporal Information

Even though exemplar-based approaches to object recognition and categorization both in psychophysics as well as in computer vision have been very successful, they still mostly rely on *static* object representations. Visual input on the retina, however, consists of dynamic changes due to object- and self-motion, nonrigid deformations of objects, and articulated object motion as well as scene changes, such as variations in lighting, occluding and re- and disappearing objects, where at any given point in time several of these changes can be interacting. The question therefore can be raised whether recognition and categorization of objects – even of static objects or scenes – is influenced by temporal information. Several psychophysical experiments, which we will briefly discuss in the following section, indeed suggest an important role for this information, both in learning and recognition of objects.

In a series of experiments conducted by (Stone 1998) the issue of temporal information for object recognition was investigated. The experiments consisted of a simple recognition test in which several novel, rotating 3-D objects had to be memorized first; in a later recognition stage, both learned and new objects were presented to participants who had to indicate whether they knew the object or not. Interestingly, when Stone reversed the order of the temporal sequence – resulting in the objects rotating in the *other* direction – participants were significantly worse than when presented in the correct temporal sequence. This is a surprising result because, even in appearance-based accounts of recognition, temporal order would not matter because both rotation sequences contain the exact same views. The results therefore provide compelling evidence that temporal information is indeed part of the object representation and that it can be used for recognition. In another series of experiments Chuang et al. (2006) used sequences of novel, *deforming* 3-D objects in a similar experimental paradigm. They also found the temporal order effect suggesting that spatiotemporal object representations not only encode rigid transformations but also nonrigid transformations.

In experiments by Wallis and Bülthoff (2001), several faces had to be learned from short image sequences that showed a rotating face. The sequence, however, did not

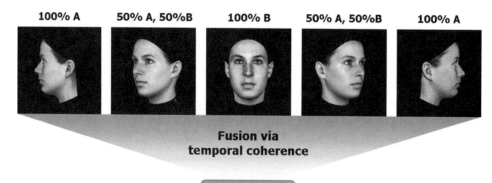

Figure 26.3. Illustration of the experiments by Wallis and Bülthoff (2001) and Wallis (2002). A sequence of morphing faces is shown to participants who integrate the different faces into one coherent representation based on spatiotemporal similarity.

contain images of a single rotating face but rather depicted a morphing face that changed identity as it rotated. When later tested for recognition, participants reported for static images of both constituent faces that they had already seen them, although they never noticed the morphing during the learning trials (see Fig. 26.3). This effect vanished as soon as the images of the sequence were presented side-by-side on the screen (rather than as a movie), showing that the effect was truly due to the temporal information contained in the sequence. In a follow-up study (Wallis 2002), the results of this experiment were replicated with different faces in the sequence rather than a slowly morphing face. These results demonstrate the importance of temporal information during *learning* of objects. Indeed, this strategy does make sense in an appearance-based framework in which the brain somehow has to decide that different images of an object belong together in order to assign those images to one object representation. Temporal contiguity – or more accurately, spatiotemporal similarity – is a powerful cue for this association, as our environment usually tends to change only by a small amount from one moment to the next.

26.2.3 Computational Implementation

Taken together, these results ask for an extension of current object recognition frameworks with a temporal component in order to arrive at truly spatiotemporal object representations. Combining methods from computer vision, psychophysics, and machine learning, Wallraven (2007) and Wallraven and Bülthoff (2001, 2007) have developed a framework that fulfills this requirement and that is able to learn spatiotemporal, exemplar-based object representations from image sequences. More specifically, spatiotemporal characteristics of the visual input are integrated into a connected view-graph representation based on tracked local features – an input sequence is divided into so-called keyframes, each of which contains information about its temporal history. In order to provide robust classification performance, machine learning techniques are used to design efficient methods for combining support vector classification schemes with these local feature representations (Wallraven et al. 2003).

In several studies it was shown that the framework achieved excellent recognition results on both highly controlled databases as well as on real-world data (Wallraven and Bülthoff, 2001; 2007; Wallraven 2007). The integration of spatiotemporal information provides characteristic information about dynamic visual input via the connection of views and the 2-D image motion of discriminative features. In addition to delivering good recognition performance, the framework was also able to model results from psychophysical experiments on face and object recognition. For example, the temporal association of the experiments by Wallis and Bülthoff (2001) found a simple explanation in spatiotemporal similarity as measured by the local feature tracking, which is used to extract the keyframes. If we consider a rotation sequence of a nonmorphing, standard face, features from the first frame will be tracked for a while, then a keyframe will be triggered as too many new features appear, and so on until the end of the sequence. For a rotation sequence of a *morphing* face, local features in subsequence frames will differ much more in their spatiotemporal similarity (i.e., the eyes will suddenly move further apart and look a little different) such that features become lost more easily. This in turn results in more keyframes for morphed than for normal faces. When using different faces in the rotation sequence such as done in Wallis (2002), this behavior becomes even more pronounced, resulting in even more keyframes due to earlier loss of features. Indeed, using similar sequences as used in the psychophysical experiments, the experimental results were fully replicated computationally (Wallraven 2007). Moreover, the computational experiments provided additional information as to which facial features might be used to drive such a spatiotemporal association of subsequent frames – predictions that could be tested in further psychophysical experiments, thus closing the loop between perception research and computer vision.

One of the major criticisms of exemplar-based approaches is that they require, in the strictest sense of the definition, too many exemplars to be able to work efficiently as they substitute computation (of elaborate features such as geons, e.g.) with memory (storing of exemplars). This leads to an explosion of storage requirements and, therefore, to problems with recognition, because retrieval cannot be done efficiently anymore. The framework described here addresses this problem in the following way:

- Local features are used to significantly reduce the memory footprint of visual representations. The extraction and modeling of stable, appearance-based local features as the basis of object representations has been shown to provide excellent generalization capabilities for categorization and very good discrimination capabilities for recognition.
- The trajectories of the tracked features provide access to the motion of objects in the image plane, leading to further generalization.
- The graph structure of the keyframes allows for self-terminating learning of object representations, connecting of different objects and events across time, access to often-recognized views (so-called canonical views),

The exemplar-based keyframe framework, therefore, *trades* (rather than substitutes) computation for memory and provides more efficient storage and retrieval options.

Figure 26.4. Changing material appearance by simple, perceptual heuristics rather than complex, physically correct calculations. The image on the *left* is the original; the image on the *right* shows a re-rendering of the object to make it look transparent. Adapted from Khan et al. 2006.

26.3 Perception of Material Properties

Returning to the image in Figure 26.1, let us focus on the elephant statue in the foreground. In addition to quickly being able to categorize this object as an elephant, another very important perceptual judgment also can be made easily: we can immediately say that the elephant is made of marble. Our ability to judge material properties using only an image of the object is surprisingly accurate given that our perceptual system has to disentangle effects of shape, material, viewpoint, and illumination in order to arrive at a satisfactory conclusion. As one might imagine, this problem is highly ill-posed, as an infinite number of combinations of the aforementioned factors are compatible with the given 2-D image. Our brain, however, has evolved to take into account natural image statistics and has learned powerful statistical priors that work surprisingly well in constraining the solution space to plausible parameter combinations.

One of the most powerful of these priors is the so-called convexity prior (Langer and Bülthoff 2001), which helps us to interpret otherwise ambiguous illumination gradients. This prior is demonstrated in Figure 26.5, which shows a sequence of a rotating hollow mask. In the fourth image in the sequence we actually look into the inside of the mask, which should therefore result in a concave face with a nose protruding into the image plane. Instead, we perceive quite vividly a "normal," convex face with the nose pointing towards us.

26.3.1 Exchanging Materials

The question now is: What kinds of priors might the brain use to tell us that object in Figure 26.4 is made of marble? An indirect answer to this question comes from recent work by Khan et al. (2006), who used simple computer graphics techniques to modify the material appearance of 2-D images without resorting to complex calculations of light-transport equations as it is done now in advanced computer graphics applications.

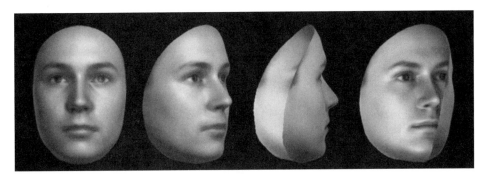

Figure 26.5. Illustration of the convexity prior, which usually helps the brain to assign a unique shape interpretation to physically ambiguous figures. A rotating hollow face mask will always seen as convex, even when we look into it from behind.

In standard computer graphics terminology, the interaction of an (idealized) object with incident illumination is governed by the so-called bi-directional reflection function (BRDF). Given a viewing angle and the angle of the incident light, the BRDF specifies the reflectance for each point on the surface of the object. Depending on the material, the BRDF can be a highly complex function, which is not easy to model analytically but instead has to be measured empirically. In order to change the material of an object in the scene, one would need to know the exact shape of the object, the viewing angle, and the remaining scene geometry. To derive such a physically correct solution, of course, is a highly ill-posed problem given a single 2-D image. The question is now: Can we derive a *perceptually correct* solution?

The core idea in the work by Khan et al. (2006) was to arrive at a reasonably exact estimation of the object geometry *taking into account the so-called bas-relief ambiguity* (Belhumeur et al. 1999). The ambiguity states that the human visual system cannot distinguish between surfaces that are affinely transformed along the line of sight and has been exploited by artists for centurys in bas-reliefs (e.g., in wood and stone carvings in churches and on temples). This ambiguity means that in a perceptually correct estimation of the shape of an object we need only the *distribution* of the surface normals but not their absolute values. Such a shape reconstruction can be achieved by a simple 2-D filtering of the (isolated) object using a bilateral filter. The output of the filter is then taken directly as the reconstructed depth map of the object. It is important to note that the scale of the filtering (i.e., the coarseness or fineness of the reconstructed depth map) needs to correspond to the desired material structure; mismatches here result in noticable artifacts.

In order to turn an object transparent, such as in Figure 26.4, it needs to reflect the background. A simple blurred pasting of random bits of the surrounding background, however, was found to be enough to convey the impression of transparency. This filling-in procedure again only needs to pay attention to the distortions in the reconstructed shape rather than its physically correct depth values. Our visual system is apparently not able to do an inverse ray-tracing to derive the physically realistic reflections.

This proof-of-concept work has shown that the human visual system is able to estimate the geometry of an object given a single 2-D image by reconstructing the

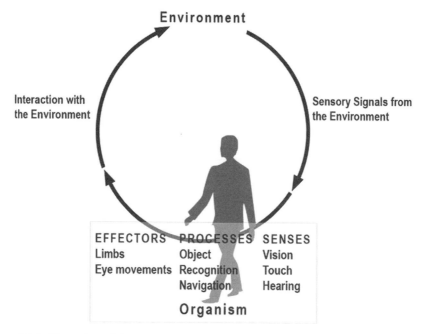

Figure 26.6. Illustration of the perception-action cycle. Information about the environment is picked up by the senses, processed by the brain, and used to interact with the environment.

relative distortions in its shape. Furthermore, material judgments of an object seem to be made taking into account simple image and material statistics such as color and texture coarseness. Referring to Figure 26.2, this is an excellent example of a fusion of perceptual research and computer graphics that results in novel approaches and findings for both fields.

26.4 Multisensory Object Processing

In the previous sections, we have mainly focused on the visual domain. The human, however, is a multisensory animal that is equipped with several sensory organs that together provide an enormous amount of specifically structured information about the environment. In addition, the human is situated in a continuous perception-action cycle (see Fig. 26.6), in which multisensory input is processed by the brain (more generally, the central nervous system); this processed input is then fed to effectors (our limbs, the eyes, etc.) in order to interact with the environment (looking around, moving an object, etc.). This interaction in turn changes the state of the environment (a different part of the scene is looked at, an object changes place, etc.), which is again taken up by our senses, and thus the cycle continues. This perception-action cycle, therefore, introduces the important concept of the *embodied agent*: this means that we are situated in a world that we can sense and with which we can interact, and at the same that we have a task/context in which we work.

Returning to our initial question of how we categorize objects, this brings up the issue of whether and how we integrate information from multiple senses for this task. In order to answer the question of how we might be able to recognize objects both from vision and from touch, a series of psychophysical experiments was conducted by Newell et al. (2001). Participants had to learn views of four simple, 3-D objects made of stacked toy bricks either in the haptic modality (when they were blindfolded) or in the visual modality (without being able to touch them). Subsequently, they were tested both within the same modality as well as across modalities. Recognition results showed that cross-modal recognition was possible well above chance. Interestingly, recognition of *rotated* objects in both within-modality conditions was severely affected by rotation in both modalities. This shows that not only visual recognition is highly view-dependent but also that haptic recognition performance is directly affected by different viewing parameters. The results from this experiment thus support the view that haptic recognition is also mediated by exemplar-based processes.

26.4.1 Visuohaptic Similarity Ratings

Consider Figure 26.4 again: beyond their visual qualities, the two types of materials seem to evoke tactile/haptic qualities. For example, both materials might be cool to the touch, they are most likely smooth, and we expect the marble elephant to feel different than the glass elephant. It is clear that in order to do this we need to connect visual input with tactile/haptic memory. Beyond their common view-dependency, visual and haptic object representations might therefore share additional commonalities. Indeed, one can ask how close sensory information is coupled in a representation of the same object.

In order to address this question, Cooke et al. (2006a) investigated how perceptual similarities and categorization vary when different sensory modalities are used to explore objects. The study used parametrically defined 3-D stimuli (see Fig. 26.7) that varied in two important perceptual parameters that are accessible by both sensory modalities: shape (or macrogeometry) and texture (or microgeometry). Participants explored the objects using vision alone, touch alone, or both vision and touch. Multi-dimensional scaling (MDS) techniques were then used to obtain perceptual spaces arising from each of these conditions. The spaces were then compared in order to test for an effect of modality. Given the close connections between similarity and categorization (Hahn and Ramscar 2001), modality-specific differences in categorization were also investigated; therefore, participants categorized the objects at the end of the similarity rating experiment.

The experiments found similarities as well as differences among the representations recovered from haptic, visual, and visuohaptic exploration. Regardless of modality, participants referred to the dimensions used to judge similarity as shape and texture, exclusively. The same ordinal relationships among stimuli in the input space were found in MDS spaces reconstructed from visual, haptic, and bimodal exploration – that is, participants were able to recover these relationships regardless of the modality used (the grid in Fig. 26.7 shows the reconstructed perceptual space, which follows closely the two dimensions of the physical parameter space). Given the complexity of the

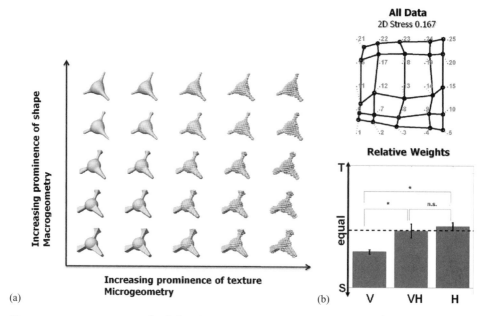

Figure 26.7. (a) Parametrically defined stimuli used to test commonalities between similarity and categorization judgments across modalities. (b) Reconstructed perceptual space for all modalities and weights given to shape (S) and texture (T) in the three experimental conditions (V = visual, VH = visuohaptic, H = haptic).

measurement space, this is not a trivial process. Despite sharing common dimensions and ordinal relationships, there were two clear differences among modality-specific perceptual spaces. First, the relative weights of shape and texture dimensions differed: on average, shape dominated texture when objects were seen, whereas shape and texture were roughly evenly weighted when objects were either touched, or both seen and touched (see Fig. 26.7). This finding agrees with the notion that vision is specialized for the extraction of object macrogeometry and that, in touch, microgeometry will be weighted more.

Interestingly, the same pattern of weights was observed in the categorization task, indicating that a relationship between similarity and categorization exists not only for stimuli perceived visually, but also for those perceived haptically and visuohaptically. A final result is particularly relevant concerning the question of multimodal integration: fitting similarity data from all three modality conditions using a single map with subject-specific weights (the one shown in Fig. 26.7) was as good as fitting data from each modality condition with three separate, modality-specific maps. This implies that, for this data set, differences across modalities can be accounted for by simply linearly scaling the dimensions of a common map – speaking in favor of a common object representation that might be very similar across modalities. Furthermore, when both similarity and categorization weights were averaged according to modality, bimodal weights turned out to be values between unimodal weights, indicating that a weighted average of unimodal weights may be used in the multimodal condition.

The results suggest close connections between visual and haptic processing, both for similarity and categorization judgments. Similar perceptual computations might be carried out in both modalities to arrive at perceptual representations that carry information about shape and texture of objects (see Cooke et al. (2006b) for computational studies on this issue). Additionally, a simple, linear weighting of cue information might be enough to explain modality-specific processing.

26.4.2 Computational Issues

The perceptual studies in this section so far have provided evidence in favor of multi-sensory object representations and shared processes across sensory modalities. Especially in the field of robotics, there have been attempts at constructing systems capable of multisensory processing. The level of integration of the different modalities, however, is usually very shallow. A promising approach that is currently being pursued in this area is "epigenetic robotics" (Berthouze and Metta 2005), which is defined as "systems, either natural or artificial, [which] share a prolonged developmental process through which varied and complex cognitive and perceptual structures emerge as a result of the interaction of an embodied system with a physical and social environment." Developments in this research area are motivated by computer vision, perceptual research, and robotics.

One example of such an integrated approach has been the continued development of the keyframe framework discussed in section 26.2.3 together with the LIRA-Lab in Genoa, Italy (Wallraven and Bülthoff 2007). The framework was implemented on a robot that was equipped with both visual input (CCD-cameras) and proprioceptive/tactile input (a fully controllable robotic arm with a five-fingered hand). Objects were learned by the robot picking up an object and executing a preprogrammed hand motion that rotated the object around three axes. The visual information, consisting of a sequence of images from the object exploration, was used to extract keyframes (in section 26.2.3). Beyond visual information, however, the robot also had access to proprioceptive information; that is, how did the hand turn to go from keyframe k_t to k_{t+1}? This information basically anchors different keyframes in a viewer-centred joint space driven by proprioceptive input coming from the joint angles. When recognizing an object, the robot again picked it up and performed the same motion; in order to make use of multisensory information, possible matches among the stored keyframes were searched for only among matching proprioceptive transformations. This simple strategy resulted in a large increase in recognition performance compared to visual-only recognition.

Although multisensory implementation is certainly limited in its generalizability, it nevertheless demonstrates how a simple augmentation of visual information by other sensory input can be used to design more efficient computational systems. More importantly, however, such an integration will be necessary for any system that performs interactions with the environment. Imagine that the robot's task is to insert an object into a slit. By using an integrated object representation such as we described, it would be able to access proprioceptive transformations given only visual input. How does the robot need to turn its hand to match a given view (keyframe) of an object?

26.5 Conclusion

In this chapter, we have discussed the issue of multisensory categorization from a combined perceptual and computational perspective. Several psychophysical experiments have demonstrated that object representations suitable for recognition and categorization

- are built on exemplar-based, spatiotemporal processing,
- are driven by and reflect the appearance-based statistics inherent in real-world images (light tends to come from above, objects have a certain size, simple histogram properties drive material recognition), and
- need to be augmented by multisensory information in order to efficiently solve real-world tasks that involve manipulation of and interaction with the environment.

Although the studies presented here have only scratched the surface of perceptual processing (e.g., we have just focused on two sensory modalities), we believe that the aforementioned results are of fundamental importance to future computational vision systems (as well as for efficient, perceptually realistic computer graphics). The challenges for computer vision, then, lie in constructing and validating vision systems that integrate these results and thus enable deeper interpretations of visual (or multisensory) input that go beyond current state-of-the-art.

Bibliography

Belhumeur PN, Kriegman DJ, Yuille AL. 1999. The bas-relief ambiguity. *Int J Comput Vis* 35(1):33–44.

Berthouze L, Metta G. 2005. Epigenetic robotics: modelling cognitive development in robotic systems. *Cognit Syst Res* 6:189–192.

Biederman, I. 1987. Recognition-by-components: a theory of human image understanding. *Psychol Rev* 94(2):115–147.

Bülthoff HH, and Edelman S. 1992. Psychophysical support for a 2-d view interpolation theory of object recognition. *Proc Nat Acad Sci* 89:60–64.

Chuang L, Vuong QC, Thornton IM, Bülthoff HH. 2006. Recognising novel deforming objects. *Vis Cognit* 14(1):85–88.

Cooke T, Jäkel F, Wallraven C, Bülthoff HH. 2006a. Multimodal similarity and categorization of novel, three-dimensional objects. *Neuropsychol* 45(3):484–495.

Cooke T, Kannengiesser S, Wallraven C, Bülthoff HH. 2006b. Object feature validation using visual and haptic similarity ratings. *ACM T Appl Percept* 3(3):239–261.

Foster D, Gilson S. 2002. Recognizing novel three-dimensional objects by summing signals from parts and views. *Proc Biol Sci* 269:1939–1947.

Hahn U, Ramscar M. 2001. *Similarity and categorization*. Oxford: Oxford University Press.

Hayward W. 2003. After the view-point debate: where next in object recognition? *Trend Cognit Sci* 7(10):425–427.

Hoiem D, Stein A, Efros AA, Hebert M. 2007. Recovering occlusion boundaries from a single image. In International conference on computer vision.

Khan EA, Reinhard E, Fleming RW, Bülthoff HH. 2006. Image-based material editing. *ACM T Graph* 25(3):654–663.

Langer M, Bülthoff HH. 2001. A prior for global convexity in local shape-from-shading. *Perception* 30:403–410.

Newell F, Ernst M, Tjan B, Bülthoff HH. 2001. View-point dependence in visual and haptic object recognition. *Psychol Sci* 12(1):37–42.

Stone J. 1998. Object recognition using spatio-temporal signatures. *Vision Res* 38(7):947–951.

Tarr M, Bülthoff HH. 1999. *Object recognition in man, monkey, and machine cognition special issues*. Cambridge: MIT Press.

Wallis G. 2002. The role of object motion in forging long-term representations of objects. *Visual Cognit*.

Wallis G, Bülthoff HH. 2001. Effect of temporal association on recognition memory. *Proc Natl Acad Sci USA*.

Wallraven C. 2007. *A computational recognition system grounded in perceptual research*. Berlin, Germany: Logos Verlag.

Wallraven C, Bülthoff HH. 2001. Automatic acquisition of exemplar-based representations for recognition from image sequences. IEEE Computer Society Press.

Wallraven C, Bülthoff HH. 2007. *Object recognition in man and machine*. Tokyo: Springer.

Wallraven C, Caputo B, Graf A. 2003. Recognition with local features: the kernel recipe. In ICCV 2003 Proceedings, Vol. 2, 257–264. IEEE Press.

CHAPTER 27

Comparing 2-D Images of 3-D Objects

David W. Jacobs

27.1 Introduction

Visual classification presents many challenges, but in this chapter we will focus on the problem of generalization. This is the ability to learn about a new class of object from some images, and then to recognize instances of that class in very different images. To do this we must somehow account for variations in appearance due to changes in viewpoint, alterations in lighting, variations in the shape of different objects within the same class, and a myriad of other causes.

At the core of this generalization is the question: how best can we determine the similarity between a small set of 2-D images? Most of our visual input comes in the form of 2-D images. Our ability to classify is based on experience with a large number of images, but if we want to know how to get the most from many images, it makes sense to begin by asking how we can get the most from just a few images.

One of the most important constraints that we can use when comparing 2-D images is our knowledge that these are images of the 3-D world. We do not need to treat images as generic 2-D signals, and to compare them as such. Rather, we can base our comparisons on knowledge derived from the 3-D world. Geometry provides strong constraints on how the 2-D appearance of a 3-D object can change with viewpoint. The physics of light and the material properties of objects that reflect this light constrain how much variation there can be in the appearance of an object as the lighting varies. The way in which the parts of 3-D objects can articulate or deform determines the variations in appearance that can occur as, for example, we bend our arms, or smile. In light of this, we take the view that our representations of 2-D images and our methods of comparing them should be informed by the fact that these are images of the 3-D world. If instead we compare images using methods that would be equally suitable to any 2-D signal, then our comparisons will not be as powerful as they could, and we will not be extracting as much as we might from our images.

In this chapter, I will give some examples of work that collaborators and I have done that illustrates this approach. For example, suppose we see an image of a face from one viewpoint. How should we compare this to an image taken from a different viewpoint? We show that we can achieve good recognition results by matching the images using a stereo matching algorithm; that is, we perform recognition based on matching the images just as we would for reconstruction. Recognition is based on matching that accounts for changes in viewpoint. Or, we show that we can match objects when there is lighting variation using representations that are insensitive to lighting changes. Deriving such representations requires an understanding of how light interacts with 3-D shapes. Finally, if we want to recognize shapes that can deform or articulate, we can do so using representations that are insensitive to deformation or articulation. Again, our comparison of 2-D images is based on a model of how transformations in the 3-D world affect appearance.

First, however, we will briefly contrast this approach with two alternatives. The first type of approach attempts to use 2-D images to reconstruct properties of the 3-D world. For example, we could use a 2-D image (or stereo, or motion) to reconstruct the 3-D shape of the object at which we are looking. Or we could attempt to compute some partial 3-D information that is invariant to viewpoint. Or we could compute intrinsic material properties of an object, such as its color, lightness, or texture, separating these from the happenstance of lighting. Or we could compute the skeleton of a shape that is not affected by articulations. Once we compute these intrinsic properties of objects, we may compare them directly, having already eliminated the effects of viewing conditions.

This is potentially a very powerful approach to classification. Early examples of this approach include the generalized cylinders research program of Binford (e.g., Binford 1971; Brooks 1981); intrinsic images work of Barrow and Tenenbaum (1978); Marr's (1982) approach to image analysis, which focused on constructing 2 1/2-D and then 3-D representations; and Biederman's (1987) geon theory of human visual classification. This approach has broad appeal, because it offers a very concrete way to cope with variability and to perform generalization.

The drawback of this approach is that it has proven difficult to extract representations of images that are 3-D, intrinsic, or otherwise invariant to viewing conditions. In some cases, this has been proven to be impossible (Burns, Weiss, and Riseman 1992; Clemens and Jacobs 1991; Chen, Belhumeur, and Jacobs 2000). Of course, all approaches to classification face serious difficulties, so this may not be a reason to abandon hope for *these* approaches. However, it may be that these approaches are trying to solve an intermediate problem (reconstruction) that is more difficult than the original problem (recognition).

For example, when we look at a person from the front, it may be very difficult to judge the length of the nose. If we attempt a 3-D reconstruction of the face from that one view, we are therefore quite likely to make mistakes that will lead to significant miscalculations in how the face will look when seeing it in profile. Formally, reconstruction may be an ill-posed problem. Instead, we can forego reconstruction and wait until we see a profile view of a face, and ask the simpler question: Are these two images consistent with a single face, seen from two viewpoints? Although a 3-D reconstruction of the nose from a single view may be difficult, the nose's frontal image still may contain a great deal of information about how the nose might or might not look when viewed in profile. This information can be used in the course of image comparison, even if it is not sufficient for reconstruction.

A second common approach to generalization is based on prior experience and machine learning. We may, for example, obtain many images of an object, and train a classifier to identify new instances of that object (e.g., LeCun et al. 1990; Cortes and Vapnik 1995; Poggio and Edelman 1990). More generally, we may attempt to learn a distance function, using many example images of objects from many different classes. With these images we can learn a distance function that produces small distances for images of objects from the same class, and larger distances for images of objects from different classes (e.g., Belhumeur, Hespanha, and Kriegman 1997; Moghaddam and Pentland 1997). This can potentially allow us to learn a new class from a small number of images, and generalize to quite different images belonging to the same class. The distance function encodes how the appearance of objects can vary. With this approach, if 3-D information is indeed important, the classifier or distance function is expected to learn that implicitly.

This approach is certainly powerful, but we feel that it has two current limitations that can be overcome by stressing the primacy of image comparison, perhaps as part of an approach that also incorporates machine learning. The first limitation is that learning approaches can be quite sensitive to the representation that is used. It is well known that there is no completely universal learning algorithm; that any effective approach to learning must begin with a reasonable set of hypotheses to consider; and that these hypotheses are, in part, specified by the representation used. When learning-based approaches treat images as arbitrary, 2-D signals, they place a heavy burden on the learning algorithm. It must discover every way in which the 3-D world constrains the sets of images that a single class of objects can produce. If instead we begin with image representations that are insensitive to variations caused by the nature of the 3-D world, we can expect much better results.

The second limitation of many learning algorithms is that they require data to be embedded into some vector space. This means, implicitly, that they require correspondence between images. For example, many machine learning approaches to face recognition convert a 2-D image into a 1-D vector, and apply some linear projection to these vectors. This implicitly assumes that it is meaningful to compare pixels in two images simply because they have the same (x, y) coordinates. One cannot expect a learning algorithm to be effective unless this implicit correspondence is meaningful. This problem is well known, and has been addressed in some approaches that preprocess images to find correspondences (Beymer and Poggio 1996). Here, we simply argue that any effective classification method must, at its heart, have methods for building representations based on meaningful correspondences, and these methods should be based on an understanding of how 3-D variations affect the appearance of an object and the position of its components in an image.

To illustrate these points, we will begin with image comparisons that handle 3-D variations in pose, in which correspondence is critical. Next, we will consider articulations and deformations. Finally, we will consider image comparisons when there is lighting variation, to demonstrate the advantages of using representations that are insensitive to lighting change.

27.2 Comparing Images with Pose Variation

As our first example, we consider the problem of face recognition based on the comparison of images taken from different viewpoints. The key issue in image comparison under these conditions is to find meaningful correspondences between points in the images. No comparison method will produce meaningful results if we have matched one person's nose to another's cheek. In Castillo and Jacobs (2007, in press) we propose using stereo algorithms to provide these correspondences. Typically, stereo matching algorithms are used to find correspondences when two images are taken from known, nearby viewpoints (similar to the way we view the world with two eyes). They match images in a way that maximizes the similarity of corresponding features, which are subject to strong geometric constraints on valid correspondences. The most important constraints are as follows:

- **The epipolar constraint:** The relative position of the cameras determines a set of epipolar lines in both images. All points on an epipolar line in one image must match points on the corresponding epipolar line in the second image.
- **The ordering constraint:** The order of points along corresponding epipolar lines is the same in both images. This constraint is not true for all scenes, including ones containing small objects in front of a distant background, but it does hold for images of faces.
- **Occlusion:** When viewpoint changes, some parts of the scene will be blocked from view, while others come into view. It is therefore important to allow for some points to go unmatched.

Decades of research have developed fast, effective stereo matching algorithms. Using these, we can find the correspondences between two images of faces that minimize the matching cost between corresponding pixels, while enforcing all valid geometric constraints.

We can use stereo matching in the following face recognition algorithm. We suppose that we have *gallery* images of a number of faces that we will compare to a new *probe* image. We compare a probe image to each gallery image in turn, identifying the probe with the gallery image that matches it best. In order to compare them using a stereo algorithm, we must first compute the epipolar geometry that relates the two images. When the viewer is at least a few feet from a face, we can show (Castillo and Jacobs, in press) that this requires a correspondence between four points in the two images. For example, if one can identify the centers of the eyes and mouth, and the tip of the nose on the probe and gallery images, these corresponding points determine the epipolar lines that we will match. We can then compare a probe image to a gallery image by running a stereo algorithm that finds the pixel correspondence that minimizes a matching cost. It is important to note that although the stereo algorithm produces correspondences, we do not use these for 3-D reconstruction, the traditional use of stereo. Instead, we just use the matching cost of the best correspondence as a measure of the similarity of the two face images.

To implement this approach, we use the stereo algorithm of Criminisi et al. (2007). This has been developed for videoconferencing applications, and is suitable for real-time matching of faces. The algorithm performs matching between pairs of

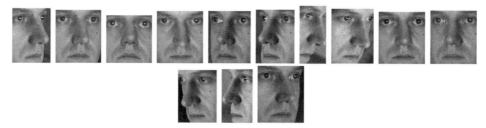

Figure 27.1. Images from CMU's PIE dataset, for one subject. In these images, pose varies, but lighting and expression are fixed. The original photos have been cropped to extract faces, based on the location of the eyes and mouth.

corresponding epipolar lines using dynamic programming. For each pair of epipolar lines, the algorithm finds the correspondence between points that minimizes the matching cost while maintaining the points' order. Such a matching can allow for foreshortening, as a large patch in one image is matched to a smaller patch in the other image. Normalized cross-correlation is used as a comparison method, providing some resistance to lighting variations.

We use the PIE images (Fig. 27.1) taken at CMU (Sim, Baker, and Bsat 2003) for our experiments. This dataset contains images of 68 individuals viewed from thirteen different viewpoints, and also contains images with variations in illumination and expression. As in previously reported experiments, we assume that the gallery images are all taken in a common pose. This will be the case in many applications. (It is an interesting and difficult problem to perform recognition when the gallery images are taken in a variety of conditions. The challenge, then, is to judge that two images of the same person taken under different conditions are more similar than two images of different people taken under the same conditions.) Some prior methods use 34 individuals to train their system, reserving the remaining 34 to form a gallery of possible matches. Other methods use all 68 individuals in the gallery. Our approach requires no training, but we report experiments with both 34 and 68 people in the gallery, to facilitate comparison. We show comparative results in Table 27.1. This table contains the average results using 156 pairs of different views for the gallery and probe images. Castillo and Jacobs (in press) contains more detailed results.

These experiments demonstrate that stereo matching leads to effective face recognition even when the viewpoint of the cameras differs by up to 180 degrees, and even when there is some variation in lighting. This may seem surprising, but there are several intuitive reasons behind this high performance. First, when stereo matching becomes difficult, as in untextured regions, it is usually because many different correspondences produce similar matching costs. Such ambiguities can lead to gross errors in 3-D reconstruction, the usual application of stereo. However, we only use stereo correspondences to determine the matching cost. Where matching is ambiguous, even incorrect correspondences will lead to nearly correct matching costs. Second, accurate matching is often difficult in small regions of the image, such as at object boundaries. Small errors here can produce troubling artifacts in reconstruction but have little effect on the matching cost we use. Third, because the face is nearly symmetric, we can flip a probe image to simulate rotation about the face's central axis. We try matching using both possibilities, and pick the one that matches with lowest cost. This means that

Table 27.1. *Our method compared to results reported in Gross et al. (2004) and Romdhani et al. (2002). Our proposed method very significantly outperforms prior approaches in cases in which the epipolar geometry is known and lighting is fixed. In particular, note that FaceIt, which is a commercial system, does not handle pose variations well. To our knowledge, the best current results are due to LiST (Romdhani et al. 2002). Our approach is significantly more accurate, and forty times faster, than LiST*

Method	Accuracy
34 Faces	
Eigenfaces	16.6%
FaceIt	24.3%
Eigen Light-Fields (3-point norm)	52.5%
Eigen Light-Fields (Multipoint norm)	66.3%
Stereo Matching Distance	**87.4%**
68 Faces	
LiST	71.6%
Stereo Matching Distance	**80.3%**

effectively a gallery view of a face will not differ by more than 90 degrees from either the probe view or its reflection. These factors motivate us to use stereo matching costs for recognition, even when viewing conditions vary considerably.

The set of correspondences allowed in our approach are exactly those that are geometrically possible due to pose change, including the possibility of occlusion. This is because the epipolar and ordering constraints together capture all possible image deformations that can occur. We can contrast this with methods that are purely 2-D and with methods based on 3-D reconstruction. First, most face recognition algorithms have been developed for situations in which there are not large pose changes; they match corresponding pixels after applying a similarity transformation that aligns two or three points, such as the eyes or mouth. This cannot account for the fact that, for example, one cheek may appear larger in one image, while the other appears larger in the second image. Some recent work uses affine transformations or other types of nonrigid warps to generate correspondences; these are more general, but may not account for occlusion, and may compute geometrically inconsistent correspondences (Gross et al. (2004) describes such approaches). Perhaps closest in spirit to our method, Beymer and Poggio (1996) use optical flow to align images before matching. However, all these approaches align images by conceptualizing them as 2-D signals that should be matched with 2-D transformations. In contrast, by considering the images as 2-D projections of a 3-D object, we can choose exactly the set of transformations for alignment that are appropriate to the viewing conditions.

In contrast, 3-D morphable models (Romdhani et al. 2002) have been used to reconstruct a 3-D model from a single image. This model can then be used effectively to generate correspondences. This approach is based on the reconstruction work of (Blanz and Vetter 1999), originally developed for graphics. This work has shown that by using a great deal of prior knowledge about faces, 3-D reconstructions can be produced that generate quite life-like, novel images. However, this process of reconstruction requires morphable models of faces that are built with painstaking care; fitting a model to an image can take minutes and requires a human to click on ten to fifteen features points, as compared to the four points required by our method. Our method is much simpler, and outperforms Romdhani et al. (2002). This is because we use 3-D knowledge to compare images without solving the difficult intermediate problem of reconstructing a 3-D object.

27.3 Deformations and Articulations

As our next example, we consider the problem of matching images when a change in shape or viewpoint may cause image deformations, or when an object has parts that articulate. We begin by finding representations of images that are invariant to deformations, and then specialize this approach to build a representation of shapes that is insensitive to articulations. The larger theme here is that one can improve image-matching methods when one has some idea of how changes in the world may affect the image.

We will define an image deformation as an arbitrary continuous, one-to-one transformation (i.e., a homeomorphism). Intensities change their position, but not their value, with deformations. To model this, we will consider an image as a 2-D surface embedded in 3-D. We will then show that as we vary the way we embed the image, geodesic distances on this surface become increasingly insensitive to deformations. This approach is described in greater detail in Ling and Jacobs (2005).

Let $I(x, y)$ denote the image intensity at point (x, y). Then we can represent the image as a 2-D surface in a 3-D space, with coordinates (u, v, w), by setting $u = (1 - \alpha)x$, $v = (1 - \alpha)y$, and $w = \alpha I(x, y)$. α is a parameter between 0 and 1 that tells us the relative value of image distance and intensities when we map them to the same space. Many previous researchers have made use of similar embeddings, but we have been particularly influenced by Sochen, Kimmel, and Malladi (1998), who use this representation to develop methods for anisotropic diffusion. They smooth images by averaging intensities weighted by their geodesic distance on the embedded surface. In this case, the geodesic distance between two image points is just the length of the shortest path connecting them on the embedded surface. The parameter α controls the extent to which intensity influences this geodesic distance. For example, when $\alpha = 0$, the geodesic distance between two image points degenerates to just the ordinary Euclidean distance between them in the image. But as α increases, two points separated by a large gradient in intensity grow further apart.

For our purposes, it is important to note that the u and v coordinates of this embedding are distorted by deformations, but the w coordinate is not. Therefore, as α increases, the geodesic distance between two points is less and less affected by deformations. In the limit, as $\alpha \to 1$, the geodesic distance between two points becomes invariant to deformations. In this case, the length of a path is just the integral of the absolute value of the change in image intensities along that path. Figure 27.2 illustrates this in 1-D. Any image representation based on geodesic distance in this embedding can therefore be made insensitive or even invariant to deformations by adjusting α.

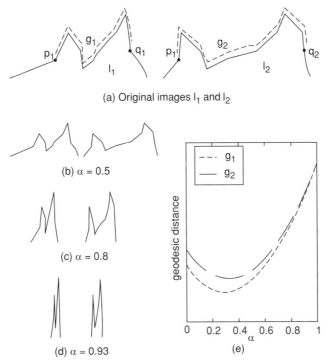

Figure 27.2. (a) Two 1-D images that are related by a deformation. $g1$ and $g2$ show geodesic paths between points p and q. (b), (c), and (d) show these images represented as 1-D surfaces (e.g., as curves), embedded in a 2-D space representing the image coordinates and intensities, for different choices of the parameter α used in the embedding. (e) shows how the geodesic distance between p and q converges to the same value in the two curves as α gets close to 1. This figure is adapted from Ling and Jacobs (2005), © 2005 IEEE.

We now discuss some possible choices of representations based on geodesic distance. We will focus on representing a region of an image in the neighborhood of a feature point, and also discuss methods of detecting such points.

Given an image point, p, perhaps the simplest representation is to construct a histogram of the intensity of all points, as their geodesic distance to p varies. This is similar to representations such as spin images (Johnson and Hebert 1999) and shape contexts (Belongie, Malik, and Puzicha 2002). To do this we can divide distances into discrete intervals. In each interval we construct a histogram of the intensities of all points whose distance to p is within that interval.

This histogram, however, is not deformation insensitive. The issue is that image deformations can alter the number of pixels that have a certain intensity. To illustrate this, suppose that the image contains a region, R, having uniform intensity. We denote one of the points in R by q, and the distance from q to p by d. In this case, as $\alpha \to 1$, the distance between any pair of points within R will go to 0, and so the distance from p to all points in R will go to d. However, the area of R can change arbitrarily due to deformation. That means that if we build a histogram of all points a distance d away from p, the number of points with the intensity of R can vary drastically due to deformation. A similar problem occurs even for nonuniform regions. To account for this, we must sample the set of points that are a distance d away from p in a way that is also insensitive to deformations. We do this by first extracting the level curve of points a distance d from p, and then sampling the intensity of points along this level curve at intervals that are uniform according to the geodesic distance. Regions of uniform intensity are sampled analogously. This ensures that the set of sample points we obtain will also be insensitive to deformations.

To demonstrate the potential of this representation, we have performed some simple experiments. In the first experiment we study the performance of our geodesic intensity histogram (GIH) in comparison with several other methods. We use both synthetic and real datasets that have significant nonlinear deformations. All methods use the Harris-Affine interest point detector to find feature points.

Mikolajczyk and Schmid (2003) provide convenient online code for several state-of-the-art local descriptors. The descriptors are normalized to enable direct comparison using sum of square differences (SSD). Benefiting from their code, we compare the geodesic-intensity histogram with steerable filters (Freeman and Adelson 1991), SIFT (Lowe 2004), moments invariants (Van Gool, Moons, and Ungureanu 1996), complex filters (Schaffalitzky and Zisserman 2002), and spin images (Lazebnik, Schmid, and Ponce 2003). A receiver operating characteristics (ROC)–based criterion is used to measure the accuracy with which we can match features in one image to features in a second one. This is similar to Mikolajczyk and Schmid (2004). Instead of using the false-positive rate, we study the detection rates among the top N matches, as N varies. Figure 27.3 shows that our new method outperforms prior ones on images with deformations.

We have also developed a closely related approach for the comparison of binary images that represent shapes (Ling and Jacobs 2007). We compute distances between points on the boundary of the shape using the length of the shortest path that remains entirely within the shape. This is analogous to using a geodesic distance with $\alpha = 1 - \epsilon$, for some small ϵ. In this case, paths that cross the boundary are always longer than paths inside the boundary. We call this distance between two boundary points the *inner distance*. We describe the shape, relative to a boundary point, using a histogram of the distance from the feature point to every other boundary point in the shape. The inner-distance representation we construct is not invariant to deformations of shape, which can change the length of a path inside a shape, but it is insensitive to articulations that affect the relative position of parts without changing their shape, as when a person bends an arm. In some sense, the magnitude of changes in the inner distance reflect the amount of deformation that has occurred in a shape. Ling and Jacobs (2007) describe a number of experiments that demonstrate that the inner distance works extremely well in shape identification tasks, on a number of large datasets.

The deformation-invariant representations described in this section are quite different from the methods described in the previous section to handle pose variation, because they do not explicitly reference the 3-D geometry of objects. However, we see both approaches as part of a common effort to understand the sorts of image transformations that can result from changes in object position or shape. These cause nonlinear changes in the position at which points on an object appear. In order to handle these variations, we must develop image comparison algorithms that can account for these changes.

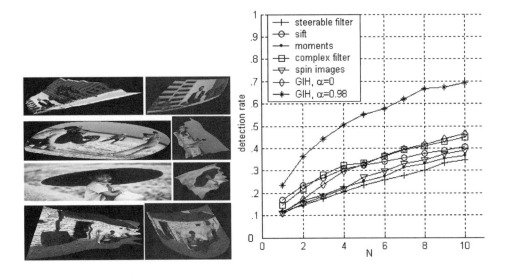

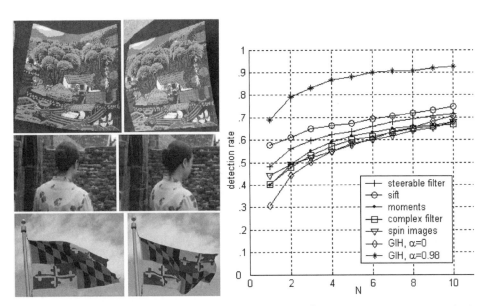

Figure 27.3. In the *top right*, we display the ROC curves for an experiment using synthetic deformations, which are shown in the *top left*. *Bottom right* shows the ROC curve for real images with deformations, shown in the *bottom left*. From the ROC curves we can see that GIH performs better than other methods. We also show results with our method using $\alpha = 0$, to confirm that when we use Euclidean distances, our approach becomes comparable to spin images. This figure is adapted from Ling and Jacobs (2005), © 2005 IEEE.

27.4 Lighting

Finally, we will discuss the effects that variations in lighting can have on the appearance of a 3-D object. Lighting variation does not create a matching problem, because changing the lighting generally doesn't change the image location of a scene point;

rather, it presents us with the challenge of determining when two portions of an image should be considered similar. In other words, when are image variations due to a change in lighting, and when are they due to a change in the identity or geometry of an object?

To understand the effects of lighting variation on the appearance of a scene, we must look at the interactions between lighting and 3-D geometry. In this section we describe two studies of this problem. First, in Chen et al. (2000) we look at how the gradient of an image will vary as the lighting changes, for different sorts of 3-D, Lambertian scenes. We show that, in general, the direction of the image gradient tends to be insensitive to lighting variation, whereas the intensity of the gradient is quite sensitive to these variations.

More specifically, we can consider three situations. First, suppose we have a planar, Lambertian object illuminated by a point source of varying intensity and direction. In this case, it is easy to show that the direction of the image gradient will be identical to the direction of the gradient of the albedo of the surface. Changes in lighting scale the image intensities and the magnitude of the image gradient but do not change its direction.

Next, consider a 3-D surface with a discontinuity in its surface orientation. An example of this would be the edge of a polyhedron. This surface discontinuity produces an image discontinuity, and near this discontinuity the image gradient will be orthogonal to its direction. Again, the direction of the image gradient is invariant to changes in lighting, whereas its magnitude is quite sensitive to lighting. Note that these two simple scenarios are the ones often used to motivate the use of edges to mitigate the effects of lighting. However, edges are highly sensitive to variations in lighting direction and intensity, because they invariably rely on the use of thresholds related to the gradient magnitude. As lighting affects the gradient magnitude, edges can appear or disappear. However, representations based only on image gradient direction garner the benefits usually ascribed to edges, without their lighting sensitivity.

Finally, Chen et al. (2000) consider the more general case. Roughly speaking, when a surface changes albedo or surface normal much more rapidly in one direction than in the other, the image intensities will tend to also change more rapidly in a direction near the projection of that direction. This will be true for most, but not all, lighting directions.

To be specific, consider a smooth shape with uniform albedo. Let l denote a unit vector in the direction of a light with unit intensity. Let $N(x, y)$ denote the surface normal at (x, y). Let $N_x(x, y)$ denote the partial derivative of this normal, as we move in the x direction. Then $N_x(x, y)$ is a vector in the tangent plane of the surface. We can similarly define $N_y(x, y)$, which is also a vector in the tangent plane, not necessarily orthogonal to $N_x(x, y)$. For a Lambertian object, the intensity is just the inner product between the light and the normal. So the intensity at (x, y) is $I(x, y) = l \cdot N(x, y)$, and the image gradient is given by:

$$(I_x(x, y), I_y(x, y)) = (l \cdot N_x(x, y), l \cdot N_y(x, y))$$

Suppose, without loss of generality, that we have chosen our coordinate system so that $N_x(x, y)$ is the direction of principal curvature of the surface, and $N_y(x, y)$ is the direction of least curvature. If the surface has much higher curvature in one direction than another, this means that $||N_x(x, y)||$ is much larger than $||N_y(x, y)||$. Then, for most lighting directions, $l \cdot N_x(x, y)$ will be much larger than $l \cdot N_y(x, y)$, and the image gradient will point nearly towards the projection of the direction of principal curvature. In the extreme case, when the surface is a cylinder, $||N_y(x, y)|| = 0$, and the direction of the image gradient is invariant to lighting. Note, however, that the magnitude of the image gradient can change wildly. This means that for a large class of surfaces with nonisotropic curvature, the direction of gradient is an effective, lighting-insensitive representation of the image.

Gradient directions have been widely used as image representations (Bichsel 1991; Brunelli 1994; Chen et al. 2000; Cootes and Taylor 2001; Fitch et al. 2002; Ravela and Luo 2000). We have also shown (Osadchy, Jacobs, and Lindenbaum 2007) that in some cases gradient directions are equivalent to methods based on normalized correlation of local windows (see, e.g., Jähne 1995 for a description of this standard method), and methods that represent images using the output of oriented filters, such as difference of Gaussians and Gabor jets (e.g., Schmid and Mohr 1997; Rao and Ballard 1995; Lades 1993). Prior work with all these methods mainly has been justified because they are all invariant to multiplicative and additive changes to images. However, our analysis shows that these methods can be used to compare images of 3-D scenes, because they are also insensitive to changes in lighting direction. In a recent paper (Ling et al. 2007), we combine gradient directions with support vector machines, to compare pairs of passport photos of faces, to determine whether they depict the same person. We show that representing images using gradient directions results in much higher performance than an identical approach using raw image intensities.

Our analysis also shows that these representations are not appropriate for comparing images of smooth, isotropic surfaces in which albedo or surface orientation tends to change similarly in all directions. In Osadchy et al. (2007) we show that these smooth surfaces can be modeled as an isotropic Gaussian random field. For such surfaces, the difference between two images, produced by two different lighting directions, can be modeled as Gaussian colored noise. The optimal method of signal detection in this case is to decorrelate (or whiten) the noise prior to image matching. We show experimentally that in fact gradient direction performs matching much better than whitening when we compare images of nonisotropic surfaces, whereas whitening works much better on isotropic surfaces.

Together, these results show that we can model the ways in which variations in lighting interact with surface characteristics to vary image intensities. Understanding these variations can help us to also understand which image representations will be most effective in the face of these variations.

27.5 Conclusion

The ability to compare images may be central to visual classification, because effective image comparisons allow us to generalize from images we have seen to quite different images that come from the same class of objects. In this chapter we argue that to find the best ways of comparing images, it is helpful to have a model of how changes in pose, lighting, or shape in the 3-D world will affect the 2-D appearance of objects.

When we know what 2-D transformations to expect, we can design algorithms and representations that take account of these transformations.

Bibliography

Barrow H, Tenenbaum J. 1978. Recovering intrinsic scene characteristics from images. In *Computer vision systems*, ed. A. Hanson and E. Riseman, 3–26. New York: Academic Press.

Belhumeur P, Hespanha J, Kriegman D. 1997. Eigenfaces vs. fisherfaces: recognition using class specific linear projection. *IEEE Trans Pattern Anal Mach Intell* 19(7): 711–720.

Belongie S, Malik J, and Puzicha J. 2002. Shape matching and object recognition using shape context. *IEEE Trans Pattern Anal Mach Intell* 24(4): 509–522.

Beymer D, Poggio T. 1996. Image representations for visual learning. *Science* 272: 1905–1909.

Bichsel, M. 1991. *Strategies of robust object recognition for the automatic identification of human faces*. PhD diss., No. 9467, ETH Zurich.

Biederman I. 1987. Recognition-by-components: a theory of human image understanding. *Psychol Rev* 94(2): 115–147.

Binford, T. 1971. Visual perception by computer. In IEEE conference on systems and control.

Blanz V, Vetter T. 1999. Face recognition based on fitting a 3D morphable model. *Pattern Anal Mach Intell* 25(9): 1063–1074.

Brooks, R. (1981). Symbolic reasoning among 3-dimensional models and 2-dimensional images. *Artif Intell* 17: 285–349.

Brunelli R. 1994. Estimation of pose and illuminant direction for face processing. AI memo No. 1499. Massachusetts Institute of Technology.

Burns J, Weiss R, Riseman E. 1992. The non-existence of general-case view-invariants. In *Geometric invariance in computer vision*, ed. J Mundy and A Zisserman. Cambridge: MIT Press.

Castillo C, Jacobs D. 2007. Using stereo matching for 2-d face recognition across pose. In IEEE international conference on computer vision and pattern recognition.

Castillo C, Jacobs D. In press. Using stereo matching with general epipolar geometry for 2-d face recognition across pose. *IEEE Trans Pattern Anal Mach Intell*.

Chen H, Belhumeur P, Jacobs D. 2000. In search of illumination invariants. In Proceedings of the IEEE conference on computer vision and pattern recognition.

Clemens D, Jacobs D. 1991. Space and time bounds on model indexing. *IEEE Trans Pattern Anal Mach Intell* 13(10): 1007–1018.

Cootes T, Taylor, C. 2001. On representing edge structure for model matching. In Proceedings of the IEEE conference on computer vision and pattern recognition.

Cortes C, Vapnik, V. 1995. Support-vector networks. *Mach Learn* 20(3): 273–297.

Criminisi A, Shotton J, Blake A, Rother C, Torr PHS. 2007. Efficient dense stereo with occlusion by four-state dynamic programming. *Int. J Comput Vis* 71(1): 89–110.

Fitch A, Kadyrov A, Christmas W, Kittler J. 2002. Orientation correlation. In British machine vision conference.

Freeman W, Adelson E. 1991. The design and use of steerable filters. *IEEE Trans Pattern Anal Mach Intell* 13(9): 891–906.

Gross R, Baker S, Matthews I, Kanade T. 2004. Face recognition across pose and illumination. In *Handbook of face recognition*, ed. SZ Li and AK Jain. Berlin: Springer-Verlag.

Jähne B. 1995. *Digital image processing.* Berlin: Springer-Verlag.

Johnson A, Hebert M. 1999. Using spin images for efficient object recognition in cluttered 3d scenes. *IEEE Trans Pattern Anal Mach Intell* 21(5): 433–449.

Lades M, Vortbrggen J, Buhmann J, Lange J, Malsburg C, von der Wrtz, RP, Konen W. 1993. Distortion invariant object recognition in the dynamic link architecture. *IEEE Trans Comput* 42: 300–311.

Lazebnik S, Schmid C, Ponce J. 2003. A sparse texture representation using affine-invariant regions. In IEEE conference on computer vision and pattern recognition vol. 2, 319–324.

LeCun Y, Boser B, Denker JS, Henderson D, Howard RE, Hubbard W, Jackel LD. 1990. Handwritten digit recognition with a back-propagation network. In *Advances in neural information processing systems 2 (NIPS*89)*, ed. D Touretzky. Denver, CO: Morgan Kaufman.

Ling H, Jacobs D. 2005. Deformation invariant image matching. In *IEEE international conference on computer vision* vol. II, 1466–1473.

Ling H, Jacobs D. 2007. Shape classification using the inner-distance. *IEEE Trans Pattern Anal Mach Intell* 29(2): 286–299.

Ling H, Soatto S, Ramanathan N, Jacobs D. 2007. A study of face recognition as people age. In IEEE international conference on computer vision.

Lowe D. 2004. Distinctive image features from scale-invariant keypoints. *Int J Comput Vis* 60(2): 91–110.

Marr D. 1982. *Vision: a computational investigation into the human representation and processing of visual information.* San Francisco: W.H. Freeman.

Mikolajczyk K, Schmid C. 2003. A performance evaluation of local descriptors. In IEEE conference on computer vision and pattern recognition, 257–264.

Mikolajczyk K, Schmid C. 2004. Scale & affine invariant interest point detectors. *Int J Comput Vis* 60(1): 63–86.

Moghaddam B, Pentland A. 1997. Probabilistic visual learning for object representation. *IEEE Trans Pattern Anal Mach Intell* 19(7): 696–710.

Osadchy M, Jacobs D, Lindenbaum M. 2007. Surface dependent representations for illumination insensitive image comparison. *IEEE Trans Pattern Anal Mach Intell* 29(1): 98–111.

Poggio T, Edelman S. 1990. A network that learns to recognize 3D objects. *Nature* 343: 263–266.

Rao R, Ballard D. 1995. An active vision architecture based on iconic representations. *Artif Intell* 78(1–2): 461–505.

Ravela S, Luo C. 2000. Appearance-based global similarity retrieval of images. In *Advances in information retrieval*, ed. WB Croft, 267–303. New York: Springer-Verlag.

Romdhani S, Blanz V, Vetter T. 2002. Face identification by fitting a 3d morphable model using linear shape and texture error functions. In European conference on computer vision, vol. 4, 3–19.

Schaffalitzky F, Zisserman A. 2002. Multi-view matching for unordered image sets, or "how do i organize my holiday snaps?." In European conference on computer vision, vol. I, 414–431.

Schmid C, Mohr R. 1997. Local grayvalue invariants for image retrieval. *IEEE Trans Pattern Anal Mach Intell* 19(5): 530–535.

Sim T, Baker S, Bsat M. 2003. The cmu pose, illumination, and expression database. *IEEE Trans Pattern Anal Mach Intell* 25(12): 1615–1618.

Sochen N, Kimmel R, Malladi R. 1998. A general framework for low level vision. *IEEE Trans on Image Processing* 7(3): 310–318.

Van Gool L, Moons T, Ungureanu D. 1996. Affine/photometric invariants for planar intensity patterns. In European conference on computer vision, 642–651.

Index

517